PRINCIPLES OF CRIMINAL PROCEDURE: POST-INVESTIGATION

Second Edition

By

Wayne R. LaFave

*David C. Baum Professor of Law Emeritus and
Center for Advanced Study Professor Emeritus,
University of Illinois*

Jerold H. Israel

*Alene and Allan F. Smith Professor of Law Emeritus,
University of Michigan
and Ed Rood Eminent Scholar Emeritus,
University of Florida, Levin College of Law*

Nancy J. King

*Lee S. & Charles A. Spier Professor of Law
Vanderbilt University*

Orin S. Kerr

*Professor of Law,
George Washington University*

CONCISE HORNBOOK SERIES®

WEST®

A Thomson Reuters business

Mat #40775860

Concise Hornbook Series and Westlaw are trademarks registered in the U.S. Patent and Trademark Office.

© West, a Thomson business, 2004
© 2009 Thomson Reuters

610 Opperman Drive
St. Paul, MN 55123
1–800–313–9378

Printed in the United States of America

ISBN: 978–0–314–19934–8

Preface

This book is intended to be used primarily by law students while engaged in the study of the subject of criminal procedure. This is one of two concise hornbooks that we have written on this subject; the other is *Principles of Criminal Procedure: Investigation*. The present book is for use in a criminal procedure course where the focus is upon the subsequent, more formal parts of the criminal process (sometimes referred to as "bail to jail," albeit including post-conviction review). The *Investigation* book, on the other hand, can alone be used in a criminal procedure course where the focus is primarily or exclusively upon that part of the entirety of criminal procedure having to do with the detection and investigation of crime. Both of these books could be used together in connection with a survey course in criminal procedure which examined both the investigation and post-investigation areas.

It has been our effort to provide as much information and analysis as is possible in a relatively short and easy to use (and carry) paperback volume. By excluding any documentation via footnotes of the various subjects considered and discussed herein (an approach requiring extraordinary self-restraint by four law professors!), we have been able to use virtually all of the space in this conveniently-sized paperback for textual elaboration of the subjects covered. Leading Supreme Court cases and, occasionally, lower court cases of special significance, are identified in the text by name and date only; full citations are available in the Table of Cases. We have provided both a very detailed Table of Contents and also an Index so that a student may easily locate topics of particular interest.

The *Investigation* and *Post–Investigation* concise hornbooks together constitute a compendious counterpart to our much more substantial undertaking, a 7–volume treatise primarily for bench and bar entitled *Criminal Procedure*. We mention that fact here only to emphasize that if on occasion a student does want to explore some topic in the present book in greater depth or to locate additional relevant cases, relevant statutes or useful secondary authorities, he or she will find it relatively easy to do so. In Westlaw, just go to the database CRIMPROC and examine the comparable material there. (Chapters 1 and 2 in the present work correspond to parts of Chapters 1 and 2 in CRIMPROC, while

Chapters 3–20 herein relate, respectively, to Chapters 11–28 in
CRIMPROC. The arrangement of sections and subsections within
comparable chapters is often but not inevitably the same. Consult
the *Table of Cross-References* herein.)

While all four of us stand responsible for the work on this book
and its companion volume, *Investigation*, as a whole, the initial
responsibility for individual chapters in these two concise hornbooks was determined according to the allocation of responsibilities
in preparation of the 7–volume treatise. Hence, as to this book
Wayne LaFave had initial responsibility for chapters 4–5, 9–10, and
13, Jerold Israel for chapters 1–3, 6–8, 11–12, and 15, and Nancy
King for chapters 14 and 16–20. Each of us would appreciate
hearing from readers who have criticisms or suggestions relating to
the chapters for which we had initial responsibility.

WAYNE R. LaFAVE
JEROLD H. ISRAEL
NANCY J. KING
ORIN S. KERR

July 2009

Table of Cross–References

The authors of this Book, *Criminal Procedure: Post–Investigation*, are also the co-authors of a seven-volume treatise, *Criminal Procedure* (3rd ed. 2007, with annual updates), available in most law libraries and readily accessible on Westlaw in database CRIM-PROC. The subjects discussed in this Book are dealt with in considerably greater detail in the Treatise. In addition, while the citation of supporting authority in this Book must of necessity be very limited, many additional citations to appellate cases, legislation and court rules, as well as articles and other secondary authorities, are available in the Treatise. Users of this Book desiring either additional discussion of a particular subject or supporting authority regarding a specific topic will thus find it useful to consult the Treatise. To facilitate such consultation, we have provided this table of cross-references, indicating for each section in this Book what section or sections in the Treatise deal with the same subject matter. (Even when the section numbers are different, the subsections will usually be identical in both works.)

Summary of Contents

Table of Contents

PRINCIPLES OF
CRIMINAL PROCEDURE:
POST-INVESTIGATION
Second Edition

*

Chapter 1

THE CHARACTER OF POST-INVESTIGATION CRIMINAL PROCEDURE

Table of Sections

For additional analysis of the above topics and citations to authorities supporting their discussion in this Book, consult the authors' 7-volume *Criminal Procedure* treatise, also available as Westlaw database CRIMPROC. See the Table of Cross-References in this Book.

---

§ 1.1 Introduction

(a) **The Subject Matter.** As an academic subject matter, "criminal procedure" (or, as some prefer, "the criminal justice process") commonly refers to the totality of the procedures through which the substantive criminal law is enforced. While some law schools offer a single course on criminal procedure, many have divided that subject matter into two courses. The first course typically is devoted to procedures that are part of the criminal investigation (i.e., the procedures though which investigating officials—usually the police, but sometimes prosecutors—gather evidence that will allow them initially to determine whether it is likely that a crime was committed, and if so determined, to then identify, apprehend, and establish the guilt of the likely offender). The second course covers the remaining procedures of the criminal justice process. That course goes by a variety of titles, none of which are entirely accurate.

The second course commonly is described as dealing with the "post-investigation" portion of the process, but the procedures considered in the course actually are initiated at the completion of what may only be one phase in the investigation. Those procedures start once the investigation has lead to a decision to arrest and charge, but quite often the investigation continues after that point (sometimes, right up to the moment of the final disposition of the filed charges). Another common title for the second course, "Bail to Postconviction Review," has led to the course's common nickname ("Bail to Jail"), but that title also is chronologically incorrect, as well as overinclusive. A major topic considered in the second course is the decision to charge and that decision often comes prior to the setting of bail. Also, the course coverage typically is less than complete as to the procedures between its starting and stopping point. In particular, pretrial motions challenging the investigative portion of the process are considered in the investigation course rather than this second course. Other course titles emphasize the adversarial character of that portion of the process that occurs after charges are filed, but that characterization could just as well be applied to certain portions of the investigative process. Similarly, titles such as "Prosecution and Adjudication" fall somewhat short because they fail to encompass the full range of the functions performed in the post-investigation procedures.

This concise hornbook is designed for that second course in criminal procedure, whatever its title. For students taking a single course covering the entire criminal justice process, it can be combined with its companion volume—*Principles of Criminal Procedure: Investigation*.

Our focus throughout is on the law governing the various post-investigation procedures. Of course, the everyday administration of the criminal justice process is shaped by far more than the formal, written law, but except for the brief discussion in subsection (d), an analysis of different administrative cultures and their bearing on the actual operation of post-investigative procedures is left to the many works of social scientists exploring that subject.

(b) Accounting for Fifty-Two Different Jurisdictions. Under the American version of federalism, each of the fifty state governments retains the authority to enact its own criminal code, applicable within the territorial reach of its legislative powers. Each state also retains the power to provide for the enforcement of that criminal code through agencies and procedures that it creates. That authority has been used in each state to establish what is basically a single, general criminal justice process applicable throughout the state. Congress has added to these fifty state criminal justice processes its two distinct federal criminal justice processes. First, it has created a separate criminal justice process for the District of Columbia, used to enforce a separate criminal code that applies only in the District. Second, it has created a criminal justice process for the enforcement of the general federal criminal code, which applies throughout the country. This process utilizes national law enforcement agencies and relies on prosecutions brought in the federal district courts.

In many fields in which both state and federal governments exercise regulatory authority, the enforcement of federal law by federal officials so clearly dominates the field that law school courses focus almost exclusively on the federal enforcement system. A similar focus would be most inappropriate in the field of criminal procedure. While the federal criminal justice system may be the most prominent of the nation's fifty-two criminal justice systems, the traditional statistical measures of criminal justice systems rank it simply as one of the larger, but hardly the largest, of our fifty-two systems. Moreover, when the federal system is compared to the state systems as a group, the combined state systems clearly dominate, as they account for a much larger portion of the nation's criminal justice workload (e.g., roughly 96% of all felony prosecutions and almost 99% of all misdemeanor prosecutions). Thus, the study of the law governing the criminal justice process must take account of the laws regulating the 50 state criminal justice processes as well as the two federal processes.

Taking account of fifty-two different criminal justice systems would be a less daunting task if the fifty-two jurisdictions were subject to a single law that mandates an exclusive, comprehensive regulation of each aspect of the process. There is, however, no such law. As discussed in Chapter 2, various provisions of the Bill of Rights of the federal constitution do apply to all fifty-two jurisdictions. Those provisions do lock the fifty-two jurisdictions into a standard foundation for the construction of a criminal justice process. They also prescribe a variety of requirements for specific procedures that all jurisdictions must meet. However, as discussed in § 1.3(b), the regulation provided by the federal constitution hardly ensures uniformity among the fifty-two jurisdictions. The Bill of Rights provisions leave large segments of the process untouched by constitutional regulation, and where the constitution does regulate, even most extensively, that still leaves each jurisdiction with leeway to impose more stringent regulations of its choice. Accordingly, the legal standards adopted by the individual jurisdiction under its own laws play a significant role in the overall regulation of the process. Indeed, as to many aspects of post-investigation procedure, each jurisdiction's own standards provide the dominant regulation, with the federal constitution having only limited influence.

With each jurisdiction regulating through its own laws, some degree of diversity is almost certain to be found among the fifty-two jurisdictions. We will not attempt in this single volume to describe all the variations that can be found in the laws of the different jurisdictions. Where major conflicts in approach exist, we will describe the basic patterns that divide one large group of jurisdictions from another. It should be kept in mind, however, that on almost any aspect of non-constitutional regulation, there will be at least a few jurisdictions that depart from what we characterize as the "general rule." Similarly, when we describe state law as divided between two or three positions, there most likely will be a few states that have adopted still other approaches.

Very often a basic pattern followed by a substantial group of states is the product of the states emulating reforms adopted in a particular jurisdiction. The federal system provides one of the most frequently emulated models. As to almost every procedural step that is part of the post-investigative process, a grouping of states, ranging from a handful to a majority, have adopted the basic features of the nonconstitutional law of the federal system. The Federal Rules of Criminal Procedure provide the most prominent illustration of this influence. While the Federal Rules are applicable only in the general federal system, they almost always reflect the basic position adopted in a substantial number of states. The same is true of leading federal statutes, such as the Federal Speedy Trial Act. Accordingly, as to most steps in the process, mention will be made of the relevant federal provisions. The American Bar Association's *Standards for Criminal Justice* provides another frequently emulated model. The ABA standards have proposed an approach distinct from the federal position as to various aspects of the process, and where that approach has been adopted by substantial number of states, the ABA Standards also will also be discussed.

(c) **Procedural Subsets.** Even within a single jurisdiction the law governing post-investigative procedures will not be the same for each and every prosecution. All fifty-two jurisdictions utilize at least a few lines of division that produce procedural subsets (i.e., different classes of cases governed by different procedural standards). The most common is the line drawn between felonies and misdemeanors. Felonies, in general, are crimes subject to a punishment of incarceration for more than one year, while misdemeanors are crimes subject to incarceration for a term of one year or less. All jurisdictions distinguish between felonies and misdemeanors as to some procedures. Indeed, some states add an additional subset for certain procedures by drawing a distinction between lower level misdemeanors (e.g., punishable by 90 days in jail or less) and higher level misdemeanors (which then may or may not be treated in the same manner as felonies). We will always take note of federal constitutional distinctions drawn between misdemeanors and felonies (or certain types of misdemeanors and more serious charges). As to distinctions drawn by state law, however, only the most significant differences in the treatment of misdemeanors will be cited. Our focus is primarily on describing the law applicable to felony prosecutions.

A similar approach will be taken as to state laws creating another procedural subset based on penalty—the distinction drawn, as to various procedures, between felonies subject to capital punishment (limited to certain types of murder) and all other felonies. Our focus will be on the processing of the non-capital case, although here again, distinctions drawn in constitutional regulation between capital and non-capital felonies will always be noted.

Within a single state, a variety of different agencies may provide the personnel who exercise the authority of the primary actors in the post-investigation processing of criminal cases—the prosecutor, defense counsel, magistrate, and trial judge. Here again state law may draw procedural subsets tied to the type of official performing the particular role. Prosecutors, for example, typically are local officials (e.g., the county prosecutor), but some states also vest prosecutorial authority in the Attorney General, and in doing so, provide authority or restrictions on authority that do not apply to local prosecutors. Since such differences are relatively minor, they will be ignored in our commentary. The same is true of distinctions that may be drawn between public defenders and other types of defense counsel, whether appointed or retained.

The distinctions are not so minor, however, as to different types of courts that perform the traditional roles of the "magistrate." These courts have trial jurisdiction only as to misdemeanors (or a limited class of misdemeanors), but they typically also preside over preliminary steps in the processing of felony cases (primarily the first appearance, see § 1.2(e), and the preliminary hearing, see § 1.2(f)). Many states have more than one type of magistrate court, allowing, for example, part-time lay judges to preside in rural areas. Very often, the standards governing basic procedures will vary with the type of court (e.g., for some courts, appellate review of misdemeanor convictions will be by a *trial de novo* in the general trial court, rather than the traditional appellate review of the trial record). Since these distinctions relate primarily to the processing of misdemeanors, rather than felonies, they too will largely be ignored in our commentary.

(d) Administrative Variations. The everyday administration of the criminal justice process is a product of both the legal regulations described in subsequent chapters and the exercise of discretion by the primary administrators of the process—police, prosecutors, judges, and defense counsel. Discretion exists where the law implicitly or explicitly allows the administrator autonomy of choice as to the exercise of authority (in the case of police, prosecutor, and judge) or the exercise of a right (in the case of the defense lawyer's exercise of the rights of the defendant). Discretion exists, for example, where: (1) the law recognizes governmental authority, but places almost no limits on the administrator's decision to exercise or not exercise that authority (e.g., holding only that the administrator cannot be influenced by a bribe); (2) the law sets forth specific prerequisites for the exercise of governmental authority, but allows the administrator to choose whether or not to exercise that authority where those prerequisites are met; and (3) the law directs an administrator to choose among several different actions, but sets forth a standard for choice so open-ended (e.g., the choice shall reflect the "interests of justice") that the administrator has great latitude in choosing among the alternatives.

Grants of discretion are found throughout the criminal justice process. The discretion of police and prosecutors tends to be broadest as to the decision not to exercise governmental power adversely to an individual (sometimes described as "ameliorative discretion"), but it also extends to decisions to taking action that control the procedural rights made available to the defendant (as where the prosecutor may determine whether felony charges are screened by a magistrate at a preliminary hearing or by a grand jury, see §§ 6.2, 7.1). Judicial discretion most frequently is of a latter type, as it usually relates to prescribed decisionmaking. The scope of the discretion granted to magistrates and felony trial court judges varies somewhat from one jurisdiction to another, but judicial discretion can readily bear upon every proceeding at which those judges preside. The discretion of the defense counsel has a somewhat different character, but it also shapes the process as applied to the individual case. Counsel, sometimes only with the consent of the defendant (see § 3.6), has the discretionary power to expand the authority of the police, prosecutor, or judge by relinquishing (through a waiver) the right of the defendant that otherwise would limit the exercise of that authority.

Although the law leaves discretionary decision-making to the individual administrator, institutional arrangements play a large role in shaping the individual's exercise of discretion. In particular, where the individual administrator is part of an administrative entity, that entity may influence the exercise of discretion in various ways. It may do so informally through a variety of devices (e.g., training programs, socialization, and incentives), or it may do so formally through written guidelines that are enforced internally.

Where judges are members of multi-judge courts or magistrates are part of a consolidated court, the influence of the judicial entity will be expressed through an organizational culture that suggests a preferred path in exercising various types of discretion. Where defense counsel are part of a public defender office (see § 3.2(c)), the office policy typically will stress the need to vary the exercise of discretion to fit the needs of the defendant in the individual case, but the organizational ethos may suggest to counsel that a particular exercise of discretion generally is to be favored. Undoubtedly, however, institutional influence is strongest as to police and prosecutor, with the prosecutor's office, in particular, likely to utilize written guidelines to channel the exercise of discretion.

Even where prosecutors' offices tightly control particular discretionary decisions by individual prosecutors, there is likely to be considerable variation in the exercise of discretion as to those decisions over the state as a whole. In all but three states, the primary responsibility for prosecutions is vested in local prosecutors (typically elected officials of counties or multi-county judicial districts). There are over 2,300 local prosecutor's offices in the United States, and each is free to develop its own policies as to the exercise of discretion. Those policies are likely to be influenced by numerous variables, including the chief prosecutor's policy preferences, the caseload pressures borne by the particular office, interactions with local police departments and local courts, and the influence of the local community. In three states (Alaska, Delaware, and Rhode Island), the Attorney General's office is the sole prosecution agency (although the staff may be assigned in part to local offices), and that provides a potential for achieving state-wide consistency (if the Attorney General so desires). In the federal system, United States Attorneys are appointed for each judicial district, but they are officials within the Department of Justice and are subject to the supervision of the Attorney General (exercised primarily through the D.O.J.'s Criminal Division). Although each U.S. Attorney's office is given a fair amount of autonomy as to many decisions, as to others, the exercise of discretion is controlled by guidelines, policy directives, and in some instances, by requiring specific approval of the Criminal Division for certain administrative actions.

§ 1.2   The Steps in the Post–Investigation Process

This section presents an overview of the non-investigatory steps that carry a case from the point of arrest to the end of the process. The basic objectives of the overview are to position each step within the typical progression of the post-investigation process, and to introduce relevant terminology. The overview follows a "typical" felony case in a "typical" state system. It thus ignores a host of variations, including : (1) procedures that are used only infrequently in felony cases (e.g., "station house bail," see § 4.1(b)); (2) procedures that are used regularly, but only in a small group of states (e.g., jury sentencing in non-capital cases, see § 18.2(b)), (3) procedures that commonly are restricted to misdemeanors (e.g., use of citations as alternatives to arrests, see § 4.5) or capital felonies (e.g., bifurcated trials); and atypical chronologies (e.g., where the accused is first charged by indictment and only later arrested).

(a) The Arrest. Where a police investigation establishes probable cause to believe that a particular person committed a crime, the police have the authority to arrest that person–i.e., to take that person into custody for the purpose of charging the person with that crime. The police may seek a court order authorizing the arrest (an "arrest warrant," typically issued by a magistrate), and in some instances, that may be required, but the vast majority of felony arrests are "warrantless arrests" (i.e., made without warrant authorization).

The arrest is part of the investigative portion of the criminal justice process; indeed certain investigative procedures flow from the arrest. However, the arrest also constitutes an initial police decision to charge the person with a crime. Following the arrest, that decision of the arresting officer is subject to internal review during the "booking process" at the police station. That process involves making a record of the arrest on the police "blotter" or "log," obtaining the arrestee's photograph and fingerprints, and having a supervising officer determine whether charges against the arrestee should be pursued. If the supervising officer decides against bringing charges (concluding, for example, that the evidence is too weak to proceed), the arrestee will be released. If the officer concludes that charges should be brought, the arrestee will remain in custody (either at the police station or a local jail), but within a period of 24 or 48 hours (depending upon the jurisdiction), the arrestee must be brought before the magistrate court and a formal charging instrument (typically designated a "complaint") must be filed with that court.

(b) The Prosecutor's Decision to Charge. The ultimate authority over charging rests with the prosecutor, rather than the police. In many jurisdictions, the initial prosecutorial decision on charging comes in a review of the police charging decision during the period between the arrest and the presentation of arrestee before the magistrate (the "first appearance"). In others, the police usually will file the complaint on their own initiative, and the prosecutor will first review that decision sometime between the first appearance and the next step in the process. Where review occurs prior to the filing of the complaint, a prosecutor decision not to proceed is often described as a "no paper decision".

As discussed in § 5.1, a variety of concerns may contribute to the prosecutor's initial charging decision, including the strength of the evidence, the equities of the case, and the availability of preferable alternative dispositions (such as diversion, see § 5.1(d), or where the arrestee currently is on probation or parole, seeking a revocation of that status).Where the prosecutor decides in favor of prosecution, other decisions also must be made. Initially, the prosecutor must determine whether the proposed charge is set at the correct level, or whether there is a need to reduce or raise the offense-level recommended by the police. In many instances, the prosecutor must also consider the potential for charging multiple separate offenses (as where the arrested person allegedly committed several separate crimes in a single criminal transaction or engaged in more than one criminal transaction). Here the prosecutor must determine whether the charging instrument should allege all offenses or simply some of the offenses (e.g., only the most serious, or only those easiest to prove). Where the prosecutor chooses to proceed on more than one charge, the governing law (see § 9.1) may give to the prosecutor another choice—whether to bring the charges in a single prosecution or in multiple, separate prosecutions. A similar choice must be made where several people have been arrested for their participation in same crime, as each can be proceeded against separately or the group can be prosecuted jointly through a single charging instrument naming multiple defendants (see § 9.2).

The prosecutor's decision to go forward remains subject to reconsideration throughout the proceeding. Changes in circumstances (e.g., a critical witness is no longer available) or a fresh perspective may lead the prosecutor to conclude that the case should not go forward. When this occurs after an information or indictment has been filed (see § 1.2(h)), the prosecutor must file a motion in the trial court requesting dismissal of the charges (a *nolle prosequi* motion), which must be approved by the court (see § 5.3 (b)). The overall rate of prosecution decisions not to proceed (including both the initial decisions not to file charges and subsequent decisions to drop filed charges) varies considerably from one prosecutor's office to another. However, in almost all jurisdictions, it will rank only behind guilty pleas in accounting for the disposition of felony arrests. Prosecution decisions not to proceed are responsible for far more disposition than, for example, preliminary hearings and grand jury review (see § 1.2(f), (g)), dismissals on defense motions (see § 1.2(j)), or trials (see § 1.2(m)).

(c) Filing the Complaint. If charges are to be brought, the next step in the process is the filing of a complaint in the magistrate court. For most offenses, the complaint will be a fairly brief document. Its basic function is to set forth concisely the allegation that the accused, at a particular time and place, committed specified acts constituting a violation of a particular criminal statute. The complaint will be signed by a "complainant," a person who swears under oath that he or she believes the factual allegations of the complaint to be true. The complainant usually will be either the victim or the investigating police officer. When an officer-complainant did not observe the offense being committed, but relied on information received from the victim or other witnesses, the officer ordinarily will note that the allegations in the complaint are based on "information and belief."

(d) Magistrate Review of the Arrest. Following the filing of the complaint and prior to or at the start of the first appearance (see below), the magistrate must undertake what is often described as the "*Gerstein* review." As prescribed by the Supreme Court's decision in *Gerstein v. Pugh* (1975), if the accused was arrested without a warrant and remains in custody (the situation in the vast majority of felony cases), the magistrate must determine that there exists probable cause for the continued detention of the arrestee for the offense charged in the complaint. This ordinarily is an *ex parte* determination, similar to that made in the issuance of an arrest warrant, based upon allegations made in the complaint or an accompanying affidavit. If the magistrate finds that probable cause has not been established, she will direct the prosecution to promptly produce more information or release the arrested person. Such instances are exceedingly rare, however. Since a judicial probable cause determination already has been made where an arrest warrant was issued, a *Gerstein* review is not required in such cases.

(e) The First Appearance. As previously noted, the arrestee who is kept in custody must be presented before a magistrate within 24 or 48 hours. This appearance before the magistrate is commonly described as the "first appearance", although the terminology varies, with jurisdictions also using "preliminary appearance," "initial presentment," "preliminary arraignment," and "arraignment on the complaint." The first appearance often is a quite brief proceeding. Initially, the magistrate will make certain that the person before her is the person named in the complaint. The magistrate then will inform the defendant of the charge in the complaint and will note various rights that the defendant may have in further proceedings. The range of rights mentioned will vary from one jurisdiction to another. Commonly, the magistrate will inform the defendant of his right to remain silent and warn him that anything he says in court or to the police may be used against him at trial. In many felony cases, the magistrate also will advise the defendant of the next step in the process, the preliminary hearing, and will set a date for that hearing unless the defendant desires to waive it.

Where the felony defendant is not represented by counsel at the first appearance, the magistrate's responsibilities include making certain that the defendant is aware of his right to be represented by counsel, including representation by an attorney funded by the state if the defendant is indigent. In some jurisdictions, the indigency determination is made at the first appearance, and the magistrates initiates the particular system used for providing state-funded counsel on a finding of indigency. In others, the delivery system will be instituted by a public defender office or a pretrial services unit prior to the first appearance (see § 3.2(c)).

One of the most important first-appearance functions of the magistrate is to fix the terms under which the defendant can obtain his release from custody pending the disposition of the charges against him. This process is still known as "setting bail," although release today often is conditioned on non-financial conditions (see § 4.1). Setting bail requires consideration of various information relating to the alleged offense and offender, which typically is collected prior to the first appearance by a unit of the court (commonly a "pretrial services" unit) or at the first appearance itself. In many jurisdictions, various classes of arrestees are drug tested (typically using a urine sample) as part of this pre-appearance information collecting process. Available statistics indicate that, in metropolitan judicial districts, a substantial portion of felony defendants (e.g., 30–40%) fail to gain their release prior to the final disposition of their case (including some subject to preventative detention, see § 4.3).

(f) The Preliminary Hearing. The procedure commonly known as a "preliminary hearing" or "preliminary examination" (discussed in Ch. 6) and the process of grand jury review (discussed in Ch. 7) are both designed to provide independent screening of the prosecution's decision to charge. As noted in §§ 6.2 and 7.1, all but a handful of states require one or the other of these screening procedures in felony cases (absent a defense waiver), and roughly a third regularly make both procedures available to the defense in a majority of prosecutions. As in the *Gerstein* review (see § 1.2(d)), the preliminary hearing review is conducted by a magistrate, but it provides a quite different review structure. The preliminary hearing is an adversary proceeding in which both the defense and prosecution may present its witnesses and cross-examine opposing witnesses. The magistrate's function is to determine, based on the evidence presented, whether there is sufficient evidence supporting the charge set forth in the complaint to "bind the case over" to the next stage in the process (either review by a grand jury or the filing of an information in the trial court).

(g) Grand Jury Review. As discussed in § 7.1, eighteen states, the District of Columbia and the federal system grant defendants in all felony cases the right to be charged only after a grand jury has found the prosecution's evidence to be sufficient to support the proposed felony charge, as reflected in the grand jury's issuance of its own charging instrument, called an "indictment". Grand jury review differs from preliminary hearing review in several respects: the screening agency here is a group of laypersons (the grand jurors) rather than a magistrate; the proceeding is closed rather than open; and the proceeding is *ex parte* rather than adversary, with only the prosecutor presenting evidence. Other differences found in some but not all indictment jurisdictions include a higher level of proof to go forward (here, to issue an indictment) and the recognition of a legal authority of "nullification" (i.e., the grand jury has the right to refuse to indict where the evidence is sufficient to support the charge, but it concludes that prosecution would be unjust).

(h) The Filing of the Indictment or Information. If an indictment is issued, it will be filed with the state's trial court of general jurisdiction (a jurisdiction that includes felony trials). The indictment will replace the complaint as the accusatory instrument in the case. Where grand jury review either is not required or has been waived, an information will be filed with that trial court. Like the indictment, the information is a charging instrument which replaces the complaint, but it is issued by the prosecutor rather than the grand jury.

(i) Arraignment on the Information or Indictment. After the indictment or information has been filed, the defendant is arraigned—i.e., he is brought before the trial court, informed of the charges against him, and asked to enter a plea of guilty, not guilty, or, as is permitted under some circumstances, *nolo contendere*. See § 13.4(a). In the end, most of those felony defendants whose cases reach the trial court will plead guilty. At the arraignment, however, they are likely to enter a plea of not guilty. Where there has not been a preliminary hearing, defense counsel probably will not be apprized of the strength of the prosecution's case (pretrial discovery not yet having started). Also, in most jurisdictions, guilty pleas in felony cases are the product of plea negotiations with the prosecution, and in many communities, that process too does not start until after the arraignment. When the defendant enters a plea of not guilty at the arraignment, the judge will set a trial date, but the expectation generally is that the trial will not be held.

(j) Pretrial Motions. In most jurisdictions, a broad range of objections may be raised by a pretrial motion. Those motions commonly present challenges to the institution of the prosecution (e.g., claims regarding the grand jury indictment process), attacks upon the sufficiency of the charging instrument, challenges to the scope, location, and timing of the prosecution (claiming improper joinder of charges or parties, improper venue, or violation of speedy trial requirements), and requests for the suppression of evidence allegedly obtained through a constitutional violation. The legal restrictions that establish the grounds for most, but not all, such motions are discussed in Chapters 5–11. While some types of pretrial motions are made almost exclusively by the small percentage of defendants who intend to go to trial, others will also be seen as advantageous by the much larger group of defendants who, in the end, anticipate negotiating a guilty plea. Nevertheless, pretrial motions are likely to be made in only a small portion of the felony cases that reach the trial court. Their use does vary considerably, however, with the nature of the case. In narcotics cases, for example, motions to suppress are quite common. In the typical forgery case, on the other, pretrial motions of any type are quite rare.

(k) Pretrial Discovery. Pretrial discovery is the process by which the prosecution and defense mutually disclose to each other some aspects of the evidence that they could possibly present at trial (if the case should go to trial). At least as to the prosecution, discovery requirements also go beyond potential trial evidence to include other information that might be useful to the defense in preparing its case. As discussed in Ch. 12, states vary considerably in the scope of the disclosure required as to both types of information.

(*l*) Plea Negotiation and Plea Acceptance. Guilty pleas account for the disposition of the majority of felony arrests. The ratio of guilty pleas to trials can readily be 12 to 1 in a metropolitan judicial districts. The guilty pleas in felony cases are usually the product of a system of plea negotiation (commonly described as "plea bargaining") in which the prosecution offers certain concessions in return for the defendant entering a guilty plea. As described in § 13.1, those concessions can take a variety of forms.

Guilty pleas must be reviewed by the court prior to their acceptance. The focus here is on ensuring that the defendant is aware of the consequence of entering a guilty plea and the terms of the plea bargaining, if any. See § 13.4. Following the acceptance of the guilty plea, the court will set a date for sentencing.

(m) The Trial. Assuming that there has not been a dismissal and the defendant has not entered a guilty plea, the next step in the criminal process is the trial. In most respects, the criminal trial resembles the civil trial. There are, however, several distinguishing features that are either unique to criminal trials or of special importance in such trials. These include (1) the presumption of defendant's innocence, (2) the requirement of proof beyond a reasonable doubt, (3) the right of the defendant not to take the stand, (4) the exclusion of evidence obtained by the state in an illegal manner, and (5) the more frequent use of incriminating statements of defendants.

Where the trial is to a jury, the trial will be preceded by a variety of procedures used in the selection of the jury. These include the *voir dire* of prospective jurors and the exercise of challenges for cause and peremptory challenges (see § 14.3). While defendants have a right to a jury trial, jurisdictions are divided as to whether they can insist on the alternative of a bench trial over the objection of the prosecutor (see § 14.1(h)). Over the nation as a whole, there are far more jury trials than bench trials in felony cases, but various individual judicial districts have a tradition of heavy use of bench trials, and bench trials are fairly common in almost all districts as to certain types of cases.

The basic requirements as to jury size (12 in most jurisdictions) and the juror vote needed for a verdict (unanimity in most jurisdictions) are discussed in § 14.1. Where the jury cannot reach the agreement needed for a verdict, it is described as a "hung jury." This non-verdict permits a retrial. After an acquittal, retrial on the same charge is precluded by the prohibition against double jeopardy (see § 17.3).

Whether a criminal case is tried to the bench or the jury, the odds favor conviction over acquittal. A fairly typical ratio for felony charges will be three convictions for every acquittal. That ratio may vary significantly, however, with the nature of the offense. In some jurisdictions, the rate of conviction at trial tends to be substantially lower (though still well above 50%) for some crimes (e.g., rape) than for others (e.g., drug trafficking).

(n) Sentencing. Following conviction by guilty plea or trial, the next step in the process is the determination of the sentence. Although the judge imposes the sentence, the character of the judge's role in setting the sentence varies with the sentencing structure established in the jurisdiction's sentencing legislation. As discussed in § 18.1, several different basic structures may be adopted for felony sentencing. Moreover, jurisdictions often vary the structure according to the sanction under consideration or the type of offense (see § 18.2). The most common structures as to sentences of incarceration are: (1) a structure that basically sets the sentence by legislation and leaves the judge to do nothing more than impose that sentence; (2) a structure that grants the judge considerable discretion in setting a sentence (e.g., setting a cap as to severity, but allowing the choice of any lesser sentence); and (3) a structure that requires the judge to consider certain types of aggravating or mitigating factors, to make findings as to the presence of those factors, and to shape the sentence (or at least give serious consideration to shaping the sentence) in accord with those factors. To a large extent, the procedures employed in sentencing will vary with the structure. The most complex procedures are associated with the third structure noted above, although those procedures still fall short of replicating a trial (see § 18.4).

Apart from the first structure described above, the court usually will need to consider information beyond that which came to its attention in the course of a trial or the acceptance of a guilty plea. As discussed in § 18.5, the primary vehicle for collecting and conveying that information is the presentence report prepared by the trial court's probation department, although the prosecution and defense will be allowed to present additional information.

(*o*) **Appeals.** A substantial majority of the states, along with the federal system, have an intermediate appellate court as well as an appellate court of last resort. In these jurisdictions, rulings of trial court are appealed to the intermediate court (typically as a matter of right), with any subsequent appeal to the higher court resting in the discretion of that court. Because of double jeopardy limitations (see Ch. 17), prosecution appeals are limited primarily to adverse pretrial rulings (typically those that result in the dismissal of the prosecution, see § 19.3). In general, the defense may not appeal at the point of an adverse pretrial ruling, but must wait until after conviction and sentence (see §§ 19.2, 19.4). At that point, the defense appeal can challenge all of the rulings that led to the conviction. As to sentence, the scope of appellate review varies with the sentencing structure, and may be limited to procedural error or may allow also challenges to the substance of the sentence (see Ch. 18).

Although all convicted defendants are entitled to appeal their convictions, appeals are taken predominantly by convicted defendants who were sentenced to imprisonment. Though the trial court's acceptance of a guilty plea may be challenged on appeal, the grounds for such appellate challenges are limited. Thus, the portion of all appeals presented by guilty plea defendants is likely to be fairly small, unless the jurisdiction permits broad review of sentencing. In such jurisdictions, appeals limited to challenging the sentence can constitute a substantial portion (e.g., 20–30%) of all felony appeals, and many of those are by guilty plea defendants.

Because of the heavy rate of guilty pleas, and the significant portion of sentences not requiring incarceration, appeals challenging convictions may readily number less than 10% of all felony convictions. State intermediate appellate courts commonly have a reversal rate on defense appeals of convictions in the 5–10% range, although those rates will be somewhat higher when reversals in part are included. Courts of last resort, with discretionary jurisdiction, tend to have a substantially higher rate of reversals than the intermediate appellate courts, as they grant review in cases presenting close questions. Where a state defendant presented unsuccessfully a federal constitutional claim in his state appeal, he may seek further review on that claim by the Supreme Court of the United States, but the Supreme Court grants review (by granting a petition for a writ of certiorari) in only a minute portion of the petitions seeking such review.

(p) Collateral Remedies. After the appellate process is exhausted, convicted defendants who remain subject to custodial restraints may be able to use special post-appeal procedures to challenge their convictions, although the available grounds for challenge tend to be limited. Since these procedures are separate from the basic criminal justice process (indeed, many are viewed as civil in nature), they are described as "collateral remedies." The writ of habeas corpus is the traditional vehicle for a collateral attack upon a conviction, but many jurisdictions have created alternative vehicles (commonly known as "postconviction remedies"). Congress has created a federal postconviction remedy that is available to state prisoners to challenge their convictions on constitutional grounds in federal courts. See § 20.2.

§ 1.3   The Laws Regulating the Process

(a) Varied Sources. In each jurisdiction, several different sources of legal regulation will combine to regulate the different steps in the criminal justice process. For cases in the federal system, the primary sources are: (1) the United States Constitution; (2) federal statutes; (3) the Federal Rules of Criminal Procedure; (4) rulings of federal courts based on their common law decisional authority or their supervisory authority over the administration of criminal justice (as contrasted to rulings interpreting the Constitution, statutes, or court rules); and (5) the internal regulations of the Department of Justice and other agencies involved in the administration of the federal criminal justice process. At the state level, an even larger group of sources come into play. The legal standards applicable to the post-investigation portion of the process will come primarily from seven different sources: (1) the United States Constitution; (2) federal statutes; (3) the state's constitution; (4) the state's statutes; (5) the state's general court rules; (6) rulings of the state's courts based on their common law authority or their supervisory authority; and (7) the internal administrative standards of those state and local agencies involved in the administration of the process. The subsections that follow discuss the general character of each of the different sources, using the larger group of sources applicable to a state system.

(b) The Federal Constitution. The natural starting point in examining the law governing a particular procedure is the federal constitution. Under Article VI, the mandates of the federal constitution are the "Supreme Law of the Land." Thus, those mandates prevail over conflicting federal law from other sources (e.g., federal statutes), and where the constitutional mandates apply to the state system, they prevail over conflicting state law as well. As discussed in § 2.1, not all of the mandates of the federal constitution relating to the criminal justice process have been held applicable to the states. However, in its application of the selective incorporation doctrine (see § 2.1(d)), the Supreme Court has held that the Fourteenth Amendment makes applicable to the states most of the specific Bill of Rights provisions that relate to the post-investigative process. Also, the Fourteenth Amendment's due process clause has an independent regulatory content that has been extended, in particular, to post-investigative procedures. See § 2.2.

As to some aspects of the process, these federal constitutional provisions, as interpreted by the United States Supreme Court, provide a comprehensive regulatory scheme. Thus, the Supreme Court has developed through the double jeopardy clause a series of standards that determine under what circumstances the granting of a mistrial will preclude further prosecution. See § 17.2. In most states, those constitutional standards represent the only law on that subject. Reprosecution is prohibited where barred by the double jeopardy clause and permitted where the double jeopardy prohibition does not apply. However, states remain free to set standards more stringent than the constitutional prohibition, and in several states, retrials are prohibited by state law even though they would not be prohibited by the Supreme Court's double jeopardy rulings. In many areas of constitutional regulation, as with retrials, only a small group of states will have imposed more stringent regulations. However, in others areas, more rigorous state requirements are commonplace. Thus, the Sixth Amendment right to jury trial does not require jury unanimity to convict or acquit, but all but a few states impose that requirement. See § 14.1(e).

For many steps in the post-investigation process, federal constitutional regulation is limited to only a few features of the particular procedure. As to the preliminary hearing, for example, the Constitution's solitary requirement is that the state provide counsel for an accused who is indigent. State law governs such issues as: when is an accused entitled to a preliminary hearing (assuming no arbitrary discrimination, such as a racial dividing line, that would violate equal protection); what evidence will be admitted at the preliminary hearing; what adversarial rights (e.g., cross-examination of witnesses) will be granted the defense; and what standard of evidentiary sufficiency will be applied in determining whether the prosecution must be dismissed or can go forward. Many other aspects of the post-investigation process, particularly pretrial stages of the process, also are only lightly regulated by the federal constitution as currently interpreted.

(c) Federal Statutes. In general, federal statutes regulating criminal procedure apply only to the federal system, and serve the role of local statutory regulation discussed in subsection (e) below. However, a limited body of federal legislation (e.g., the federal wiretap statute) applies to both the state and federal criminal justice systems. Prohibitions and restrictions contained in such statutes prevail over state provisions, and they therefore must be applied by state courts in state prosecutions even though the practices prohibited or restricted would pose no difficulty under state law alone. Such statutes are largely confined, however, to the investigative stages of the process.

(d) State Constitutions. Every state has a series of constitutional provisions that guarantee certain rights of the defendant and limit governmental authority in the administration of the criminal justice process. In large part, these state constitutional provisions cover the same ground as the criminal procedure guarantees in the Bill of Rights of the Constitution. However, a state court may read its state's constitutional guarantee as imposing a more stringent limitation upon the prosecution than the corresponding federal guarantee. Also some state guarantees are distinct from any of the federal guarantees and provide constitutional rights of a type not found in the federal constitution (e.g., a state constitutional guarantee of a defendant's right to appeal a conviction).

(e) State Statutes. The federal system, the District of Columbia, and each of the states has an extensive group of statutory provisions regulating the criminal justice process. Initially, each jurisdiction has a series of sequentially presented provisions that typically are described as the jurisdiction's "code of criminal procedure." In only about a third of the jurisdictions, however, are these statutes truly codifications of the law of criminal procedure. In those jurisdictions, the "code" does set forth all of the basic governing standards, often accompanied by considerable procedural detail, in a conceptually integrated, comprehensive pattern of regulation. Such statutes typically have provisions on various aspects of post-investigative procedure, including: jurisdictional requirements; commencement of prosecutions in magistrate courts; first appearance of arrested persons; venue; pretrial release; preliminary hearings; grand jury proceedings; pleading requirements (indictments and informations); scope of the prosecution (joinder); arraignments in the trial court; timelines of proceedings; pretrial procedures; pleas; jury procedures; securing attendance of witnesses; entry of verdict; sentencing; victim's rights; post-trial motions; appeals; and extradition and detainers.

In some states, the criminal procedure codes are little more than a loose conglomeration of criminal procedure statutes, providing coverage of only the basic structural elements of the prosecution (e.g., jurisdiction and venue). Still other states have a "code" that is more than a loose conglomeration, but less than a comprehensive, integrated code. Jurisdictions in this category, along with jurisdictions with loose conglomerations, tend to rely on court rules to cover matters not reached in the statutes.

(f) Court Rules. In the federal system, the Federal Rules of Criminal Procedure play a very significant role in the regulation of the post-investigation criminal process, covering various topics (e.g., joinder, discovery, and suppression motions) that are not treated in the U.S. Code. The District of Columbia and roughly two-thirds of the states have their own general court rules, similar in function to the Federal Rules. Indeed, in some of these states, court rules govern subjects, such as speedy trial and bail, as to which legislation dominates in the federal system. Court rules are limited to matters of "practice and procedure," but that characterization can easily encompass all of the procedures discussed in later chapters. However, in the federal system and in a substantial number of the states with court rules, the legislature has the last word in prescribing standards as to matters that could be regulated by court rule.

(g) Common Law Rulings. For over a century, common law rulings were the primary source of the law governing the criminal justice process in the states. However, the introduction of comprehensive codes of criminal procedure, followed by the adoption in many states of extensive court rules, and then by the constitutionalization of the law of criminal procedure, combined to sharply reduce the role of common law rulings. Today, for all but a few states, the legal standards governing most aspects of the criminal justice process come from a combination of the federal constitution, the state's own constitution, state statutes, and state court rules (all subject, of course, to judicial interpretation). Common law rulings still dominate, however, as to certain aspects of courtroom procedure, such as the regulation of closing arguments.

Federal courts, unlike their state counterparts, are courts of limited jurisdiction that have not been vested with "open-ended lawmaking powers," and they therefore lack authority to fashion a "general" federal common law covering the total range of substantive common law subjects. Federal courts did recognize from the outset, however, an authority to fashion common law rules of procedure where Congress had not otherwise provided. Over the years, however, federal courts have made far less use of common law rules of procedure than state courts. This has been due in part to the Supreme Court's acceptance of a concept of supervisory authority over federal criminal justice which provides a grounding for judicially imposed procedural requirements that state courts ordinarily would prescribe as common law standards. Use of this grounding avoids concerns as to federal court authority to prescribe common law rules and also allows creation of standards without having to look initially to the traditional common law standards governing the particular subject.

(h) Supervisory Authority Rulings. *McNabb v. U.S.* (1943) first announced a federal court authority to establish decisional rules of criminal procedure in the exercise of the court's "supervisory authority over the administration of criminal justice in the federal courts." At issue in *McNabb* was the admission of confessions obtained from arrestees who allegedly had been detained and interrogated by government agents for two days before being taken before a federal magistrate. The Court viewed the detention as a "flagrant disregard" of a federal statutory requirement that an arrested person promptly be brought before the nearest judicial officer. The Court acknowledged that this federal statute did not itself require exclusion of statements obtained during a detention that violated the statutory command. However, the Court had an obligation, stemming from the obligations of "judicial supervision of the administration of criminal justice in the federal courts," to maintain "civilized standards of procedure and evidence in those courts." That duty mandated exclusion of the confessions, for to allow their use as the grounding of a conviction "would stultify the policy" underlying the prompt presentment statute and make "the courts themselves accomplices in willful disobedience of law." The Court clearly did not base this ruling on the common law development of the rules of evidence. That would have required it to square its ruling with common law precedent, which had tied exclusion to the potential untrustworthiness of the individual confession and the possible invasion of some common law privilege of the accused.

The scope of the supervisory authority of the Supreme Court was not clearly defined in *McNabb*. The Court did stress that it was "not concerned with law enforcement practices except insofar as courts themselves became instruments of enforcement." Where the judicial process did become involved, however, *McNabb*'s broad description of the Court's supervisory authority suggested that the Court could shape its own standards of fairness, even apart from situations presenting a statutory violation. That came to pass in a series of later Supreme Court rulings relating to the role of trial courts in regulating the litigation process. The supervisory power was relied upon to establish general procedural standards for such matters as contempt proceedings, jury selection and disqualification, discovery and disclosure, and the permissible scope of cross-examination. However, in many of the Court's supervisory power decisions, the Court's reasoning clearly had constitutional overtones, suggesting that the procedure being required might well be constitutionally mandated. Reliance upon the supervisory power was preferred, however, as it avoided the consequences that would flow from a constitutional ruling.

U.S. v. Hasting (1983) reexamined the scope of the Court's supervisory power. It characterized "the purposes underlying the use of the supervisory powers * * * [as] threefold: to implement a remedy for violation of recognized rights * * *; to preserve judicial integrity by ensuring that a conviction rests on appropriate considerations validly before the jury * * *; and finally, as a remedy designed to deter illegal conduct." Lower courts subsequently sought to extend the judicial integrity grounding to dismiss indictments or exclude evidence based on an action of the prosecutor or police, taken apart from the judicial proceeding, that was viewed as "misconduct" although not prohibited by statute, court rule, or constitutional provision. As discussed in § 7.5(b), in *U.S. v. Williams* (1992), the Supreme Court rejected one line of such rulings and cast doubt upon the validity in general of using the supervisory authority to create misconduct standards for activities outside of the litigation process.

Williams reasoned that, in dealing with grand jury proceedings (proceedings that clearly were not part of the court's own proceedings), the court's supervisory powers could be used to implement legal restrictions on prosecutorial presentations found in a statute, court rule, or constitutional restraint, but could not be used to create additional restrictions on prosecutorial presentations. That rationale could readily be extended to bar, as a general matter, the judicial creation of prosecutorial misconduct standards for all portions of the criminal justice process in which the judiciary is not itself directly involved. However, the *Williams* opinion also stressed the institutional independence of the grand jury, and some lower courts view *Williams* as largely limited to that context insofar as it restricts integrity-grounded exercises of supervisory authority.

The first and third uses of supervisory authority noted in *Hastings* relate to fashioning remedies for violations of rights recognized elsewhere in federal law. That use of the supervisory power was established as far back as *McNabb* and *Williams* reaffirmed its legitimacy in acknowledging supervisory authority to dismiss indictments where the prosecutor violated standards set forth in a statute, court rule, or constitutional command. However, this exercise of supervisory authority has also been narrowed in post-*McNabb* rulings. Two Supreme Court rulings, *U.S. v. Payner* (1980) and *Hasting* itself, hold that, in fashioning supervisory authority remedies for constitutional violations, lower federal courts "are not free to disregard the limitations the Supreme Court has deliberately placed on constitutional remedies," and a third, *Bank of Nova Scotia v. U.S.* (1988) extended that reasoning to non-constitutional limitations.

Payner held that a federal court could not utilize its supervisory authority to bypass limitations found in Fourth Amendment remedial law. In response to a deliberate unconstitutional search, the lower court there had prohibited prosecution use of the fruits of that search against a target of an investigation whose privacy was not invaded by the search. Since that remedy was contrary to Fourth Amendment rulings that had limited the exclusionary remedy to the victim of the search, it could not be imposed under the court's supervisory power. *Hasting* similarly held that a lower court could not utilize its supervisory power to fashion a remedy of automatic reversal of a trial conviction, based on the prosecutor's persistent disregard of a constitutional prohibition against adverse comment on the defendant's failure to testify, since the Supreme Court had earlier announced that the Constitution did not require a reversal if a violation of that prohibition constituted harmless error. *Bank of Nova Scotia* (§ 7.5(e)), held that a federal court may not invoke its supervisory role to craft a remedy inconsistent with remedial limitations imposed by a statute or a Federal Rule of Criminal Procedure (here too, a prohibition against reversal if the non-constitutional violation constituted harmless error).

(i) Internal Administrative Standards. All of the major participants in the administration of the criminal process are subject to regulation by what are commonly characterized as "internal administrative standards." These largely take the form of performance guidelines issued by police and prosecutor agencies for their employees, and the professional responsibility standards of lawyer-licensing agencies, which govern both prosecutors and defense counsel.

The objective of such standards is not to create regulations to be enforced by courts within the criminal justice process, but to set performance standards for the actors that will be enforced through employment or licensing sanctions. Nonetheless, prior to the Supreme Court's ruling in *U.S. v. Caceres* (1979), some federal lower courts, relying on their supervisory power, had enforced internal administrative standards by excluding evidence obtained by the government in violation of those standards. The *Caceres* Court ruled against exclusion in an opinion that extended well beyond the facts of the particular violation of agency regulations presented there (a violation of IRS regulations requiring the advance authorization of a Justice Department official, prior to electronic recording by an undercover agent of conversations with a suspected criminal). The Court noted that "regulations governing the conduct of criminal investigations are generally considered desirable," and the courts should not discourage use of such regulations by the rigid application of an exclusionary rule to every regulatory violation. "In the long run", the Court noted, "it is far better to have rules like those contained in the IRS Manual, and to tolerate occasional erroneous administration of the kind displayed by this record, than either to have no rules except those mandated by statute, or to have them framed in a mere precatory form."

The *Caceres* opinion did not rule out the possibility that judicial relief might be available where a breach of regulations presented an exceptionally compelling case. Neither did it have before it one of those situations in which the government's failure to comply with its own regulations served to establish a constitutional violation, either because the constitutionality of the governmental action was dependent on adherence to a standard policy, or because "the individual * * * reasonably relied on agency regulations promulgated for his guidance or benefit and has suffered substantially because of their violation by the agency." Still, when Congress adopted a statute requiring that federal prosecutors abide by the state Rules of Professional Responsibility for the state in which they prosecuted, lower federal courts uniformly concluded that the statute did not create a defense right and could not be remedied through sanctions applied in the criminal justice process (e.g., quashing a subpoena or dismissing an indictment), but simply a standard to be applied in a disciplinary proceeding.

§ 1.4   The Cornerstone Objectives of the Process

As noted in § 1.1(b), considerable variation exists from one jurisdiction to another in the laws governing the criminal justice process. Nonetheless, several common objectives are reflected in the laws of all fifty-two jurisdictions. This group of "cornerstone" objectives shape the basic structure of the process and the most fundamental of its governing legal principles. Many of these cornerstone objectives are mandated by the federal constitution, but their widespread acceptance was not dependent upon that constitutional command. Almost all of the cornerstone objectives were well established in the state systems long before the states were subjected, *via* the post civil war adoption of the Fourteenth Amendment (and its subsequent judicial interpretation), to significant regulation by the federal constitution. See § 2.1(d).

While there may be some minor disagreements as to whether one or the other of the objectives discussed below properly is characterized as cornerstone objective, there clearly are extensive divisions on such issues as the appropriate scope of a particular objective, whether each objective should be weighed against other objectives in determining its scope, and if so, exactly how that balance should be achieved. Those divisions often explain, in large part, the basic differences among states in the structure and legal regulation of their criminal justice processes. Courts, in interpreting statutes, court rules, and even constitutional provisions, commonly view the judicial role as applying the basic choices as to implementing and balancing these goals that were previously made by the lawmakers who adopted the provision in question. Nonetheless, at least where ambiguity exists, the judge is likely to be influenced by his or her personal perspective on those issues. Specific disagreements as to how a cornerstone objective should shape a particular aspect of the criminal justice process will be considered in later chapters. Our purpose here merely is to identify the general character of each of the cornerstone objectives and to point to some of the major structural elements of the post-investigation portion of the criminal justice process that reflect a particular objective.

(a) Implementing the Enforcement of the Substantive Law. "Legal procedure," Roscoe Pound long ago noted, "is a means, not an end; it must be made subsidiary to the substantive law as a means of making that law effective in action." While a procedure also may promote values that are independent of the aims of the substantive law, Pound was certainly correct in characterizing the *raison d'etre* of any procedural system as the practical implementation of the substantive law. As applied to the criminal justice process, this universal starting point mandates a process that promotes effective enforcement of the substantive criminal law—that is, a process through which the government can detect, apprehend, prosecute, convict, and impose punishment upon those who have violated the prohibitions of the substantive criminal law.

While efficient enforcement provides the initial objective of any criminal justice system, it is not the only objective. Other values also contribute to the structure of a criminal justice process even though they may lessen efficiency. A major point of debate, as to the American criminal justice system, is which of the other objectives discussed below have been adopted because they are viewed as implementing effective enforcement, and which have been adopted as a result of a balancing process in which other values were held to outweigh achieving maximum efficiency. In large part, the answer to that question depends upon how one defines the concept of efficient enforcement.

One view, commonly described as presenting the "crime control" model of efficiency, proceeds from the classical utilitarian justification of punishment. Efficiency under this view seeks a rate of apprehension and conviction that will deter future criminal behavior, taking account of the limited resources available to law enforcement. A strict application of the crime control model would view as inconsistent all of the additional objectives discussed below, since the conviction of criminals could be achieved most efficiently through a an administrative determination of guilt by police and prosecutor (rendering unnecessary our current structure of adjudication). While such a system presumably would result in a greater level of "overconvictions" (i.e., convictions of the innocent) than our current adjudicative process, that presumably would not detract from the deterrent function of enforcement.

A contrary position views efficiency from the perspective of a "just deserts" theory of punishment. This position requires of effective enforcement not only the apprehension and conviction of the guilty, but also the avoidance of the conviction of the innocent. From this perspective, the objective of factfinding accuracy is not simply consistent with effective enforcement, but actually an essential element of that enforcement. Accordingly, insofar as the cornerstone objectives (e.g., an adversary process of adjudication) create a structure that best serves the end of discovery of the truth, those objective also promotes effective law enforcement. However, insofar as an objective serves other ends, particularly where those ends are truth-deflecting, it interferes with ideal enforcement (which convicts as many guilty persons as possible, without also convicting the innocent). Under this position, there is a need to engage in a balancing analysis that weighs the loss to effective enforcement only when the cornerstone objective at issue is non-truth-seeking in character.

This second position has gained the greater support among lawmakers. In considering the adoption of a new procedure designed to implement a cornerstone objective unrelated to the discovery of the truth, legislators (very often) and judges (with somewhat less frequency) refer to the need for a balancing process. They look to the likely negative impact of the proposed procedural requirement upon effective law enforcement, and will reject the proposal where they conclude that it therefore is not in the public interest. Where courts require a new procedure implementing such an objective without weighing the impact on law enforcement, they often note that balancing by the court is not needed because the legislation or constitutional provision being interpreted has already struck a balance (in favor of the cornerstone objective). In contrast, where the new procedure is viewed as implementing a truth-seeking cornerstone objective, lawmakers rarely suggest a need for a balancing analysis, but tend to focus instead on administrative feasibility and the effectiveness of the procedure in implementing the cornerstone objective.

(b) Discovery of the Truth. As applied in the criminal justice process, truth-finding has two elements (1) the uncovering of crimes and (2) the determination as to who did, and who did not, commit the crime. The Supreme Court has described the discovery of the truth as a "fundamental goal" of the criminal justice system and the "central purpose of a criminal trial," and lower courts regularly have echoed such characterizations.

Various elements of the post-investigative process are directed at promoting discovery of the truth. The basic adjudicative process is aimed, in large part, at achieving reliability in both convicting the guilty defendant and exonerating the defendant who is erroneously accused. The quest for such reliability underlies many elements of the trial, including its adversary structure, prohibitions against certain potentially deceptive actions of the adversaries, evidentiary rules promoting the production of reliable evidence, disqualification standards aimed at eliminating jurors and judges who are likely to be biased (either in favor of the state or the defendant), and restrictions on the scope of a single trial (designed to preclude a mixing of issues that could confuse a factfinder). Various pretrial procedures, such as providing pretrial discovery of the opponent's case, are aimed at supplementing the capacity of the trial procedures to produce a reliable verdict. Legal restrictions imposed upon adjudication through a guilty plea similarly serve, in part, to ensure the reliability of convictions produced by that process.

Notwithstanding its importance, the truthfinding objective will, in certain respects, be sacrificed for the benefit of other values. As one court put it: "[T]ruth, like all other good things, may be loved unwisely—may be pursued too keenly—may cost too much." Consequently, there comes a point at which factfinding accuracy must give way to other values that are truth deflecting. Most of the values prevailing over truthfinding relate to substantive norms of "fairness," such as preserving human dignity and personal autonomy. Some of the legal standards implementing those substantive norms operate to prevent the discovery of reliable, relevant evidence (or to bar the use of such evidence when discovered through a violation of those norms). Thus, the privilege against self-incrimination prohibits the state from compelling the defendant to give incriminating testimony and the Fourth Amendment both bars unreasonable searches and seizures to obtain evidence and prohibits the state's use in its case-in-chief of evidence obtained through an unreasonable search and seizure. Standards implementing other fairness norms bar conviction notwithstanding ample evidence of guilt that has been fairly obtained. Thus, the Fifth Amendment's double jeopardy prohibition and Sixth Amendment's speedy trial requirement, though they sometimes operate as a safeguard against potentially unreliable factfinding, also bar conviction even where the retrial or delay casts no doubt upon the accuracy of the conviction.

Although truth-deflecting values commonly operate to benefit the defendant, that is not always the case. Respect for such values also may operate to keep the defendant from obtaining testimony or other evidence that would be exculpatory. This often occurs, for example, where a witness potentially helpful to the defense is excused from testifying on the exercise of a testimonial privilege (e.g., the self-incrimination privilege).

(c) Adversary Adjudication. The American criminal justice process also is structured to adjudicate guilt through a process that is basically adversary in character. An adversary system of adjudication vests decisionmaking authority, both as to law and fact, in a neutral decisionmaker who is to render a decision in light of the materials presented by the adversary parties. In an adversary criminal proceeding, there often will be two such neutral decisionmakers, the jury (as to factual issues) and the judge (as to legal issues); the adversary parties are the prosecution (not the victim) and the defense. The decisionmaker in a pure adversary system operates as "a generally silent referee, determining the case as it is presented, and leaving it very much to the parties to choose the battleground." The adversary model gives to the parties the responsibility of investigating the facts, interviewing possible witnesses, consulting possible experts, and determining what will or will not be told. Each party is expected to present the facts and interpret the law in a light most favorable to its side, and through a searching counter-argument and cross-examination, to challenge the soundness of the presentations made by the other side. The judge and jury are then to adjudicate impartially the issues presented by the opposing presentations.

The American criminal justice process actually seeks a "modified" or "regulated" adversary system as opposed to the "pure" adversary model described above. It does not provide for a totally silent or inactive judge; it seeks to prohibit "excesses" in adversary presentations; and it will in certain respects impose a duty on each party to assist the other in gathering information. Even with these controls, however, the American criminal justice process remains sufficiently adversarial in its overall character to stand in sharp contrast to the "inquisitorial" or "nonadversary" structure that traditionally prevailed in continental Europe. Under that structure, the primary responsibility for the initial development of relevant facts lies with a judicial officer or a prosecutor, who is required to collect all relevant evidence (both incriminating and exculpatory) in a comprehensive dossier and to bring charges if that evidence establishes a likelihood of guilt. Once the accusation is filed, the trial court assumes responsibility for the further development of the case and the presentation of evidence, including a dominant role in questioning witnesses. Although the prosecutor and defense counsel have an opportunity to contribute, their role is far more limited than the role of counsel in the American trial.

The adversary system's supposed advantage over the inquisitorial system in achieving accurate verdicts rests on two assumptions: (1) the self-interest of each side is more likely to produce all relevant evidence, and as each side, through searching inquiry, challenges the soundness of the case presented by the other side, the strengths and weaknesses of the evidence will be more fully explored; and (2) because the decisionmakers are not themselves involved in the development of the facts, they are more likely to approach the evidence at trial in an uncommitted fashion and delay reaching a decision until the case is fully explored. The adversary system is so well established in this country that debate as to the validity of these assumptions is largely mooted, although debate continues as to the need for further regulations to curb adversary excesses and to ensure that the defense has sufficient resources to challenge the state.

Although courts commonly stress the value of the adversary system in achieving accurate verdicts, they sometimes also cite the other values promoted by the adversary system. Consistent with the premise that the individual is the source of the government's sovereignty, the adversary system treats the defendant as an equal to the prosecution. The adversary system also respects individual autonomy in its commitment to the individual's self-control over the basic mode of his participation in the adjudicatory process. The defendant may play an active role in his own defense. Indeed, if he so desires, he may decide to forego his defense and plead guilty. The adversary system recognizes, as the Supreme Court has noted, the "inestimable worth of free choices." This, in turn, is said to increase the defendant's level of confidence in the process and acceptance of even adverse results.

(d) Accusatorial Burdens. The American criminal justice process is designed to be accusatorial as well as adversarial. The concepts of adversarial adjudication and accusatorial procedure complement each other, but are not virtual equivalents. The adversarial element assigns to the participants the responsibility for developing the legal and factual issues of the case, while the accusatorial element allocates burdens as between the parties with respect to the adjudication of guilt. An accusatorial process places on the government the burden of establishing the guilt of the accused and requires it to do so without forcing the accused to assist it in that task. The accusatorial process is viewed as an important component of the protection against the possible conviction of the innocent, but it is supported also by other rationales. As the party initiating a judicial proceeding, the government is viewed as naturally assuming the proof responsibilities borne by a plaintiff in any litigation (although that does not explain all aspects of the accusatorial process). The accusatorial process also is justified as responding to a government capacity to gather and preserving evidence that far exceeds the capacity of the defense (a rationale sometimes criticized as improperly promoting a "sporting theory" of justice).

The accusatorial character of the criminal justice process is reflected in various elements of the process. The most significant of those elements are the placement upon the government of the ultimate burden of persuasion, the placement upon the government of the burden of going forward with the introduction of evidence, the presumption of innocence, and the defendant's privilege against self-incrimination.

Although an important element of an accusatorial process, the principle that the state establish its case independently, without requiring the accused to assist it, is confined largely to the historical prohibition against the state's use of coercion to prove its charge against an accused "out of his own mouth," (a prohibition reflected, in part, in the privilege against compelled self-incrimination). The accusatorial process does not prevent the state from offering the accused an opportunity to relieve the state of its burden by entering a guilty plea, from offering concessions in return for such a plea, and even from using certain types of deception or encouragement to obtain a confession that will be its primary evidence of guilt. Nor does it bar requiring the accused to participate in identification procedures and to submit to a search of his person, where the state has a proper grounding for such actions. Although such investigative procedures involve, to some extent, the assistance of the accused, they have been accepted as consistent with the basic tenets of an accusatorial process.

(e) Minimizing Erroneous Convictions. While the accusatory and adversary elements of the criminal justice process are designed in part to minimize the likelihood of erroneous convictions, protection of the innocent accused against an erroneous conviction is an important independent goal of the process. It's a goal that stands apart, as well, from reliable factfinding. While the objective of reliable factfinding is to ensure equally the accuracy of both guilty verdicts and acquittals, protection of the innocent gives priority to the accuracy of the guilty verdict. It reflects a desire to minimize the chance of convicting an innocent person even at the price of increasing the chance that a guilty person may escape conviction. Accordingly, while the Supreme Court has stated that "the basic purpose of the trial is the determination of the truth," it also has noted that impairment of the trial's "truthfinding function" is of primary concern where "serious questions [are raised] about the accuracy of guilty verdicts." For, as the Court also has observed, it is "a fundamental value determination of our system * * * that it is far worse to convict an innocent person than let a guilty man go free."

The goal of minimizing the risk of erroneous conviction is served by various legal standards that stand apart from ensuring factfinding accuracy on both sides. Included here are standards that relate to factfinding accuracy, but are aimed specifically at protecting the innocent accused. Thus, the adversarial system is modified to impose an obligation upon the prosecution to disclose to the defense material exculpatory evidence that is within its possession or control. Protection against erroneous convictions also is provided by legal standards that accord to the defendant the benefit of doubt as to his guilt. The most substantial protection of this type is provided by the requirement that the state establish guilt by proof beyond a reasonable doubt.

Like other cornerstone goals of the criminal justice process, protecting against the possible erroneous conviction of an innocent accused has its limits. The prosecution's burden of persuasion is set at proof beyond a reasonable doubt, not at a higher standard that requires absolute certainty in the mind of the jurors. So too, while eyewitness identification poses a recognized risk of mistake, convictions based upon such identifications are acceptable, subject to limited prerequisites. Similarly, though recognizing that confessions can be the product of false self-condemnation, the process permits evidentiary use of confessions, subject to constitutional safeguards.

(f) Minimizing the Burdens of Accusation and Litigation. Even if eventually acquitted, an innocent person charged with a crime suffers substantial burdens. The accusation casts a doubt on the person's reputation that is not easily erased. Moreover, even should an acquittal be accepted by the public as fully vindicating the accused, that does not respond to other burdens borne by a defendant in the course of gaining that acquittal. Unless the defendant is indigent, one such burden will be the financing of his defense, as an acquitted defendant is not thereby entitled to reimbursement of his expenses. Perhaps more significant are costs that cannot quite so readily be measured in dollars. Once accused, a defendant must await trial, and this waiting period brings with it a certain degree of anxiety and insecurity that disrupts the daily flow of life. That disruption is even greater, of course, if the accused is incarcerated pending trial. When the trial finally comes, the ordeal of litigation takes a further emotional toll.

In light of these substantial burdens, a criminal justice process concerned with the protection of the innocent cannot limit itself to ensuring against erroneous convictions. It must seek also to reduce to an acceptable level the risk that accusations will be brought against innocent persons. Because the burdens of an erroneous accusation are not as great as the burdens of an erroneous conviction, the acceptable degree of risk here can be somewhat greater. It is not necessary to limit accusations to cases thought likely beyond a reasonable doubt to produce a conviction, as that would cause the state to forego accusations in many cases in which valid convictions might eventually be obtained. Adequate protection against erroneous accusations does require, however, that accusations at least be supported by sufficient evidence to produce a fair likelihood of conviction. Thus, the prosecution's decision to proceed on a felony charge generally must survive the screening of a neutral decisionmaker (the grand jury in deciding whether to indict or the magistrate at a preliminary hearing).

The complementary goal of eliminating unnecessary litigation burdens is reflected in various other rights of the accused. Provisions for pretrial release on bail seek to avoid pretrial incarceration where there is an alternative means of reasonably assuring defendant's presence at trial. The defendant's right to a speedy trial is designed, in part, to limit the length of pretrial incarceration (where bail is not available) and to "minimize the anxiety and concern" of the accused pending trial. Venue requirements seek, in part, to ensure that the defendant will be tried in a convenient forum. The double jeopardy prohibition, supplemented by joinder requirements, also seeks to reduce the burdens of litigation by prohibiting repeated trials for the same offense.

(g) Providing Lay Participation. Another cornerstone of the American criminal justice process is the use of lay persons as decisionmakers. Traditionally, lay participation was provided through the trial jury (the "petit" jury), the grand jury, and the use of lay magistrates. Today, the trial jury stands alone as the only universally available source of lay participation. While a majority of the states continue to have some lay magistrates in their judiciaries, the vast bulk of the criminal cases in those states come before those magistrates who are lawyers. As for the grand jury, only twenty jurisdictions (18 states, the District of Columbia, and the federal system) continue to require grand jury participation (through a defense right to prosecution by indictment) for all felony cases.

Of course, the trial jury, in fact, also is not used in most criminal cases. Dismissals and guilty pleas account for far more dispositions than trials, and even as to trials, a fair number are bench trials upon election of the defendant. The defendant does have a *right* to a jury trial, however, in all jurisdictions on felony and serious misdemeanor charges, and in most states, the prosecution has an independent right also to insist upon a jury trial. Since many of the safeguards provided by lay juror participation are aimed at the exceptional case, the very availability of the jury at the election of the defendant, rather than the frequency of its use, is the critical feature in meeting most of the objectives of lay participation.

(h) Respecting the Dignity of the Individual. Perhaps the most sweeping cornerstone objective, as measured by the range of its ramifications, is the objective of ensuring that criminal justice administration is consistent with respect for the dignity of the individual. The concept of human dignity, as used in this context, is far from precise, but it may be described roughly as encompassing the basic needs of the human personality, including privacy, autonomy, and freedom from humiliation and abuse.

Requiring that criminal justice practices respect human dignity is justified on several grounds. First, it is argued that all persons, including criminals, are entitled to governmental respect for their dignity as an inherent element of the social compact which provides the foundation for a democratic society. Second, in light of the combination of the "severity of the sanctions administered by the criminal law," the "status-degrading potency of criminal proceedings," and the "community outrage" that tempts officials to solve crime at all costs, the preservation of human dignity in the administration of the criminal law is characterized as the *sine qua non* for maintaining a society that respects individual liberty. Finally, ensuring respect for individual dignity is viewed as essential in obtaining public acceptance of the process and in encouraging citizen cooperation in the enforcement of the law.

The insistence upon respect for individual dignity is reflected in numerous elements of the post-investigation portion of the criminal justice process. Many of the legal standards that implement other goals serve this objective as well. Thus, requirements promoting an adversary system of adjudication also take cognizance of individual dignity by giving the defendant an element of control over his own defense. Similarly, the privilege against self-incrimination, while an essential element of an accusatorial system, has also been described by the Supreme Court as based on "our respect for the inviolability of the human personality."

Still other legal requirements focus entirely on ensuring respect for human dignity. The prohibition against cruel and unusual punishment bars punishments which lower the honor and dignity of the individual. Insofar as the double jeopardy prohibition looks to granting the convicted defendant a sense of repose, as when it gives finality to a conviction (at the defendant's option), or restricts multiple punishments, that prohibition also limits the oppression to which the guilty can be subjected.

(i) Maintaining the Appearance of Fairness. The criminal justice process seeks not only to provide fair procedures, but also to maintain the appearance of fairness in the application of those procedures. As the Supreme Court has noted, "justice must satisfy the appearance of justice." That the criminal justice procedures are fair, in fact, is not sufficient; the procedures also must be perceived as fair (and as fairly administered) by both the public and the participants.

Legal requirements aimed primarily at maintaining a positive perception of the criminal justice process include a variety of laws guaranteeing the openness of the process. They also include various laws prohibiting practices that suggest possible bias. Here, legal standards rely on the mere possibility of prejudice (rather than proof of actual prejudice) to grant relief. One such standard, for example, requires automatic reversal of a conviction where a judge had a possible financial or other personal interest in his rulings, without inquiry as to whether that interest actually produced a biased decision. At times, the process' interest in ensuring an appearance of fairness will prevail even over the defendant's desire to forego a particular procedural right. Thus, some jurisdictions insist that the defendant be present at trial even though he would prefer to be tried in absentia, with only his lawyer present.

(j) Achieving Equality in the Application of the Process. In a society dedicated to achieving "equal justice under law," it is only natural that another goal of the criminal justice process is to achieve equality in the administration of the process. The primary concern here is that each jurisdiction be evenhanded in its treatment of persons subjected to the process. This does not mean that procedures must be applied in the same way to all persons with the same criminal justice status (e.g., all suspects, all arrestees, or all defendants), but simply that like persons must be treated alike. In other words, distinctions drawn between persons with the same status must be based on grounds that are properly related to the functions of the process.

What constitutes a proper basis for disparate treatment of persons will vary with what is being decided. In determining whether to press charges, for example, a prosecutor could rationally draw distinctions based on a variety of factors (such as differences in the past criminal records of otherwise similar arrestees) that would have no rational bearing on a determination as to which defendants will receive six-person rather than twelve-person juries. Because the function of the particular procedural step plays such an important role in determining what is relevant, the law regulating the process will allow far more room for disparity in some procedures than in others. Indeed, where the function renders relevant a broad range of factors, the process tends to grant the decisionmaker almost unlimited discretion.

Even as to those areas involving extensive discretionary authority, the range of permissible considerations is not unlimited. Certain factors, such as race, ethnicity, and religion, tend to be viewed as improper grounds for discriminating in every aspect of the process. To a large extent, indigency falls in the same category, and in some instances, the state is required to provide the indigent defendant with the assistance needed to utilize the process in the same fashion as the non-indigent defendant. Measures aimed at precluding improper discrimination include provisions that allow the defendant to challenge in court the alleged misuse of discretion, requirements of decisional transparency that make it harder to hide illicit discrimination, and the prescription of specific administrative criteria that restrain discretion even as to areas in which a broad range of factors are relevant (e.g., sentencing guidelines).

(k) Addressing the Concerns of the Victim. The shaping of the criminal justice process to address the concerns of the victim of the crime is a comparatively recent development. Yet system changes instituted with this objective in mind have been so widespread and have impacted so many different aspects of the process that addressing the concerns of victims can readily be characterized today as a cornerstone objective of the process. The federal criminal justice system and almost every state system is governed by some form of "victims' rights" legislation, and over half of the states have adopted victims' rights amendments to their constitutions. These provisions clearly do not respond to all concerns victims are likely to have. As with other cornerstone objectives, conflicting objectives will sometimes prevail. The victims' rights provisions do reflect, however, a widespread recognition that the interests of the victim may stand apart from the interests of the community (as represented by the prosecution) and that these separate interests should at least be addressed in shaping the process.

The victim is now recognized to be not simply a source of evidence, but an interested third party whose concerns must be considered (though not necessarily vindicated) by police, prosecutor, and judge. Provisions recognizing victims' concerns are far too diverse to be neatly categorized, but most of them can be characterized as seeking to achieve one or more of seven objectives: (1) making the victim whole economically; (2) developing administrative sensitivity to the plight of the victim; (3) respecting the victim's privacy; (4) providing protection against potential defendant intimidation of the victim; (5) reducing the burdens borne by victims who are willing to assist in the prosecution; (6) ensuring that the victim has the opportunity to be present at judicial proceedings relating to the offense committed against the victim; and (7) giving victims a participatory role (typically limited to providing input as to the victim's perspective) as to various enforcement and judicial decisions relating to that offense.

Chapter 2

THE CONSTITUTIONALIZATION OF CRIMINAL PROCEDURE

Table of Sections

For additional analysis of the above topics and citations to authorities supporting their discussion in this Book, consult the authors' 7-volume *Criminal Procedure* treatise, also available as Westlaw database CRIMPROC. See the Table of Cross-References in this Book.

Constitutional rulings of the Supreme Court will be discussed in all of the remaining chapters. The analysis there will focus on the Court's interpretation of particular constitutional guarantees. This chapter explores the general framework within which those rulings were made. It describes what is, in effect, the doctrinal backdrop for constitutional decisionmaking in the field of criminal procedure.

§ 2.1   Application of the Bill of Rights Guarantees to the States

(a) Introduction. As initially adopted, the Constitution said very little about criminal procedure. But once the process of obtaining state ratification produced a commitment to add amendments protecting individual rights, it became obvious that the criminal justice process would receive considerable attention in those amendments. A combination of several factors—including this country's English heritage, misuse of the criminal process against colonial dissidents, and the focus of post-revolutionary political theory upon restraining the growing authority of government where it was the antagonist of the individual—had led to a heavy emphasis upon criminal process rights in the bills of rights of the state constitutions. The individual rights amendments of the federal constitution, in what became the federal Bill of Rights (i.e., the first ten amendments), were requested by the ratifying states largely to perform the same function as the state bills of rights.

The guarantees of individual rights were placed in the first eight amendments (the ninth and tenth recognizing structural safeguards that also limited governmental authority). Of the twenty-seven guarantees established in those first eight amendments, sixteen dealt specifically with the criminal justice process. One additional provision, the due process clause of the Fifth Amendment, clearly applied to criminal proceedings, as it covered the criminal sanctions of loss of life, liberty, or property, although it also extended to non-criminal proceedings where one of those interests (typically only property) was at stake. These seventeen provisions were certain to play a significant role in the shaping of the federal criminal justice process. The Bill of Rights provisions, however, applied only to the federal government. They had no bearing on the criminal justice processes of the states.

Following the civil war, the Fourteenth Amendment included a provision that clearly did apply to the states. The second sentence of section one of that amendment provided: "No state shall make or enforce any law which shall abridge the privileges or immunities of citizens of the United States; nor shall any State deprive any person of life, liberty, or property, without due process of law; nor deny to any person within its jurisdiction the equal protection of the laws." Over the many years since the adoption of the Fourteenth Amendment, a substantial portion of the Supreme Court's workload has involved the interpretation of the provisions of this second sentence. One of the more difficult recurring issues faced by the Court has been whether, and to what extent, that second sentence encompasses (and thereby makes applicable to the states) the guarantees found in the Bill of Rights. Over the years, essentially three different positions have been advanced within the Court on this issue: (1) the "total incorporation" position, advanced in numerous dissents, but never adopted by the Court majority; (2) the "fundamental fairness" position, consistently supported by a majority prior to the 1960s; and (3) the selective incorporation doctrine that has prevailed as the majority view since the mid–1960s.

Each of these positions is discussed in the subsections that follow. Since the selective incorporation doctrine has clearly won the day, one might ask why we devote two full sections to the "defeated" positions of total incorporation and fundamental fairness. Initially, an understanding of each is needed to fully appreciate the selective incorporation position. The judicial debate between the supporters of the total incorporation and fundamental fairness positions had substantial influence on the initial articulation and eventual adoption of the selective incorporation doctrine. But more significantly, strains of that debate have current vitality. As discussed in subsection (e), the concerns that were expressed by the judicial proponents of the fundamental fairness position are advanced today, in only slightly altered form, in judicial discussions of the need for the Court not to unduly restrict the states in its application of the incorporated guarantees. So too, the criticism of the totality-of-the-circumstances approach of the fundamental fairness doctrine reappears today in discussions of the standards to be fashioned under those guarantees, as described in § 2.3. Finally as discussed in § 2.2, a basic strand of the fundamental fairness concept remains a viable and frequently used measure for regulating both state and federal criminal procedure under "free-standing" due process.

(b) Fundamental Fairness. The relationship between the Fourteenth Amendment and the Bill of Rights was first considered by the Supreme Court in the criminal procedure context in *Hurtado v. Cal.* (1884). The petitioner Hurtado had been tried and convicted of murder following the initiation of charges on a prosecutor's information and a determination of probable cause by a magistrate at a preliminary hearing. Hurtado claimed that Fourteen Amendment due process had been violated by the state's failure to initiate prosecution through an indictment issued by a grand jury. In rejecting that claim, the Court acknowledged that prosecution by indictment had a long common law history, dating back to the Magna Charta, and was required in the federal system by the Fifth Amendment's grand jury clause. However, the due process clause of the Fourteenth Amendment only carried over to the states the same content as the due process clause of the Fifth Amendment imposed upon the federal government.

Prior to the adoption of the Fourteenth Amendment, *Murray's Lessee v. Hoboken Land & Improvement Co.* (1855) had established two critical principles relating to the content of the Fifth Amendment's due process clause. First, although the concept of due process clearly was derived from the "law of the land" clause of the Magna Charta, it required more than regular adherence to preexisting law (i.e., more than requiring the Crown to follow those procedures that were established by the common law and Parliament). The due process clause also prohibited any legislative or judicial alteration of procedures that would be inconsistent with the key principles of fairness found in the common law. Second, a procedure that was well established at common law thereby was consistent with due process. *Hurtado* concluded that these two principles did not combine to make prosecution by indictment an element of due process, notwithstanding its common law pedigree and its inclusion in the Bill of Rights.

Hurtado reasoned that due process did not lock into the Constitution the common practices of the Framer's era. It encompassed only those "fundamental principles of liberty and justice which lie at the base of all our civil and political institutions," and judicial determination of its content should look to "the very substance of individual rights" rather than "particular forms of procedure." Like the common law itself, which "dr[ew] its inspiration from every fountain of justice," due process should allow the legislature to take account of "the new and various experiences of our own situation," and to look to "the best ideas of all systems and ages," so as to mold basic principles of justice into "new * * * forms." Prosecution by means other than indictment had been known to the common law, and California's charging procedure, like the indictment process itself, "carefully consider[ed] and guard[ed] the substantial interests of the accused." Accordingly, it did not violate due process.

Hurtado established both prongs of what came to be known as the "fundamental fairness" or "ordered liberty" interpretation of due process. First, the due process clause protects only these rights of the individual, procedural and substantive, that are deemed to be "fundamental." Over the years, the Court variously described the standard for determining whether a right is fundamental. Due process was said to require adherence to those rights that are "implicit in the concept of ordered liberty," that are "so rooted in the traditions and conscience of our people as to be ranked fundamental," and that "lie at the base of all our civil and political institutions." As applied to criminal procedure, it was said to require "that fundamental fairness essential to the very concept of justice" The Court also repeatedly emphasized, as in *Hurtado*, that this is a flexible standard, not frozen in history. It takes account of societal change and looks to the "essence [of] just treatment," rather than the historical familiarity of form.

Second, there is no necessary correlation between the protection afforded under the specific provisions of the Bill of Rights and due process. The concept of due process has an "independent potency," which permits it to encompass rights not mentioned in the Bill of Rights (e.g., the requirement of proof beyond a reasonable doubt). *Hurtado* suggested that, since the Fifth Amendment itself included a requirement of prosecution by indictment, that was a good indication that the due process clause did not impose the same requirement. However, later cases recognized that the independent content of due process could readily overlap in its coverage with the other guaranties included in the Bill of Rights. Because due process was a vague and fluid guarantee, the Framers could well have thought it desirable to add specific provisions on some rights that might be encompassed (perhaps in part and perhaps entirely) in due process. In the end, the key to determining the content of due process was whether the particular substantive or procedural right was fundamental, not whether it was or was not mentioned in the other Bill of Rights guarantees.

Traditional fundamental fairness analysis assessed a specific procedure as it was applied (or not applied) in the particular case, not as to the overall character of a Bill of Rights guarantee that might encompass that procedure as well as others. Nonetheless, rulings applying the fundamental fairness standard made clear that certain Bill of Rights guarantees were not in any respect, under any circumstances, required by due process. Thus, requiring grand jury and petit jury participation in the decisions to charge and convict was characterized as reflecting no more than the "restricted views of Eighteenth Century England regarding the best method for the ascertainment of facts." Other procedural guarantees, however, were seen as encompassing fundamental rights in their basic conception, but not necessarily in each aspect of the guarantee or in the full range of circumstances governed by the guarantee. Thus, the Court indicated in *Palko v. Conn.* (1937) that due process would prohibit some forms of double jeopardy (e.g. a retrial following an acquittal in an error free trial), but not others (e.g. a retrial following an appellate reversal of an initial trial acquittal due to a critical legal error in the trial). So too, *Betts v. Brady* (see § 3.7(a)) concluded that due process, like the Sixth Amendment, could require appointment of counsel to assist the indigent defendant, but only under "special circumstances" (in contrast to the Sixth Amendment's flat application to all "criminal cases").

(c) Total Incorporation. While total incorporation was always a minority position, it arguably had considerable influence in the Court's eventual adoption of the selective incorporation doctrine. The total incorporation position maintained that the Fourteenth Amendment incorporated and made applicable to the states all of the specific guarantees of the Bill of Rights. Most of its supporters also maintained that the Fourteenth Amendment's due process guarantee additionally protected fundamental rights not enumerated in the first eight amendments, although Justice Black maintained that due process additionally did no more than require governmental adherence to the previously established "law of the land". Justices advancing the total incorporation position relied in large part on their reading of the history of the Fourteenth Amendment as intended to make the Bill of Rights applicable to the states, with some arguing that purpose was reflected in the Fourteenth Amendment's privileges and immunities clause, other claiming that the Fourteenth Amendment's due process clause achieved that objective, and Justice Black looking to the Fourteenth Amendment "as a whole."

The Supreme Court first rejected a total incorporation analysis in the 1890s, but the position was pressed by dissenters again in the mid–1900s, and received four votes in *Adamson v. Cal.* (1947). The majority in each instance emphasized that the framers of the Fourteenth Amendment would have directly stated that the Bill of Rights was applicable to the states if that had been their intent. The privileges and immunities clause, as the court had early held, referred only to state abridgment of the privileges and immunities of national citizenship, which shaped the relationship of the citizen to the federal government. The due process clause was no more than one of the provisions of the Bill of Rights and not a shorthand reference to the totality of those provisions. Indeed, if the concept of due process automatically encompassed all of the Bill of Rights provisions, why did the Framers add those other provisions alongside the Fifth Amendment's due process clause?

It also was noted that total incorporation would have required significant changes in the procedures of various states, but there had been no suggestion of the need for such changes in the ratification debates, and no movement to make such changes thereafter. In particular, total incorporation would have required the states to adhere to the Fifth Amendment requirement of prosecution by grand jury amendment (in contrast to a growing movement to prosecute by information), and would have required that jury trials be provided for minor civil damage actions (the Seventh Amendment requiring juries "where the value in controversy shall exceed twenty dollars").

In the end, the most influential arguments of the supporters of total incorporation were not their arguments for that position, but their arguments against the "subjectivity" and administrative impracticability of the fundamental fairness doctrine. They argued initially that there was a need to have constitutional regulation rest on the "boundaries fixed by the written words of the Constitution" (i.e, the specific guarantees of the Bill of Rights), rather than the majority's "natural law" approach, which basically invited the Court "to substitute its own concepts of decency and fundamental justice for the language of the Bill of Rights." Supporters of fundamental fairness acknowledged that a case-by-case application of the "ordered liberty" standard was an "empiric process" for which there was no "mechanic yardstick," but argued that this fell far short of leaving judges "at large" to draw upon their "merely personal and private notions of justice." Fundamental fairness analysis required a judge to look to external evidence of permanent and pervasive notions of fairness, such as the positions taken in the federal and early state constitutions, the standards currently applied in the various states, and the viewpoints of nations with similar jurisprudential traditions. Insofar as that inquiry was "open-ended," and therefore amenable to subjective interpretation, it simply matched the inquiry into the meaning of numerous terms in specific guaranties, such as "unreasonable search" and "speedy trial". Adoption of total incorporation, it was argued, would simply shift the focus of the judicial inquiry from the flexible concept of "ordered liberty" to the equally flexible terms found in many of specific guarantees. Moreover, insofar as supporters of total incorporation acknowledged that due process would have an independent content extending beyond those guaranties, total incorporation would still require application of fundamental fairness analysis in various settings.

Supporters of total incorporation also criticized the fundamental fairness doctrine as administratively impracticable. State courts, in seeking to determine what constitutional restraints applied to state criminal procedure, could not look to the body of precedent created by the application of the various specific guarantees to the federal system, but instead had to turn to a series of fundamental fairness rulings which often emphasized the totality of the circumstances of the individual case. The result, it was argued, was a lack of consistency in state court rulings, and considerable burden on the Supreme Court, which had the task of both interpreting the specific guarantees for federal cases and developing a second-level, shadow group of standards for the states. Supporters of fundamental fairness responded that any administrative difficulties caused by the case-by-case approach of fundamental fairness were insignificant as compared to the practical consequences of applying to the state systems the full range of the Bill of Rights guarantees.

(d) Selective Incorporation. In 1961, Justice Brennan, in a dissenting opinion, advanced what is commonly described as the "selective incorporation" interpretation of the Fourteenth Amendment. *Cohen v. Hurley* (1961) (Brennan, J., dis.). This interpretation combines aspects of both the "fundamental rights" and "total incorporation" interpretations of the Fourteenth Amendment. Selective incorporation accepts the basic premise of the fundamental rights interpretation that the Fourteenth Amendment encompasses rights, substantive or procedural, that are so basic as to be ranked as "fundamental." It recognizes too that not all rights specified in the Bill of Rights are necessarily fundamental. It rejects the fundamental rights interpretation, however, insofar as that doctrine looks only to the character of the particular aspect of a specified right denied in the particular case, and evaluates that aspect with reference to the "totality of circumstances" of that case. Evaluating the fundamental nature of a right in terms of the "factual circumstances surrounding each individual case" is viewed as "extremely subjective and excessively discretionary." Limiting a decision to only one aspect of the specified right also is rejected as presenting the same difficulty. Accordingly, in determining whether a specified right is fundamental, the selective incorporation doctrine requires that the Court look at the total right guaranteed by the particular Bill of Rights provision, not merely at a single aspect of that right nor the application of that aspect in the circumstances of the particular case. If it is decided that a particular guarantee is fundamental, that right will be incorporated into the Fourteenth Amendment "whole and intact." The specified right will then be enforced against the states in every case according to the same standards applied to the federal government. With respect to those guarantees within the Bill of Rights held to be fundamental, there is, as Justice Douglas put it, "coextensive coverage" under the Fourteenth Amendment and the Bill of Rights. *Johnson v. La.* (1972).

The selective incorporation doctrine gained majority support during the 1960s. The debate as to its adoption was presented largely in concurring and dissenting opinions, as the majority opinions typically applied the doctrine without any extensive discussion as to why the focus should be on the whole of a specified right. Justices opposing selective incorporation argued that it was no more than an artificial compromise between traditional fundamental fairness and the total incorporation doctrines. Supporters of the doctrine stressed that selective incorporation reduced the potential for subjectivity and "avoid[ed] the impression of personal, ad hoc adjudication" by discarding an analysis that focused on the totality of the circumstances of the individual case. Selective incorporation was also praised as promoting certainty in the law, and thereby facilitating state court enforcement of due process standards; once a specified right was held to be fundamental, the state courts were directed to the specific language of the Bill of Rights guarantee and the various decisions interpreting that guarantee in the context of federal prosecutions. This stood in contrast to the case-by-case rulings under fundamental fairness, which left the state at sea as to whether other circumstances and other aspects of a particular right would produce a different result as to what was fundamental.

The adoption of the selective incorporation position during the 1960s was accompanied by a movement towards a broader view of the nature of a "fundamental procedural right." A right was to be judged by reference to its operation within the "common law system of [criminal procedure] * * * that has been developing * * * in this country, rather than its theoretical justification as a necessary element of a 'fair and equitable procedure.' " *Duncan v. La.* (1968). The fact that another system of justice could operate without a particular right (as the civil system operated without jury trials) did not work against finding the right to be fundamental in our system. Also, an emphasis was placed upon the very presence of a right within the Bill of Rights as strong evidence of its fundamental nature.

Applying this approach, the Supreme Court in the 1960s held fundamental (and therefore applicable to the states): (1) the Fourth Amendment's prohibition against unreasonable searches; (2) the Fourth Amendment's warrant clause; (3) the Fifth Amendment's prohibition against double jeopardy; (4) the Fifth Amendment's privilege against compelled self-incrimination; (5) the Sixth Amendment's right to a speedy trial; (6) the Sixth Amendment's right to a public trial; (7) the Sixth Amendment's right to trial by an impartial jury; (8) the Sixth Amendment right to be informed of the nature and cause of the accusation; (9) the Sixth Amendment's right to confront opposing witnesses; (10) the Sixth Amendment's right to compulsory process for obtaining witnesses; (11) the Sixth Amendment's right to the assistance of counsel; and (12) the Eight Amendment's prohibition against cruel and unusual punishment.

Thus, over a brief span of the "Warren Court era," the Supreme Court made applicable to the states all but four of the 16 Bill of Rights guarantees specifically directed to criminal procedure. As for the four, the Court simply had not been presented with cases requiring incorporation rulings on three of them; the Eight Amendment prohibition of excessive bail; the Eighth Amendment prohibition against excessive fines; and the Sixth Amendment's guarantee that the jury be selected from "the state and district where the crime shall have been committed, which district shall have been ascertained by law." Indeed, it has yet to rule on these three (although lower courts have done so, unanimously assuming that the first two are fundamental and dividing on the third). As to the one remaining guarantee, The Fifth Amendment's requirement of prosecution by grand jury indictment, the Court here reaffirmed the *Hurtado* ruling that it is not fundamental. That is only the criminal procedure guarantee held not to apply to the states under the selective incorporation doctrine.

(e) Selective Incorporation and Federalism. The opinions of the Court during the era of fundamental fairness rarely failed to note the need to respect the "sovereign character of the several states" by giving the states the widest latitude in shaping their criminal justice systems, consistent with ensuring fundamental fairness. Justices opposing the adoption of selective incorporation similarly argued that the Bill of Rights provisions had long been interpreted with only the federal government in mind, and applying those provisions and their previous interpretations to the states would be inappropriate, as the state criminal justice systems operated in settings requiring far greater flexibility than the federal system. Major differences included: (1) the broader responsibilities of local police (including order maintenance and traffic control); (2) the "far wider spectrum of laws," varying from minor infractions to major crimes, that were enforced in the state systems; (3) the much heavier caseloads of state officials; and (4) a much more fragmented enforcement structure (with heavy reliance on local units and local community control). A "jot for jot" application of standards developed in the context of federal proceedings, they argued, would put "the states, with their differing law enforcement problem[s] * * * in a constitutional straight jacket."

A few of the justices supporting selective incorporation argued for taking account of some of these federalism interests by rejecting complete parallelism in selective incorporation as to those aspects of constitutional regulation that dealt with "a system of administration," rather than a "principle of justice." They suggested, for example, that the Sixth Amendment precedent requiring a unanimous jury verdict and a twelve-person jury should continue to apply to the federal system, but not to the states. The majority, however, rejected any such departure from complete incorporation of those constitutional guarantees deemed fundamental. They concluded that the preferred approach was to reexamine such past precedent to determine whether those rulings were shaped by the "limited environment" of the federal criminal justice system, or truly reflected basic constitutional principle. This "reconsideration route" led to rulings that the Sixth Amendment did not require a twelve person jury or a unanimous verdict (although the division of the Court on the latter issue left that requirement applicable to the federal system, as the deciding vote was cast by a justice rejecting absolute parallelism.)

The Court in applying various selectively incorporated guarantees also gave weight to the resource limitations of state criminal justice systems. In some instances, the result was what arguably might be characterized as an "administrative-feasibility exception" to the application of a guiding principle underlying a particular guarantee. In *North v. Russell* (1976), for example, a two-tier system for the trial of misdemeanors, with non-lawyer magistrates the sole decision-maker at the first level (thereby pushing the right to a jury trial to the second level) was sustained as an appropriate balance of the limited resources of rural communities and the procedural rights of defendants. Similarly, in *Shadwick v. City of Tampa* (1972), recognizing the "stiff and unrelenting caseloads" borne by many municipal courts, the Court held that the Fourth Amendment was not violated by the issuance of arrest warrants for municipal ordinance violations by non-lawyer clerks of municipal courts. Justice Powell's opinion for a unanimous Court initially noted that the issuance of warrants by judges or lawyers was to be preferred, but "our federal system warns of converting desirable practice into constitutional commandment."

In *New State Ice Co. v. Liebmann* (1932), Justice Brandeis famously noted: "It is one of the happy incidents of a federal system that a single courageous State may, if its citizens choose, serve as a laboratory; and try novel social and economic experiments without risk to the rest of the country." Supporters of the fundamental fairness doctrine had argued that only that approach provided the leeway necessary for such experimentation. Some of the justices strongly supporting selective incorporation responding by arguing that Justice Brandeis' admonition of caution in restricting state experimentation should not extend to "experiment's with the fundamental liberties of citizens safeguarded by the Bill of Rights." However, in *Chandler v. Fla.* (1981), the Court in a post-selective-incorporation ruling took a contrary position. The Court there looked to the value of experimentation in holding that, subject to certain safeguards, a state could permit the televising of a trial over the defendant's objection. See § 15.1(e). The Court noted that Florida had adopted its guidelines for televising trials only after a carefully reviewed pilot program had proven successful, that eighteen other states had experimented with such guidelines, and that the issue was under study in yet another dozen states. This strong display of state interest, supported by their generally careful and cautious approach, worked in Florida's favor. The Court concluded that where, as here, it could not say that the state activity automatically violated due process, it would be guided by

Justice Brandeis' admonition in *New State Ice Co. v. Liebmann* to respect state experimentation.

The Court's willingness to take account of state resource limitations, to reexamine precedent formulated in the context of the federal system, and to give weight to the value of experimentation, all combine to provide a flexibility that may not have been anticipated with the original adoption of selective incorporation. Of course, selective incorporation clearly gives the states far less leeway than would be available under a fundamental fairness analysis. Nevertheless, there apparently remains sufficient opportunity for recognition of local variations to convince those justices who have stressed federalism concerns in other aspects of constitutional law that there is no need to seek to overturn the selective incorporation doctrine.

§ 2.2   Free–Standing Due Process

(a) **Due Process Beyond Incorporation.** Prior to the adoption of the selective incorporation doctrine, the fundamental fairness doctrine had given the Fourteenth Amendment's due process clause a content that not only overlapped in part with some of the specific guarantees of the Bill of Rights, but also included prohibitions that were not to be found in those guarantees. The selective incorporation doctrine challenged only the standard adopted by the earlier decisions in determining when and to what extent the Fourteenth Amendment's due process clause subjected the state criminal justice systems to restrictions identical to those imposed upon the federal system under the Bill of Rights' specific guarantees. It did not question the conception of due process as also reaching aspects of the process not regulated by those guarantees and imposing there additional restrictions as demanded by the concept of "fundamental fairness." Indeed, over the same decade during which it was selectively incorporating various Bill of Rights guarantees, the Warren Court also was relying upon the independent content of due process to impose new limitations upon the state criminal justice systems that stood apart from any of those selectively incorporated guarantees. Because they had a grounding apart from the incorporated guarantees, those ruling were often described as resting on "free-standing due process."

It was not until after the adoption of selective incorporation that the Supreme Court found it necessary to address the distinct roles of the specific guarantees and the independent content of due process in the constitutional regulation of the state criminal justice systems. The primary source of regulation, the Court noted in *Dowling v. U.S.* (1990), comes from those specific guarantees that have been selectively incorporated and thereby made applicable to the states. "Beyond the specific guarantees enumerated in the Bill of Rights, the Due Process Clause has limited operation." That is so because "[t]he Bill of Rights speaks in explicit terms to many aspects of criminal procedure, and the expansion of those constitutional guarantees under the open-ended rubric of the Due Process Clause invites undue interference with both considered legislative judgments and the careful balance that the Constitution strikes between liberty and order." In the "field of criminal law," the Court stated, "we have defined the category of infractions that violate 'fundamental fairness' very narrowly," recognizing that the due process clause does not "establish this Court as a rule-making organ for the promulgation of states rules of criminal procedure."

The Court's characterization of free-standing due process as a limited supplement to specific guarantees might suggest a sparing use of that grounding, but, in fact, a wide range of constitutional regulations of the criminal justice process are based on the independent content of due process. Those rulings extend to almost every post-investigation stage of the process. At the charging stage, due process prohibits unjustified extensive delay in bringing charges where that delay results in prejudice to the defense, and it also prohibits charging decisions that are the product of prosecutorial vindictiveness. At the pretrial stage, due process governs procedural elements of the motion to suppress, ensures that the defense receives reciprocal discovery when it is required to provide discovery to the prosecution, provides the indigent defendant with access to experts as needed to evaluate and present a contention resting on scientific expertise (e.g., insanity), imposes on the prosecution a duty to disclose to the defense or factfinder material exculpatory evidence that is within its possession or control, and prohibits state timing requirements for motions that are so stringent as to deny the defendant a reasonable opportunity to raise a constitutional objection.

Of course, all but a small percentage of felony prosecutions are disposed of without a trial, with the greatest portion resolved by guilty plea. Here, the due process clause is the dominant source of constitutional regulation. Due process establishes the minimum amount of information that must be given to the defendant prior to accepting his plea, requires that the record provide a factual basis for the plea under certain circumstances, restricts the pressures that can be imposed upon a defendant without rendering his plea involuntary, and determines at what point there exists a constitutionally cognizable plea agreement which requires relief when breached by the prosecutor or court.

Notwithstanding the number of specific guarantees in the Fifth and Sixth Amendment applicable to the trial, a wide variety of due process limitations add considerably to the constitutional regulation of the trial. Initially, due process governs many of the structural components of the trial. Due process imposes the requirements of an unbiased judge, and contributes to the constitutionally mandated procedures designed to ensure that the jury is not tainted by prejudicial pretrial publicity. Due process also contributes in part to the defendant's right to be present at various stages of the trial, prohibits forcing upon defendant an unnecessary physical setting that conveys a prejudicial message to the jury, and limits the trial court's authority to exclude the defendant from the courtroom because of his misbehavior and to try him in absentia when he has failed to appear for trial. The constitutional right of the defendant to testify on his own behalf is also grounded in part on due process. Constitutional standards governing defendant's competence to stand trial, including the test for competency, the necessity for a competency hearing, and applicable standard of proof on that issue, also are a product of due process. The state's authority to televise trials, notwithstanding a defense objection, is also governed by due process. The state's obligation to establish guilt at trial by proof "beyond a reasonable doubt" is still another due process requirement. It leads, in turn, to due process regulation of the use of presumptions, the shifting of the burden of proof to the defense on particular issues, the utilization of alternatives in the proof of the means or mental state of a single crime, and the explanation given to the jury of the reasonable doubt standard.

Due process also contributes to the constitutional regulation of trial presentations. Due process is violated, for example, where the prosecution introduces material testimony known to be false, fails to bring to the attention of the factfinder or defendant evidence within its possession or control that contradicts its key evidence or undercuts the credibility of its key witnesses, or presents a closing argument "so infected with unfairness" as to undermine confidence in the jury's verdict. The trial judge may violate due process by excluding evidence critical to the defendant's presentation of a defense, taking unnecessary actions that "effectively dr[ive] a [defense] witness off the stand," or tolerating courtroom behavior that produces a "carnival atmosphere" prejudicial to the defense.

When the process moves to the sentencing stage, most trial-type rights (e.g., confrontation) do not apply and due process becomes the primary source of constitutional regulation. Due process governs the range of conduct that may be considered by the sentencing judge, the need for notifying the defendant of the information that the judge will consider in making the sentencing decision, the need to ensure that information relied upon is accurate, and the need to provide the defendant with an opportunity to be heard and to offer his own evidence. Due process also sets the minimum burden of proof the government must bear where the sentencing statute calls for a mandatory minimum sentence based on a judge or jury finding of a particular aggravating circumstance as well as the minimum procedural rights that must be granted to the defense where the sentencing statute imposes an extended or alternative term upon a finding of dangerousness or recidivism. Many of the special procedural guarantees attaching to capital sentencing also are prescribed by due process.

Once the process moves beyond the conviction and sentence, due process constitutes the almost exclusive source of constitutionally mandated procedural rights. The rights of an indigent defendant to appointed counsel on a first appeal as of right and at a probation revocation proceeding are the product of due process. The independent content of due process also establishes the prohibition against the vindictive exercise of judicial or prosecutorial discretion directed at defendants who exercise their right to appeal. The Supreme Court also looked to due process in requiring that the state procedure for probation or parole revocation include a prompt preliminary hearing, a final revocation hearing within a reasonable time, a neutral and detached hearing body, advance written notice of the charges, disclosure of the evidence on which the decision maker relies, a limited right of confrontation and cross-examination, and a right to appear and present evidence on his own behalf. The decision on parole release can under some circumstances also be subject to certain procedural due process rights.

Due process rulings certainly do not take a back-seat to rulings based on specific guarantees in their reach throughout the process. The Court's emphasis in *Dowling* and other cases on a restrained use of the independent content of due process tends to be reflected more in the character of those rulings than the range of subjects regulated by due process.

Initially, the methodology applied in free-standing due process analysis, as described in subsection (b), imposes restraints that either are not applied or not as rigorously applied in the interpretation of the specific guarantees. That methodology includes a heavy emphasis on historical acceptance of a practice and the consensus of the states, both factors serving to limit what may be deemed "fundamentally unfair." The methodology rejects application of the open-ended utilitarian balancing process that determines the content of procedural due process in areas other than criminal procedure. It often refers as well to the need to give deference to the legislative judgments of the states as to how best to implement a basic principle of justice.

Secondly, free-standing due process analysis commonly focuses on the operation of the challenged practice in the individual case. As a result, there is often a focus on the impact of the challenged procedure on the defendant's conviction or sentence. Thus, most free-standing due process rulings (although certainly not all) make a defense showing of likely prejudice an element of the constitutional violation. This stands in contrast to rulings under specific guarantees, which typically describe constitutional violations without regard to their prejudicial impact in the individual case (although these violations may then be subject to harmless error analysis in appellate review). As the Court noted in *U.S. v. Gonzales* (2006), in applying due process to a trial setting, it will ask whether "the trial was, on the whole fair," but where a trial right has been specified in Bill of Rights, that establishes it as an absolute trial prerequisite and the constitutional violation is established in its denial, without considering the actual fairness of the particular trial.

The case-specific focus of free-standing due process often goes beyond requiring a showing of prejudice. It stresses the need to evaluate the challenged procedure within the context of the particular state's criminal justice process, recognizing the interconnection of the various steps in the process. In some instances, free-standing due process has adopted an even narrower focus, tying fundamental fairness to the totality of the factual circumstances of the individual case. While, as noted in § 2.6(e), a similar methodology is sometimes applied in the interpretation of specific guarantees, circumstance-specific rulings are far more common in the application of free-standing due process.

(b) Due Process Analysis. In determining what procedure is mandated by the independent content of due process, the Supreme Court in the post-incorporation era has looked primarily to guideposts that also were used in the Court's earlier applications of due process under the fundamental fairness doctrine. The most significant of these guideposts have been: (1) the acceptance or rejection of the challenged procedural practice under the English common law as it was adapted to the conditions of this country; (2) the current American consensus on the validity of the challenged practice, as reflected in the judicial decisions and statutes of the various states; and (3) whether the challenged practice is consistent with, or contrary to, the logical application of the over-arching structural elements of the American criminal justice process (particularly, its adherence to an adversary system of adjudication).

None of these guideposts are necessarily controlling. Thus, while the historical acceptance of a practice provides strong evidence that the practice is not contrary to those fundamental principles "rooted in the traditions and conscience of our people," the concept of due process, as *Hurtado* noted (see § 2.1(b)), is open to the lessons of new experiences and the teachings of a new age's "sense of fair play and decency." Thus, *Jackson v. Denno* (1964) held invalid under due process the practice, long accepted in American common law, that allowed the trial judge to give to the jury the determination of whether a confession was obtained by methods so oppressive that it should not be admissible in evidence. Nonetheless, deep common law roots are given great weight, and may well sustain a practice even though the current consensus of the states is to prohibit that practice. *Martin v. Ohio* (1987) (upholding the constitutionality of placing on the defense the burden of establishing self-defense).

(c) **Substantive Due Process.** The vast majority of free-standing due process rulings relating to the criminal justice process resolve procedural due process claims. The typical procedural claim accepts the legitimacy of restricting an individual's liberty based on a criminal conviction, but contends that the process leading to the conviction violated the fundamental fairness standard. Substantive due process claims, in contrast, challenge the government's basic justification for restricting a protected liberty, without regard to the procedures employed in establishing that justification. Those claims, in the context of the criminal justice process, typically challenge restrictions on liberty that stand apart from the imposition of the criminal sanction and the proof of criminal liability. Restrictions of that type occasionally arise in the post-investigation portion of the process, where the individual's personal liberty is restricted (as in the case of preventive detention, see § 4.3(d), or the bodily intrusion presented in *Sell v. U.S.*, discussed below). However, as illustrated in *District Attorney's Office v. Osborne* (2009), claims alleging procedural inadequacies can sometimes be presented as both procedural and substantive due process claims. As discussed in § 16.11(c), in *Osborne*, the convicted defendant's challenge to the state's refusal to grant him DNA testing of the state's biological evidence was considered a procedural due process claim insofar as it alleged a lack of fundamental fairness in the procedure made available to vindicate the convicted defendant's recognized liberty interest in avoiding further punishment by establishing his innocence through newly discovered evidence. That challenge was also treated, however, as presenting a substantive due process claim insofar as it argued for recognition of a "free-standing right to DNA evidence" as a protected liberty interest that had been arbitrarily denied.

Substantive due process claims face two significant hurdles that go beyond the limitations on due process analysis discussed in subsections (a) and (b). The first obstacle facing a substantive due process claim is the "more-specific provision" rule of *Graham v. Connor* (1989). Under the *Graham* rule, where one of the specific constitutional guarantees "provides an external textual source of constitutional protection" against a particular type of government behavior, "that Amendment, not the more generalized notion of 'substantive due process,' must be the guide for analyzing those claims." This position reflects the Court's traditional "reluctan[ce] to expand the concept of substantive due process because the guideposts for responsible decisionmaking in this unchartered area are scarce and open-ended." The *Graham* rule requires that the due process claim identify a protected interest distinct from that protected by the specific guarantee. Thus, in *Albright v. Oliver* (1994), where the petitioner claimed that the initiation of a criminal charge on clearly unreliable evidence violated his personal liberty, the Court majority concluded that the claim was cognizable under substantive due process only if the claimed liberty interest was distinct from the pretrial deprivation of liberty produced by the criminal charge, since that interest is the focus of the Fourth Amendment's requirement of probable cause for an arrest.

A second obstacle facing a substantive due process claim is the Court's general unwillingness to find a denial of substantive due process absent the most compelling case. Thus, in *Sacramento v. Lewis* (1998), involving a police officer's alleged reckless indifference in the course of a high speed chase that resulted in a death, the Court majority held that acts of a government official violated substantive due process only where so egregiously abusive as to "shock the conscience." The Court concluded that the police recklessness there fell short of that standard as the police were acting on an "instant judgment" and without "harmful purpose." The conscious-shocking standard, it noted, requires egregiousness of the character of forced stomach pumping, which had been held to violate that standard in the pre-incorporation era ruling of *Rochin v. Cal.* (1952).

The Court has noted that the conscious-shocking standard is not the only route to finding a substantive due process violation. A violation will be established where the state has violated a "fundamental liberty interest" recognized by history and tradition, as "implicit in the concept of ordered liberty." Such a right was present in *Sell v. U.S.* (2003), but even as to its invasion, the Court insisted on the absence of any state justification in finding a substantive due process violation. *Sell* held that substantive due process prohibited the involuntary administration of antipsychotic drugs for the purpose of rendering the accused competent to stand trial, absent a showing that the treatment is "medically appropriate," that it is unlikely to have side effects that may undermine the "fairness of the trial," that lesser alternatives are not available, and that the government interest in bringing the accused to trial is an "important government interest" (e.g., the offense being prosecuted was serious and the accused will otherwise be released).

§ 2.3   Guideposts for Constitutional Interpretation

A variety of considerations influence the Supreme Court's interpretations of constitutional guarantees. Some of these considerations—such as the language of the guarantee and the history underlying its adoption—are staples of all constitutional interpretation. Others tend to vary with the particular guarantee, or, as in the case of the criminal process guarantees, with the field of regulation. Discussed below are considerations that have been emphasized, at least since the advent of selective incorporation, in the Court's interpretation of the constitutional guarantees that apply to the criminal justice process. The weight given to the different considerations has varied with individual justices, and not all of the considerations can be said to have strong majority support today. However, each appeared to have such support at one time or another, and with the Court's rulings obviously impacted by shifts in its composition, those considerations given less weight by today's majority can readily become the considerations given the most weight by tomorrow's majority.

(a) **The Need for Expansive Interpretations.** At any particular point in its history, the Supreme Court has viewed certain constitutional provisions as more deserving of expansive interpretations than others. Thus, the Court over much of the last century has spoken of the need for "more exacting judicial scrutiny" in assessing governmental action that impacts the First Amendment, while over the same period no similar suggestion of a special need for liberal construction was even hinted at for the contracts clause. Although occasional earlier rulings spoke of a special need for expansive interpretations of the criminal process guarantees, it was not until the 1930s that the Court's rulings reflected a consistent pattern favoring such interpretations. That movement arguably lost some support in the 1940s, particularly as to the Fourth Amendment, but then regained strength in the 1950s and then reached the epitome of its strength in the 1960s. Over a stretch of several years in the 1960s, covering the latter half of Chief Justice Warren's tenure, the Court produced what commentators came to describe as the "criminal justice revolution" of the "Warren Court." That period was marked not only by the adoption of the selective incorporation doctrine, but also by expansive interpretations of the incorporated guarantees that went far beyond their previous applications to the federal criminal justice system. Supreme Court rulings in subsequent decades have not been as consistent in their direction, but they have included a fair share of expansive interpretations, most notably producing substantial constitutional regulation of aspects of the process never given significant consideration by the Warren Court. Moreover, over that period, at times the majority, and at times individual justices, have continued to reflect in their reasoning the view that the criminal procedure provisions present a special case for expansive interpretations.

The most extensive explanations of the special need for expansive interpretations of the Constitution's criminal procedure guarantees are found in academic commentary rather than Supreme Court opinions. Several of the rationales offered in that commentary, however, do find support in a series of comments, typically brief, made occasionally in opinions for the Court and more frequently in the opinions of individual justices. The rationales having such support look primarily to three factors, each discussed below: (1) the relationship of criminal procedure to the general protection of civil liberties; (2) the relationship of criminal procedure to the protection of minorities; and (3) the presence of various structural elements that enhance the Court's authority in exercising constitutional review of the criminal process.

The civil liberties concern. At least since the late 1930s, the Court has made the protection of civil liberties one of its primary concerns. It has shifted its focus from the protection of property rights to the protection of those liberties deemed more fundamental to the preservation of individual freedom. The Court has left no doubt that it considers the procedural rights of the accused to be among those more fundamental freedoms. It has accepted the premise that procedural fairness and regularity in the enforcement of the criminal law are essential to a free society. "In the end," it has explained, "life and liberty can be as much endangered from illegal methods used to convict those thought to be criminals as from actual criminals themselves." Indeed, it has added, the " 'quality of a nation's civilization can be largely measured by the methods it uses in the enforcement of its criminal law.' "

Protecting minorities. The decade of 1930s was also marked by the Court's tentative suggestion in *U.S. v. Carolene Products Co.* (1938) that one of its major functions is to protect against discrimination those "discrete and insular minorities" who cannot count on the protection of the political process. In later years that suggestion took on substantial force, particularly in the Court's application of the Fourteenth Amendment to instances of racial discrimination by government. Safeguarding the rights of the accused has been viewed as relating to the Court's role of protecting minorities in two respects. First, accused persons are themselves viewed as a highly unpopular minority. As Justice Frankfurter noted, it is precisely because appeals based on criminal process guarantees are so often made by "dubious characters" that infringement of those guarantees calls for "alert and strenuous resistance"; other constitutional protections, such as the First Amendment guarantees, "easily summon powerful support against encroachment," but criminal process guarantees are "normally invoked by those accused of crime, and criminals have few friends." Second, the criminal process is seen as having a special bearing upon various disadvantaged minority groups. Speaking of the Warren Court, former Solicitor General Archibald Cox noted that "[m]any purely procedural questions * * * were influenced by the realization that in another case they might affect the posture of a Negro in a hostile southern court."

"Judicial review" justifications. The special case for expansive interpretations of criminal procedure guarantees also is attributed to several factors that supposedly make the exercise of judicial review more readily supportable in the criminal justice area than in many other areas of constitutional adjudication. Initially, the structure of many of the applicable guarantees—in particular, the specificity of most of the Fifth and Sixth Amendment guarantees—is said to permit criminal procedure rulings to be more firmly rooted in the text and history of the applicable constitutional provisions. Of course, some provisions, such as the due process clause, are open-ended, but at least they present no ambiguity as to their applicability to the criminal justice process.

Adding to this supposedly firmer foundation for judicial review in the criminal procedure area is the fact that the Court only infrequently is required to overturn legislative decisionmaking. Rulings on police investigative methods generally deal with practices that have been instituted by the police without formal legislative authorization. Rulings relating to trial and pretrial procedures similarly tend to deal with practices adopted by courts on their own initiative. Criminal procedure rulings, it is argued, largely bypass the concerns raised by the anti-majoritarian character of judicial overturning of legislation.

Another factor cited as contributing to the Court's willingness to act boldly in the area of criminal procedure is its presumed expertise in dealing with at least those procedural issues that relate to the process of adjudication. The Supreme Court has not described its competence in this area in quite the same way as commentators, who claim that lawyers (and judges) have unique expertise in deciding "what procedures are needed fairly to make what decisions." Yet, the Court has clearly indicated that it views itself as exercising a special responsibility in reviewing procedures of adjudication. Those procedures, it has noted, relate directly to the integrity of the judicial process. Moreover, while the Court's rulings on adjudicatory procedure undoubtedly have a bearing on the achievement of substantive policies, they do not prohibit the legislature from setting substantive standards, but merely require that proof of violation of these standards be established in a certain way. Accordingly, as Justice Jackson noted, the determination of "procedural fairness" is treated as "a specialized responsibility within the competence of the judiciary on which they do not bend before political branches of Government, as they should on matters of policy which comprise substantive law."

(b) The Text. The language of the Constitution is a universally accepted guidepost for its interpretation. Commentators may refer to interpretations that "transcend the text," but even justices subscribing to the concept of a "living constitution" acknowledge that the text must control where it is "clear" in its meaning. Nonetheless, and not surprisingly, the Supreme Court's rulings in constitutional criminal procedure relatively infrequently rely on the "plain meaning" of the provision being applied. Challenges to procedures clearly prohibited, or clearly not prohibited, by the language of a guarantee do not present the difficult issues that merit the Supreme Court's attention. Where rulings have been based largely on the plain meaning of the text, there typically has been a dissent concluding that the meaning is not so plain and that an analysis of the language in light of the function of the provision leads to a different result.

More frequently, opinions will cite the language of a guarantee as pointing in a particular direction, which is then confirmed by some other guidepost (typically the original understanding). The influence of the language in this manner will depend, in large part, upon the individual justice's approach to constitutional interpretation. Justices who emphasize the original understanding commonly expect to find some original direction in the text.

(c) The Original Understanding. Much of the academic questioning of "originalism" has failed to persuade the Supreme Court, at least in its criminal procedure jurisprudence. As evidenced by its inquires into the historical background and legislative history of each of the Constitution's criminal process guarantees, the Court clearly has acknowledged its obligation to render decisions that are in accord with the guarantee's original design. By accepting the direction provided by that historical background and legislative history, even when its content is not entirely consistent, the Court has rejected the contention that originalism is rarely helpful because history is almost always far too ambiguous to provide helpful answers on specific interpretive issues. By treating evidence of "the intent of the Framers" as a strong indicator of the "original understanding" of the founding generation, the Court has rendered moot the distinctions that commentators have drawn between determining the common understanding of the language of the guarantees at the time of their adoption and the subjective intent (or expectations) as to content held by the drafters (or ratifiers) of the guarantees.

The one aspect of originalism that has divided the Supreme Court is the choice of the appropriate level of generality at which the guarantee's original design should be understood. That choice has particular significance in two settings: (1) where the founding generation viewed a guarantee as aimed at prohibiting a particular procedural practice and the modern day procedure being challenged is deemed analogous to that prohibited procedure; (2) where the modern day procedure being challenged is identical to, or analogous to, a procedure known to the founding generation and thought not to be prohibited by the particular guarantee. A justice adhering to what might be described as "strict originalism" would find the specific understanding of the founding generation to be controlling in both situations and rule accordingly on the counterpart modern practice. A justice following what might be described as "loose originalism" would look more to the general purpose of the guarantee, which could lead to a ruling inconsistent with the specific understanding. This broader concept of originalism (which strict originalist would describe as not originalism at all, but just a form of "value analysis") tends to be followed by justices who adhere to the concept of a "living constitution" or tend to be categorized as "pragmatists".

Whether a current practice is truly analogous to a practice clearly prohibited under the original understanding is an issue often clouded by striking differences in the modern day procedural context. Where justices are in agreement that the analogy fits, however, loose originalists are likely to agree with strict originalists that the original understanding prevails and the modern day procedure must be prohibited. Differences in judicial perspectives as to the original understanding are more likely to be critical where a particular practice clearly was deemed acceptable under the original understanding but now can be viewed as arguably inconsistent with the general objectives of the guarantee. Here, the prevailing position has varied with the modern day context in which the particular procedure is employed, the character of the guarantee at issue, and the composition of the Court at the time of the ruling.

Over the years, historical acceptance has sustained a variety of procedures that might be viewed as inconsistent with a basic function of a particular guarantee. Thus, the Court has looked to historical acceptance in holding that: the right to jury trial does not apply to prosecutions for petty offenses notwithstanding that they obviously are criminal prosecutions; the double jeopardy prohibition of successive prosecutions for the "same offence" does not apply to successive prosecutions for the same basic criminal conduct under two statutes that use different elements in defining the prohibited offense; and due process does not prohibit the forfeiture of the property of an innocent owner which had been used by others as an instrumentality of crime. In support of such rulings, the Court has noted that where a guarantee has "deep historical roots," it must be interpreted in light of its "common-law understanding." Although the general premise of the guarantee might, as a matter of logic, lead to a contrary result, there are guarantees as to which "a page of history is worth a volume of logic," and instances in which "logic * * * must defer * * * to history and experience."

On the other side, the Court has also developed a variety of countervailing rationales in holding unconstitutional various procedures with equally strong historical pedigrees which indicated that the procedures had been viewed by the Framers as constitutionally acceptable. In some instances, the Court has reasoned that changed circumstances have deprived that historical acceptance of much of its weight. Thus, in *Tenn. v. Garner* (1985), the Court noted that the common law rule allowing the use of deadly force to prevent the escape of any suspected felon, without regard to the suspect's dangerousness, originally had been deemed reasonable under the Fourth Amendment, but its acceptance came at a time when "virtually all felonies were punishable by death," and when the officer's use of deadly force typically came in hand-to-hand combat that itself posed a danger. Today's setting was quite different, with almost all crimes formerly punishable by death no longer subject to that penalty, with many crimes formerly deemed misdemeanors now lifted to the felony level, and with handguns allowing officers to use deadly force in settings where the escaping suspect poses no threat to the officer. Of course, changes of the type cited in *Garner* are not unique. With so many new developments in the criminal justice process and its administration since the adoption of the Bill of Rights (or the Fourteenth Amendment), there is almost always some change that casts upon a procedure a somewhat different light than existed at common law. Thus, the critical issue is whether the change truly alters the character of the procedure in such a way as to eliminate the characteristic that led the Framers to view the procedure as consistent with the applicable Bill of Rights guarantee. The Court has offered no clear guidelines on that issue, as evidenced by frequent disagreement over the significance of such changes.

In other instances, the Court has discounted historical acceptance of a particular procedure on the ground that the guarantee in question was designed as an "open ended provision," intended to be "molded to the views of contemporary society." Thus, the due process clause has been described as "the least frozen concept of our law—the least confined to history and the most absorptive of powerful social standards of a progressive society," and it has been applied to condemn various practices never thought to raise significant constitutional difficulties at common law. So too, the "reasonableness clause" of the Fourth Amendment has been characterized as open to interpretation "in light of contemporary norms and conditions" (leading to decisions that "ha[ve] not simply frozen into constitutional law those law enforcement practices that existed at the time of the Fourth Amendment's passage"); the prohibition against cruel and unusual punishments has been described as "draw[ing] its meaning from the evolving standards of decency that marks the progress of a maturing society"; and the equal protection clause has been held to impose a general command that requires the Court "to be open to reassessment of ancient practices." However, the extent to which a particular guarantee incorporates such an "evolving concept" is often unclear. As discussed in § 2.2(b), in recent years, in its interpretation of free-standing due process, the Court has spoken of giving great deference to historical pedigree in criminal procedure cases, notwithstanding that this guarantee supposedly is "the least confined to history."

Finally, historically accepted practices have also been rejected on the ground that the practice conflicts with a more fully developed understanding of the general principles underlying a particular guarantee. Thus, the practice of not providing court appointed counsel for indigent felony defendants was held to violate the Sixth Amendment in light of experience establishing the "obvious truth that the average defendant does not have the professional legal skill" to ensure that he receives a fair trial (see § 3.1). The analysis applied in such cases is reconciled with originalism on the assumption that the Framers would not have wanted a constitutional framework designed for the future as well as the present to lock-in their specific, immediate expectations on the application of a guarantee, without regard to what might be learned through subsequent experience in applying that guarantee to a variety of different settings. When such experience reveals that a practice originally thought to be consistent with the guarantee's core purpose is, in fact, in conflict with that purpose, requiring a choice between the Framers' specific expectation and their overall objective, they presumably would have expected coherence in effectuating that overall objective to prevail.

The concepts of changed circumstances, open-ended guarantees that absorb the "evolving gloss of civilized standards," and re-examination in light of the deeper, experienced-based understanding of a guarantee's core purpose, provide ample leeway for holding unconstitutional any historically sanctioned practice viewed by today's Court as inconsistent with the general thrust of its current interpretation of a particular guarantee. Whether that will occur depends in large part on that point within the spectrum of approaches to constitutional interpretation at which a Court majority can be formed. Over the years, individual justices have varied considerably in their general philosophy of constitutional interpretation, particularly as it bears on their analysis of "the original understanding." Thus, composition changes, even as to a single justice, have produced sometimes substantial and sometimes subtle shifts in the perspective commanding a Court majority.

(d) Policy Analysis. An analysis that looks to the general policies (sometimes described as "values") underlying a particular guarantee is most often used in considering the constitutionality of procedures that have no common law counterpart, but such an analysis has sometimes also been applied to procedures that are analogous to traditional, common law procedures. A policy analysis initially identifies the basic function of a guarantee and then decides what requirements are needed to fulfill that function. Thus, the Court, in setting standards for determining when counsel's performance undermines the Sixth Amendment guarantee to the assistance of counsel, first identified the overall purpose of the guarantee—ensuring a fundamentally fair proceeding—and then identified the level of inadequacy likely to have deprived the defendant of the guarantee's objective (see § 3.10).

Although some justices have criticized value-driven analysis as largely subjective, it remains a key methodology for many aspects of constitutional criminal procedure. For some guarantees, its use is confined largely to particular aspects of the guarantee (e.g., in the cost-benefit analysis that sets the scope of the Fourth Amendment's exclusionary rule), but as to other guarantees (e.g., the Sixth Amendment right to a jury trial), it has been used in setting the constitutional standards that govern various aspects of the guarantee.

(e) The Appropriateness of Administratively Based Per Se Rules. In many settings the Supreme Court has viewed the constitutional question at issue as naturally calling for what might be described as a "categorical" or "definitional" standard—i.e., a standard that looks to a single characteristic or event and does not adjust to the uniqueness of each case. Such a standard is imposed, for example, in determining what constitutes a criminal case for the purpose of applying the Sixth Amendment right to appointed counsel (§ 3.2(a)). In other settings, the Court has viewed the constitutional question at issue as calling for a standard requiring a fact sensitive judgment geared to a variety of circumstances that differ with each case. Such a standard is applied, for example, in determining whether the granting of a mistrial, without defendant's consent, will bar a retrial (§ 17.2(c)). In still other settings, the Court has concluded that, while the question at issue generally calls for a case-by-case balancing of a variety of circumstances, administrative concerns justify imposing a "per se" or "bright-line" test which finds a particular action to be constitutional or unconstitutional based on a single event or characteristic. Such a standard is similar in formulation to the usual categorical standard, but its grounding is different. The Court is not saying that the function of the applicable constitutional guarantee necessarily requires such a bright-line rule. Indeed, the Court is acknowledging that its per se standard is either over-inclusive or under-inclusive as compared to the application of that function to all relevant circumstances on a case-by-case basis. Nonetheless, practical considerations relevant to administration of the Court's ruling have convinced the Court of the need to adopt a shorthand generalization in the form of a per se rule even though the function of the guarantee might point to the ad hoc application of a totality-of-the-circumstances analysis.

Supreme Court decisions imposing categorical standards often suggest alternative lines of reasoning which leave unclear whether that standard is required logically by the function of the guarantee or has been adopted because the alternative of applying that function to the totality-of-the-circumstances would present unacceptable administrative difficulties. Nonetheless, a variety of rulings imposing categorical standards clearly indicate that the Court there carved out a bright-line rule, even though it might include more or less than the logic of the guarantee would require, because of the difficulties that would be presented in applying that logic via a standard calling for an ad hoc, multi-circumstance analysis. See e.g., *Cuyler v. Sullivan* (§ 3.9(d)) (incompetency of counsel established per se when an actual conflict of interest adversely affected counsel's performance in a setting of joint representation of codefendants, as Court will conclusively presume prejudicial impact upon the outcome of the proceeding rather than engage in usual case-specific inquiry into prejudicial impact); *Turner v. Murray* (§ 14.3(a)) ("because risk of racial prejudice infecting capital sentencing proceeding is especially serious in light of the complete finality of the death penalty," a capital defendant accused of an interracial crime is entitled automatically to voir dire questioning on racial bias without the usual prerequisite of showing that racial issues are "inextricably bound up with the conduct of the trial"). On the other hand, the Court also has ruled in a variety of settings that administrative concerns did not justify a bright-line rule, and some of those settings presented issues analogous to the issues presented in cases adopting administratively based-bright line standards. See e.g., *U.S. v. Cronic* (§ 3.7(d)) (rejecting a lower court ruling adopting a per se standard of ineffective assistance of counsel based upon factors such as the tardy appointment of counsel, and requiring, instead, an examination of the actual performance of counsel under the circumstances of the individual case); *Ristaino v. Ross* (§ 14.3(a)) (rejecting as to noncapital cases an automatic entitlement to voir dire questioning on racial bias where the crime is interracial, as determining the presence of a "constitutionally significant likelihood" of juror bias requires an evaluation of "all the circumstances" presented by the case).

As might be surmised from the divergence in its rulings, the Supreme Court has not issued a bright-line rule as to when administrative concerns should lead to the adoption of a per se rule. There is general agreement on the use of a per se standard where it provides an almost perfect fit with the result that would be reached by applying the logic of the guarantee on a case-by-case basis to the circumstances of each case. "Conclusive presumptions," the Court has noted, are "designed to avoid the costs of excessive inquiry where a per se rule will achieve the correct result in almost all cases." The key is to be able to say that, though " 'cases that do not fit the generalization may arise,' " they are " 'not sufficiently common * * * [to] justify the time and expense necessary to identify them.' " Some justices have suggested that unless the bright-line rule meets this standard by producing very little overinclusion or underinclusion (as compared to a case-by-case analysis), it bears the seeds of its own demise. Nonetheless, the Court's rulings suggest that at least two somewhat distinct administrative concerns may lead to the adoption of bright-lines that fall considerably short of an "almost perfect fit." Where these considerations apply, the Court has shown a willingness, at times, to adopt a bright-line standard which produces for the vast majority of cases the same result as the logical application of the function of the guarantee to the distinctive circumstances of the case, but which produces as well a substantial body of applications that result in condemning more or less than that function would otherwise require.

One setting that may lead to such an administratively based bright-line prohibition is that in which establishing a constitutional violation otherwise requires a difficult factual determination, such as assessing whether an actor was motivated by bad faith or bias. Concern that such a determination can be made accurately only by a potentially pernicious judicial inquiry can lead the Court to prefer a per se prohibition that avoids the necessity of making that factual determination. See e.g., *Peery v. Leeke* (1989) (where judicial order precluded testifying defendant's overnight consultation with counsel, prejudice component of ineffective assistance claim conclusively presumed, in part because prejudice otherwise would be determined only be reviewing the character of earlier communications between counsel and defendant). A second setting is that in which the administrator lacks the capacity, expertise, or opportunity to apply a finely tuned standard. Thus, over the past few decades, the Supreme Court frequently has extolled the virtues of bright-line standards in the constitutional regulation of police activities. The Court has noted that "a single familiar standard is essential to guide police officers, who have only limited time and expertise to reflect on and balance the social and individual interests in the specific circumstances they confront."

(f) The Appropriateness of Prophylactic Rules. The Supreme Court also has not formulated a bright-line standard as to when it is appropriate to utilize "prophylactic rules." Indeed, the Court has not yet settled on a standard definition of what constitutes a "prophylactic rule." The key apparently is the rationale underlying the rule rather than the form of the rule. In explaining decisions characterized as establishing prophylactic rules, the Court has emphasized two features of those rules—their function and their grounding.

Initially, as suggested by the term "prophylactic," the rules are characterized as preventive measures. Their purpose is to safeguard against a potential constitutional violation, rather than to identify what constitutes a constitutional violation. Prevention may be achieved (1) by imposing procedural safeguards that provide a protective shield for the underlying constitutional right, (2) by utilizing an evidentiary exclusionary remedy to take away the primary incentive for constitutional violations by law enforcement officers seeking to acquire evidence, or (3) by prohibiting a law enforcement practice that readily might be misused and manipulated to deprive a suspect of a constitutional right. Secondly, the prophylactic rule is grounded not on the conclusion that a violation of the rule invariably produces a violation of the core guarantee, but on the Court's exercise of its authority to craft remedies and procedures that facilitate its adjudication responsibilities.

The Court has emphasized two important consequences that follow from the special function and grounding of prophylactic rules. Because prophylactic rules may be violated without denying a constitutional right, those violations may be given remedial consequences which are narrower or which do not apply in as broad a range of proceedings as the remedies attaching to the actual violation of the constitutional right that the prophylactic rule is designed to prevent. So too, the non-constitutional grounding of prophylactic rules leaves the door open for Congress to replace those rules with other safeguards that serve the same preventive function.

Prophylactic rules that formulate procedural prerequisites for particular police, prosecutorial, or judicial actions do not declare that such actions would have produced a violation of the core guarantee without those prerequisites being followed. Rather, the prerequisites are described as necessary to combat what would otherwise be a substantial potential for constitutional violations in those actions. Such prerequisites were imposed in two Supreme Court rulings that have come to be viewed as paradigmatic of prophylactic procedural prerequisites—*Miranda v. Ariz.* (1966) and *N.C. v. Pearce* (§ 18.7). *Miranda* required the police to give various warnings to an interrogated suspect in order to ensure that custodial interrogation did not result in compulsion that would violate the suspect's privilege against self-incrimination. Absent such warnings, a statement obtained through custodial interrogation was automatically excluded from the prosecution's case-in-chief, without regard to what other circumstances might suggest as to whether the statement was compelled in violation of the Fifth Amendment. *Pearce* concluded that there is a significant likelihood that a judge who imposes a higher sentence on a defendant following that defendant's successful appeal (and subsequent retrial and conviction) is doing so vindictively, and thereby violating due process. Because it would be most difficult for the defendant to establish actual vindictiveness, the Court required, as a prophylactic safeguard, that the judge set forth the reasons for the higher sentence and rely upon "objective information concerning identifiable conduct on the part of the defendant." In the absence of such an acceptable statement of reasons, supported by factual data, the higher sentence cannot be accepted, without regard to whether it was or was not in fact a product of vindictiveness.

In *Dickerson v. U.S.* (2000), in responding to Justice Scalia's dissenting opinion challenging the legitimacy of prophylactic rules, the Court majority emphasized that the leading prophylactic ruling, *Miranda v. Ariz.*, was a decision "interpreting and applying the Constitution." However, as Justice Scalia noted in his dissent, the Court did not refer to the traditional explanation of prophylactic rules as flowing from the Court's authority to adopt standards that "buttress constitutional rights." Indeed, in explaining the constitutional grounding of the *Miranda* "guidelines," the *Dickerson* majority offered an analysis similar to that traditionally offered in sustaining per se standards. At the same time, however, the *Dickerson* majority also acknowledged that *Miranda* contained a feature that the Court had associated only with prophylactic rulings—the authority of Congress to replace the *Miranda* guidelines with a legislative solution that was "at least as effective" in protecting against self-incrimination violations in police interrogation.

Dickerson put to rest any question as to the constitutional legitimacy of prophylactic rulings, and at the same time, continued to recognize a distinction between those rulings and other constitutional rulings. It provided, however, no clear answers as to how such rulings were distinguishable from other constitutional rulings (particularly per se rulings), and why their special character produced unique rules as to their implementation (including possible congressional substitution of alternative measures). Commentators speculated that the failure of the *Dickerson* opinion to more completely address these issues stemmed from a division within the Court beyond that reflected by the Scalia dissent. Three years later, the several opinions in *Chavez v. Martinez* (2003) provided strong support for that speculation. There, the eight justices speaking to the issue agreed that a *Miranda* violation was quite distinct from a classic Fifth Amendment violation, and that it therefore did not provide a basis for a damage remedy under a federal civil rights statute. They were sharply divided, however, in their characterization of *Miranda's* distinctive character.

Four justices, in an opinion by Justice Thomas, characterized *Miranda* (and several rulings dealing with a witness' exercise of the self-incrimination privilege) as establishing "prophylactic rules designed to safeguard the core constitutional right protected by the Self–Incrimination Clause." Such rulings, the opinion added, "do not extend the scope of the constitutional right itself," and therefore are more limited as to remedies. Two justices, in an opinion by Justice Souter, described *Miranda* (and the other rulings cited by Justice Thomas) as establishing "law outside the Fifth Amendment's core, with each case expressing a judgment that the core guarantee, or the judicial capacity to protect it, would be placed at some risk in the absence of some complimentary protection." The special character of these "complimentary rulings" advised against their extension through recognition of a damage remedy. Two justices, in an opinion by Justice Kennedy, similarly placed *Miranda* (though not the other Fifth Amendment rulings) in a special category, as a constitutional ruling adopted to "reduce the risk of a coerced confession and to implement the self-incrimination clause". Here too, the characterization impacted the remedy.

Chavez clearly indicates that there is a class of rulings viewed as distinct from interpretations of the "core guarantee" and therefore treated different as to remedy, and presumably also as to Congressional replacement. Whether described as a "judicially created prophylactic rule" or as an "extension" providing "complementary protection" for the core guarantee, the characterization of the ruling stems from its basic function of precluding constitutional violations that otherwise might go undetected. The Court has failed, however, to came close even to the limited degree of consensus found in *Chavez* when it comes to identifying the precise conditions that justify issuance of such rulings. The range of views advanced by individual justices has extended from those who see a substantial need for such rulings to those who view such rulings as inconsistent with the judicial role. Thus, while some justices have been receptive to creating new "prophylactic rules" and extending previously established prophylactic rulings, others will do no more than tolerate the well established prophylactic ruling of the past where the considerations underlying *stare decisis* compel that they do so. In recent years, the composition of the Court has favored both refusing to adopt proposed new prophylactic rulings and restricting old prophylactic rulings.

   (g) Weighing the Impact Upon Efficiency. A new constitutional regulation often will impose a substantial burden upon the administration of the criminal justice process. That burden can take various forms, including increased expenditures for an already underfunded system, additional hearings for already congested court dockets, and perhaps even insurmountable obstacles to the solution of some crimes. The extent to which such "practical costs" should be considered by the Court has been a matter of continuing debate among the justices. In general, the Court tends to discuss the practical impact of a ruling when it views itself as having more flexibility in fashioning its ruling. Thus, discussions of practical impact are more commonly found in decisions interpreting open-ended clauses, decisions applying the more specific clauses to new settings or settings that have been altered by changed circumstances, and decisions setting forth or applying prophylactic rules. On the other side, where the Court views the text or history of a particular provision as setting forth a "constitutional command that * * * is unequivocal," the practical costs incurred in applying that command are said to be irrelevant. The constitutional command itself strikes a balance between the rights of the accused and society's need for effective enforcement of the criminal law, and the Court is bound to accept that balance. See e.g., *Smith v. Hooey* (§ 10.4(a)) (expense involved in transporting an accused incarcerated in another state would not be weighed in shaping his right to a speedy trial; as the Wisconsin Supreme Court had noted, " 'we will not put a price tag upon constitutional rights' ").

   Where the applicability of a guarantee is acknowledged to be less than clear, the justices' views on weighing practical costs ordinarily fall within the outer boundaries marked by two distinctive positions. On the one side, there is the view that, if the burden imposed would be great, the Court should hesitate to extend the guarantee unless its extension is essential to fulfilling the function of the guarantee. On the other side, there is the view that practical costs should be a decidedly subordinate concern. They should be given weight only where the burden is substantial and clear, relates to an important state interest, and cannot be offset by other measures; and even then, they need not be controlling.

As a result of these differences in viewpoint, the treatment of practical costs in majority opinions tends to be inconsistent. Many opinions discuss practical costs as a factor to be given serious consideration, and several refer to such costs as an important reason for not extending a particular doctrine. See e.g., *Scott v. Ill.* (§ 3.2(a)); *Shadwick v. City of Tampa* (§ 2.1(e)). Other opinions mention such costs, but promptly dismiss them, while still others fail to even acknowledge what are obviously significant administrative burdens imposed by a new ruling.

*

Chapter 3

THE RIGHT TO COUNSEL

Table of Sections

For additional analysis of the above topics and citations to authorities supporting their discussion in this Book, consult the authors' 7-volume *Criminal Procedure* treatise, also available as Westlaw database CRIMPROC. See the Table of Cross-References in this Book.

§ 3.1 Diverse Constitutional Groundings

Although courts commonly speak of a single constitutional right to counsel, there are in fact several different groundings for a constitutional right to counsel, and in that sense, several different constitutional rights to counsel. These rights apply at different stages of the criminal justice process. But once a particular grounding establishes a constitutional right to counsel, the requirements flowing from the right (e.g., effective assistance by counsel) commonly are the same without regard to the particular grounding.

(a) Sixth Amendment Rights. The Sixth Amendment provides that "in all criminal prosecutions, the accused shall enjoy the right * * * to have the assistance of counsel for his defense." That this provision guaranteed a right to representation by privately retained counsel was obvious from the outset; that it also included an obligation of the state to provide at public expense defense counsel for the indigent defendant (i.e., the defendant financially unable to retain a lawyer) was far less certain. Unlike the right to retained counsel, a right to appointed counsel lacked any substantial historical grounding. Nonetheless, the Court eventually came to interpret the Sixth Amendment as granting a right to representation by counsel to all defendants, with the state required to provide counsel where the defendant was indigent. Moreover, that Supreme

Court precedent also indicates that the proceedings encompassed by the Sixth Amendment right to counsel are precisely the same whether the issue is allowing representation by retained counsel or requiring the state to appoint counsel for the indigent.

The first major Supreme Court discussion of the constitutional right to counsel came in *Powell v. Ala.* (1932), which considered the rights of defendants both to utilize retained counsel and to be provided with court appointed counsel. *Powell* was not itself a Sixth Amendment case. It involved a state prosecution and was decided under the then prevailing "fundamental fairness" interpretation of Fourteenth Amendment due process (see § 2.1(a)). Nonetheless, it has had continuing significance through subsequent interpretations of the Sixth Amendment right to counsel. When the Court later discarded the fundamental fairness interpretation in favor of a selective incorporation analysis that made the Sixth Amendment directly applicable to the states (through the Fourteenth Amendment), its interpretation of the Sixth Amendment rested heavily upon *Powell*'s analysis of the need for counsel.

The Supreme Court had before it in *Powell* a prosecution that was to become a cause célèbre in the fight against racial injustice. Nine black youths had been charged with the rape of two white girls in the vicinity of Scottsboro, Alabama. Eight of the youths had been convicted, with the jury imposing the death sentence. On appeal, the defendants raised two claims relating to the right to counsel. First, they claimed that they had a constitutional right to retain counsel to represent them at trial and that the trial court had violated this right by failing to give them sufficient opportunity to seek retained counsel. Second, they claimed that, assuming arguendo that they would have been unable to employ counsel even if they had been given that opportunity, the trial court would then have had an obligation to make an effective appointment of counsel. The trial judge at their arraignment had announced that he was appointing "all of the members of the bar" to represent them, but defendants argued that this had been an empty gesture, made in such a haphazard way that the local bar member who eventually stepped forward to represent them at trial (in consultation with an outside attorney) was largely unprepared. The Supreme Court sustained both of defendants' claims, finding that each separately established a denial of due process.

The *Powell* opinion initially considered the trial court's failure to give the defendants an adequate opportunity to retain counsel. The opinion concluded that the due process clause of the Fourteenth Amendment guaranteed to defendants a right to be represented by retained counsel, and to implement that right, a trial court must give the defendant reasonable time and opportunity to secure counsel. The Court here relied heavily upon the historical developments that had led to the adoption of the Sixth Amendment and similarly worded state provisions. The practice in England had been to allow the complete assistance of retained counsel in misdemeanor trials, but to deny defendants the right to utilize their counsel at felony trials, except for arguments on legal questions. This limitation had not been accepted in many of the American colonies, which allowed defendants the full assistance of retained counsel in felony as well as misdemeanor trials. At the time of the adoption of the Constitution, twelve of the thirteen states had rejected the English rule on felony cases, and the Sixth Amendment, not surprisingly, did the same. The *Powell* opinion concluded that the right to utilize retained counsel, as reflected in these state and federal provisions, readily fit within the concept of due process. For due process guaranteed a right to a fair hearing, and such a hearing, "[h]istorically and in practice, in our country at least, has always included the right to the aid of counsel when desired and provided by the party asserting the right."

When the *Powell* opinion turned to the defendants' second claim, asserting an indigent defendant's right to appointed counsel, it did not look to the history underlying the Sixth Amendment or to the early state provisions. This was understandable since the right of the indigent defendant to counsel provided by the state had a much narrower historical base. Where the original states provided for the appointment of counsel, they usually did so only in capital cases. Similarly, Congress, shortly before the ratification of the Sixth Amendment, had adopted a statutory provision requiring an appointment of counsel that was limited to capital crimes. Indeed, at the time of the *Powell* decision, almost half of the states apparently did not provide appointed counsel in most felony cases.

A constitutional right to appointed counsel could be derived, however, if not from historical traditions, from the due process right to a fair hearing. In concluding that the right to retained counsel was an essential element of due process, the first portion of the *Powell* opinion had stressed that the "right to be heard would be, in many cases, of little avail if it did not comprehend the right to be heard by counsel." The indigent defendant, the Court reasoned, was as much entitled to a fair hearing as the more affluent defendant who could afford to retain a lawyer. The state accordingly had a due process obligation to provide the indigent defendant with a lawyer where counsel's assistance would be necessary to achieve a fair hearing. Language in the first portion of the opinion arguably also suggested that a lawyer would almost always be needed to provide a fair hearing. Even the "intelligent and educated layman," the opinion had noted, needs the "guiding hand of counsel" to cope with the intricacies of the law. The *Powell* Court's holding on appointed counsel, however, was carefully limited to the type of situation presented in the case before the Court—"a capital case, where the defendant is unable to employ counsel, and is incapable adequately of making his own defense because of ignorance, feeble-mindedness, illiteracy, or the like."

The *Powell* reasoning suggested that there were two distinct and separately grounded constitutional rights to counsel. First, as a result of the rejection of the English common law rule, the defendant had gained a right to be represented by counsel provided at his own expense. Whether or not a lawyer was needed in the particular case did not matter; that was for each defendant to decide, and the state had to respect the defendant's decision, as only his resources were involved. Second, a constitutional right to appointed counsel arose out of the state's obligation to provide a fair hearing. That obligation carried with it an affirmative duty to provide counsel for the indigent defendant where a lawyer's assistance was needed to ensure a fair and accurate guilt-determining process. This right arguably was narrower in scope than the right to retained counsel. Since public funds were being expended, the provision of counsel could be tied to cases where it was actually needed. Thus, the *Powell* ruling on appointed counsel had been restricted to the special circumstances of that case, while its ruling on the right to use retained counsel had spoken of a general right applicable in all felony cases.

Six years after *Powell,* in *Johnson v. Zerbst* (1938), the Court drew no distinction between the right to retained counsel and the right to appointed counsel in its interpretation of the Sixth Amendment. *Johnson* involved a federal prosecution in which two apparently indigent defendants, charged with the felony of counterfeiting, had been refused appointed counsel because theirs was not a capital case. The Court held that their trial without counsel violated the Sixth Amendment, which applies by its terms to "all criminal prosecutions." The *Johnson* opinion reasoned that the Sixth Amendment "embodies a realistic recognition of the obvious truth that the average defendant does not have the professional legal skill to protect himself" in a criminal trial. It therefore "withholds from the federal courts, in all criminal proceedings, the power and authority to deprive an accused of his life or liberty unless he has or waives the assistance of counsel." This constitutional prerequisite for a valid conviction applied to all defendants, including those unable to afford counsel.

For a twenty-five year period following *Johnson,* the Supreme Court refused to extend that ruling to state cases. Although *Johnson* had held that the Sixth Amendment required appointed counsel in all federal felony cases, state cases were governed by the "less rigid and more fluid" requirement of the Fourteenth Amendment's due process clause. Relying upon a fundamental fairness analysis, the Court held in *Betts v. Brady* (1942) that due process required the appointment of counsel only where the special circumstances of the particular case indicated that the indigent defendant needed a lawyer to obtain a fair trial. *Powell* and other capital cases presented one illustration of such special circumstances. In non-capital cases, the need for appointed counsel could be established by the complicated nature of the offense or possible defenses thereto, events during trial that raised difficult legal questions, and personal characteristics of the defendant, such as youthfulness or mental incapacity. The special circumstances test of *Betts v. Brady* was sharply criticized by commentators, who argued that it was virtually impossible to render a retrospective judgment that a defendant forced to proceed pro se had not been prejudiced by the lack of counsel.

In *Gideon v. Wainwright* (1963), the Court rejected the special circumstances rule of *Betts* and extended the right to appointed counsel in state cases to all indigent felony defendants. Unlike *Betts*, *Gideon* appeared to proceed from the premise, consistent with the selective incorporation doctrine (see § 2.1(d)), that the Fourteenth Amendment rendered the Sixth Amendment right to counsel directly applicable to the states as a fundamental right. However, rather than simply relying on *Johnson v. Zerbst's* holding under the Sixth Amendment, *Gideon* returned to *Powell's* discussion of the need for counsel. It concluded that "reason and reflection require us to recognize that in our adversary system of criminal justice, any person hauled into court, who is too poor to hire a lawyer cannot be assured a fair trial unless counsel is provided for him."

Gideon, like *Johnson v. Zerbst*, viewed the Sixth Amendment as prescribing the invariable prerequisites of a fair trial and including the assistance of counsel among those prerequisites. It follows from this premise that no Sixth Amendment distinction should exist between the affluent defendant's right to retained counsel and the indigent defendant's right to appointed counsel. Where a particular proceeding is deemed to be a stage in the "criminal prosecution" for Sixth Amendment purposes, both should have an automatic right to representation by counsel (in the case of the indigent, at state expense). On the other hand, where the proceeding is not within the span covered by the Sixth Amendment's reference to the "criminal prosecution," neither should have a Sixth Amendment right to counsel. Whether a Sixth Amendment right to counsel exists should depend on the nature of the proceeding and not on whether the claim relates to retained or appointed counsel.

This conception of the Sixth Amendment as a single right finds further support in later cases which determined whether particular stages in the process were encompassed by the Sixth Amendment and whether counsel's performance was so deficient as to constitute a denial of the Sixth Amendment right to counsel. In making both of those determinations, the Court has viewed as irrelevant whether the defendant's claim relates to retained counsel or appointed counsel. Of course, though the Sixth Amendment creates a single right to counsel, applicable to both retained and appointed counsel, where the Sixth Amendment does not apply, due process, as discussed below, may provide greater protection of the right to retained counsel by prohibiting an unreasonable state interference with the defendant's utilization of retained counsel in a proceeding as to which there is no constitutional right to appointed counsel.

(b) Due Process Rights. While *Powell v. Ala.* (1932) recognized due process rights to the assistance of appointed and retained counsel in the context of a proceeding that today would be subject to the Sixth Amendment, *Powell's* due process analysis did not disappear with the selective incorporation of the Sixth Amendment. Rather, it has had continuing significance for other proceedings not encompassed by the Sixth Amendment—particularly proceedings that occur after the defendant has been convicted and sentenced (and therefore is no longer an "accused" in a "criminal prosecution"). Thus, in the post-incorporation ruling of *Gagnon v. Scarpelli* (1973), a due process right to appointed counsel in parole and probation revocation hearings was found to flow logically from hearing rights previously mandated under the due process clause. Past precedent had established that the parolee or probationer was entitled to substantial procedural safeguards in a revocation hearing, including the rights to present evidence and confront opposing witnesses. *Gagnon* concluded that due process also requires the state to provide appointed counsel where, under the facts of the particular case, counsel is needed to ensure the "effectiveness of the [hearing] rights guaranteed by [due process]." The *Gagnon* Court refused to formulate "a precise and detailed set of guidelines" for determining when counsel was needed to ensure the effective operation of the hearing rights demanded by due process. It did note that counsel ordinarily should be provided where there is a significant factual dispute or the individual relies upon contentions that a layman would have difficulty presenting. At the same time, it cited other situations in which appointment of counsel ordinarily would not be necessary.

Speaking to the possibility of imposing a flat requirement of counsel in all revocation cases, the *Gagnon* Court acknowledged that such a requirement "had the appeal of simplicity." However, "it would impose direct costs and serious collateral disadvantages without regard to the need or the likelihood in a particular case for a constructive contribution by counsel." In most revocation cases, the issue presented simply did not require that expertise of a lawyer. Quite often, "the probationer or parolee has been convicted of committing another crime [which automatically establishes grounds for revocation] or has admitted the charges against him." Although he may still contend that revocation would be too harsh in light of the nature of his violation, "mitigating evidence of this kind is often not susceptible of proof or is so simple as not to require either investigation or exposition by counsel." On the other side, "the introduction of counsel" would "alter significantly the nature of the [revocation] proceeding." The state would respond by retaining its own counsel and the role of the hearing body would become "more akin to that of a judge at trial, and less attuned to the rehabilitative needs of the individual probationer." In addition, the revocation proceedings would be prolonged, and "the financial cost to the State—for appointed counsel, counsel for the State, a longer record and the possibility of judicial review—[would] not be insubstantial."

In contrast to *Gagnon*, which adopted a case-by-case approach similar to that of *Betts* (§ 3.1(a)), the Court adopted a flat "in-or-out" approach in assessing due process claims to other proceedings that occur after the criminal prosecution is ended. In *Ross v. Moffitt* (1974), the Court rejected the contention that due process required appointment of counsel to assist indigent defendants in preparing their applications for second-tier, discretionary appellate review. *Pa. v. Finley* (1987) and *Murray v. Giarratano* (1989) extended the *Ross* reasoning to hold that due process also did not require appointment of counsel for collateral challenges to a conviction (e.g., habeas corpus). *Evitts v. Lucey* (1985), on the other hand, held that due process established a right to retained and appointed counsel on a first appeal granted by state law as a matter of right. *Halbert v. Mich.* (2005) similarly held that due process established a right to appointed counsel as to a first appeal of a guilty plea conviction, even though state law granted review only at the discretion of the appellate court.

Ross, the first of these due process rulings, stressed the different position of the defendant who seeks to challenge a conviction in a postconviction proceeding, as opposed to the defendant who seeks to avoid a conviction at trial. The defendant at trial has need for an attorney "as a shield to protect him against being 'haled into court' by the State and stripped of his presumption of innocence." On appeal, in contrast, the attorney is to be utilized "as a sword to upset [a] prior determination of guilt." The defendant here is "seeking not to fend off the efforts of the State's prosecutor but rather to overturn a finding of guilt made by a judge or jury below." As one of the factors to be considered under a due process analysis is the "risk of an erroneous deprivation" of the protected liberty interest without the claimed procedural safeguard, a defendant stands in a lesser position when he claims a right to appointed counsel following a conviction.

Despite this "lesser position" of a person challenging a conviction, *Evitts* recognized a due process right to counsel for a first appeal as a matter of right. Moreover, it did so as flat rule, rather than looking to the circumstances of the case, as in *Gagnon*. This was so even though, in contrast to *Gagnon*, the Court was not building upon other due process prerequisites for the proceeding involved. Indeed, the Court had held that the Constitution imposed no obligation upon a state to grant appeals of right in criminal cases (§ 19.1(a))—a factor noted by *Ross* in explaining why the defendant on appeal occupied a lesser position than the defendant at trial (who, of course, had a constitutional right to a fair trial).

At issue in *Evitts* was a due process right to representation by a retained counsel on a first appeal as of right. Defendant had been represented by retained counsel, but he claimed that counsel rendered ineffective assistance, and such a claim depended upon having an underlying constitutional right to counsel in the particular proceeding. See § 3.7(a). Prior to *Evitts*, in *Douglas v. Cal.* (1963), the Court had recognized an equal protection right of an indigent defendant to the assistance of appointed counsel on a first appeal granted by state law as a matter of right. *Evitts* held the *Douglas* ruling also had a constitutional grounding in due process and that grounding necessarily established as well a right to be represented by retained counsel. *Douglas* had reasoned that, while the state had no constitutional obligation to establish an appellate process, once it had established such appellate review as " 'an integral part of [its] system for finally adjudicating the guilt or innocence of a defendant,' " it could not, first structure the appeal so that it was basically a "meaningless ritual" for a defendant lacking the assistance of counsel, and then fail to include a right to utilize counsel's assistance. Drawing an analogy to *Gideon*, the Court noted that under the state's appellate procedure, as under its trial procedure, "the services of a lawyer will for virtually every layman be necessary" to effectively present his case. Here too, the defendant faced an "adversarial system of justice" in which "lawyers are 'necessities,' not luxuries." Accordingly, due process, as to the first appeal of right, mandated a right to counsel parallel to the trial-level right established in *Gideon* under the Sixth Amendment. The *Gideon* argument, as *Evitts* noted, lent itself to a due process grounding, as it looked to the fairness of the adjudication process.

In contrast to *Douglas* and *Evitts*, *Ross* found that, where the lesser position of the person challenging a conviction was combined with the quite different function of a second appeal that was discretionary, adjudication fairness did not mandate the assistance of appointed counsel. The Court stressed that the defendants in this setting have already received a full appellate review, assisted by counsel, on their first appeal as of right. Accordingly, further assistance of counsel is not necessary to provide "meaningful access" to the higher appellate courts. In considering a defendant's petition for review, those higher courts will have before them the trial transcript, the intermediate court brief prepared by counsel, and in most instances, the opinion of the state's intermediate appellate court. Those materials, supplemented by any personal statement of the defendant, provide an "adequate basis" for determining whether to grant review. This is especially so because of the discretionary nature of the second-tier appellate review. The traditional standard utilized in determining whether to grant such discretionary review is whether the appeal presents issues worthy of high court consideration because of their general legal significance, rather than whether there has been a "correct adjudication of guilt" in the individual case.

Halbert held that the Michigan appellate structure on guilty plea appeals, where the first-tier appellate review was available only by leave of the appellate court, presented a situation closer to *Douglas* and *Evitts* than *Ross*, and the indigent defendant therefore had a due process right to the assistance of appointed counsel in preparing a petition seeking such review. The Court majority stressed that: (1) this discretionary appeal was "the first and likely only direct review [that] the defendant's conviction will receive"; (2) the state intermediate appellate court viewed its decision on granting review as an "error-correcting instance," and was "guided by the merits of the particular [applicant's] claims, not by the general importance of the question presented" (in contrast to traditional second-tier appellate review, as noted in *Ross*); and (3) guilty plea defendants are "generally ill equipped to represent themselves" and lack the support of a brief on the merits previously filed by appellate counsel (in contrast to *Ross*).

In *Pa. v. Finley* (1987), the majority characterized the issue before it as whether due process required the state to appoint counsel to assist the respondent in preparing a collateral attack upon her conviction under a state postconviction relief procedure. The state there had appointed counsel, but counsel had then been allowed to withdraw after concluding that the collateral attack lacked arguable merit. The Court majority reasoned that the withdrawal procedure would present a constitutional issue (see § 3.2(c)) only if respondent had an underlying constitutional right to the appointment of counsel. Turning to that question, the Court did not focus on the importance of counsel's expertise in preparing a collateral attack petition. Arguably, a stronger case could be made here than in *Ross,* as collateral challenges in state proceedings commonly assert new claims, and not simply claims previously presented (with counsel's assistance). The *Finley* Court stressed, instead, the place of the collateral attack within the totality of the proceedings for determining guilt. The majority noted that "post-conviction relief is even further removed from the criminal trial than is discretionary direct review," is not "part of the criminal proceedings itself," and "normally occurs only after the defendant has failed to secure relief through direct review of his conviction." In such a setting, the Court concluded, "the fundamental fairness mandated by the Due Process Clause does not require that the State supply a lawyer as well."

In *Murray v. Giarratano* (1989), a sharply divided Court refused to create an exception to *Pa. v. Finley* based on the special character of the particular postconviction proceeding in that case. At issue in *Murray* was the claim of Virginia's death row inmates that they were entitled to appointed counsel to assist them in preparing collateral attack challenges to their convictions and sentences. In upholding that claim, the Fourth Circuit had viewed the inmates' situation as presenting special circumstances that distinguished *Finley*. First, here, unlike *Finley,* the inmates had been sentenced to the death penalty. Second, the district court here had made special factual findings as to the inmates' need for counsel. That court had concluded "that death row inmates had a limited amount of time to prepare their petitions, that their cases were unusually complex, and that the shadow of impending execution would interfere with their ability to do legal work." While the state did assign "unit attorneys" to each penal institution, the district court had also found that those attorneys could not adequately assist the death row inmates because their role was limited to that of "legal advisor" rather than counsel for the inmate. Those district court findings were seen as providing a case-specific showing of the essentiality of counsel that had not been present in *Finley*.

Speaking for four justices, Chief Justice Rehnquist authored a plurality opinion that flatly rejected both of the distinctions cited by the lower court. The plurality emphasized the *Finley* precedent and the fact that the Court's post-*Gideon* rulings on the right to counsel "ha[d] been categorical holdings as to what the Constitution requires with respect to a particular stage of a criminal proceeding in general." This "tack" had been adopted in light of "the Court's dissatisfaction with the case-by-case approach in *Betts v. Brady* that led to the adoption of the categorical ruling * * * in *Gideon*." There was nothing in the nature of the collateral proceeding that justified departure from the continued use of categorical holdings. In response, Justice Stevens' dissenting opinion, also speaking for four justices, argued that "particular circumstances" necessarily shape the scope of the due process right to counsel. Here the circumstances cited by the lower court, as well as additional circumstances, clearly distinguished *Finley.*

With eight justices evenly divided as to the significance of the special circumstances presented by the Virginia inmates, the deciding vote in *Murray* was cast by Justice Kennedy. His very brief opinion appeared to give some weight to special circumstances, although Justice O'Connor found no inconsistency in the Kennedy and Rehnquist opinions and joined both. Justice Kennedy initially accepted Justice Stevens' analysis insofar as it established (1) that "collateral proceedings are a central part of the review process for prisoners condemned to death" and (2) that the "complexity of our jurisprudence in this area * * * makes it unlikely that capital defendants will be able to file successful petitions for collateral relief without the assistance of persons learned in the law." He noted, however, that the necessary assistance can be provided in "various ways" and there was no showing that Virginia's approach had been unsatisfactory. For "no prisoner on death row in Virginia ha[d] been unable to obtain counsel to represent him in postconviction proceedings, and Virginia's prison system is staffed with institutional lawyers to assist in preparing petitions for postconviction relief." Accordingly, Justice Kennedy concurred in the reversal of the lower court ruling based "on the facts and record of this case."

The division of the Court in *Murray* leaves open the extent to which the Court majority will give weight to the special elements of a procedural setting, as it relates to a particular type of litigant, in assessing a due process claim to appointed counsel. Arguably, the division among the justices was limited to the capital case. There was no suggestion that special circumstances could play a role on a discretionary appeal (*Ross*) or a collateral proceeding (*Finley*) in a non-capital case. Yet, there remains *Gagnon v. Scarpelli,* a case utilizing a special-circumstances approach outside of the capital offense context, which was not discussed in any of the *Murray* opinions. Certainly the thrust of the Court's rulings is not so firmly settled as to impose a significant barrier to the adoption in future cases, especially by a Court of changed composition, of an approach that more strongly favors either categorical rulings (e.g., *Evitts, Finley, Halbert,* and *Ross*) or special-circumstances rulings (e.g., *Gagnon*).

Indeed, in *Coleman v. Thompson* (1991), the Court left open the possibility of recognizing a type of special-circumstances right to appointed counsel on collateral attack, there based on a characteristic of state law. *Coleman* left open the question of whether an indigent defendant who seeks to raise on collateral attack a claim of ineffective assistance by trial counsel is entitled constitutionally to the assistance of appointed counsel in preparing that claim where state law precluded raising the ineffective assistance claim on direct appeal, insisting instead that it be presented on collateral attack.

Still another issue left in limbo is whether the due process right to utilize retained counsel may have a broader scope than the due process right to appointed counsel. Pre-*Gideon* rulings had indicated that the right to representation by retained counsel had a broader due process grounding than the right to appointed counsel. Thus, during the same period in which the accused's right to appointed counsel in a noncapital felony case was controlled by the special circumstances rule of *Betts,* the right of such a defendant to representation by retained counsel was characterized as "unqualified." Indeed, *Powell v. Ala.* (§ 3.1(a)) had suggested in dicta that due process would be denied if a court, even in a civil case, "were arbitrarily to refuse to hear a party by counsel, employed by and appearing for him." On the other hand, as previously noted, the later Sixth Amendment rulings have indicated that the rights to appointed and retained counsel are equivalent under that Amendment. The same could be true of due process. Although, one consideration presumably distinguishing a due process analysis of the right to appointed counsel would be its weighing of the burden placed upon the state in providing counsel at its expense, the due process rulings rejecting claims to appointed counsel have tended to emphasize other factors, such as the limited role of collateral challenges in ensuring reliability of verdicts. Those other factors could be deemed equally controlling in rejecting claims as to retained counsel—unless the Court recognizes an independent due process interest of the litigant not to be prevented from utilizing his own resources to present his case through counsel if he so chooses. Support for recognizing such an interest may be found in historical practice. As to almost all proceedings relating to criminal liability that are not themselves part of the criminal prosecution (e.g., appeals and collateral challenges), there is a longstanding history of allowing representation by retained counsel.

The possibility that a state could refuse to permit retained counsel where it need not appoint counsel was raised in *Gagnon.* After holding that due process required appointment of counsel in probation and parole revocation cases where the circumstances made counsel necessary to ensure the "effectiveness" of due process guaranteed hearing rights, the *Gagnon* Court cited several concerns in refusing to impose a flat requirement of appointed counsel in all revocation cases. Among those concerns was the potentially adverse impact of automatic representation by counsel upon the special nature of the revocation proceeding (where the state typically did not use counsel and the focus often was upon a "predictive and discretionary" determination as to rehabilitative potential). That impact, of course, would flow from frequent representation by retained counsel as well as by appointed counsel. The Court added a warning, however, should a state decide to restrict the use of retained counsel. It stated in a footnote: "We have no occasion to decide in this case whether a probationer or parolee has a right to be represented at a revocation hearing by retained counsel in situations other than those where the State would be obliged to furnish counsel for an indigent." In other contexts, lower courts have noted that should a state seek to bar the assistance of retained counsel in a proceeding that relates to the criminal justice process, it must at least be able to point to the pernicious impact of counsel on the special character of the proceeding. This view finds support in *Wolff v. McDonnell* (1974), where the Court held that prisoners did not have a right to "either retained or appointed counsel" in prison disciplinary proceedings as a result of various difficulties that would arise from the "insertion of counsel" into such proceedings.

(c) **Derivative Rights to Counsel.** A constitutional right to the assistance of counsel also can be derived from other constitutional guarantees besides the due process right to a fair hearing. Thus, *Miranda v. Ariz.* (1966) held that the right to consult with counsel was indispensable to the protection of the self-incrimination privilege of a person subjected to custodial interrogation. The Court there required that the police inform such a person that "he has a right to consult with a lawyer and to have the lawyer with him during interrogation," and that "if he is indigent, a lawyer will be appointed to represent him." This requirement extends beyond the Sixth Amendment right to counsel since custodial interrogation often occurs before the individual is an "accused" in a "criminal prosecution." The *Miranda* right, however, rests on a condition that, as a practical matter, is likely to be eliminated if the individual exercises that right. The *Miranda* right exists only if the arrestee is subjected to custodial interrogation, and if the arrestee refuses to waive the right to counsel, the police have the option of not pursuing the interrogation, which relieves them of the obligation to obtain counsel.

The *Miranda* approach, requiring an opportunity to consult with counsel as a means of safeguarding another constitutional guarantee, has also been advanced in other situations not encompassed by the Sixth Amendment. In *Kirby v. Ill.* (1972), this approach was urged by the dissenters in arguing that a suspect placed in a lineup should have a right to the presence of retained or appointed counsel, but it was rejected by the majority. In *U.S. v. Mandujano* (1976), two justices argued that the self-incrimination privilege of a target-witness before a grand jury carried with it a right to consult with retained or appointed counsel prior to questioning. While the Court did not find it necessary to rule on that contention, the *Mandujano* plurality opinion argued against a right to counsel, and later cases have approvingly cited that discussion. Thus, the prospects for recognition of further derivative rights to counsel, beyond that established in *Miranda,* currently appear dim.

(d) Equal Protection and Appointed Counsel. Assume that a state allows a person to be represented by retained counsel in a proceeding as to which neither due process nor the Sixth Amendment requires the appointment of counsel. Does the equal protection guarantee then require the state to provide appointed counsel for indigent persons so as to ensure equal treatment? Supreme Court precedent indicates that the equal protection guarantee may impose an independent obligation upon the state to provide appointed counsel, but also indicates that this obligation is limited largely to situations in which due process would also require appointment of counsel. The key cases in assessing the scope of the state's obligation under the equal protection clause are *Douglas v. Cal.* (1963) and *Ross v. Moffitt* (1974). An analysis of those rulings, however, must begin with an examination of the earlier case of *Griffin v. Ill.* (1956). While *Griffin* did not involve the appointment of counsel, it is the seminal ruling on the state's general obligation to provide "equal justice" in the criminal justice process.

Griffin dealt with a state law that gave every defendant the right to appeal, but then conditioned appellate review on defendant's presentation of a trial record that often could not be prepared without a stenographic trial transcript. Defendant, who was indigent, asked the state to provide him with a free transcript so that he could prepare his appeal, but the state refused to do so. The Supreme Court held that this refusal resulted in a denial of due process and equal protection. Both Justice Black's plurality opinion and Justice Frankfurter's separate concurring opinion acknowledged that the state had no constitutional obligation to provide appellate review of criminal convictions. However, once the state had granted defendants a right to appeal, it could not condition the exercise of that right upon a prerequisite that discriminated against those defendants who were indigent. "In criminal trials," Justice Black noted, "a State can no more discriminate on account of poverty than on account of religion, race, or color" since "the ability to pay costs in advance bears no relationship to defendant's guilt or innocence." Commenting generally upon this country's dedication "to affording equal justice to all," Justice Black added, in an oft-quoted statement: "There can be no equal justice where the kind of trial a man gets depends on the amount of money he has."

Notwithstanding the sweeping language in Justice Black's opinion, it was far from certain that the *Griffin* ruling would be extended to the appointment of counsel for the indigent. By requiring a transcript to perfect an appeal, the state had denied the indigent defendant access to an integral part of its process for ensuring against unjust convictions. In contrast, the indigent defendant denied appointed counsel on appeal still had his right to appellate review. However, in *Douglas v. Cal.* (1963), the Court extended *Griffin* to the right to counsel.

Douglas held invalid on equal protection grounds an intermediate appellate court's practice of refusing to appoint counsel on appeal when the court, after reviewing the trial record, concluded that "such appointment would be of no value to either the defendant or the court." The majority opinion found this practice inconsistent with the "*Griffin* principle." Here too, there was "discrimination against the indigent," with "the kind of appeal a man enjoys depend[ing] on the amount of money he has." Unlike the indigent, the more affluent defendant was not required to "run [the] gauntlet of a preliminary showing of merit" to have his case presented by counsel. As the Court saw the state's procedure, "the indigent, where the record was unclear or errors were hidden, had only the right to a meaningless ritual, while the rich man had a meaningful appeal." The *Douglas* opinion stressed, however, that it was not requiring "absolute equality" throughout the criminal justice process. What was at stake here was the first level of appeal, the "one and only appeal an indigent has as of right." The Court was not here concerned with review "beyond the stage in the appellate process at which the claims have once been presented by a lawyer and passed upon by an appellate court."

In stressing the importance of the first appeal, and in characterizing a defendant's presentation of his appeal without counsel as a "meaningless ritual," the *Douglas* opinion cited factors that arguably would have supported a due process right to appointed counsel in that case. Indeed, in *Evitts v. Lucey* (§ 3.1(b)), the Court looked to the reasoning of *Douglas* in finding a due process right to retained counsel on a first appeal as a matter of right. When *Ross v. Moffitt* (1974) refused to extend *Douglas* to indigent defendants seeking appointed counsel to prepare petitions for a discretionary second appeal, it looked to both due process and equal protection. The Court did note that each clause "depend[s] on a different inquiry which emphasizes different factors." For due process the emphasis is on "fairness between the State and the individual dealing with the State, regardless of how other individuals in the same situation may be treated." "Equal protection, on the other hand, emphasizes disparity in treatment by a State between classes of individuals."

In refusing to extend *Douglas* to the petition for second-level discretionary review, the *Ross* majority examined separately the impact of the two clauses, and found that neither lent support to the defendant's claim. In discussing the due process element, the Court stressed the quite different relationship of the defendant and the state on an appeal as opposed to a trial. As discussed in subsection (b), it reasoned that the defendant's role as the person pressing the appeal and challenging a determination of guilt reduces the strength of his claim for procedural safeguards. Accordingly, the state does not "automatically * * * act unfairly" in leaving indigent defendants to pursue on their own a discretionary determination as to second tier review. The Court concluded: "Unfairness results only if indigents are singled out * * * and denied meaningful access to the appellate system because of their poverty, [and] that question is more profitably considered under an equal protection analysis."

Analyzing the unfairness question under equal protection, the *Ross* majority found that there was no denial of meaningful access based on poverty. It stressed the ease with which an appellate court could determine whether to grant discretionary review even where the application had not been prepared by counsel. It acknowledged that "a skilled lawyer, particularly one trained in the somewhat arcane art of preparing petitions for discretionary review," could prove helpful to his client. However, the state had no "duty to duplicate the legal arsenal that may be privately retained by a criminal defendant in a continuing effort to reverse his conviction, but only to assure the indigent defendant an adequate opportunity to present his claims fairly in the context of the state appellate process." Here, unlike *Douglas,* that opportunity was available without counsel.

At times, as in *Evitts v. Lucey* and *Halbert v. Mich.* (see § 3.1(b)), the Court's discussion of due process considerations has emphasized both the limited significance of the particular proceeding in determining guilt and the presence or absence of "meaningful access" without a lawyer, with its due process analysis of meaningful access looking to the equal protection analysis in *Ross*. These discussions suggest that where the Court finds no due process right to appointed counsel, it is thereby also finding that the disadvantage faced by the indigent without counsel is not so great as to establish an equal protection claim. On the other hand, in *Pa. v. Finley* (see § 3.1(b)), the Court, as in *Ross*, distinguished the considerations applicable to due process and equal protection in the course of finding that neither established a right to appointed counsel in preparing a collateral attack petition. As to due process, the *Finley* Court stressed that here, as on an appeal, the defendant stands in the lesser position of one challenging a conviction. In its equal protection analysis, the *Finley* Court stressed that the indigent defendant was not being placed at a significant disadvantage in light of the availability of other resources that framed the legal issues for possible collateral review (the trial record and appellate briefs and opinions).

The separate equal protection analysis of cases like *Finley* and *Ross* leaves open the potential for finding an equal protection right to appointed counsel in a setting in which the particular procedure is not sufficiently significant to support a due process right to counsel, but the indigent defendant forced to proceed pro se does not have available the alternative resources found in *Finley* and *Ross* to permit adequate judicial consideration of his claim. However, the Court has offered no suggestion of any setting in which such an analysis would apply.

As discussed in § 3.2(a), the Court has found no due process or Sixth Amendment right to appointed counsel where a misdemeanor prosecution does not hold open the possibility of a sentence of incarceration. That ruling is based on limited consequences of a conviction for such offense. Although states uniformly allow for representation by retained counsel in such misdemeanor cases, and the indigent defendants in such cases face the same inadequacies in self-representation as the indigent misdemeanor defendants given appointed counsel because they face a sentence of incarceration, the Court has never suggested that there might be an equal protection right to appointed counsel in this setting. In contrast, the Court has recognized an equal protection claim to a transcript on an appeal from such a conviction where the transcript was a prerequisite to full appellate review. *Mayer v. Chicago* (1971) held that an indigent defendant convicted of an ordinance violation punishable only by a fine was entitled under *Griffin* to a free transcript of his trial where state appellate procedure made such a transcript a prerequisite to challenging on appeal the sufficiency of the trial evidence. Although extending the *Griffin* equal protection analysis to a setting in which the proceeding was not of sufficient significance to create a due process right to counsel, *Mayer* involved an absolute bar of access to that proceeding rather than a situation in which access was available to the indigent, but subject to a significant disadvantage (i.e., proceeding without counsel).

§ 3.2 Scope of the Indigent's Right to Counsel and Other Assistance

(a) Right to Appointed Counsel: Misdemeanor Prosecutions. Prior to *Argersinger v. Hamlin* (1972), all of the appointed counsel cases decided by the Supreme Court had involved felony prosecutions. Though the Sixth Amendment refers to "all criminal prosecutions," several lower courts had ruled that the Sixth Amendment right to appointed counsel, like the Sixth Amendment right to jury trial, did not apply to prosecutions for "petty offenses" (basically misdemeanors punishable by no more than six months imprisonment). That position was presented to the Court in *Argersinger,* where it was unanimously rejected. The Court could find no substantial reason for extending the petty offense exception to the counsel clause. While there was "historical support" for the jury trial exception, "nothing in the history of the right to counsel" suggested "a retraction of the right in petty offenses, wherein the common law previously did require that counsel be provided." There also was no functional basis for drawing the line at petty offenses. The "problems associated with * * * petty offenses," the Court noted, "often require the presence of counsel to insure the accused a fair trial." It could not be said that the legal questions involved in a misdemeanor trial were likely to be less complex because the jail sentence did not exceed six months. Neither is there less need for advice of counsel prior to entering a plea of guilty to a petty offense. Indeed, petty misdemeanors may create a special need for counsel because their great volume "may create an obsession for speedy dispositions, regardless of the fairness of the result."

Since the defendant in *Argersinger* had been sentenced to jail, the Court found it unnecessary to rule on the defendant's right to appointed counsel where "a loss of liberty was not involved." The opinion laid the foundation, however, for distinguishing between misdemeanor cases involving sentences of imprisonment and those in which only fines are imposed. Both *Johnson v. Zerbst* (§ 3.1(a)) and *Gideon v. Wainwright* (§ 3.1(a)) had referred to counsel's assistance as necessary to ensure "the fundamental human rights of life and liberty." The special significance of the loss of liberty to both the accused and society could not be denied. As the *Argersinger* opinion noted: "[T]he prospect of imprisonment for however short a time will seldom be viewed by the accused as a trivial or petty matter and may well result in quite serious repercussions affecting his career and his reputation."

The *Argersinger* opinion also cited to the practicability of applying an "actual imprisonment" standard. Responding to the contention that appointment of counsel for minor offenses was beyond the capacity of "the Nation's legal resources," it noted that an actual imprisonment standard would limit significantly the burden imposed upon the states. Although many jurisdictions classified traffic offenses as criminal, only a minute portion of all such offenses were likely to be "brought into the class where imprisonment actually occurs." Indeed, the opinion stated, "the run of misdemeanors will not be affected by today's ruling."

In *Scott v. Ill.* (1979), the Court refused to carry the Sixth Amendment right to appointed counsel in misdemeanor cases beyond the actual imprisonment standard suggested in *Argersinger.* The petitioner there was an indigent defendant who had been convicted of shoplifting. Although that misdemeanor offense was punishable by a maximum sentence of one year in jail and a $500 fine, petitioner had been sentenced to only a fine of $50.00. Referring to both the Sixth Amendment and the Fourteenth Amendment's due process clause, the Supreme Court concluded that the "federal constitution does not require a state trial court to appoint counsel for a criminal defendant such as petitioner." *Argersinger,* the Court stated, had rested on the "conclusion that incarceration was so severe a sanction that it should not be imposed * * * unless an indigent has been offered appointed counsel." It had thereby "delimit[ed] the constitutional right to appointed counsel in state criminal proceedings." The "central premise of *Argersinger*—that actual imprisonment is a penalty different in kind from fines or the mere threat of imprisonment"—was not altered by the fact that the misdemeanor involved here carried a potential punishment that took it beyond the petty offense category. The key for all misdemeanors is whether the judge imposes a sentence of imprisonment on conviction of the misdemeanor offense. The Court also noted that the actual imprisonment standard "had proved reasonably workable, whereas any extension would create confusion and impose unpredictable, but necessarily substantial, costs in 50 quite diverse states."

Scott was a 5–4 decision, with Justice Powell noting that he had joined the majority opinion only to provide "clear guidance" to the lower courts. However, in light of subsequent cases building upon *Argersinger* and *Scott,* the Court appears firmly committed to utilizing the actual imprisonment standard as the sole Sixth Amendment dividing line for requiring appointed counsel in misdemeanor cases. It has shown no inclination to build upon Justice Powell's reluctant concurrence, and require appointment of counsel, under a due process analysis, in a particularly compelling non-imprisonment misdemeanor case.

In *Ala. v. Shelton* (2002), the Court made clear that the actual imprisonment standard considers not only the immediate consequences of a sentence, but also any potential for subsequent imprisonment based on the sentence. Thus, a state could not sentence a person on an uncounseled conviction to a sentence of probation that could result in incarceration upon a subsequent revocation of probation. The Court distinguished *Nichols v. U.S.* (1994), which held that an uncounseled misdemeanor conviction valid under *Scott* (no term of incarceration having been imposed) could be used to enhance the imprisonment sentence for a subsequent conviction. In

Shelton, although the imprisonment would be triggered by a probation violation, the sentence was for the underlying conviction (not for the probation violation). In *Nichols*, in contrast, the sentence was for the subsequent conviction on which the defendant had counsel. There the earlier conviction was simply being considered as an element of the defendant's criminal background, in much the same way as other past behavior.

Of course, the states remain free to provide counsel in situations where the Constitution does not compel appointment. A large group of states require appointment for all offenses that carry an authorized punishment of incarceration. Many others, however, utilize a standard, as to all misdemeanors or just minor misdemeanors, that is tied in some way to actual imprisonment. Some of these states have a statutory standard requiring that counsel be appointed unless the judge declares on the record prior to trial that a sentence of incarceration will not be imposed.

(b) Right to Appointed Counsel: Stages of the Proceeding. As discussed in § 10.1, a constitutional right to the assistance of appointed counsel can be found in the Sixth Amendment, the due process clause, the equal protection clause, and as a derivative of the privilege against self incrimination. The Sixth Amendment right clearly is the most extensive in its coverage; it applies to many more of the basic steps in the criminal justice process than the other constitutional rights to counsel. Two prerequisites shape the scope of the Sixth Amendment right. First, the Sixth Amendment speaks of the right of an "accused" in a "criminal prosecution." The right attaches at the point the individual becomes the accused and carries forward through the prosecution until the individual loses that status. However, it does not extend to each and every step in the process over that period. The Supreme Court has held that the Sixth Amendment right extends only to those steps in the prosecution that constitute a "critical stage" in the defense of the accused. The Sixth Amendment grants the accused the right to the assistance of counsel "for his defense," and that assistance does not require the presence or advice of counsel as to steps in the process that will not bear upon the ability of counsel to challenge the prosecution and present the case for the defense.

The "accused" prerequisite. At what point does an individual become an "accused" in a criminal prosecution? The key here, the Court has noted, is the government's initiation of "adversary judicial proceedings" against the individual with respect to criminal charges. That action reflects the "solidified * * * [governmental] commitment to prosecute," and marks the beginning of a "prosecution." It also identifies the start of a relationship between the individual and the government that brings into play the underlying function of the Sixth Amendment right—"protecting the unaided layman at critical confrontations with his adversary."

Precisely what constitutes the initiation of "adversary judicial proceedings" is an issue most commonly considered in connection with police investigative procedures, and that issue has been discussed previously in the chapters on those procedures, see §§ 5.4(a), 6.3(a). As those discussions indicate, the initiation of adversary judicial proceedings typically requires a governmental commitment to prosecute that is that is conveyed to the court. This clearly includes the filing of a charging instrument (e.g. an indictment or information) with the court. Where that instrument is filed prior to the defendant's arrest, he is an "accused" at the time of his arrest and entitled to the assistance of counsel when subjected to subsequent investigative procedures that constitute critical stages in the prosecution (e.g. a lineup or interrogation). An arrest alone, however, is not an "adversary judicial proceeding", and the person arrested prior to being formally charged (by far the most common situation) is not an "accused." Indeed, the Court noted in *U.S. v. Gouveia* (1984), a person detained without the filing of charges does not become an accused even if he is detained for a substantial period of time and the government has every intention of filing charges when it completes its investigation.

The defendants in *Gouveia* were prison inmates who had been confined to a special Administrative Detention Unit for many months after prison officials concluded that they had murdered a fellow inmate and began to build a case against them. Defendants claimed that the government's failure to honor their request for appointment of counsel during their confinement in the ADU constituted a violation of their Sixth Amendment right to counsel. The Court of Appeals sustained their claim. It reasoned that, in prison cases, there existed a substantial possibility that the government might delay the initiation of formal charges, resulting in the loss of evidence that could have been preserved through the preindictment investigation of appointed counsel. The Supreme Court acknowledged that the concern of the Court of Appeals was legitimate, but concluded that it was a concern met by other procedural protections (the statute of limitations and the due process protection against prejudicial delay in bringing charges), rather than the Sixth Amendment right to counsel. The Court majority noted that it had "never held that the right to counsel attaches at the time of arrest," and had "never suggested that the purpose of the right * * * is to provide a defendant with a preindictment private investigator." Both the function and language of the Sixth Amendment sustained the prerequisite of the initiation of adversary judicial proceedings.

Even though the arrested person has not been charged by indictment or information, when he is brought before the magistrate for his first appearance (see § 1.2(e)), that proceeding in itself marks the initiation of adversary judicial proceedings. In *Rothgery v. Gillespie County* (2008), the lower court sought to distinguish prior Supreme Court rulings characterizing the first appearance as a point of attachment of the Sixth Amendment right to counsel, arguing that those cases presented a prosecutor's decision to charge (as reflected in the filing of a complaint authorized by the prosecutor as part of the first appearance). In *Rothgery*, the state had brought the arrestee before the magistrate on a police affidavit of probable cause, and there was no showing that such action was taken with the knowledge or involvement of the local prosecutor. Rejecting that distinction, the Supreme Court concluded that whether the first appearance reflected a sufficient commitment to prosecute should not depend on whether an officer's probable cause affidavit constituted a formal "complaint" under state law, or on the "allocations of power among state officials under state law." The first appearance functionally reflected a "sufficiently concrete" government commitment to prosecute to constitute an "adversary judicial proceeding." It involved a magistrate informing the arrestee of the charges against him (as set forth in a complaint or probable cause affidavit) and the magistrate imposing restrictions on the arrestee's liberty (in setting terms of pretrial release) "in aid of the prosecution." That was sufficient, the Court noted, to establish that the "state's relationship with the defendant had become solidly adversarial."

Once started, the Sixth Amendment's "criminal prosecution" continues through to the end of the basic trial stage, including sentencing. In the course of ruling upon due process and equal protection claims, a series of cases, as discussed in § 3.1(b), have clearly indicated that the "criminal prosecution" has ended where the defendant is pursuing an appeal from his conviction. Less clear is the status of post-sentencing proceedings before the trial judge that similarly present challenges to the conviction. The answer may depend, in part, upon the nature of issues presented. If the proceeding involves no more than an extension of a trial ruling, and occurs shortly after trial, as in a post-verdict motion for judgment of acquittal, it should be treated as subject to the Sixth Amendment. On the other hand, a motion for a new trial based on new evidence, which can occur months after the conviction, might be treated as closer to a collateral attack, which clearly is outside the criminal prosecution.

While timing is a significant factor in assessing post-trial proceedings in the trial court, it is not necessarily conclusive. Thus, a probation revocation proceeding that occurred months after defendant's conviction was held to be a part of the criminal prosecution where that proceeding also involved the setting of the defendant's basic prison term for the crime. In that case, *Mempa v. Rhay* (1967), the trial judge placed the defendant on probation without fixing the term of imprisonment that would be imposed if probation were later revoked. The Supreme Court concluded that the subsequent determination and imposition of a prison sentence at the probation revocation proceeding was as much a part of the criminal prosecution as the sentencing of a defendant immediately after trial. In contrast to *Mempa, Gagnon v. Scarpelli* (1973) held that a probation revocation hearing is not part of the criminal prosecution when a prison sentence had previously been imposed but then suspended in favor of probation. The only issue presented in such a hearing is whether to revoke probation, and that determination is based on defendant's subsequent conduct rather than the commission of the original offense.

Of course, even though a proceeding is not part of the criminal prosecution, there may still be a right to appointed counsel drawn from a constitutional provision other than the Sixth Amendment. Thus, *Douglas v. Cal.* (§ 3.1(c)) and *Evitts v. Lucey* (§ 3.1(b)) established an equal protection and due process right to appointed counsel on a first appeal provided as a matter of right, and *Gagnon* (§ 3.1(b)) established a due process right to appointed counsel under special circumstances in a probation or parole revocation proceeding. On the other hand, *Ross v. Moffitt* held that neither equal protection nor due process required appointment of counsel to assist an indigent convicted defendant in preparing an application for second-level discretionary review of a conviction, and *Pa. v. Finley* and *Murray v. Giarratano* found no constitutional basis for requiring appointment of counsel to assist an indigent prisoner in filing a habeas petition or other collateral attack upon his conviction. See § 3.1(b).

The "critical stage" prerequisite. The Supreme Court has applied critical-stage analysis to a variety of different steps in the criminal prosecution. In the course of those rulings, it has referred to several different touchstones for determining whether a particular step constitutes a critical stage (and therefore gives the accused the right to the assistance of counsel as to that step). Courts are directed to ask whether the particular procedural step was one "where available defenses may be irretrievably lost, if not then and there asserted," whether the assistance of counsel at this point is "necessary to mount a meaningful defence," and whether "potential substantial prejudice to defendant's rights inheres in the confrontation between the accused and the government" and counsel's assistance can "help avoid that prejudice." Supplemented by the analysis applied in the Court's various rulings, these touchstones would appear to require a reviewing court to ask the following questions in determining whether a particular procedure constituted a critical stage in the criminal prosecution of the defendant: (1) whether the procedure either (i) had a consequence adverse to the defendant as to the ultimate disposition of the charge which could have been avoided or mitigated if defendant had been represented by counsel at that procedure, or (ii) offered a potential opportunity for benefitting the defendant as to the ultimate disposition of the charge through rights that could have been exercised by counsel, and (2) whether that adverse consequence could have been avoided, or the lost opportunity regained, by action that subsequently provided counsel could have taken. Answering these inquiries will require a court to examine various features of the procedural rules of the particular jurisdiction. Thus as discussed below, the first appearance before a magistrate and the arraignment before the trial judge may or may not be a critical stage depending upon the state's treatment of the defense actions and the rulings made at those proceedings.

Applying "critical-stage" analysis, the Supreme Court has held that an accused person has a Sixth Amendment right to counsel's assistance at certain investigative procedures in which the accused participates, including a lineup and efforts by police, prosecutors, or their secret agents to elicit incriminating statements from the accused, but not other such procedures, such as the taking of handwriting exemplars. See *U.S. v. Ash* (1973). The Court also has held that an indigent defendant was entitled to appointed counsel at an arraignment, where state law made that proceeding a critical stage by viewing defenses not raised at that point as abandoned. *Hamilton v. Ala.* (1961) Similarly, the Sixth Amendment right applied where the defendant was asked at a first appearance to enter a plea described as "non-binding", but his plea of guilty, though it could be withdrawn, could nonetheless be used against him at trial. *White v. Md.* (1963) However, *Rothgery v. Gillespie County* left open whether a standard first appearance—involving no more than making an ex parte determination of probable cause, giving notice of charges, and setting bail (see § 1.2(e))—constitutes a critical stage. In the course of holding that the Sixth Amendment right to counsel attached at the first appearance, the Court noted that whether the first appearance also was a critical stage, entitling the indigent defendant to the presence and assistance counsel, was a distinct issue, which it need not address under the facts of that case. Statements in both the opinion for the Court and a concurring opinion suggest, however, that the standard first appearance ordinarily would not be a critical stage. The concurring opinion, in particular, stressed that whether a pretrial procedure constitutes a critical stage depends upon its potential bearing on the trial, not "to other objectives that may be important to the accused," as the accused's right to the assistance of counsel "for his defence" refers to "defense at trial."

State law. In many states, indigent defendants regularly receive the assistance of appointed counsel at stages at which there is no constitutional right to appointed counsel. In some instances, this is the product of a practice adopted by public defender agencies or local courts, rather than a clearly defined legal right. For example, state provisions on appointed counsel commonly provide for the initiation of the appointment process at the defendant's first appearance before a magistrate, but public defender offices often initiate the representation of indigents before that time (particularly where that office makes the initial indigency determination).

Various state laws also provide for assistance where not constitutionally required. Thus, statutes stating that appointed counsel's obligations extend through "appeal" have been interpreted in some states as requiring appointed counsel to prepare petitions for discretionary appellate review. All but a few of the thirty-seven states with capital punishment provide for appointment of counsel to assist capital defendants in preparing collateral challenges to their convictions. A smaller, but substantial group of states grant imprisoned indigent defendants the assistance of counsel in challenging through collateral attack their convictions for non-capital offenses (commonly on condition that the public defender determines that adequate grounds exist for pursuing such a challenge). A majority of the states go beyond the constitutionally required minimum as to probation revocation proceedings and provide appointed counsel for all such proceedings without regard to the special circumstances test of *Gagnon v. Scarpelli* (see § 3.1(b)).

(c) "Delivery Systems". The administrative "delivery system" used to provide appointed counsel varies from state to state (and often from county to county within a state). The three most common delivery systems are: (1) automatic representation by a public defender agency; (2) individual appointments of private attorneys; and (3) the "contract attorney system," which provides representation through attorneys furnished by an organization that has contracted with the local government to provide representation for a particular portion of indigent defense cases.

Public defender agencies are agencies of the county or state. Due to conflicts of interest and other factors, these agencies will be excluded from representing a small portion of the indigent defendants, so jurisdictions using a public defender agency (which includes 90% of the 100 must populous counties) will also use one or both of the other system to cover those excluded cases. In a contract system, as in a public defender system, the organization assigns the individual counsel, but here the organization is not a governmental entity (most often, it is a private law firm or a non-profit entity sponsored by the local bar association or the legal aid society). The contract may or may not create an entity that is, in effect, a "private public defender" (i.e., it may cover almost all or only a limited portion of the indigent defense caseload, and it may utilize a flat fee for all representation, similar to a defender office budget, or an hourly fee with caps, similar to an individual appointment system). Individual assignment systems often utilize a "neutral rotating" system of selection from a list of attorneys that have been approved by the local trial court. Some jurisdictions, however, continue to use the traditional system under which appointments are made at the discretion of individual trial judges.

(d) Counsel Withdrawal on Appeal. The defense attorney violates no obligation of professional responsibility in forcing the state to prove its case at trial, no matter how clear the defendant's guilt. On appeal, on the other hand, the defendant is presenting a challenge and the lawyer has an ethical obligation not to assert frivolous claims. In *Anders v. Cal.* (1967), the Supreme Court first addressed the potential tension between that professional obligation and the indigent defendant's constitutional right to appointed counsel on first appeal of right. The *Anders* Court unanimously agreed that defendant's constitutional right to appointed counsel did not preclude withdrawal where (1) counsel, after "conscientious investigation," concludes that the appeal is "frivolous" and (2) the appellate court "is satisfied that counsel has diligently investigated the possible grounds of appeal, and agrees with counsel's evaluation of the case." However, the *Anders* majority also found that the withdrawal procedure utilized in the case before it, which relied on counsel's conclusory "no merit" letter, failed to provide satisfactory safeguards against undermining the defendant's constitutional right to counsel. Describing the kind of withdrawal procedure that would protect that right, the *Anders* majority set forth the basic elements of what was later characterized as *"Anders'* prophylactic framework" for withdrawal. That framework has four elements: (1) after a "conscientious examination" of the appeal, counsel must determine that it is "wholly frivolous" and "so advise the court and request permission to withdraw"; (2) "that request must be accompanied by a brief referring to anything in the record that might arguably support the appeal"; (3) "a copy of counsel's brief should be furnished the indigent [defendant] and time allowed him to raise any points that he chooses"; and (4) the appellate court, "after a full examination of all the proceedings," must find that "the case is wholly frivolous."

Subsequent Supreme Court rulings have concluded that the *Anders* prophylactic framework was not mandated, but simply presented as an illustration of "one method of satisfying the requirements of the Constitution for indigent criminal appeals." The state has leeway to craft other methods that also guarantee a "fair opportunity to obtain an adjudication on the merits of the appeal," with that fairness judged in light of "the underlying goals that the procedure should serve—to ensure that those indigents whose appeals are not frivolous receive the counsel and merits brief required by *Douglas*, and [to allow the state] to protect itself so that frivolous appeals are not subsidized and public moneys not needlessly spend." *Smith v. Robbins* (2000). In *Smith*, a closely divided Court upheld a procedure under which counsel initially informed the court (and the client) that he had reviewed the record and found the appeal to be frivolous and attached a summary of the "procedural and factual history of the case with citations to the record," and the appellate court then independently examined the record and required counsel to brief on the merits if it found any non-frivolous issues, and if not, affirmed the conviction. The Court noted that this procedure: (1) required a determination that the appeal was "frivolous" (as contrasted to rejected state procedures that had asked counsel or court to determine only that the appeal was unlikely to prevail); (2) provided "at least two tiers of review" (by counsel and court) of the frivolity issue; (3) precluded the possibility of counsel withdrawing and the appellate court then being required to rule on the merits of a non-frivolous issue without substantive briefing; and (4) did not allow counsel to file a "bare conclusion" statement of his analysis, but required a summary of the case's procedural and factual history, which "both ensures that a trained legal eye has searched the record for arguable issues and assists the reviewing court in its own evaluation of the case." See also *McCoy v. Court of Appeals of Wis.* (1998) (requiring counsel to cite in his withdrawal brief the precedent which led him to conclude the appeal would be frivolous was consistent with *Anders*, as the function of an *Anders* brief is not to "substitute for an advocate's brief," but to ensure "that counsel has been diligent in examining the record for meritorious issues").

(e) Assistance of Experts. Relying on the independent content of due process, *Ake v. Okla.* (1985) held that, "when a defendant has made a preliminary showing that his sanity at the time of the offense is likely to be a significant factor at trial, due process requires that a State provide access to a psychiatrist's assistance on this issue, if the defendant cannot otherwise afford one." The *Ake* majority stressed that its ruling was limited to cases in which the defendant's mental condition was "seriously in question," as evidenced by the defendant's "preliminary showing."

Moreover, the state's obligation did not go beyond providing the defense with the assistance of one competent psychiatrist, and it could provide that psychiatrist as it saw fit (i.e., the defendant's constitutional right did not include the authority "to choose a psychiatrist of his personal liking or to receive funds to hire his own"). The Court noted that it had never held that "a State must purchase for the indigent all the assistance that his wealthier counterpart might buy," but due process did require that the indigent defendant be given the "basic tools" needed to present his defense. Taking into consideration the defendant's interest "in the accuracy of the criminal proceeding," the limited financial burden that would be imposed upon the state under the proposed standard, and the probable value of psychiatric assistance in presenting an insanity defense, a court appointed psychiatrist clearly was such a "basic tool." The psychiatrist was needed "to conduct a professional examination * * *, to help determine whether the insanity defense is viable, to present testimony, and to assist in preparing cross-examination of a state's psychiatric witness."

In *Caldwell v. Miss.* (1985), the Court found it unnecessary to consider whether the rationale of *Ake* extended beyond psychiatric assistance since the defendant there, who asked for the appointment of a criminal investigator, a fingerprint expert, and a ballistics expert, had offered "little more than undeveloped assertions that the requested assistance would be beneficial." Lower courts have divided on such an extension of *Ake*. Several have held that the analysis of *Ake* does not extend beyond providing the assistance of psychiatrists where the defendant's mental condition is placed in issue by the law governing culpability or punishment. Drawing the line here is justified by the special role of defendant's mental condition under that law, standing apart from such fact bound issues as whether defendant committed the act and caused the harm, and the special role of the psychiatrist (as stressed in the *Ake* opinion) in gaining a sensible and accurate determination of defendant's mental condition. However, most courts addressing the extension of *Ake* have concluded that psychiatric assistance is not so unique as to invariably exclude from the *Ake* rationale all other types of experts. The question in each case must be not what field of science or expert knowledge is involved, but rather how important the scientific issue is to the case. Applying this standard, courts have concluded that due process, in the appropriate setting, may require the state to provide: a psychiatrist or psychologist to assist on issues beyond a mental condition that is recognized as a defense or a mitigating punishment factor; a forensic expert to assist in the evaluation of physical evidence; a hypnotist needed to challenge the victim's post-hypnotic identification testimony; and an investigator to find critical evidence identified by the defense.

Of course, as *Caldwell* indicated, application of the *Ake* analysis to other types of assistance carries with it the requirement of a threshold showing of need. Courts uniformly stress that the requisite showing of need must set forth in detail what assistance is being requested and why it is needed. As to the degree of need, it is noted that the situation presented in *Ake* was unique. With insanity, once the defense can show that the defendant's mental condition is "seriously in question," the requisite need follows automatically, as the insanity defense is almost certain to be a "significant factor" at trial. As to other issues, in contrast, there may be a serious factual issue on which an expert could provide assistance, but the issue may be one that the defense could seriously contest without an expert. Moreover, if the expert is needed to contest the issue, it does not follow necessarily that the issue is one likely to affect the outcome of the case. Accordingly, a showing of need must establish why the expert is needed to contest the issue and why the issue will be important to the defense.

In the federal system and a large number of states, the issues raised by the extension of *Ake* are avoided as a result of statutes or court rules making various types of expert assistance readily available to indigent defendants. Under the Criminal Justice Act of 1964, applicable in the federal system, appointed counsel need only meet the "private attorney" standard in showing need—i.e., the circumstances of the case are such that "a reasonable attorney would engage such services for a client having the independent means to pay." In some jurisdictions, public defenders do not even have to seek court authorization to utilize an expert, as the office's budget assumes that experts will be employed in some portion of the office's cases.

§ 3.3   Waiver of the Right to Counsel

(a) **General Requirements.** Just as the right to counsel extends through various stages in the criminal justice process, waiver of that right can occur at each of those stages. In some respects, what is required for a valid waiver will vary with the particular stage. Thus, the standards for a waiver of counsel in the course of a police investigation differ in certain respects from the standards governing a waiver in a judicial proceeding. A judge accepting a waiver at trial, for example, may be required to conduct a type of inquiry as to the defendant's state of mind that simply would not be feasible for a police officer accepting a waiver prior to custodial interrogation. Our focus in this section is upon waivers in judicial proceedings, particularly before the trial court.

While the standards governing waiver vary with the nature of the proceeding, there are several general principles that apply to all waivers of the right to counsel. To be valid, a waiver of counsel must be made "knowingly, intelligently, and voluntarily." There must be "an intentional relinquishment or abandonment of a known right or privilege," and it may not be the product of governmental tactics that amount to "coercion."

The Supreme Court repeatedly has warned the lower courts against simply assuming that the defendant has the necessary knowledge and understanding to make a constitutionally acceptable waiver. It has in fact directed those courts to "indulge in every reasonable presumption against waiver." Consistent with this approach, a waiver may not be presumed from a "silent record"; the record must show that the defendant was informed specifically of his right to the assistance of appointed or retained counsel and that he clearly rejected such assistance. "No amount of circumstantial evidence that the person may have been aware of his right will suffice to stand" in place of a specific notification of rights. Having been informed of his right, the defendant's relinquishment of that right must be clear and unequivocal.

Finally, a waiver at one stage does not necessarily constitute a waiver for all stages. Thus, the defendant who waives at a preliminary hearing cannot thereby be assumed to have waived for subsequent proceedings before the trial court. Indeed, most jurisdictions place the obligation on the trial court to determine at each new stage that the defendant desires to continue with his waiver. Some, however, adhere to the constitutional minimum of requiring a new determination only if the defendant indicates that he has changed his mind or significantly changed circumstances suggest that his reexamination of the issue is in order.

(b) Waiver at Trial: The Necessary Inquiry. Assume that a defendant, having been informed by the trial court of his right to counsel (including appointed counsel, if indigent), states unequivocally that he wishes to proceed without counsel. Is that enough to establish that his waiver was made "intelligently" as well as "knowingly"? While it may be enough for a waiver in the course of a police investigatory procedure, establishing an acceptable waiver before the trial court typically requires much more. On direct appeal from a conviction, the prosecution ordinarily must be able to point to a trial court inquiry establishing the necessary level of understanding by the defendant. When a waiver is challenged on collateral attack (e.g., habeas corpus), "it is the defendant's burden to prove that he did not competently and intelligently waive his right to the assistance of counsel." *Iowa v. Tovar* (2004). Here, the lack of an adequate inquiry will not be sufficient in itself to invalidate the waiver, as the defendant must show that he actually lacked the needed understanding (which could have been obtained apart from the judicial inquiry).

The Supreme Court has refused to "prescrib[e] any formula or script to [be] read to a defendant," or questions to be directed to a defendant, to ensure that the waiver of counsel is intelligent. It has noted that "the information a defendant must possess in order to make an intelligent election * * * will depend on a range of case-specific factors, including the defendant's education or sophistication, the complex or easily grasped nature of the charge, and the stage of the proceeding." *Tovar*. Speaking to the importance of the stage of the proceeding, the Court has stressed the need for "a 'pragmatic approach to the waiver question,' one that asks 'what purposes a lawyer can serve at the particular stage of the proceedings in question, and what assistance he could provide to an accused at that stage,' in order 'to determine the * * * type of warnings and procedures that should be required before a waiver of that right will be recognized.'" *Tovar*. Thus, the Court has required the most extensive inquiry where the defendant desires to waive counsel and proceed to trial representing himself. There, it has held that the trial court must warn the defendant of the specific "dangers and disadvantages" of self-representation, so that the record establishes defendant's awareness of the general skills that counsel could have brought to the litigation process. *Faretta v. Cal.* (§ 3.5(c)).

Tovar refused to require similar warnings where the defendant sought to waive counsel and enter a guilty plea. The state court here had concluded that the waiver of counsel was inadequate under the Sixth Amendment because the trial court had: "(1) [failed to] advise the defendant that 'waiving the assistance of counsel in deciding whether to plead guilty entails the risk that a viable defense will be overlooked'; and (2) [failed to] 'admonish' the defendant 'that by waiving his right to an attorney he will lose the opportunity to obtain an independent opinion on whether, under the facts and applicable law, it is wise to plead guilty'." A unanimous Supreme Court responded:

> "[N]either warning is mandated by the Sixth Amendment. The constitutional requirement is satisfied when the trial court informs the accused of the nature of the charges against him, of his right to be counseled regarding his plea, and of the range of allowable punishments attendant upon the entry of a guilty plea."

In the guilty plea context, the "purposes a lawyer can serve" were likely to be "more obvious, requiring less rigorous warnings" to ensure that the defendant understands how the waived right "would apply in *general* in the circumstances" of his waiver.

The *Tovar* Court also noted, however, that it need not decide whether the sparse guilty plea colloquy in the case before it had been sufficient in itself to establish the understanding needed as to the assistance off counsel. That colloquy, in its discussion of counsel's assistance, consisted of the trial court noting its understanding that defendant desired to waive application for court appointed counsel and represent himself, the defendant stating that the court's understanding was correct, and the court then explaining the trial rights (including counsel's assistance at trial) relinquished by pleading guilty. There was no explicit advisement that the defendant's right to counsel included "the right to be counseled regarding [the] plea." However, defendant here was challenging the waiver on collateral attack, and the guilty plea colloquy did not stand alone. Defendant also had waived counsel at the first appearance and at a subsequent sentencing hearing ("where he could have withdrawn the guilty plea"); "the state [did] not contest that the defendant must [have been] * * * alerted to his right to the assistance of counsel in entering a plea" (assistance that the state had described as involving "working on issues of guilt and sentencing"); and the defendant had never asserted "that he was unaware of his right to be counseled prior to and at his arraignment."

The *Tovar* court had no need to explore what defendant would have to understand to be aware of "the nature of charges against him" and the "range of allowable punishments." Various lower courts have held that it is sufficient that the defendant be aware of the general character of the offense charged (which does not require knowledge of all of its elements) and the general range of the punishment. However, as *Tovar* noted, states remain free to require advisements that go beyond the constitutional minimum, and as to these elements, most jurisdictions require more advice as part of the guilty plea procedure. See § 13.4(c), (d).

(c) Competency. In *Godinez v. Moran* (1993), the Supreme Court considered the question of whether a court was required constitutionally to conduct a further inquiry into defendant's competency where there was some question about his mental state, but he had just been held competent to stand trial. The Court held that an additional competency hearing, as such, was not mandated by due process since a single standard determined both mental competency to stand trial and mental competency to waive counsel (or plead guilty). The standard for competency to stand trial requires that the defendant have a "sufficient present ability to consult with his lawyer with a reasonable degree of rational understanding" and "a rational as well as factual understanding of the proceedings against him." No greater mental capacity is required constitutionally for a waiver of counsel, the Court reasoned, as the right of the defendant to proceed without counsel does not require that he have "greater powers of comprehension, judgment and reason than would be necessary to stand trial with an attorney." On the other hand, as *Godinez* also cautions, a prior determination that a defendant is competent to stand trial does not mean that the defendant has the necessary understanding of the particular decision to waive counsel (or to plead guilty). "In this sense," the Court noted, "there is a heightened standard for pleading guilty and for waiving the right to counsel, but it is not a heightened standard for competence."

(d) Forfeiture of the Right. A long line of state and federal cases have sustained trial court rulings that forced defendants to proceed pro se because they failed to obtain counsel prior to the trial date. In these cases, defendants were advised of their right to retain counsel, given ample time to obtain counsel prior to the scheduled trial date, and nevertheless appeared in court on that date without counsel and without a reasonable excuse for having failed to obtain counsel. The courts typically have characterized such conduct by defendant as a "waiver" or "waiver by conduct" of the right to counsel. However, the circumstances in many of these cases clearly did not fit the traditional definition of a defense waiver in the right to counsel context—that is, a defendant's "intentional relinquishment or abandonment of a known right." Initially, the facts often suggested that the defendant had not intended to relinquish his right to counsel. Secondly, the trial court in some instances dispensed with even the barest inquiry that would have been needed for a true waiver. Finally, even if such an inquiry may be unnecessary where defendant's conduct unequivocally shows an intentional abandonment of his right, that characterization would appear to depend upon a prior warning as to the consequences of that conduct (here, failing to have counsel at the time scheduled for trial), and the cases do not always refer to such a warning having been given.

Most often, the analysis offered by the courts fits the category of "forfeiture" rather than "waiver." As the Supreme Court explained in *U.S. v. Olano* (1993), a forfeiture rests on the failure to make "a timely assertion of a right" rather than an intentional abandonment of the right. What these courts have held, in effect, is that the state's interest in maintaining an orderly trial schedule and the defendant's negligence, indifference, or possibly purposeful delaying tactic, combined to justify a forfeiture of defendant's right to counsel in much the same way that a defendant's physical assault upon his counsel can result in defendant's loss of the right to representation by counsel. Some courts, however, have refused to adopt such an analysis, insisting that there be at least some evidence of an intentional relinquishment in the defendant's failure to retain counsel prior to the scheduled trial date.

§ 3.4   Choice of Counsel

(a) Judicial Discretion in Selecting Appointed Counsel. Administrative systems for assignment of state-funded counsel (see § 3.2(c)) typically make that assignment without seeking input from the defendant. On occasion, indigent defendants have argued that they have a right to the assignment of a counsel of their choice if that attorney is willing to accept the assignment under the same financial terms as any other state-funded attorney. A few decisions recognize a grounding for such a claim in state law, but the possibility of a federal constitutional grounding has been firmly rejected. Courts note that the Sixth Amendment right to counsel of choice applies only to retained counsel (including those willing to represent a defendant *pro bono*). Otherwise, the federal constitution guarantees only representation by competent counsel, and allows the state to place administrative concerns over the defendant's preferences as to state-funded counsel. Those concerns include: (1) the disruption of the "even handed distribution of assignments" if defendants' preferences focus on particular attorneys; and (2) avoiding the administrative costs that would be involved if preferences were recognized, including making an inquiry into the competency and availability of the attorney preferred by the defendant and providing an explanation whenever that attorney did not receive the assignment.

(b) Replacement of Appointed Counsel. Because the indigent defendant has no right to appointed counsel of choice, he also has no right to replace one appointed counsel with another even if that can be done without causing any delay in the proceedings. The defendant has a right to substitution only upon establishing "good cause, such as a conflict of interest, a complete breakdown of communication, or an irreconcilable conflict which [could] lead * * * to an apparently unjust verdict." The mere loss of confidence in his appointed counsel does not establish "good cause." Defendant must have some well founded reason for believing that the appointed attorney cannot or will not competently represent him. Although an irreconcilable conflict establishes good cause, courts warn that defendant cannot manufacture good cause by abusive and uncooperative behavior. Indeed, such behavior may lead to the court allowing counsel to withdraw, and requiring defendant to proceed pro se on the ground that he forfeited or "waived by conduct" his right to counsel.

Similarly, the indigent defendant (unlike the defendant with retained counsel, see § 3.4(c)) has no constitutional grounding for objecting to a trial court's decision not to grant the continuance that would be required for continued representation by the originally appointed counsel, but instead to appoint new counsel. In reversing a lower court decision that found a Sixth Amendment violation where the trial court failed to grant such a continuance, the Supreme Court, in *Morris v. Slappy* (1983), noted that the lower court had erred in concluding that the indigent accused had a constitutionally protected interest in his "meaningful relationship" with his originally appointed attorney.

(c) **Choice of Retained Counsel.** *Grounding*. Where defendant has a Sixth Amendment or due process right to the assistance of counsel, that constitutional guarantee encompasses the "right to retained counsel of his choosing" as an aspect of his " 'right to spend his own money to obtain the advice and assistance ... of counsel.' " The Supreme Court has noted, however, that the "essential aim of the [constitutional right to counsel] is to guarantee an effective advocate for each criminal defendant, rather than to ensure that a defendant will inexorably be represented by the lawyer whom he prefers," and that the defendant's right to counsel of choice therefore can be "circumscribed" by appropriate governmental interests. Relying on such language, the government argued in *U.S. v. Gonzalez–Lopez* (2006) that the trial court's erroneous denial of defendant's right to representation by his counsel of choice (by improperly refusing to allow representation *pro hac vice*) did not violate the Sixth Amendment unless the defense could also show that defendant had been "prejudiced," as that term is defined in the context of ineffective assistance of counsel claims (see § 3.10(d)) (i.e., defendant would have to show that the representation by substitute counsel was sufficiently different from the likely representation by defendant's counsel of choice as to present a reasonable probability of a prejudicial impact upon the outcome of the prosecution). A closely divided Supreme Court majority rejected that contention as reflecting a failure to distinguish the separate groundings of the effective-assistance component of the right to counsel and right to representation by counsel of choice. The majority noted that the right of the accused "to be defended by the counsel he believes to be best" is part of the "root meaning of the [Sixth Amendment] guarantee," not a right derived from the "[general] purpose of the rights set forth in the Sixth Amendment * * *, to ensure a fair trial." Accordingly, "deprivation of the right is 'complete' when the defendant is erroneously prevented from being represented by the lawyer he wants, regardless of the quality of the representation he received" and its bearing (if any) on the fairness of the trial. Moreover, the majority noted, once established, a Sixth Amendment violation of the right to representation by counsel of choice requires automatic reversal of a subsequent conviction, as that is a "structural defect" (and therefore not subject to harmless error analysis, see § 19.6(d)).

Limitations. Where justified by a sufficient governmental interest, the right to counsel of choice may be circumscribed by precluding representation by a particular individual or category of individuals. Governmental interests justifying such a restriction typically are related to preserving a fundamental tenet of the adversary system—such as ensuring competent legal representation, requiring adherence to the ethical standards of the legal profession, or preserving the appearance of fairness. Common illustrations of instances in which defendant's right to retain counsel of choice is overridden on such grounds include the denial of defendant's choice to be represented by a person who is not a member of the bar, by an attorney who has a conflict of interest due to representation of other defendants or prospective witnesses, and by a former prosecutor who was involved previously in the prosecution of the same or related charges.

The defendant's capacity to retain counsel of choice also may be restricted by judicial action that is not directed at precluding representation by a particular attorney, but nonetheless has that impact. The classic illustration is the scheduling of the trial at a time when defendant's preferred counsel would be unavailable (usually due to a schedule-conflict). While the judicial interest here is not as significant as the interest in preserving fundamental elements of the adversary system, it nonetheless need not give way entirely to the defendant's preference for particular counsel. The "right to retain counsel of one's choice," appellate courts have frequently noted, "may not be insisted upon in a manner that will obstruct an orderly procedure in courts of justice and deprive such courts of their inherent powers to control the same." At the same time, the appellate courts have also recognized that, under some circumstances, the failure of a trial court to alter its preferred schedule so as to allow defendant to be represented by counsel of choice will result in a constitutional violation. While trial courts will be given considerable leeway in their determination not to alter that schedule, a substantial body of cases have found, upon the consideration of multiple factors (particularly, the degree of inconvenience and the strength of the justification offered by the defendant), that the denial of a continuance needed to ensure representation by a particular counsel resulted in a Sixth Amendment violation. Of course, if the defendant can establish that current counsel would not be able to provide competent counsel (as where a conflict of interest exists), the trial court must allow a continuance where needed to replace that counsel.

In *Caplin & Drysdale, Chartered v. U.S.* (1989), the Supreme Court upheld a quite different type of restriction on defendant's ability to retain counsel of choice. At issue there were asset forfeiture provisions directed at persons charged and convicted of specific crimes, which carried the potential of rendering a defendant unable to hire any counsel, (thereby forcing him to accept court appointed counsel). Under these statutes, the government could obtain a pretrial freezing of assets that might be subject to forfeiture, and after conviction, it could recapture funds that defendant had paid to third party recipients where those persons were aware of the pending forfeiture (which could include funds paid to an attorney after defendant had been indicted). Although a particular defendant might have other assets with which to retain counsel, the Court assessed the constitutionality of the statute under the assumption that "there will be cases" in which the end result of the forfeiture provisions would be to render a defendant "unable to retain the attorney of his choice." Justice White's opinion for the majority concluded, however, that there would be no Sixth Amendment violation even in such a situation.

Justice White's opinion initially cited the well established principle that a "defendant has no Sixth Amendment right to spend another person's money for services rendered by an attorney, even if those funds are the only way that defendant will be able to retain the counsel of his choice." Under the well accepted "taint theory," long recognized in forfeiture law generally, the defendant never had "good title" to the property, as the government obtained a "vested property interest" in the proceeds at the point at which the illegal transaction occurred. Moreover, the government's interest was not limited to simply "separating a criminal from his ill-gotten gains," although Congress obviously has a legitimate interest in "lessen[ing] the economic power of organized crime and drug enterprises" by stripping them of their "undeserved economic power" (including "the ability to command high priced legal talent"). The assets forfeited pursuant to the statute were to be deposited in a fund used to support law-enforcement efforts in various ways, and where the assets came from rightful owners, defrauded of their property, those owners could seek restitution.

The petitioner in *Caplin & Drysdale* contended that the forfeiture statute "upset the balance of forces between the accused and accuser" by allowing the prosecution, through its discretion as to the utilization of the forfeiture remedy and the pretrial restraining order, to exercise what the dissenters described as "an intolerable degree of power over any private attorney." The majority saw this claim as analogous to that rejected in *Wheat v. U.S.*, where government motions to disqualify defense counsel on conflict-of-interest grounds had been challenged as likely to be used by prosecutors to eliminate effective adversaries. Here too, an otherwise permissible procedure would not be struck down because of the potential for abuse. "Cases involving particular abuses," Justice White noted, "can be dealt with by the lower courts, when (and if) any such cases arise."

(d) The Pro Se Alternative. When a court denies a defendant's request for appointment of new counsel or for a continuance to permit the defendant to hire new counsel, it commonly will inform the defendant that he either must proceed with his current counsel or represent himself. Very often the defendant will choose the latter alternative, noting that he does so only because it is the lesser of two evils. If an appellate court concludes on appeal that the trial judge erred in failing to appoint new counsel or in denying the continuance, defendant's choice of proceeding pro se will be viewed as "involuntary" and his conviction reversed. However, if the trial court's decision is upheld, the defendant cannot complain about being "forced into" proceeding pro se. It is not inconsistent with the concept of a voluntary waiver to require a choice between waiver and another option, provided that other option is itself consistent with the protection of his constitutional rights.

Though a defendant's decision to proceed pro se made in response to a proper rejection of his motion to substitute counsel will not be viewed as involuntary, it still may be challenged successfully on appeal if it did not reflect a knowing and intelligent waiver of counsel. Where a defendant appears for trial on the scheduled date without having retained counsel (see § 3.3(c)), requiring the defendant to proceed pro se is the only option open to the court if it is to hold the trial on that date. Accordingly, the need for orderly administration may require that defendant's unreasonable failure to obtain counsel be treated as a forfeiture of his right to counsel. A forfeiture is not necessary, however, where the case can proceed either with the current counsel (for whom the defendant could not successfully substitute) or with the defendant proceeding pro se. Accordingly, courts uniformly insist that the choice to proceed pro se in this situation be tested by the traditional standards applicable to "true waivers" of counsel. See § 3.5(c).

§ 3.5   The Constitutional Right to Self–Representation

(a) The *Faretta* Ruling. In *Faretta v. Cal.* (1975), a divided Court recognized a Sixth Amendment right of the defendant to proceed pro se (i.e., to represent himself) at trial. The majority opinion relied heavily on the structure of the Sixth Amendment (which speaks of rights of the "accused," and affords to the accused the "assistance" of counsel) and the historical background of the Amendment (the right of self-representation was specifically noted in various state constitutional and statutory provisions establishing a right to counsel). The majority acknowledged that a constitutional right to proceed pro se "seems to cut against the grain" of decisions, like *Powell v. Ala.* and *Gideon v. Wainwright,* (see § 3.1(a)) that are based on the premise that "the help of a lawyer is essential to assure a fair trial." It rejected, however, the dissenters' contention that the state's interest in providing a fair trial permitted it to insist upon representation by counsel. The framers of the Sixth Amendment were well aware of the value of counsel in obtaining a fair trial, but placed on a higher plane the "inestimable worth of free choice." Since "the defendant, and not his lawyer or the State, will bear the personal consequences of the conviction," he should be free to decide whether he would better off conducting his own defense. Although his decision may not be wise, his "choice must be honored out of that respect for the individual which is the lifeblood of the law."

Having established a constitutional right to self-representation at trial, the Court then turned to the conditions under which it could be exercised. The defendant who proceeds pro se, it noted, must act "knowingly and intelligently" in giving up those "traditional benefits associated with the right to counsel." He should "be made aware of the dangers and disadvantages of self-representation, so that the record will establish that he 'knows what he is doing and his choice is made with eyes open.'" The defendant need not, however, "have the skill and experience of a lawyer in order competently and intelligently to choose self-representation." Here the record showed that the defendant was "literate, competent, and understanding, and that he was voluntarily exercising his informed free will." That he may not have mastered the intricacies of the hearsay rule, or that he lacked other "technical legal knowledge," was "not relevant to an assessment of his knowing exercise of the right to defend himself." Accordingly, the lower court had erred in forcing him to accept appointed counsel.

The *Faretta* Court reversed the defendant's conviction without considering the likely impact of the Sixth Amendment violation on the outcome of the trial. As it later explained in *McKaskle v. Wiggins* (1984): "Since the right of self-representation is a right that when exercised usually increases the likelihood of a trial outcome unfavorable to the defendant, its denial is not amenable to harmless error analysis. The right is either respected or denied; its deprivation cannot be harmless."

In *Martinez v. Court of Appeal* (2000), the Court distinguished *Faretta* in holding that there was no constitutional right to self-representation on appeal. *Faretta* had relied on the structure of the Sixth Amendment, but here any constitutional right would have to be based on due process. See § 3.2(b). From the perspective afforded by due process, the Court was "entirely unpersuaded," in light of "the practices that prevail in the nation today," that the "risk of either disloyalty or suspicion of disloyalty [in representation] is of sufficient concern to conclude that a constitutional right of self-representation is a necessary component of a fair appellate proceeding." Also, with defendant's position having shifted from that of an "accused" to a convicted defendant, the "autonomy interests" presented at this stage were "less compelling than in *Faretta*."

(b) Notification. Dissenting in *Faretta*, Justice Blackmun raised the question of whether "every defendant [must] be advised of his right to proceed pro se." The Court had held that notification of the right to counsel is essential; might not a similar requirement apply to the "other side" of defendant's Sixth Amendment right? Lower courts have uniformly assumed that there is no constitutional obligation to inform the defendant of his constitutional right to proceed pro se in the absence of a clear indication on his part that he desires to consider that option. This position is based in part on concern that notification of the right to proceed pro se might undermine the "overriding constitutional policy" favoring the provision of counsel.

Courts are not quite so uniform in describing what constitutes a sufficient indication of a defendant's interest in proceeding pro se to impose upon the trial court a duty to explore that interest. Most courts look to *Faretta*, where the Supreme Court noted that the defendant had "clearly and unequivocally declared to the trial judge that he wanted to represent himself," and hold that no action is required by the trial court absent the defendant's unequivocal expression of a desire to proceed pro se.

(c) Requisite Warnings and Judicial Inquiry. *Faretta* stressed that trial courts, before permitting a defendant to represent himself, must determine that he is knowingly and intelligently relinquishing the benefits of representation by counsel. Appellate opinions have suggested that the defendant should be informed at least of the following: (1) that "presenting a defense is not a simple matter of telling one's story," but requires adherence to various "technical rules" governing the conduct of a trial; (2) that a lawyer has substantial experience and training in trial procedure and that the prosecution will be represented by an experienced attorney; (3) that a person unfamiliar with legal procedures may inadvertently give the prosecutor a windfall by failing to make objections to inadmissible evidence, may fail to make effective use of such rights as the voir dire of jurors, and may make tactical decisions that produce unintended consequences; (4) that there may be possible defenses and other rights of which counsel would be aware and if those are not timely asserted, they may be lost permanently; (5) that a defendant proceeding pro se will not be allowed to complain on appeal about the competency of his representation; and (6) "that the effectiveness of his defense may well be diminished by his dual role as attorney and accused." If the defendant persists in his request to proceed pro se, notwithstanding the court's warnings as to the possible disadvantages of self-representation, then the preferred procedure directs the court to ascertain, through a penetrating inquiry, that the defendant understands and appreciates those disadvantages and their possible consequences.

In most jurisdictions, the preferred procedure described above, as to both warnings and inquiry, is only that; appellate courts describe the procedure as the "better" practice, but do not require that the lower courts adhere to it. However, some jurisdictions do mandate specific warnings and a particular inquiry by statute, court rule, or the exercise of the appellate court's supervisory power. In these jurisdictions, a lack of substantial compliance with the prescribed process ordinarily will result in an appellate reversal without considering whether there also was a Sixth Amendment violation. In other jurisdictions, however, trial court departures typically have forced the appellate courts to consider the extent to which the Sixth Amendment requires either or both warnings as to the disadvantages of proceeding pro se and an on-the-record inquiry as to the defendant's appreciation of those disadvantages and their possible consequences.

The *Faretta* opinion noted that the defendant "should be made aware of the dangers and disadvantages of self-representation, so that the record will establish that 'he knows what he is doing and his choice is made with his eyes open.'" Relying upon this statement, several courts have suggested that a waiver is not constitutionally acceptable unless the trial judge specifically warns the defendant of the dangers of self-representation. Other courts take the position that *Faretta* requires only that the defendant have been aware of the disadvantages of proceeding pro se, and that awareness can be established without regard to any admonitions or colloquies. A waiver is constitutionally acceptable where such factors as defendant's involvement in previous criminal trials, his representation by counsel prior to the trial, and his explanation of his reasons for proceeding pro se indicate that he was fully aware of the difficulties of self-representation. For at least some courts, such factors can serve the same function as an extensive colloquy, but only when they provide "a compelling case of circumstantial evidence that the pro se defendant knew what he or she was doing."

(d) Grounds for Denial. In the course of discussing why the defendant in *Faretta* should have been allowed to proceed pro se, the *Faretta* opinion pointed to three possible grounds for denying self-representation, notwithstanding an unequivocal request by the defendant. First, *Faretta* stressed that the request in that case was made "well before the date of trial." This suggests that, at some point, a request might be so disruptive of the orderly schedule of proceedings as to justify rejection on that ground alone. Provided defendant does not demand additional time to prepare, lower courts generally deem pro se motions to be timely as long as they are made before trial. On the other hand, the trial court is recognized as having broad discretion to reject as untimely a request made during the course of the trial.

Second, *Faretta* noted that "the trial judge may terminate self-representation by a defendant who engages in serious and obstructionist misconduct." Ordinarily, this authority would be exercised only after the defendant has begun to represent himself. However, in exceptional situations, the defendant's behavior in the course of seeking to obtain self-representation may in itself be disruptive and thereby justify denying his pro se motion.

Third, by requiring a valid waiver of counsel as a prerequisite for self-representation, *Faretta* recognized the authority of a trial court to refuse to permit self-representation when, despite its efforts to explain the consequences of waiver, defendant is unable to reach the level of appreciation needed for a knowing and intelligent waiver. *Faretta* also makes clear, however, that a defendant does not need legal expertise nor unusual intelligence to meet its standard of awareness of the dangers and disadvantages of self-representation.

Ind. v. Edwards (2008) recognized a fourth ground for denial, relating to the defendant's mental illness, but left open the precise scope of that ground. The Court there held that a state had the authority to allow its trial courts to deny self-representation to mentally ill defendants—even where those defendants (1) were mentally competent to stand trial, and (2) had the understanding of the disadvantages of self-representation required by *Faretta*—based on the trial courts properly finding that the defendants "suffer from severe mental illness to the point where they are not competent to conduct trial proceedings by themselves." The procedural setting presented in *Edwards* required the Court to address only the question of whether a state could recognize such authority, and the opinion therefore found it unnecessary to articulate a specific standard for measuring a mentally ill defendant's lack of capacity to represent himself at trial. The state asked the Court "to adopt, as a measure of a defendant's ability to conduct a trial, * * * [that the] defendant cannot communicate coherently with the court or a jury." The Court responded, however, that it was "sufficiently uncertain * * * as to how that particular standard would work in practice to refrain from endorsing it as a federal constitutional standard here." It was necessary only to acknowledge that the state had an authority which the court below had thought to be barred by *Godinez* (§ 3.3(c)), and to remand the case so that the state court could consider application of that authority under the facts before it.

The *Edwards* majority initially concluded that *Godinez* was not controlling because: (1) the defendant in *Godinez* proceeded pro se to enter a guilty plea, not to represent himself at trial, and "his ability to conduct a defense at trial was expressly not at issue"; and (2) the issue posed in *Godinez* was whether the state was required constitutionally to impose a higher standard of mental competency than the competency-to-stand-trial standard (with the Court saying it was not required to do so), while the issue here was whether the state was allowed to do so. The Court then took note of "several considerations" that led it to conclude that the "Constitution permits a state to limit * * * defendant's self-representation right by insisting upon representation by counsel at trial—on the ground that the defendant lacks the mental capacity to conduct his trial defense unless represented."

Some of the considerations discussed in the *Edwards* opinion reflected the special character of "mental illness." Thus, the Court noted that the relevant literature establishes that "mental illness itself is not a unitary concept," as it "interferes with an individual's functioning at different times in different ways"; accordingly, "in certain instances an individual may well be able to satisfy [the trial competency] standard, for he may be able to work with counsel at trial, yet at the same time he may be unable to carry out the basic tasks needed to present his own defense at trial." Other factors cited by the Court could readily be extended beyond the mental-illness situation. Thus, it noted that *Faretta* viewed self-representation as "affirming the dignity" of a defendant but that end would be defeated where defendant's inadequacies could well lead to a "spectacle * * * as likely to prove humiliating as enabling," and "in that exceptional context, [self-representation could] undercu[t] the most basic of the constitution's criminal law objectives, providing a fair trial." Moreover, the state also has an interest in ensuring not only that proceedings be "fair," but they "appear fair to all who observe them," and that appearance hardly can be achieved where a defendant "by reason of his mental condition stands helpless and alone before the court."

(e) Subsequent Challenge to Ineffective Representation. Commenting upon the limitations of self-representation, the *Faretta* opinion noted: "Neither is * * * [the right of self-representation] a license not to comply with relevant rules of procedural and substantive law. Thus, whatever else may or may not be open to him on appeal, a defendant who elects to represent himself cannot thereafter complain that the quality of his own defense amounted to a denial of 'effective assistance of counsel.' " Relying upon this statement, lower courts have consistently rejected claims of defendants that their pro se presentation was so inadequate as to result in a denial of a fair trial. The courts note that the defendant's failure to utilize even the ordinary skills of laymen may in itself be a strategic ploy of a defendant hoping to create grounds for an appellate reversal of an almost certain conviction. They also frequently point to efforts of the trial judge to assist the defendant (though noting that such efforts are not constitutionally mandated) or the availability of consultation with standby counsel (although appointment of such counsel also is not mandatory).

   (f) Standby Counsel. *Faretta* noted that "a state may—even over objection by the accused—appoint a 'standby counsel' to aid the accused if and when the accused requests help, and to be available to represent the accused in the event that termination of the defendant's self-representation is necessary." This statement was viewed by the lower court in *McKaskle v. Wiggins* (1984) as restricting the role of standby counsel, in the absence of a defendant's request for assistance, to "being seen but not heard." A divided Supreme Court disagreed, holding that the seen-but-not-heard standard was entirely too narrow. Unsolicited and undesired participation by standby counsel did present a difficulty, when it involved more than "assisting defendant in overcoming routine [procedural] obstacles." Even then, however, all such participation did not per se constitute a violation of defendant's right of self-representation. In determining whether such participation undermined defendant's *Faretta* right, the Court would apply a two-pronged test. First, did "standby counsel's participation over defendant's objection effectively allow counsel to make or substantially interfere with any significant tactical decisions, or to control the questioning of witnesses, or to speak instead of the defendant on any matter of importance"? Such action necessarily undermines the defendant's right of self-representation since it deprives him of the "actual control over the case he chooses to present to the jury." Second, even if the defendant was able to present his case in his own way, did the additional unsolicited participation of counsel "destroy the jury's perception that the defendant is representing himself"? That impact also eviscerates defendant's *Faretta* right since the "defendant's appearance in the status of one conducting his own defense" is an important aspect of the "dignity and autonomy" of the individual protected in *Faretta*. Moreover, "from the jury's perspective, the message conveyed by the defense may depend as much on the messenger as the message itself."

   (g) Hybrid Representation. Under a hybrid form of representation, defendant and counsel act, in effect, as co-counsel, with each speaking for the defense during different phases of the trial. Lower courts have consistently rejected the defense contention that *Faretta's* recognition of both self-representation and representation by counsel as "independent constitutional rights" logically establishes a constitutional grounding for hybrid representation. They have reasoned that the constitutional rights to self-representation and representation by counsel are mutually exclusive, though the trial court may permit hybrid representation, in its discretion, as "a matter of grace." Of course, since hybrid representation is in part pro se representation, allowing it without a proper *Faretta* inquiry can create constitutional difficulties. Courts often will not allow hybrid representation because of its potential tactical use by the defense. Counsel will carry most of the load, but the defendant will present an opening or closing argument to the jury that will allow him, in effect, to "testify" without being subjected to cross-examination.

§ 3.6 Counsel's Control Over Defense Strategy

(a) "Strategic" vs. "Personal" Decisions. As the Court noted in *Faretta*, a defendant who chooses to be represented by counsel thereby relinquishes to counsel the authority to make various decisions relating to the defense presentation. As to those decisions, commonly described as "strategic decisions," the client is bound by the attorney's exercise of competent professional judgment even if the attorney's action or inaction amounts to a forfeiture of a defense right. Although such forfeitures are sometimes described as "waivers," they do not require the defendant's knowledge, understanding, or agreement with the defense counsel's decision to forego the exercise of the particular right. Where the defendant is aware in advance of the defense counsel's intent to pursue a particular strategy and disagrees with that strategy, the defendant may seek to replace that counsel with one who will respect the defendant's wishes (counsel acquiescing to the defendant's wishes on strategic decisions, while not required, rarely will open the door to a successful postconviction claim of ineffective assistance of counsel). However, a client-attorney disagreement on a strategic decision does not constitute the "just cause" needed to mandate replacement of counsel. Accordingly, the indigent defendant will not be granted new state-funded counsel (see § 3.4(b)), and defendant with retained counsel may be denied the opportunity to substitute new counsel of choice if that will cause scheduling difficulties (see § 3.4(c)).

In contrast to strategic decisions, other decisions are categorized as "personal decisions"—i.e., decisions so "fundamental" that the ultimate decision-making authority must rest with the defendant. Here, the defense counsel can take action only with the approval of the defendant, and where the action amounts to a waiver of a right, the publicly acknowledged consent of the client may be required.

The Supreme Court has stated, in dictum or holding, that it is for the defendant to decide whether to take each of the following steps: plead guilty or take action tantamount to entering a guilty plea; waive the right to jury trial; waive his right to be present at trial; testify on his own behalf; or forego an appeal. Lower court rulings have added to this group: the waiver of the right to attend important pretrial proceedings; the waiver of the constitutional right to a speedy trial; the refusal (by a competent defendant) to enter an insanity plea; and the decision to withhold defendant's sole defense at the guilt/special circumstances phase of a capital case and use it solely in the penalty phrase. State provisions on waiver of the right to be charged by a grand jury indictment traditionally have also placed that decision in the hands of the defendant.

On the other side, the Supreme Court has indicated, in dictum or holding, that counsel has the ultimate authority in deciding whether or not to advance the following defense rights: barring prosecution use of unconstitutionally obtained evidence; obtaining dismissal of an indictment on the ground of racial discrimination in the selection of the grand jury; wearing civilian clothes, rather than prison garb, during the trial; striking an improper jury instruction; including a particular nonfrivolous claim among the issues briefed and argued on appeal; foregoing cross-examination; calling a possible witness (other than defendant) to testify; controlling the discovery provided to the prosecution (even where risking the possible sanction of excluding a defense witness' testimony by failing to give the prosecution timely notice relating to the witness); allowing *voir dire* and jury selection in a federal case to be conducted by a federal magistrate rather than a federal district judge; and being tried within the 180 day time period specified in the Interstate Agreement on Detainers. Lower court rulings have added to this list a variety of other determinations, including the following: whether to exercise a peremptory challenge; whether to request or consent to a mistrial; whether to request, or object to, the exclusion of the public from the trial; whether to seek a change of venue, continuance, or other relief due to prejudicial pretrial publicity; whether to seek a continuance and thereby relinquish a statutory right to trial within a specified period of days; whether to seek a competency determination; and choosing among different lines of defense that could produce an acquittal.

Taken together the various rulings produce a picture that is clear at many points but clouded at others. Thus, lower courts have divided as the proper classification of various decisions, including: whether to accept a jury of less than twelve; whether to rely upon a partial defense (i.e., a defense that challenges only the higher level of multiple charges); whether to stipulate to the introduction of prior recorded testimony on a critical issue (or all issues); and whether to pursue an "all or nothing" defense by waiving the right to a jury instruction on lesser included offenses. Some have viewed such decisions as within the control of the defendant, while others have viewed them as decisions within counsel's strategic control.

In *Fla. v. Nixon* (2004), the Supreme Court added at least one further layer of complexity to the distinction drawn between "personal rights" and lawyer-controlled rights. At issue there was the decision to concede the defendant's commission of murder at the guilt phase of a capital trial (thereby avoiding inconsistency in the presentation of mitigating evidence at the penalty phase). The decision was made by counsel, but only after the defendant was consulted and repeatedly refused to take a position on the proposed strategy (indeed, defendant refused even to discuss the matter). The lower court concluded that this was a decision belonging to the personal choice of the defendant, as the action taken was akin to entering a guilty plea. As such, it concluded, counsel's approach only could be adopted with the fully informed and publicly acknowledged consent of the client. This followed, the lower court reasoned, from ruling of the Supreme Court in *Brookhart v. Janis* (1966). The Court there had held that the defense counsel could not enter, "without the defendant's informed consent," an agreement as to the state's burden of proof that was characterized as amounting "almost [to] a guilty plea" (the defense counsel agreed "that all the state had to prove was a prima facie case, that he would not contest it, and that there would be no cross-examination of witnesses").

In reaching its ruling in *Nixon*, the Supreme Court did not address the lower court's conclusion that the strategy adopted there involved a "personal choice" decision. That issue did not have to be resolved because the waiver of rights made by counsel was constitutionally sufficient in light of the defendant's refusal to exercise his personal choice after repeated consultations. The requirement of an explicit affirmative waiver by the defendant, as applied in the case of a guilty plea, and arguably extended to the situation presented in a *Brookhart,* would not be extended to the distinguishable setting of this case. Here, unlike *Brookhart,* counsel did not accept a "truncated proceeding, shorn of the need * * * [to establish] guilt beyond a reasonable doubt." While acknowledging in his opening statement that defendant committed the murder, defense counsel: (1) did not thereby relieve the state of its obligation to present admissible evidence meeting the reasonable doubt standard; (2)

retained the authority to object to the admission of prejudicial evidence and to cross-examine witnesses; and (3) did not preclude raising an appeal any "errors in the trial or jury instructions." Where the client refused to take a position, counsel was free to adopt such a strategy.

In tying its ruling to the client's refusal to make a choice, the *Nixon* Court apparently was reserving for another day the question of whether counsel could have insisted upon the strategy adopted there if the client had opposed it. However, the opinion also appeared to reflect the assumption that, even if the client had the final word, the decision was not so personal to the client that counsel could not proceed where the client was unresponsive. Thus, while some waiver decisions subject to defendant's control require an explicit acceptance by the defendant, precluding counsel from taking that action where the client is unresponsive, others apparently allow counsel to proceed in that setting. The *Nixon* explanation of the difference between the decision made there and the decision made in *Brookhart*, however, offers only limited guidance as to how this distinction might be applied as to other types of decisions within the defendant's control.

Nixon may also have contributed to drawing a distinction among lawyer-controlled decisions with respect to the need for client-consultation. The traditional position was that, as to counsel-control issues, there was no Sixth Amendment obligation of counsel to consult with the client prior to exercising counsel's choice of strategy. In many of the cases in which the Court held that a particular decision was within the control of counsel (and the client therefore was bound by the action or inaction of counsel), the Court obviously assumed that the defendant had never been consulted. Indeed, as discussed in subsection (b), the Court, in explaining why particular decisions have been placed within counsel's control, often refers to difficulties that would be presented if consultation was required (which would be the result of holding the decision to be within the control of the client).

On the other hand, in *Strickland v. Washington* (1984), the Court's seminal ruling on the violation of the Sixth Amendment through ineffective assistance of counsel (see § 3.10), the Court spoke of counsel's "duty to consult with the defendant on important decisions and to keep the defendant informed in the course of the prosecution." *Nixon* stressed that counsel there had fully consulted, as required by *Strickland*, and did so without reaching the issue of whether counsel's decision involved a "personal right" of the defendant. The Third Circuit has concluded, in light of *Strickland*, that a failure to consult, even as to a counsel-controlled decision, may constitute ineffective assistance of counsel. The consultation obligation, the Third Circuit noted, serves four important functions even as to "issues on which counsel has the final word." Consultation will: (1) ensure that counsel receives any factual information relevant to the issue that the defendant might have; (2) give the defendant the opportunity (depending on timing) to consider the possibility of seeking substitute counsel or proceeding pro se; (3) "promote and maintain a cooperative client-counsel relationship"; and (4) give to the attorney the opportunity to shape his or her decision in light of "the client's views and desires concerning the best course to be followed." Of course, where counsel would have insisted upon exercising her authority without regard to the client's wishes, the last function obviously does not alter the character of counsel's representation. However, in particular cases, the failure to meet at least the first two functions of consultation may have an impact so significant as to meet the prejudice prong of the ineffective assistance standard.

(b) **Balancing of Interests.** The Supreme Court's explanations of why particular decisions are for counsel or client typically have been brief and conclusionary. In the course of concluding that a particular decision is within the defendant's control, the Court has emphasized that the right involved is "fundamental" (or "basic"). It has failed to explain, however, why various rights subject to counsel's authority are not equally fundamental. Arguably, the decision to plead guilty has a special quality because it involves the relinquishment of so many basic rights. But it is more difficult to distinguish the right to be tried before a jury, for example, from the right to present a particular witness or to cross-examine an opposing witness.

Gonzalez v. U.S. (2008) offers the leading explanation as to why particular decisions fall within the lawyer-control category. The Court there explained why "giving the attorney control of trial management matters is a practical necessity." It noted that most choices "affecting conduct of the trial, including the objections to make, the witnesses to call, and the arguments to advance, depend not only upon what is permissible under the rules of evidence and procedure but also upon tactical considerations of the moment and the larger strategic plan for the trial. These matters can be difficult to explain to a layperson; and to require in all instances that they be approved by the client could risk compromising the efficiencies and fairness that the trial process is designed to promote." The attorney generally will have "a better understanding of these procedural choices" than the client, "or at least the law should so assume." Moreover, "requiring personal, on-the-record approval from the client could necessitate a lengthy explanation the client might not understand at the moment and that might distract from more pressing matters as the attorney seeks to prepare the best defense."

The Court's emphasis on the strategic character of the decisions, the difficulties presented in explaining tactical considerations to clients, and the disruptive impact of such consultations would appear to be equally relevant to many of the decisions that are subject to the client's control. Concurring separately in *Gonzalez*, Justice Scalia argued that the Court's "tactical-vs-fundamental approach" was vague and subjective. "Depending upon the circumstances," he noted, "any right can be tactical"—including the "decision to plead guilty." "Whether a right is 'fundamental',," he added, is "equally mysterious," as "one would think that any right guaranteed by the Constitution would be fundamental."

Lower courts have suggested that the determination that particular decisions do or do not require defendant's personal choice has rested on a balancing of several factors including, but not limited to, the fundamental nature of the right involved and the significance of strategic considerations. Other considerations cited as bearing on that balancing include: (1) the objective of avoiding disruption of the litigation process (in particular, whether there is a ready occasion for determining that a decision was actually made by the client, as in the case of a jury trial waiver); (2) the distinction between objectives and means (with objectives, such as avoiding conviction, being for the client, and means, such as presenting certain witnesses, being for the lawyer); (3) the "inherently personal character" of the particular decision (which places it under the control of the defendant, as in the defendant's decision to testify); and (4) the need to foster a strong defense bar (reflecting a concern that if counsel is not given the control needed to avoid professionally embarrassing presentations, counsel will avoid criminal defense work, particularly court appointments).

(c) Violations of Personal Choice. As discussed in § 3.10, *Strickland v. Washington* ordinarily imposes two prerequisites for reversing a conviction based upon inadequacies in the performance of counsel: (1) a showing that the performance was incompetent as measured by an "objective standard of reasonableness"; and (2) a showing of a potential prejudicial impact, as measured by a "reasonable probability that, but for counsel's unprofessional errors, the result of the proceeding would have been different." Where counsel is alleged to have violated defendant's right to make a procedural decision within defendant's control, the application of each prong of *Strickland* presents issues unique to that claim.

Incompetency. Where counsel violated defendant's clearly expressed choice as to a decision within defendant's control, that action in itself establishes the incompetency of counsel's performance. Counsel's decision may have been tactically sound, but because the decision belonged to defendant, the failure to accept defendant's choice automatically falls below an objective standard of reasonableness. Thus, the first prong of *Strickland* is met where counsel ignores defendant's direction (as where defendant directs counsel to file a first appeal as of right, but counsel fails to do so), or where counsel uses coercion to force the client to relinquish his personal choice (as where counsel's last minute threat to withdraw forced the client to waive a jury trial).

Establishing incompetent performance is not quite so easy, however, where the defendant never was asked and therefore never expressed his choice. *Roe v. Flores–Ortega* (2000) indicates that defendant here must make a showing that he would have taken a position contrary to counsel if asked. In *Roe*, where counsel failed to consult and did not take a first appeal as of right, the Court concluded that the defendant had to establish either that (1) the circumstances of the case were such that a "rational defendant would [have] want[ed] to appeal," or (2) that "this particular defendant reasonably demonstrated to counsel that he was interested in appealing." Thus, the Court noted, a "highly relevant factor would be whether the conviction follows a trial or a guilty plea, both because a guilty plea reduces the scope of potentially appealable issues and because such a plea may indicate that the defendant seeks an end to judicial proceedings." The Court added that where there was a guilty plea, other circumstances also must be considered in assessing whether counsel should reasonably have assumed that the defendant had an interest in an appeal. Those circumstances include "whether the defendant received the sentence bargained for" and whether the plea "expressly reserved or waived some or all appeal rights."

Prejudice. The *Strickland* standard of ineffective assistance also requires a showing of prejudice, and the Court in *Roe v. Flores–Oretega* held that the failure-to-consult could not be treated as per se prejudicial. Even if "all the information counsel knew or should have known" establishes that the rational defendant would want to appeal or that this defendant demonstrated an interest in an appeal, that does not invariably establish that the failure to consult "actually caus[ed] the forfeiture of the appeal." To meet the prejudice prerequisite, the defendant must "demonstrate that there is a reasonable probability that, but for counsel's deficient failure to consult with him about an appeal, he would have timely appealed." The Court acknowledged that this inquiry "is not wholly dissimilar from the inquiry into whether counsel performed deficiently" by failing to consult. Thus, where the defendant shows nonfrivolous grounds for appeal, that will establish both that a "rational defendant would [have] want[ed] to appeal" and a "reasonable probability" defendant would have chosen to appeal after consultation. On the other hand, where the failure to consult constituted deficient performance because defendant had "sufficiently demonstrated to counsel his interest in an appeal," the defendant must also be able to establish that after consultation (where counsel might have suggested that an appeal was fruitless), he would have continued that interest and instructed his counsel to file the appeal.

The court in *Flores-Ortega* concentrated on whether the defendant would have exercised the right of appeal, not on whether the appeal would have been successful. That is consistent with the position the Court has taken where counsel failed to follow a defendant's instruction to file a first appeal as of right. There, the Court has noted, a "defendant is entitled to [an] appeal without showing that his appeal likely would have merit." This is so, the Court has explained, because counsel's deficient performance led to "forfeiture of the proceeding itself." Where a proceeding did occur, a "presumption of reliability" attaches, and to overcome that presumption, the defendant must show specific outcome prejudice. Where no proceeding occurred, there can be "no presumption of reliability" and the defendant need not show he was likely to have succeeded, just as a defendant deprived of counsel at trial need not show that the assistance of counsel would have produced a different result.

§ 3.7   The Right to Effective Assistance of Counsel: Guiding Principles

(a) **The Prerequisite of a Constitutional Right to Counsel.** The Supreme Court first recognized a constitutional right to the effective assistance of counsel in *Powell v. Ala.* (1932). *Powell* noted that where due process requires the state to provide counsel for an indigent defendant, "that duty is not discharged by an assignment at such a time or under such circumstances as to preclude the giving of effective aid in the preparation and trial of the case." Subsequent cases, involving Sixth Amendment and equal protection rights to counsel, similarly held that a right to counsel encompassed a right to effective assistance by that counsel. For "a party whose counsel is unable to provide effective representation is in no better position that one who has no counsel at all."

The Supreme Court rulings establish that a constitutional requirement of effective assistance extends to counsel's performance in any proceeding as to which there would be a constitutional right both to appointed counsel for the indigent and to retained counsel for the non-indigent. Where there is no such constitutional right to counsel's assistance, however, even the most negligent performance of counsel will not give rise to an ineffective assistance claim. Thus, in *Wainwright v. Torna* (1982), the Court rejected defendant's claim that he had been denied the effective assistance of counsel when his retained attorney failed to file a timely application for discretionary review at the state's second-level of appeal. Noting that "*Ross v. Moffitt* (§ 3.1(b)) held that a criminal defendant does not have a constitutional right to counsel to pursue [such] discretionary state appeals," the *Torna* majority opinion concluded that the lawyer's negligence therefore did not violate any constitutional right of the defendant. The Court reasoned: "Since respondent had no constitutional right to counsel, he could not be deprived of the effective assistance of counsel by his retained counsel's failure to file the application timely." While *Torna* involved retained counsel, *Pa. v. Finley* (1987) indicated that the same analysis applied to appointed counsel where the state had no constitutional obligation to provide appointed counsel (there, on a collateral postconviction proceeding).

As discussed in § 3.1(b), in proceedings in which there is no right to appointed counsel (such as that involved in *Torna*), there may be a due process right to proceed through retained counsel absent a compelling state interest for excluding counsel. Since the right to use retained counsel here would not be based on a constitutional need for counsel to ensure a fair hearing, but simply on a "state's duty to retrain from unreasonable interference with the individual's desire to defend himself in whatever manner he deems best," the right would not carry with it a state obligation to ensure that retained counsel provided effective assistance. The defendant alone would bear the consequences of his unwise choice of counsel, notwithstanding constitutional protection of his right to proceed by counsel rather than pro se.

(b) Retained vs. Appointed Counsel. Prior to the Supreme Court's 1980 decision in *Cuyler v. Sullivan* (1980), many lower courts utilized different standards for reviewing ineffective assistance claims depending upon whether counsel was appointed or privately retained. Some of the earlier cases had refused on an agency rationale to even recognize ineffectiveness claims involving retained counsel. Other courts recognized that the law of agency was misplaced as applied to criminal cases, but found a basis in the state-action requirement of the Fourteenth Amendment for applying a less stringent standard of review to the alleged incompetency of retained counsel. A constitutional violation, it was argued, required state participation at a sufficient level to render the state responsible for counsel's inadequacies. That responsibility was seen as arising automatically from the trial court's selection of appointed counsel. As for retained counsel, the state bore responsibility for counsel's inadequacies only where they were so obvious that they should have been apparent to the trial court.

Sullivan put to rest this division among the lower courts. The ineffective assistance claim in *Sullivan* was based upon a retained attorney's multiple representation of codefendants with possibly conflicting interests. Although arguing that counsel was not ineffective, the prosecution also claimed that, in any event, "the alleged failings of * * * retained counsel cannot provide a basis for a * * * [constitutional violation] because the conduct of retained counsel does not involve state action." Rejecting that contention, the Supreme Court noted that "a proper respect for the Sixth Amendment disarms [the prosecution's] contention that defendants who retain their own counsel are entitled to less protection than defendants for whom the State appoints counsel. * * * Since the State's conduct of a criminal trial itself implicates the State in the defendant's conviction, we see no basis for drawing a distinction between retained and appointed counsel that would deny equal justice to defendants who must choose their own lawyers."

(c) The Adversary System Touchstone. The companion cases of *U.S. v. Cronic* (1984) and *Strickland v. Washington* (1984) provide the general framework for analysis of ineffective assistance claims. The critical element, both opinions noted, is to evaluate the performance of counsel in light of the underlying purpose of the constitutional right to counsel. Since both cases involved challenges to the performance of counsel at the trial level, the opinions focused on the purpose of the Sixth Amendment right to counsel. However, since the Court indicated that the role of counsel under that Amendment flowed from the adversary nature of the trial process, and that the same principles would apply to other stages of the criminal justice process that are "sufficiently like a trial in its adversarial format and in the existence of standards for decision," the analysis of *Cronic* and *Strickland* also has been applied to the various stages of the process at which due process or equal protection establish a constitutional right to counsel.

The *Cronic/Strickland* analysis rests initially on the premise that the Sixth Amendment right to counsel, like other Sixth Amendment rights, sets forth one of the "basic elements of a fair trial." A key component of that fair trial was an adversarial system of litigation. The Sixth Amendment included a guarantee of assistance of counsel because "it envision[ed] counsel playing a role that is critical to the ability of the adversarial system to produce just results." The " 'very premise of our adversary system * * * is that partisan advocacy on both sides of a case will best promote the ultimate objective that the guilty be convicted and the innocent go free,' "and it was this " 'very premise' that underlies and gives meaning to the Sixth Amendment." Effective assistance therefore must be measured by reference to the functioning of the adversary process in the particular case. "The right to effective assistance," the *Cronic* opinion noted, is "the right of the accused to require the prosecution's case to survive the crucible of meaningful adversary testing. When a true adversarial criminal trial has been conducted—even if defense counsel may have made demonstrable errors—the kind of testing envisioned by the Sixth Amendment has occurred." The critical question therefore is whether counsel's performance was so deficient that the process "lost its character as a confrontation between adversaries," producing an "actual breakdown of the adversary process." Emphasizing this same point of reference, the Court stated in *Strickland:* "The benchmark for judging any claim of ineffectiveness must be whether counsel's conduct so undermined the proper functioning of the adversarial process that the trial cannot be relied on as having produced a just result."

In tying the concept of effective assistance to the functioning of the adversary process, the Court clearly rejected a measurement based solely on a comparison of counsel with his or her peers. The key was not how close counsel came to gaining for defendant the best possible result that an attorney might have realistically achieved. Neither was it the grade counsel might receive as measured against some model for attorney performance, whether theoretical or reflective of empirical data. Rather the focus was on the presence of the requisite adversarial testing. The most obvious case of ineffectiveness would be that in which counsel simply did not act as an advocate, either because he was prevented from doing so or simply did not make the effort. Where counsel sought to perform as advocate, the question would then be whether his effort provided a "meaningful adversary testing." What was "meaningful" for this purpose would be measured by reference to the operation of the adversary process to achieve its basic objective, ensuring the reliability of the adjudication. Thus, as the *Cronic* opinion noted, a failure to provide adversarial testing as to a single issue, when that issue is critical to a finding of guilt, may in itself produce a breakdown in the adversarial process. On the other hand, as *Strickland* further noted, meaningful adversarial testing hardly requires that challenges be made and investigations be directed at each and every point without regard to its likely insignificance in testing the strength of the prosecution's case.

(d) Per Se vs. Actual Ineffectiveness. The adversary system touchstone advanced in *Cronic* and *Strickland* appeared to call for a determination of "actual ineffectiveness" under the facts of the particular case. A constitutional challenge could be found only upon a determination both that counsel had actually failed in some respect to discharge the duties of an advocate in an adversarial system and that counsel's failure so affected the adversary process as to undermine confidence in the result it produced. These determinations suggest a fact-sensitized judgment that evaluates the nature and impact of counsel's representation under the circumstances of the individual case. Not all of the Court's past rulings, however, had adopted such a "judgmental" approach. Some had seemingly relied upon per se standards of ineffective assistance. In cases in which trial courts had prevented counsel from utilizing certain adversarial procedures, the Supreme Court had found ineffective assistance without looking to other aspects of counsel's performance. See § 3.8(a). In cases in which counsel had acted upon a conflict of interest, the Court had also found ineffective assistance without examining all aspects of counsel's performance. See § 3.9(d).

In *Cronic*, the Court was presented with a case in which the lower court had extended the per se approach to conclude that counsel was inherently incapable of providing effective assistance. The lower court in *Cronic* had sustained defendant's ineffectiveness claim without referring to any specific error or inadequacy in counsel's performance. Instead, it had inferred that "counsel was unable to discharge his duties" based upon five aspects of the circumstances surrounding counsel's appointment (including the lateness of the appointment, the complexity of the case, and counsel's lack of experience) Justice Stevens' opinion for the *Cronic* Court rejected this "inferential approach." It concluded that a determination of actual effectiveness is the standard prerequisite for sustaining an ineffective assistance claim, and the use of a presumption of inherent ineffectiveness therefore must be limited to unique circumstances presented in extreme cases.

Justice Stevens' opinion initially stressed that a judicial evaluation of an ineffectiveness claim must "begin by recognizing that the right to the effective assistance of counsel is recognized not for its own sake, but because of the effect it has on the ability of the accused to receive a fair trial." Accordingly, establishment of an ineffectiveness claim ordinarily requires some showing of an adverse effect on the reliability of the trial process. Moreover, because "we presume that the lawyer is competent," the burden ordinarily rests on the accused to make that showing. "There are, however, circumstances that are so likely to prejudice the accused that the cost of litigating their effect in a particular case is unjustified." In such situations, constitutional effectiveness, amounting to a "breakdown of the adversarial process," could be presumed. However, upon turning to the Court's past decisions, Justice Stevens found only three settings in which such a presumptive approach was justified.

First, there was the situation in which "counsel was either totally absent or prevented from assisting the accused during a critical stage of the proceeding." Falling in this category were cases in which the trial court had unconstitutionally refused to appoint counsel or had restricted counsel's assistance. The second situation was that in which counsel was physically present, but completely absent in effort. As the Court put it, "if counsel entirely fails to subject the prosecution's case to meaningful adversarial testing, then there has been a denial of Sixth Amendment rights that makes the adversary process itself presumptively unreliable." Finally, there were "occasions when, although counsel is available to assist the accused during trial, the likelihood that any lawyer, even a fully competent one, could provide effective assistance is so small that a presumption of prejudice is appropriate without inquiry into the actual conduct of the trial." *Powell v. Ala.* (§ 3.1(a)) was such a case. The trial court there had utilized such a haphazard process of appointment—ordering admittedly unprepared outstate counsel to proceed with whatever help the local bar, appointed en masse, might provide—that ineffective assistance was properly presumed without further inquiry.

"Apart from circumstances of this magnitude", the *Cronic* opinion noted, "there is generally no basis for finding a Sixth Amendment violation unless the accused can show * * * [counsel's inadequate performance] undermin[ed] the reliability of the finding of guilt". Conflict-of-interest cases presented only a partial exception as the Court there insists upon a showing that the conflicted counsel took action adverse to the defendant's interest before then presuming prejudice as to the outcome. See § 3.9(d).

A fact-sensitized evaluation of counsel's performance also was emphasized in *Strickland*. As discussed in § 3.10, the *Strickland* majority rejected requiring adherence to specific performance standards, stressed the "countless ways [in which a lawyer can] * * * provide effective assistance in any given case," and noted the need for deferential review. Like *Cronic*, *Strickland* conditioned reversal on a showing of likely prejudice as to outcome in light of the circumstances of the case, noting that the conflict-of-interest cases and the judicial-interference cases (see § 3.8) simply were exceptions to the general rule.

In subsequent rulings, the Supreme Court has resisted the attempt to create further exceptions to the requirement of a case-specific showing of likely prejudicial impact. In *U.S. v. Gonzalez–Lopez* (2006), the Court majority pointed to unique features of the incompetency claim that justified requiring such a showing as to that claim and not other Sixth Amendment claims. The majority cited both the historical roots of the incompetency claim in due process analysis, and the grounding of the claim as a logical derivative of the general objective of the Sixth Amendment guarantee ("ensuring a fair trial"), rather than in the directive of the guarantee itself (i.e., the directive that the defendant be allowed the choice of representation by counsel).

§ 3.8 Ineffective Assistance Claims Based Upon State Interference and Other Extrinsic Factors

(a) **Restrictions Upon Counsel's Assistance.** The "right to the assistance of counsel," the Supreme Court noted in *Herring v. N.Y.* (1975), "has been understood to mean that there can be no restrictions upon the function of counsel in defending a criminal prosecution in accord with the traditions of the adversary factfinding process." Accordingly, state action, whether by statute or trial court ruling, that prohibits counsel from making full use of traditional trial procedures may be viewed as denying defendant the effective assistance of counsel. In considering the constitutionality of such "state interference," courts are directed to look to whether the interference denied counsel "the opportunity to participate fully and fairly in the adversary factfinding process." If the interference had that effect, then both the overall performance of counsel apart from the interference and the lack of any showing of actual outcome prejudice become irrelevant. The leading cases finding such interference are: *Herring* (trial court refused to permit a closing argument in a bench trial); *Geders v. U.S.* (1976) (trial court prevented counsel from consulting with accused during an overnight recess that separated the direct examination of the accused from his forthcoming cross-examination); and *Brooks v. Tenn.* (1972) (state statute deprived the defendant of the "guiding hand of counsel" as to shaping the defense presentation where it required a testifying defendant to be the defense's first witness).

In each of the above cases, the Court arguably might also have held the particular restriction unconstitutional on the ground that it imposed an undue burden on the exercise of a constitutionally protected trial right. Whether such a ruling would have required a conviction reversal is uncertain, however, because most constitutional violations are subject to the harmless error standard of *Chapman v. Cal.* (§ 19.6(c)). The unconstitutional state imposed interference with counsel, in contrast, was presumed prejudicial and therefore required automatic reversal. In explaining why this presumption is drawn, the Court has cited the similar treatment of Sixth Amendment violations arising from the failure to appoint counsel. The key apparently is the responsibility of the state for counsel's lack of performance.

(b) State Invasions of the Lawyer–Client Relationship. State invasions of the lawyer-client relationship are unlike the direct impediments involved in cases like *Herring,* in that they do not necessarily restrict the lawyer's performance. Indeed, the circumstances surrounding the invasion may often negate any realistic likelihood that the invasion had any adverse impact upon counsel's performance. In *Weatherford v. Bursey* (1977), the Supreme Court held that, at least in some such cases, it will not find a Sixth Amendment violation. In that case, Weatherford, in order to maintain his undercover status, attended, at Bursey's request, two pretrial meetings with Bursey and his lawyer. Weatherford did not disclose to his superiors any information derived from those discussions that related to defense plans for the trial. Similarly, when Weatherford was unexpectedly called as a prosecution witness at that trial, he carefully limited his testimony so as not to touch upon anything he might have learned through the lawyer-client meetings.

The basic issue presented in *Weatherford v. Bursey* was whether the Supreme Court would adopt what it described as a "per se" or "prophylactic rule." The lower court had adopted such a rule. Relying on Supreme Court precedent, it had held that "whenever the prosecution knowingly arranges or permits intrusions into the attorney-client relationship the right to counsel is sufficiently endangered to required reversal and a new trial." A divided Supreme Court held that the lower court had misread the relevant precedent and had adopted a rule that failed to give sufficient weight to the "necessity of undercover work and the value it often is to effective law enforcement." In *Hoffa v. U.S.* (1966), another case in which an undercover agent had been present during attorney-client conversations, the Court had assumed, without deciding, that a conviction would be overturned if the informer had reported the substance of those conversations to the authorities. Here, however, as in *Hoffa,* the undercover agent had not reported the substance of the lawyer-client conversations and his trial testimony had not related to those conversations. The Court noted that "Bursey would have a much stronger case" if either (1) Weatherford had testified at trial as to those conversations, (2) the "State's evidence [had] originated from those conversations," (3) the "overheard conversations had been used in any other way to the substantial detriment of Bursey," or (4) "even had the prosecution learned from Weatherford * * * the details of the * * * conversations about trial preparations." But with "none of these elements * * * present here," there was no basis for finding a Sixth Amendment violation.

Weatherford did not answer the question of whether a per se Sixth Amendment violation might be established where the prosecutorial intrusion into the lawyer-client relationship clearly lacks any legitimate justification. The Supreme Court subsequently had such an unjustified invasion before it in *U.S. v. Morrison* (1981). In that case, D.E.A. agents, although aware that the defendant had been indicted and had retained counsel, met with defendant without defense counsel's knowledge or permission, and while seeking her cooperation, disparaged her retained attorney. The court of appeals held that defendant's right to counsel was violated irrespective of the lack of proof of prejudice to her case, and that the only appropriate remedy was a dismissal of the prosecution with prejudice. The Supreme Court unanimously reversed. The Court found it unnecessary to rule on the government's contention that a Sixth Amendment violation could not be established here without "some [defense] showing of prejudice." Even if it were assumed that there had been a Sixth Amendment violation, the remedy imposed by the lower court was incorrect because it was not "tailored to the injury suffered." Since "[r]espondent has demonstrated no prejudice of any kind, either transitory or permanent to the ability of her counsel to provide adequate representation in these criminal proceedings," there was "no justification" for such "drastic relief" as a dismissal with prejudice.

In declining to reach the government's contention that a showing of prejudice would be needed to establish a Sixth Amendment violation, the *Morrison* opinion left open the possibility that the Court might adopt a per se reversal standard for those state invasions of the lawyer-client relationship that are not supported by any legitimate state interest. The federal lower courts have divided on this issue on postconviction review of cases in which the prosecution had intentionally obtained, without any legitimate justification, information passed between the defendant and his lawyer. Some have concluded that the intentional invasion of the lawyer-client relationship producing such disclosure constitutes a per se Sixth Amendment violation, with no need to show that the defendant was prejudiced at trial as a result of the disclosure. Others have held that the defendant must show prejudice (e.g., the government's use of the obtained information to its advantage), and the First Circuit has taken a "middle position," with the government bearing the "high burden" of showing that it did not use the information against the defendant.

§ 3.9   Ineffective Assistance Claims Based Upon Attorney Conflicts of Interest

(a) The Range of Possible Conflicts of Interest. As courts have long noted, the constitutional right to effective assistance of counsel, "entitles the * * * [defendant] to the undivided loyalty of his counsel." The defendant does not receive the full efforts of counsel when the attorney's decisions are influenced by obligations owed to persons other than the defendant. Such a division of loyalty can arise from various different defense arrangements that may subject counsel's representation to conflicting interests. These include: (1) joint representation of codefendants who will be tried together; (2) joint representation of codefendants who will be tried separately; (3) defense counsel has previously represented, or is currently representing, in another matter or the same matter, a likely prosecution witness; (4) defense counsel has previously represented, or is currently representing, in another matter or the same matter, a victim of the alleged offense; (5) a third party with some interest in the case is paying the defendant's legal fees; (6) a fee arrangement that creates a possible conflict between counsel's financial interests and the defendant's interests (e.g., a compensation agreement under which counsel has an interest in royalties received from a movie or book relating to the trial); (7) counsel was involved in the same transaction and fears possible criminal prosecution; (8) counsel is under investigation or being actively prosecuted by the same prosecutor's office as to another matter; (9) counsel is facing possible criminal or disciplinary consequences as a result of questionable behavior in representing the defendant; (10) counsel has delivered, or has an obligation to deliver, to the police physical evidence that can be used against the defendant; and (11) counsel is to be called as a prosecution witness.

In many of the above situations, conflicts also arise where the potentially conflicting representation is by another attorney in the same law firm as the defendant's counsel. Under ethics codes, conflicts generally are vicariously imputed to all members of a law firm. While the Supreme Court has not ruled directly on this approach, *Burger v. Kemp* (1987) "assumed without deciding that two law partners are considered as one attorney" in analyzing the conflict potential of representing codefendants. Some courts treat the lawyers in a public defender office in much the same manner. Many other jurisdictions, however, hold the "same firm" principle generally inapplicable to public defenders, in part because "the salaried government employee does not have the financial interest in the success of the departmental representation that is inherent in private practice." Their position may also be influenced by concern that logic would require that the standard applicable to public defenders also be applied to prosecutors' offices, where the disruptive impact of disqualifying the entire staff is far greater, as providing outside substitutes for prosecutors is far more cumbersome than providing outside substitutes for public defenders.

In jurisdictions that treat defender offices differently, where the defender office's potential conflict stems from confidential information received from a past client now a prosecution witness, the common solution is to utilize a "Chinese Wall," which keeps that information away from the attorney representing the defendant. That device tends not to be viewed as sufficient, however, as to codefendants. Defender offices commonly are prohibited by state law from representing indigent codefendants, even when the codefendants seek joint representation; representation is provided through a combination of the defender office representing one codefendant and separate appointed counsel representing each of the others.

While the various conflict settings described above all create a potential for inhibiting counsel's actions on behalf of his client, none do so inevitably. Thus, under the prevailing standards of professional responsibility, situations creating a serious potential for creating a conflict of interest typically call for safeguards, but not an absolute prohibition against representation. The Model Rules of Professional Conduct, for example, provide that where the lawyer has another client whose interests are "directly adverse" to the defendant, the lawyer may nonetheless represent the defendant if the lawyer "reasonably believes the representation will not adversely effect the relationship with the other client," and each client consents after full disclosure. Such standards recognize both that (1) a directly adverse interest of another client will not necessarily be relevant to the strategy that best serves the defendant, and (2) even if that adverse interest does conflict with a particular favorable strategy, the defendant may prefer to be represented by this one attorney, notwithstanding the obligations that the attorney owes to another. In particular, codefendants may find themselves in somewhat disparate positions as to their respective roles in the charged crime and the strength of the evidence against them, but nonetheless prefer joint representation as a means of implementing what they view as their best strategy. As the Supreme Court has noted: "Joint representation is a means of ensuring against reciprocal recrimination. A common defense often gives strength against a common attack."

As one might anticipate, the courts have not been willing to adopt prophylactic rules that ban defense arrangements that carry a conflict potential when the profession itself has been unwilling to ban those arrangements. On the other hand, the courts have been willing to view many of those arrangements as suspect. They have recognized also that it is often impossible to reconstruct the precise impact of a divided loyalty upon counsel's performance. In particular, a conflict of interest may have as much bearing on matters that are not reflected in the appellate record (e.g., the failure to inter-

view witnesses or seek a plea bargain) as it does on those acts or
omissions at trial that are a part of the record. Very often the only
person who knows exactly what the conflict's full ramification
might have been is the defense lawyer herself, and courts are
naturally wary of the lawyer's disclaimers of influence (or even the
lawyer's acknowledgment of influence, which may be seen as a
"last ditch" effort to help the client). One response to these
difficulties inherent in a postconviction attempt to trace the impact
of a possible conflict has been the development of a trial court
obligation to make a pretrial inquiry into possible conflicts.

   (b) The Trial Court Duty to Inquire. *Holloway v. Ark.*
(1978) held that, where defense counsel had informed the trial
court that he would be placed in an actual conflict as a result of
joint representation (one of the defendants might testify and counsel would not be able to cross-examine on behalf the others in light
of the "confidential information" received from the different defendants), the trial court committed constitutional error when it failed
to conduct a proper inquiry into the possible conflict. The Court
rejected the state's contention that constitutional error existed only
if the defendants could now show that a conflict actually existed.
The Supreme Court in *Glasser v. U.S.* (1942) held that a trial court
had a duty not to "insist that counsel undertake to concurrently
represent interests which might diverge" (which had occurred there
in appointing one codefendant's attorney to represent the other
codefendant). The trial court had violated that duty here when it
failed to conduct an inquiry and simply directed counsel to continue
with the joint representation. Its failure "either to appoint separate
counsel or take adequate steps to ascertain whether the risk [of a
conflict] was too remote to warrant separate counsel" violated the
defendants' Sixth Amendment rights.

   Having responded to the state's claim that no constitutional
error could exist without a showing of an actual conflict, the
Holloway opinion turned to the state's claim that defendants'
convictions could not be overturned without a showing of prejudice.
Glasser, the Court noted, was to the contrary. Although the language of *Glasser* was not without ambiguity, the *Glasser* opinion
was properly read as "holding that, whenever a trial court improperly requires joint representation over timely objection, reversal is
automatic." Subsequent to *Glasser,* the Supreme Court had recognized in *Chapman v. Cal.*(§ 19.6(c)) that certain constitutional
violations could constitute harmless error. However, *Chapman* and
its progeny had also recognized that the denial of the right to
counsel is "so basic to a fair trial that * * * [it] can never be
treated as harmless error." The reasoning of *Glasser,* the *Holloway*
opinion concluded, placed in the same category the Sixth Amend-

ment violation created by a failure to inquire where there is a constitutional duty to do so. In "the normal case where [*Chapman's*] harmless-error rule is applied, * * * the reviewing court can undertake with some confidence its relatively narrow task of assessing the likelihood that the error materially affected the deliberations of the jury." But as *Glasser* had suggested, in the case of joint representation of conflicting interests, "the evil * * * is in what the advocate finds himself compelled to *refrain* from doing." While "it may be possible in some cases to identify from the record the prejudice resulting from an attorney's failure to undertake certain trial tasks," to "judge intelligently the impact of a conflict on the attorney's [total] representation of a client," including such matters as potential plea negotiations, "would be virtually impossible." An "inquiry into a claim of harmless error here would require, unlike most cases, unguided speculation." Thus, once the failure to inquire was treated as akin to judicial placement of the attorney in a conflict position, that ended the judicial inquiry and a reversal of the conviction was required.

The fact situation presented in *Holloway* was especially suited for requiring trial court action. As the lower courts later noted, the "imposition upon the state * * * is not heavy" when the trial court has before it a timely objection by counsel, and an appropriate response at that point will avoid the need subsequently for a difficult post-hoc determination as to whether counsel was inhibited by an actual conflict. A more troublesome issue, it was noted, was what "affirmative duty" should be placed upon the trial court to inquire into the propriety of multiple representation when defense counsel fails to request separate representation. That issue produced the Court's second major discussion of the duty to inquire, in *Cuyler v. Sullivan* (1980). The defendant Sullivan had been represented by two attorneys, retained by his two codefendants and paid in part by friends of the group. Each defendant had a separate trial, and Sullivan was the only one of the three convicted. Neither defense counsel nor Sullivan objected to the multiple representation. When counsels' effectiveness was challenged in a federal habeas proceeding, the court of appeals held that, in light of *Holloway,* Sullivan had established his claim for relief by showing a possible conflict of interest. The Supreme Court ruled that the lower court had misread *Holloway* and had applied an improper constitutional standard. The trial court here was not under an obligation to inquire into the possibility of a conflict of interest, and where such an obligation did not exist, a postconviction claim of ineffective assistance required a showing of an "actual" rather than a "potential" conflict.

In ruling that the trial court had no constitutional obligation to inquire into the propriety of counsels' multiple representation, the

Sullivan Court found *Holloway* clearly distinguishable as a case in which counsel had sought relief from a conflict. It noted: "Defense counsel have an ethical obligation to avoid conflicting representations and to advise the court promptly when a conflict of interest arises during the course of trial. Absent special circumstances, [with no such notification], trial courts may assume either that multiple representation entails no conflict or that the lawyer and his clients knowingly accept such risk of conflict as may exist."

The dissenters in *Sullivan* argued that the dangers of multiple representation were so grave that in every case in which two or more defendants were jointly charged or had been joined for trial, the trial court should be under an obligation "to inquire whether there is multiple representation, to warn the defendants of the possible risk of such representation, and to ascertain that the representation is the result of the defendant's informed choice." The majority acknowledged that such a procedure would be desirable. Indeed, under proposed (and subsequently adopted) Federal Rule 44(c), a similar obligation was about to be imposed upon federal trial courts. However, to so substantially extend the essentially prophylactic rule of *Holloway* as a constitutional mandate was another matter. The inquiry that the dissenters would require was not without costs. It would impose a burden on both the trial court and the lawyer-client relationship. Indeed, Chief Justice Burger in *Holloway* had warned that a trial court's attempt to explore the nature of the relationship between jointly represented codefendants, including their potential defenses, could present "significant risks of unfair prejudice" to the defense. It therefore should not be unconstitutional for the state court to seek to limit such costs by relying in general on the professional obligation of counsel to advise the court when an actual conflict arises. Where counsel has not taken that step, the trial court should have a constitutional obligation to act on its own initiative only where it has good cause to believe that counsel may have erred in assuming that there was no actual conflict. Accordingly, the controlling Sixth Amendment standard, the *Sullivan* majority concluded, would be that, in the absence of objection by counsel, an inquiry was not mandated "[u]nless the trial court knows or reasonably should know that a particular conflict exists."

The *Sullivan* opinion did not explain precisely what information would place a trial judge in a position where he "reasonably should know" that a conflict exists. The Court did explain, however, why the *Sullivan* case did not present such a situation. Relevant factors cited were the separate trials of the codefendants, an opening statement that outlined a defense compatible with the view that none of the defendants were involved in the offense, and a suggestion in that statement that counsel were willing to call all relevant witnesses. While the defense later rested without presenting those witnesses, that decision "on its face" appeared to be "a reasonable tactical response" to the weakness of the prosecution's case.

In *Mickens v. Taylor* (2002), the Court majority found no need to decide whether the trial court there had a duty to inquire under the *Sullivan* branch of that duty (i.e., the "knows or reasonably should know" standard), but it did describe an earlier ruling, *Wood v. Georgia* (1981), as presenting such a situation. *Wood* was a case in which the Supreme Court originally granted certiorari to determine whether a state could constitutionally revoke the probation of defendants who were unable to pay the fines imposed under their previous convictions. The case was remanded, however, for an evidentiary hearing on a conflict issue raised by the Court sua sponte. The defendants had been charged with an offense committed in the course of their employment and their counsel had been provided by their employer. They had been sentenced to pay substantial fines on the assumption that the employer would provide them with the necessary funds. When the employer refused to give them the funds, counsel did not immediately move for modification of the fines or ask for leniency. Instead, he pressed the argument that a revocation for the failure to pay fines that were beyond a defendant's means was unconstitutional, a contention which, if accepted, would work to the long range benefit of the employer. The Supreme Court noted that the record of the revocation proceedings was not sufficiently complete for it to determine whether a conflict actually existed. "Nevertheless," it noted, "the record does demonstrate that the *possibility* of a conflict of interest was sufficiently apparent at the time of the revocation hearing to impose upon the [state] court a duty to inquire further." All of the relevant facts relating to the employer's retention of counsel, the employer's failure to pay the fines, and "counsel's insistence upon pressing a constitutional attack" were known to the state court. Moreover, "any doubt as to whether th[at] court should have been aware of the problem [was] dispelled by the fact that the [prosecutor] had raised the conflict problem."

In *Holloway,* the Court required automatic reversal of defendant's conviction on finding a violation of the duty to inquire. In *Wood,* however, the Court remanded and directed the lower court to grant a new revocation hearing only if it found an "actual conflict" under the standard announced in a separate prong of the *Sullivan* opinion (see subsection (d) infra). *Mickens* subsequently explained that different consequences attached to violations of the *Holloway* and *Sullivan* branches of the duty to require. The *Holloway* situation presented a limited exception to the general rule that convictions would be reversed only on a finding that counsel representation in fact resulted in an "actual conflict."

The situation presented in *Holloway*, the *Mickens* majority noted, justified presuming that there had been a "disabling conflict" which "undermined the adversarial process." That situation presented an objection raised by defense counsel, who is "in the best position to determine when a [disabling] conflict exists." Moreover, that objection came in the setting of joint representation, which is "inherently suspect," and which places on counsel joint obligations that "effectively seal his lips in crucial matters and make it difficult to measure the precise harm arising from counsel's errors." A violation of the *Sullivan* branch of the duty to inquire presented neither of these factors and therefore did not justify drawing a similar presumption. Here, on postconviction review, there was no reason to depart from the general standard governing postconviction review of an alleged conflict, even though that standard was initially formulated (in *Sullivan*) as to a case in which there had been no duty to inquire.

The *Mickens* majority reasoned that requiring an automatic reversal where a trial judge violated the *Sullivan* duty to inquire "makes little policy sense." The thrust of the law of ineffective assistance is to tie reversal to a showing of likely prejudice. "The trial court's awareness of a potential conflict renders it no more likely that counsel's performance was significantly altered" by a conflict then a situation in which "the trial judge is not aware of the conflict (and thus not obligated to inquire)." Neither could it be said that the "trial judge's failure to make the *Sullivan*-mandated inquiry often makes it harder for reviewing courts to determine conflict and effect, particularly since these courts may rely on evidence and testimony whose importance only became established at the trial."

After *Mickens*, on review following a conviction, whether the trial court violated the *Sullivan* duty is an issue that need not be decided. For the same standard of review governs whether the *Sullivan* duty applied and was ignored or simply did not apply. Responding to the dissent's contention that this would lead trial courts to ignore their *Sullivan* duty to inquire, *Mickens* noted that dissent's position "rested on the unproven" presumption that judges "need the incentive of an exclusionary rule," and also ignored the "incentive" that the *Sullivan* standard already provides for making an inquiry.

(c) Waiver and Disqualification. As a result of pretrial prosecution motions raising possible defense conflicts, inquiries required under provisions like Federal Rule 44(c), and, to a lesser extent, *Sullivan's* inquiry requirement, courts have been forced in recent years to face the question of what should be done when a defendant tells the court to ignore any possible conflict because he or she desires to waive the right to conflict-free counsel. At this point, the Supreme Court noted in *Wheat v. U.S.* (1988), trial courts could "face the prospect of being 'whipsawed' by assertions of error no matter which way they rule." If the trial court disqualifies the defendant's counsel, the defendant will raise a claim (as did defendant in *Wheat*) that he was denied his Sixth Amendment right to counsel of choice. On the other hand, "if the trial court agrees to the multiple representation, and the advocacy of counsel is thereafter impaired as a result, the defendant may well claim that he did not receive effective assistance of counsel." *Wheat* recognized that some lower courts had indicated that the defendant's waiver of conflict-free counsel would automatically defeat such a claim (assuming the waiver was "knowing and intelligent"), but that position was not universal. The *Wheat* Court sought to reduce this "whipsaw" potential by setting forth the standards under which a trial court constitutionally could refuse to allow multiple representation notwithstanding defendant's waiver.

The *Wheat* majority initially rejected the defendant's contention that "the provision of waivers by all affected defendants cures any problems created by the multiple representation." "No such flat rule," the Court noted, "can be deduced from the Sixth Amendment presumption in favor of counsel of choice." The Sixth Amendment right to choose one's counsel is not absolute; because of countervailing considerations, a defendant cannot insist upon counsel who is not a member of the bar nor can he insist upon representation by an attorney "who has a previous or ongoing relationship with an opposing party, even when the opposing party is the Government." In the conflict situation also, a countervailing consideration is present. The courts "have an independent interest in ensuring that criminal trials are conducted within the ethical standards of the profession and that legal proceedings appear fair to all who observe them." In light of this interest, "where a court justifiably finds an actual conflict of interest, there can be no doubt that it may decline a proffer of waiver and insist that defendants be separately represented."

The *Wheat* majority recognized, however, that the critical situation, as a practical matter, was that in which the trial court found multiple representation to present a "potential" rather than an "actual" conflict. To find an actual conflict, a court must determine that the defense counsel is subject to an obligation or unique personal interest which, if followed, would lead counsel to adopt a strategy other than that most favorable to the defendant. Very often, whether that obligation or interest will come into play, and whether it will lead in a direction other than that most favorable to the defendant, will depend upon future events that may or may not occur (e.g., whether a particular witness testifies). Accordingly, the *Wheat* majority characterized as "rare" any case in which "an actual conflict may be determined before trial"; the "more common" case was that in which the court finds that "a potential for conflict exists which may or may not burgeon into an actual conflict." Because the likely materialization and dimensions of such potential conflicts are "notoriously hard to predict" in the "murkier pretrial context when relationships between parties are seen through a glass darkly," the Court concluded that a trial court can properly find, upon a showing of "a serious potential for conflict," that the presumption favoring defendant's choice of counsel should be overridden.

Wheat further noted that the trial court, in deciding whether to override that presumption, could take into consideration the fact that potential conflicts often reflect "imponderables" that "are difficult enough for a lawyer to assess, and even more difficult to convey by way of explanation to a criminal defendant untutored in the niceties of legal ethics." So too, it need not ignore the reality "that the willingness of an attorney to obtain such waivers from his clients may bear an inverse relation to the care with which he conveys all the necessary information to them." On the other hand, the trial court should also be aware of the possibility that the "government may seek to 'manufacture' a conflict to prevent the defendant from having a particular able counsel at his side." In the end, the trial court, in its evaluation of these and other relevant considerations, must be "allowed substantial latitude in refusing waivers" in cases of potential conflict as well as in cases of actual conflict.

Turning to the case before it, the *Wheat* majority found that the trial court had acted within its discretion in refusing defendant's request to substitute counsel who had been representing two separately charged accomplices of the defendant. The trial court had been "confronted not simply with an attorney who wished to represent two coequal defendants in a straightforward criminal prosecution: rather, [counsel] proposed to defend three coconspirators of varying stature in a complex drug distribution scheme." Moreover, one of the codefendants had pleaded to a lesser count as part of a plea agreement, and the government intended to call him as a prosecution witness at defendant's trial. The other codefendant, although previously acquitted on the drug charges, remained open to a trial on tax evasion and other charges relating to the conspiracy (his offer to plead to those charges had not yet been accepted by the district court and could still be withdrawn), with a distinct likelihood that the defendant Wheat would be called as a government witness at that trial. Thus, counsel in two different situations could have been placed in a setting where he would be cross-examining a former client. Ruling on a motion made "close to the time of trial," the trial court had relied on "instinct and judgment based on experience" in evaluating these factors, and it could not be said to have "exceeded the broad latitude which must be accorded it in making this decision."

In its discussion of the "broad latitude" that must be accorded the trial court, the *Wheat* Court emphasized that this latitude worked both ways—that it also applied to a trial court's determination to allow multiple representation with appropriate waivers. While sustaining the decision of the trial court below to deny multiple representation, the Court noted that other trial courts might have reached an opposite conclusion "with equal justification," and that it was not suggesting one conclusion was "right" and the other "wrong." Moreover, while the circumstances before the trial court here were characterized as establishing "a serious potential for conflict," the Court's discussion of the trial court's two-way discretion referred to both "potential" and "actual" conflicts.

Although *Wheat* recognized the discretion of the trial court to accept waivers and refuse to disqualify counsel, even in an actual conflict situation, that discretion does not apply to all forms of conflict. *Wheat* involved a conflict situation (the multiple representation of codefendants) in which the primary concern is that the conflict might adversely impact counsel's representation of the defendant, with that potential giving rise, in turn, to a separate "judicial-integrity" concern that the conflict will make the proceeding appear less than "fair." In other conflict situations, however, the conflict also carries with it the potential of giving the defendant an adversarial advantage by depriving the prosecution of "a level playing field," and here the prosecution apparently can insist upon disqualification. "Waiver by the defendant is ineffective in curing the impropriety * * * since he is not the party prejudiced."

The classic illustration of such a conflict situation is that in which defense counsel is a former prosecutor and acquired through that position confidential information relating to the prosecution's case against his current client. An analogous defense advantage is presented where defense counsel formerly represented a prosecution witness, and through that representation obtained confidential information that counsel now intends to use to challenge the witness (against the wishes of the witness). Lower courts also have recognized that the prosecution is placed at a disadvantage where the defense counsel either is called as a defense witness or acts, in effect, as an "unsworn defense witness" because of juror awareness of her participation in the events on which she will examine and cross-examine witnesses. So too, where the prosecution calls the defense counsel as a prosecution witness, counsel's capacity to contradict her own testimony in the course of questioning witnesses or delivering a closing statement gives the defense a weapon that would not be present as to other prosecution witnesses.

(d) Challenging Convictions. *Cuyler v. Sullivan* (1999) set forth the standard to be applied on postconviction review in determining whether a claim of defense counsel conflict of interest, not presented prior to conviction, requires reversal of the conviction. The conflict there arose from multiple representation in a situation not sufficiently indicative of conflict to impose upon the trial court a constitutional duty to inquire. *Mickens v. Taylor* (2002) held that, aside from the special situation of *Holloway*, the *Sullivan* standard also applies where the trial court had a constitutional duty of inquiry, but failed to conduct that inquiry. The Court has not spoken to the situation in which the trial court conducted an inquiry in a non-*Holloway* setting and decided not to disqualify counsel, but the defendant following conviction raised a claim of conflict of interest. Very often, that claim will be defeated by the defendant's pretrial waiver of any conflict, obtained in conjunction with the trial court's decision not to disqualify. However, if no waiver was obtained or the waiver is now determined to be faulty, it seems likely that here too the *Sullivan* standard will apply in determining whether the conviction should be reversed.

The Court in *Cuyler v. Sullivan* initially rejected the contention that a defense showing of a potential conflict was enough to require a reversal of a conviction. "A reviewing court," it noted, "cannot presume that the possibility of conflict has resulted in ineffective assistance of counsel. Such a presumption would preclude multiple representation even in cases where 'a common defense * * * gives strength against a common attack.'" Accordingly, "to establish a violation of the Sixth Amendment, a defendant must demonstrate an actual conflict of interest adversely affected his lawyer's performance."

The *Sullivan* opinion emphasized that its rejection of a potential conflict standard, in favor of requiring a showing of an actual conflict, should not be taken to suggest that the defendant must establish actual outcome prejudice. As the Court had noted first in *Glasser v. U.S.* and then again in *Holloway*, "unconstitutional multiple representation is never harmless error." Thus, under *Sullivan*, once a defendant "shows that a conflict of interest actually affected the adequacy of his representation," he is automatically entitled to relief; there is no need to also establish that the Sixth Amendment violation might have adversely affected the outcome of the case.

The *Sullivan* standard requires that the defendant presenting a postconviction challenge "demonstrate [that] an actual conflict of interest adversely affected the lawyer's performance." This requires a showing both that (1) counsel was placed in a situation where conflicting loyalties pointed in opposite directions (an "actual conflict"), and (2) counsel proceeded to act against the defendant's interests ("adversely affect[ing] counsel's performance"). Looking to the Court's explanation of *Glasser's* requirement of automatic reversal upon finding a Sixth Amendment violation, Justice Marshall, in dissent, questioned the second prong of this standard. If the impact of an actual conflict upon the outcome of the case requires an unduly speculative judgment, was not, he asked, the same true of its impact upon counsel's performance? The thrust of the Court's opinion, however, clearly was that these were two separate determinations of a quite different character. It would not be sufficient for reversal to show only that counsel had faced a situation in which action or inaction that might benefit his client would work to the detriment of another interest that divided counsel's loyalty. There would be no harm to the defendant if counsel actually pursued the route favoring his client, disregarding the conflicting interest. Moreover, even where counsel did not pursue that route, counsel's decision may have been influenced solely by a reasonable determination that the route not taken was inferior to an alternative route, which was more beneficial to his client, putting aside any concern for the conflicting interest. Having identified an actual conflict of interest, defendant should be able to establish as well precisely how counsel acted in response to that conflict. However, once it is shown that counsel was actually influenced by the conflict in one aspect of his performance, it would be inappropriate to measure the impact of that conflict solely by reference to that action or inaction. A court could not assume that counsel so motivated had not also been influenced by the conflict in various other aspects of his representation. Hence, any inquiry into outcome prejudice would be too speculative, and automatic reversal therefore would be required.

Two lines of lower court rulings have departed from the *Sullivan* standards relating to the impact of a conflict—one line limiting the presumption of prejudice and the other eliminating the "adversely affected" prerequisite. *Beets v. Scott* (5th Cir. 1995) initiated the first line of cases. A closely divided Fifth Circuit there concluded that *Sullivan-Glasser* outcome-prejudice presumption should apply only to conflicts presented by "multiple representation" situations (i.e., defense counsel represented codefendants or represented the defendant and witnesses or other interested parties), as opposed to conflicts arising from some self-interest of the attorney. In the latter situation, a claim of ineffective assistance based on a conflict should be treated no differently than any other ineffective assistance claim. Thus, the court should apply the standard of *Strickland v. Washington* (discussed in § 3.10), which requires a showing of prejudicial impact upon the outcome. The *Beets* majority reasoned that attorney ethical conflicts that do not result from obligations owed to current or former clients simply reflect another form of incompetent performance. To allow a "recharacterization of ineffectiveness claims to duty of loyalty claims," thereby importing *"Cuyler v. Sullivan's* lesser standard of prejudice" was to "blu[r] the *Strickland* standard" and undercut its role as the "uniform standard of constitutional ineffectiveness."

In *Mickens v. Taylor* (2002), the Supreme Court left open the possibility of adopting the *Beets* position and even extending it. *Mickens* involved a defense counsel who had formerly represented the person his client was charged with killing. The Court applied the *Sullivan* standard on postconviction review, requiring a defense showing of a "conflict of interest (that) adversely affected * * * counsel's performance." However, the Court majority went on to state that, "lest today's holding be misconstrued," it was important to note that the case "was argued and presented on the assumption" that the *Sullivan* standard governed if automatic reversal was not required. "That assumption," it added, "was not unreasonable in light of the holdings of Courts of Appeals which have applied *Sullivan* 'unblinkingly' to all kinds of alleged attorney conflicts, *Beets v. Scott*, * * * [including] not only when (as here) there is a conflict rooted in counsel's obligations to *former* clients, * * * but even where the representation of the defendant somehow implicates counsel's financial or personal interests, including a book deal, * * * a job with the prosecutor's office, * * * the teaching of classes to Internal Revenue agents, * * * a romantic entanglement with the prosecutor, * * * or fear of antagonizing the trial judge." "It must be said," the Court majority continued, "that the language of *Sullivan* itself does not clearly establish, or indeed even support, such expansive application." Both *Sullivan* and *Holloway* "stressed the high probability of prejudice arising from multiple concurrent representation, and the difficulty of proving that prejudice." Thus, Federal Rule 44(c), imposing a duty to inquire, was limited to that situation. Other conflict settings might not present "comparable difficulties" of proof, and therefore might not require "the prophylaxis" of the *Sullivan* standard, which was designed for a situation "where *Strickland* itself is evidently inadequate to assure vindication of the defendant's Sixth Amendment right to counsel." Whether the *Sullivan* prophylaxis should be extended "even to * * * [cases of] successive representation," as involved in *Mickens*, "remains, as far as the jurisprudence of the Court is concerned, an open issue."

The second line of lower court cases have looked in the opposite direction, creating a presumption of prejudicial impact more extensive than *Sullivan*. They reason that certain conflicts should be deemed "per se conflicts," requiring automatic reversal once the actual conflict is established, with no need to show some point at which the conflict "adversely effected" the counsel's performance. Placed in this category are conflicts viewed as flagrant and likely to have a widespread influence not focused on a particular action or inaction of counsel. This per se approach has been applied in the federal courts where the attorney is alleged to have engaged in the same criminal activity as the defendant or closely related criminal activity, and where a trial judge indicated to appointed counsel that approval of his fee and future appointments would depend upon counsel "pull[ing] his punches." State courts, perhaps relying upon state law, have applied a per se standard to such conflicts as a lawyer first prosecuting the defendant and then representing him as defense counsel in a probation revocation proceeding on the same charge, a lawyer representing the defendant while also employed by the agency involved in investigating or prosecuting, and a lawyer simultaneously representing the defendant and the victim.

Sullivan itself did not decide whether the defendant there had made a sufficient showing of an actual conflict and adversely affected performance, but it offered as illustrations of sufficient and insufficient showings those presented in *Glasser v. U.S.* (1942) and *Dukes v. Warden* (1972). In *Glasser,* the record showed that counsel had failed to cross-examine a key witness and had failed also to object to "arguably inadmissible evidence." Both omissions were held to have resulted from counsel's desire to diminish the jury's perception of the guilt of a codefendant also represented by counsel. Thus, the *Sullivan* Court noted, an "actual conflict of interest [had] impaired Glasser's defense." In contrast to *Glasser, Dukes v. Warden* had rejected an "actual conflict" claim. Defendant there had relied solely on a showing that the lawyer who advised him to plead guilty had later sought leniency for his codefendants by arguing that their cooperation with the police had induced defendant's plea. Unlike Glasser, Dukes could not "identify an actual lapse in representation" and "nothing in the record * * * indicated that the alleged conflict resulted in ineffective assistance."

§ 3.10 Ineffective Assistance Claims Based Upon Lawyer Incompetence

(a) Guiding Considerations. Prior to the Supreme Court's 1984 ruling in *Strickland v. Washington* (1984), lower courts had been divided on several issues bearing on those ineffective assistance claims that were grounded on the allegedly incompetent performance of counsel. Some courts adopted specific guidelines for judging defense counsel's performance (typically borrowed from the ABA Standards), with a departure from a guideline constituting "per se incompetency"; others eschewed guidelines and stressed a fact-sensitive analysis that looked to all the circumstances of the case. Among courts that focused on the totality of the circumstances, some applied the traditional test of whether counsel's deficiencies were so great as to have rendered the proceedings a "farce" or "mockery of justice," while others looked to whether counsel's performance fell below that of a "reasonably competent attorney." Most courts further required for reversal a defense showing that counsel's incompetence had a prejudicial impact upon the outcome, but some concluded that a showing of incompetency should shift the burden to the state to show a lack of prejudice, and courts applying categorical performance guidelines typically mandated automatic reversal.

In *Strickland v. Washington,* the Court responded to all of these divisions among the lower courts. Building upon the role of the effective assistance guarantee as discussed in *U.S. v. Cronic* (§ 3.7(c)), the *Strickland* Court held that: (1) to establish ineffective assistance requiring reversal of a conviction, a defendant must show both (i) that "counsel made errors so serious that counsel was not functioning as 'counsel' guaranteed * * * by the Sixth Amendment," and (ii) that the "deficient performance prejudiced the defense"; (2) the "proper standard for [measuring] attorney performance is that of reasonably effective assistance," as guided by "prevailing professional norms" and consideration of "all the circumstances" relevant to counsel's performance; (3) more specific guidelines in applying that standard are "not appropriate"; and (4) the proper standard for measuring prejudice is whether there is a "reasonable probability that, but for counsel's unprofessional errors, the result of the proceedings would be different."

Of a significance arguably equal to these rulings, Justice O'Connor's opinion for the Court also discussed at length the basic considerations that should guide a court's judgment on an incompetency claim. She emphasized that:

> Judicial scrutiny of counsel's performance must be highly deferential. It is all too tempting for a defendant to second-guess counsel's assistance after conviction or adverse sentence, and it is all too easy for a court, examining counsel's defense after it has proved unsuccessful, to conclude that a particular act or omission of counsel was unreasonable. A fair assessment of attorney performance requires that every effort be made to eliminate the distorting effects of hindsight, to reconstruct the circumstances of counsel's challenged conduct, and to evaluate the conduct from counsel's perspective at the time. Because of

the difficulties inherent in making the evaluation, a court must indulge a strong presumption that counsel's conduct falls within the wide range of reasonable professional assistance: that is, the defendant must overcome the presumption that under the circumstances, the challenged action "might be considered sound trial strategy." There are countless ways to provide effective assistance in any given case. Even the best criminal defense attorneys would not defend a particular client in the same way.

Although stressing this need for deference, Justice O'Connor warned that, here too, general principles could not be converted into "mechanical rules." The "ultimate focus must be the fundamental fairness of the proceeding." In every case, the court must retain its concern as to "whether, despite the strong presumption of reliability, the result of the particular proceeding is unreliable because of a breakdown in the adversarial process."

The focus on fundamental fairness, Justice O'Connor noted, logically also required that defendant make a showing of prejudice to gain relief. Since the purpose of the Sixth Amendment guarantee is "to ensure that a defendant has the assistance necessary to justify reliance on the outcome of the proceeding," any deficiency in counsel's performance "must be prejudicial to the defense in order to constitute ineffective assistance under the Constitution." Here, unlike other Sixth Amendment contexts, prejudice could not be presumed: "Attorney errors come in an infinite variety and are as likely to be utterly harmless in a particular case as they are to be prejudicial. They cannot be classified according to a likelihood of causing prejudice." The only exceptions would be the special situations identified in *Cronic*. See § 3.7(d).

The defendant's challenge in *Strickland* was to the performance of counsel in a capital sentencing proceeding. After discussing the role of counsel in the adversary adjudication of guilt, the Court noted that the same principles applied to a capital sentencing proceeding as it was "sufficiently like a trial in its adversarial format and in the existence of standards for decisions." In *Smith v. Murray* (1986), the Court later applied the "test of *Strickland v. Washington*" to the alleged incompetency of appellate counsel. *Hill v. Lockhart* (1985) similarly held that *Strickland's* two-part test applies to challenges to guilty pleas based on the alleged ineffectiveness of counsel. Thus, the *Strickland* standard would appear to govern the determination of actual incompetence in all settings where the Constitution requires the effective assistance of counsel.

Strickland involved a federal habeas review of a state conviction, and the Court considered, but rejected, applying a more lenient standard in that setting. The Court concluded that, since the ineffectiveness standards it was announcing had their focus in "fundamental fairness," they should be equally applicable on habeas review, notwithstanding the presumption of finality that "is at its strongest in collateral attacks." Subsequent to *Strickland*, Congress modified the federal habeas statute, changing the general standard of review as to state convictions. The issue for the federal habeas court was no longer whether the state court correctly interpreted constitutional standards in affirming the habeas petitioner's conviction, but whether the state court applied Supreme Court precedent (in the case of ineffectiveness claims, the standards of *Strickland*) in an "objectively unreasonable standard." Thus, today a federal court on habeas review may not overturn a state conviction on an ineffective assistance claim simply because it would conclude as a de novo determination that the *Strickland* standards were violated. It must take account of the flexibility in various portions of the *Strickland* standards, and accept a contrary state court application of those standards, unless it is deemed "objectively unreasonable." See § 20.6(f).

(b) The Competency Standard. The *Strickland* opinion, in its initial discussion of the deficient performance component of an incompetency claim, characterized that component as requiring "counsel * * * errors so serious that counsel was not functioning as the 'counsel' guaranteed the defendant by the Sixth Amendment." Since prejudicial impact was a separate component of the claim, the "seriousness" of counsel error apparently was to be measured by reference to the role of counsel in providing what *Cronic* had described as "the kind of [adversarial] testing envisioned by the Sixth Amendment." To assist lower courts in making this adversarial performance determination, the Court in *Strickland* set forth a general "standard" for assessing attorney performance. It adopted for this purpose the "reasonably effective assistance" standard that had been advanced by the federal Courts of Appeals. This same standard, it noted, had been "indirectly recognized" as the relevant measure of attorney competency in the Court's opinion in *McMann v. Richardson* (§ 13.6(a)). The Court had there stated that a guilty plea could not be challenged "as based on inadequate legal advice unless counsel was not a 'reasonably competent attorney' and the advice was not 'within the range of competence demanded of attorneys in criminal cases.' " This approach, the Court noted, utilized an "objective standard of reasonableness" for determining whether counsel's representation was "outside the range of professionally competent assistance."

Prior to *Strickland*, several commentators had suggested that the standard used to describe the expected level of counsel performance was far less significant than the attitude and concerns that a court brought to its assessment of counsel's failures. The Court's opinion in *Strickland* lent support to this view. Far more discussion was devoted to the concerns that should guide a court in applying the standard (e.g., the variation in circumstances that render inappropriate a guidelines approach, the need for "deferential" scrutiny that avoids second-guessing, and the importance of considering the totality of the circumstances) than to explaining the standard itself. The Court also refused to attach to the standard such significance as to render suspect lower court rulings that had relied on somewhat differently worded standards.

While *Strickland* characterized the applicable standard as one of "reasonableness under prevailing professional norms," it also made clear that "prevailing norms of practice" are no more than "guides" to determining what is reasonable. The ultimate point of reference is that performance by counsel needed, under the circumstances of the case, to ensure "the proper functioning of the adversarial process." It is this function of counsel that provides the "objective standard of reasonableness" and determines what is "within the range of competence demanded of attorneys in criminal cases."

The *Strickland* opinion rejected the suggestion that specific guidelines, such as the ABA Standards, should be viewed as prerequisites for a competent performance. Utilizing specific guidelines in that fashion was inappropriate because (1) "no particular set of detailed rules for counsel's conduct can satisfactorily take account of the variety of circumstances faced by defense counsel or the range of legitimate decisions regarding how best to represent a criminal defendant," and (2) "reliance on such guidelines * * * could distract counsel from the overriding mission of vigorous advocacy." The Court did add, however, that such guidelines, although not controlling, were relevant in assessing prevailing professional norms. Later cases have given varying weight to performance guidelines. In *Nix v. Whiteside* (1986), the defendant challenged his attorney's efforts to avoid the breach of professional responsibility that would have occurred through the introduction of perjured testimony. The majority suggested that counsel's action was supported by the state's ethical standards and was thereby immune from challenge, but four justices were unwilling to support any such "blanket rule." The majority also suggested that a breach of ethical standards, where aimed at benefiting the defendant, would not necessary fall below the competency standard. In *Wiggins v. Smith* (2003) (involving a failure to obtain a social history report) and *Rompilla v. Beard* (2005) (involving a failure to examine the file on a prior conviction that the prosecution intended to use as a capital-case aggravator), the Court noted that defense counsel had failed to take investigative steps prescribed by relevant

ABA standards, but it also stressed the special need for those steps in the factual context of the particular case.

(c) Applying the Reasonableness Standard. As might be expected, the many lower court rulings applying *Strickland's* competency standard are sometimes inconsistent in their treatment of roughly similar fact situations. Nevertheless, they do suggest some general patterns, at least as to those claims most likely and least likely to be successful. In general, the defendant is most likely to establish incompetency where counsel's alleged errors of omission or commission are attributable to a lack of diligence rather than an exercise of judgment. Courts will far more readily find incompetency where there has been "an abdication—not an exercise—of professional judgment." On the other side, where counsel's action or inaction was based on strategic choice, the defendant will find it most difficult to establish incompetency. Speaking to the interplay between an attorney's duty to investigate and the making of strategic decisions, the *Strickland* Court noted that "strategic choices made after thorough investigation of law and facts relevant to plausible options are virtually unchallengeable." This "virtually unchallengeable" status obviously requires great deference for strategic choices, but it comes with the important prerequisite of a "complete investigation."

Where the challenged tactical decision does not rest on an inadequate investigation (of fact or law), but simply on a claim of poor judgment, some lower courts have indicated that incompetency can still be established if the adopted strategy was so outlandish that "no competent attorney would have made such a choice." In *Yarborough v. Gentry* (2003), the Supreme warned lower courts against too readily reaching such a conclusion. In unanimously reversing a lower court ruling that counsel's closing argument constituted ineffective assistance, the Court noted that each of the weaknesses cited by the lower court had a plausible strategic justification: counsel's failure to highlight other exculpatory evidence may have reflected a strategy of "focusing on a small number of key points [rather than] * * * a shotgun approach"; counsel's mentioning of details that were legally irrelevant but harmful to his client's character arguably reflected an effort to emphasize to the jury that it could not consider such factors; and counsel's acknowledgment he too could not be sure of the truth arguably served as a "rhetorical device that personalizes the doubt anyone but an eyewitness must have."

Courts reviewing competency claims frequently stress that, even apart from tactical judgments, they do not demand that counsel's performance be flawless. It must be anticipated that the lawyer will occasionally fail to recognize that a certain course of action may be available to his client. Accordingly, an incompetency claim is most likely to be successful when the defendant can point to a long series of questionable omissions by counsel; this suggests that the lawyer's errors were not simply the product of human fallibility, but the result of a lack of conscientious effort. Very often, however, a single error which was both glaring and related to a matter of obvious significance has been held sufficient to establish incompetency. Although the court must look to the level of counsel's overall performance, clearly negligent treatment of a crucial deficiency in the prosecution's case or an obvious strength of the defense will outweigh the adequate handling of a series of minor matters. Thus, while the issues of prejudicial impact and incompetency are separate prongs of the *Strickland* test, the potential prejudicial impact of the subject dealt with by counsel reaches over into the competency determination, as that potential obviously relates to the care and effort expected from a competent adversary.

Kimmelman v. Morrison (1986) illustrates how the two prongs may overlap in evaluating a single error, so that potential impact leads to a finding of incompetency, but does not necessarily establish prejudice—which rests on actual (not potential) impact. Habeas petitioner Morrison's claim of ineffective assistance rested solely on his counsel's failure to make a timely suppression objection based on an allegedly unconstitutional search and seizure. During Morrison's trial for rape, the state had introduced a sheet seized from his bed and expert testimony concerning stains and hair found on the sheet. Defense counsel had objected on Fourth Amendment grounds, but the trial court refused to consider that objection because there had been no pretrial motion to suppress. Counsel explained that he had not previously been aware of the seizure of the sheet, but the trial judge found that to be no excuse since counsel had not asked for pretrial discovery. Counsel then sought to justify that omission by asserting that it was the state's obligation to inform him of its case against his client and that he had not expected to go to trial since he had been told that the complainant was reluctant to testify. Both justifications were rejected by the trial judge. The first represented a clear misunderstanding of the law and the second ignored the fact that it would have required a court order, not simply the victim's preference, to dismiss the rape indictment.

Rejecting the state's contention that counsel's overall trial performance reflected professionally reasonable representation, notwithstanding his mishandling of the Fourth Amendment objection, the Supreme Court concluded that counsel's failure to request pretrial discovery clearly fell below "prevailing professional norms." The state's attempt to "minimize the seriousness of counsel's errors by asserting that [its] case turned far more on the credibility of witnesses than on the bedsheet and related testimony" was not persuasive. Here, there had been a "total failure to conduct pre-trial discovery," for which counsel offered only "implausible explanations" that reflected a "startling ignorance of the law." Counsel's performance would not be measured by a "hindsight" evaluation of the "relative importance of various components of the State's case"; at the time he failed to seek discovery, counsel "did not * * * know what the State's case would be." While "the relative importance of witness credibility vis-à-vis the bedsheet and related expert testimony [would be] pertinent to the determination of prejudice" (a determination left for lower court consideration on remand), it "shed no light on the reasonableness of counsel's decision not to request discovery."

Among the incompetency claims that courts often find more difficult to evaluate are those based on counsel's failure to interview possible defense witnesses or otherwise pursue possible sources of helpful information. On the one hand, the lack of pretrial preparation is widely noted to be "the preeminent cause of poor legal performance." On the other, courts also recognize that "the amount of pretrial investigation that is reasonable defies precise measurement." What is satisfactory to meet minimum standards of competency "will necessarily depend on a variety of factors, including the number of issues in the case, the relative complexity of those issues, the strength of the government's case, and the overall strategy of counsel." The Supreme Court in *Strickland* advised that special attention be given in this regard to the "information supplied [to counsel] by the defendant." Counsel has no need to pursue a particular line of investigation, the Court noted, when "defendant has given counsel reason to believe that pursuing * * * [that line] would be fruitless or even harmful." So, too, "when the facts that support a certain potential line of defense are generally known to counsel because of what the defendant has said, the need for further investigation may be considerably diminished or eliminated altogether."

The difficulties presented in judging the adequacy of counsel's factual investigations are reflected in the sharp divisions in the Supreme Court in three cases involving investigations relating to capital sentencing—*Burger v. Kemp* (1987), *Wiggins v. Smith* (2003), and *Rompilla v. Beard* (2005). The challenged investigative errors were: counsel's failure to seek additional information as to defendant's psychological problems and troubled background in *Burger*; counsel's failure to obtain a social history report in *Wiggins*; and counsel's failure to examine the full court file on a prior conviction used by the prosecution to establish a "history-of-violence" aggravator in *Rompilla*. In each case, habeas counsel took the investigation beyond the point at which trial counsel had stopped, and uncovered significant mitigating evidence. The Court majority in *Burger* found that while "counsel could well have made a more thorough investigation," the decision not to do so reflected "a reasonable professional judgment." In *Wiggins* and *Rompilla*, Court majorities found that the investigative failures violated *Strickland's* competency standard. In each case, the majority and dissenting justice disagreed in their reading of certain factors that all agreed to be relevant, such as: whether counsel's initial investigation had suggested that further investigation would produce significant mitigating evidence; whether counsel reasonably believed that the introduction of that line of mitigating evidence would open the door to a harmful counter-attack by the prosecution; whether counsel's failure to investigate further was the product of "inattention," rather than a "reasoned strategic judgment" that took account of limited defense resources; and how easy or difficult it would have been to further pursue the investigation. The different results and even the divisions within the Court arguably can be reconciled by reference to such factors. However, the opinions in the cases also suggest that individual justices have quite different perspectives as to the influence of defense counsel's skills and efforts in determining which defendants receive capital sentences and as to the use of the Sixth Amendment to raise at least the minimum level of counsel's effort in the typical capital case.

(d) The Prejudice Element. Prior to the ruling in *Strickland,* lower courts had adopted a confusing array of standards governing the prejudice component of an incompetency claim. *Strickland* replaced those standards with a single test—whether "there is a reasonable probability that, but for counsel's unprofessional errors, the result of the proceeding would have been different." A "reasonable probability," the Court noted, was a "probability sufficient to undermine confidence in the outcome."

Application of the *Strickland* prejudice standard can call for quite difficult and subjective judgments, depending upon the character of counsel's alleged incompetency. Where counsel's performance relates to the introduction of evidence, the court can ask what bearing that evidence might have had on the jury's verdict, a question very much like that traditionally applied in harmless error analysis (although the standard is different). The Court has indicated in this regard that evidence considered must take account of the entire causal chain that would have occurred but for the counsel error constituting incompetency. Thus, in *Rompilla v. Beard*, the critical error was the failure to examine a file for the purpose of rebutting the prosecution's proof of an aggravator, but the Court found prejudice in the possible impact of the evidence found in that file as it related to showing a mitigating factor (a prejudice showing the dissent characterized as "rest[ing] on serendipity").

Where the alleged incompetency relates to some legal claim aimed at producing a dismissal or new trial, the court can readily determine whether that objection would have been successful. However, where the alleged incompetency relates to a claim that would have changed the structure of the trial, as opposed to producing a dismissal or altering the evidence before the jury, the task of determining its impact (assuming the claim had merit) is quite different from traditional harmless error analysis. Where a court erred in denying a change of venue, or rejecting a challenge to jury composition, that error results on appeal in an automatic conviction reversal. See § 19.6(d). If those claims were not presented due to counsel's incompetency, should the court then ask whether there is a reasonable probability that the outcome of the trial would have differed if the trial had been in a different district or before a different jury? Courts have divided in their approach to this issue, with some suggesting that here also prejudice should be automatic.

In light of the function of the prejudice requirement, the Court has warned against "an analysis focusing solely on mere outcome determination, without attention to whether the result of the proceeding was fundamentally unfair or unreliable." *Lockhart v. Fretwell* (1993). Prejudice does not automatically follow from a reasonable probability of a different result had counsel acted otherwise. Thus, *Nix v. Whiteside* (1986) held that the defendant, "as a matter of law," could not establish prejudice where he claimed that his counsel had improperly prevented him from presenting perjured testimony which could have swayed the jury. So too, in *Lockhart,* the Court held that there was "no 'prejudice' within the meaning of *Strickland*" where counsel's incompetence consisted of failing to present an objection that was supported by precedent at the time of trial, but later was rejected with the overturning of that precedent.

In *Kimmelman v. Morrison* (1986), counsel's incompetence was in failing to present a Fourth Amendment exclusionary rule claim, and the Court remanded for consideration of the prejudice issue. Arguably implicit in the remand was the assumption that prejudice would be established if there was a reasonable likelihood that the exclusion of the illegally seized evidence would have altered the outcome. Three concurring justices nonetheless argued that the failure to gain exclusion of evidence that clearly was reliable, though illegally seized, did not lead to "an unjust or fundamentally unfair result" and therefore could not constitute prejudice. The Court subsequently noted, however, that its references to fundamental fairness in discussing prejudice "do not justify a departure from a straight forward application of *Strickland* when the ineffectiveness of counsel does deprive the defendant of a substantive or procedural right to which the law entitles him." *Williams v. Taylor* (2000).

Finally, it should be noted that the *Strickland* discussion of prejudice must be read in light of *Cronic's* recognition of extreme situations in which prejudice will be presumed. One of these situations, as illustrated by *Powell v. Ala.*, requires circumstances of appointment so restrictive that counsel cannot possibly provide effective representation. As discussed in § 3.7(d), this exception is narrowly confined. A second exception—where counsel "entirely fails to subject the prosecutor's case to meaningful adversarial testing"—has been applied by lower courts to a variety of situations in which counsel either was not present during a critical stage in the proceeding or was present but failed to do anything. However, in *Bell v. Cone* (2002), the Supreme Court warned against expansion of this *Cronic* exception. A presumption of prejudice is permissible, the Court noted, only where the "failure is complete," and not where counsel simply failed to take particular steps (important though they might well be) in challenging the prosecution's case. Thus, the federal habeas court there erred in applying that exception to a capital sentencing proceeding because counsel failed to introduce mitigating evidence and waived closing argument. Counsel had challenged the state's case in other respects (including bringing out favorable evidence on cross-examination of the state's witness and calling the jury's attention in an opening statement to mitigating evidence that had been introduced as part of an insanity defense), and the allegations as to mitigating evidence and waiving closing argument constituted no more than claims of "specific attorney error," which were "subject to *Strickland's* performance and prejudice components."

*

Chapter 4

PRETRIAL RELEASE

Table of Sections

For additional analysis of the above topics and citations to authorities supporting their discussion in this Book, consult the authors' 7-volume *Criminal Procedure* treatise, also available as Westlaw database CRIMPROC. See the Table of Cross-References in this Book.

---

§ 4.1 Pretrial Release Procedures

(a) The Federal Bail Reform Act. The 1984 Bail Reform Act (18 U.S.C.A. §§ 3141–3151) provides that when a person charged with a crime appears before a judicial officer, the judicial officer "shall order the pretrial release of the person on personal recognizance, or upon execution of an unsecured appearance bond in an amount specified by the court * * * unless the judicial officer determines that such release will not reasonably assure the appearance of the person as required or will endanger the safety of any other person or the community." In the event of such a determination, the judicial officer is then to "order the pretrial release of the person * * * subject to the least restrictive further condition, or combination of conditions, that such judicial officer determines will reasonably assure the appearance of the person as required and the safety of any other person and the community," which may include the condition that the person

(i) remain in the custody of a designated person, who agrees to assume supervision and to report any violation of a release condition to the court, if the designated person is able reasonably to assure the judicial officer that the person will appear as required and will not pose a danger to the safety of any other person or the community;

(ii) maintain employment, or, if unemployed, actively seek employment;

(iii) maintain or commence an educational program;

(iv) abide by specified restrictions on personal associations, place of abode, or travel;

(v) avoid all contact with an alleged victim of the crime and with a potential witness who may testify concerning the offense;

(vi) report on a regular basis to a designated law enforcement agency, pretrial services agency, or other agency;

(vii) comply with a specified curfew;

(viii) refrain from possessing a firearm, destructive device, or other dangerous weapon;

(ix) refrain from excessive use of alcohol, or any use of a narcotic drug or other controlled substance * * * without a prescription by a licensed medical practitioner;

(x) undergo available medical, psychological, or psychiatric treatment, including treatment for drug or alcohol dependency, and remain in a specified institution if required for that purpose;

(xi) execute an agreement to forfeit upon failing to appear as required, property of a sufficient unencumbered value, including money, as is reasonably necessary to assure the appearance of the person as required * * *;

(xii) execute a bail bond with solvent sureties * * * in such amount as is reasonably necessary to assure the appearance of the person as required * * *;

(xiii) return to custody for specified hours following release for employment, schooling, or other limited purposes; and

(xiv) satisfy any other condition that is reasonably necessary to assure the appearance of the person as required and to assure the safety of any other person and the community.

But it is expressly stated that the "judicial officer may not impose a financial condition that results in the pretrial detention of the person."

The 1984 Act also specifies the factors that, on the basis of "the available information," are to be taken into account in determining which conditions will suffice, namely:

(1) the nature and circumstances of the offense charged, including whether the offense is a crime of violence, a violation of section 1591, a Federal crime of terrorism, or involves a minor crime or a controlled substance, firearm, explosive, or destructive device;

(2) the weight of the evidence against the person;

(3) the history and characteristics of the person, including—

(A) the person's character, physical and mental condition, family ties, employment, financial resources, length of residence in the community, community ties, past conduct, history relating to drug or alcohol abuse, criminal history, and record concerning appearance at court proceedings; and

(B) whether, at the time of the current offense or arrest, the person was on probation, on parole, or on other release pending trial, sentencing, appeal or completion of sentence for an offense under Federal, State, or local law; and

(4) the nature and seriousness of the danger to any person or the community that would be posed by the person's release.

A release order must include a written "clear and specific" statement of all conditions imposed and advise the person released of the penalties for and other consequences of violating those conditions. The judicial officer may at any time amend the order to impose additional or different conditions. On motion of either the defendant or the government, the release conditions may be reviewed by the court with jurisdiction over the offense charged, and a release order may be appealed to the court of appeals. Violation of a condition of release is punishable by contempt and, in addition, can result in revocation of the release upon a judicial finding that the person is unlikely to abide by any condition of release or that there is no combination of conditions which will assure his appearance or nondanger. A person who "knowingly fails to appear before a court as required by the conditions of release" is to incur a forfeiture of "any property" designated in his bond or forfeiture agreement and, in addition, may be subjected to fine and imprisonment.

(b) **State Practice Generally.** Typically, an arrested defendant is taken to the nearest stationhouse and then transported to the city jail within 24 hours. For defendants charged with a minor offense listed in a fixed bail schedule, the first opportunity for release comes at that time. Those defendants unable to obtain their release at the station must await their appearance before a judicial officer, often the following morning, at which time the judge will set the terms of release. Defendants who obtained their release earlier, if their cases are not immediately disposed of at their subsequent court appearance, may have the amount of their bail revised upward or downward.

Judges are inclined to give primary consideration to the seriousness of the offense charged, most likely because it is a factor that is clearcut and easy to apply. The strength of the case against the defendant, as communicated by the prosecutor or police, is also an important yardstick in practice. A third factor considered very relevant is the defendant's prior criminal record. In many localities it is unusual for the judge to determine or consider other facts about the defendant's background and character, such as whether he is employed and how long he has resided in the community, but in many major cities bail projects obtain this information and supply it to the court.

As for the methods by which a defendant may obtain pretrial release in the state courts, one frequently used procedure is cash bail raised by the defendant through personal savings or money supplied by friends and family, in which case the entire amount is usually returned to him if he appears as required. But if, as is often the case, the defendant must rely upon the services of a bail bondsman, then he will have to pay a fee usually not less than 10 per cent of the bond amount, a payment that is not recoverable by the defendant. Another method by which pretrial release may be obtained in many locales is by paying 10 per cent of the bond directly to the court, most or all of which is returned if he appears in court as scheduled. Yet another possibility is that a defendant may obtain his release on a property bond, which means he offers property as bail in lieu of cash. Still another possibility is personal bond, sometimes referred to as personal surety or release on recognizance (r.o.r.), which is used when the judge concludes the defendant is sufficiently motivated to show up that he can be released on his own signature without bail. In addition to or in lieu of these methods, some localities utilize daytime release, release to the custody of an approved individual or organization, or release on conditions.

(c) Counsel at Bail Hearing. If the defendant is represented by counsel at his bail hearing, this greatly improves his chances for either bail set in a modest amount or release on his own recognizance. One reason that the participation of a defense attorney makes such a difference is that he can bring relevant facts about his client's background to the judge's attention, as well as present reasonable alternatives to money bail and invoke available community resources for this purpose. There is thus much to be said for the contention that the Sixth Amendment right to counsel applies at that time, a conclusion that finds strong support in *Coleman v. Ala.* (1970), where the holding that a preliminary hearing is a "critical stage" for right to counsel purposes was based in part on the fact that "counsel can also be influential * * * in making effective arguments for the accused on such matters as * * * bail." But even after *Coleman* some courts have held that there is no constitutional right to counsel at a bail hearing.

(d) Proof at Bail Hearing. Information received at a bail hearing need not conform to the rules pertaining to the admissibility of evidence at trial, but this should not be taken to mean that information must be accepted by the court without regard to its reliability. Thus, whether hearsay is admissible in a bail hearing must ultimately be determined on a case by case basis by asking whether in the particular circumstances it is the kind of evidence on which responsible persons are accustomed to rely in serious affairs. It is customary for the prosecution to supply such facts as defendant's prior bad record in order to show that this defendant's bail should be higher or the conditions of his release more strict than would typically be true for a person so charged, and for the defense to supply favorable facts about defendant's ties to the community to show the contrary. The approach of the applicable bail statute may have some influence on who feels compelled to show what; a scheme based on a presumption that personal recognizance is appropriate until the contrary is shown would seem to put the prosecution in a more difficult position.

(e) Defendant's Statements. Sometimes the question has arisen whether defendant's incriminating statements made at the bail hearing are admissible against him at trial. One view of this matter is that because the law favors the release of defendants pending determination of guilt or innocence, a defendant should be encouraged to testify at a hearing on a motion to set bail without the fear that what he says may later be used to incriminate him, which is accomplished by requiring that the defendant's testimony at the bail hearing be excluded from evidence at his later trial. Whether that result is mandated by the Constitution is a more difficult matter. A negative answer was given in one case, where the defendant's claim, that he was compelled to forfeit his fifth amendment right to remain silent in order to safeguard his eighth amendment right to reasonable bail, was based largely upon the Supreme Court's decision in *Simmons v. U.S.* (1968). The *Simmons* analogy was rejected because in that case the Court emphasized that a defendant who wished to assert a fourth amendment objection has been required to show that he was the owner or possessor of the seized property or that he had a possessory interest in the searched premises, while by contrast a defendant at a bail bond hearing need not divulge the facts in his case in order to receive the benefits of the eighth amendment right to bail. But there is much to be said for the conclusion that a defendant at a bail hearing is confronted with a clearly impermissible compelled election, for the applicable constitutional guarantee is not just the right to bail, but the right to non-excessive bail, and in the case just discussed the defendant not unreasonably concluded that the recommended amount of bail would be determined to be appropriate for him unless he rebutted the government testimony portraying him as a big-time drug dealer.

(f) Victim's Right to Be Heard. As a result of the victim's rights movement, all jurisdictions have enacted provisions recognizing certain rights that crime victims possess regarding criminal prosecution of those accused of having committed offenses against them. One of the rights most frequently recognized in these provisions is the right to be heard on the matter of defendant's release on bail. The federal statute, 18 U.S.C.A. § 3771, explicitly recognizes a crime victim's right "to be reasonably heard at any public proceeding * * * involving release," and approximately two-thirds of the state constitutional provisions appear to recognize such a right. Any right of a victim to be heard at a bail hearing is sometimes strengthened by notice requirements. Thus, the federal statute declares that a crime victim also has a right "to reasonable, accurate, and timely notice of any public court proceeding ... involving ... any release ... of the accused." Most of the state constitutional provisions contain similar notice requirements, although some require that the victim actually have requested such notice.

The right to be heard at a bail hearing is best viewed as the right to contribute information having a direct bearing upon the questions before the judge on that occasion, which involve the terms and conditions of release and (in some instances) whether release should be permitted at all. It thus has been held that at a federal detention hearing a victim's statement could be relevant to (i) the strength of the case against the defendant, (ii) the seriousness of the crimes he is alleged to have committed, and (iii) the reasonable apprehension of personal danger to the victim. Presumably the bail hearing judge may limit the testimony given by the victim at the hearing to that bearing upon the decisions before him, particularly under those provisions describing the right as to be "reasonably heard" or to give "relevant" information.

§ 4.2 Constitutionality of Limits on Pretrial Freedom

(a) **Amount of Money Bail.** The Eighth Amendment to the United States Constitution, also applicable to the states through the Fourteenth Amendment due process clause, provides in part: "Excessive bail shall not be required." The traditional question raised under this provision is that of what amount of money bail may constitutionally be required of a defendant. The leading case on this point is *Stack v. Boyle* (1951), involving twelve petitioners who had been charged with conspiring to violate the Smith Act, which made it a crime to advocate the overthrow of the government by force or violence. Bail was fixed in the district court in the uniform amount of $50,000 for each petitioner. The petitioners then moved to reduce bail on the ground it was excessive under the Eighth Amendment, and in support submitted statements as to their financial resources, family relationships, health, prior criminal records, and other information. Though the only response of the government was a certified record showing that four other persons previously convicted under the Smith Act had forfeited bail, the district court denied the motion and thereafter denied writs of habeas corpus for the petitioners. The court of appeals affirmed, but the Supreme Court ruled that bail had "not been fixed by proper methods," and then concluded that "petitioners remedy is by [a renewed] motion to reduce bail" in the district court.

One respect in which the *Stack* decision is important is in its specification of the purpose underlying bail which may be legitimately taken into account in setting the amount; the Court declared that bail "set at a figure higher than an amount reasonably calculated to fulfill th[e] purpose [of assuring defendant's appearance at trial] is 'excessive' under the Eighth Amendment." In addition, *Stack* stresses that setting an amount of bail properly serving this single purpose requires an assessment of the facts of the particular case. The "traditional standards" recognized by the Court in *Stack* were "the nature and circumstances of the offense charged, the weight of the evidence against him, the financial ability of the defendant to give bail and the character of the defendant." It was relatively easy to find noncompliance with the Eighth Amendment in *Stack,* for (as the Court noted) "bail for each petitioner has been fixed in a sum much higher than that usually imposed for offenses with like penalties and yet there has been no factual showing to justify such action in this case."

As this last comment reflects, the nature of the offense and in particular the "risk" the defendant is running in terms of the potential punishment is an important factor in the Eighth Amendment equation. But *Stack* teaches that it is by no means the only factor. This would indicate that use of a bail schedule, wherein amounts are set solely on the basis of the offense charged, violates the Eighth Amendment except when resorted to as a temporary measure pending prompt judicial appearance for a particularized bail setting. Indeed, such use of a master bond schedule may be constitutionally objectionable on other grounds as well, including that procedural due process requires a hearing in various administrative proceedings, a fortiori, it requires a hearing before depriving a person of his liberty, and that the procedure violates the equal protection clause because it is based upon an irrelevant view that a poor person should post precisely the same amount of bail as a rich person.

(b) Poverty and Pretrial Release. As for the relevance of the defendant's indigency upon the Eighth Amendment bail question, *Stack v. Boyle* (1951) is itself instructive, for it expressly states that "the financial ability of the defendant to give bail" is one of the factors that must be taken into consideration. This is certainly sensible, for an impecunious person who pledges a small amount of collateral constituting all or almost all of his property is likely to have a stake at least as great as that of a wealthy person who pledges a large amount constituting a modest part of his property. But it is a substantial jump from that truism to the proposition that an amount of bail a defendant cannot meet because of his poverty is thereby "excessive" under the Eighth Amendment. Courts have refused to take that leap; they instead continue to adhere to the proposition that bail is not excessive merely because the defendant is unable to pay it.

As for an equal protection claim, note must be taken of the oft-quoted comments of Justice Douglas in *Bandy v. U.S.* (1960).

Observing that the Court had held in *Griffin v. Ill.* (1956) "that an indigent defendant is denied equal protection of the law if he is denied an appeal on equal terms with other defendants, solely because of his indigence," Justice Douglas opined that it must be similarly unconstitutional for "an indigent [to] be denied freedom, where a wealthy man would not, because he does not happen to have enough property to pledge for his freedom." Some have argued that this position has been bolstered by such cases as *Williams v. Ill.* (1970) and *Tate v. Short* (1971), deemed to provide a close analogy because they held that equal protection bars subjecting indigent defendants to sentences of imprisonment beyond that which other defendants could receive. However, *Williams* and *Tate* did not bar imprisonment for indigents merely because a wealthier defendant would likely escape such a consequence by being fined instead, and *Griffin* has since been given a rather narrow interpretation by the Supreme Court. Thus, notwithstanding the forceful argument by some commentators in support of the equal protection argument, the courts have not been inclined to accept the equal protection argument that bail is unconstitutional when set in an amount a particular indigent defendant cannot meet. But several courts, relying upon *Williams* and *Tate,* have held that failure to grant credit against a maximum sentence for presentence incarceration imposed because of a defendant's inability to post bail violates the equal protection clause.

Because of bail reform efforts in recent years, the dimensions of the debate concerning the indigent defendant have changed somewhat. Because of the general recognition that money bail is but one of several possible forms of release, a compelling argument can be made that money bail may no longer be constitutionally viewed as the sole means of pretrial release or even as the preferred means of gaining pretrial freedom. Important here is *Pugh v. Rainwater* (1977), involving a challenge to the Florida bail system, which recognized several alternative forms of release, but without (1) a presumption in favor of release on recognizance; or (2) priority for the nonfinancial alternatives. The court concluded "that equal protection standards are not satisfied unless the judge is required to consider less financially onerous forms of release before he imposes money bail." This means, as the court later put it, "that in the case of an indigent, whose appearance at trial could reasonably be assured by one of the alternative forms of release, pretrial confinement for inability to post money bail would constitute imposition of an excessive restraint."

(c) Opportunity to Prepare a Defense. While there is little reason to doubt the proposition that pretrial detention has a significant adverse impact upon the ability of a defendant to vindicate himself at trial or secure leniency in sentencing, courts have not been particularly receptive to post-conviction claims by defendants that they were entitled to relief because their pretrial incarceration in some way interfered with preparation of their defense. However, a particularized claim made during the time of pretrial detention will sometimes produce limited relief, as is illustrated by *Kinney v. Lenon* (1970). There the juvenile defendant, in custody awaiting trial on charges arising out of a schoolyard fight, alleged in support of his claim for pretrial release "that there were many potential witnesses to the fight, that he cannot identify them by name but would recognize them by sight, that appellant's attorneys are white though he and the potential witnesses are black, that his attorneys would consequently have great practical difficulty in interviewing and lining up the witnesses, and that appellant is the sole person who can do so." Convinced that there had been "a strong showing that the appellant is the only person who can effectively prepare his own defense," the court concluded that defendant's detention was infringing upon his constitutional right to compulsory process to obtain witnesses in his behalf, which "as a practical matter would be of little value without an opportunity to contact and screen potential witnesses before trial." The court thus held that release of the defendant into the custody of his parents was necessary to protect "his due-process right to a fair trial."

§ 4.3 Constitutionality of Mandating Pretrial Detention

(a) **Preventive Detention in the Federal System.** As noted earlier, the *Stack v. Boyle* (1951) interpretation of the Eighth Amendment prohibition on "excessive" bail was that in setting pretrial release conditions there is but one legitimate consideration: what is necessary to provide a reasonable assurance that the particular defendant will subsequently appear at the proceedings against him? There is no question, however, but that this legal theory is not always respected in practice and that bail determinations are sometimes influenced by such considerations as the accused's assumed danger to the community. Especially in earlier days, when there was almost exclusive reliance upon money bail and little opportunity for a defendant to obtain review of his bail setting, this could quite easily occur. Because of the sub rosa character of such action, the concept of "preventive detention" (pretrial custody of a defendant for the purpose of protecting some other person or the community at large) did not receive close scrutiny.

In recent years, by comparison, the subject of preventive detention has been much debated. This is largely attributable to bail reform activities, for from the very beginning of those efforts one of the most serious impediments to bail reform has been the fear that a greater number of pretrial releases would mean a greater amount of serious crime. And thus bail reform statutes sometimes include a preventive detention scheme, as is the case with the federal Bail Reform Act of 1984. A detention hearing is to be held, upon motion of the attorney for the government, where the case involves a crime of violence, an offense for which the maximum penalty is death or life imprisonment, certain serious drug offenses, or any felony by one with two or more convictions of the aforementioned type offenses. Also, such a hearing is to be held on motion of either the attorney for the government or the judicial officer that the case involves a serious risk that the person will flee or will obstruct or attempt to obstruct justice or interfere with a prospective witness or juror. If at the hearing the judicial officer "finds that no condition or combination of conditions will reasonably assure the appearance of the person as required and the safety of any other person and the community," then detention is to be ordered. A rebuttable presumption in support of such a finding exists in certain circumstances. The Act also makes nonviolation of any federal, state or local crime a condition of any release under the Act, and upon violation of that condition revocation of the release is required upon a finding of probable cause that such a crime was committed while on release, and also a finding that the person is unlikely to abide by any conditions of release or that there is no combination of release conditions that will assure the person will not flee or pose a danger. A person ordered detained may obtain review of the order from the court with original jurisdiction over the offense charged, and may appeal from the detention order.

(b) Preventive Detention and the State Constitutions. The practice in the fifty states regarding preventive detention is quite diverse, largely because of the remarkably different state constitutional provisions to be found on the subject of bail, which may be conveniently grouped as follows: (1) In nine states, the provision on bail is essentially the same as the Eighth Amendment in the federal constitution; that is, there is an express prohibition upon excessive bail, but not a specific declaration that defendants generally have a right to have bail set in their cases. (2) In 23 states, what might be called the traditional state constitutional approach is taken, which in its purest form is a provision declaring "All prisoners shall, before conviction, be bailable by sufficient sureties, except for capital offenses, where the proof is evident, or the presumption great." Seventeen states follow this language almost verbatim, while in six others the only difference is that instead of or in addition to the exception for capital cases is an exception for cases where the punishment was once capital, where the punishment is life imprisonment, or where specified serious offenses are charged. (3) In the remaining 18 states there is once again a constitutional declaration of a right to bail as above, typically with an exception for capital cases or some other exception as listed above, but significantly the constitutional provision then, by virtue of an amendment added thereto in relatively recent years, goes on to describe other situations in which a form of preventive detention may be utilized.

As for the states in the first of these three groups, that is, those in which the constitutional bail provision is like the Eighth Amendment in not expressly declaring a right to bail, these provisions would appear to present no greater bar to preventive detention schemes than does the Eighth Amendment itself. As for the states in the third group, it may be concluded that preventive detention of the type specifically exempted in their respective constitutions from the right-to-bail provisions contained therein are *not* objectionable on the ground that it intrudes upon that right. It is thus not surprising that virtually all of those states with either a constitutional authorization for preventive detention or no constitutional declaration of a right to bail permit such detention in some circumstances (e.g., whenever the charge is of a certain type and in addition (i) there is a finding that the defendant, if released, would present a danger to another person or the community; (ii) some condition precedent is met, typically that the defendant at the time of the alleged crime was already on bail, probation or parole, or had previously been convicted of offenses of a certain type; or (iii) a specified condition precedent was met and in addition a finding of dangerousness was made). There are many other variations among these states as well, but most of these state provisions are not as elaborate as the federal provisions discussed earlier, and because of their more abbreviated nature the matter of procedural safeguards is not always developed to the same degree. Because shortcomings in this regard can lead to the invalidation of preventive detention schemes on federal due process grounds, state courts are likely to judicially engraft such protections onto the applicable provisions in the state constitutions, statutes and court rules to forestall such an event.

What remains to be considered here are the states in the second group, that is, those with the "traditional" kind of constitutional bail provision: one expressly granting a right to bail with only a very narrow exception (usually that of a capital charge) and without any additional claim of authority to engage in preventive detention. The question here, as to cases not falling within the specified exception, is whether the state constitutional declaration of a right to bail leaves any room at all for pretrial detention of criminal defendants in the interest of protecting another or the community. Without foreclosing the possibility that some particular state *might* construe its own right-to-bail provision somewhat more narrowly, it is fair to say that the preventive detention possibilities in these jurisdictions are quite limited yet not nonexistent. These right-to-bail provisions do not permit that broader variety of preventive detention authorized in the federal system—that is, detention based upon nothing more than a finding that a certain defendant charged with a serious offense would be dangerous to some other person or the community if released. As for preventive detention based on some sort of a condition precedent, clearly one or more prior convictions of a certain type will not suffice, and probably being on probation or parole regarding a prior conviction will not either. (It is common practice, in addition to or in lieu of such new charge, to undertake proceedings to revoke the probation or parole, which would take care of the bail question, as the state-conferred constitutional right-to-bail does not extend to those individuals being held pending a hearing to determine whether probation or parole should be revoked.)

What is left for consideration against these state right-to-bail provisions are those preventive detention schemes that rest, in essence, upon the fact that the individual, while on pretrial release, apparently engaged in some form of misconduct, typically criminal conduct but sometimes noncriminal conduct deemed to violate an express or implied condition of the previous release from custody. It is sometimes said that such conduct by the defendant constitutes a forfeiture of his previously-exercised right to bail, which doubtless is the proper conclusion in at least some circumstances. Perhaps the easiest case of this kind is that in which the on-bail defendant's misconduct was an effort to obstruct the fair disposition of the charges against him, such as by witness intimidation.

What if the defendant's misconduct during pretrial release was not of that kind, but nonetheless constituted a criminal offense and/or a violation of some condition of release? Some authority is to be found indicating that a state constitutional right to bail does not stand in the way of preventive detention in such circumstances. In *State v. Ayala* (1992), for example, where "an explicit condition placed upon the defendant's release on bail was to refrain from committing any federal, state or local crimes," and "defendant was subsequently arrested on charges that, while on release, he had engaged in an unprovoked brutal assault on Mathews in broad daylight," the appellate court "agree[d] with the state that the power to enforce reasonable conditions of release is a necessary component of a trial court's jurisdiction over a criminal case," and that consequently the "fundamental right to bail guaranteed under our state constitution must be qualified by a court's authority to ensure compliance with the conditions of release." The broad language in *Ayala,* which could easily be interpreted to mean that a right to bail in the state constitution is subject to a releasing judge's "power * * * to revoke" whenever the defendant commits *any* crime or violates *any* condition of release, must be contrasted with that in *State v. Sauve* (1993), where the court concluded that the "absolute right to bail" in a state constitution means that "liberty must remain the norm" and that exceptions must thus be limited to " 'special circumstances' where the state's interest is 'legitimate and compelling,' " and that to "justify a compelling state interest * * * there must be a nexus between defendant's repeated violations and a disruption of the prosecution."

Because of the infrequency with which the issue has been reached by appellate courts, it is difficult to generalize from either *Ayala* or *Sauve* , but it does seem that the court in *Sauve* was right about one thing: if state constitutional declarations of a right to bail are not to be rendered meaningless, exceptions to that right must be extremely limited and must in every instance be grounded in a compelling state interest. This means that bail revocation can never be justified merely because a release condition has been violated or because the person has apparently committed some offense during release; rather, such events must manifest a significant threat to a compelling state interest. Just what qualifies as such an interest is a harder question. *Sauve* represents one possible conclusion, namely, that a defendant's new criminal conduct or violation of a release condition must "threaten the integrity of the judicial system, in the constitutionally limited sense that they thwart the prosecution of the defendant." But some courts have concluded that dangerousness in a somewhat broader sense should suffice when it is manifested by the released defendant's apparent commission of a serious crime or his violation of a release condition.

(c) The Eighth Amendment Ambiguity. Whether the Eighth Amendment posed a constitutional barrier to preventive detention remained unclear until the Supreme Court addressed the issue in *U.S. v. Salerno* (1987). Those holding to the view that the Eighth Amendment did *not* encompass a right to bail found it useful to trace the excessive bail provision back to a comparable provision in the English Bill of Rights of 1689. The latter provision, it was noted, was not prompted by the well established statutory provisions that carefully enumerated which offenses were bailable and which were not, but rather by judicial circumvention of the protections of the Habeas Corpus Act by setting prohibitively high bail for bailable offenses. The English excessive bail clause, therefore, was developed as a specific remedy for judicial abuse of the bail procedure as otherwise established by law and did not, in and of itself, imply any right to bail. This distinction, it was argued, was recognized in the colonies and early states, as reflected by three significant developments: (1) several states dealt with the right to bail by statute, thus indicating an understanding that the subject was open to legislative limitation; (2) several states adopted constitutional provisions that were explicitly directed to limiting the power of the judiciary; and (3) several states adopted constitutional provisions that granted a right to bail and also an excessive bail clause, manifesting a recognition that the latter did not encompass the former. Hence the view that the Eighth Amendment does not confer a right to bail was also claimed to be consistent with the contemporary understanding when the Amendment was considered and adopted.

As for those holding to the view that the Eighth Amendment *does* include a constitutional right to bail, they took a somewhat different view as to the significance of the Amendment's English antecedents. They agree that English law denied bail for some offenses, but found no evidence that such a denial was ever permitted for the purpose of protecting the community. Rather, they suggested, the underlying assumption was that certain classes of offenders, particularly those whose lives were at stake, ought to be detained simply to assure their presence at trial. Pretrial release was more readily denied during this period in cases of particularly heinous crimes, but the reason, apart from the fact that such offenses carried heavier penalties and therefore involved a greater temptation to flee, was the fear that persons guilty of especially atrocious offenses might well be killed before they could appear for trial. In any event, so the argument proceeded, the English history is not controlling here because from the very beginning the American concept of bail differed significantly from that of the English. This is reflected by the fact that most states put in their state constitutions a provision that "all persons shall be bailable." And while these state constitutional provisions contain an exception for capital cases, this hardly reflects acceptance of the concept of preventive detention. Rather, these provisions were enacted in this form because it had been thought that most defendants facing a possible death penalty would likely flee regardless of what bail was set. Those favoring a broader reading of the Eighth Amendment contended it was the only logical construction of the bail provision, for to read the Amendment as barring judicial setting of excessive bail but not legislative denial of bail would make it virtually meaningless, as well as inconsistent with the general approach taken in the Bill of Rights, which is concerned primarily with curtailing the powers of Congress.

Then came *Salerno,* involving a facial challenge to the Bail Reform Act of 1984 (meaning, the Court emphasized, that "the challenger must establish that no set of circumstances exists under which the Act would be valid"). The Supreme Court found the *Stack* language "far too slender a reed on which to rest" the argument that the Eighth Amendment grants "a right to bail calculated solely upon consideration of flight." But the Court's brief discussion of the subject concluded with the caution that

> we need not decide today whether the Excessive Bail Clause speaks at all to Congress' power to define the classes of criminal arrestees who shall be admitted to bail. * * * Nothing in the text of the Bail Clause limits permissible government considerations solely to questions of flight. The only arguable substantive limitation of the Bail Clause is that the government's proposed conditions of release or detention not be "excessive" in light of the perceived evil. Of course, to determine whether the government's response is excessive, we must compare that response against the interest the government seeks to protect by means of that response. Thus, when the government has admitted that its only interest is in preventing flight, bail must be set by a court at a sum designed to ensure that goal, and no more. * * * We believe that when Congress has mandated detention on the basis of a compelling interest other than prevention of flight, as it has here, the Eighth Amendment does not require release on bail.

Thus, there exists in *Salerno* at least the suggestion that under the Eighth Amendment the risk of future crimes by certain types of arrestees could be so insubstantial as to make preventive detention of such persons excessive.

(d) Other Constitutional Objections. The language from *Stack* quoted above has understandably prompted the argument that preventive detention schemes are unconstitutional simply because they run afoul of the presumption of innocence. But while it is now generally accepted that the presumption of innocence has constitutional stature, as currently viewed by the Supreme Court it appears to have no bearing upon the preventive detention issue. The Court in *Bell v. Wolfish* (1979) concluded that the presumption "is a doctrine that allocates the burden of proof in criminal trials" and requires the factfinder "to judge an accused's guilt or innocence solely on the evidence adduced at trial and not on the basis of suspicions that may arise from the fact of his arrest, indictment, or custody or from other matters not introduced as proof at trial," and that it has "no application * * * before his trial has even begun."

Presumption of innocence aside, it is nonetheless possible that a particular preventive detention scheme would be vulnerable to an attack on due process grounds on the theory that it amounts to an impermissible imposition of punishment. As the Supreme Court recognized in *Bell*, the Constitution "includes freedom from punishment within the liberty of which no person may be deprived without due process of law," so that generally "punishment can only follow a determination of guilt after trial or plea." But the Court in *Bell* deemed it beyond dispute that pretrial incarceration is not inevitably "punishment" within the meaning of this doctrine. As for how to draw the "distinction between punitive measures that may not constitutionally be imposed prior to a determination of guilt and regulatory restraints that may," the Court identified a series of three factors: (1) "whether the disability is imposed for the purpose of punishment or whether it is but an incident of some other legitimate governmental purpose"; (2) absent an intent to punish, whether "an alternative purpose to which [the restriction] may rationally be connected is assignable for it"; and (3) if there is such a purpose, a "legitimate governmental objective," whether the disability "appears excessive in relation to the alternative purpose assigned [to it]."

Applying these factors, the Supreme Court in *Salerno* concluded the Bail Reform Act did not violate substantive due process. The legislative history "clearly indicates that Congress did not formulate the pretrial detention provisions as punishment for dangerous individuals"; rather, they serve a legitimate function, as "there is no doubt that preventing danger to the community is a legitimate regulatory goal." As for the third *Bell* factor, the Court concluded that "the incidents of pretrial detention" were not excessive because the Act "carefully limits the circumstances under which detention may be sought to the most serious crimes," the arrestee "is entitled to a prompt detention hearing" at which "the government must convince a neutral decisionmaker by clear and convincing evidence that no conditions of release can reasonably assure the safety of the community or any person," "the maximum length of pretrial detention is limited by the stringent time limitations of the Speedy Trial Act," and the conditions of confinement reflect the regulatory purpose because detainees are, to the extent possible, to be housed separately from convicted defendants. The Court's emphasis upon these characteristics of the Act, together with the assertion that what is involved here is a balancing of the "particularized government interest" against "the individuals's strong interest in liberty," suggests that a more expansive type of preventive detention law would be vulnerable under the *Bell* test.

Next, there is the possibility that a preventive detention scheme could be questioned on equal protection grounds. The traditional standard of review under the equal protection clause requires only that the law be shown to bear some rational relationship to legitimate state purposes, though there are special instances in which a more demanding "strict scrutiny" approach is required. Even assuming the latter test is not applicable here, a matter on which there is not complete agreement, it might be argued that a preventive detention scheme which selects only from those charged with crimes is arbitrary. The reasoning is that there certainly are persons *not* charged with any crime who give every indication of being at least as dangerous as anyone awaiting trial on a pending charge, and that this being so, it is arbitrary to imprison the man who is about to be tried for a past offense while imposing no restraint on the man who is not facing trial. While *Jackson v. Ind.* (1972), holding that "pending criminal charges" provide no justification for incarcerating incompetents under less demanding standards than apply to mentally ill persons not so charged, arguably supports that conclusion, authority is to be found declaring that it is rational for a legislative body to conclude that those charged with a particular type of offense are likely to repeat their crimes and thus to authorize preventive detention as to persons so charged.

Even if a particular preventive detention scheme suffers from none of the previously discussed constitutional defects, it is nonetheless necessary that the procedures whereby it is determined which individuals will actually be confined be fair in a procedural due process sense. Even in a situation in which it is conceded that the defendant has no absolute right to bail, a fair adjudicatory procedure must be followed. Just what constitutes fair procedure for due process purposes depends to some extent upon the circumstances and matter at issue. Thus, in *Gerstein v. Pugh* (1975), concerning the judicial determination of probable cause after a warrantless arrest, the Court held that "the full panoply of adversary safeguards—counsel, confrontation, cross-examination, and compulsory process for witnesses," is not constitutionally required, while in *Morrissey v. Brewer* (1972), concerning parole revocation, the Court ruled the parolee was entitled to notice, an opportunity to present evidence, and a right to confront and cross-examine adverse witnesses. In *Salerno,* the Court briefly discussed the procedural due process question in upholding the facial constitutionally of the Bail Reform Act of 1984. The Court stressed the procedures mandated by the Act: "a right to counsel at the detention hearing," and a right to "testify in their own behalf, present information by proffer or otherwise, and cross-examine witnesses who appear at the hearing," and declared "these extensive safeguards suffice to repel a facial challenge," But the Court may or may not have intended *Gerstein* as the benchmark in stating enigmatically that these procedures "far exceed what we found necessary to affect limited post arrest detention" in that case.

(e) Detention Where Serious Offense Charged. One variety of preventive detention scheme is that which withholds the right of pretrial release for defendants charged with a certain type of serious offense. Illustrative is the right-to-bail provision in one state constitution excepting cases of "sexual offenses involving penetration by force or against the will of the victim * * * where the proof is evident or the presumption great." One court held that this provision violated the federal Constitution because it "created an irrebuttable presumption that every individual charged with this particular offense is incapable of assuring his appearance by conditioning it upon reasonable bail or is too dangerous to be granted release." Because *Salerno,* discussed above, placed great emphasis on the need for proof that the particular "arrestee presents an identified and articulable threat to an individual or the community," it does not put that analysis in doubt. Thus, such a challenge might be directed at the rather common capital offense exception in the right-to-bail provisions of state constitutions, or especially at variations thereto not so steeped in tradition, such as the constitutional provisions in a few states that go beyond the capital offense exception by including instead or as well certain named noncapital offenses or any offense punishable by life imprisonment. So the argument goes, since *Salerno* deemed it most important that the federal preventive detention statute both (i) was limited to serious offenses and (ii) as to them had careful procedures for assessing dangerousness on a case-by-case basis, these bail exception clauses (which themselves accomplish only the first of these requirements) violate the federal constitution absence procedures for making individual dangerousness assessments. But at least if the state constitutional exception is stated narrowly enough, it would appear that if (1) judicial discretion as to individual cases is preserved and (2) most of the procedural requirements highlighted in *Salerno* are followed, then (3) it is not necessary that the dangerousness inquiry be quite as focused as contemplated by the federal statute.

(f) Detention Upon Individual Finding of Dangerousness. Even if a preventive detention law requires a case-by-case determination of the defendant's dangerousness, it can be argued that there is a fundamental constitutional defect, namely, that there appears to be no simple, reliable technique for predicting which defendants are likely to be dangerous. However, the Supreme Court's decision in *Schall v. Martin* (1984), upholding a preventive detention statute for juvenile proceedings, suggests a challenge based upon this uncertainty is unlikely to prevail. The Court there declared "that from a legal point of view there is nothing inherently unattainable about a prediction of future criminal conduct," which "forms an important element in many decisions" regarding sentencing and parole and probation release and revocation. That language was relied upon in *Salerno,* discussed above, upholding the facial constitutionality of the Bail Reform Act of 1984.

This is not to suggest that all of the many state provisions of this kind to be found today would pass muster under *Salerno*, as the Supreme Court in that case recognized that any provision of this kind must meet certain substantive and procedural due process requirements. On the substantive side, the Court in *Salerno* deemed it necessary "that the government's regulatory interest in community safety * * * outweigh an individual's liberty interest," which was the case as to the federal statute because (i) "it operates only on individuals who have been arrested for a specific category of extremely serious offenses," (ii) it requires the government to "demonstrate probable cause to believe that the charged crime has been committed by the arrestee," and (iii) in addition the government "must convince a neutral decisionmaker by clear and convincing evidence that no conditions of release can reasonably assure the safety of the community or any person." As for the serious offense limitation, surely it means that a state preventive detention provision permitting denial of bail upon a finding of dangerousness with respect to *all* arrestees, without regard to the seriousness of the charge, cannot be upheld.

As for procedural due process, the Court in *Salerno* placed considerable emphasis upon the fact that "the procedures by which a judicial officer evaluates the likelihood of future dangerousness are specifically designed to further the accuracy of the determinations." Specifically enumerated in this regard were: (i) the detainee's right to counsel; (ii) his ability to testify and otherwise present information; (iii) his right to cross-examine witnesses who appear; (iv) guidance to the judicial officer in the form of a statutory list of relevant considerations; (v) the government must prove its case by clear and convincing evidence; (vi) the judicial officer must make written findings of fact and statement of reasons for detention; (vii) immediate appellate review of a detention decision. Many of the state preventive detention provisions may be vulnerable on this score, as a majority of the state detention provisions contain only some of these minimal protections.

(g) Detention for Misconduct During Release. The one form of preventive detention most likely to pass muster under the federal Constitution is that allowing revocation of pretrial release and detention until trial upon a showing that the defendant engaged in misconduct during that release. This is most obviously the case where the defendant has unlawfully tried to thwart his prosecution or conviction by such conduct as threatening, injuring, or intimidating any prospective witness, juror, prosecutor, or court officer. Notwithstanding any constitutional or statutory right to bail, a court has the inherent power to confine the defendant in such circumstances in the interest of safeguarding the integrity of its own process.

What then of the broader proposition that a defendant may have his bail revoked for any serious criminal conduct engaged in during such release? In support of such a scheme, it may argued that it lacks the defects of outright pretrial detention, where one of the main failings is the fact that the judge has no reliable indicator available by which to determine which defendants will commit further crimes, and thus it is not surprising that there exists even pre-*Salerno* authority to the effect that such a provision is constitutional. Under *Salerno*, the question is whether a requirement that the arrestee be guilty of a prior offense or be charged with committing a crime while out on parole, probation, or pretrial release obviates any need for the arrestee to be charged with an "extremely serious" crime or to be shown to be dangerous. The rationale for an affirmative answer, that the government's interest in detaining repeat criminal offenders is more significant because such individuals pose a statistically greater danger to the community upon release than do first-time offenders, weakens when the arrestee can be detained merely because he is on pretrial release rather than being on parole, probation, or having previously committed a crime. This probably means that if the defendant has been accused twice of relatively insignificant criminal conduct, this cannot be treated as a sufficient manifestation of dangerousness (though some courts permit revocation on the ground that the proper purpose of the statutory authorization is *not* protection of the public but assuring compliance with lawful orders of the court). By comparison, a statute requiring that the original charge and new conduct both be at the felony level would seem much less vulnerable.

§ 4.4 Special Situations

(a) **Capital Cases.** In 1818 the State of Connecticut adopted a constitutional provision reading: "All prisoners shall, before conviction, be bailable by sufficient sureties, except for capital offenses, where the proof is evident, or the presumption great." Since that time, forty states have adopted substantially the same clause, and it has always been generally assumed that the exception in these state constitutional provisions does not offend the Eighth Amendment. On the federal level, the Supreme Court declared in *Carlson v. Landon* (1952): "The Eighth Amendment has not prevented Congress from defining the classes of cases in which bail shall be allowed in this country. Thus in criminal cases it is not compulsory where the punishment may be death." It is less certain whether these provisions would in every instance withstand challenge on substantive or procedural due process grounds, although the chance of a successful constitutional challenge would appear to be less in those jurisdictions following the majority view that a sufficient showing of defendant's guilt of the capital offense leaves intact the discretionary power of the court to admit any defendant to bail.

In states with these provisions, legislative abolition of the death penalty has been consistently held to mean that persons charged with offenses formerly subject to capital punishment are in all cases bailable, even when the abolition of capital punishment was accompanied by legislation declaring otherwise. But there has not been agreement as to how these constitutional provisions should be applied when the legislature has provided for the death penalty but has done so in such a way that imposition of the penalty is constitutionally barred. The courts are split, depending upon whether they adopt the penalty theory or the classification theory. The former is that these constitutional provisions are based upon the strong flight urge because of the possibility of an accused forfeiting his life, and thus are inapplicable once that possibility is removed by either the legislature or the courts. The classification theory, on the other hand, is that the underlying gravity of those offenses endures and the determination of their gravity for the purpose of bail continues unaffected by the decision that the death penalty provision is unconstitutional.

Because these constitutional provisions take away the right to bail only in those capital cases where "the proof is evident or the presumption great," it is not sufficient to bring a capital case within that exception that the defendant has been charged in such a way that he could receive the death penalty. Rather, these provisions contemplate that bail should be denied when the circumstances disclosed indicate a fair likelihood that the defendant is in danger of a jury verdict of an offense punishable by death, for only in instances where such likelihood exists is his life in jeopardy and the well recognized urge to abscond present. Under the traditional grading of criminal homicide whereby the death penalty can be returned only upon a finding of guilty of murder in the first degree, this means a fair likelihood of such a verdict. But under the Supreme Court's decisions holding unconstitutional a mandatory death penalty for first degree murder but upholding the imposition of a sentence of death where the jury or judge is required to weigh statutory aggravating and mitigating circumstances, it would seem that this fair likelihood exists only if it appears likely one of the requisite aggravating circumstances is present.

Where does the burden of proof lie? One line of cases takes the view that since the defendant is entitled to bail only on application and when he so applies is trying to change the status quo, the burden is rightly on him to show that the proof is not evident or that the presumption is not great. The other and better view is that these constitutional provisions confer a right to bail except under

the limited circumstances specified and that the burden should rest
on the party relying on the exception, that is, the prosecution.
Assuming the latter approach, the next question is what probative
force the indictment has with respect to this burden. The decisions
on this issue fall into three categories: (1) the burden is on the state
to adduce some facts in addition to the indictment in order to
satisfy the court that the case against the accused meets the
constitutional requirement; (2) the indictment is *prima facie* evidence of a capital offense within the constitutional exception; and
(3) the indictment is conclusive against the allowance of bail. In
those jurisdictions permitting the institution of even capital offense
prosecutions by information rather than indictment, some courts
have ruled that the filing of the information raises such a presumption of defendant's guilt as to constitute a prima facie showing.
Such a result is inconsistent with the reasoning in *Gerstein v. Pugh*
(1975), where the Supreme Court held an information (as distinguished from an indictment) would not suffice to justify continued
custody of a defendant arrested without a warrant. As for whether
a probable cause finding by a magistrate at a preliminary hearing
should suffice, it would seem not given that it is not customary for
the defendant to present evidence at the preliminary hearing.

(b) Juvenile Cases. Because state courts have typically relied
upon juvenile code safeguards in dealing with pretrial release issues
in juvenile cases, there has for some time existed considerable
uncertainty as to what extent a constitutional right to bail exists in
this context. But under the general "fundamental fairness" approach that the Supreme Court has utilized in determining what
rights of adult defendants also apply in juvenile proceedings, it may
be concluded that there is no unqualified constitutional right to bail
for a juvenile. This is clearly reflected in the fact that the Supreme
Court, in the case of *Schall v. Martin* (1984), upheld a statutory
provision authorizing pretrial detention of an accused juvenile
delinquent based on a finding that there is a "serious risk" that the
child "may before the return date commit an act which if committed by an adult would constitute a crime." The Court, in holding
this provision conformed to the "fundamental fairness" demanded
by the due process clause, first concluded that the statute served a
legitimate state objective, "protecting the community from crime,"
deemed to be more weighty than the juvenile's countervailing
interest in freedom from restraint, which "must be qualified by the
recognition that juveniles, unlike adults, are always in some form of
custody." As for the added constitutional requirement that the
pretrial detention not constitute punishment, the Court concluded
there was "no indication in the statute itself that preventive
detention is used or intended as a punishment." *Schall* also declared that as a constitutional matter it was necessary that the

procedures afforded juveniles "provide sufficient protection against erroneous and unnecessary deprivation of liberty," deemed to be the case there, as the juvenile was entitled to a prompt adversarial determination of probable cause of a delinquent act and that the serious risk of a criminal act in the immediate future existed. Because the statute required a finding of facts and statement of reasons supporting preventive detention, the Court concluded the statute need not enumerate the specific factors upon which the juvenile court judge might rely. The Court in *Schall* also emphasized "that from a legal point of view there is nothing inherently unattainable about a prediction of future criminal conduct."

(c) During Trial. Once the defendant's trial has commenced, he is in a somewhat different posture regarding his right to be at large on bail or other form of release. As the Supreme Court recognized in *Bitter v. U.S.* (1967): "A trial judge indisputably has broad powers to ensure the orderly and expeditious progress of a trial. For this purpose, he has the power to revoke bail and to remit the defendant to custody. But this power must be exercised with circumspection. It may be invoked only when and to the extent justified by danger which the defendant's conduct presents or by danger of significant interference with the progress or order of the trial." Thus, bail may be revoked during trial where a defendant has made threats to government witnesses, or where he has engaged in obstructive misconduct during the course of the trial. But in *Bitter,* where the revocation was apparently based upon nothing more than "a single, brief incident of tardiness," there was no basis for committing the defendant to custody.

(d) After Conviction. Once the defendant's trial is completed and he has been convicted, his situation with respect to his release, even if he plans to take an appeal, changes significantly. The typical state constitutional provision guaranteeing a right to bail is limited to the time "before conviction," and this distinction is ordinarily observed in state statutes just as it is in the Federal Bail Reform Act of 1984. But the federal Act is especially strict. Pending sentence or appeal, the general rule as to a defendant who could be or has been sentenced to a term of imprisonment is that the court is to order the defendant detained unless the court finds by clear and convincing evidence that he is not likely to flee or pose a danger to the safety of any other person or the community if released under sections 3142(b) or (c). In the pending appeal situation, however, the court must also find that the appeal is not for the purpose of delay and raises a substantial question of law or fact likely to result in reversal, an order for a new trial, a sentence that does not include a term of imprisonment, or a reduced sentence less than the time served up to the point when such reduction is ordered. Because a literal reading of that provision would mean release would virtually never be available when the defendant's motion for a new trial had been denied and he was now taking an appeal, it has been construed by the courts in a less absolute fashion. Denial of bail on appeal because of an absence of a substantial question is constitutionally permissible.

The post-conviction situation is different as to a person convicted of a crime of violence, a drug offense carrying a statutory maximum sentence of 10 years or more, or an offense for which the maximum sentence is death or life imprisonment. When such a person is awaiting imposition or execution of sentence, he is to be detained unless the court finds by clear and convincing evidence that the person is not likely to flee or pose a danger to any other person or the community, and in addition one of two other events occurs. One is where the court also finds that there is a substantial likelihood that a motion for acquittal or new trial will be granted. The other is where an attorney for the government has recommended no sentence of imprisonment be imposed. But where such a person has filed an appeal or cert. petition, he is to be detained.

The United States Supreme Court first held in *McKane v. Durston* (1894) that there is no constitutional right to bail pending appeal from a conviction. The rationale is that a defendant who has been convicted and has little hope for reversal might be strongly tempted to flee, and one with greater hope for reversal might be tempted to tamper with witnesses who had been especially useful to the prosecutor so as to minimize the chances of conviction after remand. Courts have held that it is permissible for the legislature to exclude certain types of cases from judicial consideration on the question of post-conviction bail, and that it is permissible to impose conditions on post-conviction bail that might not pass muster before conviction, both of which is consistent with the generally accepted proposition that there is no federal constitutional right to bail pending appeal after conviction in a state court. But that proposition has in turn not foreclosed the holding that once a state makes provision for such bail, the Eighth and Fourteenth Amendments require that it not be denied arbitrarily or unreasonably.

(e) During Interlocutory Appeal by Prosecution. While release is a disfavored option when the defendant takes an appeal following his conviction, quite obviously such should not be the case when the defendant has *not* been convicted (and in all probability could not be convicted) because of a ruling in the defendant's favor the prosecution now seeks to challenge via an interlocutory appeal. Some jurisdictions take the position that a defendant is always entitled to be released whenever the prosecution takes such an appeal, while others utilize the same standards and procedures as apply regarding pretrial release. A few states follow an intermediate position: outright release is the strongly favored alternative, to be selected except upon a rather extraordinary showing of a need for custody.

(f) Probation or Parole Revocation. Even assuming a constitutional right to have bail set in other circumstances, it does not follow that a defendant held pending a revocation hearing for an alleged violation of probation has a right to bail. As explained in *In re Whitney* (1970): "Since a conviction has been obtained, * * * it is hardly unreasonable to use incarceration pending the revocation hearing to protect society against the possible commission of additional crimes by the probationer." The same is true of a person who is awaiting parole revocation proceedings.

(g) Material Witnesses. The federal Bail Reform Act of 1984 provides that if the testimony of a person is material in a criminal proceeding and it is shown "that it may become impracticable to secure the presence of the person by subpoena," then the release conditions otherwise provided for in that Act shall be utilized. Detention of a material witness for inability to comply with the conditions set is not allowed "if the testimony of such witness can adequately be secured by deposition, and further if detention is not necessary to prevent a failure of justice," and in such case release may be delayed "for a reasonable period of time until the deposition of the witness can be taken." In the context of increased reliance upon this authority post–9/11/01, one court has reaffirmed that the term "criminal proceedings" in the statute includes a grand jury, and that it is unobjectionable that "grand jury secrecy requires the judge to rely largely on the prosecutor's representations about the scope of the investigation and the materiality of the witness's testimony." Nearly all states have enacted similar provisions dealing with the pretrial confinement of material witnesses.

§ 4.5 Alternatives to Arrest

(a) Summons in Lieu of Arrest Warrant. Another avenue of reform in the efforts to prevent unnecessary pretrial detention, especially in minor cases, is invocation of the criminal process against a person without taking custody. One way in which this may be done is by a judicial officer issuing a summons instead of an arrest warrant, as is now authorized by the law in most jurisdictions. There is considerable variation in these laws. A few permit the magistrate to issue a summons instead of an arrest warrant only if the prosecutor so requests, while many others merely indicate that the magistrate has the option of utilizing either a warrant or a summons without in any way indicating that the latter alternative is to be preferred. Still others appear to tilt in favor of the warrant alternative by indicating that a summons may or shall be utilized only upon the finding of some specified justification. In contrast to all of these provisions are those statutes and rules of court that manifest a preference for the summons alternative, usually by asserting that a summons "shall" be utilized (at least as to lesser offenses) unless there exists a basis for concluding that one of various adverse consequences would thereby result.

Those provisions not falling into the very last category have had little impact in decreasing the number of arrests. For one thing, arrest warrants are seldom required and are seldom sought, so that the occasion for choosing between a warrant and summons rarely arises. For another, it is generally the practice (even when not required) for the magistrate to rely upon the prosecutor or police officer to ask for a summons, and such requests are seldom made. Moreover, it is unlikely that information relevant to a judicial determination of the likelihood of the person's appearance in response to a summons will be tendered to the court.

(b) Citation in Lieu of Arrest Without Warrant. Despite the success of the longstanding practice of having the police issue citations for all but the most serious traffic violations, for years there was very little movement to extend these procedures to more ordinary criminal cases. As of 1960 only four states had adopted police citation statutes that extended beyond traffic offense cases, though more recently the number has increased dramatically. Many of the relevant statutes and rules of court do not require the police to utilize the citation alternative in any particular circumstances. A great many of them do nothing more than declare that the officer is allowed either to arrest or to issue a citation for certain offenses, without any suggestion that citation is the preferred alternative. Some other provisions make issuance of a citation the disfavored alternative by setting out certain circumstances that must exist before the officer may give a citation instead of or just after making an arrest. By comparison, certain other grants of authority to utilize the citation alternative seem to encourage that alternative somewhat more by instead reciting those circumstances which, if established, would bar the citation alternative or mandate the arrest alternative. But all of the foregoing must be distinguished from the final category, that in which the statute or court rule expressly and unequivocally declares that the citation alternative "shall" be used unless certain circumstances (e.g., inability of the person to provide satisfactory identification) are present.

Because this last variety of provision is bound to have a much more profound impact in terms of ensuring that police more frequently utilize the citation alternative, the proposal has been made that what is needed in all jurisdictions is mandatory resort to the noncustody alternative in lesser cases absent unusual circumstances. The Supreme Court in *Atwater v. City of Lago Vista* (2001) declined to impose such a requirement as a matter of Fourth Amendment reasonableness, and in doing so opined that the common system in which the officer has the power to opt for "the discretionary leniency" of a citation in lieu of custodial arrest is adequate because "it is in the interest of the police to limit petty-offense arrest."

However, the situation is complicated by the fact that a warrantless arrest may and often does provide an opportunity for the officer to make a lawful search of the defendant and the surrounding area. In *U.S. v. Robinson* (1973), the Supreme Court held that a search of the person could be conducted incident to "a lawful custodial arrest," and in *Ariz. v. Gant* (2009) the Court held that the passenger compartment of an automobile may be searched incident to the "lawful custodial arrest" of an occupant when either (i) "the arrestee is unsecured and within reaching distance of the passenger compartment at the time of the search" or (ii) "it is 'reasonable to believe evidence relevant to the crime of arrest might be found in the vehicle.' " Thus, here as well it would seem that unless the right to search is somehow disentangled from the right to arrest, the need (or, in some cases, just the opportunity) to conduct a search will discourage resort to the citation alternative. A few jurisdictions have attempted to address this problem with a statutory declaration to the effect that the officer's election of the arrest-release on citation sequence does not adversely affect his authority to search.

But, as is made clear by *Knowles v. Iowa* (1998), such statutory provisions would, at best, appear to provide a basis for a search in relatively few circumstances. In *Knowles*, an officer stopped Knowles for speeding and then, pursuant to a statute authorizing but not requiring him to issue a citation in lieu of arrest for most bailable offenses, issued a citation. The officer then made a full search of Knowles' car and found a bag of marijuana. That search was upheld by the state courts on the ground that because a state statute declared that issuance of a citation in lieu of arrest "does not affect the officer's authority to conduct an otherwise lawful search," it sufficed that the officer had probable cause to make a custodial arrest. A unanimous Supreme Court reversed on the ground that the two search-incident-arrest rationales discussed in *Robinson* ("concern for officer safety" and "need to discover and preserve evidence") did not justify the search in the instant case. (*Knowles* was deemed inapplicable in *Va. v. Moore* (2008), as there the police *did* arrest defendant, albeit in violation of a state law mandating the citation alternative.)

The statute in *Knowles*, of course, was different than those alluded to previously, as the *Knowles* legislation addressed a citation-*instead-of*-arrest situation rather than an citation-*following*-arrest situation. But the rationale of *Knowles* would seem applicable in either instance, that is, in any case where a custodial arrest is lacking. This being the case, it is especially important to note that the Court in *Knowles* only passed on "the search at issue" and did not invalidate the statute the state courts had relied upon; indeed, the Court emphasized that Knowles "did not argue * * * that the statute could never be lawfully applied." As for when such a statute *might* be lawfully applied, the only possibility would seem to be the case in which the offense was one for which there *could* be evidence on the offender's person or in his vehicle. The issue there, it would seem, is whether, in the interest of not discouraging resort to the citation alternative in such cases, officers opting for the citation alternative should be given the same opportunity to discover evidence they would have by electing the more severe alternative of custodial arrest, or whether instead searches contemporaneous with use of the citation alternative should be permitted only on probable cause of finding such evidence, which will often but not inevitably be present in this kind of case.

Knowles' impact upon future use of the citation alternative is unclear. Because Iowa officers can opt for either citation or custodial arrest, they could now shift to the latter so as not to lose the search opportunities they had been afforded by the statute. But this seems unlikely; the political costs of making custodial arrest the usual choice for traffic offenses would be great, as would the cost in terms of police manpower. More likely is that the citation alternative will usually be used but that police will opt for custodial arrest on occasion when, perhaps only because of a "hunch," they want an excuse to search, apparently permissible under the *Whren v. U.S.* (1996) holding that the existence of probable cause for arrest makes any arbitrary selection of violators to be arrested irrelevant under Fourth Amendment. Another possibility is that police will attempt to circumvent *Knowles* by making searches as before, but without first manifesting any decision as to citation versus arrest, and then following productive searches with custodial arrests, so that the search can be rationalized under the *Rawlings v. Ky.* (1980) principle that a search "incident" to arrest may come before the formal making of an arrest if the grounds for arrest existed at the time the search was made.

*

Chapter 5

THE DECISION WHETHER TO PROSECUTE

Table of Sections

For additional analysis of the above topics and citations to authorities supporting their discussion in this Book, consult the authors' 7-volume *Criminal Procedure* treatise, also available as Westlaw database CRIMPROC. See the Table of Cross-References in this Book.

§ 5.1 Nature of the Decision

(a) **In General.** The charging decision, involving a determination of whether a person should be formally accused of a crime and thus subjected to trial if he does not first plead guilty, is a vitally important stage in the criminal process with serious implications for the individual involved. A decision to charge will result in the defendant's loss of freedom pending and during trial or at best release only upon financial or other conditions, and will confront him with the economic and social costs of a trial. Whatever the outcome at trial, the charge itself can be and often is damaging to reputation and imposes upon the defendant the considerable expense of preparing a defense. Charging decisions, viewed collectively, are also of obvious importance to the community. Among other things, the manner in which these decisions are made permits adjustment of the criminal justice process according to local variations in the crime problem and the community resources available to combat it.

In minor cases, most notably those involving lesser traffic offenses, this decision is commonly made exclusively by police, but even when the prosecutor does play the central role, other actors may play a significant part. The police exercise considerable influence, for the overwhelming majority of cases that reach the prosecutor are brought to his attention by police after they have made an arrest, a decision as to which they exercise vast and largely uncontrolled discretion. Another actor who may play an important part is the victim. In many locales certain crimes such as nonsupport and the passing of bad checks are unlikely to come to official attention unless reported directly to the prosecutor's office by a concerned citizen. Here again, a decision not to bring the matter before the prosecutor virtually assures no charge. While it has been asserted that the defendant and his counsel should also have some opportunity for input into the charging decision, such participation in the charging decision does not ordinarily occur on a regular basis except where the concept of a screening conference has been adopted.

As for positive influence of the victim, under the federal victims' rights statute (18 U.S.C.A. § 3771), a crime victim is granted a "reasonable right to confer with the attorney for the Government in the case," but it is nowhere specified that the conference must precede or concern the prosecutor's charging decision, and the statute goes on to specifically declare that "[n]othing in this chapter shall be construed to impair the prosecutorial discretion of the Attorney General or any officer under his direction." About half of the states have adopted constitutional or statutory provisions recognizing a right of the crime victim to "confer," "consult" or "communicate" with the prosecutor, but state courts have viewed these provisions as not limiting the prosecutor's charging discretion and not conferring upon victims any right to judicial review of the exercise of that discretion.

In most jurisdictions there are institutional checks upon the prosecutor's charging power in serious cases, so that he exercises this power affirmatively only with the concurrence of another agency. In the federal system as a Fifth Amendment requirement and in about a third of the states as a matter of state law, a felony charge must be approved by a grand jury unless the defendant has waived that right. And unless the grand jury has first acted, most jurisdictions require that a felony charge be approved by a judicial officer at a preliminary hearing, again unless the defendant has waived that protection.

(b) Evidence Sufficiency. It is not possible to state categorically how much evidence is required before the prosecutor is justified in charging a suspect with a crime, as the law does not expressly provide a distinct probability of guilt standard for the charging decision. Although the prosecutor's decision to charge is often reflected in the post-arrest issuance of an arrest warrant, and though it is clear that such a warrant may issue only upon "probable cause," it does not necessarily follow that charging would be proper on the same quantum of evidence, if for no other reason than that the prosecutor will have to consider whether his decision to charge will withstand review at the preliminary hearing and before the grand jury. As a practical matter, the prosecutor is likely to require admissible evidence showing a high probability of guilt, that is, sufficient evidence to justify confidence in obtaining a conviction.

(c) Screening Out Cases. Even when it is clear there exists evidence that is more than sufficient to show guilt beyond a reasonable doubt, the prosecutor might nonetheless decide not to charge a particular individual with a criminal offense. Such discretionary enforcement of the criminal law has traditionally been an important part of the American prosecutor's function. Whether this exercise of discretion at the charging stage is a vice or a virtue is a matter on which there is not complete agreement. It does seem fair to say, however, that something less than full enforcement of the law by the prosecutor is an absolute necessity. As one judge once noted, if every prosecutor "performed his * * * responsibility in strict accordance with rules of law, precisely and narrowly laid down, the criminal law would be ordered but intolerable." But this is not to suggest that there does not reside in the prosecutorial screening function considerable potential for abuse.

(d) Diversion. The choices for the prosecutor when making the charging decision are not merely those of prosecution or no action at all. An intermediate course, commonly referred to as deferred prosecution or pretrial diversion, may be available. Diversion is the disposition of a criminal complaint without a conviction, the noncriminal disposition being conditioned on either the performance of specified obligations by the defendant, or his participation in counselling or treatment. Typically, the effect of diversion is to stop the clock on criminal prosecution while the defendant is offered counselling, career development, education and supportive treatment services. If he participates and responds as required for a specified period of time, then the charges are dismissed without trial. But if the defendant does not meet his obligations then he may be subjected to prosecution on the deferred charge.

(e) Selection of the Charge. If the prosecutor has decided upon prosecution, there often remains the question of what the charge should be. Sometimes it is simply a matter of whether the charge should be of a greater or lesser crime—for example, felony burglary versus misdemeanor breaking and entering. This involves judgments about both evidence sufficiency (whether the greater crime can be proved at trial) and enforcement policy (whether prosecution for the greater crime would be unduly harmful to this defendant). However, sometimes the prosecutor will initially charge a defendant with a higher offense than can be proved or than would be "just," hoping to use that charge as leverage to obtain a guilty plea to a lesser crime. Sometimes the defendant's conduct will appear to violate more than one criminal statute, in which case the prosecutor will need to decide whether the defendant is to be charged with more than one offense, where the same considerations come into play. If the prosecutor ultimately decides to proceed on a lesser charge or a fewer number of charges than originally lodged against the defendant, some states require that the prosecutor consult the crime victim about such an adjustment.

§ 5.2 Discretionary Enforcement

(a) **The Prosecutor's Discretion.** The notion that the prosecuting attorney is vested with a broad range of discretion in deciding when to prosecute and when not to is firmly entrenched in American law. Prosecutors in this country have long exercised this discretionary authority, but it would be in error to assume that discretionary enforcement by prosecutors is essentially the same in all locales. The extent of and reasons for nonenforcement vary considerably from place to place, often because of factors over which the individual prosecutor has no control. It is nonetheless possible to identify the most common explanations:

(1) *Because of legislative "overcriminalization."* Included in the typical state criminal code are likely to be crimes that are over-defined for administrative convenience (e.g., the gambling statute barring *all* forms of gambling so as to confront the professional gambler with a statutory facade that is wholly devoid of loopholes); crimes that merely constitute "state-declared ideals" (e.g., the crime of adultery); and now-outdated crimes that found their way into the law because of the mood that dominated a legislature at strategic moments in the past.

(2) *Because of limitations in available enforcement resources.* No prosecutor has sufficient resources available to prosecute all of the offenses that come to his attention. To deny the authority to exercise discretion under these circumstances would be like directing a general to attack the enemy on all fronts at once. Thus, so the argument goes, the prosecutor must remain free to exercise his judgment in determining what prosecutions will best serve the public interest.

(3) *Because of a need to individualize justice.* A criminal code can only deal in general categories of conduct. Individualized treatment of offenders, based upon the circumstances of the particular case, has long been recognized in sentencing, and it is argued that such individualized treatment is equally appropriate at the charging stage so as to relieve deserving defendants of even the stigma of prosecution.

Decisions not to prosecute, when not motivated by doubts as to the sufficiency of the evidence, usually fall within one of these three broad categories. A closer look at the practice makes it possible to particularize further those situations in which prosecutors most commonly decline to prosecute. They are: (i) when the victim has expressed a desire that the offender not be prosecuted; (ii) when the costs of prosecution would be excessive, considering the nature of the violation; (iii) when the mere fact of prosecution would, in the prosecutor's judgment, cause undue harm to the offender; (iv) when the offender, if not prosecuted, will likely aid in achieving other enforcement goals, such as by acting as an informant; and (v) when the "harm" done by the offender can be corrected without prosecution.

A full appreciation of the extent of the prosecutor's power, however, requires consideration of the fact that his discretion may be exercised in the other direction. A particular individual may be selected out for prosecution notwithstanding the fact that the case is one which ordinarily would not result in an affirmative charging decision. Such selection may occur in response to press and public pressure for "law and order," to rid society of certain "bad actors" who are thought to have committed more serious crimes, and for similar reasons.

(b) Police Discretion. Discretion is regularly exercised by the police in deciding when to arrest, and such decisions have a profound effect upon prosecution policy for the simple reason that for the most part the police determine what cases come to the attention of the prosecutor. As a general matter, it may be said that the exercise of discretion by the police at the arrest stage occurs for much the same reasons as the charging discretion of the prosecutor described above. This police discretion is in a practical sense even less restricted than the prosecutor's discretion, for it is exercised at an earlier and generally less visible stage of the criminal process. But in the eyes of the law, discretion by the prosecutor is considered proper while discretion by the police is with rare exception (as in *Town of Castle Rock v. Gonzales* (2005), concluding a "well established tradition of police discretion has long coexisted with apparently mandatory arrest statutes") viewed with disfavor.

(c) Jury and Judge Discretion. The prosecutor does not function in a vacuum, and thus a decision not to prosecute is often based upon the expectation that the judge or jury would refuse to convict notwithstanding proof of guilt beyond a reasonable doubt. A full understanding of the prosecutor's discretion, therefore, necessitates an awareness of the discretion that may be exercised at the trial stage by a jury, and at a pretrial or trial stage by the judge. The jury in a criminal case has uncontrolled discretion to acquit the guilty. An empirical study has shown that juries acquit the guilty because: (1) they sympathize with the defendant as a person; (2) they apply personal attitudes as to when self-defense should be recognized; (3) they take into account the contributory fault of the victim; (4) they believe the offense is de minimus; (5) they take into account the fact that the statute violated is an unpopular law; (6)

they feel the defendant has already been punished enough; (7) they feel the defendant was subjected to improper police or prosecution practices; (8) they refuse to apply strict liability statutes to inadvertent conduct; (9) they apply their own standards as to when mental illness or intoxication should be a defense; and (10) they believe the offense is accepted conduct in the subculture of the defendant and victim.

Because there is not agreement on whether such discretionary action by a jury is a desirable safety valve in the criminal justice system or an unavoidable evil, it is a debatable point whether it is proper for the trial judge to act in a similar fashion when a case is tried before him without a jury. The law generally seems to take the view that it is not the business of a judge trying a case without a jury to act "like" the jury could be expected to act. Yet judges acquit guilty defendants for the same reasons as juries. That situation must be distinguished from one in which the judge attempts to foreclose conviction on policy rather than evidentiary or legal grounds without the defendant even standing trial. The prevailing view is that the judge does not have authority either to dismiss charges or to reduce charges merely because the prosecutor, had he been so disposed, could have dealt with the case in such a fashion at the time of charging.

(d) The "Problem" of Discretion. It is tempting to view discretionary enforcement in general and charging discretion by the prosecutor in particular as practices that need not be a matter of concern. After all, what harm can there be in the benign act of not invoking the criminal process against one who has violated an obsolete or overbroad law, one whose conduct is not serious enough to warrant the expenditure of scarce enforcement resources, or one who has committed a crime under strongly mitigating circumstances? But this vast and largely uncontrolled discretion cannot be dismissed on the notion that only acts of leniency are involved. Absent procedures that ensure that the "right" decisions are being reached regarding who should receive leniency and when, society at large and also the individuals dealt with by the criminal justice system are jeopardized. As for society at large, the fundamental point is that what is characterized as the bestowal of leniency can sometimes work contrary to the public interest in effective law enforcement. As for the individuals involved, the basic point is that the discretionary power to be lenient is an impossibility without a concomitant discretionary power not to be lenient, so that the power to be lenient is the power to discriminate. Discretion is necessary in criminal administration because of the immense variety of factual situations faced at each stage of the system and the complex interrelationship of the goals sought, and thus the issue is not discretion versus no discretion, but rather how discretion should be confined, structured, and checked.

(e) Confining the Prosecutor's Discretion. Because a major source of excess prosecutorial power is the loose drafting and overly casual definition of conduct as criminal that characterize the nation's penal codes, adequate reform of the substantive criminal law would eliminate many cases now screened out only at the option of the prosecutor. Clearly, some significant portion of the prosecutor's discretion could be rendered unnecessary if obsolete or largely unenforceable statutes were repealed. In addition, some statutes could be more narrowly drawn, again eliminating certain cases that are now screened out only at the will of the prosecuting attorney, and some statutes could be subdivided so as to reflect degrees of severity, thus providing a clear basis upon which the prosecutor could determine whether a greater or lesser charge is called for.

(f) Structuring the Prosecutor's Discretion. Three basic needs must be met before the prosecutor's charging discretion can become more structured and thus more rational. They are: (i) *The need for more information.* More detailed background information about the offender is needed so that it may be determined whether he is a dangerous or only marginal offender. In addition, most prosecutors lack sufficient information about alternative treatment facilities and programs in the community to be able to make a rational determination of whether there exists some better course than prosecution. (ii) *The need for established standards.* What is needed is for each prosecutor's office to develop a statement of general policies to guide the exercise of prosecutorial discretion, particularizing such matters as the circumstances that properly can be considered mitigating or aggravating, or the kinds of offenses that should be most vigorously prosecuted in view of the community's law enforcement needs. (iii) *The need for established procedures.* These procedures might include a "precharge conference" at which the prosecutor and defense counsel could discuss the appropriateness of a noncriminal disposition. Such a practice would make it less likely that favored defense counsel or clients will have the sole opportunity to discuss their cases with the prosecutor and receive the benefits of such exchanges, and would also provide a natural occasion for an exchange of information that might be useful to each side in deciding whether to agree on a disposition.

(g) Checking the Prosecutor's Discretion. Although the American criminal justice system has reasonably effective controls to ensure that the prosecutor does not abuse his power by prosecuting upon less than sufficient evidence, there are—as a practical matter—no comparable checks upon his discretionary judgment of whether or not to prosecute one against whom sufficient evidence exists. The prosecution function has traditionally been decentralized, so that state attorneys-general exercise no effective control over local prosecutors. Actions such as impeachment and quo warranto have only served to reach extreme cases of continued and flagrant abuse. If a specific instance of nonenforcement is challenged in the courts by way of mandamus action, the usual response is that the matter rests with the executive rather than the judicial branch of government. This is also the typical reaction if a specific instance of enforcement is challenged as being grounded in an "improper motive." Or, if a specific instance of enforcement is called into question as an arbitrary deviation from a general pattern of nonenforcement, the complaining prospective defendant can seldom overcome the several hurdles to establishing his denial-of-equal-protection claim. And while the local prosecutor is in theory responsible to the electorate, the public can hardly assess prosecution policies that are kept secret.

While it may be apparent that this is an unfortunate state of affairs, it is not so apparent how the situation might be best remedied. Some have suggested close administrative review, modeled after what is said to be the practice in Germany. But such administrative review would require a hierarchial arrangement quite different from the present structure of most state governments. Another possibility is judicial review of the prosecutor's discretionary enforcement decisions. One proposal is that decisions by a prosecutor not to prosecute be subjected to regular review by a judicial officer, who would determine whether the prosecutor's decision conformed to his pre-existing written standards. In support of such judicial screening, it is argued that it would ensure uniformity of treatment and would enhance the various benefits to be derived from giving the prosecutor's enforcement policies greater publicity. Others have suggested that judges would be unable to review prosecution policies because of the practical difficulties of evaluating the allocation of scarce prosecution resources, and would be unable to achieve meaningful review of prosecution decisions because the court would be unable to go behind the record to determine that there was an insufficient factual basis for the reasons the prosecutor has provided. The Supreme Court expressed the latter view in *Wayte v. U.S.* (1985).

(h) **Mandating the Prosecutor's Discretion.** Given the well established principle that a prosecutor possesses vast discretion in the enforcement of the criminal law, does it follow that he is obligated to exercise it? At least one court has answered in the affirmative. In *State v. Pettitt* (1980), the defendant, after his conviction for taking a motor vehicle without permission, was

charged under the habitual criminal statute pursuant to the prosecutor's "mandatory policy of filing habitual criminal complaints
against all defendants with three or more prior felonies." The
defendant, who had prior convictions for taking a motor vehicle
without permission, second degree burglary, and unauthorized use
of a vehicle, argued that "a policy which prevents the prosecutor
from considering mitigating factors is a failure to exercise discretion, which may, as in this case, result in an unfair and arbitrary
result," and the court agreed. Given the draconian nature of full
enforcement of habitual criminal laws, the result in *Pettitt* is an
appealing one. But it does not necessarily follow that full enforcement of any particular criminal statute is inevitably an abuse of
discretion. There may well be statutes that are so narrowly drawn
and that encompass conduct so serious that a prosecutor would be
justified in fully enforcing them.

§ 5.3 Challenges to and Checks Upon the Decision Not to Prosecute

(a) Mandamus. It sometimes happens that one or several
private citizens will attempt to force a reluctant prosecutor to
initiate a criminal prosecution by asking a court to issue a writ of
mandamus—an order directing the prosecutor to take affirmative
action with respect to a particular case. It is unlikely that this
effort will succeed, as mandamus is available only to compel performance of a duty owed to the plaintiff and not to direct or
influence the exercise of discretion in the making of a decision. This
means, of course, that because of the longstanding acceptance of
the notion that a prosecutor does have discretion in deciding when
to prosecute, mandamus is deemed an inappropriate remedy in this
context.

(b) Private Prosecution; Qui Tam Actions. It has sometimes been argued that private prosecution is desirable and ought
to be recognized by more jurisdictions. But the generally accepted
view is that the prosecution function should be performed by a
public prosecutor because prosecution by a private party without
authorization or approval of the prosecutor presents a serious
danger of the vindictive use of the criminal law process. Thus, even
in the face of apparent authority in the law permitting private
prosecution, it has been refused on the ground that it is desirable to
seek uniformity of prosecutorial policy. Indeed, it has often been
held that private attorneys may constitutionally be involved in a
criminal prosecution *only* if the prosecutor maintains substantial
control over the case. Even where a private citizen is allowed to file
an application for a criminal complaint, it does not necessarily
follow that the judge must issue the complaint upon a showing of

probable cause or that prosecution must be allowed to proceed over
the prosecutor's objection. A criminal prosecution brought by a
private individual must be distinguished from a *qui tam* legal
action, so called because the plaintiff in this civil action states that
he sues *as well* for the state as for himself. It is an action that may
be brought only when specifically authorized by a statute providing
a penalty for the commission or omission of a certain act and
further providing that this penalty may be recovered in a civil
action, with part of it to go to the person bringing such action and
the remainder to the state. *Qui tam* statutes were once an important part of the law enforcement scheme, but this was before the
time of organized police forces and effective conventional law enforcement procedures. They have been abolished in England, and
are seldom to be found in this country.

(c) Judicial Approval of Nolle Prosequi. An initial decision not to prosecute may be reached by the prosecutor without his
being required as a matter of course to explain his decision to or
obtain the approval of a judicial officer. The situation may change,
however, after some initial steps toward prosecution have been
taken. The common law view was that a prosecutor was free to nol
pros (from the Latin phrase *nolle prosequi*—an entry on the record
by the prosecutor declaring that he will not prosecute) even after a
formal charge was embodied in an indictment or information lodged
against the defendant. Concern over this unbridled discretion in the
prosecutor resulted in legislation or rules of court in many jurisdictions intended to restrain the nol pros power of the prosecutor.
These provisions, at a minimum, forced the prosecutor to explain
his reasons for doing so in writing, thus assuring greater visibility
of the manner in which the prosecutor acted; at a maximum they
required that he receive judicial approval to make his decision
effective. Most jurisdictions have imposed such restraints only after
formal accusation by indictment or information, but some others
apply them to all cases that have passed the preliminary hearing
stage. Doubtless the effect of these restrictions varies from place to
place, depending upon established custom, but at least in some
locales they are of little significance. A requirement of a statement
of reasons may result in boilerplate "in the interests of justice"
explanations, and where required judicial approval may be given
perfunctorily. As for the standard the judge is to apply in passing
upon the prosecutor's request where the law requires judicial
approval of a nolle prosequi, typical is the federal position that the
executive branch's exercise of its discretion with respect to the
termination of pending prosecutions should not be judicially dis-
turbed unless clearly contrary to manifest public interest.

(d) Grand Jury. Most jurisdictions permit the grand jury to
initiate prosecution by indictment even though the prosecutor

opposes prosecution. Some require only that the foreman, acting on behalf of the grand jury, sign the indictment, while others require the prosecutor's signature but view that requirement as mandating only a "clerical act" by the prosecutor. However, it takes a most unusual case for a grand jury to act as a "runaway" and indict notwithstanding the prosecutor's opposition. It is fair to conclude, therefore, that the grand jury is not a meaningful check upon the prosecutor's decisions not to prosecute.

(e) Attorney General. In most jurisdictions the state Attorney General may initiate local prosecutions in at least some circumstances. This authority ranges from power concurrent with that of the local prosecutor, to power to initiate prosecution under certain circumstances, such as at the request of certain officials or in order to enforce specified statutes. In addition, most states allow the Attorney General to intervene in a local prosecution. About half the states give the Attorney General broad authority to intervene on his own initiative, while some others allow intervention only at the direction or request of another official. In theory, at least, the power of the Attorney General to initiate a local prosecution is a check upon the local prosecutor's exercise of discretion in deciding not to undertake a prosecution. In practice, however, initiation of prosecution by Attorneys General only rarely occurs. Moreover, the great majority of interventions come at the request of the local prosecutor, though occasionally the Attorney General will prosecute where it appears the local prosecutor has failed to act because of a conflict of interest.

(f) Removal; Special Prosecutor. Various mechanisms are available in the several states by which a local prosecutor might be removed from office. Impeachment is the most common method of removal, but some states have provided for removal by the governor, removal by a court, removal on recommendation of the Attorney General, impeachment by the legislature, or recall by the electorate. The grounds for removal vary among the states, and include such causes as "malfeasance, misfeasance, nonfeasance, or nonadministration in office," "incompetency, neglect of duty or misuse of office when such incompetency, neglect of duty or misuse of office has a material adverse effect upon the conduct of such office," and "incompetency, corruption, malfeasance or delinquency in office, or other sufficient cause." Disbarment and conviction of a serious crime are other common grounds for removal. Removal proceedings are seldom utilized, and the same may be said for criminal prosecution of a prosecutor for nonfeasance, misfeasance, or malfeasance in office. The risk of such sanctions, it is fair to say, has only a limited effect upon the making of decisions not to prosecute.

Another possibility is that a prosecutor will be replaced with respect to a particular case by a special prosecutor. Considerable authority is to be found in support of the validity of an appointment of a special prosecutor under some circumstances. The need for the services of a special prosecutor may arise because the prosecuting attorney is legally precluded from proceeding due to a conflict of interest, because he is faced with a difficult case beyond his investigative and legal abilities, or because public confidence requires an "uninvolved" outsider to investigate and prosecute corruption within the judicial/governmental system. It does not appear that the special prosecutor mechanism constitutes a meaningful check upon the decision not to prosecute.

§ 5.4   Challenging the Decision to Prosecute: Equal Protection

(a) Discriminatory Prosecution. The Fourteenth Amendment to the United States Constitution prohibits any state from taking action that would "deny to any person within its jurisdiction the equal protection of the laws." Though there is no comparable language in the Constitution applicable to the federal government, it has been held that the Fifth Amendment due process clause imposes a similar restraint upon actions by the national government. This guarantee, which of course applies with respect to the enactment of laws by the legislative branches, also extends to the conduct of the executive branches in the enforcement of these laws.

Although the United States Supreme Court has never had occasion to hold that a prosecutor's charging decision was in violation of the equal protection clause, the Court has in several instances indicated that a charging decision could suffer such a defect. In *Oyler v. Boles* (1962), for example, though the Court found the defendant had not established that the state habitual criminal statute had been discriminatorily enforced against him, a distinction was drawn between the permissible "conscious exercise of some selectivity in enforcement" and an impermissible selection "deliberately based upon an unjustifiable standard such as race, religion, or other arbitrary classification." In recent years, therefore, a host of federal and state courts have entertained claims of discriminatory prosecution. These claimants have seldom prevailed because of their heavy burden to overcome the presumption of legal regularity in enforcement of the penal law by proving the three essential elements of a discriminatory prosecution claim: (1) that other violators similarly situated are generally not prosecuted; (2) that the selection of the claimant was "intentional or purposeful"; and (3) that the selection was pursuant to an "arbitrary classification."

(b) Problems of Proof. The defendant bears the ultimate burden of proof as to all three elements of a discriminatory prosecution claim. In *U.S. v. Armstrong* (1996), the Supreme Court declared that the defendant, to overcome the presumption of regularity, must present "clear evidence to the contrary." This has been read by lower courts as requiring application of the "clear and convincing evidence" standard. Some of the pre-*Armstrong* cases speak of the burden shifting to the government at some point, which has prompted some uncertainty as to when this ought to occur and exactly what kind of burden is then on the government.

If the problem is that the critical facts are often in the hands of the prosecutor rather than the defendant, an alternative approach to it is to afford the defendant more ready access to those facts. One longstanding difficulty, of course, is that prosecution policies are not reduced to writing and made available to the public. In lieu of or in addition to that information, it would be helpful to the defendant if he could require the prosecutor to give testimony concerning the reasons underlying his inaction in other cases or his affirmative action in the instant case, but courts are understandably reluctant to require prosecutors to so testify even when this might be the only way the defendant could establish his claim. Similarly, government documents about the particular case that might reveal motivation may also be very helpful, but courts are likewise reluctant to order such discovery. Here again, the result may be that the discovery will be denied even when it would be the only way the defendant could be expected to establish his claim.

Instructive on this matter of discovery is *U.S. v. Armstrong* (1996), where the Supreme Court imposed a "rigorous standard for discovery in aid of" a selective prosecution claim. The Court explained that the reasons for the presumption of regularity re the prosecutor's actions also have significance at the discovery stage, for if discovery is ordered that event itself will "divert prosecutors' resources and may disclose the Government's prosecutorial strategy." Moreover, a demanding standard re discovery was seen as "a significant barrier to the litigation of insubstantial claims." And thus the Court in *Armstrong* concluded that even to obtain discovery a defendant must first produce "some evidence tending to show the existence of the essential elements of the defense," that is, both discriminatory intent and discriminatory effect. Because of the latter element, this required threshold includes "a credible showing of different treatment of similarly situated persons."

(c) "Arbitrary Classification". In *Oyler v. Boles* (1962), the Supreme Court emphasized that "the conscious exercise of some selectivity in enforcement is not in itself a federal constitutional violation," and that to prevail on an equal protection claim a defendant would have to show that he was selected pursuant to an "arbitrary classification" such as "race" or "religion." Notwithstanding the number of appellate cases in which a discriminatory enforcement claim has been raised (usually without success), it is far from clear just what constitutes an "arbitrary classification" in this context. The lower court cases indicate that a rather limited number of classifications have been rather readily held or assumed to be "arbitrary." Included are those instances in which the selection for prosecution was based upon race, national origin, sex, political activity or membership in a political party, union activity or membership in a labor union, or more generally the exercise of First Amendment rights.

But while at least as to some of these categories it may be highly unlikely if not impossible that there could ever be a sufficient explanation for an enforcement policy so limited, it must be stressed that the classification in question cannot be looked at only in the abstract. Rather, it must be examined as it relates to legitimate law enforcement objectives. Under traditional equal protection analysis, the question that *usually* must be asked is whether there is a "rational relationship" between the classification and those objectives. (A few classifications, such as those based on race or national origin or those restricting the exercise of fundamental constitutional rights, are subjected to a more demanding strict scrutiny-compelling interest test, while a few others, such as those based on gender, are subjected to an intermediate level of scrutiny.)

Consider, for example, a classification that is or appears to be based upon the sex of the offender, sometimes challenged with respect to enforcement of the prostitution laws. With rare exception, courts have not been receptive to equal protection claims directed to enforcement practices that bring about the prosecution of female prostitutes but not their male customers. The prostitute-customer distinction, which could be made by the legislature, has been deemed appropriate in light of legitimate law enforcement interests. The use of male "decoys" to catch prostitutes without equivalent use of female "decoys" to catch persons seeking prostitutes has been upheld as a rational way to maximize the deterrent effect of the law and to utilize resources in a way most likely to lead to convictions. By comparison, if the policy was to enforce the prostitution laws against female prostitutes but not against male prostitutes, then it seems much more likely a court would conclude there was a denial of equal protection.

The broader point is that a prosecutor's enforcement classification is "arbitrary" only if people have been classified according to criteria that are clearly irrelevant to law enforcement purposes. There is certainly nothing wrong, for example, with a decision to employ the statute against only those kinds of conduct that present a threat to the central interests intended to be protected by the law. Illustrative of enforcement policies deemed to fit this description are the following: enforcement of gambling laws against bookmakers but not those placing bets with them, prosecuting draft evaders but not those who abet them, prosecuting those who violate the law against selling securities without a license only if they have sold 10 or more securities, and enforcement of the law prohibiting public officials from accepting money only against those receiving over $100. Some cases are a bit more difficult, as where it is arguable that the persons selected for enforcement were chosen because of their personal characteristics rather than the nature of their conduct. It has been held, however, that selective enforcement may be justified when a striking example or a few examples are sought in order to deter other violators, and on this basis it has been deemed permissible to proceed against the most notorious violators or the most prominent persons who are violating a particular law. Sometimes the notoriety of the person selected for prosecution is largely attributable to his public stands on issues, in which case the matter must be scrutinized more closely.

One way of looking at the issue of what constitutes an "arbitrary classification" for discriminatory enforcement purposes is to inquire whether that question is different than when it is asked whether a criminal statute employs a classification that violates the equal protection clause. Courts have sometimes upheld an enforcement classification on the ground that it would have been permissible for the legislature to draft a statute matching the actual enforcement practice, yet some decisions have held invalid enforcement policies identical to those which have been permitted when expressed in criminal statutes. Except perhaps for highly sensitive issues better left to the political-legislative process, the former is the better view. Surely if the legislature encompasses more conduct than can be reasonably reached by available enforcement resources, then those responsible for making enforcement policy must likewise be allowed to focus on those aspects of the problem that are most serious, just as the legislature could have done initially.

Another issue, essentially the reverse of that put above, is whether an enforcement scheme employed by a prosecutor is inevitably "arbitrary" whenever the applicable criminal statute could not have been lawfully drawn in a fashion that would square precisely with the enforcement practice. The answer is no. One reason that discretionary enforcement is necessary is because the inherent limitations upon the effective use of language in criminal statutes make it impossible to state exactly and completely all that is to be included and excluded. This being so, an enforcement policy is not constitutionally invalid merely because it could not have been expressed in the criminal statute without running afoul of equal protection or void for vagueness limitations. The most obvious example is the policy discussed earlier of maximizing deterrence by enforcing certain laws against notorious or prominent violators.

Yet another important issue regarding the meaning of the "rational relationship" test in this context concerns the subject matter against which the classification must appear to be rational. Is it sufficient that the classification bear a rational relationship to *some* permissible governmental purpose, or must the classification be rationally related to the purposes of the criminal law under which the defendant is charged? The answer may depend on the circumstances. Consider, for example, *U.S. v. Sacco* (1970), where the defendant objected that he was singled out, "based on his suspected role in organized crime," for investigation and prosecution under the alien registration laws. That this was the basis of selection was not disputed, yet the court unhesitantly held that it "cannot be said that that standard for selection is not rationally related to the purposes of * * * the alien registration laws." In other words, it is quite rational, considering the purposes underlying the alien registration statute, to focus upon those aliens suspected not to be law-abiding. One might well doubt whether the result would be the same were Sacco singled out on the same basis for prosecution under a generally nonenforced criminal adultery statute; there is nothing relating to the policies underlying *that* law which would explain a focus upon those suspected of organized crime. Yet, authority is to be found that would seemingly produce the same result on those facts.

(d) "Intentional or Purposeful." In *Oyler v. Boles* (1962), the Supreme Court declared that there is no equal protection violation unless "the selection was *deliberately* based upon an unjustifiable standard." In support, the Court cited *Snowden v. Hughes* (1944), wherein it is stated: "The unlawful administration by state officers of a state statute fair on its face, resulting in its unequal application to those who are entitled to be treated alike, is not a denial of equal protection unless there is shown to be present in it an element of intentional or purposeful discrimination." It is not immediately apparent, however, precisely what that language means.

In *Snowden,* the words were used in a way that implied bad faith, or awareness of the unjustifiability of the standard of selection. Given the context in which the matter arose in that case, this is not surprising. *Snowden* involved a civil suit to recover damages for infringement of civil rights, and it is understandable that the Court might not have wished to have an administrative official held personally liable in damages for a good faith mistake on his part. But this sensible notion that a nonmalicious official should not be required to pay out damages clearly has no application when a defendant in a criminal prosecution is seeking dismissal of the charges against him because of the basis upon which he was selected for prosecution. In such a case, the question ought to be whether the classification used by the prosecutor is *in fact* arbitrary, not whether the prosecutor was personally aware that it was arbitrary. This principle is unquestionably sound, but it cannot be said with assurance that it is always grasped by the courts or applied by them.

But if malice ought not be required when a discriminatory prosecution defense is interposed, then in what sense can it be said that there must be "intentional or purposeful discrimination"? The answer, which is fully consistent with the more generalized development of equal protection doctrine, is that it is not enough that a particular enforcement policy has the *effect* of singling out those who happen to be in an impermissible class; there must have been an *intent* to single out that class. A decision to prosecute black gamblers but not white gamblers would clearly be impermissible, but this is not also true of a decision to focus upon the numbers racket rather than poker in private clubs because of the former's ties to organized crime. Nor does this latter policy become arbitrary merely because it has the effect that most of the defendants prosecuted for gambling are black. By the same token, the mere fact that the latter policy would be legitimate does not mean that enforcement intended to discriminate against blacks can be "papered over" by this other reason. This highlights the significance of the earlier discussion of burden of proof, and in particular the important question of whether a defendant who has succeeded in showing a discriminatory effect should be deemed to have shifted the burden to the prosecution to establish that this effect was not deliberate but instead was an incidental consequence of a legitimate enforcement policy.

(e) Nonprosecution of Others. Many cases reflect the view that a defendant cannot prevail on a discriminatory prosecution claim unless he shows, inter alia, that the law in question is generally not enforced against others similarly situated. Whether this is a sensible limitation is a matter on which there is a difference of opinion. One view is that if a prosecutor "has a list of 1,000 known violators and reasonably exercises his discretion to enforce the law selectively by prosecuting every other person on the list, namely, even numbers," but then also prosecuted the 149th person on the list "to vent his personal prejudice against her, she has been deprived of equal protection of the laws and should be permitted to quash the prosecution." Although at least in abstract terms an appealing position, it has frequently been challenged on practical grounds. It is argued that general nonenforcement must remain an essential prerequisite of a discriminatory prosecution defense so that it cannot be too readily invoked. "Were the law otherwise all enforcement proceedings could be turned into subjective expeditions into motive without the stabilizing, objectively verifiable, element of an unequal pattern of enforcement."

§ 5.5   Other Challenges to the Decision to Prosecute

(a) **Vindictive Prosecution.** In *Blackledge v. Perry* (1974), where defendant was convicted of misdemeanor assault, exercised his right to trial *de novo*, and then was charged with felony assault based upon the same conduct, the Court held that a person "is entitled to pursue his statutory right to a trial *de novo*, without apprehension that the State will retaliate by substituting a more serious charge for the original one." The felony charge was thus barred on due process grounds. *Blackledge* emphasized that this result was necessary even absent "evidence that the prosecutor in this case acted in bad faith or maliciously," because it was the appearance of vindictiveness that would chill the right to appeal. But in *U.S. v. Goodwin* (1982), the Court declined "to apply a presumption of vindictiveness" in a pretrial setting because a realistic likelihood of vindictiveness was deemed not to exist at that stage. The Court added, however, that it did not "foreclose the possibility that a defendant in an appropriate case might prove objectively that the prosecutor's charging decision was motivated by a desire to punish him for doing something that the law plainly allowed him to do."

Does this mean that a defendant should prevail simply by showing, for example, that he was selected for charging by a vindictive prosecutor who was annoyed by the defendant's exercise of his First Amendment rights in complaining about government policy or the conduct of government officials? Where this has occurred with respect to a statutory provision not generally enforced as to those similarly situated, a prerequisite to an equal protection claim, defendants making such a showing have prevailed on a discriminatory prosecution theory. But it has been suggested that these cases truly are not so much equal protection cases as they are cases in which the defendants have been deemed entitled to relief because prosecutors have retaliated against specially protected actions by defendants, such as the exercise of First Amendment rights. If this is so, then presumably a defendant should likewise prevail upon a showing that the authorities focused upon him because of his exercise of First Amendment rights *even when* the law under which he is charged is generally enforced against others, a result the Supreme Court indicated in *Wayte v. U.S.* (1985) it did not favor.

Whether a vindictive prosecution defense this broad will ever be generally accepted by the courts is not entirely clear. There will likely be considerable resistance to such a development, primarily because of a perceived need to impose some limits on the number of criminal prosecutions in which a defendant would be entitled to put the prosecutor's motivations and intentions into issue. In the equal protection area, that objective is largely served by the requirement that the defendant show the law in question is not being enforced against others similarly situated. In the *Blackledge–Goodwin* line of vindictive prosecution cases, so the argument goes, this "stabilizing, objectively verifiable, element" is provided by the necessity of the defendant establishing an exercise of a right by him that was *both* preceded by a favorable charging decision and followed by an unfavorable one.

(b) Reneging on a Promise. In *U.S. v. Bethea* (1973), the United States attorney agreed with defendant that he would not be prosecuted for his failure to report for induction if defendant now submitted himself for induction, the defendant did so but the Army refused to induct him on moral grounds, after which defendant was prosecuted for his earlier failure to report. The defendant relied upon *Santobello v. N.Y.* (1971), holding a plea bargain enforceable against the government, but the court ruled it was not controlling here, because the "concern of *Santobello* was to protect a defendant who by pleading guilty has surrendered valuable constitutional rights in exchange for the prosecution's assurances." Under *Bethea*, then, a defendant would prevail only in limited circumstances, such as those in which the agreement is that the charges will be dropped if defendant passes a lie detector test but that otherwise defendant will plead guilty or otherwise the results of the test will be admissible against defendant at trial. The soundness of the *Bethea* rule is to be doubted, and has been rejected by those courts that have enforced prosecution agreements for charges to be dropped if the defendant passed a polygraph examination or aided a criminal investigation in some way. Sometimes this has been achieved by utilizing contract principles and focusing upon the "consideration" the defendant has supplied, and sometimes this has resulted from application of the even broader principle that a pledge of public faith is enforceable in any event. A promise not to prosecute is unlikely to be enforced if made by an official unauthorized to make such a commitment (especially if defendant's reliance can be accommodated in some other way), or if defendant failed to keep his side of the bargain (as to which the prosecutor must obtain a judicial determination unless the agreement indicates otherwise, in which case the court is limited to determining whether the prosecutor's decision in this regard was reached honestly and in good faith).

(c) Desuetude and Lack of Fair Notice. Virtually every jurisdiction has some criminal statutes that, as a practical matter, have become ineffective without any legislative or judicial action invalidating or repealing them. These statutes have been long unenforced, and are totally ignored by those charged with enforcing the law and by the public at large. But it sometimes happens that these old laws are resurrected and enforced by a prosecutor, in which case the question may arise as to whether the defendant so proceeded against can object. While there is a doctrine in the civil law called desuetude whereunder a statute is abrogated by reason of its long and continued nonuse, it is commonly assumed that the concept of desuetude has no place in American law. Such was the conclusion of the Supreme Court in *D.C. v. John R. Thompson Co.* (1953), declaring that the "repeal of laws is as much a legislative function as their enactment."

This analysis has not escaped criticism. For one thing, it has been questioned whether the prosecutor's conduct in now enforcing the long dormant law can fairly be said to be nothing more than a carrying out of the wishes of the legislative branch of government. More significant, however, for present purposes, is the argument that those prosecuted should sometimes have available a lack-of-fair-notice defense under the due process clause. The notion is that a penal enactment that is linguistically clear, but has been notoriously ignored by both its administrators and the community for an unduly extended period, imparts no more fair notice of its proscriptions than a statute that is phrased in vague terms. No case expressly recognizing such a defense has been found, although courts have occasionally suggested that given the right set of circumstances the due process lack of notice defense would prevail here.

(d) Civil Action Against Prosecutor. In the event that a defendant in a criminal case later brings a tort action for malicious prosecution against the prosecutor on the ground that the latter's decision to prosecute was improper, the action will be dismissed on the ground that the prosecutor is absolutely immune. This is the clear majority view in the state courts and is also the rule adopted by the Supreme Court for application when such a suit is brought against a federal prosecutor. This common-law immunity of a prosecutor, the Court noted in *Imbler v. Pachtman* (1976), is grounded in "concern that harassment by unfounded litigation would cause a deflection of the prosecutor's energies from his public duties, and the possibility that he would shade his decisions instead of exercising the independence of judgment required by his public trust." In *Imbler*, the Supreme Court relied upon this concern in holding that such absolute immunity also exists when a federal civil rights action is brought against a state prosecutor in federal court. The Court stressed that this did "not leave the public powerless to deter misconduct or to punish that which occurs," for the prosecutor could be criminally prosecuted for willful denial of constitutional rights and could be subjected to professional discipline. The holding in *Imbler* was confined to circumstances in which the prosecutor's activities "were intimately associated with the judicial phase of the criminal process," such as the prosecutor's actions "in initiating a prosecution and in presenting the State's case."

(e) Recoupment of Litigation Expenses. In 1997 Congress enacted legislation whereby the defendant in a federal criminal case could sometimes collect for his attorney's fees and litigation expenses, to be paid from the regular budget of the prosecuting agency. To prevail, the claimant must prove that: (1) he was not represented by assigned counsel paid for by the public; (2) he was the prevailing party; (3) the prosecution was "vexatious, frivolous, or in bad faith"; (4) the attorney's fees were reasonable; and (5) no special circumstances exist that would make such an award unjust. The most critical and difficult issue ordinarily confronted in proceedings brought under this legislation is whether there is a basis for finding the government's position to be "vexatious, frivolous, or in bad faith." The legislative history is of little help in indicating the meaning of those words in this context, except in a negative sense. For one thing, recovery is contemplated in a broader range of cases than those that would amount to the common law tort of malicious prosecution, which requires the acquitted defendant to prove there was no probable cause, as Congress indicated recovery under this legislation would not be foreclosed by a grand jury finding of probable cause to support the indictment. On the other hand, Congress clearly intended to impose a more demanding standard than the Equal Access to Justice Act, authorizing recoupment against the government in civil cases unless the government shows its position was "substantially justified," which has been interpreted as referring to a "reasonable basis in law and fact."

§ 5.6 Challenges to the Decision to Forego or Terminate Diversion

(a) The Diversion Process. For years, individual prosecutors have in a very informal and often haphazard way permitted diversion in some circumstances, agreeing not to proceed with prosecution of a defendant if he in return makes restitution to the victim or does some other act. Of primary concern here, however, is the kind of diversion that is now becoming quite common: a formalized procedure authorized by legislation or court rule whereby persons who are accused of certain criminal offenses and meet preestablished criteria have their prosecution suspended for a three month to one year period and are placed in a community-based rehabilitation program, after which the case is dismissed if the conditions of the diversion referral are satisfied. In the earlier and informal days of pretrial diversion, it was perceived as just another aspect of the prosecutor's discretion, meaning that the prosecutor's decisions on when to divert and when to terminate a diversion were largely uncontrolled. That is still the case in some jurisdictions, although there is a noticeable trend toward limiting the prosecutor's discretion in these respects as diversion programs become more formalized. In several states, a prosecutor contemplating diversion must consult with the crime victim on the matter.

(b) Statutory Standards for Diversion. One consequence of the greater attention now given to the pretrial diversion alternative is that efforts have been made to identify criteria by which to select those defendants who are the most likely candidates for diversion. Sometimes these criteria are set out in statutes or rules of court. It has occasionally been claimed that such provisions are unconstitutional attempts to limit the prosecutor's discretion, barred by the separation of powers doctrine, but such challenges have been rejected where the legislation does not destroy or unreasonably restrict the prosecutor's discretion. If the statute provides that the courts are to administer the program or if the program was adopted by rule of court, then it is clear that the setting of standards does not encroach upon the executive power because then a judicial function is involved. If a particular defendant was made ineligible for a pretrial diversion program by virtue of certain criteria in a statute or rule of court, a defendant might attack those criteria on equal protection grounds. Except in extraordinary circumstances, however, it is unlikely that such a challenge will prevail. In *Marshall v. U.S.* (1974), for example, the Supreme Court held there was no equal protection denial in the statutory exclusion from the treatment alternative under the Narcotic Addict Rehabilitation Act of those persons with two prior felony convictions. The Court reasoned that it was not "unreasonable or irrational for Congress to act on the predicate * * * that a person with two or more prior felonies would be less likely to adjust and adhere to the disciplines and rigors of the treatment program and hence is a less promising prospect for treatment than those with lesser criminal records."

(c) Decision Not to Divert. A decision by the prosecutor not to divert a particular defendant and instead to proceed with prosecution on the pre-existing charge is, in essence, a decision to prosecute, and thus at a minimum is subject to challenge in the same way as any other decision to prosecute. One possibility, therefore, is that a nondiversion decision will be contested as a discriminatory decision to prosecute violating the equal protection clause. While defendants seldom are successful in bringing such a challenge, if it is brought within the context of a formalized diversion program the defendant's chances may be somewhat better because the established criteria in a statute, rule of court or a prosecutor's policy statement may help the defendant show he was singled out on an arbitrary basis. Another possible basis upon which to challenge a decision to charge is that the prosecution is vindictive or has the appearance of vindictiveness. As earlier noted, no presumption of vindictiveness exists in a pretrial setting, and thus in such circumstances the defendant cannot prevail without proving the existence of a vindictive motive. The chances of a defendant carrying that burden would seem somewhat greater when the prosecution does not square with established diversion criteria.

Though it has been argued that the decision by the prosecutor not to divert a particular defendant should not be subject to routine judicial review, and though it seems clear that such a decision does not implicate rights entitling the defendant to a hearing as a matter of course, as a general matter it is fair to say that such decisions, at least when they occur within the context of a formalized diversion program, are likely to be subject to somewhat greater judicial scrutiny than the usual decision to charge. The extent to which this is so, however, will depend upon the exact nature of the diversion program. A program created by court rule is likely to be construed to includes judicial power to interpret and enforce the rules. Under such a scheme an "abuse of discretion" standard is likely to be used upon review, which prompts somewhat closer scrutiny than under the equal protection arbitrariness test. Greater court control is also likely if a diversion program is interpreted to be an aspect of the court's sentencing function or if the applicable statute expressly assigns responsibility for the program to the courts.

(d) Decision to Terminate by Prosecution. If a defendant is accepted into a diversion program, the operating assumption is that if he carries out his responsibilities under the program the charges against him will be dropped. But this gives rise to the question of how free the prosecutor is, on his own, to decide that the "deal is off" or to conclude that the defendant has defaulted in some respect. In *U.S. v. Bethea* (1973), which might be viewed as an unusual type of diversion case, the prosecutor promised that he would drop the charges against defendant for failure to report for induction in the Army if defendant submitted himself for induction. The defendant complied, but the Army rejected him on moral grounds, after which the prosecutor proceeded with the prosecution. Relying upon the plea bargaining case of *Santobello v. N.Y.* (1971), defendant tried to enforce the agreement in court, but the court ruled the prosecutor's decision was "not reviewable here" because, unlike the situation in *Santobello,* the defendant had not "surrendered valuable constitutional rights in exchange for the prosecution's assurances." But there is much to be said for the proposition that such contract law analysis is inappropriate here and that the government should be required to keep its word without regard to whether the defendant has supplied "consideration." And even if the premise underlying *Bethea* is sound, it would seem not to govern the more typical diversion case, where by entering into the deferred prosecution agreement the defendant waived his right to a speedy trial.

The defendant cannot complain about now being subjected to prosecution if he failed to carry out his part of the bargain, but whether there has been such a failure in a particular case may not be entirely clear. This being so, the question naturally arises as to how the prosecutor is to make that decision and whether the decision is subject to review. One view is that the prosecutor should have the discretionary authority to determine whether the offender is performing his duties adequately under the agreement and, if he determines that the offender is not, to reinstate the prosecution. Another is that the defendant is entitled to a hearing before the prosecutor to determine whether defendant violated a material term of the agreement and, if so, whether the prosecution should be reinstated or the agreement modified, and to judicial relief if the record does not support the prosecutor's decision to reinstate the prosecution. Indeed, it would seem that some sort of hearing is ordinarily required in this context as a matter of procedural due process, for revoking a person's diversion status is quite similar to parole revocation and probation revocation, as to which the Supreme Court mandated hearings in *Morrissey v. Brewer* (1972) and *Gagnon v. Scarpelli* (1973).

§ 5.7   Challenges to the Charge Selection

(a) **Duplicative and Overlapping Statutes.** Sometimes a defendant's challenge to a prosecutor's charge selection is directed to the statutory scheme under which the prosecutor acted, as when the defendant claims that the legislature has bestowed unnecessary discretion upon the prosecutor by defining the same criminal conduct in two different statutes carrying different penalties. Such a challenge reached the Supreme Court but was rejected by a unanimous Court in *U.S. v. Batchelder* (1979). The defendant in *Batchelder* was convicted under a statute making it a crime for various persons, including one who "has been convicted in any court of a crime punishable by imprisonment for a term exceeding one year," to "receive any firearm * * * which has been shipped or transported in interstate or foreign commerce." He objected to his five year prison term, the maximum under this provision, because another statute carrying a two year maximum covers any person, among others, who "has been convicted by a court of the United States or of a State or any political subdivision thereof of a felony * * * and who receives, possesses, or transports in commerce or affecting commerce * * * any firearm."

In response to defendant's vagueness objection, the Court acknowledged that lack of fair notice as to the potential punishment might well violate due process, but concluded that the provisions at issue were not deficient because, though they created "uncertainty as to which crime may be charged and therefore what penalties may be imposed, they do so to no greater extent than would a single statute authorizing various alternative punishments." As for the Court of Appeals' concern that the legislative redundancy left the prosecutor with "unfettered" discretion, the Court responded that

> there is no appreciable difference between the discretion a prosecutor exercises when deciding whether to charge under one of two statutes with different elements and the discretion he exercises when choosing one of two statutes with identical elements. In the former situation, once he determines that the proof will support conviction under either statute, his decision is indistinguishable from the one he faces in the latter context. The prosecutor may be influenced by the penalties available upon conviction, but this fact standing alone does not give rise to a violation of the Equal Protection or Due Process Clauses.

As for the defendant's claim the statute amounted to an impermissible delegation of congressional authority, the *Batchelder* Court concluded that because the provisions at issue "plainly demarcate the range of penalties that prosecutors and judges may seek and impose," this meant "the power that Congress has delegated to those officials is no broader than the authority they routinely exercise in enforcing the criminal laws."

In assaying *Batchelder*, it is useful to think about three types of situations in which a defendant's conduct may fall within two statutes. They are: (1) where one statute defines a lesser included offense of the other and they carry different penalties (e.g., whoever carries a concealed weapon is guilty of a misdemeanor; a convicted felon who carries a concealed weapon is guilty of a felony); (2) where the statutes overlap and carry different penalties (e.g., possession of a gun by a convicted felon, illegal alien or dishonorably discharged serviceman is a misdemeanor; possession of a gun by a convicted felon, fugitive from justice, or unlawful user of narcotics is a felony); (3) where the statutes are identical (e.g., possession of a gun by a convicted felon is a misdemeanor; possession of a gun by a convicted felon is a felony). The Court in *Batchelder* had before it a situation falling into the second category, but seems to have concluded that the three statutory schemes are indistinguishable for purposes of constitutional analysis. But while the first of the three is certainly unobjectionable, the third is highly objectionable. It is likely to be a consequence of legislative carelessness, as there is nothing at all rational about this kind of statutory scheme, which provides for different penalties without *any* effort whatsoever to explain a basis for the difference, and thus confers discretion that is totally unfettered and totally unnecessary. And thus the Court in *Batchelder* is less than convincing in reasoning that this third category is unobjectionable simply because in other instances, falling into the first category, the need for discretionary judgments by the prosecutor has not been and cannot be totally eliminated.

Just how broad the *Batchelder* holding is in other respects is not entirely clear. Of particular importance is the question of whether more dramatic or more certain disparities between the sentences allowed or required under the two statutes at issue makes a difference. In response to the Court of Appeals' objection that the prosecutor was given unfettered discretion in "selection of which of two penalties to apply," the Supreme Court answered that the government had not been allowed "to predetermine ultimate criminal sanctions" but instead had simply enabled "the sentencing judge to impose a longer prison sentence," for the prosecutor's choice of the statute that allowed imprisonment "not more than five years" rather than the one providing for imprisonment "not more than two years" had simply added to the judge's sentencing discretion. But what if, for example, one statute permitted imprisonment up to ten years and the other made ten years the mandatory minimum? In such a case, where the prosecutor actually makes a sentencing decision without either sentencing information or expertise in sentencing, there is more force to the equal protection argument. With the advent of strict sentencing guidelines and the increased use of mandatory minimum sentences, prosecutors virtually dictate the punishment for a given defendant when they select the charge to prosecute, but courts, relying on *Batchelder*, have nonetheless refused to restrain the discretion of prosecutors over charge selection.

(b) Discriminatory Charge Selection. Even if the statutory scheme whereunder the prosecutor selected the charge is not objectionable, the defendant might nonetheless claim that the seriousness of the charge or number of charges lodged against him are the

result of discriminatory enforcement. In *U.S. v. Batchelder* (1979),
the Court expressly noted that the prosecutor's conduct in selecting
the charge is "subject to constitutional constraints," in particular
the equal protection clause's prohibition upon "selective enforcement 'based upon an unjustifiable standard such as race, religion,
or other arbitrary classification.'" As for exactly what must be
shown to make out an equal protection claim, what was said on this
matter earlier regarding the decision to charge is generally applicable in this context as well. Here, as there, it is extremely difficult to
make out a successful equal protection claim.

(c) Vindictive Charge Selection. A defendant who cannot
make out an equal protection claim might nonetheless, given the
right sequence of events, prevail on a due process vindictiveness
theory under *Blackledge v. Perry* (1974). There, defendant was
convicted in district court of misdemeanor assault, exercised his
right to trial de novo in the superior court, and was then charged
with the felony of assault with a deadly weapon with intent to kill.
Relying upon *N.C. v. Pearce* (1969), holding that due process
prohibits a judge from imposing a more severe sentence upon
retrial for the purpose of discouraging defendants from exercising
their statutory right to appeal, defendant claimed the felony charge
deprived him of due process. The Supreme Court agreed:

> There is, of course, no evidence that the prosecutor in this
> case acted in bad faith or maliciously in seeking a felony
> indictment against Perry. The rationale of our judgment in the
> *Pearce* case, however, was not grounded upon the proposition
> that actual retaliatory motivation must inevitably exist. Rath-
> er, we emphasized that "since the fear of such vindictiveness
> may unconstitutionally deter a defendant's exercise of the right
> to appeal or collaterally attack his first conviction, due process
> also requires that a defendant be freed of apprehension of such
> a retaliatory motivation on the part of the sentencing judge."
> We think it clear that the same considerations apply here.
> * * * A person convicted of an offense is entitled to pursue his
> statutory right to a trial *de novo,* without apprehension that
> the State will retaliate by substituting a more serious charge
> for the original one, thus subjecting him to a significantly
> increased potential period of incarceration.

Because the Court in *Blackledge* did not require proof of
"actual retaliatory motive," the defendant there prevailed merely
by showing that he exercised a "right" and that this was followed
by "a more serious charge" by the same prosecutor. The right in
Blackledge was the right to appeal and the more serious charge was
lodged after he had been once tried and convicted, but lower courts
often took the same approach when the defendant's exercise of the
right and the prosecutor's escalation of the charge all occurred in a

pretrial setting. However, the Supreme Court rejected such an extension of *Blackledge* in *U.S. v. Goodwin* (1982). There, defendant was charged with several misdemeanor and petty offenses that were scheduled for trial before a federal magistrate until defendant exercised his right to have them tried by jury in district court. The case was accordingly transferred to another prosecutor, who upon review of it obtained a felony indictment. The defendant's subsequent felony conviction was overturned on appeal on the theory that the more serious charge was barred under *Blackledge* even absent proof of actual vindictiveness. The Supreme Court disagreed and reversed, concluding that a presumption was "not warranted in this case" because actual vindictiveness was so unlikely on these facts. One major consideration, the Court explained, was "the timing of the prosecutor's action in this case," in that "in a pretrial setting * * * the prosecutor's assessment of the proper extent of prosecution may not have crystallized." A second consideration was the "nature of the right asserted" by the defendant, in that, as "compared to the complete trial *de novo* at issue in *Blackledge,* a jury trial—as opposed to a bench trial—does not require duplicative expenditures of prosecutorial resources before a final judgment may be obtained," and thus provides "no reason" for prosecutorial vindictiveness. It thus appears unlikely that the *Blackledge* prophylactic rule has any application whatsoever in a pretrial setting.

In a case falling within *Blackledge,* where again the defendant is not obligated to prove actual vindictiveness, should the prosecutor be allowed to make some showing that there was a valid reason for his "adjustment" of the charges against the defendant? Yes, the Supreme Court later indicated by asserting that "the *Blackledge* presumption is rebuttable" and "could be overcome by objective evidence justifying the prosecutor's action." Three positions have emerged as to what showing by the prosecutor will suffice: (1) that the prosecutor merely needs to present a nonvindictive reason; (2) that the prosecutor must dispel any appearance of prosecutorial vindictiveness; and (3) that the prosecutor must come up with an objective explanation for his actions. The virtue of the third approach is that it (a) takes account of the due process value stressed in *Blackledge* that defendants be "freed of apprehension of such a retaliatory motivation" by the prosecutor; (b) is a realistic way to police vindictiveness, for a determination of actual motivation (as the Court said in *Pearce*) would "be extremely difficult to prove in any individual case"; and (c) allows the judge to avoid the Hobson's choice of either allowing the extra charge or making an explicit finding of prosecutorial bad faith.

In any event, the situation is quite different in a case governed by *Goodwin* rather than *Blackledge,* for the Court in the former case said that when the "presumption of vindictiveness" is not applicable it is then necessary for the defendant to "prove objectively that the prosecutor's charging decision was motivated by a desire to punish him for doing something that the law plainly allowed him to do." The Court made it quite clear that it would be most difficult for the defendant to meet this burden.

(d) Reneging on a Promise. A prosecutor's decision as to the level of the charge or the number of charges may be challenged on the ground that in so proceeding the prosecutor is reneging on a binding promise, as where defendant was improperly prosecuted for manslaughter in violation of an agreement with the state that if he admitted the conduct the charge would instead be reduced to motor vehicle homicide. The issues that can arise in this context are essentially the same as those discussed earlier in § 5.5(b).

Chapter 6

THE PRELIMINARY HEARING

Table of Sections

> For additional analysis of the above topics and citations to authorities supporting their discussion in this Book, consult the authors' 7-volume *Criminal Procedure* treatise, also available as Westlaw database CRIMPROC. See the Table of Cross-References in this Book.

§ 6.1 Functions of the Preliminary Hearing

(a) Multiple Functions. The preliminary hearing (also referred to as the "preliminary examination," "probable cause hearing," and "bindover hearing") was an early addition to the American criminal justice process, designed to provide a fairly prompt independent review of the sufficiency of the evidence supporting the prosecution's decision to charge. At that time, there was no requirement of a *Gerstein* review of a warrantless arrest (see § 1.2(d)), and the time span between arrest and grand jury review of the decision to charge could be quite extensive. As the preliminary hearing developed over the years, it came to perform several additional functions (commonly described as "incidental" or "ancillary") that often were of value to the defense. A critical legal issue today is whether those other functions (discussed below) will be taken into account by courts in shaping the procedures of the preliminary hearing and the remedies available where preliminary hearing errors are consider in a post-indictment or post-conviction setting. See e.g., § 6.4(a), (e). Whether or not recognized in judicial decisions, those other functions play a very significant role in the defense decision as to whether to waive the preliminary hearing. They explain, in particular, why defense counsel will often insist upon a hearing even though the preliminary hearing magistrate obviously will find the evidence sufficient to support the charge.

(b) Screening. The preliminary hearing is a judicial proceeding, commonly conducted by a magistrate, and generally available only in felony cases. At that proceeding, the prosecution in an open and adversary hearing must establish that there is sufficient evidence supporting its charge to "bind the case over" to the next stage in the process (either review by the grand jury or the filing of an information in the trial court). In determining whether the prosecution has made such a showing, the magistrate judge provides an independent screening of the prosecution's decision to charge. Indeed, most courts view this screening objective as the sole legally cognizable purpose of the preliminary hearing. The independent review by the magistrate is said "to prevent hasty, malicious, improvident, and oppressive prosecutions, * * * to avoid both for the defendant and the public the expense of a public trial, and to save the defendant from the humiliation and anxiety involved in public prosecution."

(c) Discovery. In meeting the evidentiary standard for a bindover, the prosecutor will necessarily provide the defense with some discovery of the prosecution's case. The defendant may obtain even more discovery by cross-examining the prosecution's witnesses at the hearing and by subpoenaing other potential trial witnesses to testify as defense witnesses at the hearing. The extent of the discovery obtained in this manner will depend upon several factors, including: (1) whether the prosecution can rely entirely on hearsay reports and thereby sharply limit the number of witnesses it presents; (2) whether, even assuming hearsay cannot be used, the bindover standard may be satisfied by the presentation of a minimal amount of testimony on each element of the offense; (3) whether, notwithstanding the ease with which the standard is met, the prosecution follows a regular practice of presenting most of its evidence; (4) whether the defendant is limited, both in cross-examination and in the calling of witnesses, to direct rebuttal of material presented by the prosecution; and (5) whether limited discovery procedures apply to the preliminary hearing or can be made applicable to the preliminary hearing at the discretion of the magistrate (in particular, whether the prior recorded statements of prosecution witnesses will be available for cross-examination of those witness).

In many jurisdictions, the positions taken on as to these factors combine to make preliminary hearing discovery quite limited, but in other jurisdictions, contrary positions produce a preliminary hearing that gives the defense a fairly good preview of the prosecution's case. Whether preliminary hearing discovery is narrow or broad, its importance to the defense will depend in large part on how that discovery compares to what is available under the jurisdiction's pretrial discovery. Another relevant consideration will be whether the defendant is willing to bear the tactical costs that may be incurred in utilizing certain tools of preliminary hearing discovery (e.g., the possible creation of adverse testimony which may be used by the prosecution at trial).

(d) Future Impeachment. Extensive cross-examination of prosecution witnesses at the preliminary hearing may be of value to the defense even though there is little likelihood of successfully challenging the prosecution's showing of evidentiary sufficiency and little to be gained by way of discovery. This is because, as the Supreme Court has noted, "the skilled interrogation of witnesses [at the preliminary hearing] by an experienced lawyer can fashion a vital impeachment tool for use in cross-examination of the State's witnesses at the trial." *Coleman v. Ala.* (1970) In many instances, witnesses are more likely to make damaging admissions or contradictory statements at the preliminary hearing because they are less thoroughly briefed for that proceeding than they are for trial. Also, with respect to some witnesses, the more they say before trial, the more likely that there will be some inconsistency between their trial testimony and their previous statements. Arguably, the jury may view such inconsistencies as more damaging to the witness' credibility when the inconsistency is with preliminary hearing testimony, as opposed to prior statements given to the police, since the preliminary hearing testimony was given under oath in a judicial setting. Moreover, in some jurisdictions, the use of the inconsistent statement is not limited to impeachment; it may be used as well as substantive evidence. On the other hand, cross-examination designed to lay the foundation for future impeachment carries with it certain tactical dangers for the defense, including educating the prosecution and the witness as to weaknesses in the witness' testimony.

(e) The Perpetuation of Testimony. Preliminary hearing testimony traditionally has been admitted at trial as substantive evidence, under the "prior testimony" exception to the hearsay rule, where the witness is "unavailable" to testify at trial (e.g., the witness has died, the witness is now beyond the reach of the subpoena, or the witness exercises a privilege which exempts the witness from testifying). Thus, the hearing perpetuates the testimony of witnesses. For reasons discussed in § 6.4(d), the defense rarely will have its own witnesses testify at the preliminary hearing. Accordingly, the perpetuation of testimony is of practical significance primarily as it relates to prosecution witnesses, and the possibility of perpetuation tends to by viewed by the defense as a negative feature of the hearing.

Cal. v. Green (1970) upheld the constitutionality of admitting the preliminary hearing testimony of an unavailable witness (there a witness assumed unavailable due to a lapse of memory). In finding that preliminary hearing testimony was well within the prior testimony exception, the *Green* Court noted: "[the] preliminary hearing testimony [of the now-unavailable witness] * * * had already been given under circumstances closely approximating those that surround the typical trial. [The witness] was under oath; [the defendant] was represented by counsel—the same counsel in fact who later represented him at the trial; [the defendant] had every opportunity to cross-examine the witness as to his statement; and the proceedings were conducted before a judicial tribunal, equipped to provide a judicial record of the hearing." A few state courts have disagreed with the *Green* conclusion as a matter of state law. They have concluded that the special restrictions their states place on cross-examination at the preliminary hearing precludes application of the prior testimony exception. Other state courts, although following *Green*, have suggested that defense may preclude application of the exception by showing that defense counsel in the particular case lacked information that would have altered the entire character of the cross-examination.

Although *Green* was uniformly read by lower courts as focusing on the defense opportunity to cross-examine rather the exercise of that authority, *Ohio v. Roberts* (1980) raised the possibility that *Green* could be limited to situations in which the opportunity to cross-examine had been extensively utilized. However, *Crawford v. Wash.* (2004), which reshaped the governing standard under the confrontation clause (see § 16.4(a)), in speaking to the admissibility of "prior trial or preliminary hearing testimony," referred only to "defendant [having] had an adequate opportunity to cross-examine."

(f) Other Functions. In a particular jurisdiction the preliminary hearing may be utilized to serve other incidental functions, such as to gain reduction of bail or other terms of pretrial release. This is particularly true where bail is set at the initial appearance largely on the basis of a schedule tied to the offense charged, and the preliminary hearing provides the magistrate court with its first extensive examination of the facts of the individual case. The preliminary hearing also may serve as an integral part of the plea bargaining process, particularly where negotiations have been undertaken prior to the hearing. The hearing may then provide a valuable "educational process" for the defendant who is not persuaded by his counsel's opinion that the prosecution has such a strong case that a negotiated plea is in the defendant's best interest. The preliminary hearing also may be utilized to establish mitigating circumstances that can then be presented at sentencing through the preliminary hearing transcript.

§ 6.2 Defendant's Right to a Preliminary Hearing

(a) The Federal Constitution. In *Hurtado v. Cal.* (1984), the Supreme Court held that the Fifth Amendment guarantee of prosecution by grand jury indictment was not a fundamental right applicable to the states through the due process clause of the Fourteenth Amendment. The procedure challenged in that case provided for charging by prosecutor's information rather than by indictment, but it also required a magistrate's determination of probable cause at a preliminary hearing. In *Lem Woon v. Or.* (1913), however, the Court was faced with a procedure permitting direct filing of an information without "any examination of commitment by a magistrate * * * or any verification other than [the] prosecutor's official oath." A unanimous Supreme Court held that the lack of a preliminary hearing caused no due process difficulties. Having held earlier in *Hurtado* that a grand jury indictment was not required, the Court was "unable to see upon what theory it can be held that an examination or the opportunity for one, prior to the formal accusation by the district attorney, is obligatory upon the States." The Court has continued to adhere to the *Lem Woon* holding, and in *Gerstein v. Pugh* (1975), the Court rejected the contention that a preliminary hearing is required by the Fourth Amendment. Though the Court in *Gerstein* did hold that a reasonably prompt "judicial determination of probable cause [is] a prerequisite to extended restraint on liberty following [a warrantless] arrest," it concluded this could be done in a nonadversary proceeding (as opposed to a preliminary hearing).

Though the Constitution does not require that the defendant be afforded a preliminary hearing, once a jurisdiction provides for a preliminary hearing, it may not then restrict the defendant's right to that hearing in a manner that would violate constitutional protections. Thus, *Coleman v. Ala.* (1970) held that a state cannot grant defendants a right to a preliminary hearing and then refuse to appoint counsel to represent an indigent defendant at that hearing. See § 6.4(a). So too, though prosecutors may control the availability of the preliminary hearing (see subsection (b)), they may not engage in discrimination that would violate the equal protection clause in determining which defendants receive a preliminary hearing.

(b) The Federal Practice. In the federal system, the Fifth Amendment requires grand jury screening (unless waived) in all felony cases. Federal law also provides for a preliminary hearing, but federal courts from the outset held that preliminary hearing screening was subordinate to grand jury screening. Thus, where a grand jury indictment was issued prior to the time set for the preliminary hearing, courts held that the defendant's right to a hearing was "mooted." The return of the indictment established probable cause, so there was nothing left for the preliminary hearing magistrate to decide. The Federal Rules of Criminal Procedure subsequently incorporated this analysis. Federal Rule 5.1(a) requires a preliminary hearing for a felony prosecution, but then recognizes an exception where the "defendant is indicted." That exception allows the prosecutor to "bypass" the preliminary hearing by simply obtaining a grand jury indictment prior to the scheduled date of the hearing.

At one time, many U.S. attorneys could not present charges to grand juries until several weeks after arrest and preliminary hearings were fairly common. Today, however, grand jury screening generally is available within the time frame allowed for a preliminary hearing, and federal prosecutors tend to follow a practice of uniformly bypassing the preliminary hearing by obtaining a prior indictment.

(c) Indictment States. Eighteen states, as in the federal system, require prosecution by indictment (unless waived) for all felonies. All of these "indictment states" also have statutes or court rules granting the defendant a right to a preliminary hearing within a specified period after his arrest. The common pattern in these jurisdictions is to allow bypassing without restriction, as in the federal system. The use of bypassing varies considerably, however, from one indictment state to another, and often from one prosecutorial district to another within a state. Districts range from those in which bypassing is the standard practice and preliminary hearings are reserved for exceptional cases to those in which the standard practice is to have preliminary hearing review first and then grand jury review, with bypassing limited to exceptional cases.

Where prosecutors ordinarily prefer to bypass, and preliminary hearings are the exception to the general rule, the decision not to bypass is usually the product of one of the following circumstances: (1) the need to perpetuate the testimony of a witness who might well be unavailable at trial; (2) some special reason for putting a prosecution witness to the test of testifying in public; (3) promoting the victim's interest in pursuing the matter by presenting it in a public forum; (4) gaining the defense perspective as to the events involved where there is some uncertainty as to what actually happened and the defense has indicated a willingness to present its side of the story at the preliminary hearing; (5) gaining a further identification of the suspect by having the victim make that identification at the hearing; and (6) promoting public confidence in a sensitive prosecutorial decision by having the evidence presented in a public forum and the decision to proceed ratified by a magistrate (or if the case is likely to be dismissed, by inviting dismissal in an open proceeding rather than a grand jury proceeding, where the prosecutor might be accused of having "dumped" the case due to political pressures).

Where the common practice is to go forward with the preliminary hearing, approaches vary in identifying those exceptional cases in which mooting will be utilized. Uniformly, the indictment will come first (with the preliminary hearing thereby precluded) on those charges that are developed through a grand jury investigation. Indeed, the indictments in such cases are often issued even before the defendant is arrested. The indictment will also come before arrest where the defendant is a fugitive or outside the jurisdiction. Beyond this, prosecutors differ as to the need for further exceptions. Some will bypass in particular cases or particular types of cases in which they find special justification for limiting the number of instances in which the victim will be forced to testify in public. Thus, a prosecutor's office may regularly bypass in all sex offense prosecutions. Some prosecutors will bypass where the preliminary hearing process would be protracted due to the number of exhibits or witnesses or the number of separate hearings that would have to be held for factually linked defendants. Thus, where a single agent is the key witness on a number of separate drug buys, the prosecutor may go directly to the grand jury (where the agent can testify as to all of the drug buys in a single presentation) rather than have the agent be forced to testify at each of the separate preliminary hearings that the individual defendants would demand. Finally, some prosecutors will bypass where they judge the discovery inherent in a preliminary examination to be too costly under the circumstances of the particular case.

(d) Information States. Almost two-thirds of the states permit felony prosecutions to be brought by either information or indictment (although several in this group allow only for indictments for capital or life-sentence felonies, see § 7.1(e)). These states are commonly described as "information states" (although technically they are "option" states) because the overwhelming choice of prosecutors is to use the information alternative. Almost all of these states also provide for a preliminary hearing, and all but a handful require a preliminary hearing bindover (or waiver) as a prerequisite to prosecution by information.

In several information states, the possibility of bypassing the preliminary hearing by first obtaining an indictment is precluded. Some have eliminated the indicting grand jury and others require a preliminary hearing even after an indictment has issued. The vast majority of the information states, however, hold open the possibility of bypassing the preliminary hearing by obtaining an indictment prior to the scheduled hearing. While there are occasional districts in information states that make frequent use of bypassing, the far more common patterns are either (1) never bypassing or (2) bypassing in very limited group of cases, as described in § 7.1(f).

A handful of information states accept what is sometimes described as the "direct filing" of an information (i.e., the prosecutor may file the information in the trial court without first obtaining a preliminary hearing bindover or a defense waiver of that screening). Some of these states have abolished the preliminary hearing. Others provide for a preliminary hearing but allow a prosecutor to bypass by a direct filing prior to the scheduled hearing. Special safeguards are added to ensure that the information so filed has adequate evidentiary support. The direct filing procedure may require, for example, that the trial court approve the filing and that the information be accompanied by affidavits establishing probable cause. Another approach is to allow the defendant, after obtaining complete discovery, to move for dismissal on the ground that the evidence available to the prosecution, even if taken as undisputed, fails to establish a prima facie case. That motion is utilized to screen cases in a fashion roughly analogous to the motion for summary judgment in civil cases.

(e) Waiver and Demand. While many states condition the defendant's right to a preliminary hearing upon a timely demand for the hearing, the majority position appears to be that the right can be lost only by an affirmative waiver reflecting a voluntary and knowledgeable choice by the defendant. To obtain a knowledgeable waiver, caution would direct the magistrate to explain the purpose of the hearing, the rights available at the hearing, and the nature of the charges on which the hearing would be held. However, in contrast to the waiver of many other rights, neither statutory provisions nor case law prescribe a particular litany for an affirmative waiver of a preliminary hearing. Statutes and court rules typically require that the magistrate advise the arrested person of the "right" to a preliminary hearing, with only a few also mandating a description of the "nature" of the hearing. Courts have held that a waiver should be judged in light of the circumstances of the individual case, including the defendant's familiarity with the criminal justice process.

In many jurisdictions, the prosecution has a right to insist upon a preliminary hearing notwithstanding a defense waiver. That right tends to be exercised only where the prosecutor desires to use the preliminary to perpetuate testimony.

§ 6.3   The Bindover Determination

(a) **The Applicable Standard.** The standard to be applied by the magistrate in determining whether the defendant will be boundover typically is set forth in the statute or court rule that establishes the right to the hearing. The dominant formulation of that standard directs the magistrate to determine whether "there is probable cause to believe that an offense has been committed and that the defendant committed it." Another common formulation directs the magistrate to determine whether "it appears that an offense has been committed and there is probable cause to believe that the defendant committed it." Although the "offense has been committed" phrasing suggests that more than probable cause is needed to establish the corpus delecti, that distinction appears to have been lost in most, if not all, of these jurisdictions.

Exactly what probable cause means in the context of the preliminary hearing has been left to judicial development. Courts typically have followed one of three approaches in their descriptions of the probable cause requirement. Perhaps the most common is to look to the Fourth Amendment standard of probable cause as formulated in cases involving probable cause to arrest. Another approach is to focus on the character of the evidence needed to establish probable cause at the preliminary hearing. Courts here note that, as to each element of the crime, there need only be "some evidence" from which a reasonable person could infer the presence of that element. Some courts using this standard may require evidence establishing no higher probability than that needed to arrest. For others, however, to infer the "presence" of an element may require more than establishing a "fair probability" as to that element. A third approach is to stress what probable cause in the preliminary hearing context does not require. Thus, courts will note that it does not require proof beyond a reasonable doubt, and some will add that it also does not require proof that meets the preponderance of the evidence standard. Again, such courts may have in mind only the arrest standard of probability, but they may all have in mind a somewhat higher showing of probability.

The use of the Fourth Amendment arrest standard in describing probable cause at a preliminary hearing indicates equivalence only in the requisite degree of probability. It does not mean that the magistrate's ruling will merely duplicate the decision made in the same case (often by the same magistrate) in the issuance of an arrest warrant or in the ex parte post-arrest finding of probable cause made pursuant to the *Gerstein* requirement (see § 6.2(a)). The difference in context will necessarily lend a different shading to the preliminary hearing determination. Here, the assessment of probable cause will be made at an adversary rather than an ex parte proceeding. Even where use of hearsay is permitted, that hearsay will be presented through the testimony of a witness, who can be cross-examined as to the source of the hearsay, rather than through a showing based entirely on affidavits. Also, the arrest standard, directed primarily at police, is expressed in terms of "the factual and practical distinctions of everyday life in which reasonable and prudent men, not legal technicians act," while the charging decision being reviewed at the preliminary hearing is, by its nature, one involving the "legal technicians" of the prosecutor's office. Under the arrest standard, considerable uncertainty must be tolerated on occasion because of the need to allow the police to take affirmative action in ambiguous circumstances, but no comparable exigencies are presented when the charging decision is made. Thus, a police officer may make an arrest where the circumstances suggest that the property possessed by the suspect may have been stolen, but the prosecutor ordinarily has no justification for proceeding to charge without first determining that a theft actually did occur.

When courts occasionally state that probable cause at a preliminary hearing requires "more" than the probable cause needed for an arrest or search warrant, they usually have in mind nothing more than the differences in the type of evidence required at each stage. However, commentators have suggested that the preliminary hearing has a "forward looking" component that logically should require a higher and different degree of probability than that applied to the review of an arrest or search. Consider, for example, the classic hypothetical in which the evidence known to the police establishes beyond a reasonable doubt that one of two independent actors committed a crime, but does not distinguish between the two. The usual view of Fourth Amendment probable cause would allow an arrest of both actors, but arguably the same should not be said for a preliminary hearing bindover, assuming no further evidence has been produced. The arrest standard looks only to the probability that the person committed the crime as established at the time of the arrest, while the preliminary hearing looks both to that probability as of the time of the hearing *and* to the probability that the government will be able to establish guilt at trial. If the police have been unable to develop further evidence pointing to the guilt of one of the actors, and there is not a reasonable likelihood that such evidence will be forthcoming, it arguably would be contrary to the screening function of the preliminary hearing to bindover either actor.

This view of probable cause as encompassing consideration of the prosecution's likely future development finds support in occasional language in appellate opinions and magistrate explanations of bindover rejections. However, a "forward looking" interpretation of probable cause finds no support in standard descriptions of the preliminary hearing's probable cause, and has been rejected by the few courts speaking directly to the issue. The statutory adoption of a probable cause standard, these courts have noted, carries with it an automatic presumption that the prosecution may be able to "strengthen its case at trial," which is not subject to reevaluation by the magistrate in the individual case.

Several states have departed from this traditional preliminary hearing perspective to apply other standards that seek to test the likelihood of the prosecution being able to succeed at trial. A few have done this by moving to a bindover standard that is roughly analogous to the standard applied by a trial judge in deciding whether the prosecutor's case is strong enough to send to the jury. These jurisdictions require that the prosecution establish a "prima facie case" at the preliminary hearing—that is, the evidence presented, taken in the light most favorable to the prosecution, must be sufficient to allow a reasonable finder of fact to convict the defendant at trial. Such a standard is also applied by the grand jury in a much larger group of states. Of course, in the grand jury context, the prima facie case standard is applied somewhat differently because the grand jury sees only the prosecution's evidence and its witnesses are not subject to cross-examination. In the preliminary hearing, where cross-examination is allowed and the defense can present its own evidence, the application of this standard comes closer to the ruling on a motion for directed verdict at the close of all the evidence.

Other states have sought to place a greater focus on likely success at trial by emphasizing the procedures used in meeting the bindover standard rather than the standard itself. These states use the traditional probable cause standard while providing what is commonly described as a "mini-trial" hearing. The prosecution is limited to use of evidence that would be admissible at trial, and the defense is allowed full scope in cross-examination and in the presentation of defense evidence. Though the mini-trial hearing fits naturally with a bindover standard requiring a prima facie case, it is seen as having value as well in a jurisdiction applying a probable cause standard requiring a degree of probability similar to an arrest warrant. A mini-trial hearing, particularly if combined with the magistrate's capacity to judge witness credibility, provides a screening procedure that arguably is much more exacting even though it requires no greater degree of probability.

A substantial majority of jurisdictions reject both the prima facie standard and the mini-trial type of preliminary hearing. Those attributes are deemed inconsistent with various provisions of the typical statute or court rule establishing the preliminary hearing. The bindover standard is described in terms of "probable cause" in the governing statutes and court rules, in contrast to provisions on the grand jury which do refer to a prima facie case standard. The timing requirements are stringent and do not suggest affording the prosecution adequate time to bring together its full case in the form of admissible evidence. Indeed, the basic thrust of reform in preliminary hearing procedure has been to shorten time periods and preclude continuances so as to ensure that no person is being held in custody or otherwise subjected to significant restraints on his liberty where the state does not have some reasonable grounding for its charge. Viewing the preliminary hearing from the perspective suggested by that objective, imposition of either a mini-trial approach or a prima facie evidence test is deemed inappropriate.

(b) Assessment of Credibility. Closely related to the definition of the applicable bindover standard is the extent of the magistrate's authority to pass judgment on the credibility of witnesses in applying that standard. Courts almost uniformly recognize that the magistrate has authority to judge credibility. If that were not so, there would be no reason for allowing the defense to cross-examine prosecution witnesses and present contradicting evidence of its own. The critical issue is how much leeway is granted to the magistrate in judging credibility.

In those jurisdictions with mini-trial type hearings, appellate courts commonly speak of the magistrate having a "duty to pass judgment on the credibility of witnesses as well as the weight and competency of the evidence." They note in this regard that a proper case for a bindover is not presented simply because the "prosecution has presented evidence on each element of the offense," as the magistrate must weigh "the whole of the matter," resting "his conclusion on what he believes". However, some of the same courts have noted that the magistrate should not assume the role of the "ultimate finder of fact" and should bind over for jury consideration where "the evidence conflicts and raises a reasonable doubt regarding the defendant's guilt."

Other jurisdictions have held that the magistrate has a very narrow capacity to judge credibility. Thus, the Colorado Supreme Court, after pointedly noting that the Colorado preliminary hearing was not a mini-trial type hearing, analyzed the magistrate's authority to judge credibility in light of the limited probability required under the traditional probable cause bindover standard. It concluded that a "judge in a preliminary hearing has jurisdiction to consider the credibility of witnesses only when, as a matter of law, the testimony is implausible or incredible. When there is a mere conflict in testimony, a question of fact exists for the jury, and the judge must draw the inference favorable to the prosecution." States with a slightly broader standard would allow the magistrate to resolve conflicts in testimony, "but only 'where the evidence is overwhelming.' "

(c) Consequences of a Dismissal. As with prosecution appeals in general, a prosecution appeal of a magistrate's dismissal at a preliminary hearing must be grounded on specific statutory authorization. Traditionally, that authorization has been lacking. Today, however, numerous states specifically provide for a prosecution appeal of a magistrate's refusal to bind over, with that appeal going initially to the felony trial court as the next highest court. In general, the appellate review standard is whether the dismissal constituted an "abuse of discretion," rather than a de novo consideration of the strength of the evidence. In the many states in which the prosecution lacks a right of appeal, appellate review may still be possible by application for an extraordinary writ (e.g. mandamus). However, the state may limit those writs to challenging a jurisdictional excess, thereby requiring the prosecution to show that the magistrate applied an incorrect legal standard.

In most jurisdictions, whether or not appellate review is available, a prosecutor will look to alternative procedures to obtain a "reversal" of a dismissal. The dismissal occurs before jeopardy has attached, and the double jeopardy prohibition therefore does not bar initiation of a new prosecution for the same offense. Where prosecutions commonly are brought by indictment, the prosecutor most often will take the same charge directly to the grand jury. The grand jury may indict notwithstanding the magistrate's refusal to bind over and the defendant may be rearrested on the indictment. Where a grand jury is not available, the prosecutor may refile the complaint and attempt to obtain a bindover at a subsequent preliminary hearing (possibly before a different magistrate).

A handful of state courts have concluded that refiling undermines the magistrate's authority and therefore should not be permitted unless the prosecution offers substantial additional evidence. The vast majority, however, permit refiling at will, including refiling on the same evidence before a different magistrate, absent proof that the prosecutor's purpose is to harass the defendant.

(d) Consequences of a Bindover. In an indictment jurisdiction, the magistrate binds over for consideration by the grand jury. The grand jury is in no way bound by the magistrate's action, but must make its own determination based on the evidence presented to it, which may not be the same evidence presented before the magistrate. Indeed, it would be inconsistent with the grand jury's independence for the prosecutor to urge it to return a charge because the magistrate had found probable cause on that charge. Should the grand jury indict on that same charge, that indictment serves as the basis for further proceedings and sufficiency of the evidence supporting the bindover is no longer in issue. If the grand jury decides not to indict, charges may not be filed, and the defendant must be released (although a resubmission to the grand jury may be possible in exceptional cases, see § 7.2(h)).

When a bindover is followed by an information, the appropriate defense vehicle for challenging the bindover usually is the motion to dismiss or quash the information. That motion ordinarily must be made pretrial, and in some states, prior to pleading to the information. Courts reviewing a bindover decision often stress that they may not substitute their judgment for that of the magistrate who saw and heard the testimony. Here too, courts often state that the magistrate's decision will only be overturned when there has been a clear abuse of discretion. Accordingly, the magistrate's decision (ordinarily not accompanied by opinion or findings of fact) is most likely to be reversed when a misinterpretation of substantive law (or perhaps oversight) resulted in a total absence of proof on a particular element of the offense.

Assume now that a magistrate binds over on a record that clearly fails to establish probable cause, after which the prosecutor files an information based on that bindover. If a timely challenge in the trial court is rejected, as to which interlocutory appeal is unavailable, and the defendant is then convicted at trial, may defendant raise again the improper bindover issue on his appeal? In several states, a proper bindover is viewed as a jurisdictional prerequisite to the filing of an information, and therefore a new trial is required if it is shown on appeal that the bindover was not supported by sufficient evidence. Most states hold, however, that the magistrate's error in binding over, and the trial court's error in failing to quash the information, are rendered harmless by the introduction of sufficient evidence to convict at trial. With the state having established guilt beyond a reasonable doubt, the probable cause issue is rendered "moot", and a claim limited only to that issue offers no suggestion of having impacted the fairness of defendant's trial. Where the state appellate courts do not readily accept defense petitions for interlocutory review, this position results, as a practical matter, in typically rendering unreviewable trial court rulings rejecting motions to quash.

§ 6.4   Preliminary Hearing Procedures

(a) **Right to Counsel.** In *Coleman v. Ala.* (1970), the Supreme Court held that the Sixth Amendment right to counsel extends to the preliminary hearing and therefore grants to the indigent defendant a right to the appointment of counsel for that hearing. The Sixth Amendment right only applies to critical stages in the proceedings (see § 3.2(b)), so the Court had to determine whether the preliminary hearing is a stage where counsel's assistance was "necessary to preserve the defendant's basic right to a fair trial." The Court majority was not persuaded by the argument of the state (and the dissenters) that counsel was not needed because state law protected the unrepresented accused by prohibiting the prosecution's use at trial of "anything that occurred" at the preliminary hearing. The majority responded by reciting the various significant steps which counsel could take at the preliminary hearing. These steps included: "exposing fatal weaknesses in the State's case that might lead the magistrate to refuse to bind the accused over"; fashioning through preliminary hearing cross-examination "a vital impeachment tool" for the trial; discovery of the prosecution's case; preserving the testimony of favorable witnesses who might became unavailable at trial; and making arguments on such matters as "the necessity for an early psychiatric examination or bail." *Coleman* was written with reference to a state in which the ultimate prosecution screening was to be by the grand jury in considering an indictment, so its first cited significant step (precluding a bindover) arguably would be even more telling in an information state. Accordingly, *Coleman* has uniformly been read as requiring the appointment of counsel at the preliminary hearing in both indictment and information jurisdictions.

(b) **Application of the Rules of Evidence.** While all jurisdictions require magistrates to recognize testimonial privileges at the preliminary hearing, from that point on they vary considerably in their treatment of the applicability of the rules of evidence. With a modest degree of over generalization, the various positions can be divided into three basic approaches: (1) full applicability; (2) inapplicability with varying magistrate discretion to exclude evidence that would not be admissible at trial; and (3) general applicability with exceptions for certain types of evidence not admissible at trial.

Only a handful of states require full application of the rules of evidence, restricting the preliminary hearing evidence to that which would also be admissible at trial. These jurisdictions will not reject a bindover, however, simply because the magistrate erroneously admitted incompetent evidence. If the reviewing court concludes that there was sufficient admissible evidence before the magistrate to meet the bindover standard, the bindover will be upheld. The magistrate's error in admitting the incompetent evidence will be treated, in effect, as per se harmless error.

A much larger group of jurisdictions, perhaps a majority, start from the premise that the rules of evidence do not apply to the preliminary hearing. Most of these jurisdictions have provisions similar to Rule 1101(d) of the Federal Rules of Evidence, which states that the evidentiary rules, "other than with respect to privileges, do not apply in * * * preliminary examinations in criminal cases." Such provisions clearly allow the magistrate to admit and rely upon evidence that would not be admissible at trial where the magistrate views such evidence as sufficiently reliable for a probable cause determination. At the same time, these provisions do not restrict the magistrate's authority to insist upon adherence to the rules of evidence where the magistrate believes that the offered incompetent evidence is not sufficiently reliable. However, in most jurisdictions with Rule 1101(d)-type provisions, separate provisions restrict that discretion by authorizing two types of evidence that would be inadmissible at trial. These provisions state that "the finding of probable cause may be based on hearsay in whole or part," and that "objections to evidence on the ground that it was acquired by unlawful means are not properly made at the preliminary hearing." They commonly are viewed as allowing prosecution reliance upon such evidence.

A third group of jurisdictions, consisting of roughly a dozen states, hold the rules of evidence generally to be applicable to preliminary hearings, but creates exceptions for certain categories of evidence that would be inadmissible at trial. The two most common exceptions relate to particular classes of hearsay (e.g., reports of scientific experts) and to evidence obtained by police methods that could lead to suppression at trial.

While the vast majority of jurisdictions have provisions prohibiting challenges to the prosecution's use of unlawfully obtained evidence, such challenges are recognized in the small group of states that limit the bindover decision to admissible evidence and in several others that largely require admissible evidence. Where the objection based upon unlawful acquisition is available at the preliminary hearing, it operates somewhat differently than the pretrial motion to suppress made in the trial court. Unlike the pretrial suppression motion, which is made in anticipation of the prosecution's use of illegally acquired evidence, the preliminary hearing objection is tied to the prosecutor's attempt to actually use that evidence at the hearing. Thus, if the prosecution has sufficient evidence to support a bindover without using the fruits of an arguably unconstitutional police activity, it can avoid an exclusionary rule challenge by limiting the evidence it uses at the hearing. Also, like all evidentiary rulings at a preliminary hearing, the ruling on a challenge to evidence as illegally acquired will not be binding upon the trial court.

(c) The Defendant's Right of Cross–Examination. All jurisdictions grant the defense a right to cross-examine those witnesses presented by the prosecution at the preliminary hearing. This right is based on local law; the Supreme Court has long held that cross-examination at a preliminary hearing is not required by the confrontation clause of the Sixth Amendment. The relevant provisions typically describe the right in general terms, leaving to the judiciary the formulation of applicable limitations. As would be expected, the courts uniformly agree that cross-examination at the preliminary hearing should at least be subject to those restrictions that the particular jurisdiction imposes on trial cross-examination. Most also apply, however, one or more additional restrictions that stem from the limited screening function of the preliminary hearing and therefore are not applicable in the trial setting.

A common restriction tied to the function of the preliminary hearing permits the magistrate to cut-off examination that seems to be aimed more at obtaining pretrial discovery than at challenging the witness' testimony. Questions most likely to be challenged on this score are those asking about other sources of evidence (e.g., the names of known eyewitnesses) or exploring the range of investigative procedures that were utilized by the police. Also, where a jurisdiction holds that a particular defense is not cognizable at a preliminary hearing, as discussed in subsection (d) infra, cross-examination apparently designed to bring forth information relating to such a defense will be prohibited either as an attempt at discovery or as failing to relate to an issue properly before the magistrate. Questions that seem to be fishing for possible lines of defense, rather than supporting a particular defense that defendant intends to present at the hearing, also may be rejected as aimed at discovery.

Since the issue for determination at the preliminary hearing is only that of probable cause, a magistrate may also have authority to bar cross-examination that clearly challenges the prosecution's case but is deemed not to carry sufficient force to upset the prosecution's showing of probable cause. Thus, courts sometimes state that while cross-examination must be permitted to challenge the witness' credibility as to the events described in his or her testimony, the magistrate may bar cross-examination aimed at challenging only the witness' "general trustworthiness." So too, where the magistrate takes the position that credibility judgments at the preliminary hearing should be limited only to apparent falsehoods, and the initial questioning indicates that the witness will not retreat from her testimony, a magistrate may cut-off all further questioning as unlikely to alter the magistrate's judgment on probable cause.

At trial, the defense has available for use in cross-examination any prior recorded statements of the prosecution witness. In some jurisdictions those statements are given to the defense as part of pretrial discovery, while others make them available under Jencks-type provisions following the witness' direct testimony. See §§ 12.2(i), 16.3(c). Where availability is tied to pretrial discovery, the prior recorded statement ordinarily is not available at the preliminary hearing. A few jurisdictions do hold that the magistrate has discretionary authority to order discovery restricted to defense needs in challenging the prosecution's showing of probable cause, but most reason that pretrial discovery cannot be ordered by the magistrate, as discovery provisions do not take effect until the prosecution reaches the trial court. Where the jurisdiction utilizes a Jencks-type provision, that provision most often will be specifically limited to trial witnesses, but several such jurisdictions, including the federal, do extend the required disclosure of a witness prior recorded statements to various pretrial proceedings, including the preliminary hearing.

(d) The Right to Present Defense Witnesses. All jurisdictions recognize at least a conditional defense right to call its own witnesses at the preliminary hearing, but the limitations placed upon that right are only infrequently tested. The conventional wisdom frowns upon defense presentation of its own witnesses at a preliminary hearing absent most unusual circumstances. Most often, the defense anticipates a bindover and is utilizing the hearing to obtain discovery of the prosecution's case and to lay the groundwork for impeachment of the prosecution's witnesses at trial. If counsel should conclude that the opportunity exists to shake the prosecution's showing, that will usually be attempted through vigorous cross-examination of the prosecution's witnesses. Producing defense testimony contradicting the prosecution's case is deemed to carry costs that ordinarily far outweigh its benefits. Unless the credibility of prosecution witnesses has been shaken substantially on cross-examination, the contrary testimony of defense witnesses is likely to be viewed by the magistrate as simply presenting the kind of credibility conflict that should be resolved by the factfinder at trial. On the other hand, by presenting the defense witness at the preliminary hearing, the defendant runs the risk of making that witness' testimony less effective at trial. Just as the defense may use its cross-examination of prosecution witnesses to gain discovery and to prepare for future impeachment, the prosecution may use its cross-examination of the defense witnesses to achieve those same goals. Much the same analysis argues against presenting witnesses whose testimony will not directly challenge the prosecution's showing as to the elements of the offense, but will point to additional factors that would excuse or justify the actor's behavior.

As with the defense right of cross-examination, the defense right to call witnesses is subject not only to the limits placed upon the trial right, but also to a broad discretion of the magistrate to restrict preliminary hearing presentations in accordance with the limited purposes of that hearing. The primary restrictions imposed under that authority relate to the calling of potential prosecution witnesses for the purposes of obtaining discovery and the refusal to hear defense witnesses upon the conclusion that further testimony would do no more than raise a credibility issue. Courts also may bar witnesses viewed as presenting an "affirmative defense." The leading decisions on this prohibition involve the presentation of an entrapment defense. These rulings are not readily extended to all defenses that are "affirmative" in the sense that the defense does not negate the basic elements of the crime. No court has suggested, for example, that a defendant can be precluded from introducing evidence of self-defense at a preliminary hearing (although such a tactic most likely will do no more than raise a credibility issue that the magistrate will not resolve). However, the entrapment rulings could readily be extended to all defenses that are "affirmative" in the sense that they place upon the defense the burden of proof.

(e) Challenging Procedural Rulings. If a magistrate makes an improper procedural ruling at a preliminary hearing and subsequently binds over, and the defendant then moves to dismiss the ensuing information because of the magistrate's procedural error, what weight should be given to the strength of the prosecution's case in determining whether that error requires rejection of the bindover? Three different approaches may be taken here. As noted previously in subsection (b), in jurisdictions holding the rules of evidence applicable to the preliminary hearing, a magistrate error in admitting incompetent evidence will be viewed as harmless if there remained sufficient competent evidence to support a bindover. A similar analysis can also be applied to other errors, such as the improper curtailment of cross-examination or the refusal to allow a defense witness. Here, however, since the defense was not allowed to proceed, the court may be required to give the defense the benefit of the doubt as to what weaknesses would have been shown if the magistrate had not erred. It can nonetheless find that the prosecution's evidence would have been adequate even with that showing and therefore sustain the bindover notwithstanding the magistrate's error.

A variation of the above approach applies a harmless error standard similar to that applied by the Supreme Court in evaluating the impact of a nonconstitutional error restricting the defense's presentation at trial. See § 19.6(b). The Court there holds that a reversal will not be required if the appellate court concludes, with fair assurance, that the jury would not have been substantially influenced in its decision if the defense had been able to do what it erroneously was prevented from doing. In the context of the preliminary hearing, the trial court would ask whether the magistrate would have been substantially influenced if the defense had made the showing that was precluded by the magistrate's error. The strength of the prosecution's case would remain significant, but the question would not be whether it merely would be "adequate" for a bindover even with the added defense showing, but whether it was so strong (or the additional defense showing so weak) that the magistrate would not have been substantially swayed by the added defense showing.

A third approach holds that automatic reversal of a bindover is required where the magistrate's erroneous ruling deprived the defendant of a "substantial right," such as his right to cross-examine or to present witnesses. In determining whether the right denied is substantial, the court will look to its potential significance and the scope of the denial. Thus, such a violation was found in the denial of the cross-examination of a key witness that went "directly to the matter at issue." The analysis here does not look to the strength of the prosecution's case, but simply to the character of the error. Applying such a standard for reversal, apparently more rigorous than the harmless error standard applied at trial, is supported by the argument that redoing a preliminary hearing imposes substantially less of a burden on the judicial system than redoing a trial.

Assume that a magistrate improperly curtails cross-examination or denies a request to present a defense witness, but an indictment is issued before the magistrate's ruling can be challenged in the trial court. Has the defendant lost his right to relief even though the magistrate's ruling clearly resulted in an erroneous bindover? The tradition rule is that all "defects" in the preliminary hearing are "cured by the subsequent indictment." The rationale here is similar to that underlying the practice of mooting the defendant's right to a preliminary hearing by obtaining a prior indictment: "Once an indictment has been issued, the preliminary hearing proceedings are no longer subject to either direct or collateral attack because the defendant has been afforded an independent determination that probable cause exists, which overrides any decision that the magistrate might render at a new preliminary hearing." However, where the alleged preliminary hearing error had an impact extending beyond the bindover itself, arguably impacting the defense's trial preparation, a few courts have suggested that the trial judge has discretion to fashion a remedy that will grant the defense similar preparatory assistance (e.g., a right to depose the witness that the magistrate refused to hear). This position stands in stark contradiction to the numerous cases stating that the only cognizable function of the preliminary hearing is determining probable cause.

Assume next that the magistrate erroneously restricts a defendant's right to cross-examination or to present evidence at a preliminary hearing. The magistrate subsequently binds over and an information is filed. The defense challenges the information as based on a defective preliminary hearing, but the trial court erroneously finds that the magistrate's rulings were proper. Interlocutory review is not available, so defendant next raises the issue on appeal following conviction. At this point, information jurisdictions are divided. Most take the view that the conviction should be treated as having automatically rendered harmless the magistrate's error. The function of the preliminary hearing, they note, is to determine whether probable cause exists, and that issue obviously is closed by a finding of guilt beyond a reasonable doubt at a fairly conducted trial. This means, as a practical matter, that relief for magistrate errors at preliminary hearings will largely be limited to trial court rulings, as interlocutory review of a trial court's acceptance of a bindover is rarely available. Courts treating the trial conviction as rendering preliminary hearing errors per se harmless recognize this procedural difficulty, but reason that it does not justify disregard "of the rule that the remedy should be appropriate to the violation." Granting the defendant a reversal of the conviction and a new preliminary hearing "would be to give him an entirely disproportionate remedy"—"a windfall * * * not in the public interest."

A closely related but distinct position agrees that preliminary hearing errors are mooted insofar as they relate only to the bindover determination, but recognizes that those errors could also impact the trial. Thus, these courts start from the assumption that the error will be harmless, but will reverse a conviction if the defendant can rebut that assumption by showing "that he was denied a fair trial or otherwise suffered a prejudice as a result of the error at the preliminary examination." The cases typically have announced this standard in the course of rejecting a defense argument for automatic reversal, so they have not had occasion to explore what would constitute an adequate showing of trial prejudice. It has been suggested that the loss of a critical defense witness would be sufficient (e.g., where the magistrate refused to allow the witness to testify at the preliminary hearing and the witness then proved to be unavailable at trial), and that the lack of additional preparation for trial through the hearing would not be sufficient. The Supreme Court's decision in *Coleman v. Ala.*, discussed below, is sometimes cited as recognizing an analogous harmless error approach in the context of a constitutional violation at a preliminary hearing.

On the other side of the spectrum, several courts, viewing a proper bindover as a jurisdictional prerequisite to the filing of an information, apparently will require a new trial whenever the preliminary hearing error could have altered the magistrate's decision to bind over. This position also has been justified as necessary to ensure that the preliminary hearing does not become "a right without an effective remedy."

In *Coleman v. Ala.* (1970), the Supreme Court spoke to the impact of a subsequent conviction upon a constitutional violation at the preliminary hearing. After defendants there had been denied unconstitutionally the assistance of appointed counsel at their preliminary hearing, they had been indicted by a grand jury and convicted at a trial in which they were represented by counsel. The state contended that the subsequent conviction at trial rendered harmless per se the failure to appoint counsel at the preliminary hearing. The defendants, in response, argued that denial of the Sixth Amendment right to counsel required an automatic reversal of any subsequent conviction, as the Court had held where counsel was denied at trial. The Supreme Court took a middle position, remanding the case for consideration as to whether the denial of counsel at the preliminary hearing had been a harmless error under the standard of *Chapman v. Cal.* (§ 19.6(c)). The Court noted in this regard that while the "trial transcript indicates that the prohibition against use by the State at trial of anything that occurred at the preliminary hearing was scrupulously observed," the record before it did not reflect "whether or not petitioners were otherwise prejudiced by the absence of counsel at the preliminary hearing." Justice Harlan, in a separate opinion, sought to add specificity to the remand order, which he viewed as "too broad and amorphous." Reversal should not follow, he argued, "unless petitioners are able to show on remand that they have been prejudiced in their defense at trial, in that favorable testimony that might otherwise have been preserved was irretrievably lost by virtue of not having counsel to help present an affirmative case at the preliminary hearing." Similarly, Justice White asserted that because "petitioners had been tried and found guilty by a jury," the denial of counsel at the preliminary hearing "was harmless beyond a reasonable doubt" (the *Chapman* standard) unless "important testimony of witnesses unavailable at the trial could have been preserved had counsel been present to cross-examine opposing witnesses or to examine witnesses for the defense." It would be inappropriate, he noted, for a lower court to hold that the constitutional error had not been harmless on the speculative assumptions either "(1) that the State's witnesses at the trial testified inconsistently with what their testimony would have been if petitioner had counsel to cross-examine them at the preliminary hearing, or (2) that counsel, had he been present at the hearing, would have known so much more about the State's case than he actually did when he went to trial that the result of the trial might have been different."

Although the failure of the *Coleman* majority opinion to respond to the concurring opinions creates some ambiguity as to the exact nature of the required harmless error inquiry, all of the opinions clearly indicated that the inquiry was to take account of at least some incidental benefits that the hearing could have provided the defense at trial. Lower courts applying *Coleman* have consistently looked to those incidental benefits in determining whether the denial of counsel at a preliminary hearing required reversal of a subsequent conviction. Most have adopted an analysis similar to that suggested by Justices Harlan and White in *Coleman*, refusing to find a reasonable doubt as to possible prejudice based on the assumption that counsel's trial presentation would have been helped if counsel had been present at the preliminary hearing and therefore able to use it as an impeachment and discovery device. A few, however, have suggested that counsel's lack of opportunity to obtain such benefits as to critical preliminary hearing witnesses automatically creates a reasonable doubt under the *Chapman* standard, absent a state showing that later procedures gave counsel that same opportunity.

As discussed above, many state courts have not looked to these same incidental benefits in determining whether errors in other aspects of the preliminary hearing should require a reversal on review of a conviction. In that context, they treat the probable cause determination as the critical function of the hearing, conclude that it is mooted by the finding of guilt beyond a reasonable doubt, and refuse to consider the loss of incidental tactical advantages as sufficient in itself to overturn an indictment or a subsequent conviction. *Coleman's* broader inquiry is treated as a special attribute of a Sixth Amendment right to counsel, which is granted to ensure a fair trial, and therefore is not controlling as to the denial of defendant's rights under local law to cross-examine prosecution witnesses and present defense witnesses, such rights have been granted simply to facilitate the screening function of the preliminary hearing.

Chapter 7

GRAND JURY REVIEW

Table of Sections

241

For additional analysis of the above topics and citations to authorities supporting their discussion in this Book, consult the authors' 7-volume *Criminal Procedure* treatise, also available as Westlaw database CRIMPROC. See the Table of Cross-References in this Book.

---

§ 7.1 Defendant's Right to Prosecution by Indictment

(a) The Fifth Amendment Right. The English grand jury originally was established to assist the Crown in uncovering crime and apprehending offenders, but by the end of the seventeenth century, it had come to be valued in England as a shield against the arbitrary initiation of prosecution by the Crown. In the American colonies, the "shielding role" of the grand jury was equally revered, in part because of colonial grand juries which had refused in several highly celebrated cases to indict persons opposed to the Crown. Not surprisingly, that important role of the grand jury was guaranteed as a constitutional command though the adoption of the first clause of the Fifth Amendment, which provides:

> No person shall be held to answer for a capital, or otherwise infamous crime, unless on a presentment or indictment of a grand Jury, except in cases arising in the land or naval forces, or in the Militia, when in actual service in time of War or public danger.

The net effect of this provision is to grant to an individual accused of an infamous crime not arising in the military the right not to be proceeded against unless that accusation has been approved by an affirmative vote of a grand jury. The individual has a right to insist that the charges against him be brought by presentment or indictment, either of which has to be issued by the grand jury. The presentment historically differed from the indictment in that it was a charge issued by the grand jury on its own initiative, commonly on the basis of the jurors' own knowledge, but sometimes based on information provided by a private complainant.

Rule 7 of the Federal Rules of Criminal Procedure restates the Fifth Amendment guarantee in modern form. It provides that "an offense (other than criminal contempt) must be prosecuted by an indictment if it is punishable: (A) by death; or (B) by imprisonment for more than one year." Federal Rule 7 does not refer to prosecution by presentment since presentments became obsolete in federal practice with the assumption of an executive branch monopoly over the prosecution function. Indeed, Rule 7(c) gives effect to an indictment approved by a vote of the grand jurors only if it is also signed by the attorney for the government (thereby indicating the prosecution's acceptance). Rule 7 extends to all offenses punishable by imprisonment for more than a year (which also defines a "felony"), as an "infamous" non-capital offense traditionally was defined by reference to potential incapacitation in a penitentiary (the case for all felonies). An exception is made for criminal contempt, as that prosecution historically could be instituted on the directive of the court whose order was violated by the contempt. *Green v. U.S.* (1958). The Fifth Amendment also speaks of a persons not being "held to answer" without an indictment, and Federal Rule 10 requires the indictment be issued prior to the felony defendant's arraignment before the federal district court (see § 1.2(i)), which is the modern version of being held to answer.

(b) Fourteenth Amendment Due Process. The Fifth Amendment imposes its constitutional command only upon the federal government. That the states were not bound by the Amendment's grand jury clause was hardly critical at the time of its adoption, since all of the original states had their own laws giving defendants a right to insist upon a grand jury charge when being prosecuted for a serious offense. It was not until the middle of the nineteenth century that a state completely did away with the right to a grand jury charge, giving the prosecution the option of proceeding by information (following a preliminary hearing bindover). That development posed no legal difficulties under the Fifth Amendment, but the post civil war adoption of the Fourteenth Amendment did present a possible constitutional bar. Indeed, the first major Fourteenth Amendment due process ruling relating to criminal procedure presented the question of whether a state could prosecute a murder charge under an information issued after a preliminary hearing bindover. As discussed in § 2.1(b), *Hurtado v. Cal.* (1884), applying a "fundamental fairness" analysis of due process, concluded that prosecution by indictment was not essential to due process.

In the years since *Hurtado* was decided, the Supreme Court has dramatically altered its approach to Fourteenth Amendment due process issues. See § 2.1(d). It has adopted the position that the very presence of a guarantee in the Bill of Rights strongly suggests that the guarantee is one of those "fundamental principles of liberty and justice which lie at the base of all our civil and political institutions." As a result, it has found Fourteenth Amendment due process to encompass almost all of the guarantees relating to criminal procedure that are in the Bill of Rights. Indeed, the only other guarantees, besides the grand jury clause, not definitely within the protection of due process are those as to which the Court has not had occasion to rule. Nonetheless the Supreme Court has reaffirmed its *Hurtado* ruling that due process does not require a state to initiate prosecution by a grand jury indictment or presentment in a capital case or any other criminal case.

(c) **Indictment Jurisdictions.** Jurisdictions are commonly described as "indictment jurisdictions" if they grant to the accused a right not to be held to answer a felony charge unless that charge has been issued by a grand jury through an indictment (or a presentment, where the jurisdiction retains the presentment process). Currently, the federal criminal justice system, the District of Columbia, and eighteen states are indictment jurisdictions. These jurisdictions vary somewhat in defining the precise scope the right to a grand jury accusation, but there is unanimity as to remedy for its violation. Where a defendant was entitled to be prosecuted on a grand jury charge but was prosecuted instead on an information, and an objection was timely raised, the remedy on review of the conviction is the automatic reversal of that conviction—the error will not be deemed "harmless."

(d) **Limited Indictment Jurisdictions.** Four states require prosecution by indictment only as to the most severely punished felonies. Although sometimes described as indictment states, they are more appropriately placed in a separate category, as they do not require grand jury screening for the vast majority of felony charges. Three of the four require indictments as to more than murder, as they include all offenses punishable by life imprisonment.

(e) **Waiver in Indictment and Limited–Indictment Jurisdictions.** The grand jury clause of the Fifth Amendment, and similar clauses in state constitutions do not refer to the possibility of waiving the requirement of a grand jury charge, but then neither do the constitutional clauses establishing other procedural guarantees, and those guarantees regularly have been held to be waivable by the defendant. A few courts have suggested that, since waiver of prosecution by a grand jury charge was not recognized at common law, it should be allowed only if authorized by the legislature, and two states, by their constitutions, provide for waiver only if authorized by the legislature. Today all of the indictment jurisdictions have constitutional, statutory, or court rule provisions explicitly authorizing waivers, but those provisions typically also restrict the use of waivers. Eleven indictment jurisdictions prohibit waivers in capital cases and several extend their waiver prohibitions to offenses punishable by life imprisonment (many of which were formerly capital offenses).

(f) Information States. Over the years, the number of states allowing felony prosecutions by information (usually only after a preliminary hearing bindover) has grown. Today, 28 states fall in this category. All 28 states also have provisions stating that prosecutions may be brought by indictment. Thus, the prosecutor is given an option to proceed by indictment or information (leading some to describe the "information" states as "information-option" states). In several information states, this option is entirely theoretical, as the prosecution has no way of obtaining a grand jury from which it can seek an indictment. In those states in which the prosecutor has a true option, there is considerable variation from one prosecutorial district to another in the use of grand jury indictments. An occasional prosecutor will make the grand jury the screening agency of choice, and will utilize the indictment almost as frequently as a prosecutor in an indictment jurisdiction. Many more prosecutors will never use the grand jury. Still others, particularly in urban districts, will use the information as the standard charging instrument, but turn to grand jury screening and prosecution by indictment in exceptional situations, where that process is thought to offer special advantages.

A variety of factors may lead a prosecutor to categorize a case as one of the exceptions that should be taken before the grand jury. In many instances of prosecution by indictment in information jurisdictions, the case was originally brought to the grand jury because the prosecutor had need for the grand jury's investigative power in developing the case. Once the grand jury investigation had developed sufficient additional evidence to support a prosecution, the proposed charge was presented to the grand jury for indictment. While the prosecutor could conceivably have asked the grand jury to do no more than investigate, and then have proceeded by information, that hardly serves to gain the cooperation of the grand jury in further investigations. Thus, once a case goes before the grand jury for investigation, it invariably will stay there through the process of determining whether or not to indict.

Where a case is fully investigated, prosecutors in information states are less likely to utilize the grand jury, but special circumstances may lead the prosecutor in that direction. In certain types of cases, for reasons of efficiency or to obtain tactical advantages, the prosecutor may desire to avoid a preliminary hearing (see § 6.2(c)), and as discussed in § 6.2(d), that can be achieved by taking the case to a grand jury and obtaining an indictment prior to the point when a preliminary hearing otherwise would be held. In politically sensitive situations, the prosecutor may turn to the grand jury to use it as a buffer against adverse public reaction. Recognizing that a decision to prosecute or not prosecute will give rise to substantial controversy, the prosecutor may seek to share the responsibility for that decision with the grand jury. Occasionally, the prosecutor may truly want the independent judgment of the jurors as to whether to proceed. Thus, the prosecutor may feel that the equities of the case are closely balanced and the final determination should rest on the grand jury's sense of community standards. Similarly, the prosecutor might have difficulty with the credibility of a key witness and not want to proceed unless the grand jurors view the witness as truthful.

§ 7.2   The Structure and Effectiveness of Grand Jury Screening

(a) **Grand Jury Composition.** The grand jury, like the petit jury, speaks as the "voice of the community," and ordinarily the legal standards governing the selection of persons called to jury service (the "venire" or "array") are the same for both grand and petit jurors. See § 14.2. However, since grand jurors commonly sit over a term of at least a few months, courts tend to be more liberal in recognizing hardship excuses, producing grand juries in many jurisdictions that tend to be somewhat less representative of the community than petit juries (although, on the other hand, the absence of peremptory challenges in grand jury selection eliminates an avenue for "jury-shaping" available as to petit jurors, see § 14.3(d)).

(b) **Control Over Proof.** The grand jury's screening function requires it to review the evidence presented by the prosecutor and to determine whether that evidence is sufficient to justify indictment. That function gives the prosecution at least the initial control over the evidence presented to the grand jury. In practice, that initial control may be converted to exclusive control, but the legal structure of the grand jury does not in itself delegate such complete authority to the prosecutor. At least theoretically, several other avenues for adding to the prosecution's evidence are available: (1) in most jurisdictions, in keeping with historical tradition, grand jurors are authorized to consider any information known to the grand jurors personally; (2) grand jurors can ask their own questions of witnesses offered by the prosecution (although prosecutors commonly request that jurors pass their questions through the prosecutor to ensure that the questions are proper in content and form); (3) grand jurors have authority to insist that additional witnesses or physical evidence be subpoenaed (seeking the assistance of the court, if the prosecutor should object); (4) many jurisdictions recognize a supervisory authority of the court to insist that the grand jury consider particular evidence where that is needed to prevent a "miscarriage of justice"; (5) in those jurisdictions that place an obligation on the prosecutor to present to the grand jury material exculpatory evidence known to the prosecutor (see § 7.6(f)), a prospective defendant may seek to take advantage of that obligation by making such evidence known to the prosecutor; and (6) although the grand jury traditionally is an ex parte proceeding, a few jurisdictions, as discussed below, give the prospective defendant a right to testify before the grand jury. Available evidence indicates that several of these vehicles for adding to the prosecution's presentation (e.g., the court's exercise of supervisory authority) are rarely used, but the additional questioning by jurors and the exercise of the potential defendant's right to testify (where available) are not so unusual.

(c) The Prospective Defendant's Testimony. In all but a handful of jurisdictions, a prospective defendant's request that he be allowed to testify before the grand jury may be granted or denied in the unreviewable discretion of the grand jury. Several information states have provisions granting to the prospective defendant a right to testify before the grand jury on a timely request, but New York is the only indictment state with such a provision. Conventional wisdom would direct a prospective defendant not to testify before the grand jury, as he would be submitting himself to cross-examination by the prosecutor in a setting in which neither the defense counsel (in most jurisdictions) nor the judge (in all jurisdictions) will be present to offer some protection. But this general rule of strategy, like any other, is subject to exceptions. At least in those jurisdictions in which a witness may be accompanied by counsel (as in New York), the potential advantages of testifying may outweigh the risks of testifying in various circumstances.

(d) Evidentiary Rules. All jurisdictions require that a witness' testimonial privileges be recognized in grand jury proceedings, but there is substantial variation as to the applicability of the remaining rules of evidence to grand jury proceedings. No more than a dozen states make the rules of evidence fully applicable to grand jury proceeding. A somewhat smaller group make most of the rules applicable, but create limited exceptions (allowing the substitution of hearsay, for example, where the witness' personal appearance is not likely to be critical, as in the case of a scientific expert reporting on physical evidence). The remainder—the vast majority—adhere only to testimonial privileges, and allow complete use of hearsay and other evidence that would be inadmissible at trial. Included in this group are the federal system and most of the indictment states.

(e) Legal Advice. The prosecutor serves not only as the state's advocate in presenting its case to the grand jury, but also as the primary legal advisor to the grand jury. The tension produced by these seemingly conflicting roles tends to be moderated, however, by the character of the legal advice that must be given as well as other features of the process. The two most significant portions of prosecutorial legal advice are the explanation of the grand jury's authority and the explanation of the required elements of the crimes that might be charged in a particular case. As to the former, the grand jury also is given extensive direction by the supervising court in its charge to the jury upon its impanelment. As to the latter, prosecutors tend to rely heavily on court-approved standard jury instructions (designed for trial use) that explain the elements of the various crimes. However, in using those instructions, the prosecutor may refer, as an advocate, to the evidence supporting each element of the offense. Most jurisdictions even allow the prosecutor to express a legal opinion as to the sufficiency of the evidence before the grand jury, although there is a division as to how far the prosecutor can carry such commentary.

(f) Quantum of Proof. There is a sharp division among the states as to the quantum of proof needed to indict. Approximately a third of the states provide for indictment upon a finding of "probable cause" to believe that the accused has committed the crime charged. A slightly smaller group of states utilize a "prima facie evidence standard," authorizing indictment only "when all the evidence taken together, if unexplained or uncontradicted, would warrant a conviction of the defendant." Another group of states, consisting largely of information states, have no clear precedent as to the applicable standard. Since the factfinder may convict only if convinced of the accused's guilt beyond a reasonable doubt, the prima facie evidence standard is a substantially more rigorous test than the traditional probable cause standard.

(g) The Indictment Decision. At common law, a decision to indict required the affirmative vote of a majority of the grand jurors. The grand jury had 23 members and at least 12 had to support a decision to indict. If the majority did not support a decision to indict, the grand jury returned a finding of "ignoramus" (we ignore it) or "no bill" in response to the proposed charge put before it by the prosecution. The federal system today still provides for a grand jury of a maximum size of 23, and requires 12 affirmative votes for an indictment. A handful of states also provide for a maximum jury size of 23 and an affirmative vote of 12 for an indictment; most, however, have smaller grand jurors and require a two/thirds or three/fourths vote for indictment.

The grand jury retains complete independence in refusing to indict. That includes the authority to refuse to indict even where the evidence presented clearly meets the quantum of proof needed for indictment. This authority of the grand jury to "nullify" the law arguably was the most important attribute of grand jury review from the perspective of those who insisted that a grand jury clause be included in the Bill of Rights. That authority and its historical grounding have frequently been noted in appellate opinions discussing the grand jury's screening function. Courts are divided, however, as to whether nullification is a "right" of the grand jurors, derived from the grand jury's screening responsibility, or simply a "power" that the grand jury possesses by virtue of the lack of judicial review of its decision not to indict. Where the former position is taken, judges sometimes will inform the grand jurors of their right to nullify in the judicial charge on their responsibilities, but that is required in no more than a few states and is, at best, a distinctly minority practice in others.

(h) Resubmission. Jeopardy not having attached, a grand jury's refusal to indict does not inherently preclude returning to a new grand jury (or even the same grand jury) to seek an indictment. Jurisdictions vary in their treatment of the prosecutor's authority to resubmit a proposed indictment to a grand jury. The division here, as in the case of resubmission following a preliminary hearing dismissal, clearly favors unrestricted resubmission, but a significant minority group of jurisdictions do impose limitations. These usually come through statutory provisions requiring judicial approval for resubmissions. Though most of these provisions do not set forth any standard as to when the court should allow resubmission, where the provisions do include a standard, they typically require a showing of newly discovered additional evidence.

(i) Secrecy Requirements. Grand jury secrecy requirements are designed in large part to strengthen the grand jury's investigative function. However, they also bear upon two aspects of grand jury screening. Initially, those requirements provide a protective shield for the grand jury which decides not to indict. Secondly, those requirements may sharply limit the capacity of the indicted defendant to learn of deficiencies in the screening process that could lead to a successful challenge to the indictment.

Grand jury secrecy requirements preclude the prosecutor, the staff assisting the prosecutor, and the grand jury from disclosing the evidence put before the grand jury except upon court order. That secrecy is said to provide a protective shield against public scrutiny (and criticism) for the grand jury when it decides against indictment. In some instances the public will not even be aware that the grand jury was considering the indictment of a particular person. More often, the public will be aware (as when the person was first arrested), but arguably will be hesitant to criticize the grand jury's decision because it recognizes that the grand jury may have received exculpatory evidence which is blocked from its view by grand jury secrecy. Grand jury secrecy also is said to help the grand jury in this regard by restricting the comments of the disappointed prosecutor. However, grand jury secrecy does not restrict the disappointed victim, and the prosecution may be able with some ingenuity to have a fair amount of its case against the individual made public.

In most jurisdictions, grand jury secrecy requirements have their most substantial bearing on screening in keeping from the indicted defendant most of the deficiencies that may have occurred in the course of grand jury screening. Where the defendant furnished evidence to the grand jury (in the form of testimony or a subpoenaed document or other tangible item), the defendant obviously is aware of the grand jury's consideration of that evidence. If other persons furnishing evidence to the grand jury are friendly to the defendant, they may be willing to share with the defendant their experiences before the grand jury. Apart from these limited sources, however, the defendant must depend upon exceptions to the general requirement of grand jury secrecy to learn what occurred in the process that led to his indictment. The two exceptions offering the most potential in this regard are those authorizing disclosure as part of pretrial discovery and disclosure in connection with a motion to dismiss an indictment.

In most jurisdictions, the defense's right to pretrial discovery of grand jury material is limited to the recorded grand jury testimony of the defendant and of the witnesses who will be called by the prosecution at trial. Such discovery has a limited potential in identifying deficiencies in the screening process. It does not encompass all of the testimony presented before the grand jury (not all grand jury witnesses will necessarily be called to testify at trial), and the recorded testimony of witnesses will not necessarily identify documents and other exhibits that were presented to the grand jury. Also, the disclosure does not include comments of the prosecutor or grand jurors except as they are made as part of the examination of the witness.

Roughly a dozen states grant to the defendant pretrial discovery of the entire transcript of the grand jury proceedings that produced the indictment of the defendant. Only four of these states, however, are indictment states; the remainder are information states in which prosecutors infrequently charge by indictment. Moreover, not all of these states require a transcription that goes beyond the "testimony of all witnesses." Thus, even with a complete transcript, the defendant will be unaware of the comments of the prosecutor.

In the federal system and in a substantial majority of the states, secrecy provisions allow disclosure of relevant grand jury material in support of a challenge to the grand jury proceedings, but only upon a special showing by the defendant. Federal Rule 6(e)(3), for example, allows a court to order disclosure upon a showing that "a ground may exist to dismiss the indictment because of a matter that occurred before the grand jury." In applying that standard, courts are fully cognizant that the defense may characterize its motion as aimed at supporting a motion to dismiss, but actually be seeking valuable pretrial discovery of grand jury testimony that is not discoverable under pretrial discovery rules (see § 12.2(i)). They also recognize that the nature of many of the irregularities that justify dismissal, along with the need to show that the irregularity had a prejudicial impact, commonly would require that any disclosure cover the entire proceeding that led to the indictment. Accordingly, they tend to be cautious in granting discovery on Rule 6(e)(3)–type motions. A typical standard for such disclosure is that the defense establish preliminarily "a substantial likelihood of gross or prejudicial irregularities in the conduct of the grand jury." Applying such a standard, courts universally find insufficient a showing that does no more than point to surrounding circumstances that evidence a "potential" for irregularities. They suggest that to be successful, the defendant must be able to produce such "hard evidence" as the affidavit of a witness who was present when misconduct occurred or the clear suggestion of impropriety in a portion of the transcript released to defendant in the course of pretrial discovery. Of course, such sources of "direct proof" are rarely available, leading courts to acknowledge that the preliminary showing requirement places the defendant in "something of a 'catch 22' [situation]."

In a substantial minority of the states (including several indictment states), the application of a Rule 6(e)(3)–type motion will be mooted in many prosecutorial districts because no transcript will be available. In these states, whether a transcript is made rests in the discretion of the prosecutor or the grand jury (which is likely to follow the lead of the prosecutor). Thus, whether the proceedings are transcribed depends upon whether the prosecutor sees the greater advantage in having available a transcript for prosecutorial use (including refreshing the witness' recollection at trial) or in not providing the defense with a transcription it could use in impeaching the witness at trial or possibly identifying flaws in the screening process.

(j) The Effectiveness Debate. The debate over the effectiveness of grand jury screening dates back at least to Benthams's challenge of the English grand jury in the mid–1800s. Today's critics include those who characterize the grand jury as a worthless "rubber stamp," and those who see grand jury screening as have some value, but being far inferior to preliminary hearing screening. Supporters acknowledge that an adversary screening process (as in the preliminary hearing) would be better for some types of cases, but contend that grand jury screening provides attributes of special importance where screening is most needed—in those cases in which special factors, e.g., the involvement of politics or ethnic animosity, are likely to produce unjust accusations. Grand jury screening is also supported as far less costly than preliminary hearing screening, and as an important avenue for lay participation in the criminal justice process.

While the debate over the effectiveness of grand jury review has been aimed primarily at legislative reform, it has not gone unnoticed by the courts. Several courts have suggested that the critics probably are correct in concluding that grand jury review is largely controlled by the prosecutor. Their response has been to downplay in various respects the significance of the indictment process. Still other courts have expressed concern as to the possible loss in effectiveness of grand jury review, but have cited that concern as a basis for insisting upon procedural safeguards designed to offset prosecutorial dominance. Finally, many other courts largely reject the criticism of grand jury screening. They view grand jury review as continuing to function effectively, although that judgment may rest upon a view of the process as designed to provide screening less finely tuned than that envisaged by many of those most critical of the process. The Supreme Court of the United States has stressed, in particular, the capacity of the grand jury to either refuse to indict or to charge in a lesser offense even when probable cause exists.

These differences in judgment as to the potential value of grand jury screening are reflected in the judicial treatment of almost all of the various grounds urged for challenging an indictment. While some opinions treating such challenges openly discuss the merits of grand jury review, most do not speak to the issue directly. Very often the court's underlying policy perspective will be obvious from the result it reaches. At times, however, the same ruling might be supported by either of two quite different judgments as to the value of grand jury review. Thus, a court rejecting a challenge to an indictment that was based in part on illegally obtained evidence may be guided by the conclusion that: (1) even if use of such evidence were prohibited, the grand jury still would almost always indict upon the prosecutor's request, so adding a prohibition against such use would simply cause delay without significant gain for an inherently weak screening process; or (2) the grand jury is functioning well as a rough screening body guided by a community sense of justice and the addition of a prohibition against the use of illegally obtained evidence is not needed for effective performance of this role.

§ 7.3 Indictment Challenges Based Upon Grand Jury Composition

(a) **Challenge Procedure.** In general, in contrast to the petit jury, where composition challenges come before the jury has acted, challenges to the composition of the grand jury come after the grand jury has acted, via a defense motion to dismiss the indictment based upon the illegal composition of the grand jury. Such challenges must be made before trial, and many jurisdictions impose more stringent requirements (e.g., that the motion be made within 30 days after arraignment). Exceptionally restrictive timing requirements may be challenged as imposing an undue burden on a defendant's right to contest selection procedures that violate the federal constitution. The Supreme Court has held that restrictive requirements are constitutionally acceptable, however, provided that, as applied, they do not deny the defendant a reasonable opportunity to raise his constitutional claim. Applying this standard, the Court held valid "on its face" a state rule requiring that objections be raised within three days after the end of the grand jury term (or before trial, if it came earlier). Although defendants indicted on the last day of the grand jury term would have only three days within which to raise the claim, that period was deemed not per se unreasonable. *Michel v. La.* (1955). However, a requirement that the challenge be made prior to indictment was held invalid as applied to an indigent defendant who was not provided with appointed counsel until the day after his indictment. *Reece v. Ga.* (1957).

(b) **Equal Protection Claims.** Not long after the adoption of the Fourteenth Amendment, its equal protection clause was held to prohibit racial discrimination by the state in the selection of grand juries, as well as petit juries. Though a defendant in a state prosecution has no federal constitutional right to grand jury review, he does have "a right to equal protection of the laws [which is] denied when he is indicted by a grand jury from which members of a racial group purposefully have been excluded." Provided a timely objection is made, an indictment issued by such a grand jury cannot stand, without regard to the sufficiency of the evidence before the grand jury, since the racial discrimination "strikes at the fundamental values of our judicial system and our society as a whole."

Under the Fifth Amendment's due process clause, the same prohibition applies to racial discrimination in the selection of grand juries in federal cases.

An equal protection challenge to the selection of the grand jury will be analyzed under the same standards as apply to equal protection challenges to the selection of the petit jury. This means that the Supreme Court rulings discussed in § 14.2(c), relating to the basic elements of an equal protection challenge to the selection of the petit jury, also set the standards for equal protection challenges to grand jury selection. The same basic elements—a discriminatory impact upon "a recognizable distinct class", and a "discriminatory purpose"—are required to establish the equal protection claim. Here as well, those elements typically are established through the combination of a statistical showing of underrepresentation of a suspect class in jury service and a showing that the selection system is susceptible to manipulation. Also, as established in *Campbell v. La.* (1998), the standing doctrine of *Powers v. Ohio* (§ 14.2(c)) applies equally to grand jury selection, allowing a defendant who is not a member of the excluded group to challenge an alleged equal protection violation in the discrimination against that group. As the Court there noted, the equal protection violation basically lies in the denial of the prospective juror's right not to be discriminated against, not in any loss of potential favoritism for the person whose case is being considered by the jury.

(c) The "Fair Cross–Section" Requirement. The Sixth Amendment right to jury trial requires that a petit jury be drawn from a "fair cross-section of the community." See § 14.2(d). This requirement overlaps to a substantial extent with equal protection restrictions upon jury selection, but the two guarantees are distinct. Equal protection prohibits discrimination against a "cognizable group," while the fair cross-section requirement prohibits the exclusion of a "distinctive" group that leaves the venire less than reasonably representative. The character of a distinctive group for cross-section purposes may be somewhat different than that of a cognizable group for equal protection purposes. Also, equal protection prohibits only intentional discrimination, while a fair cross-section objection can reach the systemic under-representation of a distinct group even where there was no intent to under-represent that group. Although the state may justify such under-representation as an incidental byproduct of serving an important governmental interest, it must show that the resulting exclusion from jury service is not broader than necessary to serve that interest.

Insofar as a federal constitutional cross-section requirement applies to the grand jury venire, it would appear to impose largely the same standards as the cross-section requirement applied to the selection of the venire for the petit jury. The critical question here is whether the Fourteenth Amendment's due process clause impos- es open the states a cross-section requirement for the grand jury venire, or whether the cross-section requirement is strictly a Sixth Amendment concept made applicable to the states only for the petit jury venire. In many states, that issue will not be reached because a cross-section requirement is included in the statute governing the selection of the venire for both the grand jury and the petit jury.

In *Hobby v. U.S.* (1984), a case involving alleged racial and gender discrimination in the selection of the grand jury foreperson, the Court spoke of the "representational value's protected by due process," noting that those values required that "no large and identifiable segment of the community [be] excluded from service." *Hobby* drew upon an opinion, *Peters v. Kiff* (1972), that had referred to such due process values in recognizing the objection of a white defendant to the exclusion of blacks from his jury (a ruling which, at the time, could not be based on equal protection, as it was pre-*Powers*). Arguably, the *Hobby-Peters* "representational values" analysis was meant to apply only to intentional discrimination that violated the equal protection clause, and to provide through due process an avenue for challenge by defendants not of the group discriminated against—an avenue no longer needed today in light of *Powers* and *Campbell v. La.* (1998).

In *Campbell*, a white defendant challenging the exclusion of blacks from the grand jury raised both an equal protection objec- tion and a due process objection based on *Hobby* and *Peters*. Finding that the court below had erroneously concluded that the defendant lacked standing, the Supreme Court remanded for con- sideration of those claims on their merits. The Court noted that it was "unnecessary here to discuss the nature and full extent of due process protection in the context of grand jury selection," and spoke of "that issue, to the extent it is still open based upon our earlier precedents," as distinguishable from both defendant's equal protection claim and a "fair cross-section claim" that had not been properly presented to the state courts. Although *Campbell* certainly leaves open the possibility that a due process objection will have a content that differs from the equal protection objection now avail- able to all defendants, it also appears to assume that the content of due process, as it relates to "representational values," differs somehow from the content of a cross-section requirement. Thus, the application of a traditional fair cross-section requirement to grand jury appears still to be an open issue under Supreme Court precedent. Indeed, if due process does not go so far in its "represen- tational values" requirement, finding a constitutional grounding for such a requirement is highly problematic.

(d) Constitutional Challenges to the Selection of the Foreperson. Typically, the foreperson of the grand jury, unlike the foreperson of the petit jury, is appointed by the court rather than elected by the jurors. Since the judge makes the appointment fully aware of the juror's race, the selection procedure is naturally suspect where the number of minority forepersons has been substantially disproportionate to the representation of minorities on the grand jury panels. Such a showing can establish a prima facie case of an equal protection violation, shifting to the prosecution the obligation of showing that there was not intentional discrimination. Of course, that presumption can then be rebutted by the prosecution showing that the impaneling court looked only to other racially neutral factors in selecting the foreperson, so there was no intentional discrimination (the disproportionate underrepresentation of a particular race constituting an incidental impact of reliance on those factors).

Assuming that there has been an adequate showing of discrimination, the question remains as to whether the appropriate remedy is dismissal of the indictment. That issue was first put to the Supreme Court in *Rose v. Mitchell* (1979). The Court there found no need to reach the issue because the defendant had failed to make out a prima facie case of discrimination. It noted as to the remedy issue only that it would "assume without deciding that discrimination with regard to the selection of only the foreman requires that an indictment be set aside, just as if the discrimination proved had tainted the selection of the entire grand jury venire." In *Hobby v. U.S.* (1984), the issue was again raised, but the context was different. *Hobby* was a pre-*Powers* ruling, and the defendant there, not being a member of the groups discriminated against (blacks and women) could not rely on equal protection. He based his claim instead on the "representational values" of due process, as discussed in the previous subsection.

The Court in *Hobby* unanimously agreed that the alleged "purposeful discrimination against Negroes or women in the selection of federal grand jury foreman is forbidden by the Fifth Amendment." It split, however, as to whether such a constitutional violation invariably required dismissal of an ensuing indictment. The *Hobby* majority concluded that dismissal there was not required, as the defendant's due process interests could not have been violated by intentional discrimination that was limited to the appointment of the foreperson. "Representational due process values" granted to the defendant a right not to be indicted by a grand jury unfairly selected through the exclusion of any "large and identifiable segment of the community." Here, however, no such exclusion had been applied to the grand jury *as a whole,* but simply to a properly selected grand jury member performing the additional duties of the foreperson.

The *Hobby* majority distinguished *Rose* on three grounds: (1) the foreman in *Rose* had been appointed from outside the randomly selected panel, while the federal foreperson was a part of that panel; (2) the foreman in *Rose* had substantial duties and powers that gave him "virtual veto power over the indictment process" (e.g., the authority to issue subpoenas for witnesses and the requirement of his endorsement for a valid indictment), while the federal foreperson performed basically ministerial duties; and (3) *Rose* did not present a due process objection, but "a claim brought by two Negro defendants under the Equal Protection Clause."

In *Campbell v. La.* (1998), only the second factor could be called upon to distinguish *Rose*. The defendant there, like the defendants in *Rose*, had raised an equal protection claim (although unlike the defendants in *Rose*, he was not a member of racial group allegedly discriminated against). As in *Rose* also, the foreperson came from outside the randomly selected grand jury panel; the foreperson was selected by the judge from the venire prior to the random selection of the remaining members of the grand jury panel. The state court had nonetheless held that *Hobby* should still control because the foreperson's duties were basically ministerial. The Supreme Court responded that the foreperson's functions were irrelevant, since the foreperson also was a member of the panel and voted on the indictment. Hence, if the judge discriminated in selecting the foreperson, there had been discrimination in the selection of the grand jury panel itself. The governing cases were those dealing with discrimination in the composition of the grand jury, not *Hobby*, and they clearly required dismissal of the indictment.

The *Campbell* ruling, like *Rose*, deals with a situation found in only a small group of states that allow for selection of the foreperson from outside the randomly selected panel. The second factor distinguishing *Rose* from *Hobby* similarly applies to only a few states. Among the many states in which the judge chooses the foreperson from the randomly selected panel, some do give the foreperson more extensive powers than the federal system, but few grant powers that reach the level found in *Rose*. Lower courts addressing the issue have uniformly concluded that the foreperson's role remains "ministerial" and *Hobby* controls, unless the foreperson has the kind of decisive authority attributed to the foreperson in the *Rose* case.

Hobby's third ground of distinction has much greater potential significance. *Campbell* did not have to consider whether that ground, when standing alone, would distinguish *Hobby*. If the foreperson is selected from the panel, has only ministerial duties, but panel members of the same distinct group as the defendant are intentionally excluded from the foreperson position by the judge, does an equal protection claim require dismissal of the indictment? Lower courts agree that, in light of *Campbell*, whether an equal protection remedy is available in this situation should not depend on the defendant being a member of the group discriminated against. They disagree, however, as to whether a defendant can challenge discrimination in the selection of the foreperson when the jury composition as a whole is not impacted and the foreperson's responsibilities would not bear on the decision to indict. One view is that an equal protection claim should fail here, just as the representational due process claim failed in *Hobby*. Another is that equal protection claims are distinguishable under the analysis offered in *Powers* (focusing on the discriminatory exclusion of the potential minority jurors), as the claim rests on more than the interests of the defendant.

(e) Juror Bias. Grand jurors are commonly advised, at the time of their impanelment, that they should not participate in the review of a particular case if their vote is likely to be motivated "on the basis of friendship or hatred or some other similar motivation." However, less than half of the states have statutes disqualifying jurors on grounds relating to bias. About half of those provisions are limited to persons who have a special relationship to the case (e.g., complainants, victims, and persons related to complainants, victims, targets, or witnesses). About half are broader provisions that disqualify based on a state of mind that will prevent the juror from "acting impartially." Not all states with disqualification statutes, however, view those provisions as authorizing a motion to dismiss. Some states read their disqualification provisions as allowing only for preindictment challenges to the juror or for discharge of the juror on the court's own motion. On the other hand, several state courts have recognized a defense right to dismissal of an indictment on bias grounds without the support of a bias-disqualification statute.

Where the motion to dismiss is available, its successful use is subject to two major hurdles. The first is establishing that the juror was disqualified. This requirement may operate in practice to largely limit the defendant to challenging jurors who have a personal relationship to some person involved in the case, even where the statute extends to all persons whose "state of mind prevent[s] him from acting impartially." Without showing such a personal relationship, courts are unlikely to allow the defendant to question the juror as to his or her state of mind, notwithstanding the bias provision. They clearly will not allow a general post-indictment voir dire since it threatens the "traditional secrecy" of grand jury deliberations. Even should the defendant establish that the juror should have been disqualified under the bias-disqualification statute, there remains the obstacle of provisions that prohibit dismissal of the indictment if there were a sufficient number of votes to indict, not counting the votes of any jurors who should have been disqualified.

The majority of jurisdictions do not have bias disqualification provisions and do not permit a challenge to an indictment based on the alleged bias of a particular grand juror. Thus, courts have refused to dismiss indictments where the grand jury included relatives of the victim, persons who had an ongoing relationship to the prosecutor's office, persons who were likely to be witnesses for the prosecution at trial, and persons who were political opponents of the accused. Those courts basically hold that the defendant has no right to an unbiased grand jury under either the law of the jurisdiction or the federal constitution. They do recognize the authority of the judge to discharge jurors who are likely to be biased. That power is said to be derived, however, not from any rights of persons subjected to grand jury screening, but from the authority of the court to ensure that jurors abide by their oath not to indict out of hatred or malice.

Courts following the traditionally position maintain that a bias objection simply is inconsistent with the function of the grand jury. They note in this regard that: (1) grand juries historically could indict based upon the personal knowledge of the jurors; (2) the Sixth Amendment refers to a right to an "impartial jury", but the Fifth Amendment includes no such impartiality provision; and (3) the role of the grand jury as an accusatory body, not making a final determination of guilt, does not demand the assurances of open-mindedness applied to a trial jury. In the leading Supreme Court case speaking directly to the issue of grand juror bias, *Beck v. Wash.* (1962), the Court noted that "[i]t may be that the Due Process Clause of the Fourteenth Amendment requires the State, having once resorted to a grand jury procedure, to furnish an unbiased grand jury." The *Beck* plurality found it unnecessary to reach that issue, but Justice Douglas, in dissent, argued that the state clearly did have such an obligation.

If the issue left open in *Beck* is eventually resolved with a ruling rejecting the traditional majority position, the Supreme Court will then have to decide what steps a court must take to ensure that a grand jury is not biased. The alleged bias in *Beck* stemmed from extensive preindictment publicity, and the issue that divided the Court was whether the judge impaneling the jury had gone far enough in determining "whether any prospective [grand] juror had been influenced by the adverse publicity." The plurality found that the judge had done so when he asked the prospective jurors whether they were conscious of any prejudice and excused three who acknowledged possible bias. Assuming arguendo that due process requires the state to furnish an unbiased grand jury, *Beck* suggests that the presiding judge nevertheless has only a limited obligation to inquire into possible prejudice.

(f) **Preindictment Publicity.** Another question that would arise with the rejection of the traditional position is whether a showing of extensive prejudicial pretrial publicity would be sufficient to establish the degree of bias necessary to require dismissal of the indictment. So far, the lower courts have uniformly rejected motions to dismiss based on the inflammatory character of preindictment publicity. Even those courts accepting the premise of a defense right to an unbiased grand jury have nevertheless concluded that such a right does not allow application of the concept of inherently prejudicial publicity, which is available at the trial stage to presume juror bias and require a change of venue. (see § 15.2(a)). In the grand jury setting, these courts insist upon a specific showing of actual bias on the part of the seated jurors. Moreover, they hold that the defendant, with no right to voir dire, must establish a significant likelihood of actual bias, based upon more than the character of the publicity alone, to justify an evidentiary hearing. With access to the grand jury transcript difficult to obtain in most jurisdictions, and not very likely to reveal juror bias in any event, this required showing has been aptly characterized as rendering preindictment publicity claims almost "inevitably doomed as a matter of law."

The imposition of such a substantial burden on defendants raising preindictment publicity claims is justified on several grounds. First, the "role of the grand jury historically has differed from that of a petit jury" in a way that does not require that it have "the same freedom from outside influences." The grand jury, as an investigative body, is allowed to look to "rumor, tips, and hearsay," which would include much of the material found in preindictment publicity. Second, "if preindictment publicity could cause the dismissal of an indictment, many persons, either prominent or notorious, could readily avoid indictment, a result detrimental to the system of justice." The impact of pretrial publicity upon the petit jury can be eliminated or alleviated by a change of venue, but an indictment can be returned only by a grand jury of the judicial district in which the offense occurred. Finally, courts note that the prospective defendant has other safeguards. In cases of extensive preindictment publicity, the prospective defendant is likely to be aware that the case against him will go to the grand jury, and he can always request that the supervising judge conduct a brief inquiry into the open-mindedness of the prospective jurors, as was done in *Beck*.

(g) Postconviction Review. Assume that a defendant makes a timely objection to the composition of the grand jury, but that objection is denied by the trial judge. Assume also that the defendant is subsequently convicted by a properly selected petit jury. On appeal from a subsequent conviction, should the illegality of the grand jury's composition be treated as harmless error? In *Rose v. Mitchell* (1979), Justice Stewart, dissenting, argued that "any possible prejudice" to a defendant from racial discrimination in the selection of the grand jury "disappears when a constitutionally valid trial jury later finds him guilty beyond a reasonable doubt." The majority rejected this contention, noting that it was inconsistent with a long line of cases and failed to give adequate consideration to the varied interests at stake in prohibiting racial discrimination in the selection of the grand jury. "[B]ecause discrimination on the basis of race * * * strikes at the fundamental values of our judicial system and our society as a whole," it was entirely appropriate to "revers[e] the conviction * * * in such cases without inquiry into whether the defendant was prejudiced in fact by the discrimination at the grand jury stage." While there were "costs associated with this approach," those costs (basically the reindictment and retrial of the defendant) were "outweighed by the strong policy the Court consistently has recognized of combating racial discrimination in the administration of justice."

In *Vasquez v. Hillery* (1986), the Court reaffirmed the *Rose* ruling and added another ground for failing to treat the conviction before a fairly selected petit jury as "curing" the racial discrimination in the selection of the grand jury. The grand jury, the Court noted, "does not determine only that probable cause exists," but also "has the power to charge * * * a lesser offense" than the evidence might support. "Thus even if a grand jury's determination of probable cause is confirmed in hindsight by a conviction on the indicted offense, that confirmation in no way suggests that the discrimination did not impermissibly infect the framing of the indictment and consequently, the nature or existence of the proceedings to come."

In *U.S v. Mechanik* (1986), which held that other errors in the grand jury process did not survive an intervening conviction at a fair trial (see § 7.5(d)), the Court distinguished the equal protection rulings in *Rose* and *Vasquez*. The Court noted that the considerations that led to the setting aside of a "final judgment of conviction" in those cases "have little force outside the context of racial discrimination in the composition of the grand jury." Those considerations were said to include a long line of precedent "directly applicable to the special problem of racial discrimination" and the belief that "racial discrimination in the selection of grand jurors is so pernicious and other remedies so impractical, that the remedy of automatic reversal was necessary as a prophylactic means of deterring grand jury discrimination in the future." This explanation of the racial discrimination cases might suggest that other constitutional objections to grand jury composition would not be subject to the automatic reversal rule of the racial discrimination cases. However, the rationale of *Rose* and *Vasquez* was not viewed as so limited in the later case of *Bank of Nova Scotia v. U.S.* (1988). In discussing *Rose* and *Vasquez,* the Court there noted that it had appropriately "reached a like conclusion in *Ballard v. United States* [1946], when women had been excluded from the grand jury." The key in such cases, the *Bank of Nova Scotia* Court noted, was that "the nature of the violation allowed a presumption that the defendant was prejudiced, and any inquiry into harmless error would have required unguided speculation."

§ 7.4   Indictment Challenges Based Upon Evidentiary Grounds

(a) The Federal Standard: The *Costello* Rule. *Costello v. U.S.* (1956) is the seminal Supreme Court ruling on defense challenges to a federal grand jury indictment based on the alleged incompetency or insufficiency of the evidence before the grand jury. The defendant there, charged with tax-evasion, unsuccessfully moved to dismiss the indictment upon learning that the prosecution had presented its case to the grand jury through hearsay (three government agents who had summarized what later became the testimony of 144 witnesses at trial). On review following defendant's conviction, the Supreme Court held that the trial court correctly denied the motion because the Fifth Amendment did not preclude an indictment based "solely on hearsay" and it would be inappropriate for the Court to impose such a prohibition in the exercise of its supervisory power over procedure in the federal courts. The Court, in an opinion by Justice Black, also spoke generally of the unavailability of any indictment challenge grounded upon the "competency and adequacy of the evidence before the grand jury."

The *Costello* opinion placed considerable stress upon the "history" and "traditions" of the grand jury. The Fifth Amendment's grand jury provision assumed a grand jury that "operates substantially like its English progenitor." The English grand jurors were not "hampered by rigid procedural or evidentiary rules," but could act on "such information as they deemed satisfactory," including "their own knowledge." They acted independently and were "free from control by the Crown or the judges." Thus, defendant's Fifth Amendment claim was contrary to "the whole history of the grand jury institution."

Justice Black also noted, partially in response to defendant's suggestion that the Court look to its supervisory authority, that allowing challenges of the type urged by the defendant would impose unacceptable administrative costs. "If indictments were to be held open to challenge on the ground that there was inadequate or incompetent evidence before the grand jury, the resulting delay would be great indeed." Such a rule would allow defendants in every case to "insist on a kind of preliminary trial to determine the competency and adequacy of the evidence before the grand jury." The indicted defendant would later obtain at trial "a strict observance of all the rules designed to bring about a fair verdict." There was no need to adopt "a rule which would result in interminable delay, but add nothing to the assurance of a fair trial."

The reasoning and language of *Costello* went far beyond the particular hearsay challenge presented there. Justice Black's opinion spoke of the grand jury's freedom to rely on incompetent evidence in general, and not simply to the use of hearsay. Moreover, it rejected challenges not only to the competency of the evidence, but also to its sufficiency to establish the quantum of proof needed for an indictment. Indeed, the *Costello* opinion was written so broadly as to suggest that federal courts would be powerless to dismiss an indictment even in the extreme case in which the grand jury had received absolutely no evidence that was probative. Thus, Justice Black noted that the judicial response to an indictment should be governed by a single, overriding principle: "An indictment returned by a legally constituted and unbiased grand jury, like an information drawn by the prosecutor, if valid on its face, is enough to call for a trial of the charge on the merits." Responding to the implications of that principle, Justice Burton concurred separately, seeking to establish a narrow exception that would justify minimal judicial review of the grand jury evidence. Noting that the Court's opinion apparently "would not preclude an examination of grand jury action to ascertain the existence of bias or prejudice in an indictment," Justice Burton contended that an indictment likewise should be quashed "if it is shown that the grand jury had before it no substantial or rationally persuasive evidence."

Subsequent Supreme Court cases have not put before the Court the situation hypothesized by Justice Burton, but they have produced general reaffirmations of the breadth of the *Costello* principle. Thus, a series of rulings have stated that an indictment will not be subject to challenge in the federal courts even when based on unconstitutionally obtained evidence. In the latest of those rulings, *U.S. v. Calandra* (1974), the Court relied upon the *Costello* principle in refusing to fashion a remedy that would preclude grand jury consideration of evidence obtained through an unconstitutional search and seizure. Citing *Costello* and the broad reading of *Costello* in later cases, the *Calandra* Court noted: "[T]he validity of an indictment is not affected by the character of the evidence considered. Thus, an indictment valid on its face is not subject to challenge on the ground that the grand jury acted on the basis of inadequate or incompetent evidence; or even on the basis of information obtained in violation of a defendant's Fifth Amendment privilege against self-incrimination."

(b) The Federal Standard: The Rise and Demise of the "Misconduct Exception" to *Costello*. Many lower federal courts were not entirely comfortable with the breadth of the *Costello* ruling. They expressed appreciation for "Mr. Justice Black's fear of minitrials for indictments," but noted that there also was a need to respond to the "growing use of the grand jury as a pawn or 'mere tool' of the prosecutor." These courts sought to establish a half-way station between full review of the competency and adequacy of the evidence and a refusal to consider evidentiary challenges under any circumstances. That half-way station was founded on the doctrine of supervisory control over prosecutorial misconduct. *Costello*, it was argued, did not take from the lower federal courts their traditional authority to "preserve the integrity of the judicial process" by dismissing indictments that were the product of a presentation of evidence before the grand jury so inappropriate as to constitute prosecutor "misconduct." While historical tradition allowed the federal grand jury to consider all types of evidence, that should not allow the prosecutor to attempt to pressure the jurors into issuing an indictment by deception or other improprieties in introducing evidence.

For roughly thirty years the Supreme Court did not speak to the issue, and during that period the lower courts developed an extensive "common law" of prosecutorial misconduct in presenting evidence. See § 7.5(b). Then in *U.S. v. Williams* (1992), the Court undercut at least a substantial portion (if not all) of the doctrinal foundation of such rulings. For reasons discussed in § 7.5(b), the *Williams* majority concluded that, "as a general matter at least," federal courts lacked the authority to independently prescribe standards of appropriate prosecutorial conduct before the grand jury. Federal courts could utilize their supervisory authority "as a means of enforcing or vindicating legally compelled standards of prosecutorial conduct before the grand jury," but those standards were to be found basically in statutes, the Federal Rules of Criminal Procedure, and any constitutional prohibitions. Federal courts were not free to create on their own initiative additional limits based on their independent judgment of what was needed to ensure the proper functioning of the grand jury.

Looking to this limited authority, the *Williams* majority held that the supervisory authority of the federal courts did not extend to imposing upon the prosecutor an obligation to disclose known exculpatory evidence to the grand jury. The Court noted in this regard that the imposition of such an obligation not only was not authorized by statute, court rule, or constitutional command, but also was contrary to *Costello*. "It would make little sense," the Court noted, "to abstain from reviewing the evidentiary support for the grand jury's judgment while scrutinizing the sufficiency of the prosecutor's presentation." This was so because "a complaint about the quality or adequacy of the evidence can always be recast as a complaint that the prosecutor's presentation was 'incomplete' or 'misleading'." As an illustration, the Court cited one of the more extensive lower court rulings on supervisory authority, which it described as directing that the "prosecutor should not introduce hearsay evidence before the grand jury when direct evidence was available." That directive, the Court noted, simply reflected a shift from "complaining about the grand jury's *reliance* upon hearsay evidence" to "complain[ing] about the prosecution's *introduction* of it."

Williams thus cast considerable doubt upon the continuing vitality of most, if not all, of the lower court rulings dismissing indictments based on prosecutorial misconduct in presenting evidence. Those rulings, in general, made no effort to tie the misconduct standards they recognized to a statutory prohibition, a court rule, or a constitutional command, but relied on precisely the authority to prescribe general standards of fairness that *Williams* rejected. Arguably, some of those misconduct standards can be preserved by reference to statutory prohibitions. The *Williams* opinion cited a list of illustrative court rules and statutory provisions that could be "enforced or vindicated" through the federal courts' supervisory power. Those statutory provisions included the provision restricting prosecutorial use of immunized testimony, the provision prohibiting grand jury use of unlawfully intercepted oral communications, and provisions described in *Williams* as "criminalizing false declarations before [the] grand jury" and "criminalizing subornation of perjury" The provision barring government use of immunized testimony against the immunized person can certainly provide the requisite statutory violation to sustain pre-*Williams* rulings that consideration of such testimony by the indicting grand jury constituted grounds for dismissing the indictment. As discussed in § 7.6(e), the provisions on false testimony and suborning perjury can do the same for the pre-*Williams* misconduct rulings justifying dismissal of an indictment on the basis of the prosecutor's knowing use of perjured testimony before the grand jury.

(c) State Standards. A substantial majority of the states agree with *Costello* that an indictment should not be subject to dismissal because the grand jury relied upon evidence that would be inadmissible at trial. Roughly a dozen states (mostly information states, but including a few indictment states) disagree. The broad rule of *Costello*, they note, can be justified only "if the institution of the grand jury is viewed as an anachronism." Changes in circumstances, including the availability of transcripts, justify providing trial-court review of the evidence before the grand jury even if such review was not available at common law.

Jurisdictions rejecting *Costello* provide review of the sufficiency of the evidence to support the charge, with "every legitimate inference" drawn in favor of the indictment decision. They also review the competency of the evidence, insofar as the rules of evidence apply in the particular state, but will not dismiss if, notwithstanding the introduction of some inadmissible evidence, there is sufficient admissible evidence to support the charge. The defendant's capacity to raise an evidentiary challenge is assured by either granting the defendant an automatic right to inspect the grand jury transcript or providing for an in camera inspection by the trial court, with inspection subsequently granted to the defense if the court finds a reasonable basis for the challenge.

Where the trial court erroneously fails to grant a motion to dismiss based on the incompetency or insufficiency of the grand jury evidence, that ruling is likely to come before the appellate court only after conviction. At that point, some non-*Costello* states treat the sufficiency of the grand jury evidence as a moot issue, as the conviction at trial has clearly established the presence of more than enough admissible evidence to meet the indictment standard. Other states, however, will consider the denial of the motion to dismiss on a postconviction appeal, and reverse the conviction if the trial judge clearly erred in that ruling. A similar division is found on postconviction review of prosecutorial misconduct challenges. See § 7.5(f).

§ 7.5 Misconduct Challenges: General Principles

(a) Prosecutorial Misconduct. In almost every jurisdiction making more than occasional use of the grand jury, appellate opinions recognize a trial court authority to dismiss an indictment, under at least some circumstances, based upon prosecutorial "misconduct" in the grand jury proceedings. Whether such authority exists in the remaining states is unclear. The lack of precedent is probably due to the infrequent use of the grand jury. However, it may also rest on the assumption that consideration of possible misconduct is precluded by the *Costello* principle that indictments valid on their face, if issued by a properly selected grand jury, are not subject to judicial review. Many states following *Costello*, however, distinguish supervisory-authority prosecutorial misconduct review from the *Costello*-prohibited evidentiary review on much the same grounds as the federal lower courts advanced in distinguishing prosecutorial-misconduct review in the pre-*Williams* era (see § 7.4 (b)).

Some states have statutes that limit dismissal motions to specific grounds, not including prosecutor misconduct. Court in these jurisdictions will allow misconduct challenges only if constitutionally grounded. Where a state has a constitutional guarantee of prosecution by indictment, a constitutional challenge to prosecutorial misconduct may be based on that guarantee. However, state cases analyzing constitutional challenges most frequently have done so under the due process clause of the state or federal constitution. Of course, due process has been held not to require a grand jury screening, but courts have assumed that the state cannot provide such a proceeding and then allow such basic unfairness as to render it worthless. They note that when the indictment mechanism is employed, it must be through a grand jury which is "unbiased", and prosecutorial misconduct can produce a grand jury which is no longer unbiased. This analysis can be challenged as reading into due process a prohibition that has been rejected in other contexts. See e.g., § 7.3(e).

Where statutes do not restrict the grounds for dismissing an indictment, state courts generally have found no need to turn to constitutional guarantees to find judicial authority to dismiss indictments deemed to be the product of prosecutorial misconduct. They have found an ample grounding for such dismissals in what is characterized as the "common law", "inherent", or "supervisory" authority of the court to protect the "integrity" of the grand jury's decision-making function. They note that, though courts must give "due deference to the grand jury's status as an independent body," courts also have a responsibility not to accept indictments that are the product of the prosecutor's subversion of that body. In describing the touchstone for the exercise of this responsibility, courts frequently speak of prosecutorial conduct that substantially undercuts the grand jury's independent decision making function. Other courts, however, speak of actions that deprive the grand jury process of its "fairness and impartiality."

(b) The Federal Standard: The *Williams* Limits. Prior to the Supreme Court's decision in *U.S. v. Williams* (1992), the lower federal courts had cited as prosecutorial misconduct, calling for an indictment dismissal, a broader range of actions than almost any other jurisdiction. Such misconduct included: various actions or inactions relating to the presentation of false evidence, misleading evidence, hearsay evidence, and exculpatory evidence; the prosecutor operating under a conflict of interest; the prosecutor giving incorrect legal advice; the prosecutor testifying as a witness; the prosecutor making inflammatory comments relating to the case; the prosecutor expressing a personal opinion as to guilt; the prosecutor presenting to a grand jury an indictment that is pre-signed (thereby indicating the prosecutor's opinion); allowing an unauthorized person to be present while a witness gave testimony; the prosecutor commenting on the exercise of the privilege against self-incrimination by the target or an allied witness, or presenting before the grand jury the target's immunized testimony; various violations of the Rule 6(e) provisions governing disclosure of grand jury matter; and a totality of circumstances analysis considering the combined impact of a variety of improprieties. However, *Williams* produced a sea change in the authority of federal courts to characterize prosecutorial actions as misconduct that can produce an indictment dismissal.

The *Williams* majority rejected a Tenth Circuit ruling sustaining a pretrial dismissal because of the prosecution's failure to present before the grand jury exculpatory evidence within the possession of the government. In so doing, the Court largely limited federal courts to misconduct challenges that involve either constitutional violations or violations of "one of those few clear rules which were carefully drafted and approved by this Court and by Congress to ensure the integrity of the grand jury's functions." It rejected the contention "that the [federal] courts' supervisory power could be used, not merely as a means of enforcing or vindicating legally compelled standards of prosecutorial conduct before the grand jury, but as a means of prescribing those standards of prosecutorial conduct in the first instance."

Williams acknowledged that the supervisory authority of the federal courts had been utilized to "establish standards of prosecutorial conduct before the courts themselves", but concluded that, "because the grand jury is an institution separate from the courts, over whose functioning the courts do not preside, * * * [it is] clear that, as a general matter at least, no such 'supervisory' judicial authority exists [as to grand jury proceedings]." In support of this conclusion, Justice Scalia cited various aspects of the grand jury's "functional independence from the judicial branch," including its broad investigative authority and its "operational separateness." While it was "true [that] the grand jury cannot compel the appearance of witnesses and the production of evidence, and must appeal to the court when such compulsion is required," that link to judicial subpoena authority had served as the grounding for only limited judicial supervision which had been directly related to the use of the subpoena power (as when a court "refuse[s] to lend its assistance when the compulsion the grand jury seeks would override rights accorded by the Constitution * * * [or] * * * testimonial privileges recognized by the common law"). A quite different challenge to grand jury independence was presented where, as here, the federal courts were being asked to use their "judicial supervisory power as a basis for prescribing modes of grand jury procedure."

The *Williams* Court did not absolutely foreclose the application of supervisory power to establish standards of prosecutorial conduct before the grand jury. The Court noted that "as a general matter at least," no such supervisory authority existed. Past Supreme Court precedent was described as "suggest[ing] that any power federal courts may have to fashion, on their own initiative, rules of grand jury procedure is a very limited one." In rejecting the defendant's contention that prosecutorial disclosure of exculpatory evidence should be recognized as "a sort of Fifth Amendment common law," the Court stated that any power of federal courts to fashion "common law" standards "certainly would not" go so far. Thus, the Court appeared to leave the door open for prohibiting prosecutorial conduct that may not be "specifically proscribed by Rule, statute, or the Constitution," but nonetheless has long been deemed contrary to "the traditional functions of the [grand jury] institution." That might well be the case, for example, of prosecutorial action that intentionally keeps from the grand jury potentially exculpatory evidence that the grand jury itself specifically requested. Yet, even should *Williams* eventually be read to sustain a prohibition of this type, federal supervisory authority seems likely to remain restricted in large part, if not exclusively, to responding to prosecutorial action that contradicts either the Constitution or the specific limitations set forth in Federal Rule 6 and in the United States Code.

Post-*Williams* lower court rulings have recognized that "*Williams* was not confined to exculpatory evidence" or even to misconduct claims that relate to the "quality" of the evidence placed before the grand jury. These rulings generally view misconduct dismissals as likely to have a sound footing "only where violations of positive law embodied in a rule of criminal procedure, a statute, or the Constitution are raised." As discussed in § 7.4(b) and § 7.6(e), *Williams* has been read as overriding various pre-*Williams* supervisory-authority rulings relating to the presentation of evidence, and the same should be the case for most of the other pre-*Williams* rulings discussed at the start of this subsection. Such "misconduct" as incorrect legal advice, conflicts of interest, inflammatory comments, and expression of personal opinions as to guilt are unlikely to involve violations of a court rule or statute.

(c) Juror Misconduct. While claims of juror misconduct are raised far less frequently than claims of prosecutor misconduct, those courts considering such claims uniformly recognize the authority of a trial court to dismiss an indictment on the basis of juror misconduct. In a jurisdiction that follows *Costello* and refuses to allow challenges to the sufficiency of the grand jury's evidence, challenges to juror misconduct may be seen as distinguishable for much the same reason that challenges to the grand jury's composition are distinguishable. The *Costello* principle, it may be argued, precludes judicial review of the correctness of a juror's judgment of the evidence, but actions by the jurors that take them outside of their role can be identified and reviewed apart from that judgment.

Since grand jurors, like petit jurors, are sharply restricted in their capacity to testify as to their deliberations (see § 16.9(f)), juror misconduct claims usually relate to juror activities outside the jury room. Thus, courts have sustained challenges to indictments where jurors engaged in off-the-record substantive discussions with witnesses during recesses or visited the site of the crime on their own initiative. Where the grand jury is limited to receiving sworn testimony, the juror who engages in such independent evidence gathering clearly engages in misconduct. But where the jurisdiction does not seek to restrict the common law authority of grand jurors to act on the basis of their own knowledge, one might question that conclusion. Of course, other "outside influences," such as threats or bribes, would be grounds for challenging an indictment in any jurisdiction.

In part because of the limitation upon the jurors capacity to testify about their deliberations, and in part because of the implications of *Costello*, courts have rejected challenges to the character of the grand jury's evaluative process in deciding to indict. Thus, indictments will be sustained without regard to the time spent by the jurors in evaluating the case. So too, a court will not stop to determine whether a careful evaluation would have required separate votes on different counts in the indictment rather than a single vote approving all of the charges together.

(d) The Requirement of Prejudice. Assuming misconduct is established, must there be some showing of prejudicial impact upon the grand jury's decision to indict before a trial court can dismiss the indictment? Prior to the Supreme Court's ruling in *Bank of Nova Scotia v. U.S.* (1986), several lower federal courts had suggested that, in the exercise of their supervisory powers, trial courts could dismiss an indictment even where the defendant clearly had suffered no prejudice. The courts had authority, they argued, to dismiss an indictment simply as a "prophylactic tool" designed to deter prosecutorial misconduct, at least where that misconduct was "flagrant and entrenched." The *Bank of Nova Scotia* ruling, as discussed in the next subsection, rejected the use of the supervisory authority in this fashion. Although the propriety of prophylactic dismissals has not been widely considered in the state courts, a similar result presumably would be reached in the vast majority of the states.

Bank of Nova Scotia concluded that prophylactic supervisory dismissals, because they operated without regard to prejudice, were inconsistent with the general statutory command of Federal Rule 52(a), which bars reversal of an adjudication based on an error that was "harmless" in its impact. All states have similar harmless error statutes or rules. However, a few state courts have suggested that a traditional Rule 52(a) harmless-error analysis should not apply to prosecutorial misconduct before the grand jury when its application would render "toothless" the prohibitions violated by the prosecutor's misconduct. In such cases, they note, a prophylactic dismissal would be appropriate to ensure that "today's harmless error" does not become "the standard practice of tomorrow."

In limited situations, states which have rejected a prophylactic dismissal authority will employ an "inherent prejudice" concept to justify misconduct dismissals without a specific showing of prejudice. That concept disposes with the need for a case-by-case showing of prejudicial impact and treats a particular type of misconduct as presumptively prejudicial and therefore automatically calling for a dismissal. Courts have offered two rationales in characterizing misconduct as inherently prejudicial. One is that the impact of the misconduct is too difficult to ascertain and the defendant therefore must be given the benefit of the doubt, with the court conclusively assuming the defendant was prejudiced. The other is that the flaw in the grand jury proceeding is so basic as to constitute a "structural defect," which deprived the grand jury of the authority to act. Misconduct treated as inherently prejudicial (under either or both rationales) in states recognizing that concept includes: prosecutorial presence when the grand jury deliberated and voted; the failure to put before the grand jury the specific indictment it supposedly approved; the presence of an unauthorized person (e.g., a jailor) during the taking of testimony; and the presentation of the case by a prosecutor subject to a conflict of interest.

Apart from limited instances of inherent prejudice, states tend to require a defense showing of prejudice to justify a dismissal. Most states have adopted a prejudice standard roughly similar to the federal *Bank of Nova Scotia* standard, discussed in subsection

(e) (with only a minority adding the *Mechanik* limitation, discussed in subsection (f), for postconviction review).

(e) The Prejudice Standard of *Bank of Nova Scotia*. The Supreme Court first spoke to the prejudice requirement, as applied to a motion to dismiss an indictment based on prosecutorial misconduct, in *Mechanik v. U.S.* (1986). As discussed in subsection (f), *Mechanik* dealt with the special context of judicial review following an intervening conviction. It left open the question of what showing of prejudice, if any, was needed when the motion to dismiss was considered prior to a conviction. That issue came before the Court in *Bank of Nova Scotia v. U.S.* (1988) as a result of a trial court's pretrial dismissal of an indictment, and a prosecutor's decision to appeal that ruling rather than seek a new indictment from another grand jury. The trial court's ruling had been based on its finding of several violations of the Rule 6 provisions governing grand jury proceedings, and its additional finding that the "totality of the circumstances," as reflected in various additional acts of misconduct, had resulted in a prosecutorial undermining of the integrity of the grand jury process.

The Supreme Court initially rejected the contention that the trial court had authority to issue a prophylactic dismissal. Federal courts could not use their supervisory power to undercut a statutory command, and Federal Rule 52(a) (the "harmless error rule") specifically directs federal courts to disregard any error or irregularity that "does not affect [the] substantial rights of the accused." As applied to the grand jury, Rule 52(a) precluded dismissal absent a finding that the prosecutorial misconduct had a sufficient potential for having prejudiced the defendant on the grand jury's decision to indict as not to be deemed "harmless."

Turning to the standard to be utilized in applying Rule 52(a), the Court adopted the following measure of the necessary showing of prejudice: "Dismissal of the indictment is appropriate only 'if it established that the violation substantially influenced the grand jury's decision to indict,' or if there is 'grave doubt' that the decision to indict was free from the substantial influence of such violations." This standard was derived from the traditional federal harmless error standard governing conviction reversals based on nonconstitutional trial errors, as set forth in *Kotteakos v. U.S.* (1946). The *Kotteakos* Court, as discussed in § 19.6(b), held that a trial error would be deemed to have affected the substantial rights of the accused (and therefore not be "harmless") only if the reviewing court could say "with fair assurance," after review of the entire record, that the jury had not been "substantially swayed" by the error.

The *Kotteakos* standard requires that influence of the error be measured by its impact on the decision of the adjudicator, regardless of the correctness of the result reached by the adjudicator. Thus, the presence of sufficient evidence to convict will not necessarily render the error harmless; the question to be asked is whether, "even so, * * * the error itself had substantial influence." The particular error may have been so influential as to have played an important role in the jury's decision to convict even though it was most likely that the same result would have been reached by another jury not exposed to the error. In the grand jury setting, the federal court similarly must go beyond the question of whether the grand jury had before it sufficient evidence to indict. Misconduct may be so influential as to make it likely that the grand jury gave it great weight in deciding to indict notwithstanding that the untainted remainder of the prosecution's presentation would have been sufficient to support indictment.

Kotteakos spoke of a court being able to say with "fair assurance" that the jury was not "substantially swayed by the error." Under *Bank of Nova Scotia*, a similar degree of likelihood apparently is needed to preclude a "grave doubt" that the grand jury's decision to indict was "substantially influenced" by the alleged misconduct. Lower courts have divided, however, as to the precise degree of likelihood suggested by *Kotteakos*' "fair assurance" standard. They do agree that a fair assurance can be present notwithstanding the minimal contrary indicators that would establish a "reasonable doubt" as to having significantly influenced the adjudication. A reasonable doubt is all that is necessary to preclude a finding of harmless error for constitutional violations under the standard of *Chapman v. Cal.* (§ 19.6(c)), but *Kotteakos* is seen as requiring a greater likelihood of prejudice to preclude such a finding for nonconstitutional trial errors. The "grave doubt" language of *Bank of Nova Scotia* similarly suggests a doubt with a more substantial basis than that necessary merely to create a reasonable doubt.

Although applying its reformulation of the *Kotteakos* standard to the full range of prosecutorial misconduct in the case before it, the *Bank of Nova Scotia* opinion contained language suggesting that this prejudice standard might not govern in all situations. At the outset of its opinion, the Court majority stated that it was holding that, "*as a general matter*, a district court may not dismiss an indictment for errors in grand jury proceedings unless such errors prejudiced the defendants" (emphasis added). Subsequently, the opinion noted that the Court did not have before it a case in which either (1) "constitutional error occurred during the grand jury proceedings," (2) the "grand jury's independence was infringed," or (3) there was a history of systemic prosecutorial misconduct spanning several cases and raising a "serious question" of "fundamental fairness." The applicability of the reformulated *Kotteakos* standard to those three situations accordingly may be treated as an open question, although the context of the discussion of the latter two situations arguably indicates that they are subject to the *Kotteakos* standard and distinctive only in providing inferences in its application.

(f) Postconviction Review. In *Bank of Nova Scotia*, the misconduct challenge was presented before trial and was considered in a preconviction context by both the trial and the appellate courts. If a misconduct challenge is rejected by the trial court, that ruling ordinarily will be reviewed by the appellate court only after the defendant has gone to trial and has been convicted. The appellate court then must consider whether the element of prejudice should be analyzed from the pre-conviction perspective of the trial court or in light of the intervening conviction. State courts are divided on this issue. Most hold that misconduct which had sufficient impact to justify a dismissal prior to trial will also require dismissal of the indictment upon review following a conviction. Under this view, the indictment must be dismissed because the grand jury process was inadequate and the conviction reversed because it was based upon an invalid indictment. Thus, even though the prosecution may have proven the offense in a fair trial, it must start over again with the issuance of a new indictment and a retrial of the charge.

A contrary position holds that the defendant's conviction at a fairly conducted trial renders "moot" or "harmless" any misconduct in the indictment process. Since the grand jury's task was to determine whether there was sufficient evidence to meet the standard for indictment, and since the trial jury has now found the evidence sufficient to meet the higher standard of proving guilt beyond a reasonable doubt, any misconduct that influenced the grand jury can no longer be said to have had a substantial bearing on the outcome of the case. Unlike a constitutional violation in the selection of the grand jury, prosecution or juror misconduct does not justify reversal of a conviction under either a theory of presumed prejudice affecting the conviction or the use of reversal as a deterrent sanction.

In *U.S. v. Mechanik* (1986), the Supreme Court held the latter approach to govern in federal cases. Whether that holding extends to all types of misconduct or only certain kinds of misconduct remains an open issue. *Mechanik* presented an alleged violation of the Federal Rule 6(d) provision that allows only specified persons, including "the witness under examination," to be present before the grand jury. The prosecutor had presented before the grand jury two government witnesses who appeared together and testified in tandem. The *Mechanik* majority "assumed arguendo" that there had been a Rule 6(d) violation, and that the trial court "would have been justified in dismissing * * * the indictment on that basis had there been actual prejudice and had the matter been called to its attention before the commencement of the trial." However, since the violation was ruled upon after the defendants had been convicted on the indictment at a fair trial, it now constituted a per se harmless error. The Court (per Rehnquist, J.) acknowledged that, "it might be argued in some literal sense that because * * * Rule 6(d) was designed to protect against an erroneous charging decision by the *grand jury*, the indictment should not be compared to the evidence produced by the Government at *trial*, but to the evidence produced before the grand jury." However, the procedural setting foreclosed relief even if that argument were accepted, for "there is no simple way after the verdict to restore the defendant to the position in which he would have been had the indictment been dismissed before trial. He will already have suffered whatever inconvenience, expense, and opprobrium that a proper indictment may have spared him. In courtroom proceedings as elsewhere, 'the moving finger writes, and having writ moves on.' "

Read broadly, the *Mechanik* reasoning would characterize as per se harmless almost all forms of prosecutorial misconduct before the grand jury where there has been an intervening conviction. The lower federal courts, however, have divided as to whether *Mechanik* should be read so broadly. Courts rejecting that reading argue that the "*Mechanik* [ruling] was carefully crafted along very narrow lines" and involved misconduct that "at worst, was technical, and at most, would have affected only the grand jury's determination of probable cause." These courts hold *Mechanik* inapplicable to misconduct that goes to "fundamental fairness," but they do not limit this concept to misconduct amounting to a denial of due process. Applying that standard, they have held postconviction review available for many of the prosecutorial misconduct claims recognized in the federal courts both pre-*Williams* and post-*Williams*. Other federal courts do not find such a broad exception in *Mechanik*. They note that the rationale of *Mechanik* did not depend on the "technical * * * nature of the rule at hand; [for] the Court assumed that the violation was sufficiently substantial to permit the dismissal of the indictment." These courts, if they would recognize any exception to the *Mechanik* approach, would limit that exception to misconduct reaching the level of a constitutional violation.

§ 7.6 Common Prosecutorial Misconduct Claims

(a) **The Range of Objections.** Any attempt to categorize misconduct objections necessarily loses sight of a substantial number of objections that fail to fit any common mold. Nonetheless, the objections discussed in the reported cases seem to cluster around certain basic categories of misconduct. The subsections that follow discuss these general types of misconduct. Not considered in this discussion are various types of misconduct that ordinarily would not have an impact upon the grand jury's evaluation of the case presented by the prosecution. Included in this category are such actions as the unauthorized disclosure of grand jury material to business associates of the target and the misuse of the grand jury process to develop civil suits or to gain discovery relevant to a pending criminal prosecution. In *Bank of Nova Scotia*, the Court found that several such acts of misconduct could not justify a dismissal because they would not, by their nature, have influenced the grand jury's decision to indict (e.g., the grand jurors would not even have been aware of the secrecy violations).

(b) Prejudicial Comments and Information. The American Bar Association standards provide that the prosecutor, in his appearances before the grand jury, "should not make statements or efforts to influence grand jury action in a manner which would be impermissible at trial before a petit jury." This standard applies both to impermissible prosecution arguments and impermissible references to prejudicial information in the examination of witnesses and the introduction of evidence. Although courts frequently have cited the A.B.A. standard with approval, their rulings suggest that its incorporation of the standards applicable to trial presentations will not be strictly applied. The prosecutor in the grand jury setting wears several hats that are not worn by the trial prosecutor, and these additional roles should be taken into consideration in determining what constitutes misconduct before the grand jury. The grand jury prosecutor serves as the legal advisor to the grand jury and her performance in that role may give her leeway to make comments that would not be permitted of a trial attorney, who acts strictly as an advocate and leaves the giving of legal advice to the trial judge. So too, the prosecutor occupies a leadership role in the exercise of the grand jury's investigative authority and that role may require a reference to matters that could not be put before the petit jury by a trial prosecutor. Finally, in the federal system, operating under the limitation of *Williams*, courts cannot look to the trial standards referred to in the ABA standards unless they reflect statutory, court rule, or constitutional standards applicable to the grand jury.

In light of the special character of grand jury screening (which includes a jury capacity to decide against charging even though the evidence is sufficient), and the grand jury's investigative authority (which includes exploring criminal charges beyond those presented by the prosecutor), courts have deemed relevant to the grand jury's inquiry information that would be deemed irrelevant and prejudicial at trial. Thus, where a defendant charged with sexual abuse claimed prosecution misconduct in presenting to the grand jury testimony regarding defendant's "other bad acts" (which clearly would not have been admissible at trial), the court responded that the grand jury had a responsibility to investigate all possible offenses, including even those suggested by rumors. So too, because the prosecutor can appropriately provide "general background and investigative information" to a grand jury, a prosecutor might find a need to refer to connected offenses committed by others that are part of the investigation (while advising the jurors as to defendant's lack of involvement in those offenses). Similarly, while a prosecutor at trial could hardly tell a testifying defendant that he just committed perjury, that comment could be appropriate in examining a grand jury witness if the prosecutor's purpose was not to convey to the jurors her personal evaluation of the witness' credibility, but to facilitate the inquiry by suggesting to the witness that he reconsider his testimony and come forward with the truth. So too, the prosecutor at trial could not tell a petit jury that this was a retrial of a case in which the previous jury convicted, but a prosecutor in a grand jury proceeding can rely on the transcripts of testimony before a previous grand jury, telling the grand jury that the prosecution is seeking "a re-indictment of a previous indictment voted by another grand jury."

Still another feature that distinguishes what is appropriately presented before a grand jury is the capacity of the grand jury to ask questions and expect answers on such matters as the thoroughness of the government's investigation. Such questioning can lead to the prosecutor revealing, for example, that the target had been given the opportunity to make a statement, but had exercised his *Miranda* rights. In another case, such juror questioning led the investigating officer to inform the grand jury that the photo of the defendant used in presenting a photo array to the two crime victims had come from the files of another police department, that the drug stolen was commonly used by heroin addicts, and that he believed defendant to be a heroin addict.

(c) The Prosecutor's Assumption of Other Rules. Many courts find misconduct in the prosecutor acting as a witness before the grand jury as well as its legal advisor. That practice not only conveys the appearance of professional impropriety, but it also creates the risk that the jury will give undue weight to the prosecutor's testimony because of the prestige of her office. Some courts have suggested, that there is no misconduct when the testimony does not come from the prosecutor's personal knowledge, as where the prosecutor merely reads to the grand jury the transcript of testimony before a previous grand jury. While the Model

Rules of Professional Conduct state that counsel should not assume the role of both advocate and witness, its provisions speak to the trial and exclude the situation in which counsel's testimony relates to an "uncontested issue." Courts note that the prohibition against giving testimony while serving as the grand jury's legal advisor should extend to unsworn as well as sworn testimony, leaving open the possibility that the prosecutor will violate the dual role prohibition through comments on evidence and questions put to witnesses that convey additional information presumably known to the prosecutor.

(d) Violation of the Defendant's Witness-Rights. Various courts have either held or suggested that a subsequent indictment can be challenged because of grand jury violations of what might be characterized as the defendant's "witness–rights"—that is, rights relating to the defendant having given testimony or having refused to give testimony before the grand jury. Perhaps the most well established of those violations involves a defendant who gives immunized testimony before a grand jury and later is indicted by the same grand jury. The federal immunity statute provides that testimony given by a witness under an order of immunity may not be "used against the witness in any criminal case" (with an exception for establishing perjury in that testimony). Relying on this prohibition and its Fifth Amendment grounding (and thereby establishing a source of authority consistent with *Williams*), federal courts have held that a grand jury indictment is subject to dismissal if the grand jury had before it the immunized testimony of the person it indicted (apart from a perjury indictment).

A few courts have suggested that where the grand jury violated the defendant's self-incrimination or other constitutional rights in obtaining his testimony as a witness before the grand jury, a dismissal of the subsequent indictment may be appropriate. They distinguish *Costello's* acceptance of an indictment based on unconstitutionally obtained evidence; here, it is argued, the grand jury itself violated the rights of the defendant. Other courts, however, have viewed the appropriate remedy for the grand jury's violation of a defendant's witness–rights to be the suppression of that testimony at trial, not a dismissal of the indictment. In *Williams*, the Supreme Court noted that, "while a grand jury may not force a witness to answer questions in violation of the Fifth Amendment's constitutional guarantee, * * * other cases suggest that an indictment obtained through the use of evidence previously obtained in violation of the privilege against self-incrimination is nevertheless valid." Arguably, even when the indicting grand jury itself obtained the unconstitutionally compelled evidence, it was "previously obtained" at the point of indictment. Taking a contrary position, it is noted, would adopt an artificial distinction between indictments

issued by grand juries which compelled the testimony and indictments issued by other grand juries based on that same testimony.

Courts also recognize as misconduct, possibly calling for dismissal of the indictment, the prosecution's adverse comment on the
defendant's refusal to testify before the grand jury. Such a comment falls within the general category of irrelevant and prejudicial
commentary by the prosecution. Thus, in *Bank of Nova Scotia*, the
Supreme Court took note of a challenge based upon a similar claim
with respect to a grand jury witness—that the prosecution had
called as witnesses several associates of the prospective defendant,
despite their "avowed intention to invoke the self-incrimination
privilege," in order to suggest that they had something to hide. The
Court found no factual support for the claim and thus did not have
to decide whether such action provided a grounding for dismissal of
an indictment in the federal courts. After *Williams*, such a dismissal could arguably be justified as an implementation of a constitutional prohibition against adverse prosecutorial comments on the
exercise of the privilege, but that would require extending to the
grand jury setting a constitutional prohibition recognized as a trial
right.

(e) Deception in Presenting Evidence. The Supreme
Court has held that the prosecution at trial has a due process
obligation to correct any material false evidence presented by its
witnesses when the prosecution knows that the evidence is false.
While the courts generally have agreed that the basic components
of this obligation also apply to the grand jury setting, their reasoning has varied. Several courts have relied upon due process, looking
to the due process rulings involving trial testimony. Many others
have preferred to treat the prosecution's knowing reliance upon
false testimony as action clearly inconsistent with the prosecutor's
roles both as advocate and legal advisor and therefore subject to the
general judicial authority to dismiss indictments based upon prejudicial prosecutorial misconduct. Some of these courts express doubt
as to whether the Supreme Court's due process rulings governing
the use of false testimony at trial can readily be carried over to the
grand jury's decision to indict. They note the limited function of the
indictment and the continued availability of the trial "to correct
errors before the grand jury."

Courts also disagree as to the precise element of scienter
needed for prosecutorial misconduct in the use of false testimony.
Prior to *Bank of Nova Scotia v. U.S.*, most federal courts found
misconduct only where the prosecution knowingly relied upon false
testimony, but several courts extended that responsibility to situations in which the prosecution clearly should have been aware that
the testimony was false. State courts similarly tend to insist upon

prosecution knowledge, although an occasional case will suggest that a dismissal can be based upon a reckless disregard as to falsity. In *Bank of Nova Scotia*, the Court appeared to require knowledge as a prerequisite for a misconduct finding in the federal courts. Moreover, in light of *U.S. v. Williams*, a misconduct claim in the federal courts, if not based on a constitutional violation, must be based on the violation of a statute or court rule. The most likely candidate in the use of perjured testimony would be statutes criminalizing the subornation of perjury or false declarations. Such provisions would appear to require actual knowledge of falsity at the time that the false testimony is being presented to the grand jury.

(f) Failure to Present Known Exculpatory Evidence. Appellate courts in over twenty states and the federal system have addressed the question of whether the prosecution has an obligation to present to the grand jury at least some types of known exculpatory evidence. As a result, roughly a third of the states now have appellate opinions recognizing such an obligation. While some of those opinions relied upon statutory provisions requiring the grand jury to consider "evidence within its reach which will explain away the charge," others relied upon a due process analysis or the court's common law authority over grand jury procedures. The due process grounding is drawn by analogy from the *Brady* line of cases requiring the prosecution to disclose known exculpatory material at trial (see § 16.3(b))—an analogy implicitly rejected by the Supreme Court in *Williams*. State courts looking to their common law authority or supervisory power often draw an analogy to the dismissal of an indictment where the prosecutor knowingly relied upon perjured testimony.

The Supreme Court's ruling in *Williams* constitutes the leading precedent rejecting a prosecution obligation to disclose known exculpatory evidence to the grand jury. *Williams* concluded that requiring disclosure of even the most substantial exculpatory evidence "would neither preserve nor enhance the traditional functioning" of the federal grand jury, but instead "alter the grand jury's historical role, transforming it from an accusatory body to an adjudicatory body." "The grand jury", the Court noted, "sits not to determine guilt or innocence, but to assess whether there is adequate basis for bringing a criminal charge". For that purpose, it traditionally has been sufficient for the grand jury "to hear only the prosecutor's side." Requiring the production of exculpatory evidence would, in effect, give the prospective defendant a voice in the proceedings, contrary to both grand jury function and history. It would surely "invite the target to circumnavigate the system by delivering the exculpatory evidence to the prosecutor, whereupon it would have to be passed on to the grand jury—unless the prosecutor is willing to take the chance that a court will not deem the evidence important enough to qualify for mandatory disclosure." Moreover, allowing a challenge to the indictment based on the prosecutor's failure to present known exculpatory evidence would undercut the *Costello* prohibition, as "a complaint about the quality or adequacy of the evidence can always be recast as a complaint that the prosecutor's presentation was 'incomplete' or 'misleading'."

State courts recognizing a prosecutorial obligation to present to the grand jury known exculpatory evidence have varied in their description of the scope of that obligation. All agree that the evidence must be "known" to the prosecutor, but some have suggested that here, in contrast to the obligation imposed at trial, the knowledge of the prosecution may be limited to the knowledge of the individual prosecutors presenting the case to the grand jury. The primary variation, however, relates to describing what falls within the category of "exculpatory evidence" for the purpose of this obligation. In general, that category has been defined much more narrowly than the due process standard of material exculpatory evidence that must be disclosed at trial. Four considerations are said to require a narrower definition in the grand jury setting. First, the prosecutor at this stage of the proceedings ordinarily does not have the advantage of defense motions identifying those items that the defense views as potentially exculpatory. It would impose an intolerable burden on the government to require it to "sift through all the evidence to find statements or documents that might be exculpatory." Second, at this preliminary stage of the proceeding, where both the possible charges and defenses may be uncertain, the prosecutor is likely to have greater difficulty in determining what evidence is exculpatory. Third, consideration must be given to the "unique role of * * * grand jury [review] as a flexible and non-adversarial process." It is a basic premise of grand jury screening that the "prosecutor does not have a duty to present defendant's version of the facts." Finally, taking a page from *Costello*, some courts have stressed the need to avoid "convert[ing] a grand jury proceeding from an investigative one into a mini-trial of the merits."

(g) Erroneous Legal Advice. As legal advisor to the grand jury, the prosecutor has an obligation to give the grand jury sufficient information concerning the applicable law "to enable it intelligently to decide whether a crime has been committed." Only a handful of states, however, have precedent dealing with that obligation. This may be due in part to practical obstacles to challenging instructions. The instructions are not transcribed in some jurisdictions, and the transcription is not likely to be available to the defense in any event, apart from the dozen jurisdictions that provide for automatic transcript disclosure. Perhaps even more significantly, in jurisdictions that adhere to the *Costello* limitation of judicial review, error in the prosecution's charge on the offense is not likely to be viewed as falling within the "misconduct exception" to that limitation as such errors rarely will involve the intentional deception that is said to justify that exception.

Among those states recognizing challenges to the prosecutor's legal instructions, all agree that the prosecutor need not give instructions even roughly approximating the comprehensiveness of the trial judge's charge to the petit jury. They also agree, however, that an instruction may be "so misleading," due to mistakes or omissions, that the ensuing indictment "will not be permitted to stand even though it is supported by legally sufficient evidence." In some states, courts ask whether the instruction was sufficient to permit the grand jury to determine whether the evidence before it was legally sufficient. In others, courts speak of whether the instructions were so erroneous or lacking in needed substance as to constitute "flagrant and overbearing misconduct", or operate to "compromise" the "fundamental integrity of the indictment process."

(h) Presence of Unauthorized Persons. Grand jury secrecy provisions commonly provide that no person other than the grand jurors may be present during deliberations and voting, while only the jurors, prosecutors, supporting personnel (e.g., stenographers) and the witness under examination may be present during any other portion of the proceedings. It is uniformly accepted that a violation of the provisions on presence may justify a pretrial dismissal of an indictment, but a division exists as to whether dismissal here should be conditioned on the usual requirement of a case-specific showing of likely prejudice. Courts requiring such a showing see no basis for distinguishing the presence of an unauthorized person from other irregularities in grand jury proceedings (e.g., improper comments by the prosecutor). In determining whether an unauthorized presence presents a sufficient likelihood of prejudicial impact, these courts look to such factors as: (1) the relationship of the person improperly present to the prosecution of the offense (e.g., whether that person was the complainant, whose very presence might impose pressure on the jurors, or merely a clerk); (2) the stage at which that person was improperly present (i.e., during deliberations and voting, or simply during the presentation of evidence or argument); (3) where a person was improperly present during the presentation of testimony, whether that person had a relationship to the witness that could have influenced the witness' testimony; (4) the length of the unauthorized presence; and (5) whether the individual made any overt attempt to influence the grand jurors or a witness.

A substantial number of state courts treat unauthorized presence as a per se ground for dismissal (a position rejected as to federal courts in *Bank* of *Nova Scotia*). A per se approach is required, these courts argue, because dismissal only upon a showing of likely prejudice would offer "too great a possibility for the exercise of undue influence to be condoned." A prejudicial impact is so difficult to determine that it often would be missed. The appropriate approach, these courts argue, is to hold that even "the slightest intrusion of an unauthorized person into a grand jury proceeding voids the indictment."

*

Chapter 8

THE LOCATION OF THE PROSECUTION

Table of Sections

For additional analysis of the above topics and citations to authorities supporting their discussion in this Book, consult the authors' 7-volume *Criminal Procedure* treatise, also available as Westlaw database CRIMPROC. See the Table of Cross-References in this Book.

---

§ 8.1 Venue: General Principles

(a) **Distinguishing Venue From Vicinage.** The term "venue" refers to the locality of the prosecution; venue sets the particular judicial district in which a criminal charge is to be filed and in which it will be tried. Like venue, "vicinage" refers to a particular district, but it is the district from which the jurors will be drawn. See § 14.2(e). It also differs from venue in that it inherently identifies a particular district. The concept of venue simply requires that a district be designated in a venue provision (constitutional or statutory); the concept of vicinage in itself identifies a particular geographical district and arguably limits the territorial scope of that district. The vicinage concept requires that the jurors be selected from a geographical district that includes the locality of the commission of the crime, and it traditionally also mandates that such district not extend too far beyond the general vicinity of that locality. Thus, while a venue provision must specify how the appropriate district for trial is to be determined (or even identify that district by name), a vicinage provision can merely state that the defendant has a right to a jury "of the vicinage." That language will be taken to designate automatically, as the appropriate district for jury selection, the judicial district that includes the place of the offense.

Since venue provisions traditionally have identified the place of the trial by reference to the place where the crime was committed, which is also the reference for vicinage, the two requirements are sometimes tied together in the same provision. That is hardly necessary, however, for each requirement to bear upon the other. Though a provision may speak only to vicinage or only to venue, it typically builds upon the assumption that the locality requirements of venue and vicinage will go hand in hand. Thus, a provision giving to the defendant a right to a jury selected from a judicial district constituting the vicinage commonly will also grant, by implication, a parallel right to be tried in that judicial district; for unless the legislature specifically provides otherwise, the prevailing assumption is that the trial should be held in the district from which the jury is selected. So too, where a venue provision provides for trial in the judicial district in which the alleged offense was committed, that district commonly will also constitute the vicinage, so the venue provisions will operate by implication to require that jurors be selected from the vicinage; for it is assumed also that the jury will be drawn from the judicial district in which the trial takes place.

The overlap of venue and vicinage, however, is not inevitable. First, there exists the possibility (largely theoretical) of prescribing different districts under the two concepts. This could be done by providing for a jury selected from the district of the crime, as required by the concept of vicinage, while setting the venue for the trial elsewhere (as the concept of venue does not inherently require reference to the place of the crime). Secondly, even where, as is almost always the case, the venue provision refers to the district in which the crime was committed, and thereby encompasses the vicinage, the vicinage concept can demand a smaller geographical unit than that required by the venue provision alone. Traditionally, the vicinage concept demands that the geographical boundaries of the district of jury selection not extend substantially beyond the general vicinity of the place of the crime. Tying a venue provision to the district of the crime, on the other hand, says nothing about the boundaries of the district except that the district include the locality of the crime.

The distinction between venue and vicinage underlies the adoption of separate jury selection and venue provisions in the federal constitution and in Congress' initial legislation implementing those constitutional provisions. Though the framers of the Constitution initially saw no need to safeguard by constitutional provision the basic rights of the individual (a position later altered with the agreement to add the Bill of Rights), they nonetheless did include in the body of the Constitution certain requirements of criminal procedure that would protect the accused. Not surprisingly, one of those safeguards guaranteed that the accused would not be forced to trial outside of the state in which the charges against him arose. Appropriate venue had been a matter of great concern to the colonists. They had fiercely opposed Acts of Parliament that allowed the Crown to take colonists to England or to another colony for trial on various capital offenses. Article III, Section 2, of the Constitution prohibited the federal government from engaging in a similar practice. It provided: "The Trial of all Crimes, except in Cases of Impeachment, shall be by Jury, and such Trial shall be held in the State where said Crimes shall have been committed; but when not committed within any State, the Trial shall be at such Place or Places as the Congress may by Law have directed."

When the Constitution came before the states for ratification, Article III was strongly criticized for failing to guarantee to the accused a jury drawn from the vicinage. Article III had two flaws in this regard. First, a district as large as an entire state was far too large to constitute a vicinage. Second, it was never anticipated that the jury would be selected from the entire state. It was anticipated that trials would take place only in one or two major cities within the state and jurors would be drawn primarily from that community. Thus, in a larger state, a defendant could be tried many miles from the county in which the crime was committed with none of the jurors selected from that county. The original version of what later became the jury selection clause of the Sixth Amendment (sometimes described as the "vicinage clause") sought to impose a true vicinage requirement by requiring that the jury ordinarily be selected from the county in which the crime was committed. That proposal was challenged as impracticable and contrary to the practice in various states. The compromise eventually adopted included the combination of the Sixth Amendment and special jury selection provisions in the first Judiciary Act.

The Sixth Amendment provision granted to the accused a right to trial "by an impartial jury of the State and district wherein the crime shall have been committed, which district shall have been previously ascertained by law." Unlike Article III, Section 2, the Sixth Amendment specifically recognized a right to have the jury selected from a particular district. That right was no longer left to the implication of a venue provision. However, the geographical boundaries of the particular district were not defined in the Constitution, nor were they left to a judicial determination that might look to the vicinage concept. Certainty was to be provided, and prosecution discretion thereby limited, by the requirement that the district be "previously ascertained" by legislation. However, the districts set by the Congress could be as large as the state itself, and in the first Judiciary Act, the districts for all but two states included the entire state (the other two states were each divided into two districts).

The Judiciary Act also spoke to the drawing of jurors. As to trials generally, jurors were to be summoned "from such parts of the district * * * as shall be most favorable to an impartial trial, and so as not to incur an unnecessary expense, or unduly to burden the citizens of any part of the district with such services." A more restrictive provision was added for capital offenses, which constituted a significant portion of all federal crimes. Here trial was to be held in "the county where the offence was committed" if that could be done "without great inconvenience." But even where such inconvenience required that the trial be moved to some other county within the district, the court was directed to summon "twelve petit jurors at least" from the county where the offense was committed.

In contrast to the Sixth Amendment, many states have constitutional vicinage provisions which are true to the common law in limiting jury selection to a geographical area that might legitimately be described as the "vicinity" or "neighborhood" of the crime. Three give the defendant a right to a jury "of the vicinage." Almost a dozen provide for a right to a trial by jury "of the county in which the crime shall have been committed." A slightly smaller number speak of a jury "of the county or the district," allowing legislative creation of multi-county districts, but with districts still much smaller than the federal districts and more consistent with the common law vicinage concept (which recognized that "the vicinity" could extend beyond a single county). Because the district from which the jurors come is assumed to be the intended place of trial (absent a legislative directive to the contrary), these constitutional vicinage provisions also operate as limitations on venue. Thus, state legislation that seemingly allows venue outside the judicial district of the commission of the crime will be challenged under the state's constitutional vicinage provision, as will be legislation that allows for a change in venue (without defense waiver) from the district of the crime.

(b) The "Crime–Committed" Formula. The standard formula for setting venue calls for dividing the territory of the political entity (i.e., the state or nation) into geographical districts and then selecting as the appropriate venue that district in which the alleged crime was committed. The "crime-committed" formula is imposed as a constitutional requirement in the federal system under Article III. Only a handful of states have constitutional venue provisions (all of which impose the crime-committed formula), but many additional states make the location of the trial in the district of the crime a constitutional command through the combination of a constitutional vicinage provision and the absence of legislation authorizing trial in a district other than that of jury selection.

Although not always followed by the English, the crime-committed formula was well established in English common law at the time of the adoption of the Constitution. It presumably grew out of the role of the grand jury as a charging body, and the restriction of the grand jury to inquiring into crimes that occurred in the county for which it was sworn. Though the crime-committed formula often facilitated use of a jury of the vicinage, that formula was commonly praised as also serving the independent value of providing a forum convenient to the accused in presenting his defense. Relevant evidence would most readily be accessible at the place where the incident constituting the alleged offense had occurred. Any witnesses to the incident were most likely to live in the vicinity and any relevant tangible evidence was most likely to be found there.

At the time of the adoption of the Constitution, mobility of individuals still was quite limited, and the place of the commission of the crime was most likely also be at or near the accused's place of residence, and this added to the convenience for the defense. Of course, there would be instances in which the accused would have traveled to another district and be accused there of having committed a crime. In that situation, the crime-committed formula would deprive him of the convenience of being tried in his home district. The choice nonetheless was made for the place where the critical events had occurred. That choice may have reflected a belief that greater convenience to the accused was in a trial where the witnesses to the events were located rather than the place of his residence. It may also have been based, however, on other considerations related less to the convenience of the accused and more to the concerns of the community in which the crime took place. If only the defendant's interests were at stake, the defense could have been given the choice of having the case tried either in the district of the offense or the district of the defendant's residence. However, the defendant was never given such a choice. The absence of such an option has been viewed by some as evidence that the crime-committed formula was grounded as much on serving the interest of the public in the fair and efficient enforcement of the criminal law as on the defendant's interest in being tried in a convenient forum.

Whether or not the crime-committed formula was designed in part to promote the public interest in law enforcement, it certainly supports that interest in several ways. Since the place in which the crime is committed typically also is the place that suffered from the crime, the crime-committed formula locates the prosecution in the community that has the greatest interest in enforcing the law. So too, since the act and its consequences are most likely to have occurred in the district of the crime, insofar as the legal system seeks to judge those acts and consequences by reference to community standards, that district has the strongest claim for utilizing its community standards (as applied by a local jury). The crime committed formula also designates the district of most likely convenience for the prosecution. Its primary witnesses (including the complainant) are likely to be located in the place where the crime occurred and therefore can more easily be presented at a trial in that district. Also, the defendant most frequently will have been arrested at the place of the offense, and a trial in the same district will avoid the necessity of transporting him a long distance.

(c) Multi–Venue Offenses. When the framers of the Constitution included the crime-committed formula in both Article III, Section 2, and the Sixth Amendment, they referred in the singular to the "state" and the "district" in which the crime "shall have been committed." This reflected the assumption that a crime ordinarily would be committed in a single place. At a time when travel was difficult and slow, and communications systems were rudimentary, all of the action constituting an offense and all of the immediate harm flowing from that action commonly occurred within a limited geographic area. Even at that time, however, there were certain federal offenses that could occur in more than one place and those two or more places would occasionally be in two different states. At the state level, where the judicial districts typically were counties, it was even more likely that some offenses would be committed in more than one judicial district.

The offenses most likely to be multi-venue offenses were those commonly described as "continuing offenses." These were offenses having basic elements that continued (or, as some would say, "repeated themselves") over a period of time as part of a single crime. A prime illustration is kidnaping, which starts when the victim is taken into custody and continues until the victim is no longer under the control of the kidnappers. If the kidnaped victim was moved from one district to another in the course of the kidnaping, the offense was committed in each of those districts. At common law, larceny was placed in the same category as the continued possession of the stolen property by the thief was viewed as a continuation of the trespassory taking.

A crime also could occur in more than one place when it had two or more distinct parts. Such offenses created a multi-venue potential when they required two separate elements that could occur at separate places. A criminal statute, for example, might define the offense as requiring first the doing of a prohibited act and then the causing of a certain victim response, with the act and response capable of occurring in two different localities. Similarly a statute may require two distinct acts by the defendant which can occur in different places. The classic example here is the crime of conspiracy where it requires both an agreement and an overt act in furtherance of that agreement. Some courts have placed forcible rape in the same category, concluding that venue can apply both in the place where the defendant placed the victim in fear through force or threats of force and the place where the defendant engaged in the sexual act involved.

Multi-venue also was possible where the offense could be committed by a single act that could start in one place and finish in another. Thus, the "making" of a false claim might start with the placing of that claim in motion and end with its actual presentation. Some courts view the act of conversion as one that can start with the decision to convert a financial account or instrument held in trust to one's own use and end when that scheme is fulfilled by obtaining funds for defendant's use. So too, the attempted evasion of tax liability might start with the arrangement of a false transaction and end with the filing of a false return utilizing that transaction. While these offenses are distinguishable from those in which the act is repetitive, such as kidnaping, they are sometimes also characterized as capable of "continuation" in the sense that the prohibited action, as it involves multiple components, may start at one place and finish elsewhere.

The possibility of a multi-venue commission of an offense was recognized as early as the sixteenth century, when Parliament adopted a provision governing homicides committed through actions in one county that resulted in death in another. Crimes committed in more than one district were rare, however, and they were limited to a small group of offenses. By the mid-nineteenth century, however, with significant advances made in transportation and communications, crimes committed in more than one judicial district became much more common. This was particularly true for the federal system, which dealt with many crimes relating to commerce. In 1867, Congress adopted a general provision governing offenses committed in more than one district. That provision, in a slightly modified form, is now contained in Section 3237 of the federal criminal code. It provides:

> Except as otherwise expressly provided by enactment of Congress, any offense against the United States begun in one district and completed in another, or committed in more than one district, may be inquired of and prosecuted in any district in which such offense was begun, continued, or completed.

Most states have adopted provisions, similar to § 3237, authorizing multi-district venue when the commission of an offense involves more than one district. These provisions typically refer to offenses "committed partly" in more than one district. Some state provisions, however, seek to provide further direction, identifying characteristics that can place the commission of a crime in more than one district. One common formulation refers to "the acts or effects thereof constituting or requisite to the consummation of the offense occur[ing] in two or more counties." Another formulation refers to "conduct or results which constitute elements of the offense occur[ing] in two or more counties." While these formulations are not without ambiguity, both would appear to preclude the strict reliance on "key verbs" that has led federal courts at times to sharply limit the application of § 3237 (see § 8.2(a)).

As will be seen in § 8.2, courts often have experienced difficulties in determining whether an offense was committed in more than one place. The legislature, however, can readily shape the offense so that it clearly will fall in the multi-venue category. For example, though the crime of "sending" an item to another state might be limited to the place at which the item was placed in the stream of transportation, the crime of "transporting" would occur in any district through which the item is carried. By defining offenses so that they can be committed in more than one place, Congress can provide for extremely flexible venue. Indeed, as to most commercial activities affecting products distributed throughout the United States, Congress may, if it so chooses, provide for what is, in effect, nationwide venue. As discussed in § 8.2(f), precisely that strategy has been employed for certain federal offenses.

(d) Special Legislation. The most common special venue legislation deals with situations in which the crime-committed formula will not produce a venue. One such situation is presented by the crime committed within the territorial reach of the government but not within the territorial boundaries of any judicial district. The federal constitution recognized that difficulty when it provided in Article III that Congress could designate the "place or places" of trial when the crime "was not committed within any State." In its exercise of that authority, Congress has adopted a special provision governing the trial of offenses committed upon the high seas "or elsewhere outside the jurisdiction of any particular state or district."

Another troubling situation under the crime-committed formula is that in which it is extremely difficult or impossible to establish exactly where the events in question occurred. Several different legislative approaches are used to meet such situations. Recognizing that the exact location of a particular event is often difficult to prove, states have adopted "either county legislation" for offenses alleged to have been committed within a specified distance (e.g., 500 yards) of the boundary between two counties. The difficulty of proving the exact location of a homicide has led to statutes allowing trial in the place where the body of the victim is found, sometimes automatically and sometimes only where the place of death or mortal wound cannot readily be determined. Similarly, because victims of crimes committed in moving vehicles often are uncertain as to where the crime occurred, several states provide as to such crimes that, if the place of the offense cannot readily be determined, venue will be in any county through which the vehicle passed on the journey in question.

Some special state legislation simply has no relationship to the crime-committed formula. Thus, a Minnesota statute provides for prosecution of child abuse "either in the county where the alleged abuse occurred or the county where the child is found," and an Illinois statute provides that "a person who commits the crime of cannabis trafficking or controlled substance trafficking may be tried in any county." Such statutes are found in states without a constitutionalized crime-committed provision. Where a state has either a constitutional venue guarantee of a right to trial in the county in which the offense was committed or a constitutional guarantee of a jury of the vicinage, special venue legislation can pose constitutional difficulties insofar as it can be seen as going beyond the implementation of the crime-committed formula. Thus, state courts have struck down provisions that allowed for venue in either county for crimes committed close to their mutual boundary when that venue option was not limited to instances in which it could not readily be determined precisely where the crime occurred.

As noted in § 2.1(d), the Supreme Court has not yet squarely ruled on whether the "vicinage clause" of the Sixth Amendment ("requiring a jury of the state and district wherein the crime shall have been committed") is applicable to the states via the Fourteenth Amendment's due process clause. Lower courts considering the issue in a venue context have split on whether the vicinage clause should be viewed as a fundamental aspect of the Sixth Amendment jury clause and therefore applicable to the states. Assuming that the clause does apply, the question arises as to what geographical unit constitutes the appropriate "district" for Sixth Amendment purposes "wherein the crime shall have been committed."

In state vicinage provisions, the county is often designated as the geographic district of the vicinage, but courts speaking to the requirement of an incorporated Sixth Amendment vicinage provision generally have not been so restrictive. They note that the Sixth Amendment "vicinage" provision is not a true vicinage requirement as it has never required a jury from the "vicinity" or "neighborhood". The original federal judicial districts typically covered the territory of an entire state, and any special venue district chosen by state legislation would be within the state. Arguably, the key to the Sixth Amendment clause as applied to the states is the prior legislative designation of the district, and that too clearly is satisfied by special venue legislation. Accordingly, application of the Sixth Amendment clause to the states is deemed to pose no significant difficulty for special legislation, even where it authorizes venue in every county in the state.

A contrary interpretation, would argue that the key to the Sixth Amendment is the use of legislatively designated "standard districts" that apply across-the-board in identifying the district in which the crime was committed. Thus, if the state ordinarily designates the county as its district, it would violate the incorporated vicinage clause to allow venue in a county other than that in which the offense was committed. Even if the vicinage clause allows districts as large as the entire state, once the state establishes a smaller district, the crime-committed standard must be applied to this district. The California supreme Court adopted this position on the assumption that the vicinage clause was incorporated, but later concluded that the clause was not incorporated.

(e) Proof of Venue. No more than a dozen states treat venue in much the same manner as other procedural prerequisites for prosecution (e.g., a valid preliminary hearing bindover, or a grand jury charge). In those jurisdictions, the defendant must put the venue prerequisite in issue by a pretrial motion to dismiss, with the court then making a determination that venue does or does not exist. Venue is viewed in these jurisdictions as a procedural prerequisite, to be treated no differently than, for example, the prohibition against double jeopardy or the requirement of a speedy trial.

The federal system and the vast majority of the states view venue quite differently. They view venue as part of the case that the prosecution must prove at trial. Indeed, all but a few of these jurisdictions treat venue as a factual question to be decided by the jury in a jury trial. The court has the responsibility for determining whether, as a matter of law, the events alleged to have occurred in a particular place could be sufficient to establish that the crime was committed at least in part in that district. The jury then decides the underlying factual issue, such as whether a particular act did occur in the district, or whether an act had the objective or other quality that the court deems necessary to characterize it as locating the commission of the crime.

Though most jurisdictions treat proof of venue as a jury issue, they ordinarily do not view venue as one of those matters that must invariably be submitted to the jury. Courts frequently state that a charge on venue is required only "when trial testimony puts venue in issue." Thus, a jury charge on venue is not required "where the entirety of the defendant's illegal activity is alleged to have taken place within the trial * * * [district] and no trial evidence is proffered that the illegal act was committed in some other place or that the place alleged is not within the * * * [district]." Courts also have concluded that the failure to charge the jury on venue should not constitute error, even when the evidence puts venue in issue, where the defendant failed to request a charge on venue.

Jurisdictions requiring prosecution proof of venue at trial are divided as to the level of persuasiveness of the prosecution's proof of venue. The federal courts and a substantial number of state courts hold that the facts supporting venue only need be established by a preponderance of the evidence. They take the position that venue is not a true element of the crime (which elements constitutionally must be established by proof beyond a reasonable doubt), as it does not relate even remotely to the issues of guilt or innocence or the level of culpability. Some states, however, require proof beyond a reasonable doubt.

§ 8.2   Applying the Crime–Committed Formula

Although venue issues arise in state as well as federal cases, the federal cases present the most extensive exploration of the application of the crime-committed formula. The federal courts have been a leader in this task, in part because federal offenses so often implicate more than one place, and at the same time, lack precise counterparts in traditional common law crimes. As discussed below, the federal precedent, over the years, has looked primarily to three different modes of analysis in identifying those aspects of an offense that are critical in establishing venue in potential multi-venue situations: (1) a literal analysis of the statutory terms that describe the prohibited conduct, looking particularly at the "key verb" (sometimes described as a "literalism" approach); (2) an analysis that looks to the "nature of the offense" as identified by certain elements of the offense; and (3) a multifaceted "substantial contacts" analysis. While the Supreme Court in its most recent opinions has placed primary emphasis on the second of these approaches, all three have been considered by state courts. In addition, state courts even more frequently have referred to the Supreme Court's discussions of "constitutional venue policy". That policy is viewed as relevant to resolving ambiguities under both the modes of analysis noted above and the state statutes that set forth specific criteria for determining whether an offense was committed in more than one district.

(a) **Literalism.** The crux of the literalist approach to the application of the crime-committed formula is the assumption that most crimes contain a key verb that describes the core of the crime and thereby identifies the act which sets venue. While all would agree that a "key verb" often helps to sets venue, the critical question is whether that verb should almost invariably be viewed as providing an answer in itself. *Travis v. U.S.* (1961) is, perhaps, the most prominent ruling supporting an exclusive "key verb" approach.

The defendant in *Travis*, a union official in Colorado, was charged under a statute applicable to any person who, "in a matter within the jurisdiction of any department or agency of the United States," knowingly "makes" any false statement. The false statements at issue were non-Communist affidavits executed and mailed in Colorado to the offices of the N.L.R.B. in Washington, D.C. The defendant contended, and the Court majority agreed, that the government had erred in bringing the prosecution in Colorado as the offense only could be committed in the District of Columbia. The majority opinion stressed that the offense required that the false statement be "within the jurisdiction" of the N.L.R.B. Section 9(h) of the National Labor Relations Act did not require union officers to file non-Communist affidavits, but provided for their voluntary filing as a prerequisite to invoking the Board's authority in the investigation and issuance of complaints against employers. Accordingly, the majority reasoned, "filing [of the affidavit] must be completed before there is a 'matter within the jurisdiction' of the Board." In *U.S. v. Lombardo* (1916), the Court had dealt with an analogous situation. The defendant there, the operator of a house of prostitution in Seattle, was charged with the failure to file with the national immigration office (located in the District of Columbia) a form relating to an alien employed as a prostitute. The *Lombardo* Court, after quoting with approval the trial court's analysis of the verb "file," concluded that a "filing" could occur only in one place, and the failure to file offense therefore had occurred only in the District of Columbia. The *Travis* majority concluded that the filing prerequisite here similarly established a single place in which the false-statement offense occurred, and that place also was Washington, D.C.

The *Travis* majority acknowledged that "Colorado, the residence of the [defendant], might offer conveniences and advantages to him which a trial in the District of Columbia might lack." It did not disagree with Justice Harlan's contention in dissent that "the witnesses and relevant circumstances surrounding the contested issues in such cases more probably will be found in the district of the execution of the affidavit than at the place of filing." Its response was that the "constitutional requirement is as to the locality of the offense and not the personal presence of the offender," and here the language of the offense set that locality in only one place. When Congress required a filing to consummate the offense, it "carefully indicated the locus of the crime," precluding reliance on either the issuance of the false statement in Colorado or the mailing of the statement from Colorado as actions that expanded venue to include both Colorado and the District of Columbia.

Even before *Travis*, the Supreme had raised doubts about complete reliance upon the key verb when, in *U.S. v. Anderson* (1946), it spoke of the "locus detecti * * * being determined from the nature of the crime alleged and the location of the act or acts constituting it." *Travis*, however, had suggested that the *Anderson* reference was irrelevant where the key verb was unambiguous. Following that lead, the federal lower courts continued to describe "examining * * * the verbs employed in the statute" as the "usual method" for determining where venue will lie. They did not accept the criticism that a key verb approach gave far too much weight to statutory phrasing that typically was the product of drafting goals that had very little to do with clearly indicating the locus of the crime. They recognized, but attributed to Congress, the responsibility for setting, through Congress' use of key verbs, different venues for functionally similar offenses (as in *Travis*, where the majority acknowledged that, if § 9(h) had mandated the submission of a non-communist affidavit, the affidavit might well have been "within the jurisdiction" of the NLRB at the time of mailing, placing venue in Colorado). Subsequently, in *U.S. v. Rodriguez–Moreno* (1999), the Supreme Court acknowledged such deficiencies in key-verb analysis when it made clear that the *Anderson* approach, stressing the "nature of the offense", should prevail over key-verb analysis in determining venue in federal courts.

At issue in *Rodriguez-Moreno* was the multi-venue potential of a criminal statute prohibiting the "use" or "carry[ing]" of a firearm "during and in relation to any crime of violence." The defendant there, who had participated in a kidnaping that extended over several districts, argued that the prosecution for this firearms offense could be brought only in the district in which he threatened the victim with a weapon, and not in other districts where the kidnaping had occurred without the weapon. Relying on what it called the "verb test," the Third Circuit sustained that contention, reasoning that venue for this part of the overall criminal transaction was tied to where the firearm was either used or carried. The Supreme Court rejected that conclusion, looking to the standard of *Anderson*. It noted that "the 'verb test' certainly has value as an interpretive tool," but should "not be applied rigidly, to the exclusion of other relevant statutory language." Such language here established that the underlying violence offense itself was another element of the firearms crime. Thus, the crime had the character of an offense with "two distinct elements." This was so even though "the crime of violence element * * * is embedded in a prepositional phrase and not expressed in verbs." Also, contrary to the dissent, the majority found nothing in the character or language of the firearm offense suggesting that it was intended to be an offense which did not begin until the two elements combined. "Congress prescribed both the use of firearm and the commission of the acts that constitute the violent crime," and either provided an appropriate venue for the crime that was the product of the two.

(b) **Nature of the Offense.** In recent years, the Supreme Court, building on *Anderson*, has emphasized a venue inquiry that focus on the "nature of the offense." The two leading applications of this inquiry are *U.S. v. Rodriguez–Moreno*, described above, and *U.S. v. Cabrales* (1998).

Cabrales involved a prosecution under a money laundering statute making it a crime to "knowing[ly] * * * conduct * * * a financial transaction which * * * involves proceeds of specified unlawful activity * * * knowing that the transaction is designed * * * to avoid a transaction reporting requirement." The prosecution was brought in Missouri, where drug trafficking had produced the criminally derived funds, but the alleged financial transactions were deposits and withdrawals made in Florida (and it was not alleged that the defendant had transported the funds from Missouri to Florida). The government argued that venue in the district of the underlying criminality (here Missouri) was proper because (1) the underlying crime producing the funds is an essential element of the money laundering offense, (2) the laundering activity impacts the underlying criminal activity by making it profitable and impeding its detection, and (3) the district of the underlying offense is a most appropriate district for trial because of the need to prove that the funds were criminally derived and the "interests of the community victimized by [the] drug dealers." The Supreme Court, in a unanimous ruling, found these arguments unpersuasive.

The *Cabrales* opinion looked to the "general guide" of *Anderson* that venue "be determined from the nature of the crime alleged and the location of the acts or acts constituting it." The money laundering offense, if noted, was "defined in statutory proscriptions * * * that interdict only the financial transactions (acts located entirely in Florida), not the anterior criminal conduct that yielded the funds allegedly laundered." To be criminally liable, "the money launderer must know she is dealing with funds [criminally] derived," but "it is immaterial whether * * * [she] knew where the first crime was committed." Admittedly, "whenever a defendant acts 'after the fact' to conceal a crime, * * * it might be said that the first crime is an essential element of the second, * * * and that the second facilitated the first," but that does not establish the venue for the second in the district of the first. The government had available to it the potential for trial in the district of drug trafficking if it charged the defendant with a conspiracy with the drug dealers and treated the money laundering as an overt act. It could not use charges of money laundering, which "describe activity" of the "[defendant] alone, untied to others," as a substitute for a conspiracy charge.

Looking to the essential character of the crime created by Congress, *Cabrales* and *Rodriguez-Moreno* found that one crime treated related criminal conduct as no more than an anterior factor giving rise to a separate offense, and the other treated such conduct as critical element of the crime itself. *Cabrales* held that the element that characterized the money laundering offense was the laundering element, and though an illegal source of the funds to be laundered also was an element, the criminal conduct creating that status was simply an anterior factor. *Rodriguez-Moreno* held that the ongoing crime of violence was a "critical" conduct element of a crime prohibiting the use of a firearm "during and in relation to" that crime; the predicate crime stood alongside the use of the firearm itself, thereby creating venue in any district on which the predicate crime occurred (whether or not the firearm also was used there).

Both *Cabrales* and *Rodriguez-Moreno* emphasize the need to look to elements of the crime in determining the "nature" of the crime. They also make clear, however, that not all elements are equal. *Rodriguez-Moreno* distinguished *Cabrales* as a case in which the government sought to base venue on a "circumstance element," rather than a "conduct element" that was an integral part of the offense. The anterior crime in *Cabrales* simply identified the source of the money; the conduct proscribed by the laundering statute occurred "after the fact" as an offense "begun and completed by others." The predicate crime in *Rodriguez-Moreno*, on the other hand, was ongoing, and one of "two district conduct elements" required of the defendant for liability. In effect, the Court viewed the crime in *Rodriguez-Moreno* as a type of aggravated crime of violence, and the crime in *Cabrales* as an offense which looked to a status created by an earlier offense, but was completely separate from that offense (akin to the relationship of the crime of dealing in stolen property to the crime of theft).

(c) Substantial Contacts. The analysis employed in *Cabrales* and *Rodriguez-Moreno* cast doubt on the continuing use in federal courts of what had come to be known as the "substantial contacts" analysis of venue. In *U.S. v. Reed* (2d Cir.1985), the leading pre-*Cabrales* discussion of the substantial contacts analysis, the Second Circuit described that analysis as "tak[ing] into account a number of factors—the site of the defendant's acts, the elements and nature of the crime, the locus of the effect of the criminal conduct, and the suitability of each district for accurate factfinding."

While the substantial contracts analysis was advanced, in part, as a means of complying with the Supreme Court's directive to examine the "nature of the crime," it offered a much broader conception of that inquiry than did *Cabrales* and *Rodriguez-Moreno*. In its third factor (the "locus of the effect"), it looked beyond the elements of the crime. The place of the harm caused by a crime became a relevant consideration even as to crimes that prohibited potentially harmful acts without requiring a showing of harm as an element of the offense. Under the second and fourth factors, courts were directed to take account of all elements of the crime, including those elements that simply described anterior circumstances.

Not surprisingly, a lower court ruling applying a substantial contacts analysis supported the position that the government advanced in *Cabrales* (i.e., that a money laundering prosecution could be brought in the district of the underlying criminal activity that produced the laundered funds). In rejecting that position, the *Cabrales* Court did not mention the substantial contacts position as such, but it clearly refused to go beyond the elements of the crime in determining its nature, and as to elements, discounted the circumstance element of anterior criminality. In a post-*Cabrales* decision, the Second Circuit noted that the nature of an offense is to be determined in light of the guidelines suggested in *Cabrales* and *Rodriguez-Moreno*, and the "substantial contacts rule [then] offers guidance on how to determine whether the location of venue is constitutional, especially in those cases where the defendant's acts did not take place in the district." State courts, of course, remain free to use a substantial contacts analysis in their application of state venue law.

(d) Constitutional Policy. The Supreme Court, in both majority and dissenting opinions, has often noted the importance of turning to the policies underlying the Constitution's venue and vicinage provisions where the language and structure of the crime does not clearly fix venue. Indeed, no statement on venue determination is more frequently cited than the admonition in one such case, *U.S. v. Johnson* (1944), where the Court stated that "questions of venue in criminal cases" should not be viewed as presenting "merely matters of formal legal procedure," but as "rais[ing] deep issues of public policy in light of which legislation must be construed." However, as both commentators and lower courts have noted, the Supreme Court has been unable to achieve a consistent consensus on the precise content of those policies.

Although the Court had referred occasionally to policy considerations in earlier opinions, the 1944 opinion in *Johnson* clearly constitutes the seminal Supreme Court discussion of the guidance provided by "constitutional venue policy" in applying the crime-committed formula. Prosecution there was brought under a statute prohibiting the "use of the mails * * * for the purpose of sending or bringing into" any state a denture the cast of which was taken by a person not licensed to practice dentistry in that state. The defendant, the sender of the dentures, objected to his prosecution in the state of delivery, arguing that the offense was committed only where the dentures were deposited in the mail. The government countered that the statute prohibited the use of the mails and the offense therefore was committed "in every state through which the dentures were carried" by the mails, including the state of delivery.

Justice Frankfurter, speaking for 5–4 majority, acknowledged that Congress, "by utilizing the doctrine of a continuing offense," could, if it so desired, "provide that the locality of a crime shall extend over the whole area through which the force propelled by an offender operates." However, the Court could not ignore that granting "such leeway," to the prosecutor in the choice of venue (1) "opens the door to needless hardship to an accused by prosecution remote from home and from appropriate facilities for defense," and (2) "leads to the appearance of abuses, if not to abuses in the selection of what may be deemed a tribunal favorable to the prosecution." The potential for the former consequence, in particular, had led the Framers to adopt Article III, § 2 and the Sixth Amendment's jury selection provision. Although a construction that "permits the trial of the sender of outlawed dentures to be confined in the district of sending" was not "required by the compulsions of Article III, § 2 * * * and the Sixth Amendment," it certainly would be "more consonant with the considerations of historic experience and policy which underlie those safeguards." Where, as here, "an enactment of Congress equally permits the underlying spirit of constitutional concern for trial in the vicinage to be respected rather than to be disrespected, construction should go in the direction of constitutional policy even though not commanded by it." Accordingly, the Court would hold that "the crime of the sender is complete when he uses the mails in Chicago," and venue would not lie in the state of delivery.

Four dissenters in *Johnson* found unpersuasive Justice Frankfurter's policy arguments. They responded that "the Court misapprehends the purpose of constitutional provisions. We understand them to assure a trial in the place where the crime is committed and not to be concerned with domicile of the defendant nor with his familiarity with the environment of the place of trial." In the years since *Johnson*, the Court has continued to divide over whether it should apply a preference for a reading of the crime-committed formula that would allow prosecution in the district where the defendant was physically present, which most often will be his "home" district—*i.e.*, the district of his residence. Thus in *Johnston v. U.S.* (1956), the Court majority held that persons charged with the failure to report to hospitals for civilian work as ordered by their local draft boards could be prosecuted only in the districts where the hospitals were located and not in the districts where they lived and their draft boards were located. Speaking for the majority, Justice Reed, a dissenter in *Johnson*, stated that the case was governed by the "general rule that where the crime charged is a failure to do a legally required act, the place fixed for its performance is the situs of the crime." Justice Reed added: "This requirement of venue states the public policy that fixes the situs of the trial in the vicinage of the crime rather than the residence of the accused." Here, it was the dissenters who responded that they would have preferred "to read the statute with an eye to history and try the offenders at home where our forefathers thought that normally men would receive their fairest trial."

Only two years later, in *U.S. v. Cores*, the Court majority, in construing an immigration law violation to be continuing in nature, noted that an advantage of that construction was to produce a result "in keeping with the policy of relieving the accused, where possible, of the inconvenience incident to prosecution in a district far removed from his residence." *Cores* involved the prosecution of an alien seaman for "willfully remain[ing]" in the United States beyond the time permitted under his landing permit. If the prosecution were limited to the district in which the seaman was located at the moment the permit expired, that often would not be the district in which he eventually took up residence. While construing the offense to be continuing in nature did not ensure that the government would bring the prosecution in his place of residence, the prosecution was most likely to be brought where the defendant was apprehended (as it was in this case) and that was most likely to be his district of residence.

In *Johnson*, Justice Frankfurter argued in favor of an application of the crime-committed formula that would both establish venue in the place of the accused's residence and avoid granting the government a broad choice of venues that would "lead to the appearance of abuses, if not to abuses," in its decision to prosecute in one district rather than another. In that case, those two values would be served by the same reading of the Federal Denture Act, as the limitation of venue to the single district of the mailing typically also would produce the district of the sender's residence. In other instances, as in *Travis v. U.S.* (discussed in subsection (a)), the two goals suggested opposite readings. If the offense were held to be committed in only one district, that district would not be the most likely site of the accused's residence. The district of residence could only be made an allowable venue by holding that the crime was committed in more than one district and thereby granting to the prosecution an opportunity to choose between districts according to its own interests. The outcomes in such cases have been mixed, reflecting no clear choice in balancing the two goals. Indeed, it is unclear whether the cases have been viewed by the Court as involving a choice between the two goals.

(e) Transportation Offenses. Congress responded to the decision in *U.S. v. Johnson* by expanding venue for all transportation offenses. It amended Section 3237 (see § 8.1(c)) by adding the following paragraph:

> Any offense involving the use of the mails, transportation in interstate or foreign commerce, or the importation of an object or person to the United States is a continuing offense and, except as otherwise expressly provided by enactment of Congress, may be inquired of and prosecuted in any district from, through, or into which such commerce, mail matter, or imported object or person moves.

In *Travis*, the Supreme Court apparently concluded that this paragraph's reference to offenses "involving the use of the mails" does not apply to the situation in which the offender happens to use the mails but such use is not a specified element of the crime. Section 3237's second paragraph could not be used there to expand the venue of a false statement prosecution, otherwise available only where the government received the false document, simply because the defendant chose to make delivery by mail. The second paragraph does provide broader venue, however, for several frequently prosecuted federal offenses, such as mail fraud, wire fraud and interstate transportation crimes. As a matter of practice, it appears rarely to be employed to place venue in a district that has no greater relationship to the offense than an item having passed through the district on its way to delivery.

(f) Multiple Participants. Where multiple parties partici-pate in a criminal transaction, venue often can be extended through the special venue rules applicable to accomplice liability and the offense of conspiracy. As to accomplices, the acts of the accomplice constituting the aiding and abetting may have occurred in a differ-ent district than the commission of the crime. In such a case, the prosecutor can choose between those districts in the prosecution of the accomplice. The abolition of the distinction between principal and accomplice means the accomplice may be treated as a principal and prosecuted where the crime occurred, but he may also be treated as an accomplice and prosecuted where the accessorial acts occurred (the traditional common law position).

As to conspiracy, the formation of the conspiratorial agreement may have occurred in one district and overt acts in furtherance of the conspiracy may have occurred in other districts. Here, the prosecution has the option of proceeding against all the conspira-tors in the district of formation or in any district in which an overt act occurred. This venue standard is sometimes described as the *Hyde* rule, based on the 1912 Supreme Court ruling that first established the standard in the federal courts. It subsequently became the prevailing standard in state as well as federal courts.

Although *Hyde v. U.S.* (1912) itself involved substantial overt acts, the *Hyde* rule has been held to impose only a few basic limitations upon the overt acts that will suffice to establish venue. The act must occur subsequent to the formation of the conspiracy agreement and prior to the completion of the conspiratorial objec-tive. It also must have been done in furtherance of the accomplish-ment of that objective, but that requirement is readily satisfied. No distinctions are drawn based on the importance of the act to the accomplishment of the objective or on the legality of the act. A simple and commonplace legal activity may be sufficient, even though the action would have been taken in any event, even had there been no illegal purpose. The act can be that of a single conspirator or even an innocent agent who is acting at his di-rection. The other conspirators need not have counseled the com-mission of the act nor even have been aware that it was to be done.

Where a conspiracy involves a large number of coconspirators spread throughout the county with each performing at least some small act in furtherance of the conspiracy, the *Hyde* doctrine can give the Department of Justice enormous opportunities for venue shopping. One practical limitation, however, is the prosecution's interest in charging along with the conspiracy the substantive offenses committed in furtherance of the conspiracy (for which all coconspirators are liable). Venue in the district of prosecution must be appropriate for each of the substantive counts as well as the conspiracy count. To gain the fullest possible joinder, the prosecution for the conspiracy count will be brought not where some unsubstantial overt act occurred, but where the greatest number of substantive offenses occurred.

§ 8.3   Change of Venue

(a) **"Fair Trial" Venue Changes on Defense Motion.** All fifty-two jurisdictions recognize judicial authority to grant a change of venue on a timely defense motion where needed to ensure that the defendant receives a fair trial. Indeed, *Groppi v. Wisc.* (1971) holds that a state is constitutionally bound to allow a change of venue if a fair trial cannot be had in the district in which the prosecution is brought. The Supreme Court there struck down a state law that prohibited venue changes in misdemeanor cases as applied to a defendant who claimed that a venue change was needed because community prejudice would preclude selection of an unbiased jury. The Court noted that "under the Constitution a defendant must be given an opportunity to show that a change of venue *is* required in *his* case." In some situations, a change of venue might be the only means of gaining a fair trial, and the defendant in such a case could not be denied that remedy.

Court rules and statutes authorizing "fair trial" venue changes vary in their description of the grounds that justify such a change. Some simply set forth the ultimate standard, stating that a change is required where "a fair and impartial trial cannot be had" in the district of prosecution. Others, like Federal Rule 21, speak of the inability to obtain a fair trial because of "prejudice against the defendant" in the district of prosecution. Some speak of the inability to obtain a fair trial because circumstances preclude selection of an impartial jury. All of the above provisions clearly encompass the ground most commonly advanced for a "fair trial" change of venue—that adverse pretrial publicity precludes selection of an unbiased jury. That ground is discussed in § 15.2(a), and as noted there, it often requires determining whether strong community sentiments may bear upon decisionmaking by otherwise fair minded jurors. However, a community uproar may operate to deprive the defendant of a fair trial apart from its impact upon the jury, e.g., by threatening disruption of the trial, violence against the accused, or the intimidation of witnesses. In light of *Groppi*, such threats should be recognized as appropriate grounds for changing venue even in jurisdictions with somewhat more narrowly drawn statutory provisions.

(b) Convenience Venue Changes on Defense Motion.

Federal Rule 21(b) authorizes the granting of a defense motion seeking a change of venue "for the convenience of the parties and witnesses and in the interest of justice." Most state venue provisions do not authorize a change on convenience grounds, but a substantial minority have provisions similar to Rule 21(b). These provisions are designed to allow transfer to a clearly more convenient forum. However, the inclusion of the phrase "and in the interest of justice" makes clear that concerns of judicial administration are to be taken into account along with the convenience of the parties and witnesses. Moreover, unlike "fair trial" venue changes, here the defendant does not become entitled to a change by making a certain showing. Provisions authorizing convenience transfers typically state that the court "may transfer" on convenience grounds, and courts recognize that such a transfer lies in the discretion of the trial court, subject only to the prohibition against arbitrary or capricious exercise of that discretion.

What factors are relevant in determining whether another district would be a more convenient forum and a transfer to that district would be in the interest of justice? In the leading Supreme Court ruling on Federal Rule 21(b), *Platt v. Minn. Mining Co.* (1964), the Court cited a ten factor list that had been considered by the district court, noting that both the parties and the appellate court had agreed that the consideration of those ten factors was "appropriate." Those ten factors, frequently relied upon in subsequent federal lower court decisions, are: "(1) location of the corporate defendant [which was the apparent counterpart of the location of one's residence for an individual]; (2) location of possible witnesses; (3) location of events likely to be in issue; (4) location of documents and records likely to be involved; (5) disruption of defendant's business unless the case is transferred; (6) expense to the parties; (7) location of counsel; (8) relative accessibility of place of trial; (9) docket condition of each district or division involved; and (10) any other special elements which might affect the transfer." In a jurisdiction with victims' rights legislation, consideration would also have to be given to any logistical difficulties that a transfer would create for a victim who seeks to regularly attend the trial.

(c) "Fair Trial" Venue Changes on Prosecution Motion.

Federal Rule 21(a) and most state provisions on "fair trial" venue changes provide for a change of venue on motion of the defendant, with no mention of a similarly granted change on motion of the prosecution. Such provisions generally are held to preclude judicial authority to grant a change of venue on motion of the prosecution. However, a substantial minority group of states recognize a prosecution authority to obtain a change of venue where it cannot obtain a fair trial in the district of prosecution. Almost all rely on statutes explicitly authorizing prosecution as well as defense motions. Also, a limited body of caselaw suggests that where the venue statute does not refer to either party in authorizing venue changes, a motion by the prosecution may be recognized as consistent with a general directive to ensure a "fair trial."

Courts in states with constitutional vicinage provisions have divided over the constitutionality of legislation authorizing a change of venue upon a prosecution showing that it cannot obtain a fair trial in the district of prosecution. A majority of the courts considering the issue have upheld such legislation as consistent with the background and objective of the state constitutional vicinage provisions. Those courts have pointed to: (1) a common law authority of courts to order a change of venue upon prosecutorial application where needed to ensure a "fair and impartial" trial; (2) the presence of the vicinage provision in a jury trial guarantee which also speaks to providing an "impartial jury" of the county or district of the offense (thereby suggesting that a transfer is permissible when such a jury cannot be obtained in that district); and (3) the principle that the Constitution not be construed so as to nullify the prosecution's authority to enforce the law, which is said to be the consequence of forcing it to trial in a district where a jury is motivated by prejudice or fear to reject any case the prosecution might present. Courts rejecting this analysis rely on what they describe as the "clear language" of the vicinage provision (describing, without limitation, the defendant's right to a jury from the district of the crime's commission), a different reading of the common law practice and its significance, a reading of the constitutional reference to jury impartiality as aimed solely at precluding a jury prejudiced against the defendant, and the view that the vicinage provision implicitly places ahead of any state interest in jury impartiality the defendant's interest in a trial in the vicinage, where he is most likely to be able to benefit from his good standing with his neighbors.

As noted in § 8.1(d), lower courts are divided on the question of whether the Fourteenth Amendment's due process clause incorporates and makes applicable to the states the Sixth Amendment's "vicinage clause" (requiring a jury "of the State and district wherein the crime has been committed"). Various federal lower courts have suggested that this Sixth Amendment clause prohibits Congress from authorizing a venue change on the motion of anyone other than the defendant. Assuming arguendo that the Sixth Amendment clause applies to the states and that lower federal courts have correctly interpreted that clause as not permitting any exceptions apart from a defense waiver, the constitutionality of the state provisions allowing a venue change on the prosecution's motion will hinge upon the definition of "district" in applying the clause. As discussed in § 8.1(d), one interpretation encompasses the entire state, and therefore could treat the legislative authorization of the venue change as a prior designation that expands the district of commission to include any county to which the prosecution might be transferred. On the other hand, if the Sixth Amendment "district" in the context of a state prosecution is limited by the state's traditional venue district (e.g., the county in which the crime was committed), such venue-change provisions would be unconstitutional.

(d) Convenience Venue Changes on Prosecution Motion. Only a few states have provisions broad enough to authorize a change of venue to further the convenience of the prosecution and its witnesses. The failure of more states to provide for a prosecutorial requested change of venue on convenience grounds is probably attributable to a combination of constitutional concerns and lack of practical need. In those states with constitutional vicinage or venue provisions, the arguments utilized to sustain a change to preserve the prosecution's ability to obtain a fair trial would not extend to a convenience transfer. The lack of a significant practical need for prosecutorial-convenience stems in large part from the general effectiveness of the crime-committed formula in identifying the district most convenient from a prosecutorial perspective. The district of the defendant's actions usually is the district in which the prosecution's evidence is located, and where that is not the case, the offense is likely to have a multi-venue potential that includes the district providing the prosecution's evidence.

(e) Selection of the Transfer District. Where a change of venue is based upon the greater convenience presented by another district, the very grounds for the change identify the district of transfer. Where the change is based, however, on fair trial grounds, there likely will be numerous districts not subjected to the influences that require the transfer. Most states simply leave the choice of the district of transfer to the discretion of the court ordering the venue change. Their provisions on "fair trial" venue changes simply state that the case shall be transferred to "any [judicial district] where a fair trial may be had." That district may or may not be a district requested by the moving party. The court is to exercise its own independent judgment in selecting the district. Of course, the first consideration is that the district be one not also subject to influences that are likely to prevent a fair and impartial trial. Beyond that, the court will consider the convenience of the parties and witnesses, and the availability of facilities that will permit a speedy trial. The trial court's discretion in this regard is broad and will not be overturned by an appellate court absent a clear showing of reliance on improper factors.

A substantial minority of the states seek to narrow the trial judge's discretion by setting forth a formula for selection of the district of transfer. Some direct the trial court to select the "nearest" judicial district that is "free from exception." Others direct that the transfer be to an "adjoining" district unless a fair trial cannot be obtained there. While such provisions reduce the potential for forum-shopping, they also fail to take account of factors beyond proximity to the original district that are relevant to sound judicial administration, (e.g., court congestion).

During the 1990s, highly publicized changes of venue in prosecutions of police officers charged with using excessive force against minority arrestees spurred a movement to have courts choose transfer districts similar in racial composition to the initial district of prosecution. The issue posed is hardly new. Scattered rulings, dating back to the 1960s, have held that a court ordering a change of venue has no obligation to consider the comparative racial composition of the original district and potential transfer districts in selecting the transfer district. Indeed, it has been suggested that a race conscious selection runs the risk of violating the equal protection clause, at least insofar as it forces the court to choose between districts that will "favor" either the race of the victim or the defendant as compared to the original district. Critics of this traditional appellate court response argue for an effort to match the total demography of the original district, with race being only one component. They argue that requiring the trial court to select a transfer district that comes reasonably close to the demographic character of the original district follows from the policy underlying the common law vicinage requirement. Demographic similarity is viewed as a means of preserving the interests of the defendant, and of the community in which the crime was committed, in having the alleged criminality judged by reference to that community's values. So far, at least one appellate court and one legislature have found this argument persuasive. In *People v. Goldswer* (N.Y. 1996), the New York Court of Appeals, in the course of upholding a "fair trial" venue change on motion of the prosecution, stressed that the venue change statute "is designed to ensure a neutral forum." "Thus," the Court noted, "within reasonable limits, the community to which the trial is transferred should reflect the character of the county where the crime was committed." Florida, in its statute on venue changes, directs a court ordering a change of venue to "give priority to any county which closely resembles the demographic composition of the county wherein the original venue would lie."

*

Chapter 9

THE SCOPE OF THE PROSECUTION: JOINDER AND SEVERANCE

Table of Sections

For additional analysis of the above topics and citations to authorities supporting their discussion in this Book, consult the authors' 7-volume *Criminal Procedure* treatise, also available as Westlaw database CRIMPROC. See the Table of Cross-References in this Book.

---

§ 9.1   Joinder and Severance of Offenses

(a) **Joinder: Related Offenses.** It is commonly provided that offenses committed at the same time and place or otherwise related to one another may be joined together so that the defendant may be prosecuted for all of them in a single trial. In the federal system, for example, offenses may be so joined if they are "based on the same act or transaction, or are connected with or constitute parts of a common scheme or plan." (The "common scheme or plan" part permits joinder of offenses not close together in a time-space sense but nonetheless properly viewed as facets of a general criminal undertaking, while the "connected with" part focuses more upon the time-space relationship between the crimes and does not require that the crimes be connected in terms of their motivation.) The overwhelming majority of states have adopted the federal language or something very close to it, while most of the other jurisdictions either use some other formulation to describe offenses which may be joined because related in their commission or else ensure related offense joinder by virtue of some much broader joinder rule. Joinder of related offenses is generally favored by both the prosecution and the defendant: the state can avoid the duplication of evidence required by separate trials, reduce the inconvenience to victims and witnesses, and minimize the time required to dispose of the offenses; the defendant can avoid the harassment, trauma, expense, and prolonged publicity of multiple trials, obtain faster disposition of all cases, and increase the possibility of concurrent sentences in the event of conviction.

(b) **Joinder: Offenses of Similar Character.** In the federal system, it is also permissible to join offenses "of the same or similar character," even though they were committed by the defendant at distinct times and places and not as part of a single scheme. About half of the states have adopted the federal language, while a few others utilize language that should produce nearly the same result.

Joinder of offenses of the same or similar character has its advantages. It also helps save judicial and prosecutorial resources, and the defendant may prefer the disadvantages of joinder to the delay, and expense of multiple prosecutions especially because disposal of all of the charges in a single prosecution may facilitate concurrent sentencing. But some object that the savings to the government are not substantial and that the joint trial of such offenses creates a significant risk that the jury will convict the defendant upon the weight of the accusations or upon the accumulated effect of the evidence.

(c) Severance: Separate Defenses. In the federal system, offenses which have been joined for trial will be severed, so that they will be tried separately, if the joinder "appears to prejudice a defendant or the government." State laws also provide for severance of offenses where otherwise a party would be prejudiced or where it would be in the interest of justice and for good cause shown. One type of prejudice is where the defendant may become embarrassed or confounded in presenting separate defenses, as where the defendant wishes to testify on one but not the other of two joined offenses which are clearly distinct in time, place and evidence. If he testifies on one count, he runs the risk that any adverse effects will influence the jury's consideration of the other count. Moreover, a defendant's silence on one count would be damaging in the face of his express denial of the other, and thus he may be coerced into testifying on the count upon which he wished to remain silent. But the burden is on the defendant to show that a joint trial would be prejudicial, so that no need for a severance exists until the defendant makes a convincing showing that he has both important testimony to give concerning one count and strong need to refrain from testifying on the other.

(d) Severance: Evidence of Other Crimes. As a general matter, the prosecution may not admit at the trial of a defendant on one charge evidence that this defendant has on another occasion committed some other crime. This established rule of evidence rests upon two very legitimate concerns: (1) that the jury may convict a "bad man" who deserves to be punished because of his other misdeeds; and (2) that the jury might infer from the defendant's other crimes that he probably committed the crime charged as well. Because the same dangers exist when two crimes are joined for trial, courts have had to confront the question of whether a defendant must be granted a severance so that the jury trying the defendant on each of the crimes charged does not have available to it evidence of these other crimes. The answer depends upon (i) whether evidence of the other crimes would be admissible even if a severance was granted; and (ii) if not, whether the evidence of each crime is simple and distinct.

As for the first of these, the essential point is that there are several limited exceptions to the other-crimes-as-evidence prohibition, and that if one of the exceptions applies to the case in question then the prejudice that might result from the jury's hearing the evidence of the other crime in a joint trial would be no different from that possible in separate trials. These exceptions are where the evidence of the other crime is offered as proof of motive, opportunity, intent, preparation, plan, knowledge, identity, or absence of mistake or accident, in which instances the evidence is admissible unless its probative value is substantially outweighed by the risk that its admission will result in unfair prejudice to the accused. The "simple and distinct" part of the inquiry rests upon the assumption that, where the crimes charged are sufficiently distinct, with a proper charge, the jury can easily keep such evidence separate in their deliberations.

(e) **Severance: Cumulation of Evidence.** Although the possibility that the joinder may have prejudiced the defendant by causing the jury to cumulate the evidence against him has been recognized in the cases, relief is seldom obtained on this basis. If the trial judge is not moved to grant a severance on this basis, it is especially unlikely that appellate relief will be forthcoming, as weighing the danger of confusion and undue cumulative inference is a matter for the trial judge within his sound discretion. Appellate courts are inclined to accept unquestionably the notion that an instruction to the jury not to cumulate the evidence will avoid any prejudice.

(f) **Severance as of Right.** Defendants generally have not fared very well under rules and statutes permitting them to obtain a severance of offenses only upon proof of prejudice. For one thing, it is very difficult for the trial judge to make a finding on the prejudice issue before trial, as it involves speculation about many things that may or may not occur. Also, judges are understandably reluctant to make a finding of prejudice during trial, after the prosecution has put in most or all of its proof. And if the trial judge denies defendant's severance motion on the ground that a showing of prejudice has not been made, it is virtually impossible for the defendant to prevail on appeal. This has given rise to the proposal, reflected in recent law reform efforts, that severance of offenses should exist as a matter of right in many instances, which some states have adopted. The need for some type of reform is highlighted by an empirical study of federal trials showing that joinder of offenses increases the chance of conviction on the highest charge by 10%.

§ 9.2 Joinder and Severance of Defendants

(a) **Joinder of Defendants.** Statutes and rules of court commonly provide for the joinder of defendants, whereby two or more persons may together be prosecuted in a single trial. For example, in the federal courts "the indictment or information may charge 2 or more defendants if they are alleged to have participated in the same act or transaction, or in the same series of acts or transactions, constituting an offense or offenses. All defendants need not be charged in each count." The statutes and court rules in over a third of the states utilize such language, while some others either add to that language or else employ wording of about the same specificity permitting either somewhat broader or somewhat narrower joinder than in the federal system. In other states, the effort has been to identify more specifically the situations in which joinder of defendants is permissible.

A brief look at the way in which the federal provision quoted above has been construed will provide some insight into the kind of joinder of defendants likely to be permitted. It is first important to understand that the previously discussed joinder-of-offenses provision cannot somehow be read into the just-quoted joinder-of-defendants provision so as to produce the result that all offenses which could be joined as to a single defendant may likewise be joined as to multiple defendants; though defendant X could be jointly charged with crimes A and B because they are of the same or similar character, defendant X and Y may not together be jointly charged with crimes A and B.

One fairly common situation is that in which the several defendants are connected by virtue of a charged conspiratorial relationship. Where the joined defendants are all charged in the conspiracy count and they or some of them are also charged with various substantive offenses alleged to have been committed in furtherance of the conspiracy, joinder is proper. But it would not be proper also to join offenses alleged to have been committed outside the conspiracy period or by defendants not parties to the conspiracy. Joinder where there are multiple conspiracies has been particularly troublesome. Such joinder is improper where nothing is shown except for a slight membership overlap between the conspiracies. But even a single common conspirator will suffice where in addition it appears that the two conspiracies are a series of acts or transactions, as where they both related to the common conspirator's gambling operations.

Even absent a conspiracy count, defendants may be joined together when their acts were part of a common plan, as where the offenses charged to less than all of the joined defendants were tied in with an underlying joint crime. Yet another basis for joining defendants is where their crimes are so closely connected in respect of time, place and occasion, that it would be difficult, if not impossible, to separate the proof of one charge from the proof of the other, even absent proof of a common scheme. Thus, where the driver of a bus and the driver of an automobile have both been charged with the negligent homicide of a motorist whose car was struck by the other vehicles, these charges are properly joined. This is not to suggest, however, that joinder is proper whenever two defendants have separately committed similar crimes at about the same time and place.

(b) Severance: Codefendant's Confession Incriminates.
Assume a case in which defendants *A* and *B* have been lawfully
joined for trial, but at that trial the prosecution intends to offer
against *A* a confession by him stating, in effect, that he and *B*
committed the crime. Although this confession is admissible only
against *A* and not against *B,* a point on which the jury will be
cautioned, is *B* entitled to a severance or some other relief? Such
was the issue in *Bruton v. U.S.* (1968), where the Court first noted
it was dealing with a constitutional right, namely, the right of
cross-examination, which it had previously held "is included in the
right of an accused in a criminal case to confront the witnesses
against him" secured by the Sixth Amendment. That right would
be violated if *A,* by his confession, was a witness against *B* but
could not be cross-examined, which was the case because the jury
could not be trusted to follow the cautionary instructions in this
context, "where the powerfully incriminating extrajudicial statements of a codefendant, who stands accused side-by-side with the
defendant, are deliberately spread before the jury in a joint trial,"
and in addition "the alleged accomplice, as here, does not testify
and cannot be tested by cross-examination."

In *Parker v. Randolph* (1979), a plurality of the Court deemed
Bruton inapplicable in the case of "interlocking inculpatory confessions." The plurality reasoned that because "one can scarcely
imagine evidence more damaging to his defense than his own
admission of guilt," "the incriminating statements of a codefendant
will seldom, if ever, be of the 'devastating' character referred to in
Bruton." But the Court later held otherwise in *Cruz v. N.Y.* (1987),
reasoning that a "codefendant's confession will be relatively harmless if the incriminating story it tells is different from that which
the defendant himself is alleged to have told, but enormously
damaging if it confirms, in all essential respects, the defendant's
alleged confession," especially when, as is usually the case, "the
defendant is seeking to *avoid* his confession—on the ground that it
was not accurately reported, or that it was not really true when
made."

Bruton, which emphasized the fact that "the hearsay statement inculpating petitioner was clearly inadmissible against him
under traditional rules of evidence," has no application when a
statement by defendant's partner in crime is received under some
exception to the hearsay rule. Illustrative are cases where the
evidence was admissible because the statement was made by a co-
conspirator during the course of and in furtherance of the conspiracy, was made in defendant's presence in circumstances where if it
were not true a person would be expected to deny it (i.e., an
"implied admission"), or fell within the admission against interest,
spontaneous exclamation or business record exceptions to the hear-

say rule. These decisions seem correct in light of *Dutton v. Evans* (1970), where the Supreme Court upheld the use of hearsay evidence in the form of a statement by a co-conspirator not on trial made during the concealment phase of the conspiracy. Distinguishing *Bruton* because the instant case did not involve evidence that was "devastating" or "a confession made in the coercive atmosphere of official interrogation," the Court in *Dutton* held the admitted statement was "sufficiently clothed with 'indicia' of reliability" that it was properly "placed before the jury though there is no confrontation with the declarant." Sometimes even an accomplice's confession has been deemed to be directly admissible against a defendant (unlike the situation in *Bruton*) because of its reliability, but this is no longer possible in light of the Court's broader reading of the Confrontation Clause in *Crawford v. Wash.* (2004). Drawing upon the historical background of the Clause, the Court in *Crawford* concluded (1) that the principal evil at which the Clause is directed is the use of testimonial evidence (a term which "applies at a minimum to prior testimony at a preliminary hearing, before a grand jury, or at a former trial; and to police interrogations"); and (2) that with respect to such evidence from a witness who did not appear at trial, it may not be admitted merely upon a judicial determination of reliability, but only if that witness was unavailable to testify and defendant had a prior opportunity for cross-examination.

Because *Bruton* is grounded upon denial of the constitutional right of confrontation, it governs only in those instances in which "effective confrontation" was not possible. Though language in that case suggested that a sufficient confrontation opportunity would exist only if the codefendant took the stand *and* "affirmed the statement as his," that position was later rejected in *Nelson v. O'Neil* (1971). There, the codefendant took the stand, denied making the confession, and asserted that the substance of it was false, which placed defendant in a "more favorable" situation than if the codefendant had affirmed the statement as his. The Court in *Nelson* thus held "that where a codefendant takes the stand in his own defense, denies making an alleged out-of-court statement implicating the defendant, and proceeds to testify favorably to the defendant concerning the underlying facts, the defendant has been denied no rights protected by the Sixth and Fourteenth Amendments."

Though the lesson of *Nelson* is that ordinarily any *Bruton* problem is avoided if the maker of the confession testifies at trial, this is not inevitably the case. For example, if the two defendants are represented by the same attorney, he can hardly engage in effective cross-examination on behalf of one client without discrediting the other, and thus his decision not to cross-examine or to do so only pro forma would constitute a violation of the *Bruton* rule. Notwithstanding *Nelson,* it has been held that a sufficient opportunity for cross-examination may have been afforded even if the maker of the confession does not testify at the criminal trial. Specifically, such opportunity has been held to be present where the confessing codefendant testified at an earlier proceeding, such as a hearing on his motion to suppress the confession, and could have been cross-examined about the confession at that time. This result is supported by *Cal. v. Green* (1970), where the Supreme Court held that a witness' "preliminary hearing testimony was admissible as far as the Constitution is concerned wholly apart from the question of whether respondent had an effective opportunity for confrontation at the subsequent trial," in that his "statement at the preliminary hearing had already been given under circumstances closely approximating those that surround the typical trial." The Court has not yet decided what the result should be where in fact there was no questioning or only de minimus questioning. But in *Lee v. Ill.* (1986), the state's argument that it was sufficient that defendant could have examined the maker of the confession at the suppression hearing was rejected; because the "function of a suppression hearing is to determine the voluntariness * * * of a confession," as to which the "truth or falsity of the statement is not relevant," there really "was no opportunity to cross-examine [the maker] with respect to the reliability of that statement."

Because the *Bruton* rule was stated in terms of "a codefendant's confession inculpating the defendant," sometimes the question is whether that has occurred. The courts are generally rather demanding in that regard, insisting that the challenged statements must be clearly inculpatory. It is not enough, the Court concluded in *Richardson v. Marsh* (1987), that the codefendant's confession provides "evidentiary linkage," that is, information which by itself does not incriminate the other defendant but which does have some tendency to link him to the crime when considered together with other evidence admitted at the trial (there, that an intent-to-kill statement was uttered by an accomplice on the way to the crime while the implicated defendant was, by his own testimony, in the car with the others). In refusing to extend *Bruton* to such a situation, the majority reasoned (i) that jury instructions, deemed insufficient in a true *Bruton* situation, would suffice as to the risk of mere "inferential incrimination"; (ii) that the pretrial redaction solution would not work in an "evidentiary linkage" case because the linkage would be apparent only at the conclusion of the case; and (iii) that the solution of severance in all cases of potential "evidentiary linkage" "would impair both the efficiency and the fairness of the criminal justice system."

Assuming now that a case falling within *Bruton* is identified in a pretrial setting, the question remaining is what alternative remedies exist. One, of course, is severance of the implicated defendant. Another is a joint trial at which the prosecution elects to make no use of the confession. Yet another possibility is a joint trial at which the confession is admitted after it has been "redacted," that is, edited so as to delete any reference to the other defendant. But this solution will often not be feasible. For one thing, the maker of the confession is entitled to object if it is edited in such a way as to change its sense to his detriment, as where the deletion would leave out his claim of a valid defense. For another, the deletion must be effective in terms of removing a reference that will be perceived by the jury as referring to the codefendant. And thus in *Gray v. Md.* (1998) the Court held that a "redaction that replaces a defendant's name with an obvious indication of deletion, such as a blank space, the word 'deleted,' or a similar symbol, still falls within *Bruton*'s protective rule." This, the Court explained, is because (i) "a jury will often react similar to a unredacted confession and a confession redacted in this way, for the jury will often realize that the confession refers specifically to the defendant"; (ii) "the obvious deletion may well call the juror's attention specially to the removed name," thus "encouraging the jury to speculate about the reference"; and (iii) "*Bruton*'s protected statements and statements redacted to leave a blank or some other similar obvious alteration, function the same way grammatically," as both "are directly accusatory."

(c) Severance: Codefendant's Testimony Would Exculpate. A situation in some respects the reverse of that just discussed involves a request by one defendant for the severance of another defendant so that the latter can be called as a defense witness in the trial of the former. Even assuming such testimony is needed, the granting of a severance may be the only way by which it can be obtained. One defendant may not compel another defendant to testify in a joint trial. Moreover, the other individual is unlikely to want to give favorable testimony for his codefendant in a joint trial, for there are many tactical reasons why a defendant would wisely elect not to take the stand.

Although some other courts have viewed such severance requests sympathetically, in the main courts have viewed such tactics as an alibi-swapping device not to be encouraged. As a consequence, most courts place a heavy burden upon the requesting defendant, typically requiring him to show that he would call the codefendant at a severed trial, that the codefendant would in fact testify, and that the testimony would be favorable to the moving defendant. This often is not an easy burden to meet. For one thing, the severance would not likely produce the testimony unless the defendant who is to give the testimony has already been tried, for if he has not yet been tried his testimony could be used against him at his later trial even if he does not then take the stand. By the simple device of declaring that a defendant seeking a severance has no right to dictate the order in which the two cases would be tried if severed, courts have been able to conclude that the requesting defendant has not carried his burden. Moreover, even if the testifying defendant *is* tried first, this alone will not inevitably wipe out any basis for his later claiming reliance upon the privilege against self-incrimination, and it does not seem that this defendant can somehow be forced to waive his privilege and promise to testify as a condition of the severance being granted.

(d) Severance: Conflicting Defenses and Strategies. The joint trial of defendants who truly have antagonistic defenses is most unfair, and thus the remedy of severance is needed to prevent a trial that is mainly a contest between the defendants. This is not to suggest, however, that a severance will necessarily be granted even when there is a rather significant difference between the defensive posture of the several defendants. It is common doctrine that a severance is necessary only if the defenses are mutually exclusive (i.e., that belief of one compels disbelief of the other), and that the mere fact that there is hostility between defendants or that one may try to save himself at the expense of another is in itself alone not sufficient grounds to require separate trials. Thus the Supreme Court in *Zafiro v. U.S.* (1993) took a strict view regarding a federal defendant's right to severance: "Defendants are not entitled to severance merely because they may have a better chance of acquittal in separate trials" or "whenever codefendants have conflicting defenses." Rather, a court should grant a severance "only if there is a serious risk that a joint trial would compromise a specific trial right of one of the defendants, or prevent the jury from making a reliable judgment about guilt or innocence." Moreover, the Court added, even if a defendant makes out a showing of "some risk of prejudice," the remedy of severance is unnecessary if that prejudice "is of the type that can be cured with proper instructions," which "juries are presumed to follow."

Another kind of conflict situation is represented by *De Luna v. U.S.* (1962), where two members of the court stated a defendant's "attorneys should be free to draw all rational inferences from the failure of a co-defendant to testify, just as an attorney is free to comment on the effect of any interested party's failure to produce material evidence in his possession or to call witnesses who have knowledge of pertinent facts," and that under such circumstances the proper result would be to permit the comment and grant severance. But *De Luna* has had a limited impact. It has been deemed not to require a severance when the defense attorney for the other defendant has merely called attention to the fact that his client had taken the stand, for in such instance it is thought sufficient that the defendant who elected not to testify could have a jury instruction in support of his exercise of the privilege. Some courts have held that *De Luna* applies only when it is counsel's *duty* to make a comment and that such duty arises only when the defenses are clearly antagonistic. Still others have rejected *De Luna* on the ground that its reasoning is defective. So the argument goes, there are no "rational inferences" to be drawn from a codefendant's silence, for, as the Supreme Court instructed in *Griffin v. Cal.* (1965), even one "entirely innocent of the charge against him" might have a good reason for staying off the stand.

(e) Severance: Guilt by Association. One of the inherent risks attending the joint trial of criminal defendants is that some defendants might be convicted only because of their association with others who were proved guilty at that trial. But a defendant who shows no more than this common risk will not have established the prejudice which would entitle him to a severance. The harm from being so tainted would seem to be greatest as to relatively minor participants, but, while they may occasionally be held entitled to relief, there is certainly no general willingness to free minor figures from the risks and burdens of standing trial with more culpable associates. A guilt-by-association claim takes on somewhat more substance when it is shown that highly prejudicial evidence admissible only against a co-defendant was or will be admitted at the joint trial. One situation is where a defendant is joined with another defendant whose substantial criminal record was admitted or will be admitted at trial. A few jurisdictions mandate severance in such circumstances, but most states approach the problem on an ad hoc basis and require the defendant to show actual prejudice before compelling severance.

(f) Severance: Confusion of Evidence. Yet another basis upon which a severance of defendants might be sought is to avoid confusion by the fact-finder. If the case is so confusing that the trier of fact cannot be expected to keep straight the evidence relating to the various defendants and counts, then surely a severance should be granted. But in face of the almost certain lack of evidence that the jury was actually confused, a defendant's complaint on appeal is likely to be dismissed as in *Opper v. U.S.* (1954): "To say that the jury might have been confused amounts to nothing more than an unfounded speculation that the jurors disregarded clear instructions of the court in arriving at their verdict."

(g) Severance as of Right. At one time, nearly half of the jurisdictions granted criminal defendants a severance as a matter of right, but now only a very few statutes so provide. Some have argued, however, that the uncertain benefits of joint trials and the mischief they so frequently work justify a statute or rule of court giving defendants rights to separate trials. One consideration is that defendants generally have not fared well under rules requiring proof of prejudice: it is difficult to ascertain the degree of prejudice in advance of trial; once the trial is under way there is great reluctance to grant a severance and allow some defendants a fresh start; and on appeal there is even greater reluctance to find the trial judge's denial of the motion erroneous.

§ 9.3 Joinder and Severance: Procedural Considerations

(a) Court's Authority to Consolidate and Sever. Whether offenses or defendants are initially joined together for trial is a matter determined by the prosecuting attorney (or, in the case of an indictment, the prosecutor and the grand jury). If a defendant believes that the prosecutor has joined together offenses or defendants beyond that permitted by law, he may by motion challenge the prosecutor's action as misjoinder. Or, as we have seen, if a defendant believes the lawful joinder would be prejudicial to him in some way, he may seek a severance of offenses or of defendants. On occasion, the prosecutor may move for severance of offenses or defendants he had originally joined.

Though the court must of course rule upon motions made by the prosecutor and defendant, the court also has authority of its own in determining what the scope of a pending trial will be. For one thing, the court will likely be empowered to consolidate existing charges. In the federal system, for example, the court "may order separate cases be tried together as though brought in a single indictment or information if all offenses and all defendants could have been joined in a single indictment or information." Many states have comparable provisions, while elsewhere case law recognizes this authority as within the inherent power of the court. Under the better view, the court also has the power to order a severance, even when such action has not been specifically requested by either the prosecution or a defendant, because of the court's responsibility for the orderly progress of the trial.

(b) Misjoinder. The term "misjoinder" refers to the inclusion within a single charge of offenses or defendants the law does not permit to be joined together. An apt illustration under the law of virtually all jurisdictions would be an instance in which a single indictment includes two offenses that are neither similar in character nor part of a single scheme or otherwise connected together in their commission. Misjoinder must be distinguished from certain other charging defects. It is different from "duplicity," the joining in a single count of two or more distinct and separate offenses, and from "multiplicity," the charging of a single offense in several counts. As to these latter two defects, the defendant is entitled upon timely demand to require the prosecution to elect which offense or which count, respectively, will be relied upon. By contrast, in the case of misjoinder the remedy is a separate trial of the misjoined offenses or defendants. What these three defects have in common is that neither duplicity, multiplicity, nor misjoinder constitutes grounds for dismissal of the charge. Where a misjoinder has been shown to exist, the trial judge has no discretion to deny a motion for severance, but failure to grant the motion (at least in the federal courts per *U.S. v. Lane* (1986)) is subject to the harmless-error rule. Many state courts have followed *Lane*.

(c) Failure to Prove Joinder Basis. The misjoinder situation discussed above must be distinguished from that in which the charge is not defective on its face but at trial there is a failure to prove some fact on which the joinder rested. This might be the case, for example, where the conspiracy charge fails completely or as to a particular defendant, the conspiracy charged turns out to be several unrelated conspiracies, or two offenses alleged to be related turn out to be independent of one another. In such circumstances, it must be asked whether an affected defendant is entitled to relief equivalent to that in the misjoinder situation, to consideration for relief under some less demanding standard, or is entitled to no relief at all.

This question split the Supreme Court 5–4 in *Schaffer v. U.S.* (1960), where at the close of the government's case the court dismissed the conspiracy count, but permitted the trial to proceed on the other counts. In affirming the petitioners' conviction, the *Schaffer* majority asserted that the validity of the joinder was to be determined solely by the allegations in the indictment and that consequently the issue was not one of misjoinder but rather whether a severance should have been ordered on grounds of prejudice. Because "the proof was carefully compartmentalized as to each petitioner," the Court concluded that the trial judge properly concluded no prejudice was present. The four dissenters, on the other hand, while stressing the potential for prejudice in such circumstances, challenged the majority's major premise. For them, an allegation in the charge is a sufficient basis for judging the validity of joinder only "at the preliminary stages," and "once it becomes apparent during the trial that the defendants have not participated 'in the same series' of transactions, it [should *not* be

concluded] that the allegation alone, now known to be false, is
enough to continue the joint trial."

The *Schaffer* situation must be distinguished from that in
which the evidence *was* sufficient to go to the jury, but the jury
then acquitted on the count that was the basis upon which the
other counts were joined. In such circumstances, it is clear that the
acquittal does not affect the propriety of joinder. As was conceded
by the *Schaffer* dissenters, in such a case there "is then no escape
from the quandary in which defendants find themselves. Once the
conspiracy is supported by evidence, it presents issues for the jury
to decide. What may motivate a particular jury in returning a
verdict of not guilty on the conspiracy count may never be known."

(d) Waiver or Forfeiture. A defendant can lose his rights
under joinder and severance law by failing to assert them in a
timely fashion. This is true even in the instances of misjoinder; a
defendant is thus well advised to raise that issue by pretrial motion,
though a motion at trial would suffice at least when the circumstances establishing the misjoinder only then emerged. Misjoinder
claims raised for the first time on appeal will not ordinarily be
considered, though an exception may be made when the record
reveals some circumstance explaining why the issue was not raised
earlier.

Likewise, a claim that a severance should have been granted to
avoid prejudice may be lost for failure to assert it in a timely
fashion. Certainly a motion for severance is appropriate in advance
of trial. However, in a pretrial setting the motion often can be
assessed only in terms of the potential for prejudice, while events
later occurring at trial may provide something more concrete in
terms of actual prejudice. Thus the fact a pretrial motion has been
denied is no reason for not renewing the motion during the course
of the trial. Indeed, failure to do so may operate to the defendant's
detriment in one of several ways. Failure to renew the motion at
trial may be treated as a waiver of any severance claim, or at a
minimum is likely to limit appellate review to the question of
whether the judge properly decided the pretrial motion on the facts
then available to him.

(e) Appellate Review of Prejudice Claim. On appeal, the
defendant has the burden of showing that he was prejudiced by the
joinder, and a reversal will ordinarily be forthcoming only if it
appears there was a clear abuse of discretion by the trial judge.
Appellate courts have traditionally relied on four dubious doctrines
to support a finding of absence of prejudice through joinder and to
justify denial of relief: (1) that the judge's instructions sufficed to
confine the evidence to one offense or one defendant; (2) that if the

jury convicted as to some counts or defendants but not as to others, this shows that the jury carefully examined each count as to each defendant and rendered its verdict accordingly; (3) that any prejudice has been cured by concurrent sentencing; and (4) that any prejudice is deemed harmless if, putting the prejudicial information to one side, defendant *could* still have been convicted on the balance of the evidence.

§ 9.4   Failure to Join Related Offenses

(a) **Collateral Estoppel.** In *Ashe v. Swenson* (1970), four armed men broke into the basement of a house and robbed six poker players and then fled in the car belonging to one of the victims. Ashe and three others were arrested shortly thereafter, and he and the others were charged with seven separate offenses—robbery of each of the poker players and theft of the car. Ashe was put on trial for robbery of victim Knight. The proof that the robbery had occurred was unassailable, but the evidence that Ashe was one of the robbers was weak. The defense never questioned the testimony about the occurrence of the robbery, but concentrated on exposing weaknesses in the identification of Ashe. The case went to the jury with instructions that if Ashe was in the group participating in this scheme he would be guilty whether or not he personally took the money from this particular victim; the jury returned a verdict of not guilty. Over his objection, Ashe was then tried for robbery of victim Roberts. The witnesses, essentially the same as in the prior trial, were now more certain of Ashe's identity, and Ashe was convicted. The Supreme Court reversed, concluding that an "established rule of federal law" known as "collateral estoppel," which means simply that when an issue of ultimate fact has once been determined by a valid and final judgment, that issue cannot again be litigated between the same parties in any future lawsuit, "is embodied in the Fifth Amendment guarantee against double jeopardy." The court then reasoned:

> Straightforward application of the federal rule to the present case can lead to but one conclusion. For the record is utterly devoid of any indication that the first jury could rationally have found that an armed robbery had not occurred, or that Knight had not been a victim of that robbery. The single rationally conceivable issue in dispute before the jury was whether the petitioner had been one of the robbers. And the jury by its verdict found that he had not. The federal rule of law, therefore, would make a second prosecution for the robbery of Roberts wholly impermissible.

This collateral estoppel defense will not often be available to a criminal defendant, for it is seldom possible to determine how the judge or jury has decided any particular issue. For example, in the not atypical criminal case in which the crime consists of elements

A, B, C and *D* and the defendant interposes defenses *X* and *Y,* and the case goes to the jury on instructions to convict only if it is found that facts *A, B, C* and *D* all exist and that neither *X* nor *Y* exist, the jury's verdict of "not guilty" will not itself reveal what the jury decided as to *A, B, C, D, X* or *Y.* In such a situation, the Court in *Ashe* instructed, it will be necessary to "examine the record of a prior proceeding, taking into account the pleadings, evidence, charge, and other relevant matter, and conclude whether a rational jury could have grounded its verdict upon an issue other than that which the defendant seeks to foreclose from consideration." But unless this inquiry shows, as in *Ashe,* that there was but one "rationally conceivable issue in dispute" at the first trial, that will be the end of the collateral estoppel claim.

In trying to determine whether a particular factual matter has been determined adversely to the prosecution, it is especially important to consider the legal theory underlying the prior trial. Illustrative is *Turner v. Ark.* (1972), where, some time after petitioner, his brother, Yates and a fourth person played poker, Yates was robbed and murdered. Turner was charged with murder on a felony-murder theory and acquitted, after which he was charged with the robbery. The state's theory was that this second prosecution was not foreclosed by the earlier acquittal, for it might have occurred because the jury concluded that both Turner and his brother robbed Yates but that only the brother actually committed the murder. But the Court responded that if the jury had "found petitioner present at the crime scene, it would have been obligated to return a verdict of guilty of murder" even in those circumstances, as revealed by the judge's instructions that any party to the felony would be guilty of felony-murder. Of course, even if it is correct to say that the jury was "obligated" to convict on such facts, it is possible that the jury in the first trial disregarded those instructions and acquitted because it believed Turner should not be convicted of murder merely because of his participation in a robbery where his brother actually did the killing. Thus *Turner* indicates, in effect, that such possibilities are not to be taken into account in applying the *Ashe* rule. By like token, *Ashe* has been applied even where the first trial involved only "an implicit acquittal," that is, where the jury returned no verdict on the offense charged but did return a guilty verdict on a lesser included offense. But, as the Court later held in *Schiro v. Farley* (1994), the "failure to return a verdict does not have collateral estoppel effect * * * unless the record establishes that the issue was actually and necessarily decided in the defendant's favor." In that case, defendant's trial for a single killing resulted in the jury being given ten possible verdicts, including three murder counts ("knowingly" killing, rape felony-murder, deviate conduct felony-murder), voluntary and involuntary manslaughter, guilty but mentally ill, not guilty by reason of insanity, and not guilty. Because the jury returned a guilty verdict as to rape felony-murder and left the other verdict sheets blank, defendant claimed the state was collaterally estopped from now showing intentional killing as an aggravated factor supporting a death sentence. The Court disagreed, concluding that because the jury (i) was not instructed to return more than one verdict but (ii) was instructed that intent was required for each variety of murder, defendant had "not met his 'burden ... to demonstrate that the issue whose relitigation he seeks to foreclose was actually decided' in his favor."

In *Ashe,* the Court made note of the fact that the prosecutor there "frankly conceded" that "it treated the first trial as no more than a dry run for the second prosecution." But this does not mean that *Ashe* is inapplicable just because the prosecution's conduct can be viewed somewhat more sympathetically. The Court so held in *Harris v. Wash.* (1971), in which the state court had declined to apply *Ashe* where the issue of identity had not been "fully litigated" at the first trial because the trial judge had excluded evidence on grounds having "no bearing on the quality of the evidence." The Court reversed, holding that "the constitutional guarantee applies, irrespective of whether the jury considered all relevant evidence, and irrespective of the good faith of the State in bringing successive prosecutions." But this last observation should not be taken to mean that a defendant who himself is responsible for the separate disposition of the several charges against him may invoke the *Ashe* rule. In *Ohio v. Johnson* (1984), where defendant, charged with both murder and manslaughter based on the same killing and robbery and theft based on the same taking, entered a guilty plea over the state's objection to manslaughter and theft, the Supreme Court held that he could not rely on *Ashe* even if those offenses were mutually exclusive of the murder and robbery charges still pending. The Court explained that "in a case such as this, where the State has made no effort to prosecute the charges seriatim, the considerations of double jeopardy protection implicit in the application of collateral estoppel are inapplicable." This means a defendant may not even take advantage of his own prior acquittal if the second trial is for an offense severed from the first trial at defendant's request.

Because the Court in *Ashe* said that once "an issue of ultimate fact has once been determined * * * that issue cannot again be litigated," it is of course necessary to consider whether the issue in the second proceedings is actually the same as the issue decided in the earlier criminal trial. This requires, for one thing, consideration of the burden and standard of proof applicable in the two proceedings, as is indicated by *One Lot Emerald Cut Stones v. U.S.* (1972). One Klementova had been acquitted on charges of smuggling certain goods into the United States, after which the government instituted a civil forfeiture action with respect to those goods. In holding that he had no valid *Ashe* defense to this action, the Court reasoned that "the difference in the burden of proof in criminal and civil cases precluded application of the doctrine of collateral estoppel," for "acquittal of the criminal charges may have only represented ' "an adjudication that the proof was not sufficient to overcome all reasonable doubt of the guilt of the accused," ' " "does not constitute an adjudication on the preponderance-of-the-evidence burden applicable in civil proceedings."

Thus, the acquittal only is a bar to a later determination that there is *not* a reasonable doubt on the same fact issue. On such reasoning, it was held in *Dowling v. U.S.* (1990) that notwithstanding a defendant's prior acquittal of a certain crime, evidence of that crime may be received in a later prosecution under some exception to the "other crimes" rule (e.g., that it helps show identity or motive in the instant case). In such a situation, proof of the prior crime is an "evidentiary fact" rather than an "ultimate fact" in the second prosecution, and as such it is not a matter the prosecution must now prove beyond a reasonable doubt but rather is a matter that, if proved by a preponderance of the evidence, can contribute to a conviction beyond a reasonable doubt for the second crime.

Burden of proof issues aside, it still must be determined whether there is an identity of issues in the two proceedings, for only if there is can *Ashe* be used as a defense. The *One Lot Emerald Cut Stones* case also provides a useful illustration of this point. At the earlier criminal trial for smuggling, the government had to prove both the physical act of unlawful importation and the mental state of intent to defraud, and in the trial to the court the judge expressly found that the government had failed to establish intent. That being so, the acquittal could in no event bar the later forfeiture proceedings at which there was no need to prove such intent. Ascertaining whether the issues in the two cases are identical is not always that easy, as is illustrated by those decisions on whether two killings were sufficiently proximate that a finding of not guilty by reason of insanity in the first murder trial foreclosed conviction in the second murder trial. The same may be said of those decisions on whether an acquitted defendant may be prosecuted for perjury based upon his exonerating testimony given at the earlier trial, where the exact nature and breadth of the testimony is likely to be determinative (although some courts deem the perjury situation not within *Ashe* in any event).

Some other limitations upon the *Ashe* collateral estoppel rule remain to be briefly noted. For one thing, there must have been a valid final judgment in the earlier case, which means, for example, that no estoppel can be based upon an informal probation-like disposition involving neither verdict nor judgment or upon a judge's dismissal on the merits beyond his power because done in the absence of a waiver of jury trial. But the judgment need not be one of acquittal as in *Ashe,* and thus a defendant may not be prosecuted for an assault occurring during a robbery after he was convicted of receiving the fruits of that robbery from another party. Perhaps the result is otherwise if the conviction is on a guilty plea, for in *Ohio v. Johnson* (1984) the Court in rebuffing defendant's collateral estoppel claim asserted that "the taking of a guilty plea is not the same as an adjudication on the merits after full trial, such as took place in *Ashe*." As for the "issue of ultimate fact" requirement, this means that a defendant cannot use *Ashe* to foreclose a ruling on an issue of law contrary to that made in the earlier case, or to prevent a factual determination contrary to one which was not of the "ultimate" kind in the first trial (e.g., that a certain witness was not credible). To qualify as an "ultimate fact," the fact must be "essential to the judgment." *Bobby v. Bies* (2009). And the "same parties" requirement means that under *Ashe* one defendant cannot take advantage of another defendant's prior acquittal, just as one sovereign cannot be barred from prosecuting because of a factual determination concerning the same defendant in a trial by another sovereign, or in a trial within the jurisdiction to which the government was not a party. And even if the government *was* a party to the prior proceedings, an *Ashe* collateral estoppel claim (because it is grounded in the double jeopardy clause) cannot be based on the outcome of those earlier proceedings, whether administrative or judicial, when they were not undertaken for the purpose of imposing of punishment, or even upon an earlier criminal prosecution, where no single court had jurisdiction over the prior and present charge.

Bobby v. Bies involved circumstances resulting from the Court's *Atkins v. Va.* (2002) ruling that mental retardation is a constitutional barrier to execution rather than only a mitigating factor. In affirming Bies' death sentence pre-*Atkins*, state courts concluded his mental retardation was entitled to "some weight" as a mitigator but was not outweighed by the aggravating circumstances. Upon Bies' post-*Atkins* challenge of the sentence, a federal court ruled *Ashe* barred the state from relitigating the mental retardation issue, but the Supreme Court held an exception to *Ashe* applied given the intervening "change in [the] applicable legal context." Unlike the current situation, prosecutors pre-*Atkins* had "little incentive" to contest retardation evidence because such evidence would likeky prompt the jury also to find the presence of the aggravating factor of future dangerousness.

Can collateral estoppel operate against the defendant, so that if defendant Ashe had been convicted at his first trial he would have been barred from making a mistaken identity defense at the second trial? The prevailing view is no, and the Supreme Court has assumed that the result in such circumstances is so apparent as not to require extended discussion. In *Simpson v. Fla.* (1971) where two men entered a store and robbed the manager and a customer, Simpson was convicted of robbing the manager; when that conviction was overturned for a defect in jury instructions he was acquitted of robbing the manager, and then he was prosecuted for robbing the customer. The state court characterized the two prior trials as presenting a "double collateral estoppel" that presumably left both sides free to dispute whether or not Simpson was one of the robbers. In rejecting that line of reasoning as "plainly not tenable," the Court noted that "had the second trial never occurred, the prosecutor could not, while trying the case under review, have laid the first jury verdict before the trial judge and demanded an instruction to the jury that, as a matter of law, petitioner was one of the armed robbers in the store that night."

(b) Double Jeopardy: Same Offense. A second way in which the Constitution prohibits a prosecution because of a failure to join the charge in an earlier trial is illustrated by *Brown v. Ohio* (1977). On November 29 Brown stole a car from a parking lot in one Ohio county and on December 8 was apprehended while driving the car in another Ohio county. Charged there with joyriding on that date, Brown pled guilty, after which he was indicted in the first county for auto theft and joyriding on November 29, and his conviction for the latter crimes was affirmed by the state court despite his double jeopardy objection. The Supreme Court first set out to interpret the double jeopardy clause of the Fifth Amendment, which states that no person shall "be subject for the same offence to be twice put in jeopardy of life or limb," and concluded that offenses could be the "same" for jeopardy purposes without being "identical." The Court then took note of the longstanding *Blockburger* test, which originated as a device for determining congressional intent as to cumulative sentencing: "The applicable rule is that where the same act or transaction constitutes a violation of two distinct statutory provisions, the test to be applied to determine whether there are two offenses or only one, is whether each provision requires proof of an additional fact which the other does not." The Court in *Brown* then concluded: "If two offenses are the same under this test for purposes of barring consecutive sentences at a single trial, they necessarily will be the same for purposes of barring successive prosecutions." Looking to the definitions of joyriding and auto theft under Ohio law, the Court determined that the former consists of taking or operating a vehicle without the owner's consent and the latter of joyriding plus intent permanently to deprive the owner of possession. The relationship of the two offenses was that of concentric circles rather than overlapping circles, and thus they were deemed the "same" under *Blockburger*.

The Court in *Brown* commented at one point that "the sequence is immaterial," and this proved to be true in the subsequent case of *Harris v. Okla.* (1977). There Harris was convicted of felony murder on proof that his companion shot and killed a clerk during a robbery of a store by two men. Though proof of the underlying felony of robbery with firearms was necessary for the felony murder conviction, Harris was thereafter tried and convicted of that felony. The Supreme Court reversed, holding that "the Double Jeopardy

Clause bars prosecution for the lesser crime after conviction of the greater one." (When only the greater offense has been charged, as in *Harris*, a well-established rule of procedure sometimes produces a joinder; under that rule, a defendant is entitled to a jury instruction on the uncharged lesser included offense whenever such an alternative disposition is rationally justified by the evidence in the case.)

With respect to the *Blockburger* test, the Court in *Brown* asserted the critical question is "whether each provision requires proof of an additional fact which the other does not." In *Brown* itself, this involved nothing more than a comparison of the statutory elements of the two crimes; as noted earlier, auto theft was simply joyriding with the additional element of intent to permanently deprive. But, does this mean that if two statutory provisions are such that violation of one does not inevitably involve a violation of the other that the offenses are not the "same" under *Brown*? No, the Court answered in *Grady v. Corbin* (1990), holding that "the Double Jeopardy Clause bars any subsequent prosecution in which the government, to establish an essential element of an offense charged in that prosecution, will prove conduct that constitutes an offense for which the defendant has already been prosecuted." This expanded version of the double jeopardy protection, the *Corbin* majority explained, was necessary to protect criminal defendants from the ordeal of multiple prosecutions that would give "the State an opportunity to rehearse its presentation of proof, thus increasing the risk of an erroneous conviction for one or more of the offenses charged."

In *Corbin*, the defendant was involved in an automobile accident in which one person was killed and another injured. He received traffic tickets for driving while intoxicated and crossing the median, pleaded guilty to those offenses a few weeks later, and then raised a double jeopardy objection when he was later indicted for, inter alia, criminally negligent homicide and reckless assault. The prosecution's bill of particulars specified the negligent and reckless acts as (1) driving under the influence, (2) crossing the median, and (3) driving too fast for conditions. The Court ruled that because the state had thus "admitted that it will prove the entirety of the conduct for which Corbin was convicted [earlier] to establish essential elements of the homicide and assault offenses," the double jeopardy clause barred the prosecution. But, the Court added, this prosecution would not be barred if the state were to amend its bill of particulars to rely "solely on Corbin's driving too fast."

Corbin was soon overruled in *U.S. v. Dixon* (1993), which involved two consolidated cases in which the defendants were charged with crimes following their trials for criminal contempt based on the same conduct. After concluding that the double jeopardy protection is applicable "in nonsummary criminal contempt prosecutions just as * * * in other criminal prosecutions," the Court decided to overrule *Corbin* because (i) it "lacks constitutional roots" by virtue of being "wholly inconsistent with earlier Supreme Court precedent and with the clear common-law understanding of double jeopardy"; (ii) it "has already proved unstable in application," as manifested by the fact that in less than two years the Court had recognized "a large exception" thereto grounded in "longstanding authority" (the reference is to *U.S. v. Felix* (1992), where defendant's double jeopardy claim failed "because of long established precedent in this area," namely, "the rule that a substantive crime, and a conspiracy to commit that crime, are not the 'same offence' for double jeopardy purposes."); and (iii) it would otherwise be "a continuing source of confusion." Four other Justices in *Dixon* wanted to retain the *Corbin* "same-conduct" test. The principal argument in favor of retention was that while the *Brown-Blockburger* focus on statutory elements was sufficient as to that branch of double jeopardy law having to do with when cumulative punishments are prohibited, it was insufficient on the issue of when successive prosecutions should be prohibited, where there is a need "to prevent repeated trials in which a defendant will be forced to defend against the same charge again and again, and in which the government may perfect its presentation with dress rehearsal after dress rehearsal." The *Dixon* majority responded to this with three points: (i) the concern expressed by the dissenters was "unjustified" because the government would be deterred from bringing successive prosecutions "by the sheer press of other demands upon prosecutorial and judicial resources"; (ii) in any event, that concern could not be met by the *Corbin* "same-conduct" test, but only by an even broader "same-transaction" test, theretofore rejected by the Court; and (iii) no departure from *Brown-Blockburger* was possible, for (contrary to the assumption of some of the dissenters) the successive prosecution strand of the double jeopardy clause cannot have a meaning different from the multiple punishment strand—it is "embarrassing to assert that the single term 'same offence' * * * has two different meanings."

Although this latter conclusion was also reached in *Brown*, in the interim significant developments occurred with respect to the cumulative punishment branch of double jeopardy law. In *Albernaz v. U.S.* (1981), the Court treated *Blockburger* as only a method for ascertaining legislative intent when nothing more concrete was available. It was said that "the question of what punishments are constitutionally permissible is not different from the question of what punishment the Legislative Branch intended to be imposed." Thus, as the Court later put it in *Mo. v. Hunter* (1983), where "a legislature specifically authorizes cumulative punishment under two statutes, regardless of whether those two statutes proscribe the 'same' conduct under *Blockburger*, a court's task of statutory construction is at an end and the prosecutor may seek and the trial court or jury may impose cumulative punishment under such statutes in a single trial." What this means, of course, is that in a case such as *Harris*, cumulative punishment for the robbery and murder would be constitutionally permissible if the legislature so provided. But if this is so, and if in addition the *Dixon* decision really means that the two strands of the double jeopardy clause must be given precisely the same meaning, then the actual holding in *Harris* would likewise be open to circumvention by such legislative action. Should this be so, then surely (as one of the *Dixon* dissenters put it) "the same-elements test is an inadequate safeguard, for it leaves the constitutional guarantee at the mercy of a legislature's decision to modify statutory definitions."

With *Corbin* gone, future battles in this area may well revolve around the question of just how it is to be determined under *Brown-Blockburger* "whether each offense contains an element not contained in the other." *Corbin* characterized *Blockburger* as permitting only "technical comparison" of the offenses and, in that connection, viewed *Harris* as inexplicable under *Blockburger*. What remains to be seen is whether, with the *Corbin* "same-conduct" test now abandoned, *Blockburger* will be interpreted more generously than it was in *Corbin*, so that at least *Harris* survives. The *Dixon* majority seems to have taken a step in that direction by rejecting the dissenters' claim that *Harris* manifested a beyond-*Blockburger* rule in operation, but the *Dixon* case also shows that the Justices are not in agreement as to just how *Brown-Blockburger* should be applied. On the fundamental question of whether it is the indictments or the statutes that are to be examined in applying *Brown-Blockburger*, lower courts often focus on the statutory elements to ensure that separate prosecutions are not unnecessary barred by averments going beyond the statutory elements, but sometimes look to the allegations in the indictments when (much like the situation in *Dixon*) one of the statutes covers a broad range of conduct.

The *Brown* rule, barring the prosecution in separate trials of several crimes that are the "same" for double jeopardy purposes, is not absolute. As noted in *Brown,* an exception "may exist where the State is unable to proceed on the more serious charge at the outset because the additional facts necessary to sustain that charge have not occurred or have not been discovered despite the exercise of due diligence." The Court cited *Diaz v. U.S.* (1912), which is an apt illustration, for there the victim died after the defendant was convicted of assault and battery. Despite the tentative nature of the language used in *Brown,* such an exception is sound, for in such circumstances the inconvenience to the defendant is clearly out-weighed by the public's interest in assuring that the defendant does not fortuitously escape responsibility for his crimes.

But a plurality of the Supreme Court has now indicated its willingness to extend this exception beyond instances of actual necessity. In *Garrett v. U.S.* (1985), the defendant, two months after pleading guilty to importing marijuana, was charged with engaging in a continuing criminal enterprise, which requires proof of three or more successive violations of a certain type within a set period of time. At trial, the government's proof in that respect included the earlier importation offense, which the plurality deemed permissible under *Brown* simply because "the continuing criminal enterprise charged against Garrett in Florida had not been completed at the time that he was indicted" on the importing charge. While the dissenters objected the exception was not applicable because all the facts needed to prove a continuing criminal enterprise of shorter duration existed prior to that indictment, the plurality deemed it irrelevant "whether the Government could [at the time of the importing charge] have successfully indicted and prosecuted Garrett for a different continuing criminal enterprise" of less expansive temporal dimensions. For them, the exception in *Brown* is not limited to instances in which the government abso-lutely could not have charged the offenses together, but rather is based also on the notion that "one who at the time the first indictment is returned is continuing to engage in other conduct found criminal" cannot complain about multiple prosecutions.

The Court also cautioned in *Brown* that the case did not "raise the double jeopardy questions that may arise * * * after a convic-tion is reversed on appeal." Stressing that in *Brown* the defendant did not overturn the first conviction but rather served the sentence assessed for that crime, the Court held in *Mont. v. Hall* (1987) that if a defendant does obtain a reversal of the first conviction, then he may thereafter be prosecuted for another crime which is the "same" offense for double jeopardy purposes. Such a case, the Court reasoned, "falls squarely within the rule that retrial is permissible after a conviction is reversed on appeal."

On the subject of exceptions, *Brown* cites to a footnote in Justice Brennan's concurring opinion in *Ashe v. Swenson* (1970) recognizing the *Diaz* type of exception and then stating: "Another exception would be necessary if no single court had jurisdiction of all the alleged crimes." But if a change of venue to the county in which both offenses occurred was a possibility, should the lack of joinder be placed at the feet of the prosecutor or the defendant? Instructive is *Jeffers v. U.S.* (1977), where defendant was charged in two separate indictments with conspiracy to distribute drugs and conducting a continuing criminal enterprise to violate the drug laws, respectively. The government moved to join the charges for trial, but defendant objected on the ground that much of the evidence admissible on the conspiracy count would not be admissible on the other charge, and thus the court denied the government's motion. In upholding defendant's subsequent separate convictions for these two offenses, the Court stated: "If the defendant expressly asks for separate trials on the greater and the lesser offenses, or, in connection with his opposition to trial together, fails to raise the issue that one offense might be a lesser included offense of the other, [an] exception to the *Brown* rule emerges." Because "he was solely responsible for the successive prosecutions," his "action deprived him of any right that he might have had against consecutive trials."

While the mandatory joinder issue under *Brown-Blockburger* usually involves two criminal charges, it will occasionally involve a criminal charge and another type of proceeding. Although it has long been clear that the Double Jeopardy Clause protects only against the imposition of multiple *criminal* punishment, the Supreme Court has experienced difficulty over the years in deciding how to go about making the civil-criminal distinction. One approach, under which the outcome depended primarily on whether the sanction imposed served the traditional "goals of punishment," namely "retribution and deterrence," was abandoned in *Hudson v. U.S.* (1997), where the Court rejected the contention of bank officers indicted for misapplication of bank funds that the prosecution was barred because monetary penalties and occupation debarment had previously been imposed upon them by the Office of Comptroller of Currency. Under *Hudson*, the controlling question is whether the legislature intended to establish a civil penalty, except upon "the clearest proof" that the statutory scheme is "so punitive either in purpose or effect" as to transform what was intended as a civil remedy into a criminal penalty. The Court in *Hudson* then set out some "useful guideposts" for making the latter determination: "(1) '[w]hether the sanction involves an affirmative disability or restraint'; (2) 'whether it has historically been regarded as a punishment'; (3) 'whether it comes into play only on a finding of scienter'; (4) 'whether its operation will promote the traditional aims of punishment-retribution and deterrence'; (5) 'whether the behavior to which it applies is already a crime'; (6) 'whether an alternative purpose to which it may rationally be connected is assignable for it'; and (7) 'whether it appears excessive in relation to the alternative purpose assigned.' "

(c) "Same Transaction" Joinder. In *Ashe v. Swenson* (1970), Justice Brennan, joined by two other members of the Court, indicated he would resolve the issue at hand (whether a defendant acquitted of one robbery on mistaken identity grounds could be tried for another robbery occurring at the same time and place and obviously committed by the same person) by redefining the "same offence" part of the double jeopardy clause to mean "same transaction" rather than "same evidence." "This 'same transaction' test of 'same offence,' " he argued, "not only enforces the ancient prohibition against vexatious multiple prosecutions embodied in the Double Jeopardy Clause, but responds as well to the increasingly widespread recognition that the consolidation in one lawsuit of all issues arising out of a single transaction or occurrence best promotes justice, economy, and convenience."

Although a majority of the Court has refused to accept the "same transaction" test as a constitutional imperative, several states have adopted that standard as a matter of local law. By statute, court rule or judicial decision, a number of jurisdictions now provide that the prosecutor must join (or, that on motion of the defendant, there must be joined) all offenses arising out of the same transaction. Problems that might arise from an unqualified application of the "same transaction" standard can be overcome by various limitations upon its use, such as: that the offenses must be within the jurisdiction of a single court; that the offenses must have been known by the prosecutor at the time he commenced the first prosecution; that as to offenses charged the burden is on the defendant to move for joinder; that entry of a plea of guilty or nolo contendere does not bar later prosecution for other offenses part of the same transaction; that the court may permit a later trial of the related offense if the prosecutor did not have sufficient evidence to try it at the time of the first trial; or that the court may permit a later trial of the related offense to serve the ends of justice.

Chapter 10

SPEEDY TRIAL AND OTHER PROMPT DISPOSITION

Table of Sections

> For additional analysis of the above topics and citations to authorities supporting their discussion in this Book, consult the authors' 7-volume *Criminal Procedure* treatise, also available as Westlaw database CRIMPROC. See the Table of Cross-References in this Book.

§ 10.1 The Constitutional Right to Speedy Trial

(a) Generally. The Sixth Amendment provides that "[i]n all criminal prosecutions, the accused shall enjoy the right to a speedy

* * * trial." This right, the Supreme Court has noted, "is as fundamental as any of the rights secured by the Sixth Amendment." The right to speedy trial has its roots at the very foundation of our English law heritage, was acknowledged in the earliest days of this nation, and today is expressly guaranteed in virtually all state constitutions. It is not surprising, therefore, that the Sixth Amendment right applies not only to prosecutions in the federal courts, but also to state prosecutions through the Fourteenth Amendment due process clause.

(b) Interests Involved. As the Supreme Court explained in *Smith v. Hooey* (1969), the constitutional right to speedy trial protects "at least three basic demands of criminal justice in the Anglo–American system: '[1] to prevent undue and oppressive incarceration prior to trial, [2] to minimize anxiety and concern accompanying public accusation and [3] to limit the possibilities that long delay will impair the ability of an accused to defend himself.' " But of the three, the most serious is the last, because the inability of a defendant adequately to prepare his case skews the fairness of the entire system, and thus in *Doggett v. U.S.* (1992), the Court held that prejudice to this third interest, standing alone, was a basis for finding a Sixth Amendment speedy trial violation.

In *Barker v. Wingo* (1972), the Court declared that the right to a speedy trial "is generically different from any of the other rights enshrined in the Constitution for the protection of the accused" because

> there is a societal interest in providing a speedy trial which exists separate from, and at times in opposition to, the interests of the accused. The inability of courts to provide a prompt trial has contributed to a large backlog of cases in urban courts which, among other things, enables defendants to negotiate more effectively for pleas of guilty to lesser offenses and otherwise manipulate the system. In addition, persons released on bond for lengthy periods awaiting trial have an opportunity to commit other crimes. * * * Moreover, the longer an accused is free awaiting trial, the more tempting becomes his opportunity to jump bail and escape. Finally, delay between arrest and punishment may have a detrimental effect on rehabilitation.

But, while this is a useful explanation of why society should be interested in the prompt disposition of criminal cases, it is rather misleading to say, as it is put in *Barker,* that this "societal interest" is somehow part of the right, for the Bill of Rights does not speak of the rights and interests of the government.

(c) When Right Attaches. In *U.S. v. Marion* (1971), the Court was called upon to determine when the speedy trial right attaches. The government appealed the dismissal of a business fraud indictment two months following its return based upon the defendants' claim that the 38–month delay between the end of the scheme charged and the indictment violated their speedy trial right. The Supreme Court reversed, noting that the Sixth Amendment on its face applies "only when a criminal prosecution has begun and extends only to those persons who have been 'accused' in the course of that prosecution," and that the defendant's position did not square with the previously noted purposes of the speedy trial guarantee:

> Arrest is a public act that may seriously interfere with the defendant's liberty, whether he is free on bail or not, and that may disrupt his employment, drain his financial resources, curtail his associations, subject him to public obloquy, and create anxiety in him, his family and his friends. * * * So viewed, it is readily understandable that it is either a formal indictment or information or else the actual restraints imposed by arrest and holding to answer a criminal charge that engage the particular protections of the speedy trial provisions of the Sixth Amendment.

Because in *Marion* "the indictment was the first official act designating appellees as accused individuals," the speedy trial right attached at the time of indictment. But, as the language quoted above makes apparent, had an arrest preceded the formal charge the right would have attached at the time of that arrest.

The general rule that the speedy trial right attaches at the time of arrest or formal charge, whichever comes first, is easy to apply in most cases, but on occasion it may be unclear exactly what point in time governs. If the first critical event is indictment but the indictment is sealed until some later time, the Sixth Amendment right attaches on the date of unsealing, as there has been neither oppressive incarceration nor public accusation until then. A charging document short of an indictment, such as a complaint, will suffice *if* it alone gives the court jurisdiction to proceed to trial. In the event of reindictment following dismissed of the charge, the prevailing view is that the date of the original arrest or charge is still controlling, but that the time between the dismissal and recharging are not counted, provided of course that the defendant is not held in custody in the interim awaiting the new charge. But if the original charge was dismissed on motion of the defendant, some courts simply begin counting again as of the date of recharging. Where after the initial charge some other charge is filed against the same defendant, the date of the first charge is more likely to be deemed controlling if the second charge by the same sovereign is a refinement of the first rather than a charge of different crimes arising out of the same incident.

When the first event is arrest, the question may be whether in a nature-of-the-offense sense that arrest is sufficiently related to the later formal charge to be viewed as part of the same criminal prosecution for speedy trial purposes. Though it would be absurd in the extreme if an arrest on one charge triggered the Sixth Amendment's speedy trial protection as to prosecutions for any other chargeable offenses, the result may well be otherwise if the crimes ultimately prosecuted really only gild the charge underlying his initial arrest. Where the initial arrest is solely for violation of state law, then it is generally accepted that this arrest does not mark the commencement of the speedy trial right as to a subsequent federal charge even if based on the same activity, a result which is consistent with the dual sovereignty limitation upon the double jeopardy guarantee. But where there is close state-federal cooperation in the investigation preceding the arrest or significant federal involvement promptly after the arrest, a contrary result may be justified.

(d) Waiver or Forfeiture of the Right. A defendant's claim that his Sixth Amendment right to speedy trial was violated must be brought before the trial court by a timely motion to dismiss the charges. If the defendant fails to so move and instead enters a guilty plea or submits to trial, he may not raise the issue for the first time on appeal. The right is that of the defendant rather than his attorney, and thus counsel cannot waive this constitutional right over his client's objection. Failure of defense counsel to raise a speedy trial objection could in some circumstances constitute ineffective assistance of counsel, which perhaps explains why appellate courts not infrequently assess speedy trial claims even when there was no timely motion for dismissal below. If a defendant made a timely motion for dismissal on speedy trial grounds but it was denied, and the defendant thereafter entered a plea of guilty or nolo contendere, then under the traditional view he may not ordinarily obtain appellate review of the speedy trial claim.

(e) Remedy for Violation. In *U.S. v. Strunk* (1973), where defendant's denial of a speedy federal trial occurred while he was serving a state prison sentence, the lower court concluded that because the defendant made "no claim of having been prejudiced in presenting his defense," "the vacation of the sentence and a dismissal of the indictment would seem inappropriate," and thus the court ordered that defendant receive credit on his sentence for the period of impermissible delay, reasoning that this would compensate him for the lost opportunity to serve part of the federal sentence concurrently with the state sentence. But a unanimous Supreme Court reversed, noting that delay even in a situation such as this "may subject the accused to an emotional stress" and that as a result "the prospect of rehabilitation may also be affected." The Court thus concluded: "In light of the policies which underlie the right to a speedy trial, dismissal must remain * * * 'the only possible remedy.' "

§ 10.2   The Constitutional Balancing Test

(a) The *Barker* Case. In *Barker v. Wingo* (1972), the Court "set out the criteria by which the speedy trial right is to be judged." Noting first the "amorphous quality of the right," the Court examined "two rigid approaches" urged "as ways of eliminating some of the uncertainty." One, the proposal that the Court "hold that the Constitution requires a criminal defendant to be offered a trial within a specified time period," was rightly rejected on the ground that it "would require this Court to engage in legislative or rulemaking activity." The other, a proposal that the Court adopt a "demand-waiver doctrine" "providing that a defendant waives any consideration of his right to speedy trial for any period prior to which he has not demanded a trial," was rejected as "inconsistent with this Court's pronouncements on waiver of constitutional rights," whereunder the test is whether there has been "an intentional relinquishment or abandonment of a known right or privilege." Mere lack of demand does not evidence such a waiver, especially because defense counsel is often "in an awkward position" in deciding whether and when to make such a demand.

The Court in *Barker* thus proceeded to adopt "a balancing test, in which the conduct of both the prosecution and the defendant are weighed," and to "identify some of the factors which courts should assess in determining whether a particular defendant has been deprived of his right." They are: (1) the length of the delay; (2) the reason for the delay; (3) whether and when the defendant asserted his speedy trial right; and (4) whether defendant was prejudiced by the delay. In finding no constitutional denial in the instant case, the Court utilized these factors as follows: (1) the delay, well over five years, "was extraordinary"; (2) there was good reason for 7 months of delay while a witness was unavailable, and some delay so that a codefendant could be tried first was proper, but a 4–year delay for the latter reason was too long given the state's failure or inability to try the codefendant promptly; (3) for a long time defendant did not assert his right, and this was a calculated tactical decision based on the hope that the codefendant would be acquitted and the case against him dropped; (4) the prejudice "was minimal," as though the defendant lived "for over four years under a cloud of suspicion and anxiety," most of this time he was free on bail, and there was no showing his defense at trial was prejudiced.

(b) The Length of the Delay. With respect to this first factor, the Court in *Barker* declared that "length of the delay is to some extent a triggering mechanism," so that "[u]ntil there is some delay which is presumptively prejudicial, there is no necessity for inquiry into the other factors that go into the balance." The reference to "delay which is presumptively prejudicial" is somewhat confusing, but viewing the case in its entirety it seems fair to say that this phrase does *not* mean a period of time so long that it may actually be presumed the defense at trial would be impaired. Nor does it mean that once a sufficient time has been shown the prosecution has the burden of establishing that in fact there was no prejudice. The Court apparently meant that a claim of denial of speedy trial may be heard after the passage of a period of time that is, prima facie, unreasonable in the circumstances.

Barker says that this length of time is "dependent upon the peculiar circumstances of the case," and by way of example it is added that "the delay that can be tolerated for an ordinary street crime is considerably less than for a serious, complex conspiracy charge." The lower courts have been inclined to apply this first *Barker* factor without any extensive assessment of the unique facts of the particular case. Rather, the courts have usually tried to settle upon some time period after which, as a general matter, it makes sense to inquire further into why the defendant has not been tried more promptly. While some courts follow an eight-month mark or even something shorter, most have settled on a somewhat longer period, such as nine months or, more commonly, a time approaching, at or slightly beyond one year.

In the usual case, this matter is determined simply by calculating the time that has elapsed from when the Sixth Amendment right attached until trial (or, until the pretrial motion to dismiss on this ground is determined). But when the situation is out of the ordinary it may be necessary, as to certain portions of this intervening period, to determine whether the circumstances then prevailing were such that the interests protected by the Sixth Amendment right were implicated. Such was the approach taken in *Klopfer v. N.C.* (1967), where defendant was indicted in February 1964 for criminal trespass but the prosecutor in August 1965 obtained a "*nolle prosequi* with leave," which served to toll the statute of limitations but left the prosecutor free to reinstate the prosecution on that indictment at some future date. Though the state court ruled that the subsequent delay was not relevant to defendant's speedy trial claim, the Supreme Court disagreed, noting that even though the defendant was free without recognizance he was nonetheless subject to "anxiety and concern" because of the continuing pendency of the indictment.

But in *U.S. v. MacDonald* (1982), the Court held that the time between dismissal of military charges and the subsequent indictment on civilian charges may not be considered in determining whether the delay in bringing the defendant to trial violated his Sixth Amendment right to speedy trial. The majority reasoned that once charges are dismissed the person is no longer a subject of public accusation and has no restraints on his liberty, a situation analogous to that in *U.S. v. Marion* (1971), holding the Sixth Amendment protection inapplicable in a pre-arrest, pre-indictment situation. *Klopfer* was distinguished as a case in which the charges were suspended rather than dismissed.

MacDonald rather than *Klopfer* was deemed controlling in *U.S. v. Loud Hawk* (1986), holding that the time during which the government appealed the district court's dismissal of the indictment, while the defendants were not incarcerated and not subject to bail (and could not have been subjected to any actual restraints without further judicial proceedings), was not to be counted. This was because there was neither public accusation nor restraint of liberty during that period; mere "public suspicion" flowing from the fact that "the Government's desire to prosecute them was a matter of public record" was not deemed sufficient to trigger Sixth Amendment protections.

(c) Reason for Delay. As for the second *Barker* factor, "the reason the government assigns to justify the delay," the Court cautioned that "different weights should be assigned to different reasons." Three categories of reasons were then listed: (1) a "deliberate attempt to delay the trial in order to hamper the defense," which "should be weighted heavily against the government"; (2) a "more neutral reason such as negligence or overcrowded courts," which "should be weighed less heavily but nevertheless should be considered since the ultimate responsibility for such circumstances must rest with the government"; and (3) "a valid reason, such as a missing witness," which "should serve to justify appropriate delay" but does not permit delay indefinitely.

The reference to "the reason the government assigns" indicates that the burden to supply the reasons in a particular case is on the government. As a practical matter, however, this is likely to mean that the prosecution is afforded an opportunity to show a reason falling in the "valid" category, failing which the case will be treated as if there was a "more neutral reason." This is because a reason that is to be heavily weighted against the government will rarely be admitted or otherwise apparent from the record. And when the government simply offers no explanation at all, it has been held that the court can presume neither a deliberate attempt to hamper the defense nor a valid reason for the delay.

In *Vt. v. Brillon* (2009), the Court, after noting the established rule that "delay caused by the defense weighs against the defendant," went on to hold that "delay caused by the defendant's counsel is also charged against the defendant," "whether counsel is privately retained or publicly assigned," as "[u]nlike a prosecutor or the court, assigned counsel ordinarily is not considered a state actor." This is a sensible conclusion, the Court reasoned, as a contrary rule "could encourage appointed counsel to delay proceedings by seeking unreasonable continuances, hoping thereby to obtain a dismissal of the indictment on speedy-trial grounds." But the Court cautioned that the above-stated general rule "is not absolute," for "[d]elay resulting from a systemic 'breakdown in the public defendant system' * * * could be charged to the State."

The reason-for-delay factor was assessed with respect to interlocutory appeals "when the defendant is subject to indictment or restraint" in *U.S. v. Loud Hawk* (1986). As for the rare case in which such an appeal may be and is taken by a defendant, the Court stated that where the defendant's claim is clearly without merit he cannot complain about appellate delay, and that even if it was "meritorious" he would have a "heavy burden of showing an unreasonable delay," for a defendant "normally" cannot complain about the very process he invoked. As for government appeal, the Court said it "ordinarily is a valid reason that justifies delay" (i.e., in *Barker* category (3)), but seemed to acknowledge that a particular case could fall into category (2) because of crowded appellate courts or into category (1) if the prosecution misused the appellate process. Thus, courts must consider "the strength of the Government's position on the appealed issue, the importance of the issue in the posture of the case, and—in some cases—the seriousness of the crime."

(d) Defendant's Responsibility to Assert the Right. Although *Barker* rejected the notion that failure to demand a speedy trial constitutes a waiver of that right, the Court hastened to add that this "does not mean, however, that the defendant has no responsibility to assert his right." The Court thus held that "the defendant's assertion of or failure to assert his right to a speedy trial is one of the factors to be considered." Assertion of the right, the Court said, "is entitled to strong evidentiary weight," but yet it was cautioned that not all demands need to be assessed in the same way; the "frequency and force of the objections" should be taken into account. Thus, a mere pro forma demand will not count for much, and even a more substantial demand is weakened where the defendant subsequently engaged in delaying tactics or indicated a desire not to be tried promptly.

The Court in *Barker* deemed it important to "emphasize that failure to assert the right will make it difficult for a defendant to prove that he was denied a speedy trial." Consequently, lower courts rather readily assume that a lack of demand indicates that the defendant really did not want a prompt trial. It is important, however, to examine carefully the circumstances of the particular case. As the Court cautioned in *Barker,* a case in which the defendant knowingly fails to object to ongoing delay is quite different from "a situation in which his attorney acquiesces in long delay without adequately informing his client, or from a situation in which no counsel is appointed." Moreover, failure to make a demand can hardly be counted against the defendant during those periods when he was unaware that charges had been lodged against him or when he was incompetent.

(e) Prejudice. As for the final factor of prejudice, *Barker* teaches that it must "be assessed in the light of the interests of defendants which the speedy trial right was designed to protect": (i) to prevent oppressive pretrial incarceration; (ii) to minimize anxiety and concern of the accused; and (iii) to limit the possibility that the defense will be impaired. As with the previous three factors, *Barker* treats prejudice as neither "a necessary or sufficient condition to the finding of a deprivation of the right of speedy trial," and thus, as the Court later held in *Moore v. Ariz.* (1973), it is a "fundamental error" to say that a defendant cannot prevail unless he makes an affirmative showing of prejudice. Just when a defendant will succeed without such a showing is a matter on which the courts are not in complete agreement. It is sometimes said that defendant must have shown bad motives by the prosecutor, sometimes that the other three factors must be in defendant's favor, and sometimes that they must weigh heavily in his favor.

As for prejudice of the first type, it is noteworthy that in *Barker* the defendant's incarceration for 10 months was not deemed sufficiently oppressive to call for a ruling in his favor. Lower courts have reached the same conclusion as to substantially longer periods of imprisonment. As for the second type of prejudice, it is always present to some extent, and thus absent some unusual showing is not likely to be determinative in defendant's favor. The third type of prejudice, as the Court stressed in *Barker,* is "the most serious." One kind of situation described by the Court is where witnesses die or disappear. As to this, some substantiation is required; generally, it may be said that the defendant must show that the witness truly is now unavailable, that he would have been available for a timely trial, and that his testimony would have been of help to the defendant. Another variation of the third type of prejudice noted in *Barker* is where "defense witnesses are unable to recall accurately events of the distant past." As to this, special note must be taken of the Court's caution that loss of memory "is not always reflected in the record because what has been forgotten can rarely be shown." This suggests, at a minimum, that courts should not be overly demanding with respect to proof of such prejudice.

Doggett v. U.S. (1992) makes it clear that, with respect to that third type of prejudice, the prejudice factor of *Barker* may sometimes be placed on the defendant's side of the scales even though the defendant "failed to make any affirmative showing that the delay weakened his ability to raise specific defenses, elicit specific testimony, or produce specific items of evidence." That is, "affirmative proof of particularized prejudice is not essential to every speedy trial claim," as "excessive delay presumptively compromises the reliability of a trial in ways that neither party can prove or, for that matter identify." The *Doggett* Court then concluded, as to the eight and a half year delay in that case, that prejudice would not be presumed had the delay been for a valid reason; that it would be presumed and "would present an overwhelming case for dismissal" if the delay had been deliberate; and that it would be presumed where, as in the instant case, the government's negligence amounted to "egregious persistence in failing to prosecute." In applying this aspect of *Doggett*, courts generally have found presumed prejudice only when the post-indictment delay lasted at least five years.

§ 10.3 Statutes and Court Rules on Speedy Trial

(a) The Need. The *Barker* speedy trial doctrine standing alone is not adequate to deal with the matter of prompt disposition of criminal cases. For one thing, *Barker* and related cases merely recognize the right of a few defendants, most egregiously denied a speedy trial, to have the criminal charges against them dismissed. Quite obviously, criminal defendants as a class need some additional basis upon which to compel the government to try them promptly. Secondly, the *Barker* balancing test, as the Court fully recognized, of necessity has an "amorphous quality" to it, for there is "no constitutional basis for holding that the speedy trial right can be quantified into a specified number of days or months." Finally, notwithstanding the articulation in *Barker* of the "societal interest" in speedy trial, this societal interest will not be sufficiently protected by the Sixth Amendment alone. All of this points up the need for and significance of statutes and court rules dealing with the subject of speedy trial. court decision has typically occurred.

(b) Federal Speedy Trial Act of 1974. The Speedy Trial Act of 1974 (18 U.S.C.A. §§ 3161–3174) imposes time requirements for the trial of criminal cases in the federal courts. Under the Act, an indictment or information is to "be filed within thirty days from the date on which such individual was arrested or served with a summons in connection with such charges," except that if in a felony case no grand jury was in session during that time the period "shall be extended an additional thirty days." As for trial, it is to "commence within seventy days from the filing date (and making public) of the information or indictment, or from the date the defendant has appeared before a judicial officer of the court in which such charge is pending, whichever date last occurs." The Act also protects the defendant from undue haste, for absent defendant's consent "the trial shall not commence less than thirty days from the date on which the defendant first appears through counsel or expressly waives counsel and elects to proceed pro se."

The Act specifies the point at which the counting of the time to charge and to trial is to be commenced in certain special circumstances. If the charge was dismissed on motion of the defendant but he is later charged "with the same offense or an offense based on the same conduct or arising from the same criminal episode," then the time is to be calculated "with respect to such subsequent complaint, indictment, or information, as the case may be." If a charge was dismissed but reinstated following an appeal, then trial must ordinarily commence "within seventy days from the date the action occasioning the retrial becomes final." As for a second trial occasioned by a mistrial, order for new trial, appeal or collateral attack, again the retrial must ordinarily begin "within seventy days from the date the action occasioning the retrial becomes final."

As for the "periods of delay" that "shall be excluded in computing the time" for charge or trial, the Act specifies the following:

(1) any "period of delay resulting from other proceedings concerning the defendant," such as examinations and other proceedings to determine competency to stand trial, trial of other charges, interlocutory appeal, transfer to another district, consideration of a proposed plea agreement, "delay resulting from any pretrial motion, from the filing of the motion through the conclusion of the hearing on, or other prompt disposition of, such motion," and delay up to 30 days "during which any proceeding concerning the defendant is actually under advisement by the court."

(2) any "period of delay during which prosecution is deferred" by agreement of the prosecutor, defendant and court.

(3) any "period of delay resulting from the absence or unavailability of the defendant or an essential witness." A person is absent "when his whereabouts are unknown and, in addition, he is attempting to avoid apprehension or prosecution or his whereabouts cannot be determined by due diligence," and is unavailable "whenever his whereabouts are known but his presence for trial cannot

be obtained by due diligence or he resists appearing at or being returned for trial."

(4) any "period of delay resulting from the fact that the defendant is mentally incompetent or physically unable to stand trial."

(5) "any period of delay from the date the charge was dismissed to the date the time limitation would commence to run as to the subsequent charge had there been no previous charge," provided the dismissal was on motion of the prosecutor.

(6) a "reasonable period of delay when the defendant is joined for trial with a codefendant as to whom the time for trial has not run and no motion for severance has been granted."

(7) a "period of delay resulting from a continuance granted by any judge on his own motion or at the request of the defendant or his counsel or at the request of the attorney for the Government," provided the judge makes findings for the record as to why "the ends of justice served by the granting of such continuance outweigh the best interests of the public and the defendant in a speedy trial." Per *Zedner v. U.S.* (2006), those findings must be put on the record by the time a court rules on defendant's motion to dismiss, and a failure to do so cannot constitute harmless error or be upheld because of defendant's prospective waiver of the Act's application. The judge is to consider whether failure to grant the continuance would likely "make a continuation of such proceeding impossible, or result in a miscarriage of justice"; whether the case is so complex "that it is unreasonable to expect adequate preparation for pretrial proceedings or for the trial itself within the time limits"; whether, as to preindictment delay, it is "because the facts upon which the grand jury must base its determination are unusual or complex"; and whether failure to grant the continuance would deny defense counsel or prosecutor "the reasonable time necessary for effective preparation, taking into account the exercise of due diligence." In addition, the statute expressly forbids the granting of a continuance "because of general congestion of the court's calendar, or lack of diligent preparation or failure to obtain available witnesses on the part of the attorney for the Government." This provision on continuances, virtually unprecedented in prior speedy trial statutes and rules, is the heart of this statutory scheme. (At least sometimes, the interests of the victim will also come into play, for the federal victims' rights statute, 18 U.S.C.A. § 3771, recognizes that a crime victim has a "right to proceedings free from unreasonable delay," which may be asserted by the "crime victim or the crime victim's lawful representative.")

(8) a "period of delay, not to exceed one year, ordered by a district court upon an application of a party and a finding by a

preponderance of the evidence that an official request * * * has been made for evidence of any such offense and that it reasonably appears, or reasonably appeared at the time the request was made, that such evidence is, or was, in such foreign country."

As for sanctions, the Act provides that if the charge is not filed within the 30 day limit extended by any excluded periods or if defendant has moved for dismissal because trial did not commence within the 70 day limit extended by any excluded periods, then the case or charge shall be dismissed. "In determining whether to dismiss the case with or without prejudice, the court shall consider, among others, each of the following factors: the seriousness of the offense; the facts and circumstances of the case which led to the dismissal; and the impact of a reprosecution on the administration of this chapter and on the administration of justice." This "with or without prejudice" provision, the result of an amendment on the floor of the House, is not only anticlimactic but also very unclear. The legislative history indicates, however, that dismissal with prejudice is permitted under circumstances which would not require dismissal under the Sixth Amendment, and that the extent of prejudice to the defendant, government "fault," and defense "fault" are other factors to be weighed in the balance. But, Congress did not intend any particular type of dismissal to serve as the presumptive remedy for a Speedy Trial Act violation.

(c) State Provisions. Virtually all states have provisions in their own constitutions safeguarding the right to speedy trial. Usually the language is identical to that in the Sixth Amendment, and thus the tendency of state courts is to use the balancing test of *Barker* in construing those provisions. In addition, all but a few states have adopted statutes or rules of court on the subject of speedy trial. These provisions usually provide protection beyond the state constitutional guarantee, and thus, to understand fully the speedy trial situation in any particular jurisdiction, it is necessary to examine the applicable court rule or statute and the case law that has developed from it.

Most of the state provisions declare that trial must commence within a specified period of time from a specified event. These time limits range up to one year, with the most common time limit being six months. As for the event that will start the specified time running, these provisions usually state that where the defendant was indicted prior to arrest or, where indictment is not required, a complaint, affidavit, or information was filed before arrest, the time runs from the date the charge was filed, and otherwise the time runs from the date of arrest or first appearance before a judicial officer; some states, however, have provided (usually shorter) limits running from some later event, such as the defendant's arraignment, plea of not guilty, or demand for trial. Some of the more elaborate speedy trial statutes and court rules specify other starting times for special situations.

In the case of the typical speedy trial provision, determining the time within which the trial must begin is not merely a matter of identifying the proper starting point for counting the time and then adding on the number of days or months specified in the applicable court rule or statute. It is also necessary to add on any excluded periods. Some of these provisions define those excluded times in some detail, usually encompassing periods of delay resulting from (1) other proceedings concerning the defendant; (2) a continuance granted at the request of the prosecution or at the request of or with the consent of the defendant; (3) the absence or unavailability of the defendant; and (4) the defendant being joined for trial with a codefendant as to whom the time for trial has not run, where there is good reason for not granting a severance. Where such detail is given, it is sometimes the case that the statutory or court rule list of exclusions constitutes the only bases for extending the time, and sometimes the case that the provision contains a residual "good cause" category conferring upon the judge in the particular case the authority to find other bases for delay. Several other states have provisions with shorter or less detailed lists of excluded periods, again either with or without a "good cause" residual category. It is a fair generalization that those provisions having very long time periods to start with or not providing for a dismissal remedy in the event the trial is not commenced on time are likely to have the fewest and narrowest excluded times. Still other speedy trial provisions are quite different; no excluded periods are defined in the statute or rule of court, which instead confers upon the judge the authority to permit delay for "good cause" or pursuant to some similar general standard. Finally, there are provisions that seem to contemplate no excluded periods because they neither set out such a general standard or describe particular situations justifying exclusion.

As for the applicable sanction when a defendant by timely motion has shown that the time specified by a statute or court rule has run, the prevailing view is that only dismissal with prejudice will suffice, meaning that the defendant may not later be charged with the same offense (or, some of the provisions specify, with any related offense). Ambiguous statutes have usually been interpreted as mandating dismissal with prejudice, and only rarely as either permitting only dismissal without prejudice or placing the choice of the form of dismissal in the hands of the judge. This last alternative is also specifically provided for in a few other states, while a few other jurisdictions provide for dismissal with prejudice only for lesser offenses. But some states do not utilize dismissal of the charges in any form. In the remaining states, the only means of relief mentioned in the applicable provisions is release of the defendant from custody upon the running of the time for trial.

§ 10.4   The Imprisoned Defendant

(a) **Constitutional Right.** Despite numerous prior lower court decisions to the contrary, the Supreme Court in *Smith v. Hooey* (1969), held that prisoners also have Sixth Amendment speedy trial rights and that consequently upon demand by the prisoner the charging jurisdiction "had a constitutional duty to make a diligent, good-faith effort to bring him before the * * * court for trial." This result was assured once the Court in *Smith* concluded that the interests protected by the constitutional right are especially threatened "in the case of an accused who is imprisoned by another jurisdiction." As for the interest in preventing undue and oppressive incarceration prior to trial, delay as to an imprisoned defendant may "result in as much oppression as is suffered by one who is jailed without bail upon an untried charge," the Court noted, as delay can deprive a prisoner of the chance for "a sentence at least partially concurrent with the one he is serving," and, if a detainer is filed, "the duration of his present imprisonment may be increased, and the conditions under which he must serve his sentence greatly worsened." As for the interest in minimizing the anxiety and concern accompanying public accusation of crime, the Court in *Smith* noted that delay could be particularly harmful to a prisoner in this respect, for it would tend to thwart efforts at rehabilitation. Likewise, the interest in preventing impairment of the ability to defend is especially strong as to a prisoner, for he "is powerless to exert his own investigative efforts to mitigate [the] erosive efforts to the passage of time."

A year later, in *Dickey v. Fla.* (1970), the Court had occasion to apply *Smith* and actually hold that a particular prisoner's speedy trial right had been violated. Although *Dickey* preceded the Court's announcement of the four-pronged balancing test in *Barker*, the holding in *Dickey* can easily be placed into the *Barker* framework. In holding that the defendant's Sixth Amendment right to a speedy trial had been violated, the Court emphasized: (1) the length of the delay, here a "seven-year period"; (2) the reason for the delay, here that "no tenable reason" was ever offered for not seeking to obtain custody of defendant from a federal prison; (3) that over this period defendant made "diligent and repeated efforts * * * to secure a prompt trial"; and (4) prejudice was apparent, for in the interval "two witnesses died and another potential witness is alleged to have become unavailable," and "[p]olice records of possible relevance have been lost or destroyed."

More recently and quite correctly, lower courts have applied the *Barker* formula to prisoner cases in much the same way as in other cases. What this means, with respect to the reason for the delay, is that the government has the burden of showing that the reason is something other than a failure (as stated in *Smith*) to "make a diligent, good-faith effort to bring him before the * * * court for trial." And *Smith*, which stresses the "increased cooperation between the States themselves and between the States and the Federal Government," makes it perfectly clear that the fact the charging jurisdiction lacks the power to compel the defendant's return is not a valid reason for failing to make the effort. While a prisoner who fails to demand a prompt trial is ordinarily unlikely to prevail, note must be taken of two special circumstances: (1) where the charging authorities have not filed a detainer against the prisoner, the prisoner may be unaware of the outstanding charge, in which case his lack of demand can hardly be counted against him; and (2) when he is aware, as is more commonly the case, the imprisoned defendant is unlikely to have the assistance of counsel, which has influenced courts to be fairly generous in deciding exactly what constitutes a demand. As for the prejudice factor, it is unlikely to weigh heavily in the prisoner's favor unless he makes the kind of showing accepted by the Court in *Dickey*; courts do not often view favorably speculative assertions of loss of concurrent sentencing.

(b) Federal Speedy Trial Act of 1974. This Act deals specially with the situation in which the prosecutor knows that a person charged with a federal offense is serving a term of imprisonment in any penal institution. In such a case, the prosecutor has the option of "promptly" doing either of two things: (1) he may undertake to obtain the prisoner's presence for trial; or (2) he may cause a detainer to be filed with the person having custody of the prisoner and request him to so advise the prisoner and to advise him of his right to demand trial. If, in the latter instance, the prisoner informs the person having custody that he does demand trial, this person is to cause that notice to be sent promptly to the prosecutor who caused the detainer to be filed. Upon receipt of that notice, the prosecutor must "promptly seek to obtain the presence of the prisoner for trial."

Because under the Act generally it does not take a demand by the defendant to start the speedy trial clock running, it might be asked why an exception has been made in this particular case. A part of the explanation is that the public interest in speedy trial is not as intense in the situation just discussed; there is no additional cost associated with such correctional custody, nor any of the risks associated with pretrial release. But more important is the fact that this exception opens up an important tactical choice for the prisoner. Absent a desire by the prosecutor to go to trial, the prisoner then retains the option of demanding trial in order to overcome whatever disadvantages may flow from the fact that a detainer has been lodged against him or her or of not making the demand in the hope that the charges will be dropped before or at the time the prisoner completes his sentence.

(c) Interstate Agreement on Detainers. Under the Uniform Criminal Extradition Act, adopted in the overwhelming majority of the states, procedures are set out whereby a person imprisoned in another state may be extradited for purposes of criminal prosecution. However, the necessity for extradition often can be avoided by proceeding under the Interstate Agreement on Detainers, a Compact adopted by the federal government and virtually all the states. The IAD provides that a prisoner against whom a detainer has been filed must be promptly notified of that fact and of his right to demand trial, and if he demands trial then trial must be had within 180 days thereafter; the request is a waiver of extradition by the prisoner, and the state by adopting the Compact has agreed to surrender the prisoner under such circumstances; if trial is not had within 180 days and good cause for delay is not shown, the charges are dismissed with prejudice.

As for the inmate's demand for trial, some courts are quite particular and thus have held that a motion for speedy trial is insufficient or that a request not sent through channels is inadequate compliance with the Compact, while others are less demanding. In *Fex v. Mich.* (1993), the Court held that the 180 days begins running "when the prisoner's request for final disposition of the charges against him has actually been delivered to the court and prosecuting officer of the jurisdiction that lodged the detainer against him." The Court reasoned the alternative construction of the IAD, that the prisoner's delivery to the custodial authorities should suffice and that their "negligence or even malice" in failing or delaying to forward the request should count against the prosecutor rather than the prisoner, would produce an "undesirable result." The 180 days can be tolled in some circumstances, as where the prisoner is standing trial in another state, and can be extended by continuances for good cause, as where a witness is unavailable. If trial of the charge is not commenced on time and defendant or his counsel has not waived the time limit, then the court is to "enter an order dismissing the same with prejudice, and any detainer based thereon shall cease to be of any force or effect." Also, if the inmate is returned to his original place of imprisonment without trial, the charge "shall not be of any further force or effect." Some courts had held that dismissal is not required if the violation of the antishuttling provision is "technical" or "harmless," but in *Ala. v. Bozeman* (2001) the Supreme Court ruled otherwise because of the absolute language in the IAD.

(d) Uniform Mandatory Disposition of Detainers Act. Seven states have adopted this Act, and several others have enacted similar legislation. The UMDDA provides that the inmate's custodian must promptly inform him of any charges against him by that jurisdiction of which the custodian has knowledge or notice and of his right to request disposition of such charges. If a detainer has been filed against the inmate, failure of the custodian to advise the inmate of the detainer within a year of the filing entitles the inmate to dismissal of the charge with prejudice. An inmate can request disposition of any outstanding charge, and this request is to be forwarded by the custodian to the appropriate court and prosecutor. Failure of the custodian to perform that responsibility would entitle the prisoner to relief. Trial is to commence within 90 days of the time the court and prosecution receive the request, though additional time can be granted for good cause. The defendant has no further burden to seek a timely trial, and if the prosecutor does not ensure that the trial starts on time the defendant is entitled to dismissal with prejudice.

§ 10.5   The Right to Other Speedy Disposition

(a) Statutes of Limitations. In *U.S. v. Marion* (1971), in the course of holding that the Sixth Amendment right to speedy trial had no application to delay preceding both arrest and charge, the Court noted that statutes of limitations provide "the primary guarantee against bringing overly stale criminal charges." As the Court earlier noted in *Toussie v. U.S.* (1970):

> The purpose of a statute of limitations is to limit exposure to criminal prosecution to a certain fixed period of time following the occurrence of those acts the legislature had decided to punish by criminal sanctions. Such a limitation is designed to protect individuals from having to defend themselves against charges when the basic facts may have become obscured by the passage of time and to minimize the danger of official punishment because of acts in the far-distant past. Such a time limit may also have the salutary effect of encouraging law enforcement officials promptly to investigate suspected criminal activity.

Other objectives are served by these statutes. They prevent prosecution of those who have been law abiding for some years, avoid prosecution when the community's retributive impulse has ceased, and lessen the possibility of blackmail. But foremost is the desirability of requiring that prosecutions be based upon reasonably fresh evidence so as to lessen the possibility of an erroneous conviction. Thus, these statutes share an important common purpose with speedy trial protections, and to that end are liberally construed in favor of criminal defendants.

All jurisdictions make a distinction between serious and minor offenses, permitting longer lapses of time for prosecution of the former. For felonies the times usually range between three and six years; for misdemeanors they are ordinarily somewhere between one and three years. It is commonly provided that a few of the most serious offenses, usually murder and treason, have no statute of limitations. Virtually all jurisdictions provide that the period of limitation begins to run with the commission of the crime, that is, when every element in the statutory definition of the offense has occurred. Certain crimes (e.g., conspiracy) are properly characterized as continuing offenses, and as to them the time begins to run only when the course of conduct or defendant's complicity therein terminates.

It is common to deal with certain special situations by provisions that allow either for tolling of the time or for the time to commence at some time later than commission of the offense. The assumption underlying the rules usually applicable is that most offenses are known at least to the victim at the time of or soon after its commission, or that the offense can be discovered by adequate investigation by enforcement officials. But this is not likely to be true of cases involving fraud or breach of fiduciary obligation or those involving misconduct by a public officer or employee, and thus some statutes provide that the times for such offenses run from the date of discovery or departure from office, respectively. Many statutes more generally provide that the time does not run when commission of the crime has been concealed; these provisions are narrowly construed, for efforts at concealment are so common that literal application of such provisions would deprive the statute of limitations of most of its effect. Limitations statutes also usually provide for tolling during the period of nonavailability of the defendant. All states have adopted tolling provisions regarding a child sex abuse victim's age or inability to report the crime. Some states also deal with the stranger-rape cases, where the perpetrator's identity might become known (most likely by DNA evidence) only after many years, often by permitting "John Doe" arrest warrants, specifying the offender only by DNA type, to toll the statute of limitations, or by extending, eliminating, or otherwise tolling the statute of limitations. The trier of fact must be convinced beyond a reasonable doubt that defendant's crime was committed within the applicable statute of limitations, but it is for the court to determine by a preponderance of the evidence whether certain facts (e.g., defendant's purported flight) have affected what the time limit is.

Though the purpose of these statutes is to ensure a timely commencement of prosecution, there is not agreement on what act will suffice to show such commencement. Some legislation expressly requires that an indictment be found or an information filed, but where this is not the case it is generally held sufficient that an arrest warrant has issued or that a complaint has been filed. Assuming diligence in arresting the defendant or notifying him of the complaint, these latter interpretations square with the assumption that the basic purpose of a statute of limitations is to insure that the accused will be informed of the decision to prosecute and the general nature of the charge with sufficient promptness to allow him to prepare his defense before evidence of his innocence becomes weakened with age.

Three different views are to be found as to the effect of the running of the applicable statute of limitations in a criminal case. One is that once the time has run the court is without jurisdiction to try the offense, which means the defendant need not raise the issue in a pretrial motion and is entitled to relief notwithstanding his otherwise valid plea of guilty or his raising of the issue for the first time on appeal. The second is that this is a matter of affirmative defense which may be waived by either the defendant's failure to raise it in a pretrial motion or the defendant's entry of a guilty plea. The third variation is that the statute of limitations is waivable, but that only an intentional relinquishment of the right will suffice.

(b) Unconstitutional Pre-accusation Delays. In *U.S. v. Marion* (1971), the Court cautioned that "the statute of limitations does not fully define the appellees' rights with respect to the events occurring prior to indictment," and noted that the government conceded that the due process clause "would require dismissal of the indictment if it were shown at trial that the pre-indictment delay in this case caused substantial prejudice to appellees' rights to a fair trial and that the delay was an intentional device to gain tactical advantage over the accused." Because the posture of the case was such that defendants' due process claims were "speculative and premature," the Court did not elaborate on this due process test.

The contours of the test were elucidated to some extent in the later case of *U.S. v. Lovasco* (1977), overturning the lower court's ruling that defendant's rights were violated where he established actual prejudice (loss of the testimony of a significant witness) and the government's explanation for the 17–month delay was the desire for further investigation notwithstanding the presence of sufficient evidence to support a charge. The Court first rejected unequivocally the contention that a due process violation exists whenever precharge delay actually prejudices the defendant. Prejudice, the court concluded, "is generally a necessary but not sufficient element of a due process claim," and its existence merely "makes a due process claim concrete and ripe for adjudication." What remains to be assessed in such circumstances are "the reasons for the delay," and so the Court in *Lovasco* turned to this question and concluded that no due process violation exists in the case of "investigative delay." As for just what is encompassed within that term, the Court explained: (1) that it unquestionably covers the case where probable cause was lacking, because "it is unprofessional conduct for a prosecutor to recommend an indictment on less than probable cause"; (2) that it also covers the case where probable cause existed, for "prosecutors are under no duty to file charges * * * before they are satisfied they will be able to establish the suspect's guilt beyond a reasonable doubt," as such charging would "increase the likelihood of unwarranted charges being filed," cause "potentially fruitful sources of information to evaporate," and "cause scarce resources to be consumed on cases that prove to be insubstantial"; and (3) that it even covers the case where there is "evidence sufficient to establish guilt," for to compel immediate charging upon such evidence "would preclude the Government from giving full consideration to the desirability of not prosecuting in particular cases."

With respect to what reasons for delay are "bad," in the sense that their coexistence with actual prejudice would entitle the defendant to prevail on his due process claim, the *Lovasco* Court declined to deal with that question "in the abstract." The Court did note that the government had renewed its concession in *Marion* that dismissal would be required if the delay was undertaken solely "to gain tactical advantage over the accused," and then in a footnote observed that the government had now broadened its concession by stating: "A due process violation might also be made out upon a showing of prosecutorial delay incurred in reckless disregard of circumstances, known to the prosecution, suggesting that there existed an appreciable risk that delay would impair the ability to mount an effective defense."

Under the two-pronged test of *Lovasco,* as interpreted by the lower courts, it will be extremely difficult for a defendant to prevail on his due process claim. As for the prejudice prong, though *Lovasco* contains the somewhat qualified statement that "proof of prejudice is generally a necessary * * * element," the lower courts take the view that prejudice must always be shown. The burden of proof is on the defendant to show prejudice by a preponderance of the evidence; actual prejudice must be established, for courts are disinclined to presume prejudice no matter what the reason for delay or length of delay, and some courts also insist that the prejudice must be substantial in degree. As for the reason-for-delay prong, it is unclear where *Lovasco* places this burden. Some lower courts have read *Lovasco* to mean that once the defendant proves prejudice, then "the burden shifts" to the prosecution to show a valid reason for the delay. This is a sensible allocation of the burden, for the reasons underlying the delay are peculiarly within the knowledge of the prosecution, but the prevailing view is that the defendant must shoulder this burden as well.

(c) Post–Trial Delays. Even if the criminal trial has commenced on time, the defendant might object to delays occurring thereafter. If the case was tried without a jury, the objection might be that the trial judge unduly delayed his findings as to defendant's guilt or innocence. In one case, where the criminal trial lasted only 14 hours but defendant was adjudged guilty more than a year after commencement of that trial, the court, though not questioning the applicability of the constitutional right to a speedy trial in this context, ruled against the defendant because of his failure "to press the trial court for a quick decision," all consistent with the later analysis in *Barker*.

As for delays in sentencing, the Supreme Court in *Pollard v. U.S.* (1957) assumed that the Sixth Amendment right to speedy trial was applicable to such delays. This is also consistent with the later analysis in *Barker,* where the Court stressed that delay in punishment "may have a detrimental effect on rehabilitation" and thus be harmful to the particular defendant and to society at large. Other courts have rather consistently held that the Sixth Amendment right applies to sentencing delay, but then have typically ruled against the defendant because of his failure at any time during the interval between conviction and sentence to request prompt sentencing.

Because appeals are not a part of the "criminal prosecutions" to which Sixth Amendment rights attach, it seems clear that a speedy trial claim may not be made with respect to delays in the appellate process. But, while the Constitution apparently does not require the states to afford a right to appellate review of a criminal conviction, when a state does provide the right it must do so in a manner meeting the requirements of due process and equal protection. As one court concluded, "due process can be denied by any substantial retardation of the appellate process, including an excessive delay in the furnishing of a transcription of testimony necessary for completion of an appellate record." Though this might suggest that *Lovasco* would provide the best analogy for purposes of analysis, the court decided that application of the four factors in *Barker* was the best way "to determine whether a denial of due process has been occasioned in any given case."

Proceedings to revoke probation or parole, while likewise not a part of the "criminal prosecutions" covered by the Sixth Amendment, are subject to due process limits. In *Morrissey v. Brewer* (1972), dealing exclusively with the due process protections attending the parole revocation process, the Court concluded a parolee is entitled to two hearings, a preliminary hearing and a final revocation hearing, and that both must be conducted in a timely fashion. Because the latter might occur after "a substantial time lag" and at a place distant from where the alleged violation of parole occurred, the Court concluded that "due process would seem to require that some minimal inquiry be conducted at or reasonably near the place of the alleged parole violation or arrest and as promptly as convenient after arrest while information is fresh and sources are available." As for the final hearing, the Court in *Morrissey* declared that it "must be tendered within a reasonable time after the parolee is taken into custody," but added that a "lapse of two months * * * would not appear to be unreasonable." Later in *Gagnon v. Scarpelli* (1973), the Court held that a probationer "is entitled to a preliminary and final revocation hearing, under the conditions specified in *Morrissey*."

An exception was later recognized in *Moody v. Daggett* (1976), holding that a federal parolee was not constitutionally entitled to a prompt parole revocation hearing under the facts of that case. The parolee killed two people while he was on parole, for which he was convicted and sentenced to two concurrent 10-year terms. A parole violator warrant was then issued and lodged with prison officials as a detainer, which thus was to be executed only at the end of the new sentences, and the parolee then unsuccessfully sought dismissal of the warrant on the ground he had been denied a prompt hearing. The Court affirmed, ruling that *Morrissey* was not controlling because the parolee was not presently in custody as a parole violator: not even his opportunity for parole on the intervening sentences was affected by the outstanding warrant, and the question of whether the new sentences should run concurrently with the balance of the old one could be addressed whenever revocation was undertaken. Moreover, the Court was strongly influenced by the fact that in this particular situation there was a "practical aspect" making delay of the revocation issue a preferable course of action. Because the parolee had been convicted of new crimes obviously amounting to a violation of his parole, "the only remaining inquiry is whether continued release is justified notwithstanding the violation." Given "the predictive nature" of such a determination, as to which "a parolee's institutional record can be perhaps one of the most significant factors," it "is appropriate that such hearing be held at the time at which prediction is both most relevant and most accurate—at the expiration of the parolee's intervening sentence."

*

Chapter 11

THE ACCUSATORY PLEADING

Table of Sections

For additional analysis of the above topics and citations to authorities supporting their discussion in this Book, consult the authors' 7-volume *Criminal Procedure* treatise, also available as Westlaw database CRIMPROC. See the Table of Cross-References in this Book.

---

§ 11.1 Pleading Functions

(a) Functional Analysis. During the mid–1900s, legislative reform produced a dramatic departure from the formalism and detail that marked common law pleading. Common law pleading requirements had been criticized as overly technical and often leading to appellate reversals of convictions notwithstanding fair trials. Earlier attempts to relax those requirements had achieved mixed results. The new reforms, however, were more extensive as they had three interrelated components: (1) a single simplified pleading standard; (2) official forms for the most commonly prosecuted crimes; and (3) an expanded waiver rule. Federal Rule 7(c) set forth the most common formulation of the simplified pleading standard—requiring that the "indictment or information * * * be a plain, concise, and definite written statement of the essential facts constituting the offense charged." The Federal Rules originally included forms for only eleven different crimes, but the states typically provided official forms for a broader range of offense. The forms were later dropped from the Federal Rules as no longer needed, but many states have retained and expanded their forms (which may cover the pleadings in a fair portion of all prosecutions in the state).

The waiver reform was designed to meet the defense tactic of "sandbagging." Recognizing pretrial a defect in the prosecution's pleading, but keeping in mind that an objection pretrial only would lead to a corrected pleading, defense counsel would not challenge the defect at that point, but instead hold the possible objection in reserve. If the trial ended in a conviction, counsel would then raise the defect, and relying on the doctrine that a defective pleading rendered the entire proceedings void, obtain a new trial with a successful pleading objection. The original version of Federal Rule 12(b) was typical of the expanded waiver doctrine adopted to preclude that tactic. It provided that "defenses and objections based on defects * * * in the indictment or information other than it fails to show jurisdiction in the court or to charge an offense must be raised only by motion before trial." Rule 12(b) further stated that the failure to present any such objection pretrial constituted a "waiver." Thus, challenges to the pleadings would be lost if not presented pretrial, with the only exceptions being the failure to show jurisdiction and the failure to charge an offense. Those defects were to "be noticed by the court at any during the pendency of the proceeding."

The three reforms of the mid 1900s were viewed as reaffirming an approach to alleged pleading errors that emphasized function, rather than technical pleading requirements. The key to the sufficiency of a pleading, under this view, would ultimately depend on whether the pleading satisfied the fundamental functions of a written charge. It was in light of those functions that a court would determine if a pleading met the new "essential facts" pleading standard, and what was needed to meet those functions was illustrated by the approved forms.

Hamling v. U.S. (1974) set forth this functional approach in describing the prerequisites of a sufficient federal pleading:

> Our prior cases indicate that an indictment is sufficient if it, first, contains the elements of the offense charged and fairly informs a defendant of the charge against which he must defend, and, second, enables him to plead an acquittal or conviction in bar of future prosecutions for the same offense.

Although sometimes described as a two-pronged test, the *Hamling* standard actually includes three requirements: (1) inclusion of the elements of the offense; (2) providing adequate notice as to the charge; and (3) providing protection against double jeopardy. These three requirements have been cited repeatedly by both federal and states courts.

The second and third requirements of *Hamling* clearly identify basic functions of the accusatory pleading. The need for notice and protection against double jeopardy are commonly accepted as pleading goals and regularly are looked to in evaluating alleged pleading deficiencies. The first requirement of *Hamling*—that the pleading set forth facts alleging each of the essential elements of the offense—is less helpful. That requirement clearly identifies what must be included in the pleading, but does not explain what function is served by including that content. Most courts refer to the "essential elements" requirement as a pleading objective in itself, without exploring what lies beneath that requirement. Where courts have explored the functions that shape the essential elements requirement, they sometimes refer to notice and protection against double jeopardy, but more often cite three additional pleading functions—(1) informing the court of the elements that the prosecution intends to prove, so that it can determine whether they are legally sufficient to constitute a crime; (2) ensuring that grand jury took all the elements into consideration in voting to indict (a function limited to indictments); and (3) providing a formal record upon which the prosecution can proceed.

(b) Double Jeopardy Protection. Protecting the defendant against multiple jeopardy for the same offense was a pleading function given considerable attention at common law. Perhaps its most obvious influence is in the prohibition against multiplicity (i.e., charging a single offense in multiple counts), a practice which could lead to multiple punishments for a single offense in violation of the double jeopardy prohibition. However, the double jeopardy function is also cited as contributing to both the essential elements requirement and the requirement that the pleading have adequate factual specificity.

In fact, as applied over the years, neither the essential elements requirement nor the requirement of adequate factual specificity have been tied to what is necessary to ensure that a court can determine, simply by comparing allegations, whether two pleadings charge the same offense. The essential elements requirement, as described in § 11.2(a), demands far more than a basic identification of the crime charged (e.g., by citation to the applicable criminal code provision), though only such an identification would be needed to determine whether the two pleadings charged violations of the same criminal prohibition. The specificity requirement, as discussed in § 11.2(b), typically does not require inclusion of such matters as the precise time and place of the offense, which often are critical in assessing whether the two pleadings refer to the same criminal episode (a prerequisite for charging the same offense). Thus, even at a time when the charging instrument was the primary record of the trial, it is questionable whether the double jeopardy function gave to those pleading requirements any special content above and beyond that demanded by other pleading functions. Today, moreover, the determination of double jeopardy—especially with the introduction of the doctrine of collateral estoppel—is no longer a matter that courts expect to resolve on the basis of matching charging instruments in the first and second prosecutions. Transcriptions of trial proceedings are available to determine exactly what was put before the jury in the first case and the prosecution can be expected, in response to a defense objection, to explain how the anticipated proof in the second case will differ.

(c) Providing Notice. Discussions of pleading functions almost invariably start by noting that the pleading must "fairly inform" the accused of the charges against him. Indeed, the notice function has been characterized by the Supreme Court as tied to the defendant's Sixth Amendment right "to be informed of the nature and cause of the accusation." Some courts therefore have suggested that all basic pleading requirements are demanded by the Sixth Amendment—e.g., a failure to include reference to an essential element in a pleading constitutes a violation of the defendant's constitutional right to adequate notice of the charge against him. However, rulings focusing on the pleading providing adequate notice typically are grounded on interpretations of a Rule 7(c)-type pleading provision, with the court having no need to rely upon the Sixth Amendment. In applying the Sixth Amendment notice requirement to defense claims of surprise, partially related to pleadings, courts have looked to (1) the actual notice provided in light of the totality of the information available to the defendant and (2) the likelihood of the defendant having actually been prejudiced in defending against the charges. These rulings suggest that compliance with the Sixth Amendment notice requirement looks beyond the face of the pleadings, which the essential elements requirement and other pleading requirements do not do.

While the Sixth Amendment may not require that the pleading in itself provide adequate notice of the offense charged, Federal Rule 7(c) and counterpart state provisions clearly do require that the charging instrument provide such notice. That function clearly underlies the pleading requirement of adequate factual specificity, as discussed in § 11.3(b). Whether it also shapes the essential elements requirement is a matter of debate, and that debate is not simply of theoretical significance. Where a pleading requirement is viewed as tied solely to the notice function, courts are more likely to treat an objection based on the pleading's alleged failure to meet that requirement as "forfeited" or "waived" by the defendant's failure to raise the objection before trial (that lack of objection suggesting that the defendant did not see the need for further notice in preparing for trial). Moreover, where notice is the key to a pleading requirement, courts are more likely to look to the availability of other means of obtaining notice, such as the bill of particulars, in determining the degree of particularity that satisfies that requirement. Finally, on appellate review following a conviction, a pleading defect based on the failure to provide notice may be treated as harmless if the trial record suggests that defendant was not surprised or otherwise prejudiced by his lack of notice (notwithstanding his objection). As discussed in § 11.3(a), traditionally none of these limitations have been applied to the essential elements requirement.

(d) Facilitating Judicial Review. The basic objective of the judicial review function is to permit the trial court to rule before trial on the sufficiency of the prosecution's theory of the statutory elements. Consider, for example, a situation in which the statute does not include a particular mens rea element, and there is some question as to the level of mens rea required. The pleading's inclusion of a specific mens rea allegation could be helpful in settling that issue in advance of trial and possibly even in avoiding an unnecessary trial. Thus, if the trial court were to decide, on a motion to dismiss, that the offense requires actual intent rather than some lower level of mens rea alleged in the pleading, the prosecution might conclude that its evidence would be insufficient and not even seek to return with a new pleading alleging the required intent.

The review function explains why courts sometimes have insisted upon more factual specificity as to those elements of a particular offense most likely to raise difficult legal questions. *Russell v. U.S.* (1962) is a classic illustration. The Supreme Court there held insufficient an indictment charging a violation of a federal statute which makes it a crime for a witness to refuse to answer before a Congressional Committee "any question pertinent to the * * * [subject] under inquiry." The indictment was held defective because it failed to specifically identify the subject of the Committee's inquiry, which had to be known to determine whether the questions asked (which were set forth in the indictment) met the statutory requirement of pertinency. The Court noted that the pertinency element had been the subject of frequent litigation, with the lower courts often beset with "difficulties and doubts" in identifying the inquiry subject. Since this "critical and difficult question could be obviated by a simple averment," the prosecution would not be allowed to simply describe the question asked as "pertinent to the subject then under inquiry"; it had to identify the particular subject under inquiry in the pleading, so the trial court could determine on a motion to dismiss whether the question could be pertinent as a matter of law.

Though the judicial review function readily explains pleading rulings in cases like *Russell,* it does not provide a satisfactory justification for the many rulings that have found charging instruments deficient for failing to clearly allege elements of the crime notwithstanding that: (1) those elements obviously were a part of the offense under prevailing law (so that both sides would have been well aware that they had to be proved), (2) the deficiency produced no pretrial objection by the defense, and (3) the jury was charged on the element and it was adequately proven at trial. Such rulings clearly have looked to other functions underlying the essential elements requirement. On the other hand, as explained in § 11.2(b), the judicial review function does explain why courts have required a greater degree of specificity in pleading some offenses than others.

(e) Providing a Jurisdictional Grounding. The common law viewed the accusatory instrument as "providing a formal basis for the judgment, so that the indictment or information * * * [was required to] set forth everything necessary for a complete case on paper." This function of the pleading has been challenged as unnecessary now that complete trial records are available. That record, whether defendant enters a guilty plea or is convicted after a trial, should contain a judicial acknowledgment of the presence of the elements that support the entry of a judgment of conviction for the particular offense.

Notwithstanding the availability of the trial record, all but a few states continue to view a pleading that "charges an offense" as a necessary precondition for a conviction. Where the pleading's failure to charge an offense was challenged below, the appellate court will reverse the subsequent conviction without considering whether that pleading defect prejudiced the defense in contesting the prosecution's proof at trial. Where the objection was not raised at trial, but is presented first on appeal following a conviction, the prosecution will receive the benefit of a liberal construction of the pleading, but automatic reversal will be required if the appellate court concludes that the pleading nonetheless does not charge an offense. The pleading defect was not lost by the failure to object, it is argued, because the defendant had a fundamental right not to be put to trial on an indictment or information that failed to include all of the essential elements of the crime (and therefore did not charge an offense). Indeed, in as many as a dozen states, the clear failure to allege an essential element will require the overturning of a conviction notwithstanding a guilty plea. The explanation here is that the guilty plea does not waive a completely deficient charging instrument, as that deficiency deprived the trial court of its basic authority to proceed.

In the federal system, largely as a result of two related Supreme Court rulings, only one of which dealt directly with pleadings, one aspect of the traditional remedial position on the failure to charge an offense has been uniformly rejected and another has produced a division in lower court rulings. The first of those Supreme Court rulings, *Apprendi v. N.J.* (2000), was a seminal ruling on the issues that must be presented to the jury. One of its side effects was a reexamination of the consequences of failing to allege an essential element of an offense.

Apprendi held that a factor which increases the allowable maximum sentence is an element of the crime, and in treating that element as a sentencing factor to be decided by the judge rather than the jury, the state violated the Sixth Amendment. The federal system had a significant group of statutes in which maximum-enhancing factors had been treated as sentencing factors, leading to a deluge of cases challenging enhanced sentences under those statutes. The defendants soon learned that they faced serious obstacles in gaining relief. Where the defendant had pled guilty, that plea eliminated the Sixth Amendment issue because the defendant had not sought a jury trial. Where the defendant went to trial before a jury, but failed to object to the court's failure to submit the maximum-enhancing factor to the jury, the error was forfeited by the lack of objection and could only be considered on appeal if it met the narrow exception of the "plain error" rule. Where the defendant had anticipated *Apprendi* and objected at trial, the appellate court could still find the error to be harmless. All of these obstacles could be avoided, however, by grounding the defense challenge on the failure of the indictment to allege the maximum-enhancing factor.

While *Apprendi* had ruled only on the jury issue, a factor that is an element of the crime for Sixth Amendment purposes should also be an essential element for pleading purposes. Indeed, Justice Thomas' concurring opinion in *Apprendi* had suggested that the failure to allege such an element in the indictment constituted a violation of the grand jury cause of the Fifth Amendment. Basing the challenge on the indictment deficiency, rather than the *Apprendi* error, the defendant could look to traditional federal remedial law as to essential elements objections to avoid all of the obstacles facing *Apprendi* claims. If the defendant objected at trial, the failure to plead an essential element required automatic reversal on appeal; it was not subject to a harmless error analysis. If the defendant was raising the issue for the first time on appeal, Rule 12(b) bypassed the difficult prerequisites and discretionary character of the plain error doctrine. It provided that the indictment's failure to charge an offense "shall be noticed by the court at any time during the pendency of the proceeding." This language had been read as requiring that an essential elements objection be considered even if first raised on appeal, without regard to the plain error rule, which was designed for objections that would otherwise be forfeited by the failure to have presented the objection in a timely fashion. As for a guilty plea, several federal courts had held that the failure to allege all essential elements was a jurisdictional type of defect and therefore survived a guilty plea.

The government offered a two-pronged response to these pleading claims. First, as to objections to the indictment that had been properly raised before the trial court (in anticipation of *Apprendi*), a harmless error analysis should apply. The government recognized that harmless error analysis traditionally had not been applied to a failure of the indictment to allege the essential elements of the charged offense. It argued initially that the failure to allege an *Apprendi*-type element was not such a failure. The indictment here did allege the essential elements of an offense, albeit an offense carrying a lesser maximum than the offense on which the defendant was sentenced The true source of the error, it argued, was in the sentencing process, and such errors were subject to harmless error analysis on appellate review. The government also contended that even if the error was viewed as a pleading error, that should not preclude application of a harmless error analysis. While previous Supreme Court rulings had reversed convictions automatically on finding that the indictment failed to allege an essential element, those rulings came before *Chapman v. Cal.* (§ 19.6(c)), at a time when all constitutional violations (including violations of the Fifth Amendment's grand jury clause) were viewed as requiring automatic reversal on appellate review. In *Chapman* and its progeny, the

Supreme Court subsequently had held that most constitutional errors were subject to a harmless error analysis.

One or the other of the above arguments were upheld in the limited number of appellate cases dealing with defendants who had anticipated *Apprendi* and made a timely objection to the indictment's failure to allege an *Apprendi*–type element. The various circuits held that this defect was subject to harmless error analysis, though some also concluded that, under the circumstances of the case, the error was not harmless.

Where the indictment challenge had not been presented to the trial court, the government argued that the standard of review should be more rigorous than the harmless error standard. Rather, reversal should be required only if the defendant could meet the prerequisites of the "plain error" standard of Federal Rule 52(b). That standard had been applied by the Supreme Court to the failure to submit an element to the jury where that objection had not been timely presented. The same should be true, the government argued, of a failure to allege an *Apprendi*-type element in an indictment. This prong of the government's position received the support of a substantial group of the federal lower courts. The Fourth Circuit disagreed, however, leading to the Supreme Court's consideration of the issue in *U.S. v. Cotton* (2002).

The defendants in *Cotton* were indicted and convicted under a federal statute making a conspiracy to distribute cocaine base a 20–year offense, but raising the maximum sentence to life imprisonment if the offense involve 50 or more grams of cocaine base. At the time of the indictment and trial, the enhancement element of drug quantity was viewed as a sentencing factor, and it therefore was not included in the indictment nor presented to the jury (although defendants knew from the outset that the prosecution intended to establish the enhancement at sentencing, which it did). On appeal, relying on the intervening Supreme Court ruling in *Apprendi*, defendants argued that their sentences in excess of 20 years were invalid because the issue of drug quantity was neither alleged in the indictment nor submitted to the petit jury. The government acknowledged both errors, but argued that, since the objections had not been timely presented before the district court, they were cognizable on appeal only if they met the prerequisites for recognition as "plain errors" under Rule 52(b) and neither error fulfilled those prerequisites. Relying basically on language in the Supreme Court's ruling in *Ex parte Bain* (1886), the Fourth Circuit held that an indictment's failure to include an essential element of an offense was a "jurisdictional" defect, and therefore the enhanced sentence had to be vacated even though not timely challenged below. Rejecting that reasoning, a unanimous Supreme Court held that the indictment defect was not jurisdictional and should be cognizable only if it met the rigorous standards of the plain error doctrine (which was not the case, here, as the evidence supporting the sentencing enhancement factor was "overwhelming" and "essentially uncontroverted").

The Supreme Court in *Cotton* rejected *Bain's* broad conception of jurisdiction as an outdated "product of an era in which the [Supreme] Court's authority to review criminal convictions was greatly circumscribed." Subsequent rulings, it noted, had properly limited the concept of jurisdictional defects (i.e., defects that "require correction regardless of whether the error was raised in [the] district court") to "defects in subject-matter jurisdiction." Thus, post-*Bain* rulings had rejected "the claim that the [district] court had no jurisdiction because the indictment does not charge an offense against the United States." Since such defects were not jurisdictional, there was no reason to exempt them from the usual rule that they were not reviewable unless they constituted "plain error."

As discussed in § 11.2(e), *Cotton's* flat rejection of a jurisdictional grounding for indictment defects, including the failure to "charge an offense," has led federal lower courts not to restrict the *Cotton* ruling to the failure to allege an *Apprendi*-type element. The "plain error" prerequisite has been applied to the appellate review of traditional essential elements objections that were not presented pretrial. As discussed in § 11.2(a), where the failure to charge an offense was timely raised but erroneously rejected by the trial court, the federal lower courts have divided as to the relevance of the *Cotton* analysis and the appropriate remedial standard. Relying in part on *Cotton*, several have rejected continued application of the traditional requirement of automatic reversal and substituted harmless error review. So too, as discussed in § 11.4 and § 11.5, *Cotton* has led to a reexamination of the consequences of a finding on appeal that a variance constituted a constructive amendment of the indictment, and it is likely to produce a similar reexamination of the consequences of a finding that the trial court allowed an impermissible amendment of an indictment. Finally *Cotton* has led federal lower courts to conclude that a guilty plea cannot be overturned based on the indictment's failure to allege an essential element of the offense charged (although at least some federal courts will overturn a guilty plea when the indictment alleged facts later held not to constitute a crime).

(f) Safeguarding Defendant's Right to Prosecution by Indictment. In indictment jurisdictions, courts have frequently noted that pleading requirements serve to protect the defendant's right to be prosecuted on the charge of a grand jury as expressed in its indictments. As the Supreme Court has noted, to allow a defendant "to be convicted on the basis of facts not found by, and perhaps, not even presented to the grand jury which indicted him" is to deprive him "of a basic protection which the guarantee of the intervention of the grand jury was designed to secure." This concern is said to be reflected in "the prohibition against the amendment of indictments except by resubmission to the grand jury, and the bar against the 'curing' of defective indictments by issuance of a bill of particulars." See § 11.4(c).

Some courts have suggested that the preservation of the defendant's right to be tried only upon a charge properly found by the grand jury underlies most of the basic requirements for a pleading. The essential elements requirement, in particular, is commonly attributed to this function. The inclusion of each of the essential elements in the indictment tends to structure the grand jury's charging decision, focusing its attention on the specific requirements for criminal liability rather than a general sense of the accused's wrongdoing. Without a specific reference to an element, the "indictment contains no assurance that the grand jury deliberated or even considered whether [the facts established that element]."

The Supreme Court has suggested that the requirement of factual specificity sufficient to provide adequate notice also serves to safeguard the grand jury's charging function. Indeed, the Court majority in *Russell v. U.S.* (§ 11.2(b)) spoke of the factual allegations in the indictment serving to preclude (through the prohibition against variance) conviction of the defendant on "the basis of facts not found by, and perhaps not even presented to, the grand jury." *Russell* stressed that the prosecution should be limited to proceeding on the same basic factual theory that was before the grand jury—i.e., using facts that are consistent with "what was in the minds of the grand jury as to the essential elements of the specific offense charged."

What the grand jury function adds to pleading requirements, above and beyond other pleading functions, is unclear, as the basic standards for pleading essential elements and providing adequate factual specifically tend to be much the same in both indictment and information states. Also, not all indictment states apply standards for the amendment of indictments more restrictive than applied to the amendment information. See § 11.4 (a), (c). Similarly, if one looks only to the grand jury function of pleading requirements, the traditional appellate remedy of requiring automatic conviction reversal for essential-elements and specificity defects becomes problematic, especially as to reversals for defects that were not timely challenged (see § 11.2(d)). As noted in § 7.4(c) and § 7.5(d), flaws in the grand jury process, even when they produced an unsupportable indictment, commonly are viewed as "mooted" by a conviction, since the petit jury's finding of guilt beyond a reasonable doubt evidences that a supportable indictment clearly could now issue. Of course, some grand jury defects are viewed as "structural," requiring automatic reversal of a conviction notwithstanding the petit jury's proper finding of guilt. See e.g., § 7.3(g). The Supreme Court's ruling in *Neder v. U.S.* (2000) indicates, however, that even a grand jury's failure to consider an essential element of the crime (as evidence by the indictment's failure to include that element) is not comparable to a complete absence of screening and therefore is not structural. In *Neder*, as discussed in § 19.6(d), the Court rejected the contention that a failure to submit an element of the charged offense to the petit jury (the trial court erroneously classified the element as an issue for the court) was structural, comparable to having no jury. The Court held instead that the error was subject to harmless error review, a position that several federal courts have viewed as equally applicable to essential-element pleading defects (see § 11.2(a)). Moreover, even structural defects, such as discrimination in the selection of the grand jury, require automatic reversal only when a timely objection was made in the trial court.

§ 11.2 Basic Pleading Defects

(a) **Failure to Allege Essential Elements.** *Necessary content.* The essential elements requirement demands that the pleading allege the presence of each of the basic elements required for the commission of the offense—in general, the elements of mental state, criminal conduct, and resulting harm. It does not demand, however, that the pleading negate exemptions, excuses, or justifications that relieve one of liability notwithstanding the presence of the basic elements.

As discussed in § 18.4(g), *Apprendi v. N.J.* (2000) held that a factor which increases the allowable maximum sentence for an offense is an element of that offense for the purposes of the Sixth Amendment's jury trial guarantee and the due process guarantee of proof beyond a reasonable doubt. In *U.S. v. Cotton* (2002) and other cases, the Supreme Court has noted that such "*Apprendi*-elements" also are essential elements for pleading purposes. Several states take a similar position, but other characterize such elements as "sentencing factors" that need not be identified in the information or indictment (although the states are bound, under *Apprendi*, to submit such "sentencing factors" to the jury). These states view *Cotton* and similar Supreme Court rulings as resting on the Fifth Amendment's grand jury clause (i.e., holding that factors which are elements of the crime for jury factfinding are also elements for grand jury factfinding, and therefore must be alleged in the indictment). Since the grand jury clause does not apply to the states via

Fourteenth Amendment due process (see § 7.1(b)), the states are not bound by such Supreme Court rulings in defining essential elements. A few state courts have suggested otherwise, as they view the Supreme Court cases as also based on the Sixth Amendment's requirement of notice, which does apply to the states. Reading the pleading cases as notice cases is challenged, in turn, on the ground that notice can be provided in various ways other than pleadings (e.g., pretrial discovery). See § 11.1 (c).

To avoid omitting a crucial element of the offense, prosecutors frequently draft pleadings that track the language of the criminal statute, adding appropriate factual references (e.g., the victim's name) along the way. Reliance upon the statutory language will be acceptable, however, only if "the words of [the statute] themselves fully, directly, and expressly, without any uncertainty or ambiguity, set forth all the elements necessary to constitute the offence." In many instances, that will not be the case, and the use of the statutory language will be inadequate. If the statute fails to refer to an essential element, such as mens rea, then that element must be added to the tracked statutory language in framing the pleading. Similarly, if courts have added a significant refinement in the interpretation of a particular statutory element, that element often must be pleaded as interpreted rather than as stated in the statutory language, especially if the judicial interpretation substantially limits the scope of the statutory language.

Implicit allegations. Most failures to allege essential elements are found in pleadings which do not track the statutory language (either because that language is not sufficient in itself or because the prosecutor prefers to set forth the substance of the statute in other terms). The critical issue presented in challenges to such pleadings often is whether a particular element, though not set forth explicitly, is nevertheless included by implication. Courts tend to be more willing to find certain elements alleged by implication than others. Thus, indictments for murder need not state that the victim was a human being; the courts have long held that the very nature of the charge of "murder" suggests the presence of that element. On the other hand, the element of mens rea ordinarily will require a more explicit allegation. For example, in a typical ruling, one court held that an allegation that defendant "unlawfully sold" a pornographic magazine was insufficient to allege that defendant acted with scienter. If the activity would have been one that inherently encompassed the *mens rea* (as in the case of "assaulting" another, which implies an intent to do bodily harm), the description of the act might have been sufficient in itself to allege the necessary mental element.

In *U.S. v. Resendiz–Ponce* (2007), the Supreme Court divided over whether an allegation that the defendant "attempted" to commit a crime implicitly alleged that defendant's actions included an overt act which constituted a substantial step toward the completion of the crime (an essential element of an attempt). The majority concluded that the overt act was implicitly alleged as the word "attempt" as "used in common parlance, * * * and more importantly as used in the law for centuries, * * * encompasses both the overt act and the intent elements." Justice Scalia, in dissent, characterized the Court's "common parlance" reference as "irrelevant" and "probably incorrect." He noted that "burglary" in common parlance connotes entry into a building with felonious intent, but a burglary indictment would fail if it did not specifically allege those elements. There was no assurance, he noted, that a grand jury, relying on nothing more than the term "attempt," recognized that the crime required a substantial step toward completion. The majority, in response, focused on the notice function, reasoning that adding the phrase "took a substantial step," would hardly give the defendant "any greater notice of the charges against him."

Element specificity. Although a pleading must contain the "essential facts" constituting the offense, the need for factual detail generally stems from the factual specificity pleading requirement (discussed in subsection (b) infra) rather than the essential elements requirement. An element of a crime very often can be pleaded without providing any specific factual reference. Thus, a defendant can be alleged to have acted with "depraved indifference" without further alleging an awareness of specific circumstances that produced that level of mens rea. So too, if the aggravated assault statute requires the infliction of a "serious bodily injury," that element can be alleged in the very terms of the statute. If the pleading should require an identification of the particular injury, that additional detail most often is seen as flowing from the factual specificity requirement rather than the essential elements requirement.

Most courts will view a somewhat different type of a failure to provide greater specificity as producing an essential elements deficiency, and that is the failure to describe an element with sufficient specificity to distinguish between alternative legal components of the element. As the Supreme Court noted in *U.S. v. Cruikshank* (1876), where the statute uses "generic terms," the accusatory instrument must go beyond those terms and "descend to particulars," and the failure to do so means the element has not been pleaded. The primary illustration of this principle is found in offenses that prohibit certain action when tied to the commission or attempted commission of another crime. Although some courts disagree, the charge here ordinarily may not simply allege in a generic form that a relationship existed to other criminality (e.g., in burglary, alleging that the illegal entry was with an "intent to commit a felony"); it must specify the particular ulterior offense that fulfills the relationship in this case (e.g., by alleging an entry with "an intent to commit theft").

Consequences of error. Should a trial court find that the indictment or information fails to allege an essential element, it must dismiss the pleading. An amendment of the pleading ordinarily is not permissible. Since no offense has been charged, an amendment adding the missing element charges a new offense, and such amendments traditionally are not allowed. See § 11.4. If a failure to allege an element of the offense could be cured by an amendment adding the missing element, a basic function of the essential elements requirement—ensuring that all elements were found to be supported by sufficient evidence by the appropriate screening agency (i.e., the grand jury in an indictment jurisdiction, and the preliminary hearing magistrate in most information jurisdictions)—would be lost. The prosecutor would be adding elements to the charge even though they were never considered by the screening agency.

Where an essential elements objection is timely raised pretrial, rejected by the trial court, and then raised on appeal, the appellate court will determine de novo whether the element was properly alleged, applying the same standard as the trial court. This standard is more rigorous than that applied when the objection was not timely raised; there, as noted in subsection (e), a standard of liberal construction is applied in determining whether the pleading failed to allege an essential element. Should the appellate court find that the charging instrument failed to allege an essential element, the traditional position is that this defect requires automatic reversal of the conviction. It matters not that the defense was in no way confused by the failure to allege the element (it being understood from the outset that the prosecution would have to prove the element), and that the element was properly presented to the jury in its finding of guilt. In recent years, there has been a movement away from this position, most notably in the federal lower courts.

In the leading federal ruling of *U.S. v. Prentiss* (10th Cir. 2001), a divided Tenth Circuit (sitting en banc) held that the failure to allege the essential elements needed to constitute a crime could be a harmless error. The defendant in *Prentiss* was convicted of the crime of committing arson in Indian country, but the indictment failed to allege the Indian/non-Indian statuses of the victim and defendant (a prerequisite for the application of the offense). Anticipating the reasoning of *U.S. v. Cotton* (§ 11.1(e)), the *Prentiss* majority noted initially that the failure to allege an essential element did not deprive the trial court of jurisdiction. Thus, harmless error analysis applied on appellate review unless the error was deemed "structural," and the Supreme Court had indicated that the only structural error relating to grand jury proceedings was discrimination in the selection of the grand jury. Moreover, the majority reasoned, the Supreme Court in *Neder v. U.S.* (§ 11.1(f)) had applied a harmless error analysis to the failure to submit an element of a crime to a petit jury. Here, the underlying analogous error was the failure to submit an element to the grand jury.

As discussed in § 11.1(e), the Supreme Court's subsequent ruling in *Cotton* agreed with *Prentiss* as to the non-jurisdictional character of pleading errors, referring not only to the failure to allege an *Apprendi*-type element, but also the failure of the indictment to "charge a crime." However, *Cotton* did not address the standard of review applicable when a challenge to the pleading had been timely presented in the trial court. The government argued in its brief that prior rulings requiring automatic dismissal for timely challenged pleading errors (as in *Russell*, § 11.2(b), and *Stirone*, § 11.5(c)) predated the introduction of harmless error analysis to constitutional errors. The *Cotton* opinion, in distinguishing *Russell* and *Stirone* from the situation before the Court, did not rely on that ground. It noted only that those were cases in which "proper objection had been made in the District Court to the sufficiency of the indictment."

Following *Cotton*, additional circuits concluded that the harmless error standard, rather than an automatic reversal standard, applies to an essential-elements defect that was timely challenged before the trial court. Although *Cotton* did not speak to that issue, it had clearly indicated that the plain-error standard of Rule 52(b) applied to appellate review of an essential-elements defect that had not been timely challenged. These circuits concluded that, since Rule 52(b) applies to essential-elements defects, Rule 52(a), which establishes harmless error review for timely raised objections, should be equally applicable to essential-elements defects. Although "structural errors" are deemed per se harmful under Rule 52(a), these circuits agreed with *Prentiss* that the reasoning of *Neder* logically characterizes an essential-elements defect as non-structural. The Ninth Circuit, however, rejected that reasoning, and continued to apply the traditional position of automatic reversal. The Supreme Court granted certiorari in *U.S. v. Resendiz–Ponce* (2007) to resolve this conflict, but found no need to reach the issue, as it held that the pleading there was not defective. Since the conflict among the circuits remains, the Court seems likely to address the issue in the near future. So far, with only a few exceptions, state courts continue to adhere to the traditional position of automatic reversal.

(b) Factual Specificity. As courts repeatedly note, "an indictment [or information] must not only contain all the elements of the offense charged, but must also provide the accused with a sufficient description of the acts he is alleged to have committed to enable him to defend himself adequately." Precisely how much factual specificity is needed to meet that standard will necessarily vary from one case to another. Relevant factors include the nature of the offense, the likely significance of particular factual variations in determining liability, the ability of the prosecution to identify a particular circumstance without a lengthy and basically evidentiary allegation, and the availability of alternative procedures for obtaining the particular information. It generally is agreed that the issue is not whether the alleged offense could be described with more certainty, but whether there is "sufficient particularity" to enable the accused to "prepare a proper defense."

The leading specificity case, *Russell v. U.S.* (1962), clearly indicates that specificity requirements can be driven by more than simply providing notice. The defendants there were charged with violating a federal statute making it a crime for a witness to refuse to answer before a Congressional Committee "any question pertinent to the * * * [subject] under inquiry." The indictments set forth the precise questions that each defendant had refused to answer before the House Un–American Activities Committee (HUAC), and alleged that those questions were "pertinent to the question [i.e., subject matter] then under inquiry," but did not identify that subject matter. In finding that the indictments were defective because they failed to specify the particular subject under inquiry, the Court relied in part on notice considerations; the record of the Committee's questioning and comments was so unclear as to the subject matter under inquiry that defendant was not likely to be apprised of the prosecution's premise as to that subject matter unless it was set forth in the indictment. However, the Court also stressed that greater specificity was needed to rule on the prosecution's legal theory in advance of trial (see § 11.1(d)) and to ensure that the government's theory of the prosecution was that upon which the grand jury issued its indictment (see § 11.1(f)).

Presumably because functions beyond notice required the additional specificity, *Russell* viewed the pleading defect in that case as akin to a failure to state an element of the offense. It noted that a bill of particulars could not have cured the defect, and relied upon the Court's earlier *Cruikshank* ruling (§ 11.2(a)). State courts, however, often view specificity objections as tied strictly to a notice requirement. Thus, they hold that the bill of particulars (or sometimes even other sources of notice) must be considered in assessing the needed degree of specificity in the charging instrument. Similarly, if the issue is not raised pretrial, it generally will be viewed as waived. On appellate review (where properly raised), the courts will look to the discovery that was given (or could have been requested), and ask whether the defendant was actually taken by surprise, and if so, whether prejudice resulted. *Russell*, in contrast, required automatic reversal, as it viewed the indictment as constitutionally deficient. Now, however, the federal appellate courts that apply harmless error analysis to essential-elements defects will apply the same standard to specificity defects, although here again the federal circuits apparently are in conflict.

In applying a notice perspective to the factual specificity of a charging instrument, courts start from the assumption that the defendant is innocent and consequently "has no knowledge of the facts charged against him." But even from the perspective of the innocent person, comparatively little information is needed to prepare a defense for some crimes. A charge of assault, for example, provides enough information if it identifies who was assaulted and when and where the assault occurred. There is no need to inform the defendant of how the assault occurred (assuming the charge is simple assault and not assault with a deadly weapon). If the defendant wasn't there, the manner of assault will be irrelevant to his defense, and if he was present, he will be aware of the circumstances. Greater specificity will be required, however, where the crime encompasses more factual variations. Thus, if the defendant is charged with fraud arising from a series of statements made to the victim, he ordinarily must be informed as to which of his representations is alleged to be false.

Factual variations will not be as significant, however, where they are likely to be concentrated in time and place. In *Resendiz-Ponce* (2007), the Court concluded that the indictment need not identify the specific overt acts that constituted the requisite substantial step in an attempted reentry into the country. The different actions taken by the defendant in an attempted bordercrossing were all part of "single course of conduct" and there was no need to do more than characterize that course of conduct as an "attempt". Unlike *Russell*, the Court noted, the precise character of the course of conduct meeting the substantial step requirement does not present a situation in which guilt " 'depen[ds] so crucially upon * * * a specific identification of fact.' "

(c) Duplicity and Multiplicity. Duplicity is the charging of separate offenses in a single count. This practice is unacceptable because it prevents the jury from deciding guilt or innocence on each offense separately and may make it difficult to determine whether the conviction rested on only one of the offenses or both. Duplicity can result in prejudice to the defendant in the shaping of evidentiary rulings, in producing a conviction on less than a unanimous verdict as to each separate offense, and in limiting review on appeal. A valid duplicity objection raised before trial will force the government to elect the offense upon which it will proceed, but will not require the dismissal of the indictment.

A multiplicitous indictment charges a single offense in several counts. It often is the product of a prosecutor's mistaken assumption that a particular statute creates several separate offenses rather than a single crime that can be accomplished through multiple means. A multiplicity issue is also presented when a series of repeated acts are charged as separate crimes but the defendant claims they are part of a continuous transaction and therefore a single crime. The principle danger in multiplicity is that the defendant will receive multiple sentences for a single offense, although courts have noted that multiple counts may also work against defendant by leading the jury to believe that defendant's conduct is especially serious because it constitutes more than one crime. Multiplicity does not require dismissal of the indictment. The court may respond to a successful objection by requiring the prosecutor to elect one count, by consolidating the various counts, or by simply advising the jury that only one offense is charged.

(d) Late Objections. As noted in § 11.1(a), a critical element of the mid–1900's pleading reforms was to provide for a "waiver" or "forfeiture" of pleading objections that were not raised before trial. That reform was not carried over, however, to what original Federal Rule 12(b) and similar state provisions describe as the "failure to show jurisdiction in the court" and the failure "to charge an offense." Those two defects, the Rule 12(b)-type provisions noted, "shall be noticed * * * at any time during the pendency of the proceeding." The caselaw applying that "waiver exception" tended to focus on the "failure to charge on offense," at it was the much more common error. That defect commonly was read as limited to a failure of the pleading to allege the essential elements of the offense.

Allowing the essential elements requirement to be raised for the first time after conviction, even though previously known to the defense, arguably provides an incentive to the defense to delay making the objection. Where made before trial, a successful objection is likely to result only in the production of a new indictment or information which cures the defect by correctly alleging all of the elements. While the delay resulting from the process of forcing the prosecution to start over again may be of value to the defense under certain circumstances, that advantage hardly compares to the value of overturning a conviction. Here too, the prosecution is likely to return with a new indictment or information that now alleges all of the elements, but the defense has gained a second opportunity to avoid a conviction (and sometimes a somewhat stronger plea-bargaining position where the prosecution prefers not to force upon the complainant and other witnesses the inconvenience of another trial).

In considering essential elements objections first raised after conviction, appellate courts are fully aware of the defense incentive to sandbag and they often react accordingly. Noting that the defense's failure to raise the objection at an earlier point suggests that the defense was hardly misled, the courts repeatedly state that the charging instrument not previously challenged "should be construed liberally in favor of sufficiency, absent any prejudice to the defendant." Indeed, it is said that the pleading will be held sufficient unless it is "so defective that it does not by any reasonable construction" charge the necessary elements. Nonetheless, there is considerable variation to be found from one appellate court to another in its willingness to stretch the language of the pleading to find that an allegedly missing element was sufficiently set forth "by implication." Thus, one will find an allegation that defendant carried and used a firearm during a drug crime sufficient to imply that he did so "knowingly and willfully," while another will find an indictment alleging a postal employee "did convert * * * without authorization of law" certain postal moneys insufficient to find implicit the element of criminal intent.

Should a pleading fail to allege an essential element of the offense of conviction, notwithstanding a liberal construction in favor of sufficiency, the traditional position is that reversal of the conviction is automatic, just as it would be if the pleading objection had been properly presented at trial and erroneously rejected there. That position continues to prevail in all but a few states. In the federal courts, however, the Supreme Court's ruling in *U.S. v. Cotton* (2002) led to a federal lower court rejection of that position.

As discussed § 11.1(e), *Cotton* presented a challenge to an indictment based upon the indictment's failure to include an *Apprendi*-element which had been utilized in increasing the defendant's maximum sentence. The defense first raised this issue on appeal, but argued that its challenge was nonetheless cognizable because the trial court had exceeded the scope of its sentencing jurisdiction as set by the indictment. Responding to the government's contention that plain error analysis should apply, the defense argued that the "discretionary nature" of such review is "logically incompatible with jurisdictional error." *Cotton's* rejection of that argument appeared to go beyond the *Apprendi*-type error presented in that case, as the Court stated generally that an indictment's "failure to charg[e] a crime" is not properly characterized as a jurisdictional error. That seemed to indicate that all essential elements objections, and not simply the type presented in

Cotton, would be subject to the "plain error" standard when first raised on appeal. Thus, it was hardly surprising that the lower federal courts discarded their earlier rulings requiring automatic reversal and applied *Cotton's* plain error analysis to pleadings that omitted more traditional elements of an offense (and thereby failed to charge any offense).

One obstacle to extending plain error to essential elements objections was the language of Federal Rule 12(b). At the time of the *Cotton* decision, Rule 12(b) stated that an essential elements defect "shall be noticed by the court at any time during the pendency of the proceedings" (language subsequently amended to "may be heard" at any time). The *Cotton* opinion did not refer to Rule 12(b), but the government's brief in *Cotton* had addressed that issue. The government argued that Rule 12(b) set forth a general rule of waiver for pleading defects not raised before trial, and the function of its provision excepting the essential elements objection simply was to indicate that the objection was not waived by being first presented on appeal. That provision, the government argued, did not address the consequence of a determination that the untimely, but not waived objection had merit, for doing so would take it into the sphere regulated by Rule 52(b). Rule 52(b) had to be accorded "equal dignity," and therefore should govern as to this objection, just as it would to any other objection not properly presented to the trial court. Rule 12(b)'s provision on exceptions merely served to make certain that the waiver provision of Rule 12(b) did not operate to preclude application of Rule 52(b), as plain error only authorizes possible review for non-waived objections. A long line of federal lower court rulings had relied on Rule 12(b) in requiring automatic reversal, but in light of *Cotton's* analysis of the applicability of plain-error review, the government's argument as to the interface of Rules 52 and Rule 12(b) found judicial support even before Rule 12(b) was amended.

§ 11.3   Bill of Particulars

(a) Nature of the Bill. The motion for a bill of particulars requests that the prosecution be directed to furnish further information (i.e., "particulars") concerning the offense charged in the information or indictment. The motion ordinarily lists a series of questions concerning the events cited in the charge that the defense would have the prosecution answer. Thus, if an indictment charging the obstruction of a public official has simply tracked the language of the statute, the motion might ask for the answers to such questions as what official duties were obstructed and how did the obstruction occur. So too, where a defendant is charged with driving under the influence of alcohol, the defense may ask for particulars relating to the exact manner of the defendant's driving.

Assuming that the defense motion is granted, the status of the prosecution's response falls somewhere between a pleading and a discovery response. The factual allegations contained in the bill of particulars will limit the government's case at trial in the same manner as factual allegations in an original charging instrument. The rules governing variance between proof and pleading apply to the bill of particulars just as they do to an indictment or information. The allegations of the bill of particulars are not treated as equivalent to those in the original charging instrument, however, when it comes to meeting basic pleading requirements. If an indictment or information does not state all of the essential elements, it cannot be cured by a bill of particulars that alleges facts establishing the missing element. In *Russell v. U.S.* (§ 11.2(b)), where the pleading lacked sufficient specificity, the Supreme Court described as "the settled rule" that "a bill of particulars cannot save an invalid indictment." However, *Russell* involved a specificity deficiency that was treated as undermining the defendant's Fifth Amendment right to prosecution by indictment. Where the issue is simply a lack of factual detail needed for notice alone, the bill of particulars commonly can cure the pleading deficiency.

(b) Standards for Issuance. Some states do not have a court rule or statute governing the bill of particulars, and recognize it as a common law motion. Others have provisions like Federal Rule 7(f), which simply notes that the "court may direct the filing of a bill of particulars," and leaves to the courts the development of standards governing issuance. Still other states have rules setting forth standards, but those standards are exceptionally flexible.

Most jurisdictions hold that the issuance of the bill of particulars is discretionary. Appellate courts accordingly give great weight to the trial court's judgment when reviewing its decision not to grant a bill of particulars. Appellate courts do, however, offer various guidelines to trial courts as to where the bill should or should not be granted. The traditional common law standard for granting the motion looks to "whether it is necessary that defendant have the particulars sought in order to prepare his defense and in order that prejudicial surprise will be avoided." Taken literally, this standard might require that defendant gain disclosure of everything in the prosecution's files, because only such broad discovery can assure that defendant will not be subjected to "prejudicial surprise." But the bill relates to the pleading, and the concern therefore should be with surprise only as to the particular acts or events that underlie the pleading, not with the manner in which they will be established at trial. Accordingly, courts also state that "a bill of particulars may not call for evidentiary matter." Matching the prohibition against disclosure of evidentiary matter—

and raising similar problems in application—is the prohibition against disclosure of the government's legal theory.

The trial court is also directed to take into consideration the scope of the pretrial discovery that will be available to the defense. The defense is likely to argue, however, that even the most complete discovery, if combined with a broadly stated accusatory instrument, is likely to be of limited use because it may suggest several different directions in which the prosecution may proceed. Only the bill of particulars, the defense will contend, serves to limit the shape of the case, and thereby allow the defense to properly focus its limited investigatory resources. To this contention the prosecution will respond that it should not be required before trial to virtually set its case in stone so that the differences that almost invariably occur between pretrial investigation and trial testimony can become the source of a constant stream of defense challenges to variances between the trial proof and the particulars.

§ 11.4 Amendments of the Pleading

(a) The Prejudice/Different–Offense Standard. The dominant standard governing amendments is the two-pronged standard that permits an amendment provided it does not either (1) result in prejudice to the accused or (2) charge a different crime. Federal Rule 7(e) applies this standard only to amendments of an information, but most states apply its two-pronged limitation on amendments to both indictments and informations.

Of the two limitations imposed under the dominant standard, the prejudice limitation clearly has produced the greater consistency in interpretation among the various state and federal courts. General agreement exists that the concept of "prejudice" here requires an inquiry that focuses on the element of surprise. Ordinarily, the defense, in opposing an amendment, must make some showing that the proposed change introduces an element of surprise that will interfere with the defense's ability to defend against the charges. Courts often note that timing is the key here, with a critical distinction drawn between amendments made before and during trial. Prior to trial, prejudice in preparation ordinarily may be avoided by granting a continuance, and courts are hesitant to find prejudice if a continuance was granted, offered and refused, or not requested. Since continuances during trial (particularly a jury trial) are less likely to be granted, the prosecution faces a much more difficult task in overcoming a defense claim of surprise as to an amendment offered during trial. Such amendments are most likely to be accepted where the prosecution can show that the amendment does not change substantially the factual basis of the offense as set forth in the original pleading, the bill of particulars, or the discovery made available to the defense. However, the critical test here is whether the defense's challenge to the prosecution's evidence and the defense's presentation of its own evidence will have the same bearing upon the amended pleading as upon the original pleading, and that may not always be the case even when the defense was previously aware of the factual basis of the amendment.

The prohibition against amendments that charge a different or additional offense has produced somewhat greater divergence in its interpretation. There is general agreement that this prohibition stands without regard to the absence of prejudicial surprise. Courts uniformly recognize also that two different types of amendments that can result in the charging of a different or additional offense. The first, producing what is commonly described as a "factually different offense," is the amendment that alters the facts alleged, but continues to allege a violation of the same substantive crime as the original pleading. The second, creating what is described as "legally separate offense," is the amendment that alters the substantive crime alleged to have been violated, usually relying upon a different code provision. Where an amendment both changes the facts alleged and the statutory violation, it must be analyzed under the standards applied to both types of changes.

In determining whether a factual change produces a new offense, most courts ask whether the amendment moves to what is basically a different factual event. Thus, a court may ask whether "the prosecution is relying [through the amendment] on a complex of facts distinctly different" from that set forth in the original pleading, or whether the crime specified in the original pleading "evolved out of the same factual situation as the crimes specified in the amended indictment or information." In applying such standards, most courts do not find critical factual shifts that would produce a separate offense for the purpose of applying the double jeopardy clause (as where each assault victim produces a different offense). If the remaining characteristics of the event (e.g., time, place, behavior, and consequence) are constant, an amendment identifying a different victim of an offense (e.g., a different owner of the stolen property) does not allege a different offense. Similarly, different offenses are not changed by amendments that change the identification of the property stolen, the description of the sexual contact with the victim of a sexual assault, or different means of committing the offense. So too, though a change in the alleged date of the offense may raise difficulties in terms of prejudice (e.g., rendering irrelevant the defendant's alibi), it will not create a different offense unless it refers to an event different than that originally alleged. Some courts suggest, however, that even though the basic incident remains the same, an amendment altering the facts alleged will be deemed to allege a different offense if it changes the "theory of the prosecution."

Where the amendment alleges violation of a different substantive criminal prohibition, most courts will apply the traditional double jeopardy standard that looks to the elements of crime in determining whether two statutes proscribe the same offense. See § 9.4(b). Under that standard, an amendment will be accepted if it merely alleges a lesser included offense, but not if it alleges a more serious offense with additional elements or even a similarly graded offense with different elements.

In some respects, however, courts do not look to a traditional application of the different elements standard. Courts have divided, for example, in applying the same offense standard to the amendment of the allegation shifting the means of commission of the crime from one statutorily prescribed alternative to another. A minority position views such a change as charging a separate offense even though the same statutory provision is relied upon. They view the alternatives, at least where distinct in character, as establishing offenses that are separate in function, though having the same consequence. The majority position rejects that analysis and views such a shift as not changing the offense charged. These courts treat the amendment as merely shifting the facts that will be relied upon to establish the same basic element of the crime.

(b) The Form/Substance Distinction. A substantial group of states adhere to the formulation that permits amendment as to "form," but not as to "substance." Some of these states allow amendments as to substance prior to trial (provided they do not allege a different or additional defense), but then permit only amendments as to form after the trial has started. Others provide only for amendments as to form, which can be made at any time before verdict. Typically, these provisions apply to the amendment of indictments as well as informations.

While provisions adopting a form/substance distinction may offer illustrations of formal defects that may be cured by indictment (e.g., miswritings, surplusage, and the failure to state time or place where "not of the essence of the offense"), they do not attempt to describe what constitutes a substantive amendment. Not surprisingly courts have varied in their interpretation of that standard. A few view substantive changes as largely limited to those which charge what would constitute a different offense under a Rule 7(e)-type standard. Most, however, find substantive changes in amendments that would be acceptable (assuming no prejudice) under the narrowest interpretation of a Rule 7(e)-type standard.

Amendments are said to be substantive if they change any "essential facts that must be proved to make the act complained of a crime." Thus, a jurisdiction adopting a restrictive interpretation of the form/substance distinction is likely to bar automatically an amendment that substantially changes the pleading's description of the criminal act, the mens rea accompanying that act, or the consequences of that act. Such rulings have prohibited amendments that changed the original allegation that defendant defrauded an automobile dealer of a dollar amount to defrauding the dealer of an automobile selling for that amount, that changed the action involved in shoplifting from altering the price tag to removing the price tag, and that added robbery by reasonably appearing to be armed to an indictment that alleged defendant was actually armed. Courts also have characterized as substantive an amendment alleging the assault was against a different victim, an amendment deleting the name of one of several named robbery victims, and even an amendment altering an allegation as to the ownership of the property that was stolen. Other courts, however, have accepted as non-substantive similar changes in the name of the victim where that change did not look to a different event and did not alter the "character" of the modus operandi.

(c) The *Bain* Rule. As previously noted, most jurisdictions treat the amendment of an indictment no differently than the amendment of an information. However, the federal courts and several states draw a sharp distinction between the amendment of the information and the indictment. While utilizing the liberal Rule 7(e) standard for amendments to the information, they apply a much more stringent standard to amendments of the indictment. The permissible scope of an amendment of an indictment in federal courts is controlled by the *Bain* rule, which is based on the Supreme Court's ruling in *Ex parte Bain* (1886). The *Bain* ruling relied on common law principles that treated the indictment as the sole product of the grand jury, subject to alteration only by that body. As originally announced, the *Bain* rule imposed a prohibition against amending indictments that arguably was more restrictive than even the most stringent interpretation of the form/substance distinction. A few states that continue to look to the same common law principles (and thus are described as "*Bain* jurisdictions") have retained that original prohibition. In the federal courts, however, the *Bain* rule is now held to allow some limited amendments to the indictment, though under a standard not nearly as broad as the Rule 7(e) standard applicable to informations. In many respects, the federal rulings on amending indictments are similar to state rulings that significantly restrict amendments under a "form/ substance" standard.

Bain was decided in 1887, at a time when several states had started to depart from the early common law rule that "indictments could not be amended." The Supreme Court noted, however, that its ruling was "not left to the requirements of the common law," but was controlled by the "positive and restrictive language" of the Fifth Amendment guarantee of indictment by grand jury. That guarantee, the Court noted, entitles the defendant to be tried on the indictment as issue by the grand jury, not as amended by the prosecutor with permission of the trial court. A trial court could not allow alteration even as to matter that it deemed "surplusage" and therefore not critical to the grand jury's decision to indict. It could not "change the charging part of an indictment to suit its own notions of what it ought to have been, or what the grand jury would probably have made if their attention had been called to suggested changes," for the charge was then that of the court rather than the grand jury.

Read broadly, Justice Miller's opinion in *Bain* would have barred any amendment to what he described as the "body of the indictment." Federal courts generally have allowed amendments that deal with matters of "form" rather than substance. *Bain* itself continues to be cited, however, as an illustration of the type of change, relating to the substance of the crime, that cannot be permitted even though there is no suggestion that the change will affect the preparedness of the defendant.

In its most recent interpretation of *Bain, U.S. v. Miller* (1985), the Supreme Court stated that *Bain* today stands only for "the proposition that a conviction cannot stand if based on an offense that is different from that alleged in the grand jury indictment." In *Miller*, the indictment had alleged that the defendant defrauded an insurance company by both arranging for a burglary at his place of business and by lying to the insurer as to the value of the loss, but the evidence at trial established only the lying. Although there was no element of surprise involved, the trial court denied the government's motion to amend the indictment by striking the allegation of the defendant's prior knowledge of the burglary. After the case was submitted to the jury on the full indictment, and the defendant was convicted, the defense challenged the conviction on the ground that the government's proof had fatally varied from the scheme alleged in the indictment by failing to cover both aspects of that scheme. In the course of rejecting that contention, the Supreme Court noted that the government's proposed amendment, which would have limited the indictment to the proof presented, would have been permissible under a proper reading of *Bain*. The Court acknowledged that language in *Bain* could "support the proposition that the striking out of part of an indictment invalidates the whole of the indictment, for a court cannot speculate as to whether the grand jury had meant for any remaining offense to stand independently, even if that remaining offense clearly was included in the original text." However, later cases had implicitly rejected that proposition by holding that, "as long as the crime and elements of the offense that sustain the conviction are fully and clearly set out in the indictment, the right to a grand jury is not normally violated by the fact that the indictment alleges more crimes or other means of committing the same crime." In light of these rulings, *Miller* noted, where an indictment alleges two separate offenses or two separate means of committing the same offense, *Bain* should not be read to prohibit dropping from the indictment those allegations concerning the one offense or one means that was not supported by the evidence at trial.

Miller had no need to discuss the application of the *Bain* rule to amendments that would add or substitute new factual allegations. It noted only that *Bain* continues to stand for the proposition "that a conviction cannot stand if based on an offense that is different from that alleged in the grand jury's indictment." The Court had no reason to explore the question of what new matter results in alleging an offense "different" from that originally charged. It described as "the most important reaffirmation" of this aspect of *Bain* the Court's ruling in *Stirone v. U.S.* (1960). In that case, as discussed in § 11.5(c), the Court found that the trial court's admission of evidence establishing a factual theory of liability at variance with that alleged in the indictment resulted in a prohibited "constructive amendment" of the indictment. The indictment there alleged that the element of interference with interstate commerce had been produced through one consequence of defendant's extortion activities while the trial evidence and jury instruction allowed for the finding of interference based on a different consequence.

In a jurisdiction that applied the dominant two-pronged standard discussed in subsection (a), the new factual theory allowed by the trial court in *Stirone* would not have been viewed as alleging a different offense. The constructive amendment simply introduced a new factual alternative for establishing one element of the crime. *Stirone*, however, viewed the new theory as an impermissible departure from the original indictment because it broadened the factual basis for liability; it mattered not that this "constructive amendment" did so without creating what would be considered a separate crime for double jeopardy purposes. The *Miller* opinion also cited language in still other federal rulings that similarly indicated that changes which would fall short of producing a new offense under a Rule 7(e)-type standard will nonetheless be prohibited under the *Bain* rule as alleging an offense "different" from that originally charged. Thus, lower federal courts applying the *Bain* rule have drawn a distinction between acceptable amendments that merely explain or expand upon factual elements originally alleged (e.g., by more specifically identifying an altered commercial draft) and impermissible amendments that alter the factual theories establishing elements of the same offense. Courts have rejected amendments that added a different drug to the list of drugs possessed by defendant with an intent to distribute, and that shifted the deadly weapon under a charge of possession during a felony from a "chair" to a "chair and/or table."

Where an appellate court finds that the trial court erred by permitting an amendment that violated the *Bain* limitation, the consequence traditionally has been a reversal of defendant's conviction, without inquiry as to whether the error had a prejudicial impact upon the trial. The rejection of *Bain's* jurisdictional characterization of pleading errors in *U.S. v. Cotton* (§ 11.1(e)) may well lead to a rejection of this position. Those lower federal courts that have found in *Cotton* support for applying a harmless error standard to a properly presented essential-elements claim (see § 11.3(a)) presumably would find the harmless error standard applicable as well to a properly presented claim that the trial court permitted an amendment prohibited by *Bain*. Those courts have already indicated that the harmless-error standard will apply in appellate review of variances that constitute constructive amendments. See § 11.5(c).

§ 11.5 Variances

(a) Challenging Variances. A variance arises when the proof offered at trial departs from the allegations in the indictment or information. A defense objection to a variance may be made initially at the point that the prosecution introduces its proof, with the defense arguing that the prosecutor's evidence is irrelevant to the charges. Very often that objection may have escaped the defense's notice, or the evidence may have had relevance to a similar happening or transaction, and the defense objection will first be raised in opposition to the prosecution's request for a jury instruction resting liability on a theory supported only by the proof which departs from the pleading. The defendant objecting at this point states, in effect: "The state may have introduced evidence sufficient to establish a crime, but it is not the crime alleged in its accusatory pleading and I therefore am entitled to an acquittal." If the state has introduced evidence covering the allegations in its pleading and the variance relates to evidence establishing an additional theory of liability, then the defense objection is to allowing the jury to find liability based on this additional theory. Frequently, the prosecution, recognizing the existence of a variance, will seek to amend the pleading to conform to the evidence. If this is permitted, and the defendant is convicted, then the issue raised on appeal will be whether the amendment was properly allowed. If the trial judge does not allow the amendment (or no request for amendment is made), and the case is sent to the jury over the defendant's variance objection, then the defendant, if convicted, will contend on appeal that allowance of the variance constitutes reversible error.

If the trial judge upholds the defense objection to a variance and does not allow an amendment, then the issue basically is removed from the case. The defense has no reason to object, and the prosecution will be unable to gain appellate review of the trial court's ruling. If there is insufficient evidence to convict without the variance, and the defendant is acquitted, the prosecution cannot challenge that verdict. The prosecution may obtain a new charge based upon the material that had been excluded on a variance theory, but if the court should then conclude that the new material sets forth the same offense for double jeopardy purposes as the prior charge, the acquittal on that charge constitutes a bar to the new prosecution. Numerous states have provisions stating that "if the defendant is acquitted on the ground of a variance between the charge and the proof, * * * it is not an acquittal of the crime and does not bar a subsequent prosecution for the same crime." These provisions seek to treat the acquittal as the equivalent of a dismissal, but that position probably is unacceptable in light of the double jeopardy definition of an "acquittal." See § 17.3(a).

(b) The *Berger* Standard. Without doubt, the most frequently cited analysis of the law governing variances is that of Justice Sutherland in *Berger v. U.S.* (1935):

> The true inquiry, * * * is not whether there has been a variance in proof, but whether there has been such a variance as to "affect the substantial rights" of the accused. The general rule that allegations and proof must correspond is based upon the obvious requirements (1) that the accused shall be definitely informed as to the charges against him, so that he may be enabled to present his defense and not be taken by surprise by the evidence offered at the trial; and (2) that he may be protected against another prosecution for the same offense.

Justice Sutherland's analysis has been adopted by various state courts as the sole measure for testing the acceptability of a variance. Under what is described as the *"Berger* standard," a variance requires reversal of a conviction only when it deprives the defendant of his right to fair notice or leaves him open to a risk of double jeopardy.

In applying the notice element of the *Berger* standard, courts look to the record to determine whether it suggests "a possibility that the defendant may have been misled or embarrassed in the preparation or presentation of his defense." A failure to object to the variance at trial generally is viewed as a waiver of a claim of prejudice, and an eleventh hour objection is taken as strong evidence belying any such claim. If the defendant was previously aware of the prosecution's proof as a result of pretrial discovery or a preliminary hearing, that factor also will weigh against a finding of prejudice. The court also will look to the relationship of the variance to the defense presented by the defendant. Thus, a variance in date or location is not likely to have misled a defendant who raised an affirmative defense or claimed a lack of mens rea, as those defenses acknowledge the defendant's participation in the alleged event.

The possibility of actual prejudice at trial is put aside when courts test a variance against the risk of exposing the defendant to double jeopardy. Most courts here will apply the traditional *Blockburger* standard as to what constitutes a separate offense for double jeopardy purposes. See § 9.4(b). Yet, some courts have barred, presumably under *Berger's* double jeopardy prong, variances that changed the offense only by alleging a different means of commission as part of the same incident or a different ultimate victim of a property offense. Such rulings may reflect the state's conversion of the second prong of *Berger* into a constructive amendment limitation as discussed in the next subsection. As noted in § 11.4, some courts prohibit under the different offense standard, and most courts prohibit under the form/substance distinction, amendments that fall short of charging a separate offense for double jeopardy purposes.

(c) The Constructive Amendment Limitation. The Supreme Court, in its treatment of variances, has looked to both the *Berger* standard and the limitations that apply to amendments of the charge, particularly as to indictments. The Court accordingly has drawn a distinction between trial court allowance of a departure in the proof from the indictment so great as to be regarded as a "constructive amendment," which constitutes a reversible error in itself, and a "mere variance," which is reversible error only if it is likely to have caused surprise or otherwise violated the *Berger* standard. The leading illustrations of the Court's analysis of "mere variances" are *Berger v. U.S.* (1935) and *Kotteakos v. U.S.* (1946). The leading illustration of a "constructive amendment" variance is that considered in *Stirone v. U.S.* (1960).

Both *Berger* and *Kotteakos* involved situations in which one large conspiracy was charged but proof at trial established a series of separate conspiracies. The Court in each case applied the *Berger* standard (described in subsection (b)). Since the variances did not create double jeopardy difficulties, the focus was on whether the distinction in proof resulted in prejudice, with the Court finding that it had in one case but not in another. *Berger* held that the variance was not prejudicial when it established two conspiracies involving contemporaneous transactions rather than a single conspiracy. *Kotteakos* held otherwise as to a situation "in which one conspiracy only is charged and at least eight having separate though similar objects are made out * * * and in which the more numerous participants in the different schemes were, on the whole, except for one, persons who did not know or have anything to do with one another." There, thirteen parties were jointly tried, and as to all but one defendant, the variance resulted in the jury having before it evidence of additional conspiracies which had no bearing on the individual defendant's liability.

Neither *Berger* nor *Kotteakos* spoke to whether, if amendments had been allowed to reshape the conspiracies to fit the prosecution's evidence, those amendments would have violated the *Bain* rule. However, the Court later suggested in *U.S. v. Miller* (1985) that the *Berger* and *Kotteakos* rulings were consistent with the amendment principle announced in *Miller*. The more confined conspiracies of which the defendants were convicted were described in *Miller* as "technically included" within the broader conspiracy originally alleged. Thus, if the variances were treated as amendments, they would have reduced the scope of the charges, rather than have added new material and therefore would not have violated *Bain* as interpreted in *Miller*. That was not the case in *Stirone v. U.S.* (1960).

In *Stirone*, the indictment charged a violation of the Hobbs Act through extortion that obstructed interstate commerce by preventing the victim (Rider) from importing sand that was shipped from another state. At trial, over the defendant's objection, the court admitted evidence (and charged the jury) on obstruction of interstate commerce that resulted from Rider's inability to supply concrete for the construction of a local steel plant which had intended to ship its product in interstate commerce. The lower court found that this variance had not been fatal since defense counsel had been prepared for the introduction of that evidence. Without disturbing this finding of no prejudice, the Supreme Court reversed. Justice Black, speaking for a unanimous Court, reasoned that the variance here was the equivalent of an amendment, and the amendment would have been prohibited under *Bain*.

The variance in *Stirone* would not have created a "new offense" for double jeopardy purposes. The act of extortion was the same under both theories, with the variation extending only to the consequences establishing the element of harm (i.e., the obstruction of interstate commerce). However, the variance altered a substantial element of the crime, providing an entirely different theory of impact upon interstate commerce. In contrast to *Berger* and *Kotteakos*, it added a new factual element rather than simply rearranging the elements alleged in the original indictment. That clearly would have barred any such amendment under *Bain*.

Stirone appeared to draw an absolute parallel between the *Bain* prohibition of amendments and the prohibition of variances as constructive amendments. A strict application of the *Bain* prohibition could certainly bar variances far less extreme than that in *Stirone*. Some federal lower courts, however, have looked to *Stirone* as the prototype of the variance that will be barred automatically, as a constructive amendment. They have suggested that the variance must change the basic character of an element of the offense, producing a modification that could possibly have affected the grand jury's assessment of the charges. Others have taken a position arguably more consistent with *Bain* and construed as a constructive amendment any variance that basically alters the prosecution's factual theory as to any element. In states that adhere to a restrictive form/substance limitation on amendments, the constructive amendment doctrine has barred even the most minor variances. Thus, one court rejected a variance where the indictment charged armed robbery with a pistol and evidence was that defendant had used a rifle.

As previously noted, a constructive amendment traditionally has called for automatic reversal on appellate review. The combination of *U.S. v. Cotton* and the federal lower court rulings applying a harmless error analysis to an indictment's failure to charge an offense has led to a reconsideration of this position. (see § 11.2(a)) While *Cotton* distinguished the automatic reversal in *Stirone*, it rejected the *Bain* perspective on the jurisdictional quality of a proper indictment (see § 11.1(e)), and that perspective also influenced *Stirone*. Also, as the government noted in its *Cotton* brief, *Stirone* was decided before the Court introduced its harmless error jurisprudence as applied to constitutional errors. Not surprisingly, several of the federal circuits that apply harmless error analysis to essential-elements defects have indicated that harmless error analysis also will be applied to constructive amendments that were timely challenged in the trial court.

*

Chapter 12

PRETRIAL DISCOVERY

Table of Sections

For additional analysis of the above topics and citations to authorities
supporting their discussion in this Book, consult the authors' 7-volume
Criminal Procedure treatise, also available as Westlaw database
CRIMPROC. See the Table of Cross-References in this Book.

---

§ 12.1   The Structure of Discovery Law

(a) **"Common Law" Authority.** American courts, relying on
the English common law, initially took the position that the judiciary lacked authority to order pretrial discovery in criminal cases
absent legislative authorization of such discovery. Over the first
half of the twentieth century, courts in many states reconsidered
the common law's prohibition and concluded that it was a rule "of
policy, not power." They recognized a discretionary authority of the
trial court, in the exercise of its inherent authority over the trial
process, to require at least the prosecution to make pretrial disclosure of specified evidence to the defense. During the 1930s and
1940s, through court rules and legislation, the vast majority of
jurisdictions adopted procedures designed to promote full and open
pretrial discovery in civil cases. Over the next few decades, the
success of this movement led to a similar legislative expansion of
pretrial discovery in criminal cases. Today, almost all jurisdictions
have statutes or court rules providing for pretrial discovery in
criminal cases. However, the court's discretionary authority to
order discovery is relied upon in some jurisdictions (including the
federal) to prescribe defense discovery standards where the statutes
or court rules leave gaps.

(b) **Court Rules and Statutes.** Although the statutes or
court rules governing discovery vary in content, they tend to be
similar in structure. Typically, the basic statute or court rule
performs the following major tasks: (1) it establishes a procedure by
which the defense and the prosecution can put into effect the other
side's obligation to make pretrial disclosure; (2) it designates those
items which shall or may (upon court order) be disclosed by the
prosecution to the defense; (3) it designates those items that shall
or may (upon court order) be disclosed by the defense to the
prosecution; (4) it establishes certain exemptions from disclosure
based upon content (e.g., work product) or, in some instances,
based on the nature of the item (e.g., recorded statements of

prospective witnesses); (5) it authorizes the trial court to issue under special circumstances a protective order that will bar or limit disclosures that would otherwise be required; (6) it imposes a continuing duty to disclose discoverable items so that the process automatically encompasses items acquired after the initial disclosure; and (7) it provides a procedure for judicial administration and enforcement of the discovery provisions, including the imposition of sanctions.

As to content, discovery provisions can be loosely categorized by reference to basic coverage patterns both as to defense and prosecution discovery. Allowable defense discovery can be helpfully categorized by comparison to the Federal Rules of Criminal Procedure (providing the narrowest discovery), the original edition of the ABA Standards (providing substantially broader discovery), and the third edition of the ABA Standards (providing even broader discovery, but followed in no more half-dozen states). Not all jurisdictions have provisions that even roughly fit one model or another. Thus, approximately a dozen states provide defense discovery that is significantly broader than Federal Rule 16 but not as broad as the original ABA Standards.

Categorizing prosecution discovery is more difficult even if one ignores the distinction between conditional and mandatory provisions. See § 12.3(f). Here again, states with provisions modeled on Federal rules provide the narrowest discovery, but many states following the original ABA Standards provide similarly limited prosecution discovery. The third edition of the ABA Standards provides considerably broader prosecution discovery, and some states have gone even beyond that model.

(c) The Operation of Discovery Provisions. In some jurisdictions the same discovery provisions apply to all criminal prosecutions, but others treat separately discovery in trial courts of general jurisdiction. In still others, the discovery provisions are tied to the level of the offense. Ordinarily, discovery provisions are broadest as to felony cases, but discovery there does not become available until charges are filed in the court of general jurisdiction (i.e., the discovery provisions do not apply in proceedings before the magistrate court, such as bail hearings and preliminary hearings).

Once the discovery provision takes effect, that discovery which is granted as a matter of right, in all but a small group of jurisdictions, is provided without resort to judicial action. A motion seeking a court order directing a party to provide discovery is required only where there is a dispute as to what must be disclosed as a matter of right or the particular item is discoverable only at the discretion of the court. Under many state discovery provisions, the prosecution has an automatic obligation to disclose the items discoverable as of right within a specified number of days following the filing of the indictment or information. Under other discovery provisions, the defense must make a request of the prosecutor. That request, however, need contain no more than a listing of those categories of items specified in the discovery provision as to which disclosure is desired. Where the prosecution's right to discovery is conditioned on the defense having received similar discovery (see § 12.3(f)), the request serves to trigger the prosecution's authority to seek parallel discovery. In some jurisdictions, the prosecution's right is not so conditioned, and the defense, like the prosecution, has an automatic obligation to provide disclosure within a specified period following the filing of the indictment or information. The obligation to disclose is ongoing, so each side must make further disclosure as new discoverable material comes into its possession or previously possessed material becomes discoverable because of its intended use at trial.

(d) **Other Discovery Vehicles.** In almost all jurisdictions there will be available to the defense, and to a lesser extent, to the prosecutor, various other procedures through which some degree of pretrial discovery may be obtained. Unlike the discovery provisions, these procedures are not designed specifically to gain disclosure of the evidence possessed by the other side, but they nonetheless reveal incidentally part of that evidence. Procedures providing such a discovery potential include the bail hearing (particularly where the prosecution seeks preventative detention), the preliminary hearing, the challenge to the sufficiency of the evidence before the grand jury (available in only a small group of states), and hearings on various pretrial motions, such as the motion to suppress. Some defense discovery may be available outside of the criminal justice process, although the primary vehicle here, the Freedom of Information Act, typically will include an exemption for records "compiled for law enforcement purposes" where disclosure could reasonably be expected to "interfere" with enforcement proceedings.

(e) **Depositions.** In civil cases, the deposition is a major discovery device. At the deposition, the witness is placed under oath, and subjected to questioning by the party taking the deposition, with the opportunity given to the adversary to cross-examine and to object to improper questions. The deposition is stenographically transcribed and in many jurisdictions may also be videotaped. In criminal cases, the form of the deposition is quite similar, but the availability of the deposition is much more restricted. Only about ten states allow for the use of depositions as a basic discovery procedure. In the vast majority of the states and in the federal system, the deposition is available in criminal cases primarily for the purpose of preserving the testimony of a witness likely to be unavailable at trial. To obtain a deposition to perpetuate testimony, a party must make a showing that the deponent is a prospective material witness and is likely not to be available to testify at trial. A typical statutory formulation requires a showing "that a prospective witness may be unable to attend or be prevented from attending a trial or hearing, that the witness' testimony is material, and that it is necessary to take the witness' deposition in order to prevent a failure of justice."

Several factors help to explain why the discovery deposition, a mainstay of civil discovery, is unavailable in criminal cases in the vast majority of jurisdictions. In many jurisdictions, the defense does not receive a listing of prosecution witnesses, and in a substantial majority, the prosecution does not receive a listing of defense witnesses. Such listings are available through interrogatories in the civil process and provide the foundation for obtaining discovery through depositions.

Still another factor is the use of the "alternative" device of disclosing the prior recorded statements of potential witnesses. In civil discovery, such statements are not generally available, as they are work product protected. In criminal discovery, where a jurisdiction require the disclosure of the names of witnesses, that disclosure, particularly as to prosecution witnesses, is accompanied by the prior recorded statements of the witness (such as the statement that a prosecution witness gave to the police). While the availability of such statements is hardly the equivalent of a deposition, it contributes to the argument that there is less need for discovery depositions in criminal cases.

The potential cost of the discovery deposition is still another concern that may have contributed in many states to the decision to limit depositions to the exceptional case requiring the preservation of testimony. In civil discovery the deposition is one of the most costly and time-consuming elements of pretrial proceedings. However, that expense presumably leads counsel to avoid unnecessary depositions. In criminal cases, with most defendants being indigent, the state would bear the cost of defense depositions, and concern for client cost would not bear upon defense counsel's decision to depose. Indeed, it is argued, counsel's use of depositions as to every potential witness might become "a part of the adequacy of representation required in the constitutional right to [effective assistance] of counsel."

§ 12.2   Defense Discovery

    (a) Prosecution Possession or Control. An element bearing on almost all portions of a typical defense discovery provision is the scope of the prosecution's obligation to obtain and make available for discovery items that are not within its immediate possession. As to each item designated as subject to discovery, apart from those obviously within the prosecution's possession (e.g., items to be used at trial), the discovery provision will attach a clause describing the necessary connection of the prosecution to the particular item. States with ABA-type discovery provisions commonly describe the prosecutor's discovery obligation as extending to specified items that are "within the possession or control of the prosecuting attorney." Federal Rule 16 applies its basic discovery provisions to items "within the government's possession, custody, or control." However, it also adds as to most items that the government does not intend to use in evidence the further requirement that "the attorney for the government knows—or through reasonable diligence should know—that the * * * [item] exists."

Courts interpreting typical "scope" clauses uniformly have held that the basic obligation to disclose extends to items within the files of those investigative agencies of the same government (federal or state) that have participated in the development of the particular prosecution. Some state courts have held that the prosecutor's "control" extends to records in the possession of "any * * * prosecutorial or law enforcement office" of the particular state, whether or not involved in the investigation or ordinarily reporting to the particular prosecutor. Courts generally agree that the prosecutor's obligation does not extend to information in the possession of government agencies that are not "enforcement agencies", even though such an agency has furnished information (e.g., a vehicle registration) to the prosecutor in the particular case.

(b) Written or Recorded Statements. Another issue that has a bearing on several parts of a typical defense discovery provision is the reach of the phrase "written or recorded statement." All discovery provisions provide for discovery of written or recorded statements of the defendant, and many also allow for discovery of written or recorded statements of codefendants and prosecution witnesses. Where the prosecution has within its possession or control information regarding the substance of statements that were not "written or recorded," that information may or may not be discoverable pursuant to separate discovery provisions.

Neither the original ABA Standards nor the Federal Rules sought to define the phrase "written or recorded statement." The drafting committees in both instances recognized the possible incorporation of the definition of "statement" used in the Jencks Act (18 U.S.C.A. § 3500). That Act, which applies only to federal courts, gives the defendant a right to inspect the prior statements of a prosecution witness, following that witness' testimony at trial, for the purpose of possible impeachment of the witness. See § 16.3(c).

The Jencks Act defines "statement" for this purpose as (1) "a written statement made by said witness and signed or otherwise adopted by him," (2) "a stenographic, mechanical, electrical or other recording, or a transcription thereof, which is a substantially verbatim recital of an oral statement made by said witness and recorded contemporaneously with the making of such oral statement," and (3) grand jury testimony. The drafters of both the original ABA Standards and Federal Rule 16 agreed that the "written or recorded statement" phrase in their respective discovery provisions should include all statements that fell within the Jencks Act definition of "statement." The unresolved issue was whether the discovery provision should have a broader scope. Since the character of a person's "written" statement is fairly clear (basically including statements actually written or signed or otherwise approved by the individual), the primary uncertainty centered upon possibly going beyond the Jencks Act limitations as to a "recording" of an oral statement—i.e., not insisting that the recording be substantially verbatim and be recorded contemporaneously with the making of the oral statement.

In the federal courts, the elements of a recorded statement have been explored in two key situations, with the courts following the Jencks Act definition in both. The first involves requests for the rough notes of investigative agents relating to their questioning of the defendant in settings where the agents were not known to be government officials (e.g., where they were undercover agents). Under Rule 16(a)(1), an agent's notes regarding a defendant's oral statement are discoverable if they reveal the "substance of the statement" and the defendant was aware that he was being interrogated by a government agent, but if he was not aware, the notes are discoverable only if they constitute a "recorded statement" of the defendant. Lower courts accordingly have held that, to be discoverable, notes on conversations in this setting must have been recorded contemporaneously and must be substantially verbatim in content, as required by the Jencks Act definition of "statement." This standard requires consideration of such factors as the extent to which the language in the notes was intended to conform to the precise language of the defendant, the length of the notes in comparison to the length of the statement, and the lapse of time between the interview and the making of the notes. The second setting involves the subsequent "memorialization" of a conversation of the defendant with a non-agent, typically by the other participant in the conversation subsequently providing his written recollection of the statement to a police officer. Courts here have held that the subsequent memorialization, even where it sought to repeat verbatim what the defendant said in the conversation, will not constitute a recorded statement of the defendant because it was not recorded contemporaneously.

In states with an ABA–type discovery provision, the definition of a recorded statement is primarily of significance as to the statements of witnesses. Because these states provide for disclosure of the substance of the defendant's oral statements, the defense will obtain disclosure of the substance contained in rough notes or subsequently memorialized oral statements of the defendant even if these items do not fit within the definition of a recorded statement. As to prospective prosecution witnesses, however, many of the states make only written or recorded statements subject to discovery. Here, state courts commonly also have adopted a Jencks-type definition of recorded statements, excluding, in particular, rough notes. Several states, however, have adopted broader definitions, extending to any writing containing "a summary of a person's oral statements."

(c) Defendant's Statements. Perhaps no item is more readily discoverable by the defense than the defendant's written or recorded statement. In the federal system and all but a handful of the states, such discovery is granted as a matter of right. All of the state discovery provisions modeled after the ABA Standards and most of those modeled after Federal Rule 16 also require disclosure of the substance of certain oral statements of defendant known to the prosecution. Where these provisions apply, they eliminate dispute over whether a particular documentation of an oral statement is sufficient in quotation and time of recording to fall within the recorded statement provision. However, in many states, the oral statement provisions are much narrower in scope than the recorded statement provisions. They will, for example, require disclosure only as to oral statements that the prosecution "intends to offer in evidence at the trial." This limitation stems from the concern that the range of oral statements known to the police, including those between the defendant and investigators and between defendant and police interviewees who recounted defendant's past statements, is too broad to impose an obligation of disclosure without regard to the possible use of those statements at trial.

A 1991 amendment of Federal Rule 16 discarded the intended use requirement as to a written record containing the substance of defendant's oral statements (although intended use remains a prerequisite for disclosing oral statements where there is no such writing). However, Federal Rule 16 here retains a second fairly common limitation—the oral statement summarized in the writing must have been made "in response to interrogation by a person the defendant knew was a government agent." This limitation allows the prosecution to keep from the defense the fact that the persons he conversed with were undercover agents or non-agent witnesses who will be testifying against him at trial. It is seen as flowing from concerns relating to the defendant's misuse of that information which are similar to those concerns—discussed in subsections (h) and (i)—that have led these same jurisdictions not to require disclosure of witness lists and to bar pretrial disclosure of witness' statements. Accordingly, the Federal Rules (and similar state provisions) apply the "known agent" limitation even to oral statements that the prosecution intends to use in its case-in-chief.

(d) Codefendant's Statements. A substantial majority of the states have provisions requiring disclosure of a codefendant's statement, and those provisions vary substantially in coverage. Many provide for the disclosure of recorded or oral statements of codefendants without limitation. Others, following the original ABA model, restrict the required disclosure of a codefendant's recorded or oral statements to cases in which the codefendants will be jointly tried. The focus here is on giving the defense that information which will be critical in its determination as to whether to seek a severance. Federal Rule 16 does not include a provision requiring disclosure of a codefendant's statement, but federal courts have held that they have the discretion to order such disclosure where it is not barred by the prohibition against disclosure of the statements of prospective government witnesses (see § 12.2(i)). In this connection, they have rejected the contention that a coconspirator's statement admitted under the hearsay exception for such statements should be viewed as defendant's own statement rather than the statement of a prosecution witness.

(e) Criminal Records. Federal Rule 16 and a substantial majority of the state discovery provisions grant the defendant a right to discovery of his criminal record. Disclosure of the prior record does not disadvantage the prosecution, while the contents of the record are important to the defense on various issues (e.g., whether the defendant should testify at trial, or should move to restrict the use of prior convictions for impeachment purposes). The prior record also will show whether the defendant faces sentencing under enhanced sentencing provisions. In general, pretrial discovery provides a very limited vehicle for making a sentencing assessment. Much of the material that would be considered relevant under sentencing guidelines will be unrelated to the proof of the crime charged and therefore not be discoverable pretrial under even the broadest discovery provisions. Since the primary function of the disclosure of the criminal record relates to potential impeachment, jurisdictions which provide for disclosure of the names of prosecution witnesses commonly also require disclosure of their criminal records.

(f) Scientific Reports. Federal Rule 16 and all state discovery provisions provide for prosecution disclosure of various reports of medical and physical examinations, scientific tests, and experiments. Most jurisdictions encompass all such reports that were "made in connection with the particular case." Several limit required disclosure to reports that the prosecution intends to use at trial, and several follow the federal standard limiting required disclosure to reports that are either "material to preparing the defense" or intended to be used by the government "in its case-in-chief at trial." Automatic disclosure of scientific reports is justified on several grounds. Once the report is prepared, the scientific expert's position is not readily influenced, and therefore disclosure presents little danger of prompting perjury or intimidation. Very often such disclosure is needed to "lessen the imbalance which results from the State's early and complete investigation in contrast to [defendant's] * * * late and limited investigation." Also, a scientific report typically cannot be challenged adequately at trial without the opportunity to examine it closely and seek the assistance of defense experts, which requires disclosure well in advance of trial. These justifications have led many jurisdictions to go beyond preexisting scientific reports and require a written summary of anticipated expert testimony where the expert will testify from notes, without a report.

(g) Documents and Tangible Objects. The federal system and a substantial majority of the states have mandatory disclosure provisions governing documents and tangible objects. The remaining jurisdictions allow for disclosure at the discretion of the trial court with allowance of disclosure decidedly favored. All provisions encompass at least two categories of documents and tangible objects: (1) items "which the prosecution will use at trial", and (2) items "which were obtained from or purportedly belong to the defendant."

The Federal Rules, state provisions modeled after the Federal Rules, and some ABA-type provisions include a third category of discoverable documents and objects—those "which are material to preparing the defense." Here the burden is on the defendant to demonstrate the requisite materiality. Moreover, the use of the term "material" suggests that more than a showing of potential relevancy is demanded. Where a specific document is requested, the trial court may, if it so chooses, examine the requested item in camera to determine whether it has that potential significance. Of course, the court must be wary of underestimating the possible bearing of the evidence at it relates to a defense posture still to be developed (and not yet fully disclosed), but it can determine whether the item deals with the particular subject matter or otherwise has the type of content on which the defense bases it claim of materiality. Where the defense makes a general request for "material" documents, failing to identify materiality by document function (e.g., "sales receipts") or specific document content, and subsequently claims a Rule 16 violation during or after trial based on the prosecutor's failure to disclose a particular document, courts tend to impose a very high standard of materiality. Indeed, it has been stated that a violation will be found only where there was "some indication that disclosure of the disputed evidence would have enabled the defendant significantly to alter the quantum of proof in his favor."

In *U.S. v. Armstrong* (1996), the Supreme Court held that Rule 16 "materiality" requests do not go beyond documents material to a "defense against the government's case-in-chief." Thus, discovery of documents desired to establish a defense of discriminatory prosecution was not governed by Rule 16, but standards arising out of the law shaping that constitutional objection to the initiation of prosecution. See § 5.4(b). Rule 16 apparently also would not govern disclosure of documents helpful in raising the broad range of other objections that are not "substantive" in nature, but challenge the institution of the prosecution (e.g., vindictive prosecution).

(h) Witness Lists. State provisions patterned after the original ABA Standards generally require the prosecution to provide the defense with "the names and addresses of persons whom the State intends to call as witnesses." A small group of states, in accord with the third edition of the ABA Standards, require the prosecution to list the names and addresses of all persons "known by the government to have knowledge of relevant facts," without regard to whether the person will be called as a witness. Most of the mandatory disclosure provisions require the prosecution to list only those witnesses that it expects to present in building its case-in-chief. In other jurisdictions, however, the prosecution must also list rebuttal witnesses when it can anticipate who they will be.

The states that do not mandate pretrial disclosure of witness lists generally allow the trial court to order such disclosure at its discretion. In some jurisdictions, discovery provisions specifically recognize this discretionary authority, while other jurisdictions rely upon the inherent discovery authority of the trial court (see § 12.1(a)). Disclosure of witness lists in the federal courts, aside from capital cases (where a statute requires such disclosure), rests on the latter authority.

In many of these "discretionary jurisdictions," including the federal system, the burden placed on the defendant is especially heavy, with the courts starting from the presumption that witness-list disclosure generally is not available. To obtain disclosure, the defendant typically must point to circumstances establishing a compelling need (e.g., the defendant is suffering from a memory loss and cannot recollect what persons were involved in the events in question) and the absence of circumstances indicating a potential for intimidation of the witness (e.g., the crime charged did not involve violence and the defendant has no history of violence).

The primary objection to presumptive or mandatory disclosure of witness lists is the potential for intimidation of witnesses. The basic response of the proponents of broad discovery is that a realistic potential of such intimidation exists in only a relatively small portion of all cases and the proper response therefore is the " 'scalpel' of the protective order," which would allow disclosure in the vast majority of cases, rather than a policy that allows disclosure only in the most exceptional cases. Opponents of the regular disclosure of witness lists reply that the protective order is not a sufficient answer. They note that the protective order procedure puts the government in the position of having to make a special showing, which itself creates difficulties in protecting witnesses, and that the judicial emphasis upon using protective measures short of denying disclosure often produces an insufficient safeguard. Another concern is that allowing disclosure as a regular matter, even with a broad exception for cases presenting any threat of intimidation, would inevitably reinforce the natural reluctance of many persons to willingly come forward and testify in criminal cases.

(i) Witness Statements. In roughly half of the states (all of those with ABA-type provisions and a few others), the discovery provision provides for disclosure of the written or recorded statements of prospective prosecution witnesses (or all persons with relevant information in states with provisions similar to the third edition of the ABA Standards). Slightly less than half of these states also provide for disclosure of the substance of oral statements made by these witnesses. In those jurisdictions that do not provide for disclosure of the statements of prospective prosecution witnesses, such discovery (in contrast to witness names) tends to be prohibited (i.e., not within the trial court's inherent discretionary authority). Some jurisdictions, however, recognize a discretionary authority to order disclosure of the recorded statements of prosecution witnesses. In general, they start from a presumption against such disclosure. To be successful, the defense must make a showing of special need for the statement of a particular witness and convince the trial court that the later disclosure of that statement at trial (for use in cross-examination) is not a satisfactory alternative.

Jurisdictions barring pretrial discovery of witness statements ordinarily include in their discovery rules a specific prohibition similar to that found in Federal Rule 16(a)(2). That provision states that Rule 16 "does not authorize the discovery or inspection of statements made by prospective government witnesses except as provided in 18 U.S.C. § 3500." The cited exception is to the Jencks Act (18 U.S.C. § 3500), which was designed to ensure that prior recorded statements of witnesses are available for impeachment use, but not subject to pretrial discovery. The Jencks Act provides that, after a government witness testifies on direct examination, the government shall make available his prior recorded statement insofar as that statement relates to the subject matter of the defendant's testimony, but it also adds: "[N]o statement * * * in the possession of the United States which was made by a Government witness or prospective Government witness (other than the defendant) shall be the subject of subpoena, discovery, or inspection until said witness has testified on direct examination in the trial of the case."

The division among the states in their treatment of witness statements follows in part from their division on the disclosure of witness lists. A jurisdiction that does not grant witness lists as a matter of right will not make witness statements available as a matter of right. However, there are jurisdictions that grant discovery of witness lists as a matter of right but do not do the same for witness statements. One factor said to support a narrower position on witness statements is the defendant's potential misuse of that information to fashion false testimony that takes advantage of any gaps in the witness' account of critical events. Advocates of a complete bar on discovery of witness statements also argue that: (1) defendant has an ample opportunity to challenge the testimony of prosecution witnesses at trial since the witness' prior recorded statement may be obtained at that point under state provisions similar to the Jencks Act or common law rules on witness impeachment; (2) where witness lists are available or the defense is otherwise aware of likely prosecution witnesses, defense counsel has ample opportunity for pretrial preparation by interviewing those witnesses, and it will be in the best interests of defendant to encourage defense counsel to conduct his own investigation through such interviews rather than rely on the prosecution's investigative efforts; and (3) recorded statements of witnesses ordinarily are within the work product privilege since they are obtained by prosecutors or their agents (police officers) "in anticipation of litigation," and a blanket exemption avoids the need to litigate the work product issue on a case-by-case basis.

Proponents of disclosure respond that: (1) the perjury contention is based on "untested folklore," rejected by the experience of jurisdictions with broad discovery; (2) disclosure at trial hardly permits adequate preparation; (3) the opportunity to interview the

witness is of little value since witnesses often refuse to speak to
defense counsel, and (4) work product should be limited to "opinion" work product, which does not cover the typical prior recorded
statement (see § 12.2(j)).

(j) The Work Product Exemption. States with provisions
requiring the prosecution's mandatory pretrial disclosure of a prospective witness' recorded statement commonly also include a specific exemption for "work product." Where courts have discretionary authority to order disclosure, a common law work product
exemption similarly restricts the exercise of that discretion. As
developed in civil discovery, the work product doctrine seeks to
preserve against discovery materials developed in the course of
preparing for litigation. The underlying purpose of the doctrine, as
set forth in the leading case of *Hickman v. Taylor* (1947), is to
preclude "unwarranted inquiries [through discovery] into the files
and mental impressions of an attorney." *Hickman* did not absolutely bar civil discovery of "written materials obtained or prepared by
an adversary's counsel with an eye toward litigation," but it did
recognize a "general policy" against discovery of such "work product" of counsel. As incorporated in the Federal Rules of Civil
Procedure, Rule 26(b)(3), the *Hickman* work product doctrine (1)
encompasses documents and tangible things prepared in anticipation of litigation, (2) allows discovery of such items only upon a
showing of "substantial need" and the inability without "undue
hardship" to obtain equivalent materials, but (3) also requires the
court ordering such discovery to "protect against disclosure of the
mental impressions, conclusions, opinions, or legal theories of an
attorney or other representative of a party concerning the litigation."

Commentators have argued that a work product exception is
inappropriate as to the trial preparation material of the prosecutor.
The prosecutor, they note, is not simply an adversary, but a
representative of the people who bears a duty to "promote justice,"
which points toward full discovery and avoidance of trial by surprise. Both courts and legislatures have consistently rejected the
view that the prosecutor's broader role renders the work product
doctrine irrelevant. Thus, the Supreme Court, in *U.S. v. Nobles*
(1975), expressed no qualms in holding that the work product
doctrine applies in federal criminal cases as a common law doctrine.
Indeed, the Court noted that the work product doctrine was "even
more vital" in the criminal justice system than in civil litigation,
for "the interests of society and the accused in obtaining a fair and
accurate resolution of the question of guilt or innocence demand
that adequate safeguards assure the thorough preparation and
presentation of each side of the case."

In civil cases, the work product doctrine protects, subject to a showing of special need, what is commonly described as "fact" or "ordinary" work product—i.e., the content of a trial preparation document apart from that which reflects counsel's mental processes. Thus, discovery of a witness' prior recorded statement is available only on a showing, at the least, that the alternative of deposing the witness is unavailable or otherwise unsatisfactory. In the criminal justice system, of course, the deposition process ordinarily is not available as a discovery tool, but there remain other alternatives, such as interviewing the witness. In jurisdictions providing for discretionary discovery of a prosecution witness' recorded statement, the showing required to gain discovery often will parallel if not surpass the showing of need mandated in civil cases to obtain fact work product. Jurisdictions with ABA-type provisions, however, view the witness' recorded statement as so important to defense preparation that they simply dispatch with a showing of need and automatically make it available insofar as the record of the statement contains no more than "fact" work product.

All jurisdictions allowing disclosure of witness statements do protect, however, "opinion" work product. One issue here is whether what is to be protected is solely the mental impressions of the prosecution's legal staff, or also the mental impressions of their investigators—the police. In civil cases, as the Supreme Court noted in *Nobles,* the work product doctrine has developed "as an intensely practical one, grounded on the realities of litigation," and one of those realities is that "attorneys often must rely on the assistance of their investigators." *Nobles* concluded that the federal work product rule in criminal cases should also extend to statements taken by investigators. Many states do likewise, often with specific reference made to "police officers," but other states follow the ABA model, which limits work product to the opinions, theories, or conclusions of the "prosecuting attorneys or members of his legal staff." The difference in coverage is unlikely to have great practical significance, however, as applied to most prior recorded statements of witnesses. Statements obtained by police officers ordinarily will not reflect a significant amount of "opinion" work product. Very often, the statement will consist of little more than the witness' narrative of events in response to an open-ended question. On occasion, the interrogator's questions may reflect some legal theory or factual judgment, but such material often can be deleted without detracting from the flow of the witness' statement. Indeed, courts have held that even a prosecutor's notes on a witness interview, selectively recording particular comments or summarizing the substance of the witness' statement, do not constitute opinion work product.

Various state provisions do not contain a work product provision as such. Instead, they have a provision modeled on the 1975 version of Federal Rule 16, which exempts from discovery "reports, memoranda, or other internal government documents made by the attorney for the government or any other government agent investigating or prosecuting the case." This provision clearly covers all opinion work product and most fact work product as well. It does not recognize an exception based upon a showing of need as to either, and it covers internal reports of police officers as well as prosecutors. It is not tied to the traditional definition of work product, and presumably is not subject to traditional work product exceptions such as waiver. Accordingly, it renders unnecessary the inclusion of a work product provision. In the federal system, however, a 2002 "stylistic" revision of Rule 16, exempting disclosure under the Rule's documents provision from the internal reports prohibition, may necessitate reference to common law work product where internal reports would be "material to preparing the defense" (see § 12.2(g)).

(k) Police Reports. Police investigative reports may fall in one or more of several categories of discoverable material. Where the report contains a recital of the comments of a defendant, codefendant or witness sufficiently complete to constitute a recorded statement of that person, that portion of the report may be subject to discovery under the appropriate provision for recorded statements. So too, an abridged description of a statement may be subject to discovery when state law requires disclosure of summaries of oral statements of defendants or codefendants. Most often, the police report will contain considerable additional information that would not fall under the provisions governing recorded or oral statements. This would include the officer's own observations and comments and references to conversations with persons whose statements are not subject to disclosure. In many jurisdictions, one or more discovery provisions could conceivably reach this portion of the report. These include: (1) provisions for discovery of documents "which are material to the preparation of the defense"; (2) provisions requiring disclosure of statements of persons having knowledge of relevant facts; (3) provisions requiring disclosure of statements of prosecution witnesses where the officer himself will testify at trial; and (4) provisions authorizing discretionary disclosure of "relevant material and information" not otherwise listed in the discovery rule.

Several states, viewing police reports as a critical source for defense preparation, consider discovery under the above provisions too problematic, and specifically require the automatic disclosure of police reports. Other states, in contrast, specifically exempt police reports from pretrial discovery under all or most of the above provisions. Many do so under provisions that protect from discovery "reports, memoranda, or other internal documents" made by government agents in connection with "the investigation or prosecution of the case." Others have provisions that specifically exempt police reports from discovery except for that portion of the report that is discoverable as a recordation of a defendant's or witness' statement.

(*l*) **Protective Orders.** All jurisdictions with an extensive statute or court rule governing discovery include a provision authorizing the issuance of a protective order. In common law jurisdictions, the trial court's discretionary authority similarly permits it to defer or deny discovery for protective purposes. Federal Rule 16(d) and various state protective-order provisions authorize the trial court to "deny, restrict, or defer" discovery otherwise available. Other states, however, limit protective orders to restricting or deferring discovery and add the requirement that "all material and information to which a party is entitled must be disclosed in time to make beneficial use thereof."

What constitutes appropriate grounds for the issuance of a protective order? Federal Rule 16(d) simply notes that the order shall be issued "for good cause." Several state provisions list various interests that may be weighed against the value of disclosure to the defendant. These include: protection of witnesses and others from "physical harm, threats of harm, bribes, economic reprisals and other intimidation"; maintenance of secrecy regarding informants; and "protection of confidential relationships and privileges recognized by law." In the end, the court must determine "that the disclosure would result in a risk or harm outweighing any usefulness of the disclosure."

(m) **Constitutional Overtones.** The major portion of defense discovery focuses on avoiding "trial by surprise" by giving the defense advance notice of the evidence that the prosecution intends to use at trial. This aspect of defense discovery has been viewed as a matter to be determined by local legislative or judicial policy, with the Constitution imposing no significant requirements as to what must be disclosed before trial. The Supreme Court has noted, for example, that while it may be the "better practice" to grant the defendant pretrial discovery of his confession where the prosecution intends to use it at trial, the failure to follow that practice does not violate due process. So too, in a case in which the prosecution failed to inform defendant that his associate and codefendant had become an informant and would testify for the police, the Court, in rejecting defendant's constitutional objection, noted: "There is no general constitutional right to discovery in a criminal case."

As discussed in § 16.3(b), the Supreme Court, in a series of cases starting with *Brady v. Md.* (1963), has established a constitutional obligation of the prosecution to disclose exculpatory evidence within its possession when that evidence might be material to the outcome of the case. Since the Supreme Court's *Brady* rulings have presented situations in which exculpatory material was not disclosed at any time during the prosecution, the Court has not spoken to precisely when a *Brady* disclosure must be made. Lower courts generally have agreed that the prosecutor's *Brady* obligation is satisfied if the exculpatory material is disclosed "in time for its effective use at trial," and that for many types of exculpatory evidence, disclosure at trial itself will be satisfactory. They note that the ultimate issue under *Brady*, where the exculpatory evidence is produced at trial, should be whether delay in production resulted in a violation of the *Brady* "materiality standard"—that is, whether there is a reasonable probability that, had the evidence been disclosed to the defense pretrial (assuming it was then within the prosecution's possession or control), the "result of the proceeding would have been different."

The range of possible *Brady* material is so broad that it can readily encompass material that the discovery rule either implicitly or explicitly excludes from pretrial disclosure. Thus, *Brady* may reach impeachment material to be found in the prior recorded statement of a prospective government witness, but the jurisdiction's "Jencks Act" provision may preclude disclosure of that statement until the witness testifies at trial. *Brady* would also require disclosure of incentives given to prosecution witnesses, but requiring pretrial disclosure of the relevant documents (e.g., plea agreements) would be contrary to the protection of internal documents and would be inconsistent with a discovery provision that ordinarily seeks to withhold pretrial the identity of the prosecution's witnesses, Federal courts have divided in treating such potential conflicts between *Brady* and the limits placed on federal pretrial discovery. Many conclude that no conflict is presented since *Brady* will be satisfied by producing such exculpatory material at trial. Others have argued that disclosure at trial could be insufficient, and the trial court therefore has the authority to "trump" the Jencks Act and order disclosure pretrial of prior statements of witnesses insofar as they contain exculpatory material. Some would do this automatically and others would do so based on the character of the exculpatory evidence and the likely need for pretrial disclosure to permit the defense to use it effectively (distinguishing in this regard between impeachment material and other exculpatory material). One court has suggested, however, that even assuming arguendo that *Brady* may be violated by failing to reveal until trial exculpatory material within a witness' prior recorded statement (notwithstanding the court's capacity to grant a recess at that point if the defense needs more time to explore that material), the *Brady* doctrine does not thereby give the trial court the authority to override Jencks and order pretrial disclosure. *Brady* imposes an obligation upon the prosecution and leaves to the prosecution the initial determination of when to disclose. If it fails to comply adequately, "it acts at its own peril." See also § 16.3(b).

(n) Exculpatory Material Provisions. Over half of the state discovery provisions require, either on defense request or automatically, that the prosecution disclose exculpatory material within its possession. The descriptions of the material that must be disclosed include: "any matter or information * * * which tends to create a reasonable doubt of the defendant's guilt as to the crime charged"; "material or information which tends to negate the guilt of the accused as to the offense charged or would tend to reduce the accused's punishment"; and "exculpatory evidence". Most of the descriptions, unlike *Brady*, do not introduce an element of "materiality," which looks to the impact of the evidence upon the outcome of the case, but focus instead on whether the material simply has an exculpatory character. Similarly, most of the descriptions do not suggest that the "information" or "material" must itself be admissible in evidence. These provisions may also go beyond the coverage of *Brady* by including police agencies that would not be covered by the *Brady* doctrine but are nonetheless within the reach of the discovery rule. On the other hand, these provisions, as enforced, may not add considerably to *Brady* itself. On a pretrial motion, they do permit a court to order pretrial disclosure not otherwise within the discovery rule. Most often, however, defense will not be aware of exculpatory material pretrial, and the prosecutor's failure to disclose pretrial will first become apparent during trial or after conviction. The key then will be, as discussed in § 20.6, whether the prosecution's violation of the duty to disclose pretrial exculpatory material will produce some remedy, particularly following a conviction, even though the discovery violation fell short of a *Brady* violation.

§ 12.3 Constitutional Limitations Upon Pretrial Discovery for the Prosecution

(a) Due Process. The constitutionality of pretrial discovery for the prosecution was first considered by the Supreme Court in *Williams v. Fla.* (1970). That case considered a challenge to a typical alibi-notice provision. It required the defendant, on written demand of the prosecutor, to give notice in advance of any claim of alibi, to specify the place where he claims to have been at the time of the crime, and to provide the names and addresses of alibi witnesses. The prosecution was required, in return, to notify the defense of any witnesses it proposed to offer in rebuttal of the alibi. The possible sanction for violation of these disclosure obligations by the prosecution or defense was the exclusion of its alibi witnesses (although the defendant himself remained free to testify as to the alibi). The defendant in *Williams* had complied with the alibi-notice requirement, providing the prosecution with the name and address of his alibi witness. The prosecution then deposed that witness, and when she testified at trial, used that deposition to challenge her alibi testimony. The prosecution also introduced the testimony of an investigator who stated that the witness herself had been at still a different place during the time when she claimed to have been with the defendant.

The defense challenge to the alibi-notice rule in *Williams* rested on three grounds: violation of due process by altering the balance of the adversarial process; violation of the Fifth Amendment privilege against self-incrimination by forcing the defendant to furnish the state with information (the name and address of his alibi witness) that was useful to the state in convicting him; and violation of the Sixth Amendment's compulsory process clause by providing for a sanction of exclusion under which the defendant could be denied the right to present alibi witnesses if he failed to provide pretrial notice as required by the alibi rule. The Supreme Court found it unnecessary to consider the Sixth Amendment issue since the defendant had complied with the alibi-notice requirement and the exclusion sanction had not been applied in his case. The constitutionality of that sanction was later upheld in *Taylor v. Ill.* (discussed in § 12.5) as applied to the circumstances there presented. The *Williams* Court considered and rejected the defendant's due process and self-incrimination arguments.

As for due process, the *Williams* Court saw nothing in the Florida alibi-notice rule that unfairly affected the adversarial process. Given "the ease with which an alibi can be fabricated," the government's interest in "protecting itself against an eleventh hour defense" was characterized as "both obvious and legitimate." The adversary system was not "a poker game in which players enjoy an absolute right always to conceal their cards until played." There was "ample room in that system" for a notice requirement "designed to enhance the search for truth * * * by insuring both the defendant and the State ample opportunity to investigate certain facts crucial to the determination of guilt or innocence." The Florida rule, the Court stressed, was fairly constructed to meet that end. Florida law generally provided liberal discovery to the defendant and the alibi rule was "carefully hedged with reciprocal duties requiring state disclosure to the defendant." The critical nature of the reciprocal disclosure provided by the Florida alibi rule was subsequently brought home in *Wardius v. Or.* (1973). Distinguishing *Williams*, the Court there held that an alibi rule which failed to provide reciprocal discovery by the prosecution of its rebuttal alibi witnesses violated due process.

(b) Self–Incrimination: Non–Defendant Disclosures. Consistent with standard self-incrimination doctrine, a compelled disclosure will not violate the defendant's privilege against self-incrimination unless it requires a testimonial disclosure by the defendant. Although the Supreme Court's ruling in *U.S. v. Nobles* (1975) did not involve pretrial discovery, its reasoning clearly establishes that many types of prosecution discovery do not present self-incrimination difficulties because they do not demand a testimonial communication by the defendant. *Nobles* upheld the required defense disclosure at trial of a prior recorded statement of a defense witness. When the defense there called its investigator to testify to his conversations with two prosecution witnesses, the trial court granted the prosecutor's request to inspect that portion of the investigator's written report that had recorded the essence of those conversations. The Supreme Court, in an unanimous ruling, held that the inspection order had not violated the defendant's privilege against self-incrimination. The defendant had not "prepared the report, and there [was] no suggestion that the portions subject to the disclosure order reflected any information that he conveyed to the investigator." Although the witnesses' recorded statements "were elicited by a defense investigator on defendant's behalf," that "did not convert them into defendant's personal communications."

(c) Self–Incrimination: Defendant's Testimonial Disclosure. In *Williams v. Fla.* (1970), the Court treated the Florida alibi-notice provision before it as requiring a testimonial disclosure of the defendant. That provision imposed an obligation upon "a defendant" who intended to offer a defense of alibi to give pretrial notice of (1) "his intention to claim such alibi," (2) "specific information as to the place at which the defendant claims to have been," and (3) "the names and addresses of the witnesses by whom he proposes to establish such alibi." Justice White did comment in a footnote that "it might be argued that the 'testimonial disclosures' protected by the Fifth Amendment include only the statements relating to the historical facts of the crime, not statements relating solely to what a defendant proposes to do at trial." There was no need to further explore this possibility because (as discussed in subsection (d) infra) the Court found no element of compulsion. Moreover, the defendant in a alibi notice clearly is being asked to cite an historical fact in identifying the place at which he claims to have been at the time of the crime.

The alibi-notice provision in *Williams* required disclosure by the defendant, but many discovery provisions place the obligation of disclosure on the defense counsel. Of course, if the defense counsel can respond based on his or her own knowledge obtained in the course of the investigation, then the response may be subject to challenge on grounds other than self-incrimination (e.g., as demanding work-product), but it would not require the testimony of the defendant. On the other hand, if the disclosure can be made by counsel only by obtaining the information from the defendant, the formal structure of the disclosure obligation should not alter the treatment of the disclosure as a testimonial communication of the defendant. Indeed, in jurisdictions that treat a defendant's discovery response as a party admission, a response will be treated as an admission by the defendant, even though made by counsel and not invariably based upon information provided by the defendant. Surely any compelled statement of the attorney that will be treated as a party admission by the client must also be viewed, for Fifth Amendment purposes, as the compelled statement of the client.

(d) Self–Incrimination: The Acceleration Doctrine. Although the disclosure under the alibi-notice rule challenged in *Williams v. Fla.* clearly required a testimonial communication by the defendant, the Court there rejected defendant's self-incrimination claim. It concluded that the alibi-notice rule did not meet an additional prerequisite for a successful self-incrimination claim. The pressure imposed to disclose was not the kind of "compulsion" against which a person is protected by the Fifth Amendment privilege.

Speaking for the *Williams* majority, Justice White reasoned that the alibi-notice provision imposed no greater compulsion than would be present at trial when the defendant eventually had to decide whether or not to raise the alibi defense. At that point, if the defendant decided to present his alibi witnesses, he would be forced to "reveal their identity and submit them to cross-examination which in itself may prove incriminating or which may furnish the State with leads to incriminating rebuttal evidence." In deciding whether to take this risk, the defendant might be subject to "severe pressures" generated by the strength of the government's evidence, but such pressures had never been viewed as prohibited by the Fifth Amendment. The alibi-notice requirement simply imposed "very similar constraints" upon the defendant. It did no more than "accelerate the timing of his disclosure, forcing him to divulge at an earlier date information which * * * [he] planned to divulge at trial." Moreover, it was only the disclosure, rather than the final choice, that was accelerated. The defendant could give an alibi notice before trial, but then decide not to raise the defense at trial.

Nothing in the Florida procedure prevented him "from abandoning the defense" in his "unfettered discretion."

The defendant in *Williams* argued that the accelerated disclosure in itself violated the privilege because it forced him to make his decision before the state had presented its case-in-chief. The majority responded, however, that the defendant had no constitutional right to insist that his decision to disclose be delayed until trial. It noted: "Nothing in the Fifth Amendment privilege entitles a defendant as a matter of constitutional right to await the end of the State's case before announcing the nature of his defense, any more than it entitles him to await the jury's verdict on the State's case-in-chief before deciding whether or not to take the stand himself." The Court pointed out that the Constitutional would "raise no bar" to granting the state a continuance after the alibi witness was called, so as to allow the State to investigate the witness' background. Here the state was just accomplishing "the same result * * * through pretrial discovery."

The key to the *Williams* ruling clearly was its conclusion that accelerated disclosure did not violate the Fifth Amendment. How far that ruling extends has been a subject of considerable debate among commentators and, to a much lesser extent, among lower courts. Justice Black suggested in dissent that accelerated disclosure gave the state an advantage that might not materialize under the Court's hypothetical continuance alternative. There existed the possibility of forcing the defendant pretrial to make a choice that he otherwise would never have to face at trial. That could occur where the prosecution would otherwise not be able to establish a prima facie case on its case-in-chief (resulting in a directed acquittal and no need for the defendant to present any defense), but the pretrial disclosure by the defendant gives the prosecution leads that allow it to sufficiently bolster its case-in-chief to avoid a directed acquittal. Here, the defendant is not simply being asked to accelerate a decision that otherwise must be assessed at trial, but to risk assisting the state in fulfilling its basic obligation of establishing a prima facie case. The disclosure requirement is not being used simply to avoid the element of surprise that might make it more difficult for the prosecution to rebut the defendant's defense, but to allow the state to shore up a weak prosecution case on the basic elements of the offense.

Williams itself quite clearly did not present a situation in which pretrial disclosure forced a choice that would otherwise never have to be made because the prosecution, without the leads provided by the defense disclosure, would not have established a prima facie case on its case-in-chief. In describing the prosecution's use of the alibi disclosure, the *Williams* opinion noted only that the prosecution had followed-up on the disclosure by laying the groundwork for impeaching the alibi witness and establishing by independent evidence the falseness of her testimony. However, the *Williams* opinion did not suggest that this limited use of the disclosure was critical to its ruling. It did not take note of Justice *Black*'s suggestion that an accelerated disclosure might be used to enhance the strength of the prosecution's case-in-chief, and respond that such a case might be treated differently. Rather, it used broad language suggesting that, as long as the defense is given broad discovery of the prosecution's case, as was true in Florida, it can be required to make a reasoned tactical judgment before trial, just as it would at trial. The choice may be somewhat more difficult at an earlier stage, but that did not so alter the nature of the pressure exerted as to justify characterizing as Fifth Amendment "compulsion" at the pretrial stage the same type of pressure, produced by the strength of the prosecution's case, as had long been accepted at the trial stage.

In assessing the scope of *Williams'* accelerated disclosure doctrine, commentators sometimes look to *Brooks v. Tenn.* (1972), a case decided shortly after *Williams*. The Court there held unconstitutional, as imposing an impermissible burden on defendant's right not to testify, a state rule that defendant could testify on his own behalf only if he testified before any other defense witnesses gave testimony. The majority in *Brooks* did not refer to *Williams*, but the dissent cited *Williams*, among other cases, in arguing that the burden imposed upon the defendant by shifting the time of his decision was no worse than the analogous burdens upheld in past cases. Some commentators see in the majority's failure to refer to *Williams* (despite the dissent's reliance on that case) the limitation of the accelerated disclosure doctrine to the special situation presented in the alibi-notice context. Others see *Brooks* as presenting a situation quite distinct from any discovery requirement. What was involved, they note, was not compulsion that forced the defendant to disclose a prospective defense witness who might also be a source of incriminatory evidence, but a restriction on defendant's unfettered choice in deciding whether to exercise his personal right to testify. Moreover, the defendant there was not asked to make an initial decision from which he could withdraw (as in *Williams*), but an accelerated final decision on whether to testify.

Initially, some lower courts were cautious in their reading of *Williams*, particularly in its application to provisions requiring the disclosure of all defense witnesses. Such provisions were challenged on self-incrimination grounds in light of their potential for requiring disclosure of the names of defense witnesses who were likely to have knowledge that might help the prosecution in its case-in-chief (e.g., witnesses on a claim of self-defense). Though rejecting such challenges, which sought to have the discovery provision held unconstitutional on its face, these courts left open the possibility of exempting the defense from its discovery obligation upon a showing that the prosecution "was seek[ing] information that might serve as an unconstitutional link in a chain of evidence tending to establish the accused's guilt." A still growing group of subsequent rulings, however, have sustained reciprocal disclosure requirements without regard to the possibility that the information provided might assist the prosecution in building its case-in-chief. They have accepted the accelerated disclosure rationale of *Williams* as refuting self-incrimination claims with respect to all aspects of the advance disclosure of evidence the defendant intends to introduce at trial (except for the defendant's own testimony). Thus, the narrower reading of *Williams* advanced by the commentators has virtually no support in the more recent case law. State courts, looking to *Williams*, have accepted without limitation the constitutionality of reciprocal discovery provisions requiring pretrial defense disclosure of various elements of its intended trial presentation, including documents and tangible items, expert witnesses and their reports, witnesses generally, and the general character of likely defenses (see § 12.4).

(e) Sixth Amendment Limitations. Sixth Amendment right-to-counsel challenges to prosecution discovery have been raised primarily where (1) the defense is required to disclose information it does not intend to offer at trial, (2) that information was developed by defense counsel or defense investigative agents but is not exempted from discovery under the particular jurisdiction's work-product exemption, and (3) the information does not reveal lawyer/client communications and therefore is not protected against discovery by the attorney-client privilege. The discovery orders that most often have caused courts to give serious consideration to Sixth Amendment challenges have been those directing the defense to produce for prosecution inspection items such as the following: the reports of non-testifying experts who were consulted on a scientific issue that the defense intends to raise at trial through different experts; recordations of statements made by prospective defense and prosecution witnesses during interviews by defense investigators; and potentially adverse physical evidence relating to the crime that was either given to counsel or was discovered in the course of counsel's investigation, often apart from any communication by the client.

The basic rationale of the Sixth Amendment objection to required pretrial disclosure of such information is that the disclosure has a chilling effect upon the investigative efforts of counsel and therefore undermines the defendant's right to the effective assistance of counsel. Defense counsel, it is argued, must be afforded the "maximum freedom" to pursue various avenues of inquiry, including consultation with experts, interviews of possible prosecution and defense witnesses, and the collection of physical evidence, without fearing that any unfavorable material thereby obtained will be used against the defendant. If the attorney cannot be ensured of the absolute confidentiality of the fruits of such efforts, then she may very well refuse to pursue such avenues and miss the opportunity to uncover exculpatory evidence.

Judicial responses to such a Sixth Amendment contention have varied with the court and the type of disclosure demanded. Lower courts are divided on requiring defense disclosures of the reports of non-testifying experts. Courts sustaining a Sixth Amendment challenge have argued that the "confidentiality and loyalty of expert consultants traditionally enjoyed by defendants and defense counsel is a crucial element in the effective legal representation of the defendant." Courts on the opposite side have emphasized the defendant's responsibility in calling into issue the scientific claim on which the non-testifying expert reported. The state, in the interest of having objective scientific evidence freely available to all sides, may insist that the defense, once it raises the issue, make all of its experts available, just as it allows the defense discovery of the reports of all experts consulted by the prosecution, including those that the prosecution may later decide not to use at trial. This rationale, which is commonly described as resting on a "waiver" by the defense, would not extend to the situation in which the defense has decided (perhaps as a result of the expert's negative report) not to challenge on a certain issue, but the prosecution still wants disclosure because it must prove each element of crime, whether or not challenged by the defense, and the defense expert's report might be helpful in that regard.

Sixth Amendment challenges have been considerably less persuasive outside of the context of disclosure of non-testifying defense experts. The tendency here is to look to the work-product exemption and the attorney-client privilege as providing sufficient protection of defense counsel's role and not to impose further limitations upon otherwise prescribed disclosures through the Sixth Amendment. Thus, where counsel discovers and takes possession of physical evidence of a crime even as a result of a confidential communication with his client, disclosure will be required. The communication will be protected, perhaps even by prohibiting any reference to counsel as the source of the evidence, but the tangible item itself will be treated no differently than if it were in the hands of some third party. The adversary role of counsel, the courts note, may not turn counsel's office into a sanctuary for evidence that the government could otherwise have obtained from its original location by seizure or subpoena. So too, courts have uniformly rejected

Sixth Amendment challenges to the required production of the defense's prior recorded statements of witnesses (other than defendant) who will testify at trial.

(f) Conditional Discovery. Many state discovery provisions give the prosecution an automatic right to discovery of specified items, similar to the automatic right given to the defendant. In the federal system and in roughly half of the states, prosecution discovery, apart from that on insanity and alibi, is "conditional"—i.e., dependent upon the defendant's exercise of a right to discovery rather than existing as an independent right of the prosecutor. Unlike the defense, the prosecutor cannot simply institute a demand for disclosure of the items specified in the applicable discovery provision. The prosecutor may only insist upon disclosure if the defendant has demanded and received disclosure of material within the possession or control of the prosecution. Federal Rule 16(b)(1), for example, permits the prosecution to seek from the defense scientific reports made in connection with the case only after the defendant has used the corresponding provision in 16(a)(1) to obtain scientific reports from the government.

Conditional discovery is not needed to meet the reciprocity requirement of *Wardius* (§ 12.3(a)). That requirement is satisfied if the discovery available to the defense (as opposed to that used by the defense) is as broad as the discovery the defense must provide to the prosecution. Supporters of conditional discovery contend that, by giving the defendant the capacity to foreclose prosecution discovery, conditional discovery minimizes the risk that prosecution discovery will be held to violate defendant's constitutional rights. They argue that defendant's decision to seek discovery from the prosecution may be treated as a waiver of his privilege against self-incrimination or of any other constitutional objection to reciprocal discovery. Defense has no constitutional right to discovery of the prosecution's evidence, and the state can appropriately condition the grant of such discovery to the defense on a defense obligation to make reciprocal discovery.

Although a substantial number of jurisdictions utilize conditional discovery, the courts have said very little about the impact of the conditional element upon the constitutionality of mandating defense disclosure to the prosecution. Decisions in conditional discovery jurisdictions that have considered constitutional challenges to prosecution discovery usually have moved directly to the constitutional question without reference to the conditional nature of the discovery. Since those courts then upheld the discovery provisions, they never had to decide whether the conditional nature of the discovery provision would have saved the provision where a compelled disclosure would have been unconstitutional. Their failure to turn initially to the conditional feature may reflect doubts as to whether discovery being conditional actually makes a difference on the constitutional issue. One court has expressed such doubts based upon a series of Supreme Court rulings holding unconstitutional governmental action that operates to penalize the exercise of a constitutional right (e.g., the disbarment of lawyers who have exercised the self-incrimination privilege). Here, however, the state is not telling the defendant that the exercise of a constitutional objection in response to some governmental inquiry will result in the deprivation of some governmental benefit the individual otherwise would receive. Rather, it offers to the defendant an advantage he otherwise would not receive on condition that the defendant, in turn, relinquishes any constitutional restraint that would keep the prosecution from receiving a reciprocal advantage. One possible analogy is the process of plea bargaining, which accepts the state's offering of sentencing or charge inducements in return for the defendant's waiver of trial rights. However, the waiver process involved in plea bargaining finds support in its tradition and necessity, as well the requisite judicial inquiry to ensure that the waiver has been made knowingly and voluntarily. The "discovery bargain" arguably is distinguishable on all three counts.

§ 12.4 Prosecution Discovery Provisions

(a) **Variations in Approach.** Few courts or legislatures would disagree with the general proposition that, consistent with restraints imposed by constitutional limitations, discovery should be a "two way street" that accords neither party an "unfair advantage" and seeks to promote the determination of the truth. The difficulty arises in determining precisely what this proposition should produce in the way of prosecution discovery from the defense. As suggested in the preceding section, some disagreement exists over the extent to which the defendant's constitutional rights preclude granting the prosecution full reciprocity in discovery. But even more substantial disagreements arise in deciding how much reciprocity is needed to provide a fair adversarial balance as to the prosecution. Some argue that, even where the defense receives exceptionally broad discovery, the prosecution need be given very little discovery since it already has an "advantage over the accused through its use of the subpoena power, the grand jury, and the right to make reasonable searches and seizures for discovery purposes and through the use of the police as an investigative resource to obtain statements." Others disagree both with this conclusion and with the suggestion that an unfair advantage exists unless each party can precisely match the other in its investigative authority. They note that the government, even with all of its investigative resources, cannot be expected to uncover on its own every relevant piece of information that the defense might learn from its special resources (even apart from the defendant), so the prosecution is placed at a disadvantage where required to disclose almost all relevant information within its file without being given full reciprocity. Moreover, they argue, even if the prosecution has uncovered on its own all relevant factual information, it cannot make use of that evidence, to best ensure determination of the truth, without pretrial notice of the evidence that the defendant will use at trial. Here, they argue, the value of complete disclosure to both sides, so as to avoid a battle by surprise, stands apart from any balancing of investigative capacity.

As might be expected, the division on these issues has led to considerable variation in the comparative scope of prosecution and defense discovery. While one court rule or statute will allow the prosecution discovery that roughly parallels defense discovery, at least as to the evidence that the defense intends to use at trial, another will provide the prosecution with far less disclosure than is granted the defense. Moreover, these differences in coverage most often will not be subject to modification by the trial judge's inherent authority to grant discovery beyond that specifically authorized in the discovery provision. In the area of prosecution discovery, in contrast to defense discovery, statutory provisions commonly are viewed as preemptive. The failure of the state's discovery provisions to specifically authorize a particular type of disclosure is taken as evidencing an intent not to allow the prosecution such discovery.

(b) Alibi Defense Provisions. Unlike the practice in civil pleadings, the criminal law traditionally has not required the defendant to plead specifically his defense. A plea of "not guilty" ordinarily brings into issue all possible defenses to the substantive charge. However, the federal system and more than forty states require the defendant to give advance notice of his intent to raise an alibi defense. Most alibi provisions are similar in procedure and scope to Federal Rule 12.1. Initially, the government must issue a demand for notification, stating therein the time, date, and place of the alleged offense. If the defendant intends to raise the alibi defense, he is required to respond within a specified number of days. His response must state the specific place or places where he claims to have been at the time of the alleged offense and the names and addresses of the witnesses upon whom he intends to rely to establish his alibi. The prosecution is then required, within a specified period, to list those witnesses who will be used to establish the defendant's presence at the scene of the crime and any other witnesses who will be used to rebut the alibi defense. For good cause shown, the trial court may grant an exception or modification to any of the above requirements. Good cause exceptions most often are requested by the prosecution on grounds similar to those that would justify a protective order under the general discovery provisions.

Federal Rule 12.1 also provides that "evidence of an intention to rely on an alibi defense, later withdrawn, or of a statement made in connection with that intention, is not * * * admissible against the person who gave notice of the intention." Such provisions also have been viewed as prohibiting the prosecution from commenting upon the defendant's failure to call a listed witness in presenting the alibi defense at trial. Courts have held, however, that the notice of alibi can be used to impeach a defendant who testifies as to an alibi defense inconsistent with that contained in the notice of alibi. Here, the defendant has violated the notice requirement by failing to give notice of the alibi he is now claiming, and the court is allowing impeachment as a remedy.

(c) Insanity and Related Defenses. The federal system and almost all of the states have provisions requiring the defendant to give advance notice if he intends to rely upon the defense of insanity. In many states, as under Federal Rule 12.2(b), the obligation of notice is extended beyond insanity to encompass the introduction of expert testimony "relating to a mental disease or defect or any other mental condition of the defendant bearing on either (1) the issue of guilt or (2) the issue of punishment in a capital case." Such provisions have been held to apply to the use of psychiatric experts to support such defense claims as diminished responsibility, "brainwashing," and the innate lack of aggressiveness needed to purposely place another in fear. Indeed, it seems unlikely that any psychiatric testimony would escape its reach except that which is utilized only as to non-capital sentencing. Where the defendant enters a notice of insanity or other mental condition defense, he remains free to change his mind and proceed at trial with another defense.

(d) Identification of Defenses. Approximately a dozen states require the defendant to give notice in advance of trial of various defenses beyond alibi and insanity that defendant intends to raise at trial. These provisions sometimes are designed to encompass all defenses and sometimes are limited to a series of enumerated offenses. Even when all defenses are included, the statutory provision may include an illustrative listing of the types of defenses which a defendant is expected to identify. Typical examples cited are a claim of authority (such as ownership of the property involved), the justifiable use of force, entrapment, duress, intoxication, and the lack of the requisite mens rea. The defense-notice provisions are interpreted as encompassing only those defense claims on which testimony will be offered. The defendant need not include matters on which the state's case simply will be challenged as insufficient on its face. The function of the defense-notice requirement is to make the prosecution aware of the areas as to which the defense is likely to introduce evidence and the prosecution therefore might need to look for rebuttal evidence. Where jurisdictions provide prosecution discovery as to defense witnesses, they commonly assume that discovery is sufficient to give the prosecution notice as to likely defenses, but other states add defense-identification provisions to cover cases in which defense witnesses will not submit to prosecution interviews and the defense disclosure does not include any prior statements by those witnesses.

(e) Witness Lists. Roughly half the states authorize court-ordered defense disclosure of the names and addresses of the witnesses that the defendant intends to introduce at trial. In some of these jurisdictions, the prosecution has an independent right to such discovery. In some, discovery is conditioned upon the defense having first sought discovery, and in still others, the trial court has discretion as to whether to order witness-list disclosure. In all of these jurisdictions, the defendant is entitled to a listing of the witnesses that the prosecution intends to call.

(f) Witness Statements. Most of the states requiring defense disclosure of witness lists also require defense disclosure of its recorded statements of those witnesses. In general, a "recorded statement" for this purpose follows the Jencks Act definition, but some states utilize broader definitions that encompass written summaries of a defense witness' oral statement to a defense counsel or defense investigator. Where prosecution disclosure of recorded statements will include statements obtained from potential defense witnesses as well as prosecution witnesses (e.g., when the discovery provision extends to all persons known by the prosecution to have "knowledge of relevant facts", see § 12.2(h)), a reciprocal discovery obligation may be imposed on the defense, but it is unlikely to extend beyond those recorded statements of prosecution witnesses that the defense intends to use at trial to impeach those witnesses. See *Commonwealth v. Durham* (Mass. 2005).

Depending upon the scope of the jurisdiction's view of work product (see § 12.2(j)), that exemption may or may not commonly relieve the defense of the obligation to make pretrial disclosure of prior recorded statements under a witness-statement provision. In *U.S. v. Nobles*, the Court held that a defense investigator's recorded interview of a defense witness constituted work product, although that did not bar disclosure at trial because the exemption was waived once the investigator testified at trial as to those statements. Such a broad reading of work product could be advanced to bar pretrial disclosure even as to statements that are limited to "fact" work-product. *Nobles*, however, took a far broader view of work product than the many states with ABA-type provisions, which encompass only documents reflecting "the opinions, theories, and conclusions" of defense counsel. See § 12.2(j).

(g) Documents and Tangible Objects. Almost all of the jurisdictions with general discovery provisions authorize prosecution discovery of documents and tangible objects which the defense intends to introduce in evidence. In some jurisdictions, the prosecution has an independent right to such discovery, while in others, discovery is conditioned on the defendant first requesting discovery from the prosecution. The types of items encompassed are the same as under similar provisions authorizing defense discovery of documents and tangible objects. The primary difference between the defense and prosecution provisions is that the prosecution's obligation to disclose often goes beyond items the prosecution intends to use as evidence. See § 12.2(g).

(h) Scientific Reports. Almost all jurisdictions with general discovery provisions allow for prosecution discovery of reports and results of medical and physical examinations, scientific tests, and experiments made in connection with the particular case. Most of these provisions, like Federal Rule 16(b)(1), apply "only if the defendant intends to use the item in the defendant's case in chief at the trial or intends to call the witness who prepared the report and the report relates to the witness's testimony." Defense discovery of scientific reports in the possession of the prosecution typically extends beyond that material the prosecution will use at trial. It commonly encompasses all reports and results on scientific tests and examinations made in connection with the case, whether or not they will be used at trial. Similar prosecution discovery from the defense is specifically authorized in only a handful of states, but also may be ordered under catch-all provisions allowing the trial court to order additional discovery as to items that are material and not otherwise available to the prosecution. As discussed in § 12.4(e), in some jurisdictions, such orders have been successfully challenged on Sixth Amendment grounds.

§ 12.5 Sanctions

(a) Range. Federal Rule 16(d)(2) provides that, "if a party fails to comply with Rule 16", the court may (1) order the party to permit discovery or inspection as specified by the court, (2) "grant a continuance", (3) "prohibit that party from introducing the undisclosed evidence," or (4) "enter any other order that is just under the circumstances." State statutes or court rules authorizing discovery contain similar provisions, and common law jurisdictions recognize that appropriate sanctions or remedies may be imposed as part of the trial court's inherent authority to order discovery. The measures noted in Rule 16(d)(2)—ordering immediate disclosure, granting a continuance, and excluding evidence—are the three most commonly imposed remedies. However, judicial opinions and statutory provisions also recognize several other sanctions or remedies, including (1) a charge directing the jury to assume certain facts that might have been established through the nondisclosed material, (2) granting a mistrial, (3) holding in contempt the party responsible for the nondisclosure, and (4) dismissal of the prosecution.

(b) Prosecution Violations. *Violations discovered before or at trial.* Perhaps no defense claim relating to discovery is more frequently raised on appeal than the claim that the trial court failed to utilize the proper remedy when the defendant discovered shortly before or during trial that the prosecution had breached a discovery order. The claim usually relates to the prosecution's presentation of a witness who was not endorsed on its witness list or its introduction into evidence of a previously undisclosed statement of the defendant or a scientific report. On occasion, it will be based upon the late disclosure of discoverable material that was not used as prosecution evidence, but which might have been helpful to the defense, if disclosed earlier, in developing its own case or in impeaching a prosecution witness. The usual defense complaint is that the trial court should have excluded the evidence or declared a mistrial as opposed to granting some lesser remedy, such as simply ordering immediate disclosure, or combining such disclosure with a brief continuance. Appellate courts frequently note that a trial court must be given "broad latitude" in its selection of an appropriate remedy. Nevertheless, they also have advanced certain guidelines for the exercise of that discretion, and reversals for the failure to follow those guidelines are not infrequent.

Once the trial court learns of the prosecution's non-compliance, it is expected initially to conduct an inquiry into the background, character, and impact of the nondisclosure. In some jurisdictions, the trial court's failure to conduct an appropriate inquiry (e.g., by not offering the defense counsel an opportunity to show possible prejudice) will constitute a sufficient ground in itself for an appellate reversal. The standard directive to trial courts, in conducting the needed inquiry, is to "take into account the reasons why disclosure was made, the extent of prejudice, if any, to the opposing party [here the defendant], the feasibility of rectifying the prejudice by a continuance, and any other relevant circumstance."

In general, the concept of "prejudice" in this context is limited to an adverse impact upon the defense's ability to prepare and present its case. Some courts, moreover, will not give weight to all types of adverse impact. In particular, they will not consider harm to the defendant's presentation that flows from a defense choice of a strategy designed to mislead the jury. The function of discovery, these courts note, is to permit the defense to marshall its evidence so as to challenge the possible falsity of the prosecution's evidence. Prejudice, they argue, therefore should be limited to restrictions on the defense's capacity to present such a challenge, and should not encompass self-inflicted wounds resulting from the defendant's unsuccessful attempt to use a fabricated defense. Thus, where the prosecution negligently failed to disclose pretrial that it possessed a document written by defendant, and the defendant then gave apparently false testimony that was clearly contradicted by that document, the defense was not allowed to look to the harm it obviously suffered when the prosecution subsequently used the document to impeach the defendant.

Decisions holding that the prejudice element will not encompass the prosecution's contradiction of a fabricated defense through evidence that should have been disclosed pretrial have not dealt with instances of purposeful prosecutorial "sandbagging." The discovery violations involved could be characterized as resulting from negligence or good faith misreadings of discovery obligations. Arguably a different result would be reached where the defendant was lured into "ensnaring himself in his self-made trap" by a purposeful prosecutorial nondisclosure. Indeed, other courts have indicated that the defense should be viewed as prejudiced and entitled to relief whenever a position taken by the defense is contradicted by prosecution evidence that was not properly disclosed during pretrial discovery, even though the defendant was fully aware that reliable evidence contradicted that position and proceeded because he assumed that the prosecution was unaware of that evidence. These courts note that while defendant has no right to fabricate a defense, the purpose of discovery is to avoid "trial by surprise," and to simply allow the trial to proceed, with the defense suffering from a presentation it would not have made with proper discovery, is to undercut that objective.

Very often, the discovery violation is called to the attention of the trial court during the prosecution's case-in-chief. Commonly, the prosecution will attempt to introduce a document or a witness that was not noted in pretrial discovery, with either the prosecutor acknowledging a discovery violation or the court determining that disclosure should have been given under the general discovery provision or the court's specific discovery directive. At other times, the defense will learn in cross-examining the witness that there exists some relevant evidence that should have been made available to it under the applicable discovery standard. The likely prejudice here ordinarily flows from the defense lacking sufficient time to digest and prepare either to meet or to use the previously undisclosed evidence. Many courts therefore view the continuance as playing a critical role in assessing the potential for prejudice. Indeed, the preferred remedy, at least where the prosecution has acted in good faith, is to order immediate compliance with discovery requirements, and offer the defense a continuance so that it can take advantage of the delayed discovery.

Where the defense is truly surprised, it will be expected to demand a continuance or at least accept a court offer of a continuance. Thus, the lack of a demand, or the rejection of the trial court's offer, is often taken as strong evidence that the discovery violation has not been prejudicial. Courts also recognize, however, that there are exceptional situations in which the defense can legitimately contend that a continuance will not be enough to eliminate prejudice. Thus, the defense may already have committed itself—in opening statement or cross-examination—to a line of attack that it would not have utilized if aware of the information that is the source of the discovery violation. Such a predicament is not limited to the situations, discussed above, in which the defendant sought to fabricate a defense now shown to be false. While the defense here may not be placed in the embarrassing position of having the defendant's testimony revealed to be false, its shift in approach in light of the newly disclosed material may create the impression that it simply is fishing for a line of attack, moving from one unfounded ground to another.

Consistent with their advice to trial courts to first look to the continuance as a remedy, appellate courts frequently warn against the unnecessary use of the preclusion sanction. The trial court, it is noted, "should seek to apply sanctions that affect the evidence at trial and the merits of the case as little as possible." Sanctions generally should not have "adverse effects on the rights of the parties rather than the offending attorneys themselves," and preclusion necessarily has such an adverse effect on the interests of the community, the party represented by the prosecutor. Accordingly, some courts treat preclusion as a remedy that should be available only where there was actual prejudice and where no other remedy will respond adequately to that prejudice. Other jurisdictions, while viewing preclusion as a remedy to be used sparingly, will not place the trial court in a position where it can exclude previously undisclosed prosecution evidence only upon finding that lesser sanctions could not eliminate the prejudice to the defense. Here, the trial court is given considerably greater leeway. It may, for example, chose preclusion over a continuance where a continuance is deemed to impose substantial burdens on an already congested docket or the continuance simply would not provide the same degree of assurance that the prejudice would be eliminated. Prosecution bad faith might also justify selection of preclusion over a continuance even though the continuance would be equally effective in responding to a prejudicial impact.

The jurisdictions also are divided as to the possible use of preclusion simply as a deterrent, without regard to the presence of prejudice. Some courts would allow such use where the trial court finds that the discovery violation was intentional or reflects a recurring disregard for discovery obligations. Other jurisdictions would allow exclusion to be used only where needed to respond to prejudice. Where the trial court believes that there is need for a deterrent measure, it is directed to make use of contempt orders directed against the offending prosecutor. A sanction, these courts note, should "not be regarded as a bonus awarded without regard to its need in the furtherance of fair trial rights."

Violations discovered post-trial. When the prosecution has an obligation to disclose information or matter other than that which it will use at trial, its failure to comply with that discovery obligation may be uncovered only after the trial is completed. At this point, the analysis adopted in determining the appropriate remedy is somewhat different than that applied to a discovery violation uncovered shortly before or during trial. Standard remedies like ordering immediate disclosure and providing a continuance or excluding evidence no longer are available. The issue before the court is whether the defendant's conviction must be overturned and a new trial granted, with the defense now having the benefit of the discovery to which it is entitled.

Since the undisclosed discoverable matter was not used by the prosecution at trial, the defense is likely to argue that it would have had an exculpatory rather than incriminating potential. This brings into consideration the possibility of a violation of the prosecutor's constitutional obligation under *Brady v. Md.* to disclose exculpatory evidence. While the *Brady* doctrine often does not mandate pretrial disclosure, it does require that exculpatory evidence which meets the requisite test of materiality at least be disclosed at trial. See § 16.3(b). Accordingly, a court ruling on a discovery violation uncovered only after trial must first determine whether there also has been a *Brady* violation, which would require a new trial as a matter of due process. If it is determined that the nondisclosure did not constitute a *Brady* violation, then whether a new trial will be granted is said to rest on a balancing of the likely prejudice to the defense against "the extent of the Government's culpability" for its failure to have complied with the discovery rules. Since the court has already determined that the nondisclosed information was not sufficiently exculpatory to establish a *Brady* violation, the potential for prejudice is not likely to be substantial enough to require relief where the government's omission was "merely inadvertent or negligent." On the other hand, if the nondisclosed matter was potentially favorable, though not so significant as to meet the *Brady* standard of materiality, that potential may well be sufficient to require a new trial where the failure to disclose was "deliberate" or the result of "gross negligence."

(c) Defense Violations. In many jurisdictions, the judicial treatment of sanctions is quite similar for discovery violations by both the defense and the prosecution. Of course, differences will exist as to violations first uncovered after trial, due to the prosecutor's quite different procedural posture in the post-verdict setting. Unlike the defense, if the trial resulted in an adverse verdict to the prosecution (i.e., an acquittal), the prosecution will not be able to challenge that verdict even if it can be attributed in part to the defense's discovery violation. At this point, the only sanction available to the court will be holding the responsible person in contempt if the violation was purposeful.

Where the defense's discovery violation is brought to the court's attention before or during trial, the court can look to the same sanctions that are imposed for prosecution violations. The one major distinction is the bearing of the Sixth Amendment upon the sanction of precluding defense use of the evidence that it should have disclosed pretrial under its discovery obligations. The Supreme Court addressed that issue in *Taylor v. Ill.* (1988). Although *Taylor* rejected the contention that a preclusion sanction constituted a per se violation of the defendant's Sixth Amendment right to compulsory process, and upheld that sanction as applied in the circumstances of that case, it also indicated that the preclusion sanction may not be used against the defendant quite as freely as some courts have used it against the prosecution.

Taylor involved the exclusion of the testimony of a defense witness after defendant had failed to list that witness in responding to a prosecution discovery request (the state discovery rule authorizing the request had not been challenged). The facts there, as recounted by the Court, revealed a clear discovery violation by a counsel who sought to mislead the trial judge, apparently in a last ditch effort to gain admission of dubious testimony that might save a failing defense. After having listed four witnesses in response to a witness-list request, and having called only two of those witnesses, who testified favorably but were obviously afraid of the defendant, defense counsel, on the second day of trial, sought to add two additional witnesses. Defense counsel initially claimed that he had just been informed about the witnesses and that they had probably seen the shooting incident upon which the charge against defendant was based. Responding to an inquiry by the trial judge, counsel then acknowledged that defendant had told him about the witnesses, but said he had been unable previously to locate one of them (Wormley). The judge then directed counsel to bring both witnesses to court on the next day, at which time he would decide whether they could testify. Counsel appeared the next day only with witness Wormley, who was then voir dired in an offer of proof. Wormley's testimony revealed that he had been visited by counsel during the week before the trial began, and that he had not actually seen the shooting incident. He stated that prior to the incident, he had "run into" the defendant and had warned him that the victim was armed and seeking the defendant (although he also stated on cross-examination that he had first "met" the defendant over two years later). The trial judge concluded initially that the failure to list the witness was a "blatant" and "willful" violation and exclusion would be required. He also noted: "For whatever value it is, because this is a jury trial, I have a great deal of doubt in my mind as to the veracity of this young man."

The Supreme Court in *Taylor* initially rejected the claim of the defendant that the compulsory process clause established an "absolute bar" to the exclusion of a witness. While it was true that clause embraced the right to have the witness' testimony heard (and not simply the right to compel the witness' attendance by subpoena), that right was not without limits (as evidenced by the fact that "the accused does not have an unfettered right to offer testimony that is incompetent, privileged, or otherwise inadmissible under standard rules of evidence").

The petitioner Taylor also argued that exclusion might be permissible in other settings but not as to an unlisted defense witness. Here, "a less drastic sanction" would always be available: where a disclosure is made, though late, prejudice to the prosecution "[can] be minimized by granting a continuance or mistrial * * * [and] further violations can be deterred by disciplinary sanctions against the defendant or defense counsel." The Court responded that, while "it may well be true that alternative sanctions are adequate and appropriate in most cases * * *, it is equally clear that they would be less effective than the preclusion sanction" and would sometimes "perpetuate rather than limit the prejudice to the State." A primary purpose of discovery rules, the Court reasoned, is to "minimize the risk that fabricated testimony will be believed." Quite often, it is "reasonable to presume that there is something suspect about a defense witness who is not identified until after the eleventh hour has passed." Where "a pattern of discovery violations is explicable only on the assumption that the violations were designed to conceal a plan to present fabricated testimony, it would be entirely appropriate to exclude the tainted evidence regardless of whether other sanctions would also be merited."

To reject petitioner's claim "that preclusion is never a permissible sanction," the Court noted, it was "neither necessary nor appropriate * * * to attempt to draft a comprehensive set of standards to guide the exercise of discretion" as to the permissible use of that sanction. It was sufficient to recognize that, while "a trial court may not ignore the fundamental character" of the defendant's right to present evidence, the "mere invocation of that right cannot automatically and invariably outweigh countervailing public interests." Also to be "weigh[ed] in the balance" were: "the integrity of the adversary process, which depends both on the presentation of reliable evidence and the rejection of unreliable evidence; the interest in the fair and efficient administration of justice; and the potential prejudice to the truth-determining function of the trial process." Thus, where the defense failed to comply with a discovery requirement and "that omission was willful and motivated by a desire to obtain a tactical advantage that would minimize the effectiveness of cross-examination and the ability to adduce rebuttal testimony, it would be entirely consistent with the purposes of the Confrontation Clause simply to exclude the witness' testimony." That was the case here, and the exclusion therefore did not violate the Sixth Amendment.

The *Taylor* opinion arguably raises as many questions as it answers. At the least, it lacks the kind of clear directive that is necessary to shape a lower court consensus on the bounds of the constitutionally permissible use of the preclusion sanction. Lower courts have had the least difficulty with cases that fit the *Taylor* description of a "willful [violation] * * * motivated by a desire to obtain a tactical advantage." Such willful misconduct is seen as sufficient in itself to justify the preclusion sanction. It calls upon the combined judicial interests of deterring willful violations of discovery rules and avoiding a possible affront to the integrity of the trial process through the offering of probably perjured testimony.

Some courts suggest that the tactically motivated willful violation may be the only situation in which preclusion is constitutionally acceptable. Others, noting the broad range of interests cited by *Taylor* as relevant to the constitutional balancing process, have looked to several additional factors that may justify imposing the preclusion sanction. They would consider the degree of fault in a violation that was not intentional (asking, for example, whether the discovery requirement was clear and whether compliance was relatively simple), the degree of prejudice suffered by the prosecution, the impact of preclusion upon the total evidentiary showing (including consideration of factors suggesting that the precluded evidence is unreliable), and the degree of effectiveness of less severe sanctions. The balance struck by reference to these factors could conceivably justify preclusion in a case that did not involve a willful violation designed to gain a tactical advantage.

*

Chapter 13

PLEAS OF GUILTY

Table of Sections

For additional analysis of the above topics and citations to authorities
supporting their discussion in this Book, consult the authors' 7-volume
Criminal Procedure treatise, also available as Westlaw database
CRIMPROC. See the Table of Cross-References in this Book.

---

§ 13.1   The Plea Negotiation System

(a) **Forms of Plea Bargaining.** The great majority of criminal cases are disposed of by plea of guilty rather than by trial. Some
involve implicit plea bargaining (the defendant enters his plea
merely because it is generally known that this is the route to a
lesser sentence), but more common is explicit bargaining (the
defendant enters a plea of guilty only after a commitment has been
made that concessions will be granted, or at least sought, in his
particular case). One common form of plea agreement is where the
defendant is permitted to plead guilty to a charge less serious than
is supported by the evidence. This kind of "deal" may seem
advantageous to the defendant (1) because the less serious offense
carries a lower statutory maximum penalty, thus limiting the
judge's sentencing discretion; (2) because the defendant may thereby avoid a high statutory minimum sentence or a statutory bar to
probation; or (3) because the defendant may thereby avoid a record
of conviction on the offense actually committed, thus avoiding a
repugnant conviction label or certain undesirable collateral consequences of a felony conviction. A second form of plea agreement is
where the defendant pleads to the original charge in exchange for
some kind of promise from the prosecutor concerning the sentence.
The prosecutor may agree in a general way to seek leniency, may
promise to ask for some specific disposition, or may do no more
than promise that he will refrain from making any recommendation
or will not oppose a request for leniency by the defendant. The
prosecutor may even be so bold as to promise a certain sentence
upon a guilty plea, a promise he may know he can fulfill because of
the trial judge's practice of following the prosecutor's recommendations. Another form of plea agreement, in the not uncommon
instance of multiple charges (actual or potential) against a single

defendant, is where the defendant pleads guilty to one charge in exchange for the prosecutor's promise to drop or not to file other charges.

(b) Development of Plea Bargaining. The practice of plea bargaining, though not limited exclusively to the United States, is more firmly established here than elsewhere. It began to appear during the early or mid-nineteenth century, and became a standard feature of American urban criminal courts in the last third of the nineteenth century. One common explanation is that plea bargaining exists because of crowded court dockets, but plea negotiation practices have developed at times and places where there was no serious court congestion. Other important reasons why the plea negotiation system has reached its present proportions in this country are: (1) the rise of professional police and prosecutors who developed and selected their cases more carefully, resulting in few genuine disputes over guilt or innocence; (2) the rise of specialization and professionalism on the defense side plus broadening of the right to counsel, meaning more attorneys assisting their clients at the pretrial stage; (3) changes in the jury trial process to one so cumbersome and expensive that our society refuses to provide it; (4) the due process revolution, which made additional demands on the prosecutor's office and gave the defendant additional rights strengthening his bargaining position; (5) expansion of the criminal law, particularly new criminal legislation lacking full community backing; (6) changes in sentencing practices concerning the certainty and size of the penalty for going to trial; and (7) the desire of prosecutors and judges to reach a sentence more appropriate for the individual offender than otherwise permissible under rigid sentencing statutes.

(c) Administrative Convenience. The most commonly asserted justification of plea bargaining is its utility in disposing of large numbers of cases in a quick and simple way. The assumption is that the system can function only if a high percentage of cases are disposed of by guilty plea and that this will happen only if concessions are granted to induce pleas. Some object that society should and can pay the price for whatever increase in the number of trials would be brought about by ending plea bargaining, but it has sometimes been questioned whether an increase in funding and staffing for this purpose would, in the broad view of things, be beneficial. The issue is further complicated by the fact that it is unclear whether bringing plea negotiations to an end would significantly increase the burdens on the criminal justice system, or whether most defendants would plead guilty any way.

(d) Accurate and Fair Results. Another concern which has been expressed about the plea negotiation system is that, by its nature, it is likely to produce results which are unfair or inaccurate. The objection is that the disposition of cases is influenced by factors irrelevant to the correctional needs of the defendant or the requirements of law enforcement, such as court and prosecutor workload or the aggressiveness of the lawyers, so that either of two undesirable consequences may occur: (1) a serious offender may escape with undeserved leniency; or (2) an innocent person may be convicted. The possibility of the first of these consequences is somewhat greater in those urban centers where the pressures to move the docket are most intense. As for the second of these consequences, the fear is that even an innocent person might be tempted to plead guilty and receive the tendered concessions rather than risk conviction at trial and a more severe penalty. But we just do not know how common such a situation is, nor do we know how often innocent persons are convicted at trial.

Indeed, it has been argued that in some instances plea negotiation leads to more intelligent results than could be obtained at trial. The premise is that the categories of guilt and innocence are not always simple and clear-cut, that instead of a black-or-white dichotomy there are many gray areas at the boundaries of criminal culpability, so that in a case in which the defendant's conduct falls into one of these gray areas it is preferable to achieve an intermediate judgment via plea bargaining than to undertake a trial at which only an all or nothing result is possible. Opponents of plea bargaining offer two responses: that unjustifiably harsh provisions in the substantive law can be avoided without plea bargaining by the simple expedient of more careful and considerate initial charge selection; and that unjustifiably harsh and otherwise unavoidable provisions of the substantive criminal law should be applied strictly in order to influence changes in the formal law producing greater flexibility.

(e) **The Problem of Disparity.** Because the plea negotiation system is grounded in the granting of concessions in exchange for guilty pleas, it raises the fundamental question of whether the fact that the defendant has pleaded guilty should have any legitimate bearing on the punishment he receives. One view is that dispositional disparity between guilty plea and trial defendants, arising out of and essential to a plea negotiation system, is proper so long as it is achieved without being unduly harsh to the latter category of defendants. Thus, it is argued that it is proper for guilty plea defendants to receive concessions so long as a court does not impose any sentence in excess of that which would be justified by any of the protective, deterrent, or other purposes of the criminal law upon a defendant who has chosen to require the prosecution to prove guilt at trial rather than to enter a plea of guilty. Others object that the normal sentence is the average sentence for all defendants, so that if we are lenient toward those who plead guilty we are by precisely the same token more severe toward those who do not.

The disparity in treatment of guilty plea and trial defendants has sometimes been explained on the ground that the circumstances of a trial are often such as to justify a more severe sanction than would have been imposed had the defendant entered a guilty plea (e.g., because the brutal circumstances of the crime are more vividly portrayed if there is a trial). Still another approach is to explain the disparity in terms of factors likely to call for leniency when a guilty plea is entered. There is considerable disagreement, however, as to the legitimacy of various factors that have been put forward, such as this list of six factors in the original ABA Standards: "(i) that the defendant by his plea has aided in ensuring the prompt and certain application of correctional measures to him"; "(ii) that the defendant has acknowledged his guilt and shown a willingness to assume responsibility for his conduct"; "(iii) that the concessions will make possible alternative correctional measures which are better adapted to achieving rehabilitative, protective, deterrent or other purposes of correctional treatment, or will prevent undue harm to the defendant from the form of conviction"; "(iv) that the defendant has made public trial unnecessary when there are good reasons for not having the case dealt with in a public trial"; "(v) that the defendant has given or offered cooperation when such cooperation has resulted or may result in the successful prosecution of other offenders engaged in equally serious or more serious criminal conduct"; and "(vi) that the defendant by his plea has aided in avoiding delay (including delay due to crowded dockets) in the disposition of other cases and thereby has increased the probability of prompt and certain application of correctional measures to other offenders."

It has been forcefully argued that plea bargaining is legitimate and noncoercive only if responsive to a substantial uncertainty concerning the likely outcome of a trial because, as stated in *Scott v. U.S.* (1969): "To the extent that the bargain struck reflects only the uncertainty of conviction before trial, the 'expected sentence before trial'—length of sentence discounted by probability of conviction—is the same for those who decide to plead guilty and those who hope for acquittal but risk conviction by going to trial." Whether one accepts or rejects this line of reasoning is likely to depend upon how one views some rather fundamental questions about the plea negotiation process. One such question is that of what kinds of cases are best disposed of by plea; some see plea bargaining as a device to screen out those cases where there is no real dispute, but under the *Scott* approach bargaining would be limited to cases in which there is a substantial uncertainty concerning the likely trial outcome. Moreover, if the *Scott* theory is otherwise valid, there is the troublesome question of whether it should make any difference *why* there is a substantial uncertainty concerning the likely outcome of a trial—whether the tendering of concessions should be limited to instances in which guilt is fairly certain but unprovable (e.g., where defendant's accomplice, having made a full, substantiated confession implicating the defendant, cannot now be found), or may be legitimately extended to cases in which guilt is in real doubt (e.g., where there has been a shaky eyewitness identification of the defendant)?

(f) Other Attributes and Consequences. Even if the plea negotiation process is seen as having certain positive attributes, there remains the difficult question of whether those attributes are outweighed by certain undesirable consequences, such as (1) an unhealthy relationship between the prosecutor and defense counsel, especially when the latter is the public defender; (2) the effect on the criminal defense bar, i.e., serious temptations to disregard their clients' interests; and (3) defendants are left with an image of corruption in the system, or at least an image of a system lacking meaningful purpose and subject to manipulation by those who are wise to the right tricks.

(g) Prohibiting Plea Bargaining. In the eyes of some, the practice of plea bargaining as it has developed in this country is undesirable and ought to be abolished entirely. What is not known is whether, assuming the plea negotiation process could be and was entirely eliminated, we would end up with a criminal justice system better (or worse) than we have now. It is unclear whether abolition would produce intolerable congestion in the courts and unsatiable demands upon available resources, and it is not known whether without any form of plea bargaining to mitigate mandatory or excessive sentencing laws, the dispositions as to some types of criminal defendants would be unduly harsh. Also, some fear that if plea bargaining were prohibited, the result would be increased pre-indictment plea adjustments. The notion is that eliminating discretion at one stage of the process fosters it at others, so that efforts to eliminate plea bargaining will be counterproductive by serving to shift the discretion to some other, usually less visible stage.

In a few jurisdictions, the law forbids the prosecutor from engaging in plea bargaining in certain circumstances or with regard to certain offenses. If the defendant enters a guilty plea pursuant to a bargain the prosecutor has struck in violation of such a statute, courts are disinclined to allow the defendant to overturn his plea because of the prohibition.

(h) Plea Bargaining and the Federal Sentencing Guidelines. In the federal system, there are two varieties of sentence bargaining: (1) an agreement between the parties "that a specific sentence or sentencing range is the appropriate disposition of the case," which the court may then accept or reject, though if it is rejected then the defendant must be allowed to withdraw his plea; and (2) an agreement that in exchange for the defendant's plea the government will "recommend, or agree not to oppose the defendant's request, that a particular sentence or sentencing range is appropriate," which is not binding on the court, necessitating a warning to the defendant that if the court imposes a different sentence the defendant nevertheless may not withdraw his plea. As to both, the Federal Sentencing Guidelines provide that the court may impose the sentence contemplated by the agreement only if it is satisfied that such sentence is either "within the applicable guideline range" or "departs from the applicable guidelines range for justifiable reasons." Though there is inter-circuit disagreement on this point, under one view this means that the existence of the plea agreement is not itself a mitigating circumstance and that in determining the proper sentence the court must, for the most part, proceed just as it would had the defendant pled not guilty and been convicted after a trial. If the guilty plea defendant gets a lighter sentence, this is most likely to occur by application of at least one of two sentencing factors with special significance in the guilty plea context: (i) a decrease in the offense level by two levels because the defendant "clearly demonstrates acceptance of responsibility for his offense," which in the case of a prompt guilty plea can actually result in a decrease by a total of three levels because of defendant's conduct in "timely notifying authorities of his intention to enter a plea of guilty, thereby permitting the government to avoid preparing for trial and permitting the court to allocate its resources efficiently"; and (ii) a departure from the Guidelines because of a "motion of the government stating that the defendant has provided substantial assistance in the investigation or prosecution of another person," though not all defendants who believe such a motion will be forthcoming in fact benefit from this provision.

Where the defendant enters a plea of guilty to one count in exchange for the government's promise that it will "not bring, or will move to dismiss, other charges," it is said to have the advantage that the defendant can pick the crime with the most favorable sentencing scheme under the Guidelines, thereby determining the sentence range. To some extent this is true, but the opportunities to affect the sentence via plea bargaining are limited by the Guidelines instructions to judges that such an agreement should be accepted only upon a determination "for reasons stated on the record, that the remaining charges adequately reflect the seriousness of the actual offense behavior and that accepting the agreement will not undermine the statutory purpose of sentencing or the sentencing guidelines." While this provision appears to give sentencing courts wide latitude in deciding whether to accept charge bargains, there are other provisions in the Guidelines that further limit the opportunities for the judge to reduce the defendant's sentence as a result of the dropping of some counts. The above quoted provision goes on to say that dismissal of a charge "shall not preclude the conduct underlying such charge from being considered" as relevant conduct. What this means is that whenever "the offense level is determined largely on the basis of the total amount of harm or loss, the quantity of a substance involved, or some other measure of aggregate harm, or if the offense behavior is ongoing or continuous in nature and the offense guideline is written to cover such behavior," then such matters as the base offense level, specific offense characteristics and adjustments are to be determined on the basis of "all acts and omissions * * * that were part of the same course of conduct or common scheme or plan as the offense of conviction." This includes conduct underlying counts dismissed pursuant to a plea bargain. For example, in a drug case involving five counts of distributing heroin, the offense level is determined primarily by the quantity of drugs involved, thus if a plea agreement is reached involving a plea to one count, the offense level will still be calculated based on all the drugs of that common drug scheme.

In *U.S. v. Booker* (2005), on 5-Justice majority held that the federal Sentencing Guidelines violated the Sixth Amendment jury trial principle that "[a]ny fact (other than a prior conviction) which is necessary to support a sentence exceeding the maximum authorized by the facts established by a plea of guilty or a jury verdict must be admitted by the defendant or proved to a jury beyond a reasonable doubt." But another 5-Justice majority concluded the proper remedy was to make the guidelines advisory. While this means sentencing judges are now free to give as much or as little weight as they choose to the defendant's willingness to plead guilty, to the presence of serious criminal conduct which would be unpunished under the plea agreement, and to other factors, so long as the sentence is "reasonable," in practice *Booker* appears to have produced little change in these respects.

§ 13.2 Kept, Broken, Rejected and Nonexistent Bargains

(a) Statutory Inducements to Plead Guilty. One troublesome aspect of the plea negotiation system, the disparity that can result between the sentences imposed upon defendants who plead guilty and those given to defendants who go to trial, is by no means limited to situations in which bargaining on a case-by-case basis occurs. It is possible for the disparity to be facilitated or mandated by sentencing laws, as occurs when a sentencing provision requires or allows a certain kind or degree of sentence to be imposed upon a defendant who stands trial but does not require or allow that same punishment to be inflicted upon a likewise-charged defendant who enters a trial-avoiding plea. Under such a statutory scheme, it may legitimately be asked: (1) whether a defendant who elects to go to trial is being punished to an unconstitutional extent or in an unconstitutional manner; and (2) whether a defendant who elects to forego trial has, by virtue of the statute, entered a coerced and thus involuntary plea.

The first of these issues reached the Supreme Court in *U.S. v. Jackson* (1968), where a defendant who had not opted to plead guilty challenged the Federal Kidnaping Act because of its provision that the punishment of death could be imposed only "if the verdict of the jury shall so recommend." This meant, the Court noted, that "the defendant who abandons the right to contest his guilt before a jury is assured that he cannot be executed; the defendant ingenuous enough to seek a jury acquittal stands forewarned that, if the jury finds him guilty and does not wish to spare his life, he will die." Because the legitimate goal of this statute, "limiting the death penalty to cases in which a jury recommends it," could be accomplished in other ways, and because the "inevitable effect" of the provision was "to discourage assertion of the Fifth Amendment right not to plead guilty and to deter exercise of the Sixth Amendment right to demand a jury trial," the Court in *Jackson* concluded that the death penalty provision in the statute "needlessly penalizes" the assertion of those constitutional rights and thus was unconstitutional. The Court went on to explain that "the evil in the federal statute is not that it necessarily *coerces* guilty pleas and jury waivers but simply that it needlessly *encourages* them," and thus "the fact that the Federal Kidnaping Act tends to discourage defendants from insisting upon their innocence and demanding trial by jury hardly implies that every defendant who enters a guilty plea to a charge under the Act does so involuntarily."

This language suggested, as the Supreme Court subsequently held, that a defendant who challenged a guilty plea entered under such a sentencing scheme would not necessarily prevail. In *Brady v. U.S.* (1970), a defendant who had entered a guilty plea under this same Act prior to the *Jackson* decision and who had been sentenced to a 30 year term, unsuccessfully claimed that his plea was invalid. Declaring that *Jackson* "neither fashioned a new standard for judging the validity of guilty pleas nor mandated a new application of the test theretofore fashioned by courts and since reiterated that guilty pleas are valid if both 'voluntary' and 'intelligent,' " the Court concluded (a) that a guilty plea is not rendered unintelligent merely "because later judicial decisions indicate that the plea rested on a faulty premise"; and (b) that a guilty plea is not rendered involuntary "merely because entered to avoid the possibility of a death penalty."

Although *Brady* did not involve a bargained plea in the true sense of that term, it appears that the Court was influenced to some degree by a perceived need to reach a result not casting doubts upon the plea negotiation process. The same may be said of the later case of *Corbitt v. N.J.* (1978), which unlike *Brady* and like *Jackson* involved a defendant who had elected to stand trial. Defendant was tried and convicted of first degree murder and sentenced to the mandatory punishment of life imprisonment. Had he entered a plea of non vult or nolo contendere (see § 13.4(a)), then by state law the punishment would have been "either imprisonment for life or the same as that imposed upon a conviction of murder in the second degree," i.e., a term of not more than 30 years. The defendant thus claimed that this scheme was unconstitutional under *Jackson,* but the Court responded that the more recent case of *Bordenkircher v. Hayes* (1978) provided the better analogy. For one thing, there were deemed to be "substantial differences between this case and *Jackson"* in that the instant case (a) did not involve the death penalty and (b) did not involve a scheme whereby the maximum penalty was reserved exclusively for those who insisted on a jury trial. For another, the *Corbitt* majority saw "no difference of constitutional significance" between the instant case and *Bordenkircher,* approving a prosecutor's conduct in having defendant charged and convicted as a habitual criminal and subjected to the mandatory sentence of life imprisonment because the defendant refused to plead guilty to the original forgery charge punishable by 2–10 years. Here, as there, the defendant was free to choose either "to go to trial and face the risk of life imprisonment" or to enter a plea making possible a lesser penalty.

Lying at the heart of the *Corbitt* decision, it appears, is the debatable assumption that no constitutional distinction can be drawn between the tendering of concessions for pleas as a result of negotiations on a case-by-case basis and the wholesale tendering of concessions by statute. The majority saw both as serving a legitimate function, "the encouragement of guilty defendants not to contest their guilt," and declared that the Court could not permit bargaining by a prosecutor "and yet hold that the legislature may not openly provide for the possibility of leniency in return for a plea." To this, the author of *Bordenkircher*—Justice Stewart— objected that "there is a vast difference between the settlement of litigation through negotiation between counsel for the parties, and a state statute such as is involved in the present case," for the prosecutor "necessarily must be able to settle an adversary criminal lawsuit through plea bargaining with his adversary," while "a state legislature has a quite different function to perform." That is, while it cannot be said that authorizing plea bargaining "needlessly penalizes" the assertion of constitutional rights under the *Jackson* test, it hardly follows, as the *Corbitt* majority assumed, that this statutory scheme "is at the very heart of an effective plea negotiation program." Moreover, as the three *Corbitt* dissenters noted: "In the bargaining process, individual factors relevant to the particular case may be considered by the prosecutor in charging and by the trial judge in sentencing, regardless of the defendant's plea; the process does not mandate a different standard of punishment depending solely on whether or not a plea is entered."

Just how far *Corbitt* undercuts *Jackson* is unclear. The majority cautioned it was not suggesting "that every conceivable statutory sentencing structure" would be constitutional, and upheld the challenged statute because it was "unconvinced" that it "exerts such a powerful influence to coerce inaccurate guilty pleas that it should be deemed constitutionally suspect." Certainly there is such a "powerful influence" when it is the risk of the death penalty, "unique in its severity and irrevocability," that is involved, but the Court in *Corbitt* denied it was holding "that the *Jackson* rationale is limited to those cases where a plea avoids any possibility of the death penalty being imposed." Lower courts continue to apply *Jackson* even where the death penalty has not been involved. *Corbitt* also distinguished *Jackson* because there "any risk of suffering the maximum penalty could be avoided by pleading guilty," but it is debatable whether this ought to be determinative. It is far from apparent that a may/cannot system (i.e., defendant *may* get the maximum if he goes to trial, but *cannot* if he pleads guilty) is more coercive than a must/may system (i.e., defendant *must* get the maximum if he goes to trial, and *may* if he pleads guilty). This is especially true when, as was the case under the New Jersey statute challenged in *Corbitt,* the statutory scheme is accompanied by an established practice of not giving the maximum to a pleading defendant. Moreover, there is a sense in which the must/may system is more pernicious, for under it the price for exercising constitutional rights is the total loss of any chance of sentencing leniency.

The *Corbitt* decision may actually reflect a broader point, namely, that statutory inducements to plead guilty are to be assessed in terms of the extent to which they make the choice between plea and trial determinative and remove discretion from the prosecutor and court. This would mean that Justice Stewart was correct in asserting it would be "clearly unconstitutional" for a state legislature to provide "that the penalty for every criminal offense to which a defendant pleads guilty is to be one-half the penalty to be imposed upon a defendant convicted of the same offense after a not guilty plea."

(b) Inducements by the Prosecutor. The plea bargaining system as it has developed in this country depends not upon such statutory inducements but rather upon inducements frequently put forward by prosecutors in individual cases. In *Brady v. U.S.*, upholding as voluntary and intelligent a guilty plea entered under the statutory scheme found unconstitutional in *Jackson,* the Court cast its decision in terms that appeared calculated to lend support to some forms of plea bargaining:

> We decline to hold, however, that a guilty plea is compelled and invalid under the Fifth Amendment whenever motivated by the defendant's desire to accept the certainty or probability of a lesser penalty rather than face a wider range of possibilities extending from acquittal to conviction and a higher penalty authorized by law for the crime charged.
>
> The issue we deal with is inherent in the criminal law and its administration because guilty pleas are not constitutionally forbidden, because the criminal law characteristically extends to judge or jury a range of choice in setting the sentence in individual cases, and because both the State and the defendant often find it advantageous to preclude the possibility of the maximum penalty authorized by law. For a defendant who sees slight possibility of acquittal, the advantages of pleading guilty and limiting the probable penalty are obvious—his exposure is reduced, the correctional processes can begin immediately, and the practical burdens of a trial are eliminated. For the State there are also advantages—the more promptly imposed punishment after an admission of guilt may more effectively attain the objectives of punishment; and with the avoidance of trial, scarce judicial and prosecutorial resources are conserved for those cases in which there is a substantial issue of the defendant's guilt or in which there is substantial doubt that the State can sustain its burden of proof. It is this mutuality of advantage which perhaps explains the fact that at present well over three-fourths of the criminal convictions in this country rest on pleas of guilty, a great many of them no doubt motivated at least in part by the hope or assurance of a lesser penalty than might be imposed if there were a guilty verdict after a trial to judge or jury.

That theme was sounded by the Court on other occasions, but again in circumstances where the prosecutor's bargaining tactics were not directly at issue. Moreover, the Court gave no indication it was extending wholesale approval to all forms of prosecutorial inducements. In *Brady,* for example, the Court spoke approvingly only of the prosecutor allowing the defendant "to plead guilty to a lesser offense included in the offense charged" or "with the understanding that other charges will be dropped," but indicated a guilty plea could not stand if "induced by threats (or promises to discontinue improper harassment), misrepresentation (including unfulfilled or unfulfillable promises), or perhaps by promises that are by their nature improper as having no proper relationship to the prosecutor's business (e.g., bribes)."

But this left unsettled exactly where the line should be drawn between the permissible tender of concessions and impermissible "threats." What if the prosecutor confronted the defendant with dramatically different punishment consequences depending upon whether or not he entered a guilty plea? What if the prosecutor indicated that failure of the defendant to plead guilty would result in the filing of more serious charges against the defendant? Such were the issues in *Bordenkircher v. Hayes* (1978), for there the prosecutor carried out his threat that if the defendant did not plead guilty to the existing charge of uttering a forged instrument, punishable by two to 10 years, he would be indicted under the Habitual Criminal Act, which would subject defendant to a mandatory sentence of life imprisonment by reason of his two prior felony convictions. On federal habeas corpus, the court of appeals had held that defendant's prosecution and conviction under that Act violated the principles of *Blackledge v. Perry* (1974), where a prosecutor's escalation of charges against a defendant who had exercised his right to appeal was held to violate due process because there was a "realistic likelihood of 'vindictiveness'" in such circumstances (see § 5.5(a)).

The Supreme Court, in a 5–4 decision, reversed the court of appeals. The majority reasoned that while in *Blackledge* and related cases "the Court was dealing with the State's unilateral imposition of a penalty upon a defendant who had chosen to exercise a legal right to attack his original conviction," that situation was "very different from the give-and-take negotiation common in plea bargaining between the prosecution and the defense, which arguably possess relatively equal bargaining power." In the latter circumstances, the Court asserted, "there is no such element of punishment or retaliation so long as the accused is free to accept or reject the prosecution's offer." And consequently, the Court concluded, "the course of conduct engaged in by the prosecutor in this case, which no more than openly presented the defendant with the unpleasant alternatives of foregoing trial or facing charges on which he was plainly subject to prosecution, did not violate the Due Process Clause of the Fourteenth Amendment." The majority treated this result as a foregone conclusion in light of the Court's earlier favorable words concerning the institution of plea bargaining. Because "acceptance of the basic legitimacy of plea bargaining necessarily implies rejection of any notion that a guilty plea is involuntary in a constitutional sense simply because it is the end result of the bargaining process," it was said by way of explanation, it "follows that, by tolerating and encouraging the negotiation of pleas, this Court has necessarily accepted as constitutionally legitimate the simple reality that the prosecutor's interest at the bargaining table is to persuade the defendant to forego his right to plead not guilty."

Given the fact that this left the defendant with the life sentence he had received for failing to plead guilty to a charge carrying a 10–year maximum, the Court's decision in *Bordenkircher* is, at best, unsettling. The tensions that contributed to this troublesome result can best be seen by considering the alternative courses the Court might have taken: (1) the original charge could be presumed to reflect the prosecutor's judgment of an appropriate disposition in the case, so upon a subsequent enhancement of the charge the prosecutor would have to justify his action on some basis other than discouraging the defendant from exercising his constitutional rights, but such a ruling would merely prompt prosecutors to bring the greater charge initially in every case; (2) judicial scrutiny of the motives underlying even initial charging decisions could be undertaken with a view to determining whether the charges brought were filed to gain bargaining leverage, but this is not feasible because it is virtually impossible to show that this is what the prosecutor was doing; (3) the focus could be upon sentences that technically lie within the legal range of sentence options but violate our sense of fairness, but this would involve the judiciary in the sensitive and difficult task of making judgments about the constitutionality of legislative action in setting the permissible range of imprisonment for a variety of offenses; and (4) the prosecutor's conduct in *Bordenkircher* could be deemed outside the boundaries of permissible plea bargaining tactics because of the degree of leverage utilized by him (which is where Justice Powell came out), but such a holding would have plunged appellate courts into a review of innumerable other sentences that defendants had received after rejecting prosecutorial offers of lenient treatment in exchange for pleas of guilty.

Bordenkircher should not be read as declaring that a defendant who refuses to plead guilty and then is convicted on added charges is never entitled to relief. The Court emphasized that it did not have before it a case "where the prosecutor without notice brought an additional and more serious charge after plea negotiations relating only to the original indictment had ended with the defendant's insistence on pleading not guilty," and the holding in the case was stated in terms of the prosecutor having "openly presented the defendant with the unpleasant alternatives" he faced. This suggests that if the prosecutor fails to tell the defendant that there is a price attached to his refusal to plead guilty or only makes an unspecified threat of increased criminal liability, so that defendant has no means by which to weigh the potential liabilities of that refusal, the prosecutor might be barred from thereafter upping the ante because the defendant refuses to plead guilty.

Another way to look at *Bordenkircher* is to ask what significance the case has, if any, in a situation where the defendant *does* plead guilty. That is, what if the defendant in that case, upon being confronted with the prospect of life imprisonment from an added charge under the Habitual Criminal Act, had entered a guilty plea to the forgery charge and then later challenged that plea as coerced? Strictly speaking, *Bordenkircher* should not be viewed as foreclosing a finding of involuntariness, for the Court was only addressing the vindictive prosecution issue raised by a defendant who did not give in to the pressure. Yet, a reading of *Bordenkircher* with *Brady* indicates the defendant is not likely to prevail. The former case establishes that the prosecutor's conduct does not involve an improper threat or promise, and the latter seems to say that in such circumstances the plea is voluntary if the defendant was aware of "the actual value of any commitments made to him." But that phrase, together with the strong emphasis in *Bordenkircher* upon the prosecutor having charging discretion "so long as the prosecutor has probable cause," indicates the defendant's attack would be strengthened if the threatened charge in fact could not have been brought.

Bordenkircher should not be read as manifesting approval of any type of threat or promise made by the prosecutor in a plea bargaining context. In a footnote the Court cautioned that the case did not "involve the constitutional implications of a prosecutor's offer during plea bargaining of adverse or lenient treatment for some person *other* than the accused, which might pose a greater danger of inducing a false guilty plea by skewing the assessment of the risks a defendant must consider." It has been forcefully argued that such inducements present a special risk that an innocent defendant will plead guilty and that a guilty defendant will receive treatment that does not meet his correctional needs, but the courts have rather consistently held that there is no intrinsic infirmity in broadening plea negotiations to permit third party beneficiaries. However, guilty pleas made in consideration of lenient treatment to third persons pose a greater danger of coercion than purely bilateral plea bargaining and thus deserve close scrutiny.

A prosecutor's bargaining tactics may come under attack because of commitments exacted from the defendant in addition to the guilty plea. Illustrative is a plea bargain that included a promise by defendant to leave the state for ten years, a commitment held unenforceable because contrary to public policy; one that included a promise by defendant not to testify in favor of a codefendant, unenforceable because a violation of the codefendant's right to compulsory process; or one that required defendant to testify in another's case consistently with statements previously given the police, unenforceable because they taint the truth-seeking function of the courts. Courts are not in agreement concerning a prosecutor-induced commitment by the defendant not to take an appeal. The prevailing view is that such a bargain is a proper method of making a plea agreement enforceable, while another treats the right to appeal as non-negotiable because otherwise plea bargains could be insulated from appellate review. A middle view is that such a waiver is neither inherently coercive or fully enforceable, so that a defendant remains free to file a timely appeal, which relieves the state of its part of the bargain.

(c) Inducements by the Judge. As discussed later (see § 13.3(d)), there exists a considerable difference of opinion as to how the plea negotiation process should be structured in terms of judicial involvement, and in particular with whether it is better that the judge participate directly in negotiation sessions or remain completely aloof from them. Some jurisdictions have adopted the latter position; the federal rule is that the "court must not participate in these discussions," and several states are in accord. If in one of those jurisdictions a defendant brings his guilty plea into question by showing that it was preceded by some inducements from the judge, the case might well be disposed of in the defendant's favor without any determination of whether the judge's involvement in the particular case was so extreme as to make the plea involuntary. That is, it might well be concluded that this absolute prohibition upon judicial involvement can best be enforced by permitting a defendant to withdraw his plea without first showing that actual prejudice resulted from the judge's participation.

In a jurisdiction not taking that view, the question then to be considered is whether the nature and circumstances of the judge's participation was such that the defendant's plea was coerced and thus invalid. The generally accepted view is that such participation, in and of itself, does not require setting a guilty plea aside as a constitutional matter. Rather, there must be a more particularized assessment of the individual case, during which the trial judge's participation in the plea bargaining process must be carefully scrutinized. There remains considerable uncertainty, however, as to exactly what kind of involvement by the judge will make the defendant's plea involuntary. The Supreme Court has not had occasion to address the issue directly, though in *Brady v. U.S.* (1970), indicating approval of prosecutor bargaining, the Court in a cautionary footnote observed that those remarks were not intended to encompass a case "where the prosecutor or judge, or both, deliberately employ their charging and sentencing powers to induce a particular defendant to tender a plea of guilty." Of course, the Court has since approved such action by the prosecutor, but it is unclear whether that has any significance as to judicial involvement. One view is that judicial participation has a substantially different effect than negotiations between the parties because of the unequal positions of the judge and the accused and the judge's awesome power to impose a substantially longer or even maximum sentence if the defendant rejects the court's proposals. In response, it may be argued that this assertion is inconsistent with the Supreme Court's teachings as to what is a voluntary plea, and also with the fact that because the prosecutor has many means not available to the judge of putting pressure upon the defendant, this disparity of positions may be even greater between prosecutor and defendant.

Examination of the decisions assessing the voluntariness of a plea entered subsequent to some judicial involvement in the negotiation process sheds some light on the factors that may influence a determination that the plea is or is not valid. Certainly the defendant's plea cannot be upheld where the judge significantly overstated the defendant's predicament were he to stand trial, as where the judge erroneously indicated that in such circumstances he would have no choice but to sentence defendant to prison. Also, a plea is likely to be held involuntary where the judge was the moving force in pressing for a guilty plea after defendant had manifested a desire not to so plead or where the judge indicated conviction at trial was a foregone conclusion. On the other hand, the judge's involvement is not likely to be deemed coercive where the bargaining was not initiated by the judge, where the judge merely said he would abide by the agreement previously reached by the parties, or where the judge only suggested a compromise position between the different sentencing proposals of the defendant and prosecutor. Nor is it coercive for the judge, after jury selection had begun, to put a time limit on how long thereafter the parties had to negotiate a plea agreement, as eleventh hour settlements are properly discouraged.

Assume now a different scenario, one in which again there has been judicial involvement in the bargaining process (e.g., a promise of a 5 year sentence if defendant pleads guilty) but the defendant elected to stand trial, was convicted, and then received a more severe sentence (e.g., a 7 year sentence). Even if we are prepared to say that this defendant's plea would have been voluntary had he accepted the judge's proposal, it does not necessarily follow that the defendant in the above scenario lacks a valid constitutional claim, for the Supreme Court in a related context has made it unmistakably clear that the two situations are different and necessitate different analysis. In the above scenario the defendant's argument will be that these events amount to a violation of due process because of the vindictiveness—or, at least, the appearance of vindictiveness—against the defendant for his exercise of his constitutional right to stand trial. So the argument goes, if, as the Supreme Court held in *N.C. v. Pearce* (1969), due process "requires that vindictiveness against a defendant for having successfully attacked his first conviction must play no part in the sentence he receives after a new trial," then surely the same is true as to a defendant's exercise of a constitutional right. That argument, of course, bears a distinct similarity to that made with respect to prosecutorial inducements and rejected by the Supreme Court in *Bordenkircher v. Hayes* (1978). The defendant's position there was that if, as the Court had previously held, the prosecutor could not ordinarily escalate the charges after defendant had exercised his right to appeal, then he likewise could not do so after defendant had rejected the prosecutor's plea inducements and exercised his constitutional right to trial. But, as we have seen (see § 13.2(b)), the Court declined to apply the vindictiveness concept to plea negotiations, reasoning that "in the 'give-and-take' of plea bargaining, there is no such element of punishment or retaliation so long as the accused is free to accept or reject the prosecution's offer."

Whether that analysis carries over to cases of judicial involvement is a matter on which there is a difference of opinion, as is revealed by the en banc decision in *Frank v. Blackburn* (1980). Prior to and during defendant's state trial the trial judge conducted plea bargaining sessions in his chambers at which he stated the sentence would be 20 years if defendant were to plead guilty, but defendant rejected those offers and was convicted of armed robbery, after which the judge sentenced him to a term of 33 years. On federal habeas corpus, a majority of the court of appeals read *Bordenkircher* as making "it clear that a state is free to encourage guilty pleas by offering substantial benefits to a defendant, or by threatening an accused with more severe punishment should a negotiated plea be refused," necessitating the finding that the rule in *Pearce* is "completely inapplicable to post-plea bargain sentencing proceedings." But the dissenters in *Frank* reasoned that *Bordenkircher* had merely declined to apply the vindictiveness doctrine to plea bargaining between the parties because a contrary result would have, in effect, foreclosed what the Court had repeatedly said was a necessary aspect of the criminal process. Judicial participation, they reasoned, had no such credentials and thus was not equally deserving of exemption from the *Pearce* rule. The dissenters also noted that the opinion in *Bordenkircher* had been carefully crafted to make it unmistakably clear that it did not extend to judicial involvement. Specifically, the Supreme Court emphasized that the *Pearce* rule had been applied in situations "very different from the give-and-take negotiations common in plea bargaining between the prosecution and the defense, which arguably possess relatively equal bargaining power." Be that as it may, a defendant today would find it difficult to prevail in this setting on a *Pearce* theory, for it now appears such a defendant would not have available the *Pearce* presumption and thus would have the burden of establishing actual vindictiveness. In *Ala. v. Smith* (1989) (see § 18.8(c)), the Supreme Court ruled that because there does not exist a "reasonable likelihood" of vindictiveness in the case of a vacated guilty plea and higher sentence after a subsequent trial and reconviction, no presumption of vindictiveness exists in such circumstances.

Even assuming the majority is correct in *Frank,* there remains here (as with prosecutorial inducements) the troublesome question of whether certain inducements are improper simply because of the substantial disparity between the contemplated disposition depending upon whether the defendant opts to plead guilty or go to trial. In the *Frank* case, for example, one might well ask what legitimate objective of the plea bargaining system is served by a sentencing differential of 13 years. An even more dramatic illustration is provided by *People v. Dennis* (1975), where the judge offered defendant a term of either 2–4 or 2–6 years if he would plead guilty, the defendant elected to stand trial and was convicted, and that judge then sentenced him to a term of 40–80 years. The appellate court, noting that the judge at sentencing had before him no relevant facts of which he had been unaware at the time of his plea offer, reduced defendant's sentence to 6–18 years. One critic then asked whether this means a defendant may be penalized for exercising his right to trial by a sentence three times more severe than that he could have secured by pleading guilty, but not by a sentence twenty times more severe. Certainly this is an important question, central to the entire plea negotiation process, but it is one that courts are understandably reluctant to address.

(d) The Broken Bargain. In *Santobello v. N.Y.* (1971), the Supreme Court ruled that it was constitutionally impermissible to hold a defendant to his negotiated plea when the promises upon which it was based were not performed. The defendant in that case entered a guilty plea to a lesser included offense upon the prosecutor's promise to make no recommendation as to sentence, but at the sentencing hearing some months later that prosecutor's successor recommended the maximum sentence, which the judge imposed. After speaking approvingly of the plea negotiation system, the Court concluded that this system "must be attended by safeguards to insure the defendant what is reasonably due in the circumstances," meaning "that when a plea rests in any significant degree on a promise or agreement of the prosecutor, so that it can be said to be part of the inducement or consideration, such promise must be fulfilled." The Court thus remanded the case to the state court for a determination of whether the defendant should be given the relief he sought, withdrawal of his plea, or whether instead he should be granted specific performance by resentencing before another judge. (The Court in *Santobello* declined to find harmless error because of the sentencing judge's statement that the prosecutor's recommendation did not influence him.)

The first step in applying the *Santobello* rule is to determine if promises were made and, if so, precisely what they were. If the plea agreement is ambiguous, then courts are inclined to apply the law of contracts to resolve the ambiguity. However, because the defendant's "contract" right is constitutionally based, the prosecution is held to a greater degree of responsibility than the defendant for ambiguities, especially when the prosecutor has proffered the terms or prepared a written agreement.

One kind of promise is a commitment by the prosecutor that he will recommend or at least not oppose a particular sentence sought by the defendant. If the prosecutor does recommend or not oppose that sentence but the judge imposes a more severe sentence, the defendant is not entitled to relief under *Santobello,* for the promise to seek or not oppose the lesser sentence has been kept. However, some jurisdictions as a matter of state law have adopted the contrary position apparently on the assumption that there is an element of unfairness in holding the defendant to his plea when there was such uncertainty as to the actual result. If as a part of the plea agreement the prosecutor has promised to recommend a particular disposition, then certainly there has been a broken bargain if the prosecutor fails to make that recommendation or makes a contrary recommendation.

Some lower courts had held that such agreements include an implied promise of effective advocacy of the recommendation that, should it not occur, would also entitle the defendant to relief. But in *U.S. v. Benchimol* (1985), where the prosecutor engaged in no advocacy of and gave no reason for his promised probation recommendation, the Supreme Court rejected the court of appeals' conclusion that there had been a breach. It "was error," said the

Court, "for the Court of Appeals to imply as a matter of law a term which the parties themselves did not agree upon." The Court in *Benchimol* emphasized that the instant case was not one in which the government had made an express commitment either to make the recommendation enthusiastically or to state reasons for it, and distinguished those lower court cases in which "the Government attorney appearing personally in court at the time of the plea bargain expressed personal reservations about the agreement to which the Government had committed itself." If the prosecutor promises to recommend a certain sentence and does so, he has not breached the bargain by also bringing all relevant facts to the attention of the court.

If, on the other hand, the plea bargain was that the prosecutor would not recommend a sentence or would not oppose defendant's recommendations, it may be claimed that the prosecutor did too much. Certainly if the prosecutor promised to make no recommendation, there is a breach of the agreement when the prosecutor later recommends that the defendant be given the maximum possible sentence. By contrast, it is generally accepted that a promise of this limited nature is not broken merely by the prosecutor's conduct in supplying relevant facts at the sentencing hearing. But if the prosecutor has entered into a broader commitment, stated in terms of remaining silent or taking no position whatsoever with regard to the sentence, this may be construed as meaning that the prosecutor is barred from volunteering any information detrimental to the defendant. However, there is a disinclination to interpret such promises as commitments to remain silent under all circumstances, and thus it has been held that the prosecutor is free to speak for the purpose of correcting misstatements by the defense or in response to a question from the court.

In the case of charge bargaining, where the defendant enters a guilty plea to a lesser charge or fewer charges than originally brought, the more obvious types of broken bargain situations rarely occur because typically the more serious or additional charges are dismissed at the very time of defendant's plea. But defendants sometimes claim a violation of the *Santobello* rule when either the court or parole agency takes into account an aspect of defendant's conduct encompassed within a charge dropped pursuant to a plea bargain. Illustrative is a case in which the negotiated plea was to robbery in lieu of the original charge of armed robbery, but at sentencing the judge considered the fact that the defendant had been armed. In these and like circumstances (including when dismissed counts are used to determine the offense level under the federal sentencing guidelines), courts have consistently held that there has been no breaking of the plea bargain. It is emphasized that these facts have obvious and direct relevance to the matters to be decided, so that it would be detrimental to the sentencing and parole release processes if it were necessary to disregard them totally. Moreover, permitting their use is deemed not inconsistent with the terms of the agreement, as a bargain that involves dropping charges is attractive to a defendant primarily because the total length of time to which he can be sentenced is reduced.

Some authority is to be found to the effect that a defendant may be disentitled from prevailing on a broken bargain claim because of his own misconduct. One type of situation is that in which the defendant was able to obtain a promise of concessions by misrepresenting the material facts. Thus, it has been held that where a defendant claiming to have no prior convictions was promised probation but it was later determined he had an out-of-state felony conviction, making him ineligible for probation as a matter of state law, a sentence of imprisonment was properly imposed on the basis of the guilty plea. (If the defendant enters a plea to a lesser offense before his misrepresentation is discovered, some courts treat this as a "misplea," a guilty plea equivalent to a "mistrial" that permits the plea to be rescinded and the higher charge reinstated.) A second situation is that in which additional criminal conduct by the defendant occurs prior to the time of sentencing, which has been held to be a sufficient change in circumstances to justify the state in retreating from the promised recommendation. Certainly the defendant should not be entitled to enforce the bargain in this latter situation, but it is less apparent that permitting withdrawal of the plea would be inappropriate.

Yet another variation of the changed circumstances problem is that in *State v. Thomas* (1971), where the defendant was initially charged with atrocious assault and battery, assault with intent to rob, and robbery of one Murray. A negotiated plea was entered to the first count in exchange for the prosecutor's promise to dismiss the remaining counts, and they were subsequently dropped, but after Murray died the defendant was charged with murder. On defendant's motion to dismiss, the court ruled that under the collateral estoppel rule of *Ashe v. Swenson* (1970) the defendant could not be prosecuted on a felony-murder theory. The court reasoned that the "dismissal of the two counts must be treated as a general verdict of acquittal" and that "two issues can be deemed already litigated and decided—defendant did not assault Fannie Murray with intent to rob her nor did he rob her." But this analysis is faulty. Collateral estoppel, as defined in *Ashe,* "means simply that when an issue of ultimate fact has once been determined by a valid and final judgment, that issue cannot again be litigated between the same parties in any future lawsuit," but the dynamics of plea bargaining are such that the dropping of the two counts can hardly be said to rest upon a factual determination that the defendant did not commit the robbery or assault with intent to rob. Moreover, even the concurring Justices in *Ashe,* who preferred a considerably broader rule, acknowledged that any double jeopardy requirement that related crimes be disposed of together did not apply "where a crime is not completed or not discovered, despite diligence on the part of the police, until after the commencement of a prosecution for other crimes arising from the same transaction."

Finally, there is the case in which the government is relieved of the obligation to carry out its promise (or, in some circumstances, is entitled to the remedy of specific performance) because the defendant failed to carry out some obligation under the plea agreement beyond entering the plea. Illustrative is *U.S. v. Simmons* (1976), where part of the agreement was that the government would recommend a sentence of 15 years "in exchange for the defendants' full, complete, and truthful cooperation regarding this bank robbery." The court held that "in a plea bargain the government's obligation to make a recommendation arises only if defendant performs his obligation (in this instance, full disclosure)," but then added the important caveat that under *Santobello* "the question whether defendant did in fact fail to perform the condition precedent is an issue not to be finally determined unilaterally by the government, but only on the basis of adequate evidence by the Court." Indeed, even if the agreement expressly declared that the government had "sole discretion" to decide whether defendant had cooperated, the court which approved the bargain has a duty to inquire whether the terms have been followed, and should not permit the government to use its "sole discretion" to disregard its contractual commitments. And even assuming it is clear that the defendant has failed to perform, *Simmons* does not mean that the government will inevitably be able to forego its own obligations under the plea agreement *and* in addition hold the defendant to his plea. Illustrative is *U.S. v. Fernandez* (1992), where a plea agreement specified the sentence to be imposed as a 6–year term of imprisonment but added that if the defendant did not cooperate as specified "the agreement shall be null and void." When the defendant failed to cooperate, the prosecutor took the position that a sentence over 6 years was now possible and that defendant could not then withdraw his plea. The court disagreed, noting that the defendant "could only have reasonably understood [the above quoted language] to mean that if he failed to live up to his end of the bargain, the entire plea agreement would be null and void."

However, cases of this genre arising under the federal sentencing guidelines, which per § 5K1.1 recognize that the prosecution may make a downward departure motion because of the defendant's substantial assistance to the government, have received somewhat different treatment. This is attributable to the Supreme

Court's decision in *Wade v. U.S.* (1992), where it was held (i) that a sentencing court may not grant defendant a downward departure under § 5K1.1 in the absence of a government motion for same, and (ii) that whether to make such a motion is discretionary with the government, so that even a defendant who provides substantial assistance is not entitled to a remedy unless an unconstitutional motive underlies the government's refusal to so move. But the Court then made an important qualification, namely, that the government could sacrifice its discretion and obligate itself to move for downward departure in exchange for a plea, and cited as an example *U.S. v. Watson* (1993), where the plea agreement said that if defendant gave substantial assistance the government "would" so move. After *Wade*, it has become common procedure for federal prosecutors drafting plea agreements with a cooperation-by-defendant ingredient to specifically state therein that the government reserves the "sole discretion" whether or not to file a downward departure motion. Faced with such language, the courts have simply applied the *Wade* holding, meaning that a guilty plea defendant who enters into such an arrangement may receive concessions via downward departure, no matter what the quality and extent of his cooperation, only if the prosecutor later decides to make the requisite motion. This is, at best, an unsettling state of affairs, for under such one-sided agreements the defendant might well provide the promised substantial assistance and still end up with nothing in return. (After *United States v. Booker* (2005) made the sentencing guidelines advisory, *Wade* is still followed as to 5K1.1 departures, and thus absent a motion by the government the judge may not sentence below the statutory minimum to reflect defendant's substantial assistance, although without such a motion the judge apparently could take defendant's cooperation into account in deciding to vary beneath the advisory guidelines sentence.)

The defendant may not escape the consequences of his nonperformance merely because the quid pro quo was a concession already given up by the prosecution, such as allowing the defendant to enter a plea to a lesser offense. In *Ricketts v. Adamson* (1987), where defendant, charged with first degree murder, was allowed to plead guilty to second degree murder in exchange for his promise to testify against his confederates, and the agreement specified that if defendant refused to testify "this entire agreement is null and void and the original charge will be automatically reinstated" and the parties "returned to the positions they were in before this agreement," the Court held there was no double jeopardy barrier to vacating the second degree murder conviction and prosecuting defendant for first degree murder. This is because "the Double Jeopardy Clause * * * does not relieve a defendant from the consequences of his voluntary choice." Though that conclusion is

not objectionable, the manner in which the Court applied it in
Ricketts is troublesome. The defendant *did* testify against his
confederates and they were convicted, but after their convictions
were reversed he refused to testify a second time on the not totally
implausible contention that he had already fulfilled completely his
part of the bargain. Once the state supreme court ruled defendant's
construction of the agreement was in error, defendant offered to
testify in the pending retrial of his confederates, but the prosecution rejected that offer in favor of prosecuting defendant for first
degree murder. As the four dissenters cogently reasoned, the "logic
of the plea bargaining system requires acknowledgment and protection of the defendant's right to advance against the State a reasonable interpretation of the plea agreement." Thus, if the defendant
and state disagree as to how the agreement is to be interpreted, the
state should not be allowed to treat this as a breach by the
defendant, permitting the state to revoke the agreement; rather, at
that point "either party may seek to have the agreement construed
by the court in which the plea was entered." In light of *Ricketts,*
defense counsel would be well advised to insist that plea agreements of this type include an express provision mandating judicial
construction of it in the event of a disagreement.

(e) Remedy for Broken Bargain. Assuming now a broken
bargain not excused because of the defendant's misconduct or
subsequent events, the next question concerns the relief to which
the defendant is entitled. This is a matter of some uncertainty, for
while the Supreme Court was unequivocal in ruling in *Santobello v.
N.Y.* (1971) that there was a constitutional right to relief, that
decision is less explicit on the constitutional source of that right
and on what remedy is required under what circumstances. The
opinion of the Court, joined in by three Justices, makes reference to
the requirement that guilty pleas be "knowing and voluntary" and
says defendant was entitled to relief in the "interests of justice."
The choice of remedy was left to the state court in the first
instance, but there is an unexplained intimation that either specific
performance or plea withdrawal might be "required" by the "circumstances of the case." Justice Douglas, concurring, indicated
that the choice of remedy was itself a constitutional matter, and he
asserted that the defendant's preference should be given "considerable, if not controlling, weight." The three remaining members of
the Court were no more certain as to the source of the right. They
claimed that a breaking of the bargain constitutes "ample justification for rescinding the plea" if the defendant wishes and that if he
prefers "it may be appropriate to permit the defendant to enforce
the plea bargain."

As for the source of the right, most certainly it is not the requirement that guilty pleas be voluntary, for without regard to subsequent events a plea is either voluntary or involuntary at the time it is made. Perhaps the source is the constitutional requirement that guilty pleas be intelligent, for that requirement reflects the notion that the defendant has a constitutional interest in making an informed choice and that the state cannot mislead the defendant into making a disadvantageous choices. But if this is all there is to *Santobello,* then the intimation therein that a particular remedy might be required in certain unspecified circumstances cannot be taken seriously. By affording the defendant an opportunity to choose again on the basis of accurate information, the court fully protects the defendant's opportunity to make a meaningful choice, while the remedy of specific performance gives the defendant the full benefit of his original choice and thus suffices to vindicate his constitutional interest in deciding what course is best. This suggests another interpretation of the case: that it extends constitutional protection to the personal expectations created in defendants by plea agreements, on the notion that it is fundamentally unfair for the state to create and then destroy a defendant's expectations.

Although federal courts finding a *Santobello* violation on habeas corpus by a state prisoner ordinarily give the state court the opportunity to decide which remedy is more appropriate, federal courts ruling on claims by federal prisoners and state courts ruling on claims of state defendants rather regularly opt for the remedy of specific performance. This may be taken as some support for the protection-of-expectations theory noted above, which would generally call for such a remedy, or it may only reflect that these courts have perceived that as a policy matter specific performance is usually the most appropriate remedy, one which serves the state's interest in the continued vitality of the process of plea negotiation. Whichever is the case, clearly specific performance is usually the remedy to be preferred, which may be seen by a closer look at two situations: that in which the defendant's preference for vacatur of the plea is contested; and that in which his preference for specific performance is challenged.

Assume first a case in which the plea bargain was not kept and consequently the defendant asks that he be allowed to withdraw his plea, but the prosecution counters that withdrawal should not be permitted because it is prepared to carry out the remedy of specific performance. Four members of the Court in *Santobello* appeared to conclude that in such circumstances withdrawal of the plea and trial on the original charges should be ordered, but their explanations for this conclusion are less than compelling. Justice Douglas offered only the non sequitur that because it is the defendant's rights which were violated it must be the defendant's choice of remedy which is given preference, while the three dissenters asserted that the breaking of the bargain "undercuts the basis for the waiver of constitutional rights implicit in the plea" and thus allows those rights to be reclaimed by the defendant. But whether the constitutional basis for *Santobello* is to protect defendants from entering guilty pleas that are not intelligent or to enforce their state-created expectations, the defendant need not be given an option to rescind if the state agrees to give him the benefit of the original bargain. Both the intelligent-plea interest and the protection-of-expectations interest can be satisfied by specific performance because it gives the defendant everything on which he relied in entering the plea.

Assume now the reverse situation, where again the plea bargain was not kept but the defendant wants specific performance while the prosecution takes the position that only withdrawal of the plea should be permitted. When the breach was a failure by the prosecutor to carry out a promise that was fulfillable, then certainly the defendant's request for specific performance should be honored. This is most certainly the case when the defendant has relied on the promise to his detriment, as where a prosecutor failed to keep his promise as to what sentence recommendation he would make if the defendant first were to plead guilty and spend 60 days at a correctional center for evaluation. Though it has occasionally been held that withdrawal is the preferred remedy in the absence of such irrevocable prejudice, that position is unsound. Even absent a showing of prejudice, there is no reason why a prosecutor who has failed to keep his fulfillable plea bargain promise should be allowed to force the defendant into a withdrawal of the plea and thus, presumably, a permanent breach of the bargain. The same may be said of the case in which the breach is by the court in reneging on its earlier acceptance of a lawful plea agreement, or in which the court exceeded its authority in not permitting the prosecutor to carry through on a charge bargain.

Much more difficult are those cases in which the promise that was made by the prosecutor or some other agent of the state is "unfulfillable" in the sense that it is a commitment to produce a result not authorized by law or beyond the power of the promisor to produce. Illustrative of the latter are where the prosecutor makes commitments as to the sentence actually to be imposed, the time of release on parole, nonprosecution outside his county or district or even in another jurisdiction, nonextradition to another country, termination of civil proceedings against the defendant, or favorable action by an administrative agency. In such circumstances the court faces an unpleasant choice: order specific enforcement of the unauthorized promise and thus bind officials who took no part in the plea negotiations, or merely allow withdrawal of the guilty plea and thereby ignore defendant's reliance on the bargain. But when that reliance is nothing more than an expectation that the promise would be kept and withdrawing the plea will approximate the *status quo ante,* there is good reason to deny the defendant his desired remedy of specific performance. Otherwise there would be unnecessary encroachment upon established doctrine on the allocation of authority, such as that the prosecutor cannot bind the judge as to the sentence and cannot bind decisionmakers in another jurisdiction as to charging, sentencing, or release from incarceration. When the defendant's reliance is more substantial, then a more delicate balancing process is required. One factor that must be considered is the precise nature and extent of the detrimental reliance. If the defendant has served a period of imprisonment under the plea, has provided information to the authorities as part of the plea agreement, or has been jeopardized as to his defense by the turn of events, a court may be more willing to turn to specific enforcement even though the necessary consequence is to limit the discretion of persons who were not even parties to the plea agreement. A second factor that appears to enter into the resolution of these cases is the extent to which it is important to preserve the independence of the other agency that would be required to act in a certain way if specific performance were ordered.

When the breach was by the *defendant* and the question is what remedies are available to the *prosecution,* it is generally accepted that the prosecution has the option to either seek specific performance of the agreement or treat it as unenforceable. The latter alternative (sometimes called "cancellation") might involve voiding defendant's guilty plea, so that defendant must decide whether to plead guilty again or stand trial, or might simply involve holding the defendant to his original guilty plea without the prosecution now providing the concessions contemplated by the plea agreement the defendant breached. While the second course is proper where the defendant wants to keep his original guilty plea intact, when this is *not* the case it would seem that under ordinary contract principles the prosecution should have to (i) seek specific performance of the original agreement notwithstanding defendant's breach, or (ii) allow defendant to withdraw his guilty plea.

(f) The Withdrawn Offer. The prevailing doctrine is that the state may withdraw from a plea bargain agreement at any time prior to, but not after, the entry of the guilty plea by the defendant or other action by him constituting detrimental reliance upon the agreement (e.g., giving a self-incriminating deposition). While it has occasionally been contended on right-to-counsel and due process grounds that unless the prosecutor's plea proposal is properly conditioned it is enforceable by a defendant who, prior to the prosecutor's withdrawal of the offer, had neither entered a guilty plea nor relied to his detriment on the bargain, a unanimous Supreme Court rejected that approach in *Mabry v. Johnson* (1984). As for the right to counsel argument, the Court stated it failed "to see how an accused could reasonably attribute the prosecutor's change of heart to his counsel any more than he could have blamed counsel had the trial judge chosen to reject the agreed-upon recommendation, or, for that matter, had he gone to trial and been convicted." Moreover, there was no guilty plea obtained in violation of due process. When his agreement to accept the prosecution's offer of a 21–year concurrent sentence for a murder plea resulted in that offer being withdrawn as "a mistake" and replaced by an offer of a 21–year consecutive sentence, the defendant accepted the second offer after the trial began. Noting that this plea "was in no sense induced by the prosecutor's withdrawn offer," the Court concluded that defendant's "inability to enforce the prosecutor's offer is without constitutional significance" because that offer "did not impair the voluntariness or intelligence of his guilty plea." (Because there was neither a guilty plea *nor* any other form of detrimental reliance in *Mabry*, that decision does not address the question whether reliance short of a plea or other waiver of constitutional rights would be the basis for a due process objection.) As for the prosecutor's possible negligence or culpability in making and withdrawing the first offer, the Court deemed that irrelevant because the due process clause "is not a code of ethics for prosecutors" but is concerned "with the manner in which persons are deprived of their liberty."

(g) The Unrealized Expectation. As a general matter, it may be said that a guilty plea defendant is not entitled to relief merely because the sentence which he received is greater than he had hoped or anticipated would be imposed in his case, and this is so even if the defendant's hope or anticipation was attributable to comments made by his attorney (unless the defense attorney's "prediction" was stated in more definite terms and was significantly inaccurate, in which case the defendant might prevail on the ground that he was denied the effective assistance of counsel). Such cases must be distinguished from those in which the defendant is led to believe, most likely because of comments made by defense counsel, that a plea agreement has actually been reached with the prosecutor or the judge, but in fact there is no such agreement and the defendant does not thereafter receive the concessions contemplated under the nonexistent plea agreement. Because the defendant is entitled to credit his attorney's representation as to the fact of such an agreement, he is entitled to relief if his guilty plea was induced by such a representation. But if the defendant had a belief that there existed a plea bargain including certain concessions he did not thereafter receive, but that belief was erroneous and was based upon comments by the defense attorney or others not specifically stating that a plea agreement with those concessions had been reached, the prevailing view is that the defendant must in addition show that his belief was a reasonable one under the circumstances.

(h) Admission of Statements Made During Bargaining. The modern trend to hold inadmissible the defendant's offer to plead guilty, the plea agreement or statements made in the course of plea negotiations when no guilty plea is subsequently entered or if entered is withdrawn makes obvious sense, for a contrary rule would discourage plea negotiations and agreements. The current federal rule on this subject covers only statements made by the defendant in court when a plea is tendered or during plea discussions with the prosecutor, on the theory that confrontations between suspects and law enforcement agents are best resolved by that body of law dealing with police interrogations. Because this view fails to provide protection for defendants who plea bargain under the reasonable belief that the agent has bargaining authority, some states follow the broader view.

The rule regarding statements made during plea negotiations must be distinguished from that concerning statements made subsequent to a plea later withdrawn, as in *Hutto v. Ross* (1976). The holding below was that defendant's confession, given subsequent to a negotiated plea agreement from which the defendant later withdrew, was involuntary because it would not have been made "but for the plea bargaining." Noting that "causation in that sense has never been the test of voluntariness," the Supreme Court concluded: "The existence of the bargain may well have entered into respondent's decision to give a statement, but counsel made it clear to respondent that he could enforce the terms of the plea bargain whether or not he confessed. The confession thus does not appear to have been the result of 'any direct or implied promises' or any coercion on the part of the prosecution, and was not involuntary." A different result has been reached with respect to post-plea statements made by the defendant in compliance with a commitment made in the plea bargain or on the representation of defense counsel that they were necessary to comply with the plea agreement.

Assuming now a statement made during plea discussions under circumstances that would as a general matter make it inadmissible against the defendant, a question may arise as to whether the rule of inadmissibility is absolute. What, for example, if the statement is offered for the limited purpose of impeachment? Although it has been argued by analogy to *Harris v. N.Y.* (1971), holding admissible for impeachment purposes a voluntary statement obtained in violation of *Miranda,* that the answer should be yes, the courts have quite properly rejected that argument. *Harris* has no application in a plea bargaining context in which a waiver of the privilege against self-incrimination is an aspect of the plea obtained by active participation of the prosecution. A contrary rule in the plea bargaining context, even if constitutionally permissible, would be unwise, for it would have a strong chilling effect on plea negotiations. But the rule of inadmissibility is *not* absolute in another sense, for in *U.S. v. Mezzanatto* (1995) the Court held the aforementioned federal plea-statement rule does not "depart from the presumption of waivability" that exists as to "legal rights generally, and evidentiary provisions specifically"; hence, the Court concluded, a defendant at the outset of plea discussions could agree that any statement he made could be used to impeach any contradictory testimony if the case went to trial.

§ 13.3   Plea Negotiation Responsibilities of the Attorneys and Judge

(a) **Right to Counsel During Plea Bargaining.** The Sixth Amendment right to counsel in criminal cases applies not only at the criminal trial, but also at other "critical stages" of the criminal process occurring at or after the point at which that right has "attached." Unquestionably, this means that the defendant has a right to counsel at the arraignment, the occasion upon which the defendant is called upon to enter his plea. As for a right to counsel at a plea bargaining session with the prosecutor or his agents, the first question is whether such an activity is properly characterized as one of the "critical stages," which the Supreme Court described in *Rothgery v. Gillespie County* (2008) as "proceedings between an individual and agents of the State (whether 'formal or informal, in court or out' * * *) that amount to 'trial-like confrontations,' at which counsel would help the accused 'in coping with legal problems or . . . meeting his adversary.' " The courts have consistently answered that in the affirmative. As for attachment of the Sixth Amendment right, the Court in *Rothgery* pegged commencement to " 'the initiation of adversary judicial proceedings—whether by way of formal charge, preliminary hearing, indictment, information, or arraignment,' " with the term arraignment is this context referring to the defendant's initial appearance before a judicial officer, the point at which the magistrate informs the defendant of the charges against him and sets the terms of pretrial release, without regard to whether a "public prosecutor (as distinct from a police officer) [was] aware of that initial proceeding or involved in its conduct." The overwhelming majority of plea bargaining sessions occur after the Sixth Amendment right has attached, and consequently as to such sessions the defendant is indeed constitutionally entitled to the assistance of counsel at that time. But if, as has become increasingly common under the federal Sentencing Guidelines, a plea bargaining session involves a pre-initial appearance prospective defendant not yet charged, it is unfortunate but true that the prosecutor may reach an agreement directly with that unrepresented prospective defendant without offending the Sixth Amendment.

As for waiver of the constitutional right to counsel in the plea bargaining context, it has been argued that such waiver should not be permitted because (unlike the possible tactical advantage at trial) there is nothing for a defendant to gain by being unrepresented in the guilty plea context. This may explain why a few jurisdictions, at least in the past, have taken the position that felony defendants may not plead guilty without counsel. But in light of the Supreme Court's recognition in *Faretta v. Cal.* (1975) of a constitutional right to proceed pro se, which presumably is applicable in the guilty plea context as well, it appears that waiver must be permitted. Waiver of counsel, to be effective, must be "intelligent and competent." A defendant who is contemplating waiver of his constitutional right to counsel, *Faretta* says, "should be made aware of the dangers and disadvantages of self-representation," which would appear to require an especially careful procedure in a guilty plea context because of defendant's likely ignorance of what assistance counsel can provide even if there will be no trial. But in *Iowa v. Tovar* (2004), the Court concluded that the "constitutional requirement is satisfied when the trial court informs the accused of the nature of the charges against him, of his right to be counseled regarding his plea, and of the range of allowable punishments attendant upon the entry of a guilty plea," so that a valid Sixth Amendment waiver does *not* necessitate a warning to the defendant that waiver of counsel in deciding whether to plead guilty (i) entails the risk that a viable defense will be overlooked and (ii) deprives him of the opportunity to obtain an independent opinion on whether it is wise to plead guilty.

(b) Effective Assistance by Defense Counsel. The Sixth Amendment right of a guilty plea defendant to is to the *effective* assistance of counsel, which is to be determined not by a hindsight assessment of whether the attorney's actions and conduct were right or wrong, but rather by an inquiry into whether they fell "within the range of competence demanded of attorneys in criminal cases." There is an additional requirement that the defendant have been prejudiced by the ineffective assistance, which means in a guilty plea context that the defendant must show "a reasonable probability that, but for counsel's errors, he would not have pleaded guilty and would have insisted on going to trial." If the ineffective assistance resulted in the defendant *rejecting* a plea bargain and not pleading guilty, then, of course, the prejudice question is whether, absent the ineffective assistance, the defendant *would* have entered a guilty plea.

As for the proper remedy in the latter situation, several courts have held that the defendant must now be given another opportunity to accept the previously-tendered plea bargain. Some courts, however, limit the remedy to a new trial (hardly a satisfactory result, as a new trial does not remedy the lost opportunity to accept the plea bargain), and some others have even concluded that if the defendant received a fair trial after counsel's misadvice, then there has been no prejudice.

The better view is that it is the responsibility of the defense attorney to conduct a prompt investigation of the circumstances of the case and to explore all avenues leading to facts relevant to the merits of the case and the penalty in the event of conviction. This responsibility to investigate is related to defense counsel's broader obligation to confer with his client and to give him advice. It is essential that the attorney advise the defendant of the available options and possible consequences, though there is not complete agreement on the extent of a defense attorney's responsibilities in this regard, e.g., when, if ever, a defense attorney is responsible for alerting an alien defendant of the fact that conviction could result in deportation. But in any event, gross misinformation from defense counsel about some collateral consequence amounts to ineffective assistance if the defendant based his decision to plead guilty on that advice. It is quite proper for the attorney to express a view on the appropriate course of action, including whether a particular plea appears to be desirable, but it is for the client to decide what plea should be entered. Courts have held that defense counsel coerced defendant's plea where he threatened to withdraw from the case if a guilty plea was not entered and where the lawyer's advice was so strongly worded as to constitute a threat.

Sometimes the question is whether the particular recommendation of defense counsel constitutes ineffective assistance under the circumstances of the case. For example, what of a recommendation to accept a plea bargain made to a defendant who has asserted his innocence? One view is that it is unreasonable for counsel to recommend a guilty plea to a defendant without first cautioning him that, no matter what, he should not plead guilty unless he believed himself guilty, for our judicial system has so many safeguards that it may not be assumed that an innocent person will be convicted. The contrary view is that if a fair assessment of the prosecution's case indicates a substantial likelihood of conviction and severe sanctions, then defense counsel should not be barred from recommending the negotiated plea route merely because the defendant might in fact be innocent or because the defendant cannot bring himself to acknowledge his guilt. The latter position draws support from *N.C. v. Alford* (1970) (see § 13.4(f)), where the Supreme Court ruled it was constitutionally permissible to accept a guilty plea from a defendant who claimed to be innocent if there was a "strong factual basis for the plea."

Where the defense attorney has failed to communicate to the defendant a plea offer, it has been held that just as a defendant has the right to make a decision to plead not guilty, he also has the right to make the decision to plead guilty, which has been denied if his attorney has not informed him of the concessions offered. As for whether in the absence of such overtures by the prosecutor defense counsel is obligated to sound out the prosecutor as to what concessions would be granted in exchange for a plea of guilty by his client, one view is that at least when the lawyer concludes that under controlling law and the evidence, a conviction is probable, he should so advise the accused and seek his consent to initiate plea discussions. Another position is that such plea discussions should be considered the norm and that failure to seek them is excusable only when defense counsel concludes that sound reasons exist for not doing so, but just when a failure of defense counsel to take the initiative in this way constitutes ineffective assistance is not entirely clear.

Yet another aspect of the Sixth Amendment right to the effective assistance of counsel is that defendant is entitled to be represented by an attorney who is not hampered by a conflict of interest. Joint representation is not per se a violation of the constitutional guarantee of effective assistance by counsel, but conflicts most frequently arise out of such arrangements. Illustrative are these situations: (1) where there was a "package deal" in which defense counsel could obtain a favorable disposition for one client only if the other defendants in the case, also represented by him, also plead guilty; (2) where defense counsel was representing one client who implicated others in the hope of favorable treatment, and also one of those implicated, whose plea of guilty as recommended by counsel served to build a record of cooperation by the first client; (3) where defense counsel, representing two persons charged with joint possession of marijuana, stressed the relatively minor role of one defendant and consequently made the other appear more culpable; and (4) where defense counsel advised against a plea bargain contemplating the defendant would then testify at the trial of another defendant, also represented by this attorney.

If a defense attorney has brought about a negotiated plea, does he nonetheless have an obligation to apprise the defendant of his right to appeal following his guilty plea? At least sometimes, for the Court in *Roe v. Flores–Ortega* (2000) held that an obligation to give such advice exists when either (1) the defendant has reasonably demonstrated to counsel his or her interest in filing an appeal, or (2) a rational defendant would want to appeal under the circumstances. A "highly relevant factor" in making this determination, the Court added, is that there was a plea of guilty, for "a guilty plea reduces the scope of potentially appealable issues and * * * may indicate that the defendant seeks an end to judicial proceedings."

(c) The Prosecutor's Bargaining Tactics. In considering the prosecutor's role in the plea negotiation process, a logical first inquiry is whether there is some obligation upon the prosecutor to engage in bargaining with defendants. The courts have rather consistently answered in the negative. As the Supreme Court declared in *Weatherford v. Bursey* (1977), "there is no constitutional right to plea bargain; the prosecutor need not do so if he prefers to go to trial. It is a novel argument that constitutional rights are infringed by trying the defendant rather than accepting his plea of guilty." This is because plea bargaining is an aspect of the prosecutor's broad charging discretion whereunder he is permitted to decide when and whether to institute criminal proceedings, or what precise charge shall be made, or whether to dismiss a proceeding once brought. Of course, the prosecutor's refusal to bargain could be so arbitrary as to constitute a denial of equal protection of the laws under the Fourteenth Amendment, but a defendant is likely to prevail on such a claim only rarely and in extraordinary circumstances.

If a prosecutor were to bring a greater charge against the defendant than is supported by the evidence in order to increase his plea bargaining leverage, this would unquestionably be improper. More controversial, however, is the not uncommon practice of "overcharging" in another sense, as where the prosecutor files a felony charge supported by the evidence in the hope of inducing a plea to a misdemeanor when, as a matter of general prosecutive policy, the case would actually be tried only on a misdemeanor charge. Although the Supreme Court held in *Bordenkircher v. Hayes* (1978) that such conduct was not unconstitutional, there is a division of opinion as to whether this charging practice is ethical and proper.

Yet another practice a prosecutor may engage in during plea negotiations is some degree of "bluffing" concerning the strength of his case against the defendant at the present time. The range of possibilities here is substantial, all the way from withholding exculpatory evidence to not volunteering the immediate unavailability of a certain witness, though most prosecutors feel obligated to produce evidence indicating factual innocence. The Supreme Court, when dealing with cases which *had* gone to trial, has held that it is a violation of due process for a prosecutor to withhold favorable evidence whenever "there is a reasonable probability that, had the evidence been disclosed to the defense, the result of the proceeding would have been different," but in *U.S. v. Ruiz* (2002) concluded that at least *some* of the constitutionally-based disclosure requirements existing as to those cases do not likewise apply to guilty plea cases. In *Ruiz*, the prosecutor offered the defendant a plea bargain, by which she could have obtained a reduction in sentence, but she rejected the bargain because she would not agree, as the plea agreement necessitated, to waive her right to receive "impeachment information relating to any informants or other witnesses" as well as her right to receive information supporting any affirmative defense. The defendant later entered a guilty plea without any plea agreement, and then appealed when she did not obtain a reduction in sentence like that the prosecutor had included in the rejected plea agreement. The court of appeals concluded that the prosecutor's disclosure obligations at trial were equally applicable in a guilty plea context, and that consequently the prosecutor's proposed plea agreement was unlawful, but the Supreme Court disagreed.

In holding that the Constitution does not require the pre-guilty plea disclosure of impeachment information, the Court reasoned: (1) that "impeachment information is special in relation to the *fairness of a trial*, not in respect to whether a plea is *voluntary*," for rights may be waived (as by guilty plea) even by those who "may not know the *specific detailed* consequences" of invoking them; (2) that the Court's prior cases make it clear that a court may "accept a guilty plea, with its accompanying waiver of various constitutional rights, despite various forms of misapprehensions under which a defendant might labor"; and (3) that, as to the due process considerations of the value of the purported right and its adverse impact on the government's interests, it may be concluded (a) that the risk was slight that "in the absence of impeachment information, innocent individuals, accused of crimes, will plead guilty," considering the "guilty-plea safeguards" in Fed.R.Crim.P. 11 and the fact that the proposed plea agreement expressly incorporated a continuing duty on the prosecutor to provide "any information establishing the factual innocence of the defendant," while (b) "premature disclosure of Government witness information * * * could 'disrupt ongoing investigations' and expose prospective witnesses to serious harm." The Court then concluded that most of the foregoing reasons also applied to information regarding "affirmative defenses." Because it was the above-stated "considerations, taken together," that the Court felt supported its result, *Ruiz* hardly settles what the prosecutor's disclosure obligations are as to other types of withheld information.

In further considering the impact of *Ruiz* upon the prosecutor's disclosure responsibilities in the guilty plea context, as compared to the trial context, it is necessary to take into account the fact that a violation of the due process disclosure requirements, when occurring in the former context, has sometimes been characterized in terms of a guilty plea constitutionally defective because not intelligently made. Especially if, as the Supreme Court once intimated, for a guilty plea to be valid the defense must be aware of "the actual value of any commitments made," which is not possible if there exists a significant misperception of the likelihood that the prosecution could succeed at trial, then it may be that the prosecutor is obligated to make disclosures during plea bargaining beyond those otherwise mandated, in order to satisfy the intelligent plea requirement. To put the matter somewhat differently, if (as seems to be indicated from the Supreme Court's decisions) the legitimacy of the negotiated plea process rests upon the consent of defendants to surrender their chance of acquittal at trial in exchange for concessions, then it is essential that the defendant have had a meaningful opportunity to make a rational prediction of what the outcome at trial would be. From this would derive a broad pre-plea duty to disclose to the defendant all information bearing on the likelihood of trial conviction.

While *Ruiz* certainly indicates that there is no obligation on the prosecutor to disclose "all information" bearing on the likely outcome at trial, *Ruiz* does *not* assert that the prosecutor can withhold important information from the defendant when, as a consequence, the defendant will be misled into thinking that the "concessions" offered by the prosecutor are valuable when, in fact, they are not. *Ruiz*, after all, was *not* a case involving a defendant who *had* accepted a plea agreement and who *had* in fact been misled because such information was withheld. Consequently, that decision ought not be viewed as foreclosing a defendant's claim that a prosecutor offered illusory concessions and then concealed their true character by withholding information from the defendant. In any event, there is much to be said for more openness in plea negotiations; it would permit the defendant to play a more meaningful role in the negotiation process, produce fairer bargains, and minimize the risk of duress and mistake.

Another question about the prosecutor's bargaining procedures, concerning charge bargaining, is how far afield from the actual offense committed the prosecutor may roam in finding a charge carrying with it what the parties agree would be an appropriate sentence. When states have specifically addressed this question by statute or court rule, they have said that it is sufficient that the lesser offense to which defendant is allowed to plead is "related" (or, "reasonably related") to defendant's actual conduct, meaning it is not necessary that the offense be either included within or a lesser degree of the offense committed.

(d) Judicial Involvement in Negotiations. Some years ago there was a general consensus that trial judges should not participate in the pretrial negotiations which influence a great many defendants to plead guilty. But as a matter of current practice, considerable variation is to be found. Four different kinds of plea bargaining systems have been identified: (1) no judicial involvement of any kind, (2) involvement through unannounced but known sentencing breaks to those who plead guilty, (3) involvement by the judge in sentencing discussions in an occasional, vague, and inconsistent manner, and (4) direct participation in which the judge makes a sentence commitment before the defendant pleads. There is also considerable variation among jurisdictions as to the legal position on judicial involvement in plea negotiations. Some jurisdictions have by statute or court rule absolutely prohibited such involvement, and it is claimed that these provisions have in fact substantially deterred judicial involvement. These provisions mean the sentencing judge is to take no part whatever in any discussion or communication regarding the sentence to be imposed prior to the entry of a plea of guilty or conviction, or at least the submission to him of a plea agreement. The law in some states gives express approval to at least limited involvement by the judge in plea negotiations, and further movement in this direction can be expected. This reflects growing acceptance of the view that the "evils" of judicial participation are not as substantial as had once been commonly assumed and that they are, in any event, outweighed by certain benefits that can be achieved by having the judge more actively involved in the negotiation process. Judicial guidance is more likely to pass muster if it is limited in nature and occurs only after the parties tendered a plea bargain to the court that the court found unacceptable.

The reasons often given for keeping the judge out of the negotiation process are: (1) that his participation would have a coercive effect upon the defendant because of the unequal positions of the judge and the accused, one with the power to commit to prison and the other deeply concerned to avoid prison, to which some respond that the prosecutor has many means not available to the judge of putting pressure upon the defendant, and thus the disparity of positions may be even greater between prosecutor and defendant than between judge and defendant; (2) that if a judge was involved in the bargaining but the negotiations did not result in a guilty plea, then it would be difficult for that judge to conduct a fair trial thereafter, to which some respond that any actual or perceived risk of unfairness could be overcome by having the judge who participated in the bargaining recuse himself from the trial; (3) that such activity is inconsistent with the judge's responsibilities at the arraignment, to which some respond that the judge's presence at the negotiations rather than his after-the-fact inquiry into them provides greater assurance of voluntariness; (4) that judicial participation to the extent of promising a certain sentence is inconsistent with the theory behind the use of the presentence investigation report, to which some respond that this problem can be solved by ordering the preparation of a presentence report prior to the initiation of plea bargaining, as is the practice in some jurisdictions; and (5) that the procedure leads defendants to think of the judge as just one more official to be bought off, to which some respond that it is better for judges to administer the system than to leave it entirely to prosecutors.

Because the reasons given for nonparticipation in plea negotiations by the judiciary are not entirely without merit and substance, another important consideration is that of what is to be gained by greater judicial involvement. These benefits have been identified: (1) it would restore the sentencing function to the judiciary, in contrast to the prevailing practice that causes some judges to ratify agreements they would not have formulated had they participated in the negotiations; (2) it would facilitate the flow of information relevant to sentencing to the judge; (3) it would remove the cloak of uncertainty whereby the defendant is required to plead in the dark in the sense of not knowing whether the judge will grant the concessions the prosecutor has promised to seek; (4) it would cause the prosecutor to open his file and to freely discuss the strength of his case; (5) it would ensure that the various sentencing provisions applicable are discussed and understood; and (6) it would permit the judge to perform as an effective check on prosecutorial power, police behavior, and defense counsel effectiveness, and thus equalize the opportunity of all defendants to negotiate.

(e) Judicial Evaluation of Contemplated Concessions. While the judge is under no obligation to grant the contemplated concessions merely because the parties are agreeable, just how much "consideration" should be given to the disposition agreed to by the prosecutor and just how "independent" the judge should be in these circumstances is a most difficult issue, seldom addressed in the cases. Rather unique is *U.S. v. Ammidown* (1973), where defendant appealed his first degree murder conviction, based upon proof that he hired the man who killed his wife, because the trial was necessitated by the judge's rejection of a plea bargain contemplating defendant would enter a plea to second degree murder and testify against the killer. In reversing and remanding for acceptance of a plea to second degree murder, the court seemed to view the judge as having a rather limited function to perform with respect to charge reduction bargains. Noting that this was "a matter in which the primary responsibility, obviously, is that of the prosecuting attorney," the court concluded the "question is not what the judge would do if he were the prosecuting attorney, but whether he can say that the action of the prosecuting attorney is such a departure from sound prosecutorial principle as to mark it an abuse of prosecutorial discretion." As for "protection of the sentencing authority reserved to the judge," the court declared "that the judge is free to condemn the prosecutor's agreement as a trespass on judicial authority only in a blatant and extreme case." But now, as elaborated earlier (see § 13.1(h)), federal trial judges have somewhat greater authority in this respect, as the Sentencing Guidelines permit a judge to accept a plea agreement including a government commitment to dismiss or not bring certain charges only "if the court determines, for reasons stated in the record, that the remaining charges adequately reflect the seriousness of the actual offense behavior and that accepting the agreement will not undermine the statutory purposes of sentencing or the sentencing guidelines."

If the plea bargain agreed to by the prosecution and the defendant were to deal directly with sentence concessions, rather than charge concessions as in *Ammidown,* it is beyond dispute that the trial judge is in a quite different position. (This is particularly true in the federal system, where the judge can decline to even consider contemplated sentence concessions, or may, except as to a type (C) plea agreement, grant more generous sentencing concessions than are recommended in the agreement.) Critics of *Ammidown* point out that to distinguish between charge bargains and sentence bargains in determining the range of the judge's discretion in deciding whether the contemplated concessions should be granted assumes a difference that does not exist, as the primary significance of the charge-reduction process plainly lies in its effect on the sentence the defendant will receive. This being so, the argument proceeds, *Ammidown* is in error because it, in effect, amounts to a formal recognition of the prosecutor's authority over sentencing. Decisions are to be found on both the state and federal level accepting this latter view and thus recognizing broader discretion in the judge to determine whether a charge bargain with sentencing consequences should be approved.

(f) Responsibilities to the Victim. The victims' rights movement has given rise to two common requirements: (1) that the prosecutor consult with the victim about any contemplated plea bargain; and (2) that the judge receiving the plea first allow the victim to communicate to the court his views about the bargain. The provisions on prosecutor/victim consultation often leave something to be desired, given the combined impact of failures to specify (i) that the consultation is to be about plea bargain, (ii) that the consultation should include the victim stating his views about a possible disposition, and (iii) that the consultation is not about a deal already finalized. The victim's right to confer has proved difficult to enforce, although a few states require the judge, before receiving the defendant's guilty plea, to make inquiries of the prosecutor showing that the prosecutor has complied with his obligations under the victims' rights laws. The thrust of the prosecution consultation provisions is that the prosecutor is obligated to consider the stated views of the victim, but is entitled in the final analysis to reject them.

The victim's right to be heard at the guilty plea hearing belongs to the victim and not the state, and thus cannot be plea bargained away without the victim's consent. Absent such consent, the prosecutor's promise in the plea agreement to forego certain arguments with respect to the sentence cannot be construed as covering arguments thereafter presented independently by the victim. If a victim's right to be heard is violated, this is unlikely to provide a basis for later reopening the plea hearing, as victims' rights provisions commonly provide that failure of a victim to receive all his rights does not invalidate any agreement between the state and defendant, any plea, sentence, conviction or judgment, or, indeed, any decision or any disposition whatsoever. Absent such a provision, double jeopardy considerations would come into play, certainly after sentencing and perhaps as well merely after the plea and plea bargain have been accepted.

§ 13.4   Receiving the Defendant's Plea

(a) Arraignment; Pleading Alternatives. When the defendant is called upon to enter his plea at arraignment, he may enter a plea of (1) not guilty, (2) guilty, (3) guilty but mentally ill (in a few jurisdictions where such a plea permits a sentenced defendant to receive mental health treatment), (4) not guilty by reason of insanity (in a few jurisdictions where such a plea is a prerequisite to the presentation of an insanity defense at trial), or (5) nolo contendere (in the federal system and about half of the states). A plea of nolo contendere—sometimes referred to as a plea of non vult contendere or of non vult—is simply a device by which the defendant may assert that he does not want to contest the issue of guilt or innocence. Such a plea may not be entered as a matter of right, but only with the consent of the court. Although the prevailing view is that the consent of the prosecutor is not also required, it is common practice for the court to determine the views of the prosecutor and to give them considerable weight in deciding whether to accept the nolo plea.

Although some minor variations are to be found from jurisdiction to jurisdiction, a plea of nolo contendere usually has the following significance: (1) Unlike a plea of guilty or a conviction following a plea of not guilty, a plea of nolo contendere may not be put into evidence in a subsequent civil action as proof of the fact that the defendant committed the offense to which he entered the plea. (2) Judgment following entry of a nolo contendere plea is a conviction, and may be admitted as such in other proceedings where the fact of conviction has legal significance (e.g., to apply multiple offender penalty provisions, to deny or revoke a license because of conviction, or to claim double jeopardy in a subsequent prosecution). (3) When a nolo contendere plea is accepted, it has essentially the same effect in that case as a guilty plea. The procedures for receiving the plea are the same, the defendant may receive the same sentence, and the nolo plea is like a guilty plea in terms of its finality, its effect as a waiver of claims unrelated to the plea, and the circumstances in which withdrawal of the plea would be permitted.

In the material that follows, the concern is with what procedures are appropriate when a judge conducts an arraignment at which the defendant enters a plea of guilty or nolo contendere. Statutes or rules of court often prescribe a set of procedures for such a situation. At least some of those procedures are constitutionally required, though it remains unclear in many respects just how much of the usual plea-receiving process is constitutionally mandated.

(b) Determining Voluntariness of Plea and Competency of Defendant to Plead. When a defendant tenders a plea of guilty or nolo contendere in court at arraignment, one important responsibility of the court is to determine whether the plea is voluntary. Consistent with the Supreme Court's standard as to what constitutes a voluntary plea, this means the court will inquire whether the tendered plea was the result of any threats or promises. At an earlier time, when the legitimacy of plea bargaining was in doubt, the general practice was not to reveal in court that a bargain had been struck, but today the prevailing practice is for the voluntariness inquiry to include a determination of whether a plea agreement has been reached and, if so, what it is. Depending upon the nature of the agreement, the judge will then advise the defendant of the effect of the agreement. The voluntariness determination does not include, as a matter of course, an inquiry into the defendant's competency to plead. However, in much the same way that a trial judge has a constitutional responsibility to act upon circumstances suggesting a defendant is not competent to stand trial, a judge must defer acceptance of defendant's guilty or nolo plea whenever he has a reasonable ground to doubt the defendant's competence. Then he must put into motion the process whereby the defendant's mental condition may be inquired into and determined. In *Godinez v. Moran* (1993), the Court held the standard for competence to stand trial—whether the defendant "has sufficient present ability to consult with his lawyer with a reasonable degree of rational understanding, and whether he has a rational as well as factual understanding of the proceedings against him"—also applies in this context. Thus the Court rejected a lower court holding that in a guilty plea context a defendant's competency was to be tested by the higher standard of whether he had "the capacity for 'reasoned choice' among the alternatives available to him." In support of a single standard for both trial and guilty plea cases, the Court stressed that a "defendant who stands trial is likely to be presented with choices that entail relinquishment of the same rights that are relinquished by a defendant who pleads guilty" (e.g., to jury trial, right of confrontation, privilege against self-incrimination).

(c) **Determining Understanding of Charge.** Yet another responsibility of the judge at an arraignment at which a guilty or nolo plea is tendered is to determine that the defendant understands the charge to which he is pleading. In federal court, "the court must address the defendant personally in open court" and "must inform the defendant of, and determine that the defendant understands, * * * the nature of each charge to which the defendant is pleading." Similar requirements are to be found in state procedure. As the Supreme Court explained in *Henderson v. Morgan* (1976), a plea of guilty "cannot support a judgment of guilt unless it was voluntary in a constitutional sense. And clearly the plea could not be voluntary in the sense that it constituted an intelligent admission that he committed the offense unless the defendant received 'real notice of the true nature of the charge against him, the first and most universally recognized requirement of due process.' "

The better practice is for the judge to inform the defendant of the nature and elements of the offense to which the plea is offered, that is, the acts and mental state and attendant circumstances that the prosecution would have to prove in order to establish guilt at trial. However, *Henderson* indicates that the constitutional requirement does not in all instances go this far. The defendant there was indicted for first degree murder; his attorneys unsuccessfully sought to have the charge reduced to manslaughter, but were able to obtain a bargained plea to second degree murder; the attorneys did not tell defendant that the new charge had a required element of intent to kill; and no reference was made to this element at the time of the defendant's plea. While the Court concluded that this oversight constituted a violation of due process where, as in the instant case, there was no indication that the defendant was otherwise aware that the offense to which he was pleading had an intent-to-kill element, a cautionary footnote stated: "There is no need in this case to decide whether notice of the true nature, or substance, of a charge always requires a description of every element of the offense; we assume it does not. Nevertheless, intent is such a critical element of the offense of second-degree murder that notice of that element is required."

Just what makes an element "critical" within the meaning of *Henderson* is far from clear, though it appears that the Court in that case deemed the "design to effect the death of the person killed" critical because it was the element which differentiated the offense of second degree murder from that of manslaughter. Lower courts, in declaring a certain element to be critical in the *Henderson* sense, have often rested this conclusion upon the fact that the omitted or unexplained element was one elevating the degree and seriousness of the crime to which the plea was offered above some other offense. Courts have also taken into account whether or not the charge is a self-explanatory legal term or so simple in meaning that it can be expected or assumed that a lay person understands it. With regard to possible affirmative defenses, the judge is not obligated to mention or explain them unless made aware of facts that would constitute such a defense.

Even if the defendant was presumptively informed of the charge sufficiently via the indictment, a constitutional violation of the notice requirement may occur if prior to defendant's plea the trial court *mis*informs the defendant regarding an element of the offense. Due process is denied only if the defendant was actually unaware of the nature of the charge. Thus, essential to the result in *Henderson* was the fact that defendant's attorneys did not tell him that intent to kill was required for second degree murder or "explain to him that his plea would be an admission of that fact." On the other hand, the Court asserted in *Bradshaw v. Stumpf* (2005), where "a defendant is represented by competent counsel, the court usually may rely on that counsel's assurance that the defendant has been properly informed of the nature and elements of the charge to which he is pleading guilty." *Henderson* adds that "even without such an express representation, it may be appropriate to presume that in most cases defense counsel routinely explain the nature of the offense in sufficient detail to give the accused notice of what he is being asked to admit." Though lower courts have sometimes entertained such a presumption in order to defeat a defendant's *Henderson* claim, this is a highly questionable result.

Yet another troublesome aspect of the Court's opinion in *Henderson* is the assumption that if a defendant admits facts amounting to an element of the offense to which he entered his plea, then he cannot complain about not being told that the offense contained that element. From this, lower courts have understandably concluded that factual statements or admissions by the defendant necessarily implying the existence of unexplained elements of the crime are sufficient. To the extent that the due process requirement of notice of the charge is grounded upon a need, absent some other showing of guilt, for defendant to admit that he committed the crime, this is an understandable result. But it would seem that the notice requirement serves another important function, one of particular significance in a system authorizing plea bargaining: it ensures that the defendant understands that if he pleads not guilty the state will be required to prove certain facts, thus permitting the defendant to make an intelligent judgment as to whether he would be better off accepting the tendered concessions or chancing acquittal if the prosecution cannot prove those facts beyond a reasonable doubt. If that is so—which would seem to be what the Supreme Court meant when it said in *McCarthy v. U.S.* (1969) that a guilty plea cannot be voluntary "unless the defendant possesses an understanding of the law in relation to the facts"—then admissions by the defendant are not an adequate substitute for advice from the court as to the elements of the offense.

(d) Determining Understanding of Possible Consequences. If the defendant offers a plea of guilty or nolo contendere at arraignment, yet another responsibility of the judge is to advise the defendant of certain consequences that could follow if the plea is accepted. The conventional wisdom is that this obligation extends to those consequences that are "direct" but not to those that are only "collateral" in nature, a distinction sometimes said to turn on whether the result represents a definite, immediate and largely automatic effect on the range of the defendant's punishment. That is a useful albeit not foolproof test, and considerable variation is to be found in both federal and state cases on the direct-collateral dichotomy.

Matters concerning the nature of the sentence that could be imposed are most likely to be viewed as direct consequences. Traditionally, the emphasis in the case law has been upon the requirement that the judge inform the defendant of the maximum possible punishment, which under the better view includes punishment possible by virtue either of the sentence provisions of the statute under which the charge is brought or of other statutes that authorize added penalties because of special circumstances in the case (as where a statute provides for added punishment of persons who commit crimes while armed). But the current requirement in federal practice is that the judge advise the defendant not only of "any maximum possible penalty, including imprisonment, fine, and term of supervised release," but also "any mandatory minimum penalty," and several states have adopted comparable requirements. It has also been suggested that the defendant should be expressly warned in multiple charge situations of the possibility of consecutive sentences, but the cases reflect a split of authority on this point. The courts are even less demanding with respect to possible elaboration of how low the sentence might be; it has been held that the defendant need not be told that some of the multiple charges might be merged for sentencing purposes or that there is an included offense carrying a lesser penalty of which he might be convicted were he to stand trial.

As for the collateral consequences of which the defendant need not be warned, they include such matters as the possible evidentiary use of defendant's plea in later proceedings, the diminished reputation or other adverse social consequences that may follow conviction, loss of the right to vote, loss of a passport and the opportunity to travel abroad, loss of the right to possess a firearm, and loss of public employment, a business license or driver's license. The majority view is that deportation is a collateral consequence and that consequently an alien defendant is not entitled to be advised by the judge of that consequence, but some states (often by statute) view deportation as such a serious consequence that the alien defendant is entitled to be aware of it before entering his plea.

If a judge fails to advise the defendant of certain direct consequences of his plea and thus violates the obligation imposed upon him by statute, court rule, or court decision, does it follow that this failure amounts to a violation of due process? Although some courts have answered in the affirmative, the prevailing view is to the contrary, which accords with the Supreme Court's position on the matter. Thus, while due process might be violated because of the failure of the judge taking the plea to tell defendant of the maximum sentence or any mandatory minimum sentence, the constitutional issue can be resolved only by considering other matters. Certainly there is no due process violation if the defendant was otherwise aware of the sentencing possibilities. If he was not aware, then the question is whether the defendant was prejudiced by the lack of information or by misinformation, which usually comes down to whether having the accurate information would have made any difference in his decision to enter the plea. If the defendant received a sentence longer than he knew could be imposed, then surely the judge's failure does amount to a due process violation.

(e) Determining Understanding of Rights Waived. *Boykin v. Ala.* (1969) concerned a defendant who had pleaded guilty in state court to five armed robbery indictments and thereafter received the death penalty. At arraignment, "so far as the record shows, the judge asked no questions of petitioner concerning his plea, and petitioner did not address the court." The Supreme Court reversed, concluding that it "was error, plain on the face of the record, for the trial judge to accept petitioner's guilty plea without an affirmative showing that it was intelligent and voluntary." Noting that it had earlier established in another context the "requirement that the prosecution spread on the record the prerequisites of a valid waiver," the Court in *Boykin* concluded "that the same standard must be applied to determining whether a guilty plea is voluntarily made." The Court added that "several federal constitutional rights are involved in a waiver that takes place when a plea of guilty is entered in a state criminal trial" (namely, the privilege against compulsory self-incrimination, the right to trial by jury, and the right to confront one's accusers), and that "we cannot presume a waiver of these three important federal rights from a silent record." (In *Mitchell v. U.S.* (1999), the Court later clarified that, at least in federal procedure, the waiver of rights occurring upon entry of a guilty plea is a "waiver of a right to trial with its attendant privileges" and "not a waiver of the privileges which exist beyond the confines of the trial," so that the defendant's guilty plea did not amount to "a waiver of the privilege [against self-incrimination] at sentencing.")

In the wake of *Boykin,* most jurisdictions revised their procedures for taking pleas so that defendants were specifically warned of the constitutional rights lost by entry of a plea other than not guilty. Although this is a desirable procedure, does *Boykin* mean that a guilty plea is constitutionally defective whenever the judge failed to articulate specifically the constitutional rights listed in the *Boykin* case? Some courts have answered in the affirmative, reasoning that there cannot be a knowledgeable waiver of those rights unless the defendant was so informed of them. But most courts, often stressing the uniqueness of *Boykin* in that the defendant had been sentenced to death and his plea had apparently been accepted without any admonishments or inquiry whatsoever, have reached the contrary conclusion. The latter view is supported by Supreme Court decisions subsequent to *Boykin*: *Brady v. U.S.* (1970), citing *Boykin* but upholding a guilty plea even though defendant had not been specifically advised of the three rights discussed in *Boykin*; and *N.C. v. Alford* (1970), stating that in determining the validity of guilty pleas the "standard was and remains whether the plea represents a voluntary and intelligent choice among the alternative courses of action open to the defendant."

(f) Determining Factual Basis of Plea. In recent years, many jurisdictions have imposed an added obligation upon the judge receiving a plea of guilty, which is to make a determination regarding the accuracy of the plea. In federal procedure, for example, "[b]efore entering judgment on a guilty plea, the court must determine that there is a factual basis for the plea." Many states have adopted a comparable provision. Generally, these provisions leave the judge free to decide in the particular case how this determination can best be made; the factual basis is most commonly established by inquiry of the defendant, inquiry of the prosecutor, or defense counsel, examination of the plea agreement, presentence report or preliminary hearing transcript, testimony by police, or a combination of those methods. Nor do these provisions attempt to establish a precise quantum of evidence that must be met.

In the previously-discussed *Mitchell* case, the Supreme Court focused upon the self-incrimination aspects of inquiry of the defendant to establish, at least in part, the factual basis for a plea. For one thing, because (as noted above) *Mitchell* holds the entry of the plea is itself not a waiver of the privilege other than as an at-trial right lost by not standing trial, a defendant to whom a factual basis inquiry is made *could* decline to answer on Fifth Amendment grounds, but by doing so he "runs the risk the district court will find the factual basis inadequate." Secondly, the guilty plea and statements made in the plea colloquy, including the factual basis inquiry, "are later admissible against the defendant," for example, at sentencing. Thirdly, the fact the defendant has made incriminating statements at the factual basis inquiry does not itself constitute a waiver of the privilege at later proceedings such as sentencing. This is so, the Court explained, because that situation is unlike the case of a witness at a single proceeding, who "may not testify voluntarily about a subject and then invoke the privilege against self-incrimination when questioned about the details," thereby "diminishing the integrity of the factual inquiry." Such a concern is "absent at a plea colloquy," as "the defendant who pleads guilty puts nothing in dispute regarding the essentials of the offense" but rather "takes those matters out of dispute, often by making a joint statement with the prosecution or confirming the prosecution's version of the facts," in which case "there is little danger that the court will be misled by selective disclosure."

This inquiry into the factual basis serves a number of worthwhile functions. Most importantly, it should protect a defendant who is in the position of pleading voluntarily with an understanding of the nature of the charge but without realizing that his conduct does not actually fall within the charge. As the cases indicate, this does happen on occasion. In addition, the inquiry into the factual basis of the plea provides the court with a better assessment of defendant's competency and willingness to plead guilty and his understanding of the charges, increases the visibility of charge reduction practices, provides a more adequate record and thus minimizes the likelihood of the plea being successfully challenged later, and aids correctional agencies in the performance of their functions.

Although as a general matter the determination of a factual basis for the plea is not constitutionally required, the situation is otherwise in one special set of circumstances as a result of *N.C. v. Alford* (1970). Alford, indicted for first degree murder, pleaded guilty to second degree murder but then took the stand and declared he had not committed the murder and was pleading guilty to avoid the risk of the death penalty. Because he persisted in his plea and because a summary of the state's case indicated Alford had taken a gun from his house with the stated intention of killing the victim and had later returned with the declaration that he had carried out the killing, the judge accepted the plea. The Supreme Court upheld the plea, reasoning that "an express admission of guilt * * * is not a constitutional requisite to the imposition of criminal penalty," for one "accused of crime may voluntarily, knowingly, and understandingly consent to the imposition of a prison sentence even if he is unwilling or unable to admit his participation in the acts constituting the crime." The Court did not state just how strong this factual basis must be, but it would appear that when a pleading defendant denies the crime the factual basis must be significantly more certain than will suffice in other circumstances. In an oft-quoted footnote, the Court declared that states remain free to "bar their courts from accepting guilty pleas from any defendants who assert their innocence." This language has been cogently criticized on the ground that it would permit a trial judge for no good reason to deny a defendant such as Alford the opportunity to obtain concessions via plea bargaining unless he misrepresents his own perception of the circumstances.

(g) Acting on the Plea Bargain. In any case in which the tendered plea of guilty or nolo contendere is the result of a plea bargain, the judge receiving the plea will have added responsibilities. In some circumstances, at least, he will have to advise the defendant of the legal effect of the bargain, and he will of course have to decide whether or not to approve the terms of the bargain to which the parties have agreed. In federal procedure, for example, there are three recognized types of plea bargains. The parties may agree that if

> the defendant pleads guilty or nolo contendere to either a charged offense or a lesser or related offense, the plea agreement may specify that an attorney for the government will:
>
> (A) not bring, or will move to dismiss, other charges;

(B) recommend, or agree not to oppose the defendant's request, that a particular sentence or sentencing range is appropriate or that a particular provision of the Sentencing Guidelines, or policy statement, or sentencing factor does or does not apply (such a recommendation or request does not bind the court); or

(C) agree that a specific sentence or sentencing range is the appropriate disposition of the case, or that a particular provision of the Sentencing Guidelines, or policy statement, or sentencing factor does or does not apply (such a recommendation or request binds the court once the court accepts the plea agreement).

A critical distinction, which determines the nature of the judge's responsibilities in a particular case, is that an agreement of the (B) type involves only a promise by the prosecution to seek or not oppose a certain result, while an agreement of either of the other two types involves a promise to actually bring about a certain result. This means that when the judge learns that an agreement of the (B) type has been made, he must tell the defendant of his precarious position; "the court must advise the defendant that the defendant has no right to withdraw the plea if the court does not follow the recommendation or request." No such caution is required as to the other two types of agreements, for they do not carry this risk. Rather, as to them the court may simply proceed to "accept the agreement, reject it, or defer a decision until the court has reviewed the presentence report." But if the court ultimately rejects a type (A) or type (C) agreement, it must so advise the parties, "give the defendant an opportunity to withdraw the plea," and "advise the defendant personally that if the plea is not withdrawn, the court may dispose of the case less favorably toward the defendant than the plea agreement contemplated."

Somewhat similar procedures are required by state law, though some variation exists as to when the defendant is to be informed that if he persists in his plea he has no assurance of the anticipated concessions and when he is to be told that he retains the right to withdraw his plea if those concessions are not granted. In large measure, the disparity is attributable to the fact that the states are not in agreement on how to deal with what in federal practice is known as a type (B) agreement. In some states that type of agreement is recognized as a situation in which the defendant assumes the risk that the prosecutor's recommendation will not be followed, which means that the judge is obligated to advise the defendant of the risk he is taking. In some other states, however, that type of agreement is not viewed as calling for different treatment. In those jurisdictions no advance warning is required; if the judge ultimately decides not to accept the prosecutor's recommendation, the defendant must then be so advised and be given an opportunity to withdraw his plea.

Under either system, of course, the judge has an independent responsibility to pass upon the merits of all plea bargains contemplating certain consequences that can be achieved only by the judge or with his approval. If the bargain goes to the sentence to be imposed, quite obviously this is a matter ultimately to be decided by the judge. If the bargain necessitates the dropping of other charges where, as is common, this can be accomplished only with the judge's approval, there is at least a limited role for the judge to perform here as well (see § 13.3(e)).

Assume a case in which the judge acting on the plea bargain, if he were to impose a sentence higher than contemplated by the plea agreement, would be required to allow the defendant to withdraw his plea. In these circumstances, may the judge impose a *lower* sentence than the agreement contemplates without affording the prosecution an equivalent opportunity to withdraw? At least in the federal system regarding type (C) agreements, the answer clearly is no, for the legislative history unequivocally shows that this was the intent of the revision of rule 11 allowing type (C) agreements. The situation is not as clear at the state level. One view is that the state, if it is to bargain freely and on equal terms with the defendant, must also be allowed to timely withdraw from a plea agreement when it is apparent that the court does not wish to abide by its terms. The contrary view rests upon the conclusion that though notions of fairness apply to each side, the defendant's constitutional rights and interests weigh more heavily on the scale.

When the defendant's plea of guilty is inextricably connected to a specific disposition contemplated by the plea agreement, does the court's statement that it "accepts" the plea constitute an irrevocable decision to accept the plea agreement terms as well, so that the judge is bound to that disposition even if the presentence report later reveals that such a disposition would be inappropriate? There are many situations in which it is clear that the answer is no. One is where the trial judge has cautiously conditioned the plea acceptance upon his later agreement with the terms of the plea agreement, and another is where the law of the jurisdiction declares that a plea of guilty is not deemed to be "accepted" until certain other specified events have transpired. But the answer should be no in other situations as well under any modern system in which the judge's responsibility is recognized to include acceptance or rejection of both (i) the plea, and (ii) the plea agreement. On the other hand, once the court has accepted the plea agreement, it may not— absent a fraud on the court—change its mind because of the discovery of new facts. Were courts free to re-examine the wisdom of plea bargains with the benefit of hindsight, the agreements themselves would lack finality and the benefits that encourage the government and defendants to enter into pleas might prove illusory.

§ 13.5 Challenge of Guilty Plea by Defendant

(a) **Withdrawal of Plea.** The prevailing view is that plea withdrawal between the time of the guilty plea and sentencing is not granted as a matter of right. But it is also clear that a defendant may withdraw a guilty plea as a matter of right before it is accepted by the court, which naturally gives rise to the question of whether a guilty plea should be deemed "accepted" when the judge who received the defendant's plea has not yet decided whether to accept the underlying plea agreement, especially when the plea agreement contemplates a specific disposition and not just a recommendation. This was the nature of the question confronting the Supreme Court in *U.S. v. Hyde* (1997), where the court of appeals reasoned that the guilty plea and plea agreement are "inextricably bound up together," so that deferral of the decision whether to accept the plea agreement constitutes deferral of acceptance of the plea as well. A unanimous Supreme Court reversed, noting that the court of appeals' reasoning runs counter to language in federal rules expressly stating that in the case of a type (A) or type (C) agreement (i.e., for a specific sentence or dropping of charges) the judge may defer acceptance of the agreement in order to consider the presentence report, and then permitting plea withdrawal *only* in the event that the court ultimately rejects the plea agreement. Moreover, the Court added, the court of appeals' holding "also debases the judicial proceeding at which a defendant pleads and the court accepts his plea," and "would degrade the otherwise serious act of pleading guilty into something akin to a move in a game of chess." Some states have taken the contrary position, while others are in accord with *Hyde*.

Even when a plea cannot be withdrawn as a matter of right, a defendant who enters a plea of guilty is not foreclosed from subsequently challenging that plea or his disposition pursuant thereto. Procedurally, one means commonly employed in an effort to "undo" a plea of guilty is a motion to withdraw the plea. Contrary to earlier practice, such a motion may now be made in the federal system only before sentencing, when withdrawal is permitted for "a fair and just reason." There is considerable variation on the state level. In some jurisdictions plea withdrawal is allowed only before sentence or only before "judgment" (which may refer to the time of sentencing or some earlier time). Many states follow the former federal approach and thus recognize that withdrawal of a plea is possible both before and after sentence and judgment. In these latter jurisdictions, there has been a distinct trend in the direction of utilizing the terminology that had been used in the federal cases. Where the defendant seeks to withdraw his guilty plea before sentence, he is generally accorded that right if he can show any fair and just reason, but where the guilty plea is sought to be withdrawn by the defendant after sentence, it may be granted only to avoid manifest injustice. The prevailing approach of utilizing a more demanding standard after imposition of sentence is based upon (i) the fact that after sentence the defendant is more likely to view the plea bargain as a tactical mistake and therefore wish to have it set aside; (ii) the fact that at the time of sentencing, other portions of the plea bargain agreement will often be performed by the prosecutor (e.g., dismissal of additional charges), which might be difficult to undo if the defendant later attacks his plea and (iii) the policy of giving finality to criminal sentences resulting from a voluntary guilty plea.

As for the presentence "fair and just reason" test, some courts proceed as if any desire to withdraw the plea before sentence is "fair and just" so long as the prosecution fails to establish that it would be prejudiced by the withdrawal, but the sounder and prevailing view is that there is no occasion to inquire into the matter of prejudice unless the defendant first shows a good reason for being allowed to withdraw his plea. Under the "fair and just" test, whether the movant has asserted his innocence is an important factor to be weighed, as is the explanation for why the reason now asserted was not put forward at the time of the original pleading, and the amount of time that has passed between the plea and the motion. The "manifest injustice" test is not self-defining, and doubtless does not mean precisely the same thing in every jurisdiction, but courts commonly treat the "manifest injustice" test as being no broader than the available grounds for relief upon collateral attack. If the defendant shows a manifest injustice, under the better view it is unnecessary that he also assert his innocence.

(b) Other Challenges to Plea. A defendant who has entered a plea of guilty might also challenge that plea by resorting to certain procedures likewise utilized by defendants convicted at trial, such as appeal, habeas corpus or a statutory post-conviction hearing. In federal procedure, a defendant may take a direct appeal from a guilty plea conviction. Direct appeal offers the plea-convicted defendant a significant advantage over collateral attack, as the appeal is reviewed by a three-judge panel of the court of appeals that can overturn the plea conviction on a finding of error less than of constitutional, jurisdictional, or fundamental magnitude. The states also generally allow an appeal to be taken from a guilty plea, where again there is this advantage. But the appeal alternative is more limited in that the appeal must be taken promptly after the plea, and the only matters properly raised are those that can be resolved on the basis of the record in the case—mainly the transcript of the proceedings at which the defendant's plea of guilty was received. A state guilty plea defendant will also have available state habeas corpus or a statutory post-conviction hearing procedure in lieu thereof. These avenues, in contrast to direct appeal, provide an opportunity for a hearing at which additional facts supporting (or refuting) defendant's claim may be adduced, but relief is unlikely to be available unless any defect shown is of constitutional magnitude. A federal defendant resorting to the post-conviction procedures provided for in 28 U.S.C.A. § 2255 will prevail only by showing "a fundamental defect which inherently results in a complete miscarriage of justice" or "an omission inconsistent with the rudimentary demands of fair procedure." A state defendant may ultimately end up in federal court raising constitutional objections via federal habeas corpus.

(c) **Significance of Noncompliance With Plea–Receiving Procedures.** One issue that arises with some frequency when a defendant moves to withdraw or otherwise challenges his guilty plea is whether a failure to comply fully with the established procedures for receiving the plea is inevitably a basis for relief. The answer may turn to some extent upon the procedural context in which that issue is raised. If, for example, that question is asked regarding a federal defendant's attack upon his guilty plea in a § 2255 proceeding, the answer given by the Supreme Court in *U.S. v. Timmreck* (1979) is no. In *Timmreck,* the judge at the rule 11 hearing told defendant that he could receive a sentence of 15 years imprisonment but failed to add that there was a mandatory special parole term of at least 3 years, and he then accepted defendant's guilty plea and sentenced him to 10 years imprisonment plus a special parole term of 5 years. The district court concluded the rule 11 violation did not entitle defendant to § 2255 relief because he had not suffered any prejudice, as his sentence fell within that described to him when the plea was accepted, but the court of appeals disagreed and concluded that "a Rule 11 violation is per se prejudicial." A unanimous Supreme Court rejected the latter view. Noting that relief under § 2255 is available only when "the error resulted in a 'complete miscarriage of justice' or in a proceeding 'inconsistent with the rudimentary demands of fair procedure,'" the Court concluded this could hardly be the case when there has been merely "a technical violation of the rule" rather than one which "occurred in the context of other aggravating circumstances." The Court added that this result made good sense, given the fact that "the concern with finality served by the limitation on collateral attack has special force with respect to convictions based on guilty pleas." (States have often reached the same result as a matter of state post-conviction hearing practice.)

Timmreck intimated the result might have been otherwise had the defendant raised the claim on direct appeal, citing *McCarthy v. U.S.* (1969) in support. In *McCarthy,* the trial judge failed to address the defendant personally and determine that his plea was made voluntarily and with an understanding of the nature of the charge, as required by rule 11, and defendant raised that omission on appeal. In rejecting the government's contention that in such circumstances the government should still be allowed to prove that defendant in fact pleaded voluntarily and with an understanding of the charge, the Court concluded

> that prejudice inheres in a failure to comply with Rule 11, for noncompliance deprives the defendant of the Rule's procedural safeguards, which are designed to facilitate a more accurate determination of the voluntariness of his plea. Our holding that a defendant whose plea has been accepted in violation of Rule 11 should be afforded the opportunity to plead anew not only will insure that every accused is afforded those procedural safeguards, but also will help reduce the great waste of judicial resources required to process the frivolous attacks on guilty plea convictions that are encouraged, and are more difficult to dispose of, when the original record is inadequate.

Read narrowly, *McCarthy* says that a defendant's violation-of-rule-11 complaint on appeal cannot be defeated by the government's claim that *if* it could produce more facts by an evidentiary hearing it could show the violation was insignificant. But the above language was given a broader reading by some courts, namely, that on direct appeal a defendant's conviction *must* be reversed whenever the there was not full adherence to the procedure provided for in rule 11, while other federal courts took the harmless error approach, a position now incorporated into the federal rules. (Although that change in rule 11, unlike the more general harmless error provision in rule 52, does not also contain a plain-error provision, this does not relieve a guilty plea defendant who raises a rule 11 issue for the first time on appeal of the burden of showing plain error affected his substantial rights, as the rule 11 change did not implicitly repeal Rule 52 so far as it might cover a rule 11 case. To carry that burden, the defendant "must show a reasonable probability that, but for the error, he would not have entered the plea." *U.S. v. Dominguez Benitez* (2004).)

In *McCarthy,* the Supreme Court at one point stated that "[t]here is no adequate substitute for demonstrating *in the record at the time the plea is entered* the defendant's understanding of the nature of the charge against him." This language, the Court conceded in *U.S. v. Vonn* (2002), "ostensibly supports" the position of the court of appeals in the instant case, namely, that in considering defendant's challenge to his guilty plea on the ground the judge had skipped required advice about the right to assistance of counsel, only the record at "the plea proceeding" would be considered. But the Supreme Court then noted that in *McCarthy* the "only serious alternative" to the plea record would have been "an evidentiary hearing for further factfinding by the trial court," while in the instant case "there is a third source of information," namely, that "part of the record" showing defendant was advised on his right to counsel "during his initial appearance" and "at his first arraignment." "Because there are circumstances in which defendants may be presumed to recall information provided to them prior to the plea proceeding," the *Vonn* Court concluded that third source should have been considered by the court of appeals

States are not obligated to grant relief whenever a failure to follow plea-receiving procedures has been established. True, in *Boykin v. Ala.* (1969) the Court noted that "so far as the record shows, the judge asked no questions of petitioner concerning his plea, and petitioner did not address the court," and then concluded that it "was error, plain on the face of the record, for the trial judge to accept petitioner's guilty plea without an affirmative showing that it was intelligent and voluntary." But in *N.C. v. Alford* (1970) the Court explained that it would suffice if at a hearing on a postconviction petition it was established that defendant's plea was in fact knowing and voluntary. It of course follows that this is the case if a state defendant challenges his plea by federal habeas corpus.

(d) Significance of Compliance With Plea–Receiving Procedures. An issue in a sense the converse of that just discussed is whether full compliance with all the established procedures for taking a plea of guilty should foreclose any subsequent attack upon the plea that would necessitate a factual determination contrary to the one made when the plea was taken. The Supreme Court has confronted this question on two occasions, first in *Fontaine v. U.S.* (1973). The Court there held that upon a federal defendant's § 2255 motion to vacate his sentence on the ground that his plea of guilty had been induced by a combination of fear, coercive police tactics, and illness (including mental illness), a hearing was required "on this record" notwithstanding full compliance with rule 11, as § 2255 calls for a hearing unless "the motion and the files and records of the case conclusively show that the prisoner is entitled to no relief." The Court, in concluding such was not the case, noted that the objective of rule 11 "is to flush out and resolve all such issues, but like any procedural mechanism, its exercise is neither always perfect nor uniformly invulnerable to subsequent challenge calling for an opportunity to prove the allegations." But because one of the defendant's allegations in *Fontaine* concerned whether he had been mentally ill, a matter not routinely explored in a rule 11 proceeding, the case does not settle whether a hearing would be required if defendant's factual allegations were in all respects contrary to what had been determined at the time the plea was received.

In the second case, *Blackledge v. Allison* (1977), Allison had pled guilty to attempted safe robbery in North Carolina, answered that he understood the judge's advise that he could receive 10 years to life, and responded in the negative when asked by the judge if anyone "made any promises or threats to you to influence you to plead guilty in this case." The only record of the proceedings was the executed form from which the judge had read those and other questions. Allison, later sentenced to 17–21 years, sought relief via federal habeas corpus; he claimed that his lawyer had told him that the prosecutor and judge had agreed to a sentence of 10 years but that he should nonetheless answer the questions at the arraignment as he did. The district court denied the petition on the ground that the form "conclusively shows" no constitutional violation and thus met the *Fontaine* standard, but the court of appeals' reversal was upheld by the Supreme Court. The Court declared: "In the light of the nature of the record of the proceeding at which the guilty plea was accepted, and of the ambiguous status of the process of plea bargaining at the time the guilty plea was made, we conclude that Allison's petition should not have been summarily dismissed." The Court in *Allison* clearly signaled that if the plea had been received at another time with a more complete record, the result would be otherwise. It was emphasized that the plea here was entered in 1971, at a time when there were "lingering doubts about the legitimacy of the practice" of plea bargaining and thus reason not to disclose bargains in court, and that the only record was the printed form, which did not disclose whether the judge "deviated from or supplemented the text of the form" or what others at the hearing had said regarding promised sentence concessions. Most significantly, the Court observed that the state "has recently undertaken major revisions of its plea bargaining procedures" so that "specific inquiry about whether a plea bargain has been struck is * * * made not only of the defendant, but also of his counsel and the prosecutor," and "the entire proceeding is to be transcribed verbatim," and then concluded: "Had these commendable procedures been followed in the present case, Allison's petition would have been cast in a very different light."

Although lower courts before *Allison* were inclined to give little credence to the record made when the guilty plea was received, this is much less true today. Of course, there are still some circumstances in which a court must conduct an evidentiary hearing to resolve a challenge to a guilty plea even when the earlier proceedings were flawless. This is certainly true when the allegation goes to a matter, such as incompetence in representation by defense counsel, which is not likely to be disproved by the record made when the plea is received, or to unusual or extreme pressures that could be expected to "carry over" to the plea proceedings and influence the defendant to give false or incomplete responses. But in the more common situations in which the defendant asserts a prior misperception of the possible consequences of his plea, of whether there was a bargain, or of the terms of the bargain, and the record of the plea proceedings clearly indicate otherwise, courts are now inclined to hold that relief can be denied without an evidentiary hearing.

(e) **Effect of Withdrawn or Overturned Plea.** If a defendant entered a plea of guilty in exchange for certain concessions (for example, reduction of the charge from murder to manslaughter) but thereafter managed to withdraw or overturn that guilty plea, so that the matter will now go to trial, is the prosecutor somehow "bound" by the concessions given earlier? Although the Supreme Court in *Santobello v. N.Y.* (1971) assumed that the answer was no, some lower courts have found this issue to be a very difficult one. Two conflicting points of view have been expressed. One is that by his earlier action in giving the defendant concessions the prosecutor vouched that the ends of justice will be served by such a disposition, so that he is now foreclosed from asserting the contrary. The other and prevailing view is that holding the prosecutor to his end of the bargain while allowing the defendant to extricate himself from his plea, so that the defendant takes nothing more than a "heads-I-win-tails-you-lose" gamble, would restrain prosecutors from entering plea bargains, and judges from exercising their discretion in favor of permitting withdrawal of a guilty plea. It has occasionally been held that when in a guilty plea context a judge finds a factual basis for the lesser offense to which the defendant is pleading and dismisses the higher charge at the state's request, this provides defendant with the same double jeopardy protection as a jury verdict. But the great weight of authority is to the contrary, and rightly so. The other view ignores the importance of the plea milieu and the fact that acceptance of the guilty plea does not constitute an inferential finding of not guilty of the higher charge, in that no trier of fact was presented with a choice between the greater and lesser charge.

Yet another line of attack is to assert that trial on the greater charge after the guilty plea is withdrawn or overturned amounts to a violation of due process under *Blackledge v. Perry* (1974). In that case, where defendant was prosecuted on a felony assault charge after he exercised his right to trial de novo on a misdemeanor assault charge based upon the same incident, the Court held it was constitutionally impermissible for the state to respond to defendant's invocation of his statutory right to appeal in that way. Without regard to whether the prosecutor was acting in bad faith, due process "requires that a defendant be freed of apprehension of such a retaliatory motivation." But surely *Blackledge* has no application when all that the prosecutor has done is to return to the original charge, for there is no appearance of retaliation when a defendant is placed in the same position as he was before he accepted the plea bargain (though it may be that this "same position" must include a continuing opportunity for the defendant to enter a guilty plea to the same reduced charge as before). But what if the prosecutor really does "up the ante" after defendant withdraws or overturns his guilty plea, now filing more charges or a more serious charge than had been brought originally? Here, courts are more likely to find that *Blackledge* applies and that due process has been violated, in that the charge enhancement has the appearance of vindictiveness in response to defendant's successful challenge of his guilty plea. As discussed elsewhere herein (see § 5.7(c)), there exists considerable uncertainty as to what kind of showing by the prosecutor will suffice to justify the escalation of charges. But, even assuming some such limits otherwise govern, it is unclear whether they are applicable in a plea bargaining context. In *Bordenkircher v. Hayes* (1978), where the prosecutor carried out his threat to prosecute defendant as a habitual offender because of his unwillingness to plead guilty to a forgery charge, the Court concluded that this conduct was not barred by *Blackledge* because the vindictiveness rationale of that case had no application to "the 'give-and-take' of plea bargaining." If that is so, then it would seem to follow that if the defendant had instead entered a guilty plea on the original forgery count but then later overturned that plea, the prosecutor would again be free to threaten prosecution under the habitual offender law and to carry out the threat if defendant did not again plead guilty to forgery.

In some cases, the due process objection may be stated somewhat differently and be grounded in *N.C. v. Pearce* (1969). In that case, two defendants who had successfully challenged their original convictions were reprosecuted and convicted of the same offense but received higher sentences the second time around. The Court held that due process bars vindictive sentencing in response to exercise of the statutory right to appeal and also necessitates that defendants be free of "the fear of such vindictiveness," and thus concluded that a higher sentence could be imposed only if "based upon objective information concerning identifiable conduct on the part of the defendant occurring after the time of the original sentencing proceeding." In the guilty plea context, *Pearce* has not been read as barring a higher sentence where the prosecutor properly filed a higher charge after vacation of the guilty plea. As for when the sequence was plea of guilty, a setting aside of that plea, prosecution and conviction on the same charge to which the plea was entered, and imposition of a higher sentence, there was a split of authority until the Supreme Court decision in *Ala. v. Smith* (1989). The Court held that the *Pearce* presumption, limited to circumstances presenting a " 'reasonable likelihood' that the increase in sentence is the product of actual vindictiveness," did not apply in this situation for two reasons: (i) because plea bargaining may "be pursued * * * by providing for a more lenient sentence if the defendant pleads guilty"; and (ii) because of "the greater amount of sentencing information that a trial generally affords as compared to a guilty plea." By contrast, the *Pearce* presumption *is* applicable if the defendant also pleads guilty the second time around but receives a higher sentence than he received after the first plea.

(f) Admissibility of Withdrawn or Overturned Plea and Related Statements. In the past, some courts have held that if a defendant's plea of guilty is subsequently withdrawn or otherwise vacated, the fact of that plea may nonetheless be admitted into evidence against the defendant at his later trial because it constitutes conduct inconsistent with innocence and is comparable to an extrajudicial confession to the crime. The federal rule has long been otherwise, and the more recent state decisions have consistently held that such a plea is not admissible. This is as it should be, as the privilege extended to withdrawing the plea would be an empty one if the withdrawn plea could be used against the defendant on his trial.

It is not uncommon for a defendant to make incriminating statements in connection with the entry of a guilty plea, especially when he is called upon to supply information establishing a factual basis for the plea. If that plea has been vacated, then those statements are not admissible in evidence against the defendant either. When the nature of the statements is such as to make it evident that a guilty plea was entered, then this result is an inevitable consequence of the rule that the vacated plea is itself inadmissible. But the result is just as compelling when the statements are incriminating but do not disclose that they were given in connection with a plea of guilty. A contrary rule would discourage the giving of information needed by the court in the plea receiving and sentencing process.

§ 13.6   Effect of Guilty Plea

(a) **Rights Waived or Forfeited by Plea.** A valid plea of guilty generally bars the defendant from subsequently raising objections that might well be a basis for overturning his conviction had he gone to trial. Why this should be so and the extent to which it is so was first addressed by the Supreme Court in *McMann v. Richardson* (1970) and two companion cases. In *McMann,* a federal court of appeals ordered evidentiary hearings for three petitioners who had entered pleas of guilty some years earlier in New York but now asserted their pleas had been motivated by confessions coerced from them. Although those pleas had been received prior to the Court's decision in *Jackson v. Denno* (1964), holding unconstitutional the New York procedure requiring submission of the admissibility-of-a-confession issue to the jury, and though *Jackson* had been applied retroactively to the benefit of defendants who had gone to trial, the Court nonetheless concluded these petitioners were not entitled to relief:

> A conviction after trial in which a coerced confession is introduced rests in part on the coerced confession, a constitutionally unacceptable basis for conviction. * * * The defendant who pleads guilty is in a different posture. He is convicted on his counseled admission in open court that he committed the crime charged against him. The prior confession is not the basis for the judgment, has never been offered in evidence at a trial, and may never be offered in evidence.

The Court added that a contrary rule "would be an improvident invasion of the State's interest in maintaining the finality of guilty plea convictions which were valid under constitutional standards applicable at the time," and concluded: "It is no denigration of the right to trial to hold that when the defendant waives his state court remedies and admits his guilt, he does so under the law then existing; further, he assumes the risk of ordinary error in either his or his attorney's assessment of the law and facts."

In the companion case of *Brady v. U.S.* (1970), defendant had entered a guilty plea to violating the Federal Kidnapping Act, later held to contain an unconstitutional penalty provision whereby only those exercising their constitutional right to jury trial could receive the death penalty. Although assuming "that Brady would not have pleaded guilty except for the death penalty provision," the Court ruled he was not entitled "to withdraw his plea merely because he discovers long after the plea had been accepted that his calculus misapprehended the quality of the State's case or the likely penalties attached to alternative courses of action." In the third case in the trilogy, *Parker v. N.C.* (1970), both the death penalty and coerced confession issues were held to be foreclosed by defendant's guilty plea. Similarly, just a few years later the Court in *Tollett v. Henderson* (1973) held that a defendant who had pled guilty to murder could not subsequently challenge the racial composition of the grand jury that had indicted him, as "a guilty plea represents a break in the chain of events which has preceded it in the criminal process. When a criminal defendant has solemnly admitted in open court that he is in fact guilty of the offense with which he is charged, he may not thereafter raise independent claims relating to the deprivation of constitutional rights that occurred prior to the entry of the guilty plea."

Any thought that this was an absolute rule, extending to *all* constitutional rights, was soon dispelled. In *Blackledge v. Perry* (1974), holding that escalation of the charge against defendant from misdemeanor to felony following defendant's assertion of his right to trial de novo violated due process, the Court explained why defendant's guilty plea to the felony was no bar: while "the underlying claims presented in *Tollett* and the *Brady* trilogy were of constitutional dimension, none went to the very power of the State to bring the defendant into court to answer the charge brought against him," "the right that [defendant] asserts and that we today accept is the right not to be hailed into court at all upon the felony charge." Thereafter, in *Menna v. N.Y.* (1975), defendant's previously asserted claim that his indictment should be dismissed on double jeopardy grounds was held not to be "waived" by his guilty plea. The Court explained in a footnote "that a counseled plea of guilty * * * simply renders irrelevant those constitutional violations not logically inconsistent with the valid establishment of factual guilt and which do not stand in the way of conviction if factual guilt is validly established."

One commentator has articulated the *Blackledge–Menna* exception as follows: "a defendant who has been convicted on a plea of guilty may challenge his conviction on any constitutional ground that, if asserted before trial, would forever preclude the state from obtaining a valid conviction against him, regardless of how much the state might endeavor to correct the defect. In other words, a plea of guilty may operate as a forfeiture of all defenses except those that, once raised, cannot be 'cured.'" Where an error can be cured, the entry of the plea itself may have impaired the state's ability thereafter to prove the defendant guilty at trial. And it is not unfair to assume that the state relied on the plea to its detriment, particularly because the entry of the plea has itself made the issue so difficult to resolve later. But when the constitutional error is incurable the state is in precisely the same position after the entry of the guilty plea as it occupied beforehand with respect to its ability to prove the defendant guilty at trial: the error would always have prevented it from obtaining a valid conviction at trial. This reasoning conforms to the results in the Supreme Court's decisions. In *Tollett* the alleged defect could have been cured by reconstituting the grand jury and obtaining a proper indictment, but the due process claim in *Blackledge* and the double jeopardy claim in *Menna* involved errors that could not be cured. Other constitutional defenses of this character, which likewise should not be deemed forfeited by a guilty plea, include the Sixth Amendment right to speedy trial, the right not to be convicted of conduct that cannot constitutionally be made criminal, and perhaps the right not to be selectively prosecuted in violation of the equal protection clause.

This is not to suggest, however, that a constitutional defense of that special character will in all instances survive a guilty plea, for *U.S. v. Broce* (1989) holds to the contrary. The defendants pleaded guilty to two conspiracy indictments charging the rigging of bids on two highway projects but later, relying on a ruling re other defendants who did *not* plead guilty, interposed the double jeopardy claim that only one conspiracy was involved. The Court ruled that "a defendant who pleads guilty to two counts with facial allegations of distinct offenses concede[s] that he has committed two separate crimes," and thereby has relinquished any "opportunity to receive a factual hearing on a double jeopardy claim." The *Broce* Court distinguished *Blackledge* and *Menna* as cases that "could be (and ultimately were) resolved without any need to venture beyond [the] record," while in the instant case the defendants "cannot prove their claim by relying on [the] indictments and the existing record" or, indeed, "without contradicting those indictments, and that opportunity is foreclosed by the admissions inherent in their guilty pleas."

Even if the constitutional violation has produced an incurable defect so that the right is not automatically forfeited by a plea of guilty, there still might occur an enforceable waiver of that same right in a particular case. For example, what if a defendant is charged with count one (as to which he has a colorable speedy trial defense) and with count two (as to which he has no apparent defense), but as a result of negotiations with the prosecutor he agrees to plead guilty to count one, which carries a lower sentence, in exchange for dismissal of count two? Because the state has given up something of value, in that its prosecutorial position on count two would have deteriorated because of its reasonable assumption that it would never have to go to trial on that charge, the state's interest in preserving its opportunity to prosecute the defendant justifies foreclosing him from asserting his constitutional claim. This conclusion conforms to the Supreme Court's declaration in *Menna* that it was not holding "that a double jeopardy claim may never be waived."

If the right in question is one that *is* subject to forfeiture under the line of Supreme Court cases discussed above, this does not inevitably mean the defendant's attack upon his guilty plea will be unsuccessful. As the Court emphasized in *McMann,* it means that to prevail the defendant must "allege and prove serious derelictions on the part of counsel" not "within the range of competence demanded of attorneys in criminal cases." As the Court later concluded in *Hill v. Lockhart* (1985), the two-part ineffective assistance of counsel test of *Strickland v. Washington* (1984) (see § 3.10) applies in a guilty plea context. The first half is "nothing more than a restatement of the standard of attorney competence" stated in *McMann* above, while the second or "prejudice" part "focuses on whether counsel's constitutionally ineffective performance affected the outcome of the plea process." What the defendant must show is "a reasonable probability that, but for counsel's errors, he would not have pleaded guilty and would have insisted on going to trial," which means if the error was a failure to discover potentially exculpatory evidence, that the question is whether "discovery of the evidence would have led counsel to change his recommendation as to the plea." This in turn depends on "whether the evidence likely would have changed the outcome of a trial." Similarly, if the error was failure to advise defendant of an affirmative defense it must be asked "whether the affirmative defense would likely have succeeded at trial." In *Hill,* where the error was a failure by counsel to advise defendant correctly on his parole eligibility under the plea bargain, prejudice was not shown because it did not appear defendant "placed particular emphasis on his parole eligibility in deciding whether or not to plead guilty."

Finally, it must be emphasized that the forfeiture rule discussed above has no application to defects going directly to the guilty plea itself. This includes not only defects concerning advice of counsel, as just noted, but also defects in the procedure by which the plea was received or circumstances making the plea other than voluntary, knowing and intelligent. As the Court noted in *McMann,* it is beyond dispute that "a guilty plea is properly open to challenge" if, for instance, "the circumstances that coerced the confession have abiding impact and also taint the plea." Moreover, a defendant after his plea of guilty remains free to raise objections regarding the sentence subsequently imposed, at least when the sentence now objected to was not itself a part of the plea agreement.

(b) Conditional Pleas. There are many defenses and objections that a defendant must ordinarily raise by pretrial motion, and if that motion is denied interlocutory appeal of the ruling by the defendant is seldom permitted. As noted above, a plea of guilty is with rare exception treated as a waiver or forfeiture of such claims. This is also true of a plea of nolo contendere, which means that in most jurisdictions a defendant who wishes to preserve his pretrial objections for appeal must go to trial. A few jurisdictions have provided for a contrary result by court rules or statutory provisions to the effect that, upon a properly conditional plea, certain pretrial motions, such as suppression motions, may be reviewed upon appeal from an ensuing conviction notwithstanding the fact that such judgment is based upon the defendant's plea rather than a finding of guilty after trial. As the Supreme Court put it in *Lefkowitz v. Newsome* (1975), holding that such a provision has the effect of preserving the claim for federal habeas corpus review as well, it constitutes a "commendable effort to relieve the problem of congested trial calendars in a manner that does not diminish the opportunity for the assertion of rights guaranteed by the Constitution."

(c) Trial on Stipulated Facts. Yet another device sometimes utilized to avoid both the necessity for a full trial and the waiver-forfeiture consequences attending a nolo or guilty plea is a trial on stipulated facts. Under this procedure, the defendant enters a plea of not guilty, after which the case is submitted to the judge for decision upon the preliminary hearing transcript or other statement of facts agreed to by the parties. If the judge finds the defendant guilty, the defendant will have retained his usual right to appeal. But the conditional plea is a better procedure: it saves time by avoiding the need for even a short trial; it is more likely to be understood by the defendant; and there is a risk that in some circumstances the stipulation procedure will be viewed by an appellate court as foreclosing the very issue the defendant sought to preserve.

*

Chapter 14

TRIAL BY JURY AND IMPARTIAL JUDGE

Table of Sections

> For additional analysis of the above topics and citations to authorities supporting their discussion in this Book, consult the authors' 7-volume *Criminal Procedure* treatise, also available as Westlaw database CRIMPROC. See the Table of Cross-References in this Book.

§ 14.1   The Right to Jury Trial

(a) **Generally; Applicable to the States.** The Sixth Amendment provides that in "all criminal prosecutions" the defendant is entitled to trial "by an impartial jury of the State and district wherein the crime shall have been committed." The Supreme Court on several occasions indicated that this Sixth Amendment right was not applicable to the states via the Fourteenth Amendment due process clause, but when, as the Court put it in *Duncan v. La.* (1968), it was deemed more appropriate to settle the incorporation question by asking whether the right "is necessary to an Anglo–American regime of ordered liberty," then it was apparent that the Sixth Amendment right to jury trial was also applicable to the states. As the Court explained in *Duncan*: "[p]roviding an accused with the right to be tried by a jury of his peers [gives] him an inestimable safeguard against the corrupt or overzealous prosecutor and against the compliant, biased, or eccentric judge." The *Duncan* majority conceded that jury trial has "its weaknesses and the potential for misuse," but concluded it was well established that in criminal cases "juries do understand the evidence and come to sound conclusions in most of the cases presented to them."

The right recognized in *Duncan* is to have a jury pass on the ultimate question of guilt or innocence. This means that though it is for the judge to "instruct the jury on the law and to insist that the jury follow his instructions," "the jury's constitutional responsibility is not merely to determine the facts, but to apply the law to those facts and draw the ultimate conclusion of guilt or innocence." The right to jury trial does not include the matter of sentencing. As stated in *Spaziano v. Fla.* (1984), the Sixth Amendment "never has been thought to guarantee a right to a jury determination" of "the appropriate punishment to be imposed on an individual." The Court there held that this was so even as to the death penalty, and that consequently there was no constitutional prohibition upon a sentencing scheme permitting a trial judge to override a jury's recommendation of a life sentence instead of the death penalty. But the Supreme Court later held in *Apprendi v. N.J.* (2000) that any fact (other than the fact of a prior conviction) that increases the penalty for a crime beyond the prescribed statutory maximum is, in effect, an element of the crime, which must be submitted to a jury and proved beyond a reasonable doubt. So where the death penalty may be imposed only upon a finding of enumerated aggravating factors operating as "the functional equivalent of an element of a greater offense," then the Sixth Amendment requires that they be found by a jury, *Ring v. Ariz.* (2002). And where in a sentencing guidelines system an enhanced sentence must be based upon facts other than those established by the conviction, as in *Blakely v.*

Wash. (2004), their existence must be found by a jury if not admitted by the defendant.

(b) Petty Offenses. The Court in *Duncan* noted in passing that "there is a category of petty crimes or offenses which is not subject to the Sixth Amendment jury trial provisions and should not be subject to the Fourteenth Amendment jury trial requirement here applied to the States." Shortly thereafter, in *Baldwin v. N.Y.* (1970), where appellant had been denied a jury trial when convicted of a misdemeanor punishable by imprisonment up to one year, the Court held that "no offense can be deemed 'petty' for purposes of the right to trial by jury where imprisonment for more than six months is authorized." It was emphasized that in the federal system petty offenses had long been "defined as those punishable by no more than six months in prison and a $500 fine," that "crimes triable without a jury in the American States since the late 18th century were also generally punishable by no more than a six-month prison term."

Baldwin used the word "punishable," meaning the right to jury trial is to be determined on the basis of the punishment that *could* be imposed rather than that which it turns out is actually imposed in the particular case. This is because the maximum penalty authorized by the legislature is a truer indicator of society's judgment as to the seriousness of the crime charged. But where the legislature has not set any maximum penalty, as is typically the case as to criminal contempt, the "petty offense" distinction must be made on the basis of the penalty actually imposed. In *Frank v. U.S.* (1969), where petitioner was convicted of criminal contempt without a jury and received a suspended sentence and probation for three years, and the government conceded that he could receive not more than six months imprisonment if he violated the terms of probation, the contempt was deemed a petty offense, for conditional release is a much lesser imposition than incarceration.

The Court in *Blanton v. City of North Las Vegas* (1989) declared: "The judiciary should not substitute its judgment as to seriousness for that of a legislature, which is 'far better equipped to perform the task, and [is] likewise more responsive to changes in attitude and more amenable to the recognition and correction of their misperceptions in this respect.'" The focus, therefore, is upon the various penalties that the legislature has attached to the offense in question. As explained in *Blanton*, while it is *not* the case "that an offense carrying a maximum prison term of six months or less automatically qualifies as a 'petty' offense," a "defendant is entitled to jury trial in such circumstances only if he can demonstrate that any additional statutory penalties, viewed in conjunction with the maximum authorized period of incarceration, are so severe that they clearly reflect a legislative determination that the offense in question is a 'serious' one." This standard, albeit somewhat imprecise, should ensure the availability of a jury trial in the rare situation where a legislature packs an offense it deems "serious" with onerous penalties that nonetheless "do not puncture the 6–month incarceration line."

The penalties in *Blanton* were not serious enough to trigger the jury right: the maximum authorized prison sentence did not exceed six months; the mandatory 90–day license suspension "will be irrelevant if it runs concurrently with the prison sentence, which we assume for present purposes to be the maximum of six months"; the alternative sentence of 48 hours community service while dressed in clothing identifying the defendant as a DUI offender "is less embarrassing and less onerous than six months in jail"; and the possible additional penalty of a $1,000 fine was "well below the $5,000 level set by Congress in its most recent definition of a 'petty' offense," and is not "out of step with state practice for offenses carrying prison sentences of six months or less."

Offenses involving solely monetary sanctions may also require a jury. In *Muniz v. Hoffman* (1975), where a labor union contended it was entitled to a jury trial in a criminal contempt proceeding for violating temporary injunctions, which resulted in the imposition of a fine of $10,000, the Court disagreed. Later in *International Union, UMW v. Bagwell* (1994), the Court concluded that contempt penalties against a union of over $64,000,000 were sufficiently serious to trigger the right to a jury trial. The penalty was not compensatory in nature, and punished neither conduct in the court's presence nor the failure to take affirmative action. With this rather loose guidance, lower courts have allowed fines well in excess of $10,000 to be imposed without a jury trial, at least when the defendant's illicit activity produced substantial revenue.

Finally, there is the question of whether in the joint trial of several petty offenses there is a right to jury trial if the cumulative penalty that could be imposed exceeds the petty offense limits. One aspect of this problem reached the Supreme Court in *Codispoti v. Pa.* (1979), holding that in the case of post-verdict adjudications of various acts of contempt committed during trial, the Sixth Amendment requires a jury trial if the sentences imposed aggregate more than six months, even though no sentence for more than six months was imposed for any one act of contempt, as "the salient fact [is] that the contempts arose from a single trial, were charged by a single judge and were tried in a single proceeding." But *Lewis v. U.S.* (1996) distinguished *Codispoti* and concluded: "Here, by setting the maximum authorized prison term at six months, the legislature categorized the offense of obstructing the mail as petty. The fact that the petitioner was charged with two counts of a petty offense does not revise the legislative judgment as to the gravity of that particular offense, nor does it transform the petty offense into a serious one, to which the jury-trial right would apply." Under *Lewis*, if a petty offense is joined with a nonpetty offense, there is no inherent barrier to having the guilty/not guilty determination made, respectively, by the judge and the jury, although due process considerations require both charges go to the jury whenever the petty offense is a lesser included offense of the joined nonpetty offense.

(c) **Noncriminal Trials.** Although the Sixth Amendment right to jury trial by its own terms extends only to "criminal prosecutions," it has been argued from time to time that the right extends also to other proceedings bearing some similarity to criminal trials. Courts have generally not been receptive to this contention. It has been held, for example, that this right does not extend to suits by the government to collect civil penalties, sexual psychopath proceedings, or paternity actions. In *McKeiver v. Pa.* (1971), the Supreme Court held that "trial by jury in the juvenile court's adjudicative stage is not a constitutional requirement," reasoning that compelling jury trial might make the proceeding fully adversary and deprive it of its informal and protective character.

(d) **Size of Jury.** Although the Supreme Court had originally ruled that the right guaranteed by the Sixth Amendment was a trial by the traditional jury of 12 persons, in *Williams v. Fla.* (1970) the Court held that the Sixth Amendment was not violated by use of six–person juries. The Court explained that "the essential feature of a jury," "interposition between the accused and his accuser of the common-sense judgment of a group of laymen, and in the community participation and shared responsibility which results from that group's determination of guilt or innocence," only required a number of jurors "large enough to promote group deliberation, free from outside attempts at intimidation, and to provide a fair possibility for obtaining a representative cross section of the community." This was deemed to be the case "when the jury numbers six," "particularly if the requirement of unanimity is retained." Later, in *Ballew v. Ga.* (1978), it was held that petitioner's trial before a five–member jury deprived him of his constitutional right to jury trial. Although the Court did "not pretend to discern a clear line between six members and five," it concluded that "any further reduction" in jury size "attains constitutional significance," especially in light of the fact that there is "no significant state advantage in reducing the number of jurors from six to five."

(e) **Unanimity.** In *Apodaca v. Or.* (1972), where petitioners had been convicted of felonies by 11–1 and 10–2 votes, the Supreme

Court held that the Sixth Amendment does not require jury unanimity. As in *Williams,* the Court began the analysis with the assertion that "the essential feature of a jury obviously lies in the interposition between the accused and his accuser of the common-sense judgment of a group of laymen," and then concluded that a "requirement of unanimity, however, does not materially contribute to the exercise of this commonsense judgment," as "a jury will come to such a judgment as long as it consists of a group of laymen representative of a cross section of the community who have the duty and the opportunity to deliberate, free from outside attempts at intimidation, on the question of a defendant's guilt." The Court acknowledged that "requiring unanimity would obviously produce hung juries in some situations where nonunanimous juries will convict or acquit," but concluded that "in either case, the interest of the defendant in having the judgment of his peers interposed between himself and the officers of the State who prosecute and judge him is equally well served."

The plurality opinion in *Apodaca* also rejected the contention, raised without success in the companion case of *Johnson v. La.* (1972), that unanimity was required to effectuate the constitutional requirement that the defendant be proved guilty beyond a reasonable doubt. It noted that the reasonable doubt standard developed separately from the jury trial right and that, in any event, lack of unanimity was not the equivalent of a reasonable doubt. As for the claim that unanimity was a necessary precondition for effective application of the requirement that jury panels reflect a cross section of the community, the *Apodaca* plurality opinion rejected the assumption that "minority groups, even when they are represented on a jury, will not adequately represent the viewpoint of those groups simply because they may be outvoted in the final result." The Court did not say in *Apodaca* and *Johnson* how great a departure from unanimity would be tolerated, but in a brief concurring opinion Justice Blackmun, noting the assertion in *Johnson* that "a substantial majority of the jury" are to be convinced, declared that "a 7–5 standard, rather than a 9–3 or 75% minimum, would afford me great difficulty." Justice Powell, who supplied the critical fifth vote in *Apodaca,* explained in his concurrence that he based it upon his conclusion that unanimity was a part of the Sixth Amendment's jury trial right but was not incorporated by the due process clause. This meant that *Apodaca* authorized non unanimous verdicts in state but not federal trials.

With *Williams* having declared that there is no right to a jury of 12 and *Apodaca* that there is no right to unanimity, it was perhaps inevitable that the Court would ultimately have to consider the extent to which both variations from the traditional jury could be simultaneously permitted. *Burch v. La.* (1979) presented such a question, for at issue there was a provision that misdemeanors punishable by more than six months "shall be tried before a jury of six persons, five of whom must concur to render a verdict." A unanimous Court struck down that provision. Noting "that lines must be drawn somewhere if the substance of the jury trial right is to be preserved," the Court concluded that the "near-uniform judgment of the Nation," reflected by the fact that only two states allowed nonunanimous verdicts by six–person juries, "provides a useful guide in delimiting the line between those jury practices that are constitutionally permissible and those that are not."

(f) Jury Nullification. The function of the jury is commonly said to be that of ascertaining the facts and then applying the law, as stated by the judge, to those facts. Indeed, it is not at all unusual for a jury in a criminal case to be instructed that it has the "duty" to proceed in such a fashion. But a jury in a criminal case has the power to acquit even when its findings as to the facts, if literally applied to the law as stated by the judge, would have resulted in a conviction. This is because a jury verdict of not guilty is not subject to reversal or to review in any manner whatsoever. On occasion, juries exercise this power by acquitting defendants who are charged with violating an unpopular law and defendants otherwise viewed sympathetically.

Some have argued that this practice, usually referred to as jury nullification, is part of the right to jury trial guaranteed by the Sixth Amendment. However, there is not complete agreement on this point. In *U.S. v. Thomas* (1997), holding that a juror's intent to acquit regardless of the evidence constitutes a basis for the juror's removal during the deliberations, the court used strong language to the contrary: "Nullification is, by definition, a violation of a juror's oath to apply the law as instructed by the court * * * We categorically reject the idea that, in a society committed to the rule of law, jury nullification is desirable or that courts may permit it to occur when it is within their authority to prevent." The prevailing view is that the jury may not be told specifically that it has this power. This view is often attributed to *Sparf and Hansen v. U.S.* (1895), upholding a jury instruction that "a jury is expected to be governed by law, and the law it should receive from the court." But *Sparf* did not settle the jury nullification issue, for the Court did not address the specific question whether jurors should be told they can refuse to enforce the law's harshness when justice so requires, though lower courts have rather consistently ruled that no such instruction should be given. In support of that position, it is argued that the jury system has worked out reasonably well overall without resort to a nullification instruction, and that a nullification instruction would upset the existing balance and produce many more hung juries. In opposition, it is contended that there is no reason to assume that juries will act in a less desirable way if informed about their nullification power, that there are political advantages to be gained by not lying to the jury, and that a nullification instruction would serve to discourage acquittals based on prejudice instead of encouraging them because it sets justice and conscience as the standards for acquittal rather than leaving the jurors to use their own biases as standards.

(g) **Waiver of Jury Trial.** Contrary to earlier practice, waiver of jury trial is now generally permitted except when expressly prohibited by a constitutional or statutory provision, as is the case in a few jurisdictions. A major influence in bringing about this shift was *Patton v. U.S.* (1930), settling that waiver of jury trial was permissible in a federal criminal trial. In support of this conclusion, the Court in *Patton* pointed out that: (1) constitutional provisions as to jury trials are primarily for the protection of the accused, and thus waiver by the party sought to be benefited should be possible; (2) absence of a jury does not affect the jurisdiction of the court; (3) the argument that public policy requires jury trials is fallacious, as a defendant may plead guilty and thus dispense with trial altogether; and (4) the common law rule not permitting waiver was justified by conditions that no longer exist. The Court in *Patton* emphasized that for a waiver of jury trial to be effective there must be "the express and intelligent consent of the defendant"; it is not merely a tactical decision that may be left to defense counsel. Waiver cannot be presumed from a silent record, and thus the better practice is for the defendant to be specifically advised by the court of his right to jury trial and for the waiver to be by the defendant personally either in writing or for the record in open court. If a "jury waiver agreement" is entered into contemplating concessions to the defendant for his jury waiver, questions of alleged breach of the agreement are dealt with in essentially the same way as with plea bargains.

However, only a minority of states give the defendant an unconditional right to trial without a jury; elsewhere the defendant must also obtain the consent of the court, the consent of the prosecution, or both. In the federal system the defendant must have "the approval of the court and the consent of the government." In *Singer v. U.S.* (1965), the Court found "no constitutional impediment to conditioning a waiver of this right on the consent of the prosecuting attorney and the trial judge when, if either refuses to consent, the result is simply that the defendant is subject to an impartial trial by jury—the very thing that the Constitution guarantees him." The Court emphasized that there was no common law right to trial by the court, that generally the "ability to waive a constitutional right does not ordinarily carry with it the right to insist upon the opposite of that right," and that jury trial is the "normal and * * * preferable mode of dispensing of issues of fact in criminal cases." But the Court concluded with the cautionary note that it did "not determine in this case whether there might be some circumstances where a defendant's reasons for wanting to be tried by a judge alone are so compelling that the Government's insistence on trial by jury would result in the denial to a defendant of an impartial trial." Experience has shown that defendants relying upon this passage have generally been unable to convince the court that their reasons for wanting a trial by the court alone are sufficiently "compelling" that defendant's waiver motion must be granted despite the prosecution's opposition.

Patton actually involved a "partial" waiver of the right to jury trial, for the waiver upheld there concerned only the requirement that the jury consist of 12 persons. Some states expressly provide for pretrial election by the defendant to be tried by a smaller jury. Waiver of the number of jurors also occurs when the defendant agrees in advance or at the time of the event that the trial may continue with some lesser number of jurors when otherwise a mistrial would be necessitated by the excusal of some jurors during the trial or deliberations. In contrast to the situation in *Patton*, courts are generally not inclined to permit waiver by a defendant of his right to a unanimous verdict.

§ 14.2   Selection of Prospective Jurors

(a) **Federal Jury Selection Procedures.** Jury selection in the federal courts is governed by the Federal Jury Selection and Service Act of 1968 (23 U.S.C.A. §§ 1861–1869), the purpose of which is to ensure that juries are "selected at random from a fair cross section of the community in the district or division wherein the court convenes" and that "[n]o citizen shall be excluded from service as a grand or petit juror in the district courts of the United States on account of race, color, religion, sex, national origin, or economic status." Each district court is required to devise and implement a jury selection plan designed to achieve those objectives. Each plan must, inter alia, (1) specify whether the names of prospective jurors are to be selected from voter registration lists or the lists of actual voters of the political subdivisions within the district or division, and prescribe other sources when necessary to achieve the objectives stated above; (2) specify those groups of persons or occupational classes whose members shall on individual request be excused from jury service because such service would entail undue hardship or extreme inconvenience; and (3) specify that active members of the armed forces, members of fire or police departments, and members of the executive, legislative or judicial

branches of government who are actively engaged in the performance of official duties are barred from jury service on the ground
that they are exempt.

From time to time as directed by the district court, the clerk or
a district judge is publicly to draw at random from the jury wheel
the names of as many persons as may be required for jury service.
A juror qualification form is to be sent to each person drawn. A
district judge is to determine whether a person is unqualified for, or
exempt, or to be excused from jury service. A person is deemed
qualified unless he "(1) is not a citizen of the United States
eighteen years old who has resided for a period of one year within
the judicial district; (2) is unable to read, write, and understand the
English language with a degree of proficiency sufficient to fill out
satisfactorily the juror qualification form; (3) is unable to speak the
English language; (4) is incapable, by reason of mental or physical
infirmity, to render satisfactory jury service; or (5) has a charge
pending against him for the commission of, or has been convicted in
a State or Federal court of record of, a crime punishable by
imprisonment for more than one year and his civil rights have not
been restored."

The names of all persons drawn from the master jury wheel
who are determined to be qualified as jurors and not exempt or
excused are to be placed in a qualified jury wheel, from which the
names of persons to be assigned to jury panels are to be publicly
drawn from time to time. Summonses for those persons are then to
be issued. A person drawn is not to be disqualified, excluded,
excused or exempted from service except as indicated above, provided that a person summoned may be "(1) excused by the court, upon
a showing of undue hardship or extreme inconvenience, for such
period as the court deems necessary * * *, or (2) excluded by the
court on the ground that such person may be unable to render
impartial jury service or that his service as a juror would be likely
to disrupt the proceedings, or (3) excluded upon peremptory challenge as provided by law, or (4) excluded pursuant to the procedure
specified by law upon a challenge by any party for good cause
shown, or (5) excluded upon determination by the court that his
service as a juror would be likely to threaten the secrecy of the
proceedings, or otherwise adversely affect the integrity of jury
deliberations."

(b) State Jury Selection Procedures. Largely as a result of
changes adopted in recent years, states now follow procedures
similar to those described above in an effort to select jurors at
random from some standard list. A high percentage of those persons whose names are drawn for state jury service seek to be
excused, and in many states excuses are rather readily granted.

Statutes in many states list occupational exemptions from jury service (e.g., doctors, pharmacists, teachers, clergy, and certain public employees).

(c) Denial of Equal Protection. Long before the Sixth Amendment right to jury trial was applied to the states, state jury selection procedures were subjected to constitutional challenge on the ground that they violated the Equal Protection Clause of the Fourteenth Amendment. Just a few years after the Amendment was adopted, the Supreme Court held in *Strauder v. W. Va.* (1880) that it was a denial of equal protection for a state to try a black defendant before a jury from which all members of his race has been excluded pursuant to a statute limiting jury service to "white male persons." A year later, in *Neal v. Del.* (1881), the principle was extended to the discriminatory administration of ostensibly fair jury selection laws to achieve the same result.

An equal protection challenge can succeed only upon a sufficient showing of intentional or deliberate discrimination. For many years, defendants seldom succeeded in making the requisite showing; the state action was presumed constitutional and the lower court findings were presumed to be true. But then came *Norris v. Ala.* (1935), where the Supreme Court held that a defendant in a criminal case could make out a prima facie case of discriminatory jury selection by showing (i) the existence of a substantial number of blacks in the community, and (ii) their total or virtual exclusion from jury service. Once such a prima facie case is established, the burden then shifts to the state to prove that the exclusion did not flow from intentional discrimination, which is not met merely by testimony from a jury commissioner that he did not intend to discriminate or that he did not know any qualified blacks.

Much of the litigation that followed *Norris* concerned the question of what constitutes a "prima facie case" of discrimination and what the government must do to rebut such a case. While the Court has declined to hold that a statute is unconstitutional merely because it requires jury commissioners to apply rather subjective criteria providing some opportunity for discrimination, that opportunity plus a significant statistical disparity will constitute a prima facie case. The Court in *Castaneda v. Partida* (1977) emphasized that "an official act is not unconstitutional *solely* because it has a racially disproportionate impact." Discriminatory intent must be shown, but a prima facie case of such intent may be shown by "substantial underrepresentation," for when "a disparity is sufficiently large, then it is unlikely that it is due solely to chance or accident, and, in the absence of evidence to the contrary, one must conclude that racial or other class-related factors entered into the selection process." Because, as the Court also noted, "a selection procedure that is susceptible of abuse or is not racially neutral supports the presumption of discrimination raised by the statistical showing," it would seem that a somewhat smaller disparity will suffice when it occurs within a selection process containing subjective selection criteria.

It was long accepted that the constitutional challenge could be made only by a defendant who was a member of the excluded class. But in *Powers v. Ohio* (1991) the Court held that the defendant in a criminal case has standing to raise the equal protection rights of excluded jurors, who would themselves confront "considerable practical barriers" to challenging their exclusion. Thus, a white defendant may challenge the exclusion of black jurors on equal protection grounds because discrimination in jury selection "causes a criminal defendant cognizable injury, and the defendant has a concrete interest in challenging the practice."

(d) The "Fair Cross Section" Requirement. In *Glasser v. U.S.* (1942), the Court declared that because "the proper functioning of the jury system, and, indeed, our democracy itself, requires that the jury be a 'body truly representative of the community', and not the organ of any special group or class," jury officials "must not allow the desire for competent jurors to lead them into selections which do not comport with the concept of the jury as a cross-section of the community." Once *Duncan* was decided, it appeared very likely that this meant the cross-section requirement was now applicable to the states as a part of the right to jury trial, as was later held in *Taylor v. La.* (1975). The Court in *Taylor* declared that the purpose of a jury, "to guard against the exercise of arbitrary power," is not served "if the jury pool is made up of only segments of the populace or if large, distinctive groups are excluded from the pool." To prevail under *Taylor*, the Court later elaborated in *Duren v. Mo.* (1979), the defendant must show "(1) that the group alleged to be excluded is a 'distinctive' group in the community; (2) that the representation of this group in venires from which juries are selected is not fair and reasonable in relation to the number of such persons in the community; and (3) that this underrepresentation is due to systematic exclusion of the group in the jury-selection process."

Several points must be emphasized concerning the fair cross section requirement adopted in *Taylor*. For one thing, the requirement is simply that juries "must be drawn from a source fairly representative of the community"; the earlier rule that defendants are not entitled to a jury of any particular composition still obtains. Secondly, this fair cross section requirement is a right of *all* defendants; in *Taylor* a male defendant prevailed though the constitutional violation was the exclusion of women, just as in *Peters v. Kiff* (1972) a white man was entitled to claim that blacks had been systematically excluded. Thirdly, in contrast to the limitations that exist when there is an equal protection challenge, a defendant raising a cross section objection can prevail without showing purposeful discrimination; he "need only show that the jury selection procedure 'systematically exclude[s] distinctive groups in the community and thereby fail[s] to be reasonably representative thereof.' " But the "systematic exclusion" requirement would seem to mean that a constitutional violation is not made out by a showing that on a particular occasion a member of a distinct group happened to be mistakenly excused. On the other hand, a cross section violation can occur without there being total exclusion of a distinct group, though even total exclusion is not necessarily "systematic."

Next, it would appear that exclusion of only certain kinds of groups conflicts with the cross section objective. However, the Court in *Taylor,* while concluding that women were such a class, did not establish with clarity just what the nature of the excluded group must be. Reference is made to "large, distinctive groups" and "identifiable segments playing major roles in the community," and the Court asserts that "women are sufficiently numerous [53% of the citizens eligible for jury service] and distinct from men that if they are systematically eliminated from jury panels, the Sixth Amendment's fair cross section requirement cannot be satisfied." This suggests that some groups may be so small as to not come within *Taylor* and that some groups may be insufficiently "distinct" to fall within the cross section requirement. As for the nature of the required distinctness, the Court in *Taylor* indicated that it is not necessary that the members of the group "act or tend to act as a class," but only that by their absence "a flavor, a distinct quality is lost." The Court has since declined "to precisely define the term 'distinctive group,' " but has declared that exclusion of a particular group was unobjectionable where it did not contravene the three purposes of the cross-section requirement: (i) avoiding "the possibility that the composition of juries would be arbitrarily skewed in such a way as to deny criminal defendants the benefit of the common-sense judgment of the community," (ii) avoiding an "appearance of unfairness," and (iii) ensuring against deprivation of "often historically disadvantaged groups of their right as citizens to serve on juries in criminal cases." Lower courts have developed several criteria to determine whether a particular group is distinctive for cross-section analysis: (1) the group must be defined and limited by some clearly identifiable factor (such as race or sex), (2) there must be a common thread or basic similarity in attitude, ideas or experience which runs through members of the group, and (3) there must be a community of interest among the members of the group to the extent that the group's interest cannot be adequately represented if the group is excluded from the jury selection process. Racial, religious, and ethnic groups meet this distinctiveness standard.

Even if there is a systematic exclusion of a distinct group, this is not a constitutional violation if the exclusion is no broader than is necessary to serve a valid governmental interest. In *Taylor*, where the defective procedure was that women were not selected for jury service except when they filed a written declaration of a desire to so serve, the Court rightly concluded that this practice could not be justified on the ground than many women would find jury service unduly burdensome. Similarly, in *Duren v. Mo.* (1979), where any woman could decline jury service by so indicating on the jury-selection questionnaire, by returning the jury duty summons or simply by not showing up, the Court concluded that "exempting all women because of the preclusive domestic responsibilities of some women is insufficient justification for their disproportionate exclusion on jury venires." The Court added that "a State may have an important interest in assuring that those members of the family responsible for the care of children are available to do so," and suggested that an exemption "appropriately tailored to this interest would * * * survive a fair-cross-section challenge." In cases decided before and after *Taylor*, the lower courts have upheld statutory provisions or excusal procedures resulting in exclusion or underrepresentation of young people, old people, persons not registered to vote, certain occupational groups, aliens, persons lacking proficiency in English, and convicted felons.

(e) Vicinage. The concept of "vicinage" is frequently confused with that of "venue" The former refers to the place from which the jurors must be selected, while the latter makes reference to the place at which the trial must be held. The right to have juries drawn from the vicinage is guaranteed by that part of the Sixth Amendment assuring a jury "of the State and district wherein the crime shall have been committed, which district shall have been previously ascertained by law." Vicinage provisions are also found in state constitutions, commonly declaring a right to a jury "of the county in which the offense is alleged to have been committed." Courts have had few occasions to construe the vicinage requirement in the Sixth Amendment. As for its application in federal trials, the Supreme Court has decided that there is no constitutional right to have jurors drawn from the entire district in which the crime occurred. Lower courts have extended this proposition a bit farther by holding that the Sixth Amendment confers no right to have a jury drawn in whole or in part from that portion of the district encompassing the location of the crime. As for application of the Sixth Amendment vicinage requirement to state prosecutions, the courts have generally assumed that it is applicable for the most part. But there is not complete agreement as to what the vicinage requirement of the Sixth Amendment means in a state trial context. One view is that it merely requires that the petit jurors be drawn from within the state and federal judicial district in which the crime was committed, so that it would be permissible for a state to draw a jury and try the defendant in a county other than that in which the crime occurred so long as the two counties were in the same federal district. Another is that it is sufficient that the jurors are selected from the county, and that they need not be from the particular state judicial district where the crime occurred.

§ 14.3   Voir Dire; Challenges

(a) **Nature of Voir Dire.** If the defendant has not waived jury trial, then it is necessary to select from the panel of prospective jurors those individuals who will actually serve as jurors in his case. The examination of prospective jurors for this purpose is commonly referred to as the voir dire, an ancient phrase literally meaning "to speak the truth." This process, by which both the defense and the prosecution try to eliminate certain prospective jurors, is a very important part of trial procedure. Prospective jurors can be challenged in two ways during voir dire: by a challenge for cause, which requires the challenging party to satisfy the judge that there is a sufficient likelihood that the prospective juror is biased in some way, or peremptory challenge, which may be exercised in specified numbers without giving any reason and without control by the court. The latter is used to eliminate those prospective jurors suspected of being biased or believed, by virtue of their backgrounds and experience, to be more likely to favor the trial opponent.

One important and legitimate function of the voir dire examination of prospective jurors is to elicit information establishing a basis for challenges for cause. A second is to facilitate the intelligent use of peremptory challenges. A third function of the voir dire, albeit one which many would not view as legitimate, is that of indoctrinating the potential jurors on the merits of the case and developing rapport. The trial judge has considerable discretion in deciding what questions may be asked of the prospective jurors. He must be free to exclude those questions that are intended solely to accomplish some improper purpose or which are not phrased in neutral, non-argumentative form, to restrict the examination of jurors within reasonable bounds so as to expedite the trial and on occasion to restrict questioning in order to give some protection to the privacy of prospective jurors.

An appellate court is unlikely to reverse a trial judge's decision not to permit certain questions unless it seems likely that as a result of the limited voir dire the jury was prejudiced. Illustrative is *Rosales–Lopez v. U.S.* (1981), concluding the failure to honor the defendant's request for inquiry into racial or ethnic prejudice "will only be reversible error where the circumstances of the case indicate that there is a reasonable possibility that racial or ethnic prejudice might have influenced the jury." which is the case when "such an inquiry [was] requested by a defendant accused of a violent crime and * * * the defendant and the victim are members of different racial or ethnic groups." A defendant is even less likely to prevail if he makes a constitutional challenge to the limited scope of the voir dire. In *Ham v. S.C.* (1973), where a black civil rights worker was convicted of possession of marijuana, during voir dire the trial judge asked general questions as to bias, prejudice or partiality, but declined to ask more specific questions tendered by defense counsel which sought to elicit any possible prejudice against the defendant because of his race. The Court concluded that "since a principal purpose of the adoption of the Fourteenth Amendment was to prohibit the States from invidiously discriminating on the basis of race, we think that the Fourteenth Amendment required the judge in this case to interrogate the jurors upon the subject of racial prejudice." But *Ham* has had a rather limited impact. For one thing, the Court has as yet declined to extend the doctrine to matters other than racial prejudice. In *Ham* itself, the Court rejected petitioner's claim that the trial judge should have also inquired about possible prejudice against defendant because of his beard, in light of "the traditionally broad discretion accorded to the trial judge in conducting voir dire, and our inability to constitutionally distinguish possible prejudice against beards from a host of other possible similar prejudices." More significant is the fact that the Supreme Court and lower courts have applied *Ham* narrowly even on the question of racial prejudice. In *Ristaino v. Ross* (1976), the Court declined to find that "the need to question veniremen specifically about racial prejudice also rose to constitutional dimensions in this case," reasoning that the "mere fact that the victim of the crimes alleged was a white man and the defendants were Negroes was less likely to distort the trial than were the special factors involved in *Ham*."

The trial court has less discretion over questions asked during voir dire to select a jury in a capital case than in other criminal cases. In *Turner v. Murray* (1986), the Court held "that a capital defendant accused of an interracial crime is entitled to have prospective jurors informed of the race of the victim and questioned on the issue of racial bias." Parties must also be permitted to identify prospective jurors who would be unable to apply the law concerning the death penalty, a process known as "death-qualifying" the jury, discussed in connection with challenges for cause, below.

As for the manner in which the voir dire should be conducted, in the federal system the "court may permit the defendant or his attorney and the attorney for the government to conduct the examination of prospective jurors or may itself conduct the examination." But in the latter event "the court shall permit the defendant or his attorney and the attorney for the government to supplement the examination by such further inquiry as it deems proper or shall itself submit to the prospective jurors such additional questions by the parties or their attorneys as it deems proper." One study showed that over half of the federal judges questioned the jurors by themselves, about a third allowed the attorneys to ask supplemental questions, and the rest allowed the attorneys to ask all of the questions. There is also considerable variation in the permitted practice at the state level.

(b) Prosecution and Defense Access to Information. Most states have adopted statutes providing for defendants in criminal cases to receive in advance of trial a list of prospective jurors. Some of these enactments confer this right upon all defendants, while some are limited to felony cases or capital cases. Even in the absence of such legislation, it has sometimes been held that the defendant upon timely motion is entitled to obtain that list in advance of trial. On the federal level, a statute declares that one "charged with treason or other capital offense shall at least three entire days before commencement of trial be furnished with * * * a list of the veniremen, * * * stating the place of abode of each venireman," which has been interpreted to mean that there is no such right in other cases. However, it is provided in the Federal Jury Selection and Service Act that a defendant "shall be allowed to inspect, reproduce, and copy" those "records or papers used by the jury commission or clerk in connection with the jury selection process" at "all reasonable times during the preparation and pendency" of a motion to stay the proceedings because of noncompliance with the Act. This latter provision has been characterized by the Supreme Court as giving the defendant "essentially an unqualified right to inspect jury lists," but it is important to note that this statute is limited to instances in which a challenge to the entire panel is being made and thus is inapplicable where the list is desired only for purposes relating to conducting the voir dire.

In limited circumstances in which there is good reason to believe the jury needs protection, the names of the jurors and their addresses and places of employment may be withheld in advance of trial and even during the jury selection. The generally-accepted rule is that a so-called anonymous jury is a permissible precaution where (1) there are strong grounds for concluding that it is necessary to enable the jury to perform its factfinding function, or to ensure juror protection; and (2) reasonable safeguards are adopted by the trial court to minimize any risk of infringement upon the fundamental rights of the accused.

When the identity of the prospective jurors is known, the prosecution or the defense or both may undertake a pretrial investigation of them. As a general matter, the prosecution is in a better position to conduct such a pretrial investigation. Because members of the prosecution staff may have conducted earlier trials involving members of the same panel, the prosecution may be able to compile information on the voting habits of particular jurors. The prosecution will likewise have more ready access to the arrest and conviction records and other government records relating to the prospective jurors. Moreover, the prosecution may utilize the investigative services of local police or the FBI in acquiring background information. Wealthy defendants and those in so-called political cases often have pretrial investigation conducted on their behalf. The traditional view is that discovery of juror information from the other party by either the prosecution or defense is not allowed. However, a few courts have viewed sympathetically the proposition that the jury selection process is harmed when the parties have dramatically disparate amounts of information about the prospective jurors, and thus have allowed a defendant who lacks funds to investigate prospective jurors to inspect prosecution jury records and investigations.

(c) Challenges for Cause. Both the defense and the prosecution may challenge an unlimited number of jurors for cause, but no juror can be removed on this ground unless the judge agrees that one of the bases for such a challenge is present. The grounds for a challenge for cause are commonly set out by statute, and are typically stated in terms of a series of specific situations: that the person lacks the legal qualifications for jury service; that he has previously served as a juror on some related matter, such as on the grand jury which indicted the defendant, on the petit jury which formerly tried defendant on this charge, or on a jury which tried another person charged with the same offense; that he has served or will serve as a witness regarding the subject matter of the pending trial; or that he is related in some degree to the defendant or others directly involved in this case. In addition, a more general ground for challenge is typically stated in terms such as the following:

> That the juror has a state of mind in reference to the cause or to the defendant or to the person alleged to have been injured by the offense charged, or to the person on whose complaint the prosecution was instituted, which will prevent him from acting with impartiality; but the formation of an

opinion or impression regarding the guilt or innocence of the defendant shall not of itself be sufficient ground of challenge to a juror, if he declares, and the court is satisfied, that he can render an impartial verdict according to the evidence.

If the prospective juror is found to have the "state of mind" described above, then this is a case of actual bias requiring that the challenge for cause be granted. But, as the language quoted above indicates, this is not to suggest that a prospective juror must be excused merely because he knows something of the case to be tried or has formed some opinions regarding it. This actual bias is not limited to specific bias, that is, a bias grounded in personal knowledge or a personal relationship. Virtually all courts authorize the questioning of jurors in areas of nonspecific bias, such as actual prejudice grounded in the prospective juror's feelings regarding the race, religion, and ethnic or other group to which the defendant belongs.

If during the voir dire a certain prospective juror actually admits to such a "state of mind," he will of course be challenged and excused. But such admissions are infrequent, as a prejudiced juror is unlikely to recognize or admit his own personal prejudice. This raises the important question of whether, at least in some circumstances, bias should be implied and the prospective juror excused notwithstanding his claim of impartiality. One way in which this issue arises is when there has been extensive pretrial publicity. In *Irvin v. Dowd* (1961), for example, there had been extensive publicity announcing that defendant had confessed to six murders and 24 burglaries and that he had offered to plead guilty. On voir dire, 8 of the 12 jurors selected expressed the opinion that defendant was guilty, but all said they would render an impartial verdict. In overturning the defendant's conviction, the Supreme Court concluded that "such a statement of impartiality can be given little weight" where, as here, the voir dire reflected a "pattern of deep and bitter prejudice" in the community. But in *Murphy v. Fla.* (1975), the Court rejected the contention that *Irvin* or the Court's other prior decisions stood "for the proposition that juror exposure to information about a state defendant's prior convictions or to new accounts of the crime with which he is charged alone presumptively deprives the defendant of due process," so that bias should be implied in such circumstances notwithstanding the juror's claim of impartiality.

The implied bias issue has also been raised when prospective jurors are employees of the governmental unit undertaking the prosecution. But in *Dennis v. U.S.* (1950), the Court held that in a case where the federal government is a party, its employees are not challengeable for cause solely by reason of their employment. The ruling of the Court, that a "holding of implied bias to disqualify jurors because of their relationship with the Government is no longer permissible," continues to be followed. Lower courts are not in agreement as to whether bias may be implied because the prospective juror is employed by the victim of the crime, but are generally disinclined to imply bias because of a prospective juror's membership in some special interest organization.

Sometimes, as in *Witherspoon v. Ill.* (1968), a defendant will object that the trial court was too generous in granting challenges for cause made by the prosecution. In selecting jurors for a murder trial at which the jury would have the responsibility for deciding on the death penalty if a guilty verdict was returned, nearly half of the panel was eliminated pursuant to a statute declaring it a cause for challenge that a prospective juror states "that he has conscientious scruples against capital punishment." The Court concluded that "when it swept from the jury all who expressed conscientious or religious scruples against capital punishment or all who opposed it in principle, * * * the State produced a jury uncommonly willing to condemn a man to die," and thus no "defendant can constitutionally be put to death at the hands of a tribunal so selected." Although several lower courts, relying upon language in *Witherspoon*, concluded that veniremen could be constitutionally excluded only if it was "unmistakably clear" they would "automatically" vote against the death penalty, in *Wainwright v. Witt* (1985) the Court opted for a less demanding standard: "whether the juror's views would 'prevent or substantially impair the performance of his duties as a juror in accordance with his instructions and his oath.' " Requiring unmistakable clarity, the Court observed, is unrealistic, for "many veniremen simply cannot be asked enough questions to reach the point where their bias had been made 'unmistakably clear.' " And the "automatically" language was now inappropriate because it could not "be squared with the duties of present-day capital sentencing juries," who now are typically asked to respond to factual inquiries bearing on whether death is the appropriate penalty. In *Gray v. Miss.* (1987), the Court rejected a variety of contentions made in support of the proposition that a single deviation from the *Witherspoon-Witt* standard would not inevitably nullify the sentence of death.

In what is sometimes referred to as the "reverse-*Witherspoon*" situation, the defense in a capital case will wish to have prospective jurors questioned on voir dire in order to discover and challenge any of them who would automatically vote for the death penalty in every capital case. Relying upon "the requirement of impartiality in the Due Process Clause of the Fourteenth Amendment," the Court in *Morgan v. Ill.* (1992) held that on a defendant's request specific inquiry into such views was constitutionally mandated. Responding to the state's claim that the trial judge's "general fairness and 'follow the law' questions" sufficed, the Court asserted that the state's "own request for questioning under *Witherspoon* * * * belies this argument." Any prospective juror found to have such views should be excused, as such a person has already formed an opinion on the merits of the case and has manifested an inability to follow jury instructions to consider mitigating circumstances. The Court warned: "If even one such juror is empaneled and the death sentence is imposed, the State is disentitled to execute the sentence."

Because the proposition was put that way, *Morgan* does not disturb the earlier decision in *Ross v. Okla.* (1988), where the trial judge erred in denying such a reverse-*Witherspoon* motion, but the defendant then used one of his nine peremptories to strike that juror. The Court held the defendant had not been denied an impartial jury, as that juror "was thereby removed from the jury as effectively as if the trial court had excused him for cause," and the loss of a peremptory was likewise no such denial because "peremptory challenges are not of constitutional dimension." As for the defendant's claim it constituted a violation of due process to deprive him, in effect, of a full complement of peremptories as provided by statute, the Court in *Ross* answered that "peremptory challenges are a creature of statute," meaning the state may "define their purpose and the manner of their exercise." Here, by state law the grant of nine peremptories in capital cases "is qualified by the requirement that the defendant must use those challenges to cure erroneous refusal by the trial court to excuse jurors for cause."

Errors in death qualification will invalidate a resulting death sentence, but not the underlying conviction. Despite "substantial empirical support for the conclusion that a death-qualified jury is more likely to convict than a non-death-qualified," in *Lockhart v. McCree* (1986) the Court held that the Constitution does not "prohibit the removal for cause, prior to the guilt phase of a bifurcated capital trial, of prospective jurors whose opposition to the death penalty is so strong that it would prevent or substantially impair the performance of their duties as jurors at the sentencing phase of the trial." As for defendant's claim he had been denied his constitutional right to an impartial jury, the Court responded this was not so because the exclusion complained of "serves the State's entirely proper interest in obtaining a single jury that could impartially decide all of the issues in McCree's case." *McCree* was deemed controlling in *Buchanan v. Ky.* (1987), holding defendant was not deprived of his Sixth Amendment rights when the prosecution was permitted to "death-qualify" the jury at his joint trial where the death penalty was sought against his codefendant. Defendant's reliance on the cross-section requirement was again unavailing because it "applies only to venires," and his impartial jury argument was rejected on the ground that "a balancing of jurors with different predilections" is not required.

(d) Peremptory Challenges. A peremptory challenge generally requires no reason. These challenges permit the parties some say in who sits on the jury, as well as a means to exclude jurors that perhaps should have been excluded for cause. In the federal system, each side has 20 peremptories in a capital case and each has 3 in a misdemeanor case, while for a felony trial the defendant has 10 and the prosecution 6. Similar provisions are found in the states, where the prosecution usually has the same number of peremptories as the defendant. There is considerable variation in the practice where more than one defendant is being tried, all the way from giving each defendant the usual number of peremptories to be exercised individually to requiring all defendants collectively to exercise the number of peremptories a single defendant would have. In some jurisdictions the parties are required to exercise their peremptories as to each juror as he is individually selected, which deprives them of the opportunity intelligently to compare several veniremen before exercising any challenges. Another approach is for the prosecutor to call and examine 12 veniremen, exercise his challenges for cause and such peremptory challenges as he then wishes to use, replace those excused with others, and then tender a group of 12 to the defendant. The defendant then follows a similar procedure with this group and tenders a jury of 12 back to the prosecutor, and they continue on in this manner until both parties have exhausted their challenges or indicated their satisfaction with the jury. By contrast, under the so-called struck jury system jurors are first examined and challenged for cause by both sides, excused jurors are replaced on the panel, and the examination of replacements continues until a panel of qualified jurors is presented. The size of the panel at this time is 12 plus the number of peremptory strikes allowed all parties. The parties then proceed to exercise their peremptories in some order that will result in all exhausting their strikes at approximately the same time. This latter system, while perhaps more time consuming because in every case it is necessary to examine and qualify a large group of jurors, allows more intelligent exercise of peremptories because each party, at the time he exercises each peremptory challenge, is confronted with the total number of persons from whom the final jury will be formed, and thus is always in a position to exclude the person most objectionable to him.

In *Swain v. Ala.* (1965), the Court rejected the defendant's claim that the prosecutor's conduct in using his peremptory challenges to remove all six blacks from the jury constituted a denial of equal protection. But the Court did hold that if the prosecutor always challenges blacks, without regard to the nature of the crime or the defendant or the victim, then "it would appear that the purpose of the peremptory challenges is being perverted" and thus "the presumption protecting the prosecutor may well be overcome."

The *Swain* standard proved nearly impossible for defendants to meet. Finally, in *Batson v. Ky.* (1985), the Court rejected this "crippling burden of proof," and held "that a defendant may establish a prima facie case of purposeful discrimination in selection of the petit jury solely on evidence concerning the prosecutor's exercise of peremptory challenges at the defendant's trial." Under *Batson*, the defendant upon timely objection was required to show "that he is a member of a cognizable racial group" and "that the prosecutor has exercised peremptory challenges to remove from the venire members of the defendant's race." Most courts took this to mean that a white defendant could not object to the exclusion of blacks from his jury by the prosecutor's use of peremptories, but in *Powers v. Ohio* (1991), the Supreme Court rejected such a limitation. The Court first reasoned, as to the substantive guarantees of the equal protection clause, that under *Batson* the harm to be avoided is not merely trial of a defendant by a jury from which members of his own race have been eliminated, but also the harm to the community at large and to excluded jurors by excluding persons from jury service "solely by reason of their race, a practice that forecloses a significant opportunity to participate in civic life." Moreover, the Court concluded in *Powers*, the defendant in a criminal case has standing to raise the equal protection rights of excluded jurors, who would themselves confront "considerable practical barriers" to challenging their exclusion. As for the emphasis in *Batson* on racial identity between the defendant and the excused jurors, the Court noted such racial identity simply "may provide one of the easier cases to establish both a prima facie case and a conclusive showing that wrongful discrimination has occurred."

Following from the principle that the equal protection rights of jurors are violated when excluded on the basis of their race, *Batson* has not been limited to the situation where members of *minority* racial groups are excused. The constitutional protection extends to all race-based challenges, including the exclusion of potential jurors because they are white. It also extends to challenges based on nationality and ethnicity. Gender, too, is an impermissible basis on which to base the challenge. In *J.E.B. v. Ala.* (1994) the Court held "that gender, like race, is an unconstitutional proxy for jury competence and impartiality." The central consideration in *J.E.B.* was that "discrimination in jury selection, whether based on race or on gender, causes harm to the litigants, the community, and the individual jurors who are wrongfully excluded from participation in the judicial process." *J.E.B.*'s emphasis on the fact that both race and gender classifications are subject to "heightened equal protection scrutiny" suggests *Batson*'s broadest application would be to other classifications likewise receiving such scrutiny. Lower courts have divided over whether the *Batson* principle prohibits challenges based on religion, with the better view banning challenges based on membership alone but allowing challenges based on activities or articulated beliefs. Attempts to extend *Batson* to bar challenges based on age, sexual orientation, political affiliation, and a host of other characteristics, have proved less successful.

In addition, *Batson* violations are not limited to the peremptory challenges exercised by government attorneys. A *Batson* violation may be raised by the prosecutor if the *defendant* seeks to exclude members of the venire based on their race or gender. In *Ga. v. McCollum* (1992) the Court held *Batson* applicable where a prosecutor sought to prevent white defendants, charged with assaulting blacks, from striking black prospective jurors because of their race. The Court reasoned that (i) "a criminal defendant's exercise of peremptory challenges in a racially discriminatory manner inflicts the harms addressed by *Batson*," denial of prospective jurors' right to serve as jurors, and loss of public confidence in the fairness of jury verdicts; (ii) such exercise of peremptories "is performing a traditional governmental function"; (iii) "the State has standing to challenge a defendant's discriminatory use of peremptory challenges," as "its own judicial process is undermined" thereby and there are significant barriers to the excluded jurors themselves obtaining relief; and (iv) the interests served by *Batson* need not "give way to the rights of a criminal defendant," as a defendant's rights to a fair trial, counsel and an impartial jury do not include "the right to discriminate against a group of citizens based upon their race." The *McCollum* extension of *Batson* does *not* mean that a defendant in a criminal case can have his conviction overturned on equal protection grounds because of the discriminatory use of peremptories by his own attorney, though it does mean that one defendant may challenge peremptories separately exercised by a codefendant joined with him for trial.

As for the procedure that must be followed in determining whether relief under *Batson* is warranted, the Court has been quite specific. A *Batson* challenge is a process with three distinct steps. A defendant making a *Batson* challenge "must show that these facts and other relevant circumstances raise an inference that the prosecutor used that practice to exclude veniremen from the petit jury on account of their races," which is an "inference of purposeful discrimination." It is then for the trial court, considering "all relevant circumstances," such as a pattern of exercising strikes from the venire on the basis of race and the nature of the prosecutor's questions and statements on voir dire, to decide if the showing "creates a prima facie case of discrimination." If it does, then "the burden shifts to the State to come forward with a neutral explanation for challenging black jurors," which requires more than a denial of a discriminatory motive or the explanation "that he challenged jurors of the defendant's race on the assumption—or his intuitive judgment—that they would be partial to the defendant because of their shared race." As the Court later elaborated in *Purkett v. Elem* (1995), at this second stage it is not necessary that the prosecutor's explanation also be "at least minimally persuasive," for such a requirement would violate "the principle that the ultimate burden of persuasion regarding racial motivation rests with, and never shifts from, the opponent of the strike."

The final and third stage of the *Batson* analysis requires the trial court to decide if the opponent of the challenge carries "the ultimate burden of persuasion regarding racial motivation." An attorney's race-neutral reason will be rejected if it appears whites were not challenged on the same basis, as in *Miller-El v. Dretke* (2005). Other evidence deemed by the Court in *Miller-El* to be indicative of the absence of a valid reason included (1) statements by the prosecutor regarding the excused prospective juror's views which "mischaracterized [his] testimony"; (2) the prosecutor's failure "to engage in any meaningful voir dire examination" on the subject of the prosecutor's purported concerns underlying the strike; (3) unexplained utilization of state law, allowing "shuffling" of the order in which prospective jurors are examined, when many blacks were at the top of the list; (4) "contrasting voir dire questions posed respectively to black and nonblack panel members"; and (5) use of a jury selection manual encouraging exclusion of minorities from jury service. A reason which is grounded largely in speculation, hunches, or other subjective reactions rather than upon facts uncovered in the voir dire examination or otherwise is not likely to be deemed acceptable.

Experience under *Batson* has shown that it is ordinarily not difficult for prosecutors to come up with an acceptable reason; this is why some have viewed the *Batson* procedures as less an obstacle to racial discrimination than a road map to disguised discrimination, and why this experience is deemed to lend support to the view (expressed by Justice Marshall in *Batson*) that the only effective solution is to ban peremptory challenges.

While the Supreme Court declined "to formulate particular procedures to be followed" in the event of a *Batson* challenge, it would seem that adversarial hearings are the appropriate method for handling most *Batson* type disputes, as defense counsel can perform two crucial functions in such a setting: pointing out to the judge where the government's stated reason may indicate bad faith;

and preserving for the record and possible appeal facts bearing on the judge's decision. The Court in *Batson* declined to say whether, upon a finding of discrimination, it is better to start jury selection over with a new venire or simply to reinstate improperly challenged jurors onto the present venire. When there has been an uncorrected *Batson* violation at the trial level preserved for appeal, the appropriate appellate remedy is automatic reversal.

(e) **Alternate Jurors.** The rule at common law was that if there was some reason for discharging a juror during trial, then it was necessary to discharge the entire jury and begin the trial anew. To avoid this undesirable result, statutes and court rules now provide for the selection of alternate or additional jurors during protracted trials. Two different types of statutes and rules are to be found. The most common is the alternate juror or substituted juror type, under which one or more persons specifically identified at the outset as alternates are chosen in advance of trial. If a regular juror is discharged prior to the time the jury retires (or, in a few jurisdictions, prior to the time of verdict), an alternate juror is then designated to take his place. By contrast, under the additional juror or eliminated juror system, more than 12 jurors are selected in advance of trial. If a juror must be discharged during the trial, this is done without any further action at that time. Should more than 12 jurors remain at the time the jury is to retire, the 12 who are to participate in the deliberations are selected by lot. In the federal system as many as six alternates may be selected, while in the states the number is typically one or two.

Many states follow the former federal rule that alternates could replace regular jurors only "prior to the time the jury retires to consider its verdict." A growing body of authority recognizes that substitution of an alternate during deliberation is constitutionally permissible, at least if the substituted juror had not theretofore been relieved of the obligations of a juror or otherwise become tainted and if in addition the jury was carefully instructed to begin its deliberations anew when its composition changed. Another possible solution, now authorized in federal practice, is simply proceeding with a jury of eleven should it become necessary to excuse one of the jurors during the course of the deliberations.

§ 14.4 Challenging the Judge

(a) **Right to Impartial Judge.** Just as the defendant's right to jury trial is to an "impartial" jury, he also has a constitutional right to an impartial judge. As the Supreme Court held in *Tumey v. Ohio* (1927), "it certainly violates the Fourteenth Amendment and deprives a defendant in a criminal case of due process of law to subject his liberty or property to the judgment of a court, the judge of which has a direct, personal, substantial pecuniary interest in reaching a conclusion against him in his case." The Court concluded that such was the case in *Tumey,* where the mayor, authorized to try certain offenses, in addition to his regular salary, received the fees and costs levied by him against violators. In *Ward v. Monroeville* (1972), the Court held that the pecuniary interest does not necessarily have to be personal in order for *Tumey* to apply; in that case it was enough that the mayor before whom defendant was compelled to stand trial for traffic offenses was responsible for village finances, and the mayor's court through fines, forfeitures, costs and fees provided a substantial portion of the village funds.

Impartiality in the constitutional sense may also be lacking because the judge is involved in a very personal way in the matter at issue, as is reflected in the contempt cases. In *Mayberry v. Pa.* (1971), for example, where a criminal defendant repeatedly insulted and vilified the trial judge during trial and at the conclusion of the trial was pronounced guilty of 11 contempts and sentenced to 11–22 years, the Court vacated the judgment of contempt. The Court first noted that as the separate acts or outbursts occurred, the trial judge "could with propriety, have instantly acted, holding [defendant] in contempt, or excluding him from the courtroom." But when the judge waits until the end of the trial, due process requires that "another judge, not bearing the sting of these slanderous remarks, and having the impersonal authority of the law," sit in judgment on defendant's conduct.

(b) Challenge for Cause. Trial judges, like jurors, are subject to challenge for cause. Grounds for challenge usually are set forth in a statute or rule of court. These provisions sometimes include specific situations, such as where there is a family relationship between the judge and the defendant, counsel, or the victim of the crime, but in any event refer more generally to situations of bias. Under some statutes it is enough that the party seeking a substitution of a judge has filed an affidavit which sufficiently states the facts and the reasons for the belief that bias or prejudice exists, while in other jurisdictions a hearing must be held on the matter and the facts showing prejudice judicially determined. Under the latter circumstances the better practice is for the matter to be heard by a judge other than the one challenged.

(c) Recusal by Judge. It is not sufficient for a judge to proceed on the assumption that he may serve in any trial except when a party has successfully alleged or proved, as may be required, that he is actually biased. As a matter of judicial ethics, the judge has a responsibility to recuse himself under certain circumstances, including whenever the judge believes his impartiality can reasonably be questioned. Because one concern here is with the appearance of impropriety, this ethical obligation of the judge clearly extends beyond instances of actual bias. Especially where this recusal responsibility is accepted as part of the law of the jurisdiction and is recognized as not merely a self-enforcing duty on the judge but as a matter that may be asserted also by a party to the action, the obvious result is a broader basis upon which to bring into question whether a particular judge may try a particular case. If the judge does not recuse himself and the basis for recusal is discovered by the defendant only after conviction, a special and narrow harmless error rule applies.

(d) Peremptory Challenge. About one-third of the states have provisions allowing a party to challenge an assigned judge without alleging or proving the precise facts that lead him to believe he cannot get a fair trial. In some states, this peremptory challenge of the judge may be exercised merely by filing a notice or motion requesting transfer of the matter to another judge. Elsewhere an affidavit of prejudice, alleging that a fair trial cannot be had before the judge and that the motion is made in good faith and not for delay, will suffice. But unlike the type of provision discussed earlier, specific facts need not be alleged, and thus the provision is properly characterized as permitting a peremptory challenge. When peremptories are allowed in criminal cases, they are almost always available to both the defendant and the prosecution.

(e) Substitution of Judge. The provisions discussed above must be distinguished from those permitting substitution of a judge because of death, sickness or other disability of the judge before whom the trial commenced. In the federal courts, such substitution is permissible if the case is being tried by a jury and if the substituted judge certifies "that he has familiarized himself with the record of the trial." Similar provisions are to be found in some states, while some other jurisdictions allow substitution even when the case is being tried without a jury. The better view, however, is that if a judge is also the trier of facts, the same judge should hear all the witnesses, unless the parties consent to substitution.

Chapter 15

FAIR TRIAL AND FREE PRESS

Table of Sections

For additional analysis of the above topics and citations to authorities supporting their discussion in this Book, consult the authors' 7-volume *Criminal Procedure* treatise, also available as Westlaw database CRIMPROC. See the Table of Cross-References in this Book.

---

§ 15.1 Preventing Prejudicial Publicity

The possible adverse impact of news coverage on the fairness of the criminal trial can be limited in various ways. One is through procedural safeguards designed to offset the potentially pernicious influence of the coverage. Section 15.2 discusses the most prominent of those safeguards, which focus on the selection of the jury and the timing and place of the trial. Another approach is to seek to reduce or eliminate that news coverage most likely to have a prejudicial influence. The subsections that follow discuss the major procedural devices aimed at that objective.

(a) **Restricting Public Statements.** In *Sheppard v. Maxwell* (1966), the Supreme Court held that defendant was deprived of his due process right to a fair trial "because of the trial judge's failure to protect Sheppard sufficiently from the massive, pervasive and prejudicial publicity that attended his prosecution." In discussing

529

the various ways in which the trial court could have exercised its "power to control the publicity about the trial," the Court asserted that "the court should have made some effort to control the release of leads, information, and gossip to the press by police officers, witnesses, and the counsel for both sides." It noted in this regard that "the trial court might well have proscribed extrajudicial statements by any lawyer, party, witness, or court official which divulged prejudicial matters, such as the refusal of Sheppard to submit to interrogation or take any lie detector tests; any statement made by Sheppard to officials; the identity of prospective witnesses or their probable testimony; any belief in guilt or innocence; or like statements concerning the merits of the case." Also, "being advised of the great public interest in the case, the mass coverage of the press, and the potential prejudicial impact of publicity, the court could * * * have requested the appropriate city and county officials to promulgate a regulation with respect to dissemination of information about the case by their employees."

Despite this strong language in *Sheppard*, there continues to be considerable uncertainty as to the extent to which a trial judge may restrict public statements of persons who are not traditionally regulated by the court in their activities relating to a case. As a result, the major focus in restricting statements has been upon the extrajudicial statements of defense counsel and prosecutors. Here, the standards of professional responsibility in every state include a provision placing limits on the content of the attorneys' statements under specified circumstances. Those provisions operate as a general restraint, imposed in every case, and are enforced primarily through lawyer disciplinary proceedings. In addition, they provide the framework commonly incorporated by judges in the issuance of "gag orders" directed at counsel in individual cases and enforced through contempt sanctions.

The vast majority of state professional responsibility provisions follow verbatim or with minor variations, one of three models: (1) Disciplinary Rule 7–107 of the American Bar Association's Model Code of Professional Responsibility; (2) the original (1983) version of Model Rule 3.6 of the ABA's Model Rules of Professional Conduct; or (3) the 1994 revision of Model Rule 3.6. Although only a handful of states retain provisions based on Disciplinary Rule 7–107, that Rule and the constitutional difficulties it was thought to present explain in large part the content of the two versions of Rule 3.6.

The three ABA models have several common elements. First, they apply only to extrajudicial statements made in a setting where the lawyer reasonably can anticipate dissemination by the media. The cases have almost uniformly involved press conferences or interviews by reporters. Second, each imposes a general limitation on extrajudicial statements tied to the statement's likely impact upon the criminal proceedings, rather than to any specific objective of the lawyer to alter the outcome of those proceedings. Requiring proof of an outcome-influencing objective would undermine the effectiveness of the provision since extrajudicial statements that might have that impact almost invariably can be characterized by the defense counsel or prosecutor as aimed at other, nontrial-related functions (e.g., a prosecutor keeping the public aware or a defense counsel preserving the defendant's reputation). Moreover, even where such other objectives are in fact the lawyer's exclusive objective, the lawyer's statement may still carry a strong potential for interfering with the fair administration of justice, particularly by prejudicing prospective jurors.

Third, under each model, the potential impact upon the criminal proceeding that brings the limitation into play is not simply the influencing of prospective jurors (although that undoubtedly is the primary concern). The standard of likely impact is not restricted to jury trials and does not create an exception for statements made after a jury has been sequestered. While the fact that the trial was to the bench, or that the jury had been sequestered, may be important in determining whether the particular standard of likely impact is met, all three models hold open the possibility of considering other types of interference with the due administration of justice, such as the publicity bringing pressure to bear upon the judge or potential witnesses. Finally, all three models seek to provide specifics to assist the lawyer in determining what content a statement to the media may and may not include. Disciplinary Rule 7–107 and the original version of Model Rule 3.6 seek to do both in the text of their respective provisions. The 1994 version of Model Rule 3.6 discusses only in its commentary the content of statements likely to be barred, but continues to include in the text a listing of the content that would be acceptable.

In *Gentile v. State Bar of Nev.* (1991), the Supreme Court had before it the application of a state professional responsibility rule (Nevada Rule 177) that followed largely verbatim the original version of Model Rule 3.6. The petitioner there, a defense attorney, had been disciplined for statements made at a press conference held shortly after his client's indictment (and six months before the anticipated trial). The client had been charged, following a highly publicized investigation, with the theft of cocaine and travelers' checks from a safety deposit box, rented from the client's vault company, that had been used in a police undercover operation. At the press conference, the petitioner made statements to the effect that: (1) his client was innocent and was "being used as a scapegoat"; (2) the evidence pointed to a named police undercover officer as the true thief; (3) the defense had a video tape which showed the officer in a physical condition described as implicitly suggesting cocaine use; and (4) the other vault customers who alleged safety deposit thefts were not credible, as most were drug dealers or money launderers who had accused the defendant in response to police pressure when they tried to "work themselves out of something." In concluding that petitioner had violated Nevada Rule 177, the state disciplinary board found that: (1) the petitioner expected both the named police officer and the other vault customers to be prosecution witnesses; (2) the petitioner's admitted purpose for calling the press conference was to influence public sentiment and the possible venire by offsetting information that had been released by the prosecutor and police (relating, in particular, to the lack of culpability of the police officer); (3) although the subsequent trial revealed there was no actual prejudice, the content, purpose, and timing of petitioner's press conference (when public interest was "at its peak") established that petitioner, in making his statements, "either knew or should have known that there was a substantial likelihood that his statements would materially prejudice the anticipated trial" (the basic prohibition of Rule 177); and (4) petitioner's comment went beyond the safe-harbor provision of Rule 177, which exempts merely "stat[ing] without elaboration * * * the general nature of the * * * [client's] defense."

Before the Supreme Court, the petitioner claimed that the State Bar's disciplinary sanction (a private reprimand) should be overturned because: (1) Nevada Rule 177 on its face violated the First Amendment; (2) the application of the Rule 177 prohibition to the facts of his case violated the First Amendment; and (3) Rule 177 was "void for vagueness" as interpreted by the Nevada authorities in their application of the Rule to his case. A Supreme Court majority (per Rehnquist, C.J.) rejected the first claim, and a differently composed majority (per Kennedy, J.) sustained the third claim. The Court was evenly divided (4–4) on petitioner's second claim of a First Amendment violation in the application of Rule 177.

Petitioner's First Amendment challenge to the facial validity of Rule 177 centered on the Rule tying the prohibited commentary to a standard of creating a "substantial likelihood of material prejudice," rather than a standard of creating "a 'clear and present danger' of 'actual prejudice.'" Chief Justice Rehnquist's opinion for the majority acknowledged that the First Amendment had been held, in cases such as *Nebraska Press* (discussed in subsection (c) below), "to require a showing of clear and present danger that a malfunction in the criminal justice system will be caused before a State may prohibit media speech or publication about a particular pending trial." However, statements in *Sheppard* and other cases "rather plainly indicat[ed] that the speech of lawyers representing clients in pending cases may be regulated under a less demanding standard than that established for regulation of the press." This was so because (1) lawyers, "[a]s officers of the court, * * * have a fiduciary responsibility not to engage in public debate that will redound to the detriment of the accused or that will obstruct the fair administration of justice," and (2) as "lawyers have special access to information through discovery and client communications, their extrajudicial statements pose a [special] threat to the fairness of a pending proceeding, since lawyers' statements are likely to be received as especially authoritative."

Chief Justice Rehnquist concluded that the Model Rule 3.6 standard on potential prejudice, incorporated in Nevada Rule 177(1), fully satisfied that "less demanding" First Amendment restriction upon state regulation of lawyer speech. The opinion noted: "We agree with the majority of the States that the 'substantial likelihood of material prejudice' standard constitutes a constitutionally permissible balance between the First Amendment rights of attorneys in pending cases and the state's interest in fair trials." That test served "to protect the integrity and fairness of a state's judicial system," while imposing "only narrow and necessary limitations on lawyers' speech * * * aimed at two principal evils: (1) comments that are likely to influence the actual outcome of the trial, and (2) comments that are likely to prejudice the jury venire, even if an untainted panel can ultimately be found." The second concern alone justified limiting lawyer speech because, even if a fair trial by "impartial" jurors can ultimately be ensured through "voir dire, change of venue, or some other device, these measures entail serious costs * * * and [t]he State has a substantial interest in preventing officers of the court, such as lawyers, from imposing such costs on the judicial system and on the litigants."

Though a Court majority in *Gentile* sustained the facial validity of Rule 177's basic prohibition, a differently composed majority (per Kennedy, J.) concluded that, as applied in the case before it, the Rule's safe-harbor provision was unconstitutionally vague. Prior to holding the press conference, the petitioner in *Gentile* had studied Rule 177 and what he considered to be the applicable case law. Relying on both constitutional cases governing the seating of jurors exposed to pretrial publicity and the safe-harbor provision, he had concluded that a limited press conference would not violate Rule 177. At his press conference, while making the statements previously described, he also told reporters that there were certain areas he could not further explore "because ethics prohibits me from doing so." Justice Kennedy pointed to both petitioner's actions and the special concerns presented by a statute that used very general terms in regulating speech. His opinion concluded that "the right to explain the 'general' nature of the defense without 'elaboration' provides insufficient guidance because 'general' and 'elaboration' are both classic terms of degree, * * * [and] have no settled usage or tradition of interpretation in law." The "fact [that petitioner] *Gentile* was found in violation of the Rules after studying them and making a conscious effort at compliance demonstrates that [the safe-harbor provision] creates a trap for the wary as well as the unwary."

Justice Kennedy cited several factors as contributing to the Court's vagueness ruling. The opinion noted that Nevada had offered no prior explication of the safe-harbor provision. Arguably, a state standard that looked to the content of some analogous descriptions of defenses (e.g., in jury charges) in defining the character of an acceptable safe-harbor statement would fill that void. The *Gentile* opinion also cited the efforts of counsel to stay within the safe-harbor provision, including his rejection of reporter requests for further commentary as likely to violate the Nevada Rule. Arguably, a vagueness challenge would not be available to a lawyer who made absolutely no effort to fit his statement within a possible reading of a safe-harbor provision. Also, of obvious importance to Justice Kennedy was the application of the safe-harbor provision in the context of a defense attorney countering adverse publicity that had been initiated by the government. Arguably, the vagueness concerns would be less pressing where the statement in question was that of a defense counsel who initiated media coverage in a previously unpublicized case.

With these uncertainties attaching to the Court's opinion, it is not surprising that many states retain the Rule 3.6 safe-harbor provision at issue in *Gentile*. Others have moved to the 1994 revision of Rule 3.6 which removed the words "without elaboration" and "general" from the safe-harbor provision. The 1994 revision also includes a controversial new safe-harbor "right of reply." It provides that a "lawyer may make a statement that a reasonable lawyer would believe is required to protect a client from the substantial undue prejudicial effect of recent publicity not initiated by the lawyer or the lawyer's client."

The role of the defense counsel in responding to adverse publicly was one of the factors that divided the opinions on either side of the *Gentile* Court's 4–4 split on the First Amendment challenge to the application of Rule 177 in *Gentile*. Justice Kennedy's opinion for four justices concluded that the record "reveal[ed] no basis for the Nevada Court's conclusion that the speech presented a substantial likelihood of material prejudice," while Chief Justice Rehnquist's opinion for four justices concluded that the finding below had enough support in the record so that it could not be deemed "mistaken." Justice O'Connor joined neither opinion on this issue.

The Kennedy opinion stressed that in this First Amendment area, the Supreme Court was called upon to make its own independent review of the record. It found various factors in the record that made unsupportable a "substantial likelihood" finding, if that term was to be given "any meaningful content." The Kennedy opinion noted that: (1) the press conference was held six months before the trial; (2) the community from which the venire would eventually be drawn exceeded 600,000 in population; (3) petitioner's statement lacked "any of the more obvious bases for a finding of prejudice" (such as mention of confessions); (4) petitioner held the press conference to respond to information that had been released in the press by the police and prosecutor (including repeated press reports that the police had "complete trust" in their undercover officers and that those officers had been officially cleared after passing lie detector tests); (5) petitioner had acted with the primary motivation of merely "counter[ing] publicity already deemed prejudicial"; and (6) when the case came to trial, the jury was empaneled with no apparent difficulty, all material information disseminated at petitioner's press conference was admitted in evidence, and the jury acquitted petitioner's client.

The Rehnquist opinion agreed that "we must review the record for ourselves," but also noted that "respectful attention" should be given to the findings below because the Nevada disciplinary board and the Nevada Supreme Court were "in a far better position than we are to appreciate the likely effect of petitioner's statements * * * in a highly publicized case like this." Petitioner's strongest points were "that the statement was made well in advance of trial, and that the statements did not in fact taint the jury panel," but the Nevada Supreme Court had responded adequately to both. It had noted that the timing of the statement, "when public interest * * * was at its height," and the highly inflammatory portrayal of prospective government witnesses presented a substantial likelihood of prejudicing the prospective jury, even though that did not in fact happen. The Chief Justice noted that there was evidence pro and con on this point, and he found it "persuasive" that the petitioner, by his own admission, called the press conference "for the express purpose of influencing the venire." The Chief Justice rejected in this regard the suggestion of the Kennedy opinion that this purpose was irrelevant because the attorney was seeking to combat adverse publicity on the other side. Such an approach would place upon a court the difficult test of trying to distinguish between publicity that would influence by neutralizing and that which would create an affirmative bias. But "more fundamentally, it misconceives the constitutional test for an impartial juror," for a "juror who may have been initially swayed from open mindedness by publicity favorable to the prosecution is not rendered fit for service by being bombarded by publicity favorable to the defense." The proper defense remedies for adverse publicity are voir dire, change of venue, jury instructions, and "disciplining of the prosecutor, but not self-help in the form of similarly prejudicial comments by defense counsel."

Lower courts have viewed the *Gentile* rulings as also governing, at least in part, the constitutionality of trial court orders (commonly called "gag" orders) directing the prosecutor and defense counsel not to speak to the media. Where the order takes the form of simply directing counsel to abide by the limitations of the jurisdiction's professional responsibility provision on extrajudicial statements, the constitutionality of imposing contempt or other sanctions for violation of that order is tested simply by reference to the *Gentile* rulings. Where, however, the order takes the form of directing counsel not to give any statements to the media concerning the case (or not to give statements concerning specified aspects of the case), and the challenge is presented by counsel rather than the media, courts view the order as imposing a prior restraint and therefore subject to special requirements derived from *Nebraska Press Association v. Stuart* as well as the *Gentile* rulings. *Nebraska Press*, discussed in subsection (c) infra, involved gag orders imposed upon the press, arguably distinct from gag orders imposed upon participating lawyers, who were viewed in *Gentile* as subject to a special responsibility to ensure that their extrajudicial statements do not threaten the fair administration of justice. Nonetheless, lower courts have viewed *Nebraska Press* as equally applicable to prior restraints imposed upon counsel except insofar as it imposed a higher standard as to likely prejudicial impact ("clear and present danger") than did *Gentile*.

Courts applying a combination of *Gentile* and *Nebraska Press* insist upon three prerequisites for the issuance of a gag order directed at counsel: (1) potential statements to the media by counsel must present a "substantial likelihood" of prejudicing the criminal trial; (2) the order must be "narrowly tailored" to proscribe only those statements that present that potential; and (3) other, less restrictive alternatives (such as voir dire, jury instructions, jury sequestration, postponement of the trial, or change of venue) must be inadequate to prevent the threatened harm. In applying the first standard, courts recognize that anticipating the impact of statements not yet made necessarily involves "some 'speculation' and the weighing of 'factors unknown and unknowable.' " For that reason, the strongest cases appear to be those in which counsel previously have made statements that were widely publicized and dealt with matters likely to sway prospective or selected jurors. Closely related to the required showing is the requirement that the order be "no broader than necessary" to preserve trial by an impartial jury. Thus, an order that bars comment "on anything to do with this case" will invariably fail. Gag orders are most likely to be sustained if they refer to highly prejudicial specifics, such as the criminal record of the defendant.

The final requirement—that the trial court consider and find insufficient less restrictive alternatives—suggests a significant departure from the approach of *Gentile.* The Court there indicated that an attorney could be disciplined for statements presenting a substantial likelihood of imposing significant administrative costs on the court in ensuring the selection of an impartial jury. The attorney was not relieved of liability because the court could manage though such procedures as extensive voir dire and change of venue to obtain an untainted jury. The prohibiting of a gag order if such procedures can respond successfully to a prejudicial impact places the total focus here on ensuring that the jury is untainted rather than avoiding the imposition of significant administrative costs. Some courts, however, have taken those other costs into consideration in evaluating the effectiveness of alternatives. Thus, in responding to defense counsel's claim that the alternative of sequestration precluded extending a gag order past the point of jury selection, one court noted that sequestration was not an acceptable alternative in what promised to be a long trial because of the "negative effects of sequestration." In general, courts appear more willing to find that alternatives are not adequate in considering gag orders imposed upon counsel than gag orders imposed upon the press.

(b) Restricting the Media. The teaching of *Nebraska Press Association v. Stuart* (1976) is that a prohibition upon the media publishing information which might be prejudicial to a criminal defendant will seldom, if ever, be a permissible means for preventing prejudicial pretrial publicity. At issue in that case were orders entered prior to the trial of a mass murder, which barred the publication of "any testimony given or evidence adduced" in court and which also barred the reporting of any confessions or incriminating statements made by the defendant to the police or to any third parties (except members of the press) or of "other facts 'strongly implicative' of the accused." The Supreme Court (per Burger, C.J.) first unequivocally concluded that the bar on reporting what happened "at the open preliminary hearing * * * plainly violated settled principles," namely, that "once a public hearing had been held, what transpired there could not be subject to prior restraint."

As for the prohibition upon publication of information from other sources, the Chief Justice concluded that findings below clearly did not satisfy the stringent prerequisites for securing a prior restraint. To justify a prior restraint on the press ("the most serious and least tolerable infringement on First Amendment rights"), the trial judge had to give adequate consideration to: "(a) the nature and extent of pretrial news coverage; (b) whether other measures would be likely to mitigate the effects of unrestrained pretrial publicity; [and] (c) how effectively a restraining order would operate to prevent the threatened danger." The judge here had failed on all three factors. With respect to the first, the trial judge's finding was "only [as to] 'a clear and present danger that pretrial publicity could impinge upon the defendant's right to a fair trial,'" and his "conclusion as to that possible impact" was of necessity speculative, dealing as he was with "factors unknown and unknowable." As to the second, the record did not reflect careful consideration of "the alternatives to prior restraint discussed with obvious approval in *Sheppard v. Maxwell*," that is, change of venue, continuance, voir dire, and admonitions to the jurors. These must be so ineffective that "12 [jurors] could not be found who would, under proper instructions, fulfill their sworn duty to render a just verdict exclusively on the evidence presented in open court." And as to the third, the trial took place in a very small community where "it is reasonable to assume" that rumors "could well be more damaging than reasonably accurate news accounts."

Although the Chief Justice declined to "rule out the possibility of showing the kind of threat to fair trial rights that would possess the requisite degree of certainty" to justify a prior restraint of the press, the other opinions in the case suggested that this possibility was a highly unlikely one. Justice White expressed "grave doubt" that a prior restraint "would ever be justifiable," while Justice Powell emphasized the "unique burden" resting on one who would justify a prior restraint. Three other justices, in an opinion by Justice Brennan, concluded that a prior restraint simply "is a constitutionally impermissible method for enforcing" the right to a fair trial. Justice Stevens agreed with that conclusion as to "information in the public domain," and indicated he might reach the same conclusion in other circumstances as well.

Nebraska Press characterized a prior restraint as involving "an immediate and irreversible sanction," in contrast to a "criminal penalty or a judgment in a defamation case [which] is subject to the whole panoply of protections afforded by deferring the impact of the judgment until all avenues of appellate review have been exhausted." This might suggest that it would be constitutionally permissible for a state to adopt criminal statutes prohibiting certain identifiable prejudicial reporting, such as reporting a defendant's prior criminal record or his confession not yet ruled admissible. But other rulings of the Court indicate that criminal sanctions are not permissible except to "further a state interest of the highest order" which cannot be adequately protected by less stringent measures. Indeed two key rulings hold unconstitutional criminal prosecutions for the publication of court information normally deemed confidential. In *Smith v. Daily Mail Pub. Co.* (1979), the Court struck down a state statute making it a misdemeanor for a newspaper to publish, without written order of the juvenile court, the name of any youth charged as a juvenile offender. In *Landmark Communications, Inc. v. Va.* (1978), the Court held unconstitutional a state criminal statute prohibiting divulgence of information regarding proceedings before a state judicial tenure commission, where applied to a newspaper that lawfully acquired such information.

(c) Closed Proceedings: First Amendment Right of Access. With the Supreme Court having rejected efforts to restrain the press from reporting on an open hearing, attention naturally turned to the possibility of excluding the press and public from a hearing (or a portion of a hearing) as a means of precluding the pretrial exposure of the public to prejudicial information presented at that hearing. The constitutionality of thus closing pretrial proceedings would depend upon whether there is a press/public constitutional right of access to such proceedings and, if so, whether a weighing of that right against the defendant's right of a fair trial would permit closure under some circumstances.

As for the contention that a constitutional right of access is to be derived from the Sixth Amendment's "public trial" provision, it was rejected in *Gannett Co. v. DePasquale* (1979). The Court there concluded that, "in conspicuous contrast with some of the early state constitutions that provided for a public right to open civil and criminal trials, the Sixth Amendment confers the right to public trial only upon a defendant and only in a criminal case." *Gannett* found it unnecessary to decide whether there existed a First Amendment right of access to criminal proceedings, but shortly thereafter such a right was established in *Richmond Newspapers v. Va.* (1980), a case involving the closing of a trial.

Although there was no opinion of the Court in *Richmond Newspapers*, seven Justices recognized that a press/public right of access is embodied in the First Amendment and is applicable to the states through the Fourteenth Amendment. As a majority later explained in *Globe Newspaper Co. v. Superior Court* (1982), the First Amendment seeks to protect the "discussion of governmental affairs," and a right of access to criminal trials was part of ensuring that this "constitutionally protected discussion * * * is an informed one." *Globe Newspaper* added that there were two features of the criminal justice system which "together serve to explain why a right of access to criminal trials in particular is properly afforded protection by the First Amendment": (1) such trials have historically been open to the press and public; and (2) the right of access plays a particularly significant role in the functioning of the judicial process, for public access not only enhances "the quality and safeguards the integrity of the factfinding process, with benefits to both the defendant and to society as a whole," but also "fosters an appearance of fairness, thereby heightening public respect for the judicial process."

Richmond Newspapers and *Globe Newspaper* both recognized that the First Amendment right of access was not an absolute right, but rather a "qualified" or "presumptive" right. Closure of the proceeding was possible under a sufficient showing of a compelling need. Moreover, the protection of the defendant's interest in obtaining a fair trial could be such a need, at least theoretically. Thus, the impact of recognizing a First Amendment right of access was to take away the trial court's authority to close the proceeding as a matter of discretion, and to substitute rigorous procedural and substantive prerequisites, which narrowly confined closure, as discussed in subsection (d).

While *Richmond Newspapers* and *Globe Newspaper* firmly established a First Amendment right of access to the trial itself, there remained the question of whether such a right also applied to proceedings outside of the trial. In *Press–Enterprise Co. v. Superior Court* (1984) (*Press-Enterprise I*), the Court suggested that possibility in holding that the First Amendment right was applicable to the voir dire examination. The Court's opinion there stressed the two factors cited in *Globe*—an historical tradition of openness and the functional value of openness for the particular proceeding—rather than any characterization of the jury selection process as a part of the trial itself. In *Press–Enterprise Co. v. Superior Court* (1986) (*Press-Enterprise II*), the Court again relied upon those two factors, but this time held that a public right of access extended to a proceeding that clearly was not part of the trial—the preliminary hearing.

Turning to whether there existed as to preliminary hearings a "tradition of accessibility" (which would imply the "favorable judgment of experience"), the *Press-Enterprise II* Court adopted a focus quite different from that suggested in *Gannett*. In discussing the possibility of a Sixth Amendment right of the public to attend a suppression hearing, the *Gannett* majority had concluded that "there exists no persuasive evidence that at common law members of the public had any right to attend pretrial proceedings; indeed there is substantial evidence to the contrary." The *Press–Enterprise II* opinion looked more to the common practice (which was to have open preliminary hearings) than to the existence of some specifically recognized legal right of access. While the code that was dominant when the preliminary hearing came into prominence in the

1880s (the Field Code of New York) allowed such hearings to be closed on motion of the accused, the hearing had always been treated as "presumptuously open to the public and * * * closed only for cause shown." The history of the preliminary stood in contrast to that of the grand jury which had a long history of secrecy as a critical element of its structure. As for the functional value of openness, its advantages in this trial-type proceeding were much the same as in the trial itself. Admittedly, the preliminary hearing, unlike a trial, cannot result in a conviction; but with so many cases being resolved without a trial, the preliminary hearing would often be the most significant stage at which the public could observe the criminal justice process.

Press–Enterprise II firmly established a two part inquiry for determining whether a particular proceeding is one to which the First Amendment right of access applies. The proceeding is to be tested by reference to "experience" and "logic." The experience prong asks "whether the place and process have historically been open to the press and the general public." The logic inquiry asks "whether public access plays a significant positive role in the functioning of the particular process in question." *El Vocero de Puerto Rico v. Puerto Rico* (1993) addressed one possible ambiguity in the application of the "experience" prong. The Court there held that, in assessing the historical record for a "tradition of accessibility," a court "does not look to the particular experience of any one jurisdiction, but instead 'to the experience in that type or kind of hearing throughout the United States.'" Ambiguity remains, however, as to another aspect of the "experience" prong.

In *Richmond Newspapers*, *Press–Enterprise I*, and *Press–Enterprise II*, the Court pointed to traditions of openness that were clearly established and at least a century old. Some courts view such an historical tradition, showing "clarity, generality and duration," as an absolute prerequisite for meeting the "experience" standard, at least as to procedures which are not recent innovations. Other courts find no need for such a clearly established, lengthy tradition, even as to longstanding procedures, where they can point to a shift in the significance of the particular procedure. In dealing with pretrial procedures, for example, they note "the relative importance of pretrial procedure to that of trial has grown immensely in the last two hundred years" and stress that the "First Amendment must be interpreted in the context of current values and conditions."

In applying the "logic" prong of *Press–Enterprise II*, lower courts look to various functional enhancements that public access would contribute to the particular procedure. Opening a judicial proceeding, it is noted, can serve one or more of the following six "societal interests": "[1] promotion of informed discussion of governmental affairs by providing the public with the more complete understanding of the judicial system; [2] promotion of the public perception of fairness which can be achieved only by permitting full public view of the proceedings; [3] providing a significant community therapeutic value as an outlet for community concern, hostility and emotion; [4] serving as a check on corrupt practices by exposing the judicial process to public scrutiny; [5] enhancement of the performance of all involved; and [6] discouragement of perjury." Virtually every proceeding in the criminal justice process that impacts upon decisionmaking would be enhanced by contributing to one or more of these societal interests. Thus, the "logic" issue becomes whether the unique function of the proceeding in question inherently creates a special need for denying public access (as in the case of the grand jury), thereby rejecting the enhancements of openness.

Lower courts have held that the *Press–Enterprise II* standards extend the First Amendment right of access to a wide range of pretrial, mid-trial, and post-trial proceedings. These include: suppression hearings, bail hearings, entrapment hearings, change of venue hearings, competency hearings, hearings on the disqualification or withdrawal of counsel, judicial recusal hearings, plea hearings, and hearings on a motion to reduce a sentence. A post-trial hearing on allegations of juror misconduct has been placed in the same category, but a mid-trial inquiry has been held not to meet the *Press–Enterprise II* standard because it has a special function inconsistent with public access—minimizing the risk that the inquiry will "destroy the effectiveness of the [sitting] jury as a deliberative body."

Concurring in *Richmond Newspapers*, Justice Brennan noted that "the presumption of public trials" should not be "incompatible with reasonable restrictions imposed upon courtroom behavior in the interests of decorum. * * * Thus, when engaging in interchanges at the bench, the trial judge is not required to allow public or press intrusion upon the huddle." Relying upon Justice Brennan's comments, lower courts consistently have held that they do not violate any right of First Amendment access when they allow presentations to be made in chambers or in sidebar conferences for appropriate administrative purposes (e.g., to ensure that the jury does not overhear the discussion), even though the press and public is thereby excluded. However, there is less certainty as to whether an administratively justified use of the sidebar or in-chambers conference renders inapplicable a First Amendment right of access in its entirety or only as to contemporaneous presence. The media representatives commonly argue that the First Amendment operates to require disclosure of the transcripts of sidebar or in-chambers conferences "contemporaneously or at the earliest practicable times," absent a judicial finding of a need to seal such transcripts under the rigorous First Amendment standards of *Press–Enterprise II*. Some courts have suggested that such a claim has merit as to "sidebar or chambers conferences in criminal cases at which evidentiary or other substantive rulings have been made." Other courts have suggested, to the contrary, that where a sidebar or in-chambers conference falls within the traditional use of such conferences, even though it produces an evidentiary ruling, that tradition negates not only a First Amendment right to presence at the conference, but also a First Amendment right of access to the transcript of the proceeding.

(d) Closing Proceedings and Placing Documents Under Seal: Restricting the First Amendment Right. A proceeding may be closed and a document sealed even though subject to a First Amendment right of access. As the Court declared in *Globe Newspaper Co. v. Superior Court* (1982), the right of access "is not absolute." The Court cautioned, however, that the circumstances under which the First Amendment right can be withheld "are limited"; "it must be shown that the denial is necessitated by a compelling governmental interest, and is narrowly tailored to serve that interest."

An illustration of the need to narrowly tailor any closure to meet an offsetting privacy interest is provided by *Press–Enterprise I*. The Court there acknowledged that a prospective juror's privacy interests regarding the personal matters inquired into on voir dire could outweigh public trial interests, but concluded that the court below had erred in not considering alternatives to closure and, in any event, in closing virtually all of a six week voir dire. The proper procedure, as outlined in *Press–Enterprise I*, would have been for the trial judge to inform prospective jurors of their opportunity to raise with the judge in camera (but on the record and with counsel present) concerns about embarrassing questions, after which the judge would decide if "there is in fact a valid basis for a belief that disclosure infringes a significant interest in privacy." If such a finding was made, then the judge could either excuse that juror or order limited closure.

"Compelling governmental interests" recognized by the Supreme Court include the juror privacy interests recognized in *Press–Enterprise I*, and the preservation of the defendant's right to a fair trial, by precluding publicity that might taint a prospective or sitting jury, recognized in *Press–Enterprise II*. Lower court rulings have added several other interests that arguably could justify closure orders as to pretrial proceedings or papers filed in connection with those proceedings. These include: (1) privacy interests of both defendants and "innocent third parties," as recognized in

Title III provisions authorizing sealing of wiretaps and related documents; (2) the chilling effect that disclosure of pretrial motion papers may have on the filing of such motions; (3) the privacy interests of victims, defendants or other persons (e.g., unindicted coconspirators); (4) the need to preserve the integrity of an ongoing investigation; and (5) danger to persons (e.g., informants) or property.

Where the closure is justified as protective of the accused's right to a fair trial, and is narrowly tailored to serve that interest, just how likely must it be that the publicity resulting from an open proceeding will prejudice that right? In *Press–Enterprise II*, the Supreme Court adopted a standard less stringent than the clear and present danger standard of *Nebraska Press*, but more stringent than the "reasonable likelihood" standard imposed by the lower courts there. The Court stated:

> If the interest asserted is the right of the accused to a fair trial, the preliminary hearing shall be closed only if specific findings are made that first, there is a substantial probability that the defendant's right to a fair trial will be prejudiced by publicity that closure would prevent and second, reasonable alternatives to closure cannot adequately protect the defendant's free trial rights.

Although this standard was stated in the context of the preliminary hearing, it has been viewed as the appropriate standard for "fair-trial" closures of all parts of the criminal process to which the First Amendment right of access applies.

Perhaps the most critical aspect of the *Press–Enterprise II* standard is the weighing of alternatives. In *Press–Enterprise II*, the Court said very little about how this should be done, except to note that the lower court should have taken into account the possibility that "voir dire, cumbersome as it is in some circumstances," would permit a trial court to identify and exclude any prospective jurors who might have become biased upon learning of prejudicial information disclosed in an open preliminary hearing. The Court did not indicate whether it meant to impose a consideration of alternatives akin to that adopted in *Nebraska Press*, where alternatives were said to prevail over use of a media gag order unless so ineffective that they could not produce an untainted group of 12 jurors. Unlike *Nebraska Press*, there was no reference in *Press-Enterprise II* to the change of venue alternative, with its high costs for the defendant.

The requirement that the closure order be narrowly tailored to the accused's fair trial interest typically imposes two mandates— that the closure be appropriately limited in scope and that the transcript of the closed proceeding be available to the media and public promptly after those fair trial needs have been met. In meeting the first requirement, the court must consider whether part of the proceeding can be kept open without disclosing the information that could prejudice potential jurors. Thus, in a suppression hearing, it might be possible to have an open proceeding as to the grounding for conducting the challenged wiretap without reference to the content or character of the conversations recorded. As for timing, release of the transcript of the closed proceeding after the prosecution is terminated by trial, plea, or dismissal is almost invariably required if the only compelling interest was defendant's fair trial right. In *Gannett*, the trial court released the suppression hearing transcript shortly after the defendants pleaded guilty, and that action was cited as essential to meeting the trial court's First Amendment obligations.

(e) **Televising Proceedings.** Courts uniformly have held that the First Amendment right of access does not include a right of the media to photograph or broadcast. Courts reason that such procedures involve administrative costs that the judicial system can find too burdensome to permit, and are hardly essential to serving the objectives of having an open proceeding. Indeed, at one time, the Supreme Court suggested that the televising of a trial over the objection of the defendant was constitutionally unacceptable. In *Estes v. Tex.* (1965), pretrial hearings were televised and were seen by some of the persons selected as jurors, and much of the trial was also televised. In a 5–4 decision, the Court reversed the defendant's conviction on the ground that the "[broadcast] procedure employed by the State involves such a probability that prejudice will result that it is deemed inherently lacking in due process." The Court added that "there are numerous situations in which * * * [televising] might cause actual unfairness—some so subtle as to defy detection by the accused or control by the judge," and then proceeded to enumerate some reasons why televising a trial could cause unfairness: (1) it could have an impact upon the jurors by distracting them and making the case appear a cause celebré; (2) it could have an impact upon witnesses and decrease the quality of testimony received; (3) it could have an impact upon the judge by adding to his responsibilities and by subjecting him to greater political pressure; and (4) it could have an impact upon the defendant because it could be distracting to him and might reduce the effectiveness of his attorney's representation.

It was unclear, at best, whether *Estes* announced a constitutional rule barring television coverage in all cases and under all circumstances, for the fifth vote of the majority was by Justice Harlan, who in a separate opinion concluded only that televised trials should be banned "in cases like this one." The Court's subsequent references to *Estes* arguably indicated that *Estes* was not viewed as having announced a per se rule, and the Supreme Court so held in *Chandler v. Fla.* (1981). *Chandler* upheld a regulated state practice that allowed electronic media and still photography coverage of public criminal proceedings over the objection of the accused. The unanimous Court emphasized that "no one has been able to present empirical data sufficient to establish that the mere presence of the broadcast media inherently has an adverse impact on that process," and stressed that in the instant case the televising was done pursuant to carefully crafted guidelines designed to ensure that the excesses found in the *Estes* case were avoided. Thus, the guidelines included restrictions on the type and manner of equipment used, designed to keep the recording unobtrusive, and a prohibition against the filming of the jury itself. Moreover, the guidelines "placed on [the] trial judges positive obligations to be on guard to protect the fundamental right of the accused to a fair trial." It is still open to a particular defendant, the Court added, "to show that the media's coverage of his case * * * compromised the ability of the jury to judge him fairly" or to "show that broadcast coverage of his particular case had an adverse impact on the trial participants sufficient to constitute a denial of due process." But such prejudice is not established by merely showing "juror awareness that the trial is such as to attract the attention of broadcasters."

Currently, a substantial majority of the states authorize the televising of open trial court proceedings. However, a significant number of these states bar televising of criminal trials where the defendant objects, and the remaining states grant the trial judge discretion to refuse to permit televising in that situation. Typically, the discretion granted the trial judge is broad, so the judge need not make a showing as to good cause in order to refuse to permit televising.

§ 15.2 Overcoming Prejudicial Publicity

(a) **Change of Venue on a Defense Motion.** Where prejudicial publicity has already occurred, a trial court will turn to the procedures available for ensuring that the defendant receives a fair trial, notwithstanding that publicity. One possibility is a change of venue—that is, a removal of the case to another judicial district, which hopefully is beyond the reach of the publicity. The statutory and rule provisions governing "fair trial" venue changes on a defense motion are discussed in § 8.3(b). This section considers the application of those provisions to cases involving significant publicity, adverse to the defendant, published prior to the selection of the jury. The "fair trial" grounding for a change of venue in such cases is that the publicity has so tainted prospective jurors that an unbiased jury may not be obtainable in the district of prosecution.

Whether this grounding prevails is not determined solely by the standards prescribed in the venue-change statute or court rule. The federal constitution may also play a significant role.

The seminal Supreme Court ruling on the constitutionally required change of venue is *Rideau v. La.* (1963). There, two months prior to trial, a local TV station broadcast three different times a 20–minute film of defendant admitting in detail the commission of the various offenses with which he was charged. The parish had a population of about 150,000 and the estimated audiences for these broadcasts were 24,000, 53,000 and 29,000, respectively. Defendant's change of venue motion was denied, and he was convicted and sentenced to death. The Supreme Court held that due process was denied by the failure to grant a change of venue "after the people of [the] Parish had been exposed repeatedly and in depth to the spectacle of Rideau personally confessing in detail to the crimes with which he was later to be charged."

In *Rideau*, the record indicated that three members of the jury had seen the TV broadcast, and had been seated after testifying on voir dire that they "could lay aside any opinion, give the defendant the presumption of innocence as provided by law, base their decision solely upon the evidence, and apply the law as given by the court." But the Supreme Court declared that it did "not hesitate to hold, without pausing to examine a particularized transcript of the voir dire examination of the members of the jury, that due process of law in this case required a trial before a jury drawn from a community of people who had not seen and heard Rideau's 'interview.'" This language, and that quoted in the previous paragraph, would seem to mean that Rideau would have prevailed even if all of the seated jurors had stated on voir dire that they had neither seen nor heard about the television interview.

The apparent premise of *Rideau* is that prejudicial publicity may be so inflammatory and so pervasive that the voir dire simply cannot be trusted to fully reveal the likely prejudice among prospective jurors. As a result, a change of venue will be constitutionally mandated even though the voir dire of the seated jurors does not contain sufficient signs of the jurors having been influenced to establish an "inference of actual prejudice" under the due process standards of *Irvin v. Dowd* and its progeny (discussed in subsection (d) infra). Publicity may so affect the community that individual jurors will not be able to openly acknowledge the community pressures placed upon them. Those pressures may lead them to answer with less than full candor voir dire questions concerning their familiarity with the case, but perhaps even more significantly, may impose upon them, notwithstanding their best intentions, "a sense of obligation to reach a result which will find general acceptance in the [community]." Indeed, those pressures open the possibility of reaching even that juror who truly had never previously heard of the case. Accordingly, the *Irvin v. Dowd* standard, though it does not automatically accept juror claims of impartiality, and is quite likely to identify partiality in seated jurors who acknowledge awareness of the adverse publicity, is not deemed sufficient.

Rideau itself presented a most compelling fact situation for concluding that there was no need to look to the voir dire to conclude that an impartial jury almost certainly could not have been produced without a change of venue. That fact situation included the following: the information conveyed was as inflammatory and prejudicial as might be conceived—what the Court characterized as the equivalent of a guilty plea combined with a detailed description of the crimes involved; the medium of a 20–minute television program, with the defendant himself speaking on camera, was the most likely to make a lasting impression on all who saw it; there was a saturation of the community, with such a large portion of the populace viewing the film (even taking account of possible repeat viewers) that those who did not view it were almost certain to have heard about it; and the nature of the case (involving robbery, kidnapping, and murder) and the size of the community obviously made the trial an event of major importance.

Looking to the special features of the *Rideau* case, lower courts have characterized the "presumptive prejudice" standard of *Rideau* as "rarely applicable," reserved for "extreme situations," and setting a "high threshold" for the defendant to overcome. They note that it requires massive publicity and "bitter prejudice," reflecting such a pervasive and inexpressible "hostile attitude" as to render unreliable the usual safeguards for ensuring fairness in the selection and decisionmaking of jurors. In determining whether a case meets this standard, the lower courts look to the following factors: "(1) the nature of pretrial publicity and the particular degree to which it has circulated in the community, (2) the connection of government officials with the release of publicity, (3) the length of time between the dissemination of the publicity and the trial, (4) the severity and notoriety of the offense, (5) the area from which the jury is to be drawn, (6) other events occurring in the community which affect or reflect the attitude of the community or individual jurors toward the defendant, and (7) any other factor likely to affect the candor or veracity of the prospective jurors on voir dire." In evaluating these factors on appellate and habeas review, state and federal courts have found only a sprinkling of cases where a refusal to grant a change of venue violated the *Rideau* standard. *Rideau* has been held not to reach even the most highly publicized cases that are covered step-by-step and scoop-by-scoop in evening newscasts and front page stories. One possible explanation for the hesitancy of state courts to extend *Rideau* much beyond its extreme facts is the limited value of a venue change in many of the smaller states. If publicity is held to be of such a nature as to require a presumption of prejudice, a court in a small state simply may have nowhere to move the case, as the same level of publicity often is found throughout the state.

Not surprisingly, the standard practice of trial judges in both federal and state courts is to postpone ruling on a change of venue, even where the defendant claims that the presumed prejudice standard of *Rideau* is applicable, until after an attempt to seat an impartial jury is made. Moreover, once jury selection is started, there is a tendency to pursue it through as many potential jurors as is deemed necessary to seat a jury believed to be immune from a successful constitutional challenge under the *Irvin v. Dowd* standard of actual prejudice. This may be due to the inconvenience associated with the change to another location, the concern that the citizens of the community should not be lightly treated as incapable of giving the defendant a fair trial, and the feeling that the community most directly impacted by the crime should be the place of the trial. Moreover, on an appeal following a conviction, a reviewing court is likely to be quite deferential to the trial judge's decision not to order a change of venue, provided the jury selection process passes muster under the standard of *Irvin v. Dowd*.

(b) Change of Venire. A small group of states provide by statute for a "fair trial" change of venire. Under this procedure, the trial remains in the judicial district of original venue, but the jury is selected from another judicial district. The change of venire is viewed as an alternative to the change of venue and is available under the same standard—a determination that a "fair and impartial jury cannot be impaneled" in the district of venue. In some jurisdictions, choice of this alternative requires an additional determination that it is more economical than a change of venue (a concern arising from the need to pay the travel and housing costs of the impartial jury, which is usually sequestered). Aside from that requirement, the choice between a change of venire and change of venue ordinarily lies in the discretion of the trial court. Of course, one factor to be considered is whether the local district presents a "charged atmosphere" likely to impact the fairness of the trial even with a jury selected from another district.

(c) Continuance. Doubtless there are a number of cases in which the granting of a continuance is not the solution to prejudicial pretrial publicity, as where the publicity has aroused antagonism so intense that there is no reason to suppose that it would subside by any delay which would not put off the trial indefinitely. But a continuance is a useful technique when the hostility can be expected to fade within a reasonable time, as where the problem has arisen because of some event or disclosure occurring on the eve of the time set for trial. Another kind of situation is that noted by the Court in *Sheppard v. Maxwell* (1966), where the trial began two weeks before a hotly contested election at which both the judge and chief prosecutor were candidates for judgeships. The Court noted that "a short continuance would have alleviated any problem with regard to the judicial elections."

(d) Jury Selection. Yet another way to overcome the prejudicial impact of pretrial publicity is by a voir dire that identifies those prospective jurors influenced by the publicity and a challenge procedure that eliminates all persons in that group who actually have been biased by the publicity. The theory here is that the voir dire examination of prospective jurors will reveal which of them have actually been exposed to the pretrial publicity and what effect that exposure has had upon them. If the voir dire reveals that a prospective juror is biased, then that juror may be challenged for cause. Even if the voir dire does not establish bias to the satisfaction of the judge, the defense counsel who nonetheless believes that the pretrial publicity might have affected the prospective juror can still eliminate that juror if the defense has remaining peremptory challenges. Primary reliance is placed on the voir dire and the challenge for cause, but the peremptory challenge serves as a safety net.

As noted above, when courts refuse to adopt measures designed to avoid prejudicial publicity (e.g., closing proceedings) or to shift the venue or venire, they commonly assume that the combination of voir dire and challenges will provide an effective remedy. That assumption rests, in large part, on the assumed effectiveness of voir dire in uncovering prejudice among potential jurors, but there is reason to question whether voir dire always has that capacity. Thus, the ABA, in its commentary to the second edition of the Criminal Justice Standards on Fair Trial and Free Press, cited three "distinct but interrelated factors" that called for "caution" in trusting voir dire to screen effectively for bias: "(1) inadequate understanding of the way pretrial publicity influences the thought process of prospective jurors; (2) the tendency among a significant number of prospective jurors to underplay the importance of exposure to prejudicial publicity and to exaggerate their ability to be impartial; and (3) persistent concern about the ability of attorneys and trial judges to discern bias, particularly at the subconscious level, even when the prospective juror is being completely candid."

The ABA Standards seek to make voir dire more effective, in part, by avoiding the risk that counsel, in questioning the prospective jurors as a group, may "contaminate" jurors previously unaware of the publicity. The Standards therefore mandate the separate examination of each prospective juror outside of the presence of the others where the case presents "a substantial possibility that individual jurors will be ineligible to serve because of exposure to potentially prejudicial material." Though that procedure has been adopted in some jurisdictions, many others give the trial judge broad discretion to insist upon group voir dire. So too, many jurisdictions give the trial court broad discretion in limiting the length and depth of the voir dire as it relates to pretrial publicity. In *Mu'Min v. Va.* (1991), the Supreme Court considered the bearing of the Constitution on granting such discretion to the trial judge. The end result was a 5–4 decision, with the majority's ruling apparently limited to the special circumstances presented there.

In *Mu'Min*, 16 out of 26 prospective jurors (including 8 of the actual panel) answered affirmatively when asked if they had acquired any information about the case from the news media or any other source. The defense had asked that each of the prospective jurors be questioned out of the presence of the other jurors and be asked to respond to 64 proposed questions, but the trial court concluded that it was satisfactory to question the prospective jurors in groups of four and to put to them only some of the proposed questions. The judge did ask the prospective jurors whether any information acquired from outside sources would affect their impartiality and whether they had formed an opinion in the case. None of the persons eventually seated were among those who stated that they had an opinion or were no longer impartial or who otherwise indicated possible prejudice in their answers. The defense contended that this was not constitutionally sufficient because the judge had refused to ask of those jurors who had acquired outside information additional questions concerning the content of what they had learned.

Writing for the majority in *Mu'Min*, Chief Justice Rehnquist acknowledged a content inquiry might well "be helpful in assessing whether a jury is impartial." The issue before the Court, however, was whether the failure to conduct such an inquiry "must render the defendant's trial fundamentally unfair." Traditionally, trial judges had been given "great latitude" in voir dire questioning, and while some jurisdictions had restricted that discretion by requiring content-based questions as to pretrial publicity, others had not. One difficulty posed by such questions is that they basically required the questioning of each prospective juror in isolation so that the others not be exposed to content that had not previously come to their attention. In any event, the Chief Justice noted, whether or not the judge decides to put content questions to potential jurors, the ultimate issue remains the same—whether there is a sufficient basis for the judge's assessment that the juror is credible in stating that he or she has not formed an opinion and would be impartial. In making that assessment, the judge would have to evaluate the "depth and extent of news stories that might influence a juror," and where that publicity engendered a "wave of public passion," that "might well * * * requir[e] more extensive examination of potential jurors than under[taken] here." However, the publicity in this case, though "substantial," was not of that nature. Accordingly, the judge could constitutionally make a finding of juror impartiality in light of the responses given, without further questioning.

In her separate concurring opinion in *Mu'Min*, Justice O'Connor, who supplied the critical fifth vote for affirmance, further developed the significance of the content of the adverse publicity and the responses of the jurors actually seated. While it was true that the trial judge "did not know precisely what each juror had read," he was aware "of the full range of the information that had been reported." With this information in mind, and with each juror having indicated that no opinion had been formed, the trial judge could not be said to have violated the Sixth Amendment in accepting the jurors' assurances of impartiality. Justice O'Connor, as did Chief Justice Rehnquist, found support for this conclusion in *Patton v. Yount* (1984). The Court there had drawn a distinction between two types of issues presented in prejudicial publicity cases. One was the basically legal question as to whether the adverse publicity had reached a point where a presumption of prejudice required the trial court to reject assurances of impartiality by jurors exposed to that publicity. Where that presumption was not applicable, the trial judge's determination as to credibility was basically a factual judgment, and such credibility determinations were "entitled to 'special deference,' " allowing for reversal "only for 'manifest error.' " That was the kind of determination that was presented in this case, and while a content inquiry would have been helpful in making such an assessment, the judge's determination could not be viewed as manifest error because he decided "to evaluate a juror's credibility instead by reference to the full range of potentially prejudicial information that had been reported."

In light of the various weaknesses of voir dire in uncovering possible juror prejudice, it might be thought that, as a matter of caution, the defense should be allowed to exclude automatically all jurors who have any prior information about the case. But that quite obviously is not feasible. Indeed, as far back as 1878, the Court warned that "every case of public interest is almost, as a matter of necessity, brought to the attention of all the intelligent people in the vicinity, and scarcely any one can be found among those best fitted for jurors who has not read or heard of it, and who has not some impression or some opinion in respect to its merits." *Reynolds v. U.S.* (1878). That fact of life does not preclude, however, distinguishing between cases on the basis of the nature of the publicity, and finding certain types of publicity so inherently preju-

dicial as to exclude any juror familiar with that publicity. In
Marshall v. U.S. (1959), the Supreme Court appeared to adopt such
a position, but not as a constitutional standard.

The *Marshall* Court held that a federal district judge had erred
in allowing the trial to continue even though some of the sitting
jurors had read newspaper articles citing defendant's two prior
felony convictions and other background information of a type that
the district judge had refused to allow in evidence because of its
prejudicial character. Although the district judge had questioned
the jurors and had been convinced of their credibility in assuring
him that they would not be influenced by the news articles, the
Court found that unsatisfactory. Relying on its supervisory power
over federal court practice, the Court reversed defendant's conviction. The *per curiam* opinion accepted the proposition that "persons who have learned from news sources of a defendant's prior
record are presumed to be prejudiced." However, in *Murphy v. Fla.*
(1975), the Court later rejected the defendant's reliance upon
Marshall in a state case. It pointed out that a different standard
applied where reversal was allowed only for a constitutional violation rather than on the Court's exercise of its supervisory authority
over federal courts.

Irvin v. Dowd (1961), sets forth the basic constitutional framework for determining whether the jury selection process was inadequate to combat the prejudicial impact of adverse pretrial publicity
and thereby deprived the defendant of his constitutional right to an
impartial tribunal. The Court noted initially that, consistent with
the position taken in federal cases dating back to *Reynolds*, the
quest for juror impartiality under the Constitution certainly did
not require the automatic exclusion of all prospective jurors who
were aware of adverse pretrial publicity. Indeed, it also did not necessarily require the exclusion of persons who had a "preconceived
notion" based on that publicity, although at that point, the Constitution did require a careful examination of the totality of the circumstances. Justice Clark's opinion for a unanimous Court reasoned:

> [T]o hold that the mere existence of any preconceived
> notion as to the guilt or innocence of an accused, without more,
> is sufficient to rebut the presumption of a prospective juror's
> impartiality would be to establish an impossible standard. It is
> sufficient if the juror can lay aside his impression or opinion
> and render a verdict based on the evidence presented in court.
> * * * The adoption of such a rule, however, "cannot foreclose
> inquiry as to whether, in a given case, the application of that
> rule works a deprivation of * * * due process." [T]he test is
> "whether the nature and strength of the opinion formed are

such as in law necessarily * * * raise the presumption of partiality."

The issue thus posed under *Irvin* is whether the adverse pretrial publicity and the circumstances surrounding its dissemination created "such a presumption of prejudice * * * that the jurors' claims that they can be impartial should not be believed." The *Irvin* Court found the case before it to be one requiring such a presumption. The media reports, described by the Court as a "barrage of newspaper headlines, articles, cartoons and pictures," had contained prejudicial and inflammatory information, including defendant's confession to six homicides, his past criminal record, and his alleged willingness to enter a guilty plea in return for a life sentence. These reports had been widely disseminated, creating a "pattern of deep and bitter prejudice" in the community. As a result, over half of the 430 venire members were excused on challenges for cause because they admitted to fixed opinions, almost 90% of those examined on the point entertained some opinion as to defendant's guilt, and eight of the twelve jurors seated had said they thought defendant was guilty. Though those jurors also said they could put aside that opinion and judge the case impartially, "where so many, so many times, admitted prejudice, such a statement of impartiality * * * [could] be given little weight." The Court concluded that, "with his life at stake, it is not requiring too much that petitioner be tried in an atmosphere undisturbed by so huge a wave of public passion and by a jury other than one in which two-thirds of the members admit, before hearing any testimony, to possessing a belief in his guilt."

Irvin did not find constitutional error in the failure to grant a change of venue, but in the seating of the particular jury. Its analysis came to be described as focusing on "actual prejudice," rather than the "presumptive prejudice" which required a change of venue in *Rideau.* To succeed under an actual prejudice analysis, the defendant must "show that * * * the selection process permitted an inference of actual prejudice." That was done in *Irvin,* but not in two later cases *Murphy v. Fla.* (1973) and *Patton v. Yount* (1984). In both of these cases, the Court distinguished *Irvin* and held that the selection process did not present circumstances that would warrant presuming partiality and thereby overriding the trial judge's assessment that the seated jury was impartial.

The Court in *Murphy* found insufficient the defendant's notoriety (due to previous, highly publicized criminal activities) and the fact that 20 of 78 persons questioned were excused because they indicated an opinion as to his guilt. The Court noted that the news articles about defendant's prior crimes had appeared seven months before jury selection and were "largely factual in nature." The voir dire, moreover, evidenced no hostility towards petitioner by the jurors who were seated. There was only one "colorable claim of partiality," relating to one juror's concession that his prior impression of the defendant would "dispose him to convict." Moreover, the Court could not attach "great significance to this statement * * * in light of the leading nature of counsel's questions and the juror's other testimony indicating that he had no deep impression of petitioner at all."

Patton v. Yount appeared to come closer to *Irvin* than *Murphy*. It presented, like *Irvin*, a notorious murder case tried in a small community. Here too, the reports had made reference to damaging inadmissible information, including a prior conviction for the same crime, a prior confession, and a prior plea of temporary insanity. Also, the percentage of persons in the jury panel who acknowledged having some opinion was high (77%), and eight of the fourteen seated jurors (including two alternates) admitted that at some time they had formed an opinion as to guilt. The Court noted, however, that the "extensive adverse publicity and the community sense of outrage" were "at their height" prior to defendant's first trial. The jury selection at the second trial, which was all that was before it, came four years later, at a time when "prejudicial publicity was greatly diminished and community sentiment had softened." While "a number of jurors and veniremen" had made reference to opinions earlier held, "for many, time had weakened or eliminated any conviction they had had." In the end, it could not be said that the trial judge was manifestly incorrect in concluding that the jury was impartial.

Although the Court stressed in *Murphy* and *Patton* that each case rested on the totality of its circumstances, the primary factors that appeared to distinguish *Murphy* and *Patton* from *Irvin* were: (1) the strength of the voir dire responses of the jurors with reference to their previously developed opinions, (2) the nature of the pretrial publicity, and (3) the time elapsed between the height of the publicity and the trial. As for the first factor, the Court has indicated that the responses of both the jurors actually seated and all prospective jurors examined are relevant. The responses of those not seated casts light on the credibility of those seated jurors who were familiar with the same publicity. However, *Patton* strongly indicates that the responses of the total venire, even if it includes a substantial portion who must be excluded because of preconceptions they cannot readily lay aside, will not be as significant as the responses of seated jurors which strongly substantiate their impartiality. *Patton* noted that 126 of 163 veniremen there "admitted they would carry an opinion into the jury box" ("a higher percentage than in *Irvin*"), but it concluded that the extensive voir dire and challenges "resulted in selecting [as jurors] those who had forgotten or would need to be persuaded again." It added that "the relevant question is not whether the community remembered the case, but whether the jurors at Yount's trial had such fixed opinions that they could not judge impartially the guilt of the defendant."

With respect to the character of the publicity, *Murphy* noted the need to "distinguish * * * largely factual publicity from that which is invidious or inflammatory" and *Patton* arguably drew a similar distinction in characterizing certain articles "as merely report[ing] events without editorial comment." As for timing, *Patton* emphasized that the publicity in *Irvin* had been intensive for a period of 6–7 months leading up to the trial, while the most extensive publicity in the case before it had ended four years earlier with the termination of the defendant's first trial.

Chapter 16

THE CRIMINAL TRIAL

Table of Sections

For additional analysis of the above topics and citations to authorities supporting their discussion in this Book, consult the authors' 7-volume *Criminal Procedure* treatise, also available as Westlaw database CRIMPROC. See the Table of Cross-References in this Book.

---

§ 16.1 The Right to a Public Trial

(a) Nature of the Right. The Sixth Amendment provides that "In all criminal prosecutions, the accused shall enjoy the right to a * * * public trial." This fundamental right was one of the first sixth amendment rights held by the Supreme Court to be an essential element of due process and therefore applicable in state proceedings under the Fourteenth Amendment. The sixth amendment right to a public trial belongs to the defendant rather than the public; a separate first amendment right governs the interests of the public and the press in attending a trial, see § 15.1(d). The sixth amendment guarantee extends to all criminal trials, including criminal contempt trials, and it covers the entire trial, including the impaneling of the jury, and the return of the verdict. It also extends to certain pretrial proceedings that bear a resemblance to a trial, such as suppression hearings.

A defendant can benefit from a public trial in several ways. Most importantly, it is a "safeguard against any attempt to employ our courts as instruments of persecution. The knowledge that every criminal trial is subject to contemporaneous review in the forum of public opinion is an effective restraint on possible abuse of judicial power." In addition, a public trial makes the proceedings known to potential material witnesses who might otherwise be unknown to the parties and assures that witnesses who do testify will testify truthfully by inducing the expectation that any false testimony would be detected. In resolving issues relating to the scope of the sixth amendment right courts often look to these functions. For example, in holding the right applicable to a suppression hearing, the Court reasoned in *Waller v. Ga.* (1984) that the usual public trial interests of ensuring that the judge and prosecutor carry out their duties responsibly, encouraging witnesses to come forward, and discouraging perjury "are no less pressing in a hearing to suppress wrongfully seized evidence."

The defendant's right to a public trial is adequately protected so long as there is free public access to the trial. Although it is not necessary to accommodate everyone who wants to attend, the trial must be held at a place where there are no significant inhibitions upon public attendance. Denial of the right to a public trial establishes grounds in itself for a new trial, the defendant need not establish that he was prejudiced in any specific way by the exclusion. Predictably, the exclusion of spectators is upheld when the defendant fails to object to closure. However, the fact that the defendant can waive or forfeit his right to a public trial does not entitle him to compel a private trial.

(b) When Closure Justified. Closure of a criminal trial may be constitutional under limited circumstances. The defendant's interest in a public trial may be balanced against other interests which might justify closing the trial. Generally, the best course of action is for the trial judge to hold an evidentiary hearing on the issue of closure whenever it arises, though in some circumstances the judge will be able to take judicial notice of the essential facts. As the Court stated in *Waller,* "(1) the party seeking to close the hearing must advance an overriding interest that is likely to be prejudiced, (2) the closure must be no broader than necessary to protect that interest, (3) the trial court must consider reasonable alternatives to closing the proceeding, and (4) it must make findings adequate to support the closure." Narrow tailoring in this context requires on-the-record consideration of alternatives to closure. The trial court's failure to make such findings led the Court in *Waller* to conclude that the court clearly erred in closing an entire 7–day suppression hearing to protect the privacy of persons named in tapes that played for two and one-half hours.

Some lower courts have applied a less stringent test for "partial" or "trivial" closures, where, for example, some but not all members of the public are excluded. These courts require only a "substantial" or "important" rather than a "compelling" reason for limiting access in order to justify closure. This effort to narrow the class of cases subject to the strict requirements of *Waller* is not surprising given the inability of appellate courts to employ harmless error analysis to avoid retrial in such cases.

Trials of charges of sexual assault often prompt disputes over closure. It is not uncommon for a judge to close a portion of the trial of a sex offense for the protection of the victim, especially when the victim is a minor. Primary justification for this practice lies in protection of the personal dignity of the complaining witness. The ordeal of describing an unwanted sexual encounter before persons with no more than a prurient interest in it aggravates the original injury. Mitigation of the ordeal is a justifiable concern of the public and of the trial court. It does not follow from this, however, that a court may automatically close trials to the public whenever a minor victim testifies about a sexual assault. Rather, a court should "determine on a case-by-case basis whether closure is necessary" to protect the state's compelling interest in the welfare of the victim, taking into account "the minor victim's age, psychological maturity, and understanding, the nature of the crime, the desires of the victim, and the interests of the parents and relatives."

Limited exclusion of spectators is also permissible when there is a demonstrated need to protect a witness from threatened harassment or physical harm. Exclusion has been upheld when the witness had been subjected to pretrial threats and also when actions by spectators at the trial were understandably perceived by the witness as threatening. Similarly, exclusion during the testimony of an undercover agent engaged in ongoing investigations is proper when exposure would imperil the agent and render him useless for further investigative activities. Finally, exclusion of spectators is also permissible when necessary to preserve order in the courtroom.

§ 16.2 Presence of the Defendant

(a) Origins and Scope of the Right to be Present. The Sixth Amendment provides that "In all criminal prosecutions, the accused shall enjoy the right * * * to be confronted with the witness against him." This Confrontation Clause, which is applicable to the states via the Fourteenth Amendment, encompasses the very basic right of a defendant in a criminal case to be present in the courtroom at "every stage of his trial." While the right to be present is rooted in the Confrontation Clause of the Sixth Amendment, it also has a due process component. Accordingly, it is not restricted to situations where the defendant is "actually confronting witnesses or evidence against him," but encompasses all trial-related proceedings at which defendant's presence " 'has a relation, reasonably substantial, to the fullness of his opportunity to defend against the charge.' "

The right has been held to extend to jury selection and to communications between the judge and jury, including the giving of jury instructions, the replaying of taped testimony during deliberations, and an in-chambers conversation with a single juror that is substantive in nature. A defendant has the right to be present at the return of the verdict and at sentencing. On the other hand, the right has been held not to extend to in-chambers pretrial conferences, to brief bench conferences with attorneys conducted outside the defendant's hearing, and to various other conferences characterized as relating only to the resolution of questions of law. The constitutional right to presence does not extend to misdemeanor prosecutions.

In determining whether the constitutional right to presence extends to a particular proceeding apart from the trial itself, the Court has examined whether or not exclusion of the defendant interfered with the defendant's opportunity to test the evidence introduced against him, and whether or not it otherwise affected his opportunity to defend himself at trial. This approach is illustrated by the rulings in *Ky. v. Stincer* (1987), and *U.S. v. Gagnon* (1985). In *Stincer*, the defendant (but not his counsel) was excluded from an in-chambers hearing at which the trial court made a preliminary determination as to whether the two children who were the alleged victims of the charged sex offense had sufficient understanding of their obligation to tell the truth and sufficient intellectual capacity to be competent to testify. The Court initially noted that even though a particular hearing might be characterized as a "pretrial proceeding," it could still be a "stage of the trial" for confrontation clause purposes. That was true of the competency hearing since it "determines whether a key witness will testify." Under the circumstances of this case, however, the defendant's exclusion from the hearing did not interfere with his opportunity to confront the witnesses through cross-examination. The questions asked at the competency hearing did not relate to the crime itself many were repeated at trial, the children were subject to "full and complete" cross-examination at trial, and the judge's preliminary ruling at the in-chambers hearing was subject to reconsideration in light of the witnesses' trial testimony. In addition, the due process component of the defendant's right of presence was not violated as defendant's personal participation in the limited hearing would not have borne "a substantial relationship to [the] defendant's opportunity better to defend himself at trial."

In *Gagnon*, after a juror expressed concern that one of the defendants was sketching portraits of the jurors, the judge directed the defendant to desist. At the request of defendant's counsel, the judge also announced that he would conduct a brief in camera inquiry (with defendant's counsel present) to ensure that the sketching had not prejudiced the jurors. Counsel for the defendant did not request that his client be present during this inquiry. In chambers, the judge explained to the juror who had been the subject of defendant's artistic efforts that the defendant simply was an artist and received assurance from the juror that he was willing to proceed as an impartial juror. The Court concluded that due process "does not require that all the parties be present when the judge inquiries into such a minor occurrence." It noted that the four defendants "could have done nothing had they been present nor would they have gained anything by attending."

Consistent with the objectives of the right of presence, the right is not fulfilled where the defendant is present but lacks competency or ability to understand the language of the forum. Accordingly, *Drope v. Mo.* (1975) imposes a constitutional obligation upon a trial judge to "always be alert to circumstances suggesting a change that would render the accused unable to meet the standards of competence to stand trial" and to cause "further inquiry on the question" to be held whenever the circumstances indicate "a sufficient doubt" of defendant's competence. A similar obligation exists to provide an interpreter when an accused does not understand the English language.

With the development of sophisticated video conferencing equipment, prosecutors have asked courts to accept a defendant's virtual presence on screen as a substitute for his actual presence in the courtroom. Not having to transport an incarcerated defendant to the courthouse saves the government money, and avoids security risks. It is hard to imagine how this sort of arrangement at the trial itself, without an express waiver by the defendant, could be consistent with the Confrontation Clause and with due process. Nevertheless, the constitutionality of substituting teleconferencing for the defendant's presence is an open question at pre-and post-trial stages of the prosecution, such as sentencing, where a defendant cannot claim confrontation rights. Whatever the proceeding, a defendant must not be forced to settle for virtual communication with his own lawyer.

(b) Harmless Error and Waiver. Where the particular proceeding is one at which the defendant had a clear right to be present (as at trial), but the defendant was absent for only a brief period, that absence will not invalidate a conviction if the error is harmless beyond a reasonable doubt. If a verbatim record was made during the defendant's absence and it shows that defendant's attorney was present and that no legal error was committed in defendant's absence, then it is likely that the error will be found to be harmless.

The defendant's constitutional right to be present is one of those "basic rights that the attorney cannot waive without the fully informed and publicly acknowledged consent of the defendant." Nevertheless, waiver, or rather forfeiture, of the right by the defendant is commonly found in at least three situations. First, where defendant is present but makes no effort to attend a bench or in-chambers examination when counsel leaves the defense table to participate, this may be taken as an intentional relinquishment of the right to be present, at least where the court in no way suggests that the defendant cannot accompany counsel. Proceedings may also go forward without the defendant's presence when the defendant forfeits his right to be present by his misbehavior in the courtroom. Finally, a defendant who voluntarily remains away from trial forfeits his right to be present. These circumstances are discussed in the two subsections that follow.

Although a defendant may forfeit his right to participate in the proceedings a defendant has no contrasting right to be absent from trial, even when his absence might assist his defense. In capital cases, for example, many jurisdictions prohibit the defense from waiving presence.

(c) Forfeiture by Conduct. In *Ill. v. Allen* (1970), the Supreme Court held the right to be present could be lost by the defendant's disruptive behavior. In concluding that the trial judge acted lawfully in excluding Allen from the courtroom following his repeated outbursts, the Court declared that "there are at least three constitutionally permissible ways for a trial judge to handle an obstreperous defendant like Allen: (1) bind and gag him, thereby keeping him present; (2) cite him for contempt; (3) take him out of the courtroom until he promises to conduct himself properly." Because the first two responses were properly rejected by the trial court, the defendant could not complain when his own behavior had cost him his right to be present at his trial.

Removal is preferable to gagging or shackling the disruptive defendant. Not only is it possible that the sight of shackles and gags might have a significant effect on the jury's beliefs about the defendant, but the use of this technique is itself something of an affront to the very dignity and decorum of judicial proceedings that the judge is seeking to uphold. Moreover, a less visible form of restraint—the "stun belt"—has been used in some courts to deter misbehavior by defendants who otherwise would be removed from court. Other courts ban its use. When restraints would unfairly prejudice the defendant, and contempt would be ineffectual, removal is likely to be the only realistic alternative.

The *Allen* ruling can best be explained as involving a "forfeiture" rather than a "waiver" of a constitutional right. Thus, whether or not the defendant actually made a "knowing and intelligent" decision to relinquish his right is not critical. Two factors, present in *Allen*, are essential: (1) Allen was "repeatedly warned by the trial judge that he would be removed from the courtroom if he persisted in his unruly conduct"; and (2) he was "constantly informed that he could return to the trial when he would agree to conduct himself in an orderly manner." Finally, as Justice Brennan noted in his *Allen* concurrence, if a defendant is excluded "the court should make reasonable efforts to enable him to communicate with his attorney and, if possible, to keep apprised of the progress of his trial."

(d) Forfeiture by Voluntary Absence. In *Taylor v. U.S.* (1973), the Court held that the defendant can also lose his right to be present by absenting himself during the trial:

> It is wholly incredible to suggest that petitioner, who was at liberty on bail, had attended the opening session of his trial, and had a duty to be present at the trial, * * * entertained any doubts about his right to be present at every stage of his trial. It seems equally incredible to us * * * "that a defendant who flees from a courtroom in the midst of a trial—where judge, jury, witnesses and lawyers are present and ready to continue—would not know that as a consequence the trial could continue in his absence."

The Court in *Taylor* relied upon the much earlier case of *Diaz v. U.S.* (1912), which declared that "if, after the trial has begun in his presence, [the defendant] voluntarily absents himself, this does not nullify what has been done or prevent the completion of the trial." That language "gave birth to the notion that a defendant who took flight *before* the trial commenced could not be tried in absentia." One grounding for such a distinction is that the judicial system has a greater interest in continuing what has been started than it has in proceeding with a trial that was never underway. Lower courts, however, have held that no constitutional violation results when the trial of a defendant who has voluntarily stayed away is commenced without him, so long as he knew when trial was to begin and there was an important interest in avoiding delay, such as avoiding prejudice to several co-defendants ready to proceed. Commencing a trial without the defendant present may violate statute or court rule.

(e) Prejudicial Circumstances of Presence. The right to a fair trial is a fundamental liberty secured by the Fourteenth Amendment, and a "basic component" of that right is the presumption of innocence. Because that presumption is likely to be impaired if the defendant is required to stand trial in prison or jail clothing, courts have consistently held that such a procedure is improper. The Supreme Court reached that conclusion in *Estelle v. Williams* (1976), where it was emphasized (1) "that the constant reminder of the accused's condition implicit in such distinctive, identifiable attire may affect a juror's judgment," (2) that "compelling an accused to wear jail clothing furthers no essential state policy," and (3) "that compelling the accused to stand trial in jail garb operates usually against only those who cannot post bail prior to trial."

As a general rule, a defendant in a criminal case also has the right to appear before the jury free from shackles or other physical restraints. This right also springs from the fundamental notion that a person accused of crime is presumed innocent until his guilt has been established beyond a reasonable doubt. The defendant also has a right to have his witnesses appear without physical restraints. Though shackling witnesses does not directly affect the presumption of innocence, it nonetheless may harm his defense by detracting from the credibility of his witnesses. As a divided Court explained in *Deck v. Mo.* (2005), physical restraints visible to the jury may not be used "absent a trial court determination, in the exercise of its discretion, that they are justified by a state interest specific to a particular trial." Security concerns could support the use of shackles, but any such determination must be case- and defendant-specific, and must appear in the record. This rule recognizes the potential for shackling to cause physical suffering, to undermine the the fairness of the fact-finding process, and to interfere with the accused's ability to participate in his own defense and communicate with his lawyer. Shackling also poses an "affront" to the "dignity and decorum of judicial proceedings that the judge is seeking to uphold."

Although much of the justification for limiting the use shackles at trial is to preserve the presumption of innocence, the Court in *Deck* extended constitutional scrutiny of these measures to the sentencing phase of the capital trial after that presumption no longer applied. The dangerousness of the defendant, the Court reasoned, is relevant to the death sentencing decision and shackles may affect adversely the jury's perception of the character of the defendant. This rationale would appear to be limited to those measures that convey to the jury the state's judgment that the defendant is considered by the state to pose a risk of harm to others. Unlike shackles, the mere presence of jail clothing does not convey a threat of dangerousness.

Unlike the appearance of the defendant in jail clothes and restraints, which are practices that have the potential to be so "inherently prejudicial" that they "must be justified by an 'essential state' policy or interest," the conspicuous use of identifiable security officers at trial is treated somewhat differently. In *Holbrook v. Flynn* (1986), the Supreme Court acknowledged that the courtroom presence of a substantial number of uniformed officers could present constitutional difficulties in an extreme case, but concluded that the state generally did not have to make a specific showing of a special security need to sustain the constitutionality of deploying several such officers. Since the deployment of uniformed officers "need not be interpreted as a sign that [defendant] is particularly dangerous," but may just as readily be viewed as a measure intended to "guard against disruptions emanating from outside the court room," or as "mere elements of an impressive drama," it was not "the sort of inherently prejudicial practice that, like shackling, should be permitted only where justified by an essential state interest specific to each trial." The Court also concluded that, since the deployment of the security guards was "intimately related to the State's legitimate interest in maintaining custody during the proceeding," it "did not offend the Equal Protection Clause by arbitrarily discriminating against those unable to post bond or to whom bail has been denied."

Courts generally do not apply the same scrutiny when the use of restraints is known only to a judge and not the jury. Yet there may be some conditions of presence that so inhibit a defendant's ability to meaningfully participate in the proceeding that their use even before a judge could be justified by only the most extraordinary circumstances. For example, the use of a "stun belt" to restrain a dangerous defendant may not risk adverse jury inferences if it is invisible to the jury, but requires the same on-the-record justification as other forms of visible restraint.

Questions sometimes arise concerning the location of the defendant in the courtroom during the trial. Placement of the defendant in a separate docket as a security measure may not be viewed as stigmatizing under the analysis of *Holbrook* when routine. Nevertheless, past cases indicate that it would still be unconstitutional because it places the defendant in a position where he cannot freely communicate with counsel. It is also necessary that the defendant be situated where he can see and hear the witnesses and they can see him. In *Coy v. Iowa* (1988), the Supreme Court held that the right of confrontation extends beyond cross-examination and encompasses also the right to a "face to face meeting with the witnesses appearing before the trier of fact." *Coy* held that the defendant's confrontation rights were infringed when a state trial court, seeking to protect two juvenile victims of alleged sex abuse from the emotional trauma of viewing the defendant when giving their testimony, placed between the witnesses and the defendant a screen that blocked the defendant from their sight, without first making any individualized findings of witness trauma.

Subsequently, in *Md. v. Craig* (1990), the Court upheld on its face a state procedure that allowed the use of one-way closed circuit television to present the testimony of a child victim in a sex abuse case, who remained outside the courtroom. The Court in *Craig* stressed that the statute required a case-specific finding that the child would suffer from such extreme emotional trauma, due to the presence of the defendant, that he or she could not "reasonably communicate," and that the placement of the witness could have been viewed by the jury as suggesting that the witness was fearful of testifying in the courtroom setting rather than fearful of testifying while looking at the defendant. Justice Scalia had dissented in *Craig*, and subsequently authored the majority opinion in *Crawford v. Wash.* (2004), a case that rejected the Court's earlier reliability test for the admission of hearsay under the Confrontation Clause. Some language in *Crawford* that endorses categorical rules rather than balancing tests is at odds with the Court's opinion in *Craig*. Nevertheless courts have continued to apply *Craig*, noting that the *Crawford* decision did not mention *Craig*, and addressed when confrontation is required, not what procedures constitute confrontation.

§ 16.3 The Defendant's Right of Access to Evidence

(a) Constitutional Grounding. Various statutes, common law rules, and constitutional commands combine to shape the capacity of the defense to gain access to evidence that it might use at trial. The Supreme Court has established several standards for access to evidence, including: (1) the prosecution's duty to disclose evidence within its possession or control that is exculpatory and material; (2) the prohibition against the government's bad faith destruction of such evidence; (3) the state's duty to provide the defense with the power through subpoena to gain the production of witnesses and physical items at trial; (4) the state's duty to provide certain types of assistance or information to the defense that will allow it to use the power of subpoena to gain evidence; and (5) the prohibition against certain governmental actions that interfere with the defense use of the subpoena power. The constitutional directives listed above, each discussed in subsections that follow, have been grounded on either or both of two basic constitutional guarantees—the Fifth and Fourteenth Amendment guarantee of due process and the Sixth Amendment's command that the accused "shall have compulsory process for obtaining witnesses in his favor."

The Compulsory Process Clause naturally suggests some constitutional entitlement to trial evidence. What is surprising is how rarely the Court has relied upon that provision in its discussions of a right of access to evidence. As the Supreme Court noted in *Pa. v. Ritchie* (1987), it "has had little occasion to discuss the contours of the Compulsory Process Clause." Instead, it has addressed under the Due Process Clause claims that the government failed to assist in identifying and locating defense witnesses, or improperly interfered with the defense's use of subpoenas.

As an additional source of a constitutional right of access, commentators and occasional judicial opinions have looked to the Confrontation Clause of the Sixth Amendment. The premise here is that the right of confrontation includes not only a right to cross-examine witnesses but also a right of access to material that could serve as a basis for effective cross-examination. The state's failure to provide or facilitate access to that material would be treated in the same fashion as the denial or restriction of cross-examination itself. As the following cases suggest, this theory has yet to gain a majority on the Court. Instead the Court has continued to rely upon due process rather than the Confrontation Clause when evaluating access to evidence claims.

(b) Due Process Duty to Disclose Evidence Favorable to the Accused. *The Origins of the Brady rule.* In *Mooney v. Holohan* (1935), the Supreme Court first held that a prosecutor's use of false testimony could constitute a violation of due process. The defendant there alleged that the prosecutor had fabricated the case against him by procuring and introducing perjured testimony at trial. The Supreme Court had little difficulty in finding that defendant's claim had constitutional dimensions. A per curiam opinion noted that due process is not satisfied by "the pretense of a trial which in truth is but used as a means of depriving a defendant of liberty through a deliberate deception of court and jury by the presentation of testimony known to be perjured."

As discussed in § 16.3(d), a series of later rulings extended the "*Mooney* principle" to require that the prosecution not suborn perjury, not purposefully use evidence known to be false, and not allow the known false testimony of its witnesses to stand uncorrected. In *Brady v. Md.* (1963), the Supreme Court extended the *Mooney* principle to the prosecution's failure to disclose exculpatory evidence within its possession to the defense. The defendant Brady and a companion, Boblit, had been convicted of felony murder and sentenced to death. Prior to Brady's separate trial, defense counsel had asked to examine all of the statements that Boblit had given to the police. Counsel was shown several of Boblit's statements, but failed to receive one statement in which Boblit admitted that he had done the actual killing. At trial, defendant claimed that he had not himself killed the victim. Defense counsel stressed this claim in his closing argument, asking the jury to show leniency and not impose the death penalty. Following defendant's conviction, defense counsel learned of the undisclosed statement and sought a new trial based on discovery. The Supreme Court held that the prosecutor's nondisclosure of Boblit's statement had resulted in a denial of due process on the punishment issue, reasoning that the fact finder is equally deceived when the prosecutor "withholds evidence on demand of an accused which, if made available, would tend to exculpate him or reduce the penalty." Summarizing its ruling, the Court stated that "the suppression by the prosecution of evidence favorable to an accused upon request violates due process where the evidence is material either to guilt or to punishment, irrespective of the good faith or bad faith of the prosecution."

The Court has continued to develop the *Brady* rule in a series of subsequent cases: *U.S. v. Agurs* (1976), *U.S. v. Bagley* (1985), *Kyles v. Whitley* (1995), *Strickler v. Greene* (1999) and *Banks v. Dretke* (2004). In *Strickler*, the Court summed up the "essential components" of a *Brady* violation. Failure by the prosecution to disclose evidence to the defense, regardless of whether the defense requested the evidence, violates due process where (1) that evidence is "favorable to the accused, either because it is exculpatory, or because it is impeaching"; (2) the evidence was "suppressed by the [government], either willfully or inadvertently;" and (3) "prejudice * * * ensued." Prejudice in this context is interchangeable with the concept of materiality, explored below.

Materiality. In *Bagley*, the Court articulated the materiality standard that it employs today. Before trial in that case, the defense had requested notification of "any deals, promises, or inducements made to [government] witnesses in exchange for their testimony." The government produced signed affidavits of its two principal witnesses, private security officers, which detailed their undercover activities and concluded with the statement that the affidavits were given without any promises of reward. Following defendant's trial and conviction, it was discovered that both witnesses had signed contracts with the federal investigating agency stating that they would be paid "a sum commensurate with services and information rendered." The prosecuting attorney testified that he would have furnished the contracts if he had known of their existence, and the trial judge agreed that this should have been done. The trial judge refused to order a new trial, however, reasoning that the impeachment evidence would not have affected the outcome of defendant's bench trial. The Ninth Circuit reversed, viewing the government's failure to disclose as impairing defendant's right of confrontation, and concluded that the violation therefore required automatic reversal. The Supreme Court rejected that conclusion and remanded for reconsideration. The Justices agreed that any constitutional violation here was to be judged under the due process standard of *Brady*, rather than the Confrontation Clause. Evidence is material the Court held, "only if there is a reasonable probability that, had the evidence been disclosed to the defense, the result of the proceeding would have been different." A reasonable probability is a probability "sufficient to undermine confidence in the outcome."

Although adopting a single standard of materiality for all nondisclosure cases, regardless of whether the evidence was specifically requested by the defense, Justice Blackmun noted that specific request cases presented special considerations in applying the "reasonable probability" standard. "[A]n incomplete response to a specific request not only deprives the defense of certain evidence, but has the effect of representing to the defense that the evidence does not exist." Relying on "this misleading representation, the defense might abandon lines of independent investigation, defenses, or trial strategies that it otherwise would have pursued."

In *Kyles v. Whitley* (1995), the Court noted that "four aspects of materiality under *Bagley* bear emphasis." First, "a showing of materiality does not require demonstration by a preponderance that disclosure of the suppressed evidence would have resulted ultimately in the defendant's acquittal * * *. *Bagley's* touchstone of materiality is a 'reasonable probability' of a different result, and the adjective is important. The question is not whether the defendant would more likely than not have received a different verdict with the evidence, but whether in its absence he received a fair trial, understood as a trial resulting in a verdict worthy of confidence." Second, the "*Bagley* materiality [test] * * * is not a sufficiency of evidence test. A defendant need not demonstrate that after discounting the inculpatory evidence in light of the undisclosed evidence, there would not have been enough to convict." Third, "once a reviewing court applying *Bagley* has found constitutional error there is no need for further harmless-error review." Fourth, "*Bagley* materiality" is to be judged by reference to the "suppressed evidence considered collectively, not item-by-item," with the focus on the "cumulative effect of suppression." While the *Kyles* ruling rested on a fact-intensive analysis that has limited precedential value (especially in light of Court's close division as to that analysis), its discussion of the general character of "materiality" under *Bagley* suggests a standard that is more easily met by the defense than some lower courts had previously assumed.

Strickler v. Greene is a further illustration of the Court's application of the materiality standard. In that case, notes of a police interview of an eyewitness and letters written by the witness were not disclosed, although the prosecutor followed an open file policy. These undisclosed documents cast serious doubt on significant portions of the witness's testimony. The District Court had concluded that without the witness's testimony, the jury might have been persuaded that another man, not the defendant, was the "ringleader" and would have convicted him of first degree rather than capital murder. The Supreme Court found this possibility unsupported and, more importantly, insufficient to meet the materiality standard. Reviewing the evidence in the case, and noting that the prosecutor did not rely upon the testimony at issue during the closing argument at the penalty phase, the Court concluded that the "petitioner has not convinced us that there is a reasonable probability that the jury would have returned a different verdict if [the witness's] testimony had been either severely impeached or excluded entirely."

In a somewhat similar case, *Banks v. Dretke* (2004), the Court found that the petitioner had established the materiality of the evidence kept from him by Texas prosecutors in his capital case. The Court distinguished *Strickler*, where "considerable forensic and other physical evidence" supported guilt and where the testimony at issue was not used by the government to establish the defendant's eligibility for the death sentence. The withheld impeachment evidence in *Banks* was material, the Court explained, because it would have undermined the testimony of a witnesses who proved "crucial" to the state in securing the death sentence, serving as "the centerpiece" of the prosecution's penalty-phase case.

The timing of the disclosure. The *Brady* rule does not impose a general requirement of pretrial disclosure of exculpatory evidence that is material to the issue of guilt. Due process requires only that exculpatory evidence be disclosed at a time sufficient to permit defendant to make effective use of that evidence. Depending upon the nature of the evidence, this standard may sometimes require pretrial disclosure. Thus, where the prosecution has the statement of a witness who could present exculpatory testimony and does not intend itself to call that witness, disclosure before trial would be necessary to ensure that the defense has an opportunity to subpoena that witness for trial. Insofar as such disclosure exceeds what is permitted under local provisions for pretrial discovery or Jencks statutes regulating the timing of the disclosure of witness statements, the constitutional obligation will prevail over those provisions. For most exculpatory evidence, the prosecution should be able to satisfy its constitutional obligation by disclosure at trial. The burden rests with the defendant to establish that the "lateness of that disclosure so prejudiced [defendant's] preparation or presentation of his defense that he was prevented from receiving his constitutionally guaranteed fair trial." Moreover, if the defendant fails to request a continuance when disclosure is first made at trial, that failure may be viewed as negating any later claim of actual prejudice.

Although pretrial disclosure may not be required, prosecutors commonly respond to pretrial requests for specific exculpatory evidence by disclosing *Brady* material before trial. In some jurisdictions, discovery statutes or court rules contain a *"Brady* provision," which brings such disclosure within the formal discovery apparatus. If the prosecutor refuses to respond to a specific pretrial request, stating that the material need not be disclosed under *Brady*, the defense may ask the trial court to examine the requested items in camera and order disclosure if it should find the items to be exculpatory and material. Courts tend to be reluctant to undertake a pretrial review of *Brady* requests, and ordinarily will not provide in camera inspection unless the request is limited to no more than a few items of evidence and the defendant can show some strong basis for believing that the material may be favorable to the defense.

Addressing pre-guilty-plea disclosure for the first time in *U.S. v. Ruiz* (2002), the Court held that the Constitution does not require disclosure of impeachment information prior to a guilty plea. In *Ruiz*, the prosecutor offered the defendant a plea bargain with a reduced sentence, but she rejected the bargain because she would not agree to the term in the agreement waiving her right to receive "impeachment information relating to any informants or other witnesses" as well as her right to receive information supporting any affirmative defense. The defendant later entered a guilty plea without any plea agreement, and then appealed when she did not obtain the reduced sentence that the prosecutor had included in the rejected plea agreement, arguing that the government had an obligation to disclose impeachment evidence before a plea bargain, and that demanding a waiver of disclosure was unlawful. The Court disagreed, finding that due process did not compel disclosure of impeachment information before a guilty plea. A court may "accept a guilty plea, with its accompanying waiver of various constitutional rights, despite various forms of misapprehension under which a defendant might labor," the Court reasoned. In concluding that due process would not require pre-guilty-plea disclosure of impeachment information, the Court considered the "nature of the private interest at stake," "the value of the additional safeguard of disclosure," and "the adverse impact of the requirement upon the Government's interests." Impeachment evidence may or may not be valuable to a defendant, depending upon how much he already knows about the government's case, and there was only a small risk that without it, "innocent individuals, accused of crimes, will plead guilty," considering the "guilty-plea safeguards" in Fed.R.Crim.P. 11. An obligation to disclose impeachment information could seriously interfere with the government's interest in obtaining guilty pleas, disrupt investigations, expose potential witnesses to serious harm, and "require the Government to devote substantially more resources to trial preparation prior to plea bargaining, thereby depriving the plea-bargaining process of its main resource-saving advantages," the Court concluded.

Certainly this reasoning could support a later ruling that the Constitution does not require pre-guilty-plea disclosure of other sorts of *Brady* material either. But in *Ruiz*, the Court did not address information other than impeachment material. Indeed, the plea agreement offered to Ruiz included a provision that "any [known] information establishing the factual innocence of the defendant" "has been turned over to the defendant" and that acknowledged the government's "continuing duty to provide such information."

The Court has also suggested that the *Brady* line of cases does not apply after trial. In *District Attorney's Office v. Osborne* (2009) the Court summarily rejected the argument that the failure of the state to turn over DNA evidence for testing post-conviction violated Osborne's due process right to exculpatory evidence under *Brady*. *Brady* is a "trial right," the Court explained, and because Osborne had "already been found guilty at a fair trial," *Brady* "is the wrong framework."

The character of favorable evidence. The prosecution's duty to disclose is limited by most courts to matters that would be admissible in evidence, as only such information could be relevant to the jury's decision. Other courts view admissibility as a critical end-product, but note that the duty to disclose could encompass inadmissible material where that material appears likely to lead the defense to the discovery of admissible evidence. Several decisions of the Court support restricting *Brady* violations to admissible evidence. The nondisclosed material in *Brady* was not relevant to the issue of guilt and the Court relied on that factor in holding that the element of materiality was not satisfied as to that issue. The *Agurs* Court specifically rejected the view that the standard for judging materiality "should focus on the impact of the undisclosed evidence on the defendant's ability to prepare for trial, rather than the materiality of the evidence to the issue of guilt or innocence." That the due process duty to disclose extends only to evidence, not strategy, was reaffirmed in *Weatherford v. Bursey* (1977). The Court there rejected the contention that the government had violated *Brady* when it used as a prosecution witness an informant who had previously assured defendant that he would not testify against him. *Brady*, the Court noted, relates only to concealing evidence favorable to the accused, not to providing the defense with notice that will improve its preparation for meeting the government's evidence. In *Wood v. Bartholomew* (1995), also, the Court again emphasized the importance of admissibility, when it reasoned that because polygraph results from a test taken by a government witness could not have been introduced as evidence, the prosecutor had no *Brady* obligation to disclose those results to the defense.

Courts sometimes have been troubled by the question of whether evidence that does not point directly to the defendant's innocence nevertheless is "favorable to the accused." Most agree that evidence can be favorable even though it does no more than demonstrate that "a number of factors which could link the defendant to the crime do not." Thus, where the circumstances of the crime suggested that the offender's clothes might have been stained, and defendant's clothes were found not to have been stained, the laboratory report on the examination of his clothes were treated as "favorable" rather than "neutral" evidence. Under some circumstances, however, the rejected links may be so unlikely that the nondisclosed evidence is truly neutral. Thus, where robbers wore loose-fitting coveralls and their faces were masked, the inability of the eyewitnesses to positively identify the defendants was viewed as not really helpful to the defense and therefore not subject to *Brady*. Of course, where the question is close as to whether the evidence is "favorable" or "neutral," the nondisclosure most likely will not meet the *Bagley* test for materiality even if it is determined that the evidence is favorable.

Prosecution control over the evidence. In *Brady* and *Agurs*, the items not disclosed were within the prosecutor's files. The nondisclosed contracts in *Bagley* apparently were in the files of the investigative agency that had been assisted by the security guards, but the Court saw no reason to even comment on that factor in discussing the prosecution's responsibility. In *Kyles v. Whitley*, the Court rejected the state's contention that a "more lenient" standard of materiality should apply where the "favorable evidence in issue * * * [was] known only to police investigators and not to the prosecutor." While "no one doubts that police investigators sometimes fail to inform a prosecutor of all they know," the Court reasoned, "neither is there any serious doubt that 'procedures and regulations can be established to carry [the prosecutor's] burden and to insure communication of all relevant information on each case to every lawyer who deals with it.'"

The prosecution's obligation under *Brady* extends to the files of those police agencies that were responsible for the primary investigation in the case. Information available to other members of the "prosecution team" in the particular case, including even caseworkers from social service agencies, is included in a prosecutor's obligation as well. On the other hand, the prosecution's obligation has been held not to extend to independent agencies not involved in the investigation of the case, such as a probation department.

Defense diligence. The prosecutor's constitutional obligation is not violated, notwithstanding the nondisclosure of apparently exculpatory evidence, where that evidence was known to the defense and no request for disclosure was made. Before holding the defense responsible for its lack of diligence, courts have insisted on proof that the defense was aware of the potentially exculpatory nature of the evidence as well as its existence. Similar to the approach to measuring due diligence in the context of newly discovered evidence, courts tend to measure the knowledge of the defense by reference to what is known to either counsel or client.

Still another troublesome issue raised by the due diligence concept is how far the defense must go to obtain the material. If the defense makes a request and the prosecutor fails to furnish the item, does the defense have the further obligation to obtain the item by subpoena (assuming that process is available), or can it proceed without the item and raise a *Brady* claim after conviction? Several decisions suggest that the defense must exhaust all efforts to obtain the item where it knows of its existence. This includes obtaining the item from an alternative source where it would be available (e.g., as to a matter of public record).

(c) Disclosure of Witness Statements—Jencks Act. Where the prosecution has within its control the prior recorded statements of its witnesses, the defense will desire to obtain those statements for use in impeaching the prosecution witnesses. Under limited circumstances, *Brady* may require that the prosecution make such statements available to the defense, but the failure to disclose impeachment material will constitute a due process violation only where the lost opportunity for impeachment is so critical that there is a reasonable probability that a different result would have been reached if the statement had been made available for that purpose. For most jurisdictions, the only avenue providing assurance that the defense will receive the prior recorded statements of prosecution witnesses is a statute, court rule, or common law ruling modeled upon the federal Jencks Act, which provides for disclosure after the witness testifies at trial.

The Jencks Act was adopted by Congress in 1957 in response to the Supreme Court's ruling earlier that year in *Jencks v. U.S.* (1957). The statute establishes a right of access that is not conditioned on showing of materiality but permits a court to order disclosure only after the direct testimony of a government witness. The trial court, on application of the defense, must direct the government to disclose any "statement" of the witness "in the possession of the United States" that "relates to the subject matter as to which the witness testified." If the government contends that the entire statement or any portion of it does not relate to the subject matter of the witness's testimony, it submits the statement to the trial court for an in camera review. The court then excises such material as it finds not to relate to the witness's testimony, orders disclosure of the remainder, and preserves the excised material so that its decision to excise can be reviewed in appeal if the case should result in a conviction. If the government elects not to make the statement available as ordered by the court, the testimony of the witness is stricken, with a mistrial declared where the court views that as appropriate. In 1975, the federal rule was expanded to require disclosure by both sides of the statements of its witnesses, excepting only the defense witness who is also the defendant. Many states have adopted provisions or procedures similar to those included in the Jencks Act.

(d) **The Duty to Correct False Evidence.** The prosecutor's due process obligation with respect to false evidence builds upon the Supreme Court's seminal ruling in *Mooney v. Holohan* (1935). In that case, the Court found that the prosecutor's knowing procurement and use of perjured testimony rendered defendant's trial no more than a "pretense" in which the government utilized a "deliberate deception of judge and jury" to obtain a conviction—a result no more consistent with the "rudimentary commands of justice * * * [than] obtaining a like result by intimidation." *Mooney* involved a knowing and intentional use of perjured testimony that related directly to the defendant's commission of the offense charged. Subsequent Supreme Court rulings established that *Mooney* also encompassed the prosecution's failure to correct testimony, known to be perjured, that the witness had advanced on his own initiative. Thus, in *Alcorta v. Tex.* (1957), where the defendant claimed that he killed his wife in the heat of passion after discovering her kissing the witness, and the witness denied that he had kissed the deceased and claimed that they had been no more than casual friends, the prosecutor violated due process by allowing that testimony to stand when the prosecutor knew, from previous conversations with the witness, that the witness and the deceased had an ongoing sexual relationship.

The knowledge element of the *Mooney* principle is assessed by examining the collective knowledge of the prosecution, not the knowledge of the individual prosecutor. Thus, in *Giglio v. U.S.* (1972), where a critical prosecution witness testified falsely that he had not received a promise that he would not be indicted, the state was not excused from correcting that statement by virtue of the trial attorney's belief that the witness was telling the truth. A promise of immunity had been made by another prosecutor who handled the case at an earlier stage, that promise was attributable "to the Government," and the due process obligation of *Mooney* was that of the prosecutor's office as a whole, for it operated as an entity in serving as "the spokesman for the Government."

Taken together, *Mooney* and its progeny establish a constitutional obligation of the prosecution as an entity not to deceive the fact finder or allow it to be deceived by the prosecution witnesses. This obligation requires that it not suborn perjury, not use evidence known to be false, and not allow known false testimony of its witnesses to stand uncorrected. Where the government fails to fulfill that obligation, it matters not whether its failure is attributable to negligence or an intent to deceive. Similarly, as lower courts have noted, it matters not whether the witness giving false testimony is mistaken or intentionally lying. If the prosecution knows that the witness's statement is untrue, it has a duty to correct it.

Because the *Mooney* principle is based upon the defendant's right to a fair trial, the Court has refused to go so far as to hold that the knowing failure to correct false testimony produces a due process violation without regard to whether the false testimony was likely to have had an impact upon the outcome of the trial. As Justice Blackmun explained in his plurality opinion in *U.S. v. Bagley*, a *Mooney* violation requires the reversal of conviction unless that error was "harmless beyond a reasonable doubt; it can only stand if there was no reasonable likelihood the false testimony could have affected the judgment."

(e) The Government's Obligation to Preserve Evidence. In *Ariz. v. Youngblood* (1988), the Court examined the due process implications of the government's loss of evidence where the defendant could not obtain "comparable evidence by other reasonably available means." In *Youngblood*, the defendant, convicted of the sexual molestation and kidnapping of a 10–year-old boy, had protested the state's failure to properly preserve evidence so as to permit testing for blood group identification. A hospital physician had obtained semen samples from the victim's rectum and the police had collected the victim's clothing, but due to the inadvertent failure of police criminologists to promptly perform tests on the samples and to refrigerate the clothing, it later proved impossible to perform blood group testing that could have been matched against defendant's blood. The lower court had held that because the main issue at trial was identity and because the government was responsible for the destruction of evidence that could have conclusively eliminated the defendant as the perpetrator, a conviction was precluded by due process. Rejecting that reasoning, the Supreme Court majority held that "unless a criminal defendant can show bad faith on the part of the police, failure to preserve potentially useful evidence does not constitute a denial of due process of law."

The Court focused on two factors in explaining why the due process standard governing the failure to preserve evidentiary material required a showing of bad faith, though "good or bad faith" was admittedly "irrelevant" under the due process standard of *Brady*. First, "whenever potentially exculpatory evidence is permanently lost, courts face the treacherous task of divining the import of materials whose contents are unknown, and, very often, disputed." Second, the Court was "unwilling * * * to read the fundamental 'fairness requirement' of the Due Process Clause as imposing on the police an undifferentiated and absolute duty to retain and to preserve all material that might be of conceivable evidentiary significance in a particular prosecution." Requiring a defendant to show bad faith would appropriately restrict the constitutional obligation of police to preserve evidence to "that class of cases where the interests of justice most clearly require it, i.e., those cases in which the police themselves by their conduct indicate that the evidence would form a basis for exonerating the defendant." The significance of this limitation, the Court added, was illustrated by the facts in *Youngblood*. The police there had collected the rectal swab and the clothing on the night of the crime, a full six weeks before the defendant was taken into custody. Moreover, one of the tests that the state criminologist later found he could not use (because the clothing had not been refrigerated) was a protein molecule test that the police department had only recently started to use. The suggestion of the lower court that the state had some due process obligation to employ a particular investigatory tool was mistaken: "The situation here is no different than a prosecution for drunk driving that rests on police observation alone; the defendant is free to argue to the finder of fact that a breathalyzer test might have been exculpatory, but the police do not have a constitutional duty to perform any particular tests." A defendant convicted of possessing cocaine, for example, will be unable to obtain relief under *Youngblood* for the destruction of the substance alleged to be cocaine, if he cannot show the destruction was in bad faith. *Ill. v. Fisher* (2004) was just such a case. There police tests indicated that the substance seized from the defendant was cocaine, but before trial the defendant jumped bail, ten years elapsed, and the cocaine was destroyed "in good faith and in accord with ... normal practice." The presence of a pending discovery request for the substance did not itself demonstrate bad faith, concluded the Court. Because the evidence was at best potentially useful to the defense, relief was unavailable without a showing of bad faith.

Years later, a sample from Youngblood's case was found and tested with new DNA analyses. The test exonerated Youngblood and implicated another man in the crime. The due process test established in Youngblood's case remains good law, despite his subsequent exoneration. Many states have rejected *Youngblood's* requirement of bad faith in interpreting their own constitutional provisions.

The remedies most often sought by defendants alleging the loss of exculpatory evidence are dismissal of the prosecution or, if the lost or destroyed evidence would have been relevant only to challenge particular evidence of the prosecution, exclusion of that evidence. Such steps are regarded by most courts as extreme. In determining whether the government's failure to preserve discoverable materials requires some form of relief benefitting the defense, lower courts have tended to adopt what one court described as a "pragmatic balancing approach." The sanction depends upon a case-by-case assessment of the government's culpability for the loss, the significance of the lost evidence when viewed in light of its nature, its bearing upon critical issues in the case, and the strength of the government's untainted proof. Under this approach, either extreme culpability or a highly likely impact upon outcome may justify relief. If the evidence was destroyed for the very purpose of hindering the defense, such conscious impropriety may be enough without any further showing as to the likely impact of the destroyed evidence, as the prosecution's motivation in destroying the evidence carries with it a sufficient inference of prejudice. Relief is often limited to informing the jury that the evidence was lost and should be assumed to have the exculpatory characteristics claimed by the defense.

(f) Defense Use of Subpoenas. All jurisdictions have statutes or court rules authorizing the defense to use the trial court's subpoena power to compel persons to appear as witnesses at trial or to produce at trial designated documents or other objects. Availability of such subpoenas commonly is automatic. Where a defendant in a state case seeks to direct a subpoena to a person in another state, then the applicable Uniform Act will require the defendant (and the prosecution as well when it is using the Act) to show that the designated witness is "material and necessary."

Where the defendant is financially unable to pay the witness fee, the state will bear that cost although the issuance might then require more than a mere request. For example, Federal Rule 17 requires the defendant to show both that he is unable to pay the fee and that the presence of the witness is necessary for an adequate defense. In light of the defendant's sixth amendment right to compulsory process and his fifth amendment right not to be subject to disabilities because of his financial status, necessity under the Rule has been construed to mean "relevant, material, and useful to an adequate defense." Even under this liberal construction, however, courts have denied numerous defense requests, usually on the ground that the witness would only be cumulative or would not have personal knowledge that would allow him to give relevant testimony. Other jurisdictions grant to the indigent defendant the automatic authority to subpoena a certain number of witnesses at state expense (although a showing of need is required if the defense goes beyond that number).

A primary limitation on a subpoena is that it must be for "evidence," that is, information that will be admissible at trial. This limitation will rarely be called into question on a subpoena directing a person to testify. More frequently, a question of privilege is raised in a motion to quash directed at a subpoena duces tecum. A court assessing the evidentiary character of subpoenaed testimony, documents, or other items must look beyond the local law defining witness competency, privileges, and other evidentiary limitations or immunities because the Constitution can override state law and declare admissible that which would otherwise not be admissible.

(g) Assisting the Defense in Obtaining Evidence. In some situations, the prosecution may have a duty to assist defense efforts to obtain evidence. Perhaps the most common illustration is the prosecutor's duty, imposed under discovery rules in various jurisdictions, to make its physical evidence available to the defense so that the defense may conduct its own scientific tests on that evidence. Some courts, relying on *Brady*, have held that the defense has a constitutional right to such assistance where it can establish a reasonable basis for believing that the test results may be both "favorable" and "material." The government may have an obligation in some jurisdictions to extend its power to hold line-ups to assist the defense. While the defendant has no constitutional right to a line-up, several courts have held that due process may require the prosecution to honor a line-up request under special circumstances. Ordinarily, the defense must establish that eyewitness identification will be a material issue in the case and that "there exists a reasonable likelihood of a mistaken identification which a lineup would resolve."

In some circumstances, the prosecution may have an obligation to assist the defendant in finding potential defense witnesses. In *Roviaro v. U.S.* (1957), the defendant charged with (1) an illegal sale of heroin to "John Doe," and (2) illegal transportation of that heroin, sought before and during trial to ascertain Doe's identity. Those efforts were rejected on the ground that Doe was a government informer and his identity was protected by the "informer's privilege." Defendant was convicted on both counts on the basis of testimony by two police officers. One testified that, while keeping Doe under surveillance, he observed Doe drive defendant to a location where defendant first retrieved a package (later found to contain narcotics) from under a tree then transferred that package to Doe, then departed. The second officer testified that he had been hiding in the trunk of Doe's car and had heard defendant discuss with Doe the proposed transfer of the package. Before the Supreme Court, the government conceded that the nondisclosure of Doe's identity was improper as to the illegal sale charge, for as to it Doe had been an "active participant," but contended that the transportation charge did not require disclosure. The Supreme Court disagreed. What was at stake was "in reality the Government's privilege to withhold from disclosure the identity of persons who furnish information of violations of the law," a privilege limited in scope by "fundamental requirements of fairness." Thus, "where the disclosure of an informant's identity * * * is relevant and helpful to the defense of an accused, or is essential to a fair determination of a cause, the privilege must give way" and the government must choose between disclosing the informant's identity or dismissing its prosecution. "The problem is one that calls for balancing" of the interests involved on a case-by-case basis, "taking into consideration the crime charged, the possible defenses, the possible significance of the informant's testimony, and other relevant factors."

In *Roviaro*, the balancing process tipped in favor of requiring disclosure of the informer's identity. The defendant was placed in the position of explaining his alleged possession of narcotics. Unless he waived his constitutional right not to take the stand on his own defense, Doe was "his one material witness." Doe's testimony "might have disclosed an entrapment" or "might have thrown doubt upon petitioner's identity or the identity of the package." He was "the only witness who might have testified to petitioner's possible lack of knowledge of the contents of the package." Doe was, in sum, "the only witness in a position to amplify or contradict the testimony of the government witnesses" and the "unfairness" of denying defendant access to Doe was "emphasized" by the government's use itself of testimony regarding an alleged conversation between defendant and Doe.

Although *Roviaro* was based on the Court's supervisory authority over the federal courts, lower courts have viewed the decision as "constitutionally compelled." Lower courts have applied *Roviaro* where police undercover agents were additional eyewitnesses to the alleged crime and thus were in essentially the same position vis-a-vis the offense as the informant, but have consistently held that disclosure is not required where the informant merely provided information concerning the offense, such as by telling the police of the location of contraband. So long as the informant was more than a "tipster," and arranged for the illegal transaction, disclosure is called for should the defendant claim entrapment.

(h) Government Interference with Defense Access. The teaching of *Webb v. Tex.* (1972) is that due process limits courts and prosecutors from undermining the defense's ability to utilize the subpoena authority to gain testimony at trial. In that case, the trial judge on his own initiative warned the defendant's sole witness, an inmate with an extensive criminal record, against committing perjury. The judge said that if he lied he could "get into real trouble," that any lies would be "personally" brought to the attention of the grand jury by the judge, and that a perjury conviction was "probably going to mean several years," and "will be held against you * * * when you're up for parole." After hearing those remarks and the judge's comment to defense counsel that the witness could "decline to testify," the witness refused to give any testimony. The Court in *Webb* reversed defendant's conviction on due process grounds. "In the circumstances of this case," said the Court, the judge's remarks violated defendant's right to a fair trial because they had been cast in "unnecessarily strong terms" and "effectively drove that witness off the stand." The same principle is applied to prosecutorial efforts to discourage prospective witnesses from testifying for the defense. Threatening the prospective witness with prosecution (either for perjury or for some other offense) if he should testify, or isolating the prospective witness during the trial, can amount to a due process violation.

Though some lower courts had concluded that the *Webb* principle produced a per se due process violation, when the government charged a defendant with smuggling aliens into the country and then deported many of those aliens before defendant even had an opportunity to interview them, the Supreme Court in *U.S. v. Valenzuela–Bernal* (1982), declined to go that far. Stressing that the government was responsible both for enforcing the criminal law and faithfully executing the congressional policy favoring prompt deportation of illegal aliens, the Court concluded it was proper for the government to undertake "the prompt deportation of illegal-alien witnesses upon the Executive's good-faith determination that they possess no evidence favorable to the defendant in a criminal prosecution." Accordingly, the mere act of deportation would not in itself constitute a violation of either the due process or compulsory process clauses. To establish a violation, the defense would have to show "that the evidence lost would be both material and favorable to the defense." The defense would not be expected to render "a detailed description of their lost testimony." It would be satisfactory to make "a plausible showing that the testimony of the deported witness would have been material and favorable to the defense in ways not merely cumulative to the testimony of available witnesses."

(i) Defense Witness Immunity. *Roviaro* required the government to sacrifice a governmental interest relating to effective law enforcement in order to assist the defense in gaining access to a potentially critical witness. Commentators have argued that the same principle should mandate that the government make available to the defense the testimony of witnesses who refuse to answer questions by the defense based on their fifth amendment privilege against self-incrimination. This situation is distinguishable from instances in which a witness's exercise of another privilege stymies the defense in obtaining testimony, it is argued, because here, the interests underlying the privilege can be preserved and the testimony can be made available if the government grants the witness immunity.

Lower courts have for the most part rejected these arguments and have held that the Constitution does not entitle a criminal defendant to have immunity granted to witnesses so that they can testify on the defendant's behalf. No such right has been found in the Sixth Amendment's Compulsory Process Clause, for the subpoena is made fully available by the trial court and the compulsory process clause has been held not to override the exercise by witnesses of privileges as significant as the self-incrimination privilege. Finally, the due process obligation of *Brady* is held not to apply, for that deals only with the disclosure of evidence in the government's possession, not with the extraction of evidence from others. Nevertheless, "fundamental fairness" may require a trial court to dismiss a case if the prosecution refuses to grant immunity to a defense witness under particularly egregious circumstances. For example, one court has held that a trial judge is required to order the government to grant immunity or face dismissal when the court finds (1) that the government has "engaged in discriminatory use of immunity to gain a tactical advantage"; (2) the witness's testimony is "material, exculpatory, and not cumulative;" and (3) the testimony is "unobtainable from any other source." Apart from the case reflecting this type of deliberate distortion of the fact-finding process, the judiciary is bound by legislation governing the granting of immunity, which typically entrusts to the executive branch discretion as to whether to grant immunity. As one court argued, judges should not be propelled into "unchartered waters" where they are required to weigh "public interests" that are not always apparent from the record or readily measured.

§ 16.4   The Presentation of Evidence

(a) The Rules of Evidence and Cross Examination. The legal standards that govern the admissibility of evidence and the questioning of witnesses, usually regulated by evidence rules and statutes, are the subject of separate treatises and will not be examined here. However, the defendant's constitutional rights of confrontation may affect their application. For example, the Confrontation Clause can preclude admission of hearsay evidence by the prosecution that is otherwise admissible under local law. As the Court explained in *Crawford v. Wash.* (2004), "Where nontestimonial hearsay is at issue, it is wholly consistent with the Framers' design to afford the States flexibility in their development of hearsay law. Where testimonial evidence is at issue, however, the Sixth Amendment demands what the common law required: unavailability and a prior opportunity for cross examination." The defendant's right to testify, to compulsory process, or to fundamental fairness may override privileges or rules of exclusion recognized under state law and require the admission of defense evidence that would otherwise be inadmissible. Thus, assessing the admissibility of both prosecution and defense evidence requires examination of the possible bearing of constitutional guarantees as well as the rules of evidence.

In addition, rules of exclusion designed to promote other goals of criminal procedure may affect admissibility. Thus, the rule governing guilty pleas may preclude admissibility of statements made during plea negotiations, the rules on discovery may allow exclusion of evidence due to discovery violations, and rules requiring pretrial notice of intent to use evidence may be enforced through exclusion. Statements made in the course of pretrial suppression hearings may be excluded at trial so that defendants are not forced to choose between giving up a valid fourth amendment claim or waiving the privilege against self-incrimination.

A witness's fifth amendment privilege against self-incrimination may also bar certain cross-examination questions that would otherwise be acceptable impeachment under state law (e.g., inquiring about immunized testimony or a coerced confession). The assertion of the privilege against self-incrimination by the defendant is addressed in § 16.5; the problem of obtaining testimony from a defense witness who claims the privilege is addressed in § 6.3(g) and in § 8.3(i); and the following subsection examines the ability of a litigant to elicit a claim of privilege from a witness.

(b) Forcing a Claim of Privilege by a Witness. A witness, in contrast to a defendant, has no right not to be called to testify, but must exercise the privilege in response to each individual question. However, to force the witness to claim the privilege in open court is often to invite the jury to draw an inference unfavorable to the other side based on the witness's refusal to testify. Thus where the prosecution calls a person that the jury is likely to associate with the defendant (such as an alleged accomplice) and that person exercises the privilege, the jury might well draw the inference that the witness is guilty and, by implication, that the defendant is guilty as well (particularly where the defendant exercises his own fifth amendment right not to testify). On the other side, where the defense calls a person who has been antagonistic to the defendant and asks that person about his role in the events in question or in his assistance of the police, and that witness then claims the privilege, that could well lend credence to a defense suggestion that the witness actually committed the crime or, at least, "framed" the defendant.

In *Namet v. U.S.* (1963), the Court suggested that reversible error could occur in two situations: (1) where the prosecutor, in calling a witness he knows will assert the privilege, made "a conscious and flagrant attempt to build [the prosecution's] case out of inferences arising from the use of the testimonial privilege"; and (2) where the facts of the particular case strongly suggest that inferences from a witness's refusal to answer did, in fact, add "critical weight to the prosecution's case" in a form not subject to cross-examination and thereby prejudiced the defense. While these two grounds were set forth as standards applicable to federal cases, at least the second appears to have gained constitutional status.

Notwithstanding *Namet's* suggestion that bad faith alone would support reversal of a conviction in the federal courts, both federal and state courts have indicated that some showing of likely prejudice is also needed. Often the same circumstances on the part of the prosecution that establish bad faith will suggest likely prejudicial impact. These factors include prosecutorial misrepresentations to the court concerning the witness, the failure of the prosecutor to alert the court to the potential problem, and attempts by the prosecution to draw inferences from the witness's exercise of the privilege. In assessing prejudice courts also consider whether any inferences from the witness's assertion of privilege (1) related to central issues or collateral matters; (2) were cumulative as to a point strongly established by the prosecution's evidence; (3) were opposed by the defense through timely objection; or (4) were countered by warnings by the trial court.

(c) Sequestration of Witnesses. Witnesses on both sides of a criminal case are often sequestered in order "to lessen the danger that their testimony will be influenced by hearing what other witnesses have to say, and to increase the likelihood that they will confine themselves to truthful statements based on their own recollections."

The failure to sequester prosecution witnesses does not necessarily violate any right of the defendant to cross-examine those witnesses in particular or to a fair trial generally. Until recent decades, for example, judges in most courts possessed the discretion to withhold an order sequestering witnesses. Yet even where sequestration is required upon request, as in federal courts, not all government witnesses will be sequestered.

Every jurisdiction provides exemptions from sequestration orders for particular witnesses. The four categories of witnesses most commonly exempted by court rule or decision are (1) parties; (2) party representatives (e.g., an investigating officer for the state); (3) victims; and (4) witnesses "whose presence is * * * essential to the presentation of [a] party's cause." Obviously the defendant must be able to attend his own trial, even if he plans to testify on his own behalf. Corporate defendants may be represented throughout the trial at the defense table although a court may require that the representative be someone who is not a witness. A representative of the state, too, may be present at trial. This person is almost always an agent who has assisted in the investigation of the case. Some states, however, have made no provision for the presence of such a representative, and have allowed an investigative officer to remain in the courtroom only if that officer's presence falls within the exception for persons "essential" to the presentation of the government's case. This exception may also allow expert witnesses to remain in the courtroom during the testimony of others.

A number of jurisdictions have also limited the circumstances under which judges may exclude victims or their family members from the courtroom.

§ 16.5 Defendant's Rights to Remain Silent and to Testify

(a) **Right Not to Take the Stand.** The Self–Incrimination Clause of the Fifth Amendment, applicable to the states through the Fourteenth Amendment's Due Process Clause, provides that no person "shall be compelled in any criminal case to be a witness against himself." But the constitutional privilege against compelled self-incrimination has been interpreted by the Court to be much broader than those words would suggest. Assertion of the privilege is not limited to defendants, nor is it limited to criminal trials. The privilege entitles a witness not to answer specific questions posed in a criminal trial or in any other proceeding where he is under compulsion to answer if his answers would furnish a "link in the chain of evidence" needed to prosecute him for a criminal offense. The privilege entitles the criminal defendant to even greater protection. The defendant need not even appear as a witness. The right of the defendant is not only to avoid being compelled to give incriminating responses to particular inquiries, but also to resist being placed in a position where the inquiries can be put to him while he is under oath.

There is good reason for applying the privilege so broadly in this particular context. As the Supreme Court explained in *Wilson v. U.S.* (1893):

> It is not every one who can safely venture on the witness stand though entirely innocent of the charge against him. Excessive timidity, nervousness when facing others and attempting to explain transactions of a suspicious character, and offences charged against him, will often confuse and embarrass him to such a degree as to increase rather than remove prejudices against him. It is not every one, however honest, who would, therefore, willingly be placed on the witness stand.

This privilege, however, cannot be invoked selectively. The Supreme Court in *Brown v. U.S.* (1958) explained that the defendant has the choice, after weighing the advantage of the privilege against self-incrimination against the advantage of putting forward his version of the facts and his reliability as a witness, not to testify at all. He cannot reasonably claim that the Fifth Amendment gives him not only this choice but, if he elects to testify, an immunity from cross-examination on the matters he has himself put in dispute. It would make of the Fifth Amendment not only a humane safeguard against judicially coerced self-disclosure but a positive invitation to mutilate the truth a party offers to tell. Thus, once a defendant testifies he becomes liable to cross-examination on matters "reasonably related to the subject matter of his direct examination." At a minimum, this means that he may be questioned concerning all facts relevant to the matters he has testified to on direct examination. In addition, he is subject to searching cross-examination for impeachment purposes, for by testifying he places his credibility in issue and opens the door to fair comment upon considerations affecting his veracity. A defendant does not completely waive his fifth amendment privilege at trial by testifying solely on collateral or preliminary matters, however, such as the appointment of counsel.

In *Brooks v. Tenn.* (1972), the petitioner questioned the constitutionality of a statute requiring that a defendant "desiring to testify shall do so before any other testimony for the defense is heard," a rule related to the ancient practice of sequestering prospective witnesses in order to prevent them from being influenced by other testimony in the case. The Court majority held that the statute "violates an accused's constitutional right to remain silent," as a defendant "cannot be absolutely certain that his witnesses will testify as expected or that they will be effective on the stand" and thus "may not know at the close of the State's case whether his own testimony will be necessary or even helpful to his cause." This statute, the Court added, "may compel even a wholly truthful defendant, who might otherwise decline to testify for legitimate reasons, to subject himself to impeachment and cross-examination at a time when the strength of his other evidence is not yet clear." The Court then went on to rule that the statute also infringed upon the defendant's right of due process, for "by requiring the accused and his lawyer to make [the choice of whether to testify] without an opportunity to evaluate the actual worth of their evidence," it deprives the accused "of the 'guiding hand of counsel' in the timing of this critical element of his defense."

Not all procedures that operate to make more difficult the defendant's exercise of his choice between testifying and remaining silent are barred. For example, only a year before *Brooks*, in *Crampton v. Ohio* (1971), the Court rejected in a different procedural setting an "undue-burden" argument very much like that which won the day in *Brooks*. The defendant in *Crampton* contended that Ohio's law providing for the jury determination of the death penalty option in the proceeding in which it determined guilt created "an intolerable tension" between his constitutional right not to be compelled to be a witness against himself on the issue of guilt and his constitutional right to be heard on the issue of punishment. He argued further that the tension readily could have been avoided by the state's adoption of the bifurcated trial procedure used by other states, whereby the jury decides the issue of guilt before presentation and argument on the issue of punishment. In finding no constitutional need for a bifurcated trial, the Court concluded that "the policies of the privilege against compelled self-incrimination are not offended when a defendant in a capital case yields to the pressure to testify on the issue of punishment at the risk of damaging his case on guilt" and that a state is not "required to provide an opportunity for [a defendant] to speak to the jury [on the issue of punishment] free from any adverse consequences on the issue of guilt." The Court acknowledged that it might well be that "bifurcated trials * * * are superior means of dealing with capital cases," but from "a constitutional standpoint," it could not "conclude that * * * the compassionate purposes of jury sentencing in capital cases are better served by having the issues of guilt and punishment determined in a single trial than by focusing the jury's attention solely on punishment after the issue of guilt has been determined." Also, a court does not offend the Constitution by denying a defendant's motion to sever multiple counts for separate trials whenever the defendant wishes to testify on one count but not the other. As discussed in § 9.1(c), before granting severance in this situation, most courts first require a showing that the testimony is significant to the defense of one charge, as well as a showing that the defendant has a strong need to remain silent on the other charge.

(b) Comment and Instruction on Defendant's Silence. In *Griffin v. Cal.* (1965), the Court concluded that comment by the court or the prosecutor regarding the defendant's failure to take the stand was constitutionally impermissible. The Court characterized comment on defendant's silence as "a penalty imposed by courts for exercising a constitutional privilege" in that it "cuts down on the privilege by making its assertion costly." As for the state's claim that "the inference of guilt for failure to testify as to facts peculiarly within the accused's knowledge is in any event natural and irresistible," the Court responded that this is not inevitably the case, as where a defendant declines to testify merely because his prior convictions would then be admissible for impeachment purposes.

The Court limited *Griffin* somewhat in two decisions, *Lockett v. Ohio* (1978), and *U.S. v. Robinson* (1988). In *Lockett*, where the prosecution repeatedly referred to the state's case as "unrefuted" and "uncontradicted," the Court concluded these comments did not "violate constitutional prohibitions [as] Lockett's own counsel had clearly focused the jury's attention on her silence, first, by outlining her contemplated defense in his opening statement and, second, by stating * * * near the close of the case, that Lockett would be the 'next witness.' " Similarly, in *Robinson*, where defense counsel had noted at several points that the government had never allowed the defendant to explain his side of the story, the Supreme Court held that *Griffin* did not bar the prosecutor's response that the defendant "could have taken the stand and explained it to you." The prosecutor's reference did not treat the defendant's silence as "substantive evidence of guilt," but was a "fair response" to a claim by defense counsel.

Griffin also bars a sentencing judge from drawing an adverse inference from a defendant's silence at sentencing. The "concerns which mandate the rule of [*Griffin*] against negative inferences at a criminal trial apply with equal force at sentencing," stated the Court in *Mitchell v. U.S.* (1999). The *Griffin* rule "has become an essential feature of our legal tradition" and a "vital instrument for teaching that the question in a criminal case is not whether the defendant committed the acts of which he is accused," but "whether the Government has carried its burden to prove its allegations while respecting the defendant's individual rights."

Griffin has spawned an immense body of case law addressing when a statement that does not refer directly to a defendant's failure to take stand is nonetheless an impermissible comment on that failure. Courts agree on the general standard for resolving that issue—"whether the language used was manifestly intended or was of such character that the jury would naturally and necessarily take it to be a comment on the accused's failure to testify." Appellate courts often avoid the need to decide whether the statement was prohibited by *Griffin* by holding that any constitutional error was harmless beyond a reasonable doubt. The defense is most likely to be successful where the comment was repeated several times, included a pointed reference to the defendant, or was made in a case in which the prosecution's evidence was such that only the defendant himself could have contradicted it.

The Court in *Griffin* reserved decision on whether a defendant can require that the jury be instructed that his silence must be disregarded. The matter was settled in *Carter v. Ky.* (1981):

> A trial judge has a powerful tool at his disposal to protect the constitutional privilege—the jury instruction—and he has an affirmative constitutional obligation to use that tool when a defendant seeks its employment. No judge can prevent jurors from speculating about why a defendant stands mute in the face of a criminal accusation, but a judge can, and must, if requested to do so, use the unique power of the jury instruction to reduce that speculation to a minimum.

Somewhat the reverse problem reached the Court in *Lakeside v. Or.* (1978), where petitioner argued "that this protective instruction becomes constitutionally impermissible when given over the defendant's objection" because it "is like 'waving a red flag in front of the jury.'" The Court rejected that argument because it "would require indulgence in two very doubtful assumptions," namely, "that the jurors have not noticed that the defendant did not testify and will not, therefore, draw adverse inferences on their own," and "that the jurors will totally disregard the instruction, and affirmatively give weight to what they have been told not to consider at all."

(c) The Defendant's Right to Testify. Although at an earlier time a criminal defendant could plead his cause in person and therefore as a practical matter—though not in theory—could furnish evidence in his own behalf, in eighteenth century England there took hold the rule that a defendant was incompetent to give testimony. This rule was based on the fear that a person so directly interested in the case was likely to testify falsely. The English rule was inherited by American jurisprudence as a part of the common law but was rejected thereafter. On the federal level, for example, the Supreme Court first abrogated the general rule of incompetency based on interest and then specifically acknowledged the right of a federal defendant to testify. There were similar developments at the state level so that by the end of the nineteenth century all but one state (which later changed its practice) granted criminal defendants a right to testify. As a result of the recognition of that right under local law, the Supreme Court did not find it necessary to squarely rule on the defendant's constitutional right to testify until the mid–1980s.

In *Rock v. Ark.* (1987), the Court held that there was, indeed, a constitutional right "to testify on one's own behalf at a criminal trial." That right was said to stem from three sources: (1) the guarantee of due process (which ensures a "fair adversary process," including a "right to be heard and to offer testimony"); (2) the Sixth Amendment's Compulsory Process Clause (which "logically include[s]" defendant's "right to testify himself"); and (3) the Fifth Amendment's guarantee against compulsory self-incrimination (a "necessary corollary" of which is the defendant's right to testify "in the unfettered exercise of his own will").

The defendant's right to testify is not without limitation. It may be restricted to accommodate other "legitimate interests in the criminal trial process." For example, the Court has sustained sentence increases for false testimony. The right to testify is not a license to lie. Also, in *Portuondo v. Agard* (2000), the Court rejected the defendant's claim that his rights to be present and testify at trial were burdened impermissibly by the prosecutor's argument that his presence during the testimony of other witnesses allowed him to tailor his testimony to theirs. Writing for the Court, Justice Scalia characterized the inference the prosecutor asked the jury to draw as "natural and irresistible." The prosecutor's comments were "in accord with the longstanding rule that when a defendant takes the stand, 'his credibility may be impeached and his testimony assailed like that of any other witness.' "Allowing this argument to be made to the jury is "appropriate" and "sometimes essential to the central function of the trial, which is to discover the truth." As the dissenting opinion noted, however, some state courts have forbidden accusations of tailoring based on presence at trial.

Rock's clear recognition of the right to testify as constitutionally grounded has led to several successful challenges to restrictions placed on the exercise of the right. Restrictions "may not be arbitrary or disproportionate to the purposes they are designed to serve." *Rock* itself involved a ban on hypnotically refreshed testimony. The Court held that even though the state has a legitimate interest in imposing evidentiary restrictions designed to exclude unreliable evidence, that interest could not justify a per se exclusion of a defendant's hypnotically refreshed testimony. Such a rule was excessive because it operated without regard either to procedural safeguards to reduce inaccuracies employed in the particular hypnosis process or to the availability of corroborating evidence and other traditional means of assessing the accuracy of the particular testimony.

§ 16.6 Trial Court Evaluation of the Evidence

(a) **Bench Trials.** A significant portion of felony trials in state and federal court are conducted without juries. For much of the nation's history, bench trials in felony cases were unusual. Courts rejected the idea that defendants could waive a jury and be tried before a judge alone. Under common law "the accused was not permitted to waive trial by jury, as generally he was not permitted to waive any right which was intended for his protection." In *Patton v. U.S.* (1930), the Court paved the way for felony bench trials, holding that a defendant could waive his right to a trial by jury in any criminal case. Most states require the agreement of the prosecutor, while a few require only the consent of the judge. Conditioning the defendant's ability to forego a jury on the consent of the court or the prosecutor denies the defendant no constitutionally protected advantage, the Court explained in *Singer v. U.S.* (1965). If either refuses to consent, the result is simply that the defendant is subject to an impartial trial by jury—exactly what the Constitution guarantees him.

When the trial is to the bench, the judge sits as the finder of fact and makes all the judgments with respect to the credibility and weight of the evidence that a jury would make. However, unlike a jury, which merely renders a general verdict on each count, a judge sitting as the trier of fact often makes special findings. Indeed, in many jurisdictions, the judge is required to make such findings upon request of either party. Although the principal usefulness of findings is to facilitate appellate review where the defendant is convicted, findings may also be made in cases in which the defendant is acquitted (and perhaps later used by the defendant in advancing a claim of collateral estoppel if later prosecuted for a related offense).

(b) **Motions for Directed Acquittal.** A trial court may not direct a verdict of guilty, in whole or in part, no matter how conclusive the evidence might appear. To do so would invade the defendant's constitutionally protected right to trial by jury. A directed verdict of acquittal, however, is another matter, as the Supreme Court explained in *Jackson v. Va.* (1979):

> [T]he traditional understanding in our system [is] that the application of the beyond-a-reasonable-doubt standard to the evidence is not irretrievably committed to jury discretion. To be sure, the factfinder in a criminal case has traditionally been permitted to enter an unassailable but unreasonable verdict of

"not guilty." This is the logical corollary of the rule that there can be no appeal from a judgment of acquittal, even if the evidence of guilt is overwhelming. The power of the factfinder to err upon the side of mercy, however, has never been thought to include a power to enter an unreasonable verdict of guilty.

Jackson held that a defendant has a constitutional right not to be convicted "except upon evidence that is sufficient fairly to support a conclusion that every element of the crime has been established beyond a reasonable doubt." All states provide that at some stage of the trial proceedings the trial court will have authority to review the sufficiency of the evidence and enter an acquittal if it does not meet the *Jackson* standard. When the review comes at the end of the prosecution's case-in-chief or at the close of all evidence, the trial court may order the jury to return a verdict of acquittal commonly described as a "judgment of acquittal," "directed acquittal," or "directed verdict." Trial courts also possess authority to review the sufficiency of evidence should the jury convict. This power to enter an acquittal notwithstanding a guilty verdict is known as a judgment *n.o.v.* On appeal from a conviction, the appellate court will again review the sufficiency of the evidence under the *Jackson* standard, provided that issue was properly raised at trial.

In one state, statute precludes the court from entering a pre-verdict judgment of acquittal even when it believes that the prosecution has completely failed to prove its case. Such a position reflects the concern that allowing trial judges to enter pre-verdict acquittals will allow judicial abuse, since double jeopardy would bar the prosecution from appealing the judge's decision.

The vast majority of jurisdictions have not chosen to force the defendant to await review of the sufficiency of the evidence until after the jury reaches its decision. They provide for a motion for judgment of acquittal that can be presented at the end of the prosecution's case, at the end of the presentation of evidence by both sides, *and* after the discharge of the jury. Typically, that motion is made at the end of the prosecution's presentation of its case-in-chief and must state specifically the deficiency in the government's proof.

(c) The Sufficiency Standard. Although the evidence before the court will differ depending on when the motion for directed acquittal is made, the basic standard for review is the same:

> [A] trial judge, in passing upon a motion for directed verdict of acquittal, must determine whether upon the evidence, giving full play to the right of the jury to determine credibility, weigh the evidence, and draw justifiable inferences

of fact, a reasonable mind might fairly conclude guilt beyond a reasonable doubt. If he concludes that upon the evidence there must be such a doubt in a reasonable mind, he must grant the motion; or, to state it another way, if there is no evidence upon which a reasonable mind might fairly conclude guilt beyond a reasonable doubt, the motion must be granted. If he concludes that either of the two results, a reasonable doubt or no reasonable doubt, is fairly possible, he must let the jury decide the matter.

The formulation set forth in the above quote was characterized in *Jackson v. Va.* as "the prevailing criterion for judging motions for acquittal in federal criminal trials," a standard sufficient to fulfill the defendant's constitutional right to be convicted only where "the record evidence could reasonably support a finding of guilt beyond a reasonable doubt." The Court stressed also that "the critical inquiry on review of the sufficiency of the evidence * * * does not require a court to 'ask whether *it* believes that the evidence at the trial establishes guilt beyond a reasonable doubt,' " but "simply whether, after viewing the evidence in the light most favorable to prosecution, any trier of fact could have found the essential elements of the crime beyond a reasonable doubt."

(d) Summary and Comment on the Evidence. The common law jury trial included the privilege of the trial judge to comment to the jury about his opinion of the evidence presented, a practice thought to give to the jurors "great light and assistance." While the federal courts have retained this power, in the overwhelming majority of states this function of the trial judge was removed by constitutional provision, statute, or judicial decision. In support of the federal rule authorizing judicial comment, it is asserted that the judge's discussion of the evidence will serve to assist the jury and thereby to aid it in arriving at a just result. Those opposed object that the trial judge may abuse the privilege of comment and engage in "partisan advocacy." To remedy such abuse, the power to comment is subject to review in jurisdictions where it is permitted. For example, the Court in *Quercia v. U.S.* (1933), reversed the conviction of a federal defendant whose judge had advised the jury to observe that the defendant "wiped his hands during his testimony" and added "that is almost always an indication of lying." A judge may comment on testimony, the court explained, but "he may not assume the role of a witness. He may analyze and dissect the evidence, but he may not either distort it or add to it."

§ 16.7   The Arguments of Counsel

(a) Opening Statements. Prior to the presentation of evidence, both sides may present opening statements. The prosecutor presents the initial opening statement. As for the statement by defense counsel, there is a variation in practice; in some states the defense must present its opening statement immediately following the prosecutor's statement, while elsewhere the defense may reserve its opening statement until after the close of the prosecutor's case. Most defense attorneys prefer to provide a rebuttal to the state's story before the jury hears the evidence, in order to assist the jury in evaluating that evidence.

The Court has explained that the opening statement is "not an occasion for argument," but an opportunity to "state what evidence will be represented, to make it easier for the jurors to understand what is to follow, and to relate parts of the evidence and testimony to the whole." Because the purpose of the opening statement is a narrow one, counsel is limited to a brief statement of the issues and an outline of what counsel believes can be supported with competent and admissible evidence. Indeed, it is unprofessional conduct for the prosecutor or defense attorney "to allude to evidence to be presented unless, in good faith, there is a reasonable basis for believing that such evidence will be tendered and admitted in evidence." The prohibitions applicable to the closing argument, discussed in subsection (c) below, are binding upon the opening statements as well.

(b) Closing Argument. The special significance of closing argument was recognized in *Herring v. N.Y.* (1975). Although the trial there was to the bench rather than a jury, the Supreme Court held that there had been an unconstitutional interference with defendant's right to counsel when the trial judge announced his decision convicting the defendant without giving defense counsel the opportunity to present final argument. Justice Stewart noted that even when other aspects of fair procedure, such as compulsory process and confrontation, were in their infancy, the English criminal trial recognized the need for argument between the adversaries. The further development of those other rights, moreover, did not result in a dilution of the system's commitment to argument, but simply resulted in "shifting the primary function of argument to summation of the evidence at the close of trial, in contrast to the 'fragmented' factual argument that had been typical of the earlier common law." The result was to give such argument a central role in the adversary system:

> Closing argument serves to sharpen and clarify the issues for resolution by the trier of fact in a criminal case. It is only after all the evidence is in that counsel for the parties are in a position to present their respective versions of the case as a whole. Only then can they argue the inferences to be drawn from all the testimony, and point out the weaknesses of their

adversaries' positions. * * * The very premise of our adversary system of criminal justice is that partisan advocacy on both sides of a case will best promote the ultimate objective that the guilty be convicted and the innocent go free. In a criminal trial, which is in the end basically a factfinding process, no aspect of such advocacy could be more important than the opportunity finally to marshall the evidence for each side before submission of the case to judgment.

Herring also noted that, as with other aspects of the adversarial process, there was room as well for some degree of judicial control over argument. The trial judge should be given "great latitude in regulating the duration and limiting the scope of closing summaries." Balanced against this authority, however, is the recognition that persuasion is a matter of style as well as content, and counsel must be given considerable room to shape his or her own style in presenting argument. The closing argument traditionally has been the one place in the trial where counsel is given greatest leeway in manner of expression even as the courts strive also to bar the excesses of the overzealous advocate.

The prevailing view with respect to the order of closing arguments is that followed in the federal system: the prosecution opens the argument, the defendant is then permitted to reply, and the prosecution then is allowed to reply in rebuttal. This structure is grounded in the notion that the fair administration of justice is best served if the defendant knows the arguments actually made by the prosecution for conviction before being faced with the decision whether to reply and what to reply. In response to the contention that it is unfair to allow the prosecution to make both the first and the last arguments in the case, courts have observed that the prosecution and not the defendant carries the burden of proving guilt beyond a reasonable doubt. Statutes prescribing this order of argument have been upheld against due process challenges.

Although closing arguments are quite clearly a time for advocacy, the prosecutor is often said to be under special restraints because of his unique role in the criminal process. In the oft-quoted language of *Berger v. U.S.* (1935):

> The United States Attorney is the representative not of an ordinary party to a controversy, but of a sovereignty whose obligation to govern impartially is as compelling as its obligation to govern at all; and whose interest, therefore, in a criminal prosecution is not that it shall win a case, but that justice shall be done. As such, he is in a peculiar and very definite sense the servant of the law, the twofold aim of which is that guilt shall not escape or innocence suffer. He may prosecute with earnestness and vigor—indeed, he should do so.

But, while he may strike hard blows, he is not at liberty to strike foul ones. It is as much his duty to refrain from improper methods calculated to produce a wrongful conviction as it is to use every legitimate means to bring about a just one. * * * It is fair to say that the average jury, in a greater or lesser degree has confidence that these obligations, which so plainly rest upon the prosecuting attorney, will be faithfully observed. Consequently, improper suggestions, insinuations, and, especially, assertions of personal knowledge are apt to carry much weight against the accused when they should properly carry none.

(c) Prohibited Argument. The traditional formulations of prohibited categories of argument are often so general that they require further definitional content through case-specific rulings if they are to provide any guidance to courts and counsel. Reported decisions discussing improper argument focus almost entirely on challenges to arguments by the prosecution since, as noted above, appellate courts rarely rule directly on the propriety of a defense counsel's argument. Appellate opinions that reject challenges to alleged forensic misconduct by prosecutors are sometimes less than clear as to whether the argument of the prosecutor was (1) appropriate without regard to the argument of defense counsel, (2) appropriate only in light of defense counsel having opened the door, or (3) not prejudicial and therefore not requiring reversal even if inappropriate. Finally, appellate opinions deal with such a variety of prosecutorial comments, both upheld and rejected, that a complete description of what has been held to fall within and without a particular prohibition risks drowning the reader in a flood of endless detail. The description that follows therefore provides a far less than exhaustive review of the different categories of arguments, is limited primarily to prosecution arguments, and includes only rulings that clearly addressed the propriety of the particular comment apart from the issue of prejudice.

Going beyond the record. The prosecutor may not refer to evidence that is not within the record. To do so not only violates accepted trial norms, but also deprives the defendant of the right to cross-examine a person (the prosecutor) who is, in effect, testifying against him. The question often is presented, however, as to what is argued as evidence beyond the record, what is argued as inference from record evidence, and what is argued as common knowledge. Prosecutors are not prohibited from drawing inferences from the record, and although it is often said these factual inferences must be "reasonably" based on the record evidence, the latitude given prosecutors is very broad. The prosecutor also is not prohibited from referring to matters of common public knowledge or basic human experience. References to common sayings about behavior to classic illustrations of commonplace behavior escape the "non-record facts" prohibition.

Misrepresentation of the law. As with misrepresentations of the evidence, misrepresentations of the law also constitute improper argument. Counsel may anticipate jury instructions and tie the facts of the case to the elements of the law that will be set forth in those instructions. Because the jury is informed that the law comes from the court, and not from the attorneys, this commonly causes no significant difficulties even if an attorney should misstate somewhat the law as presented in the instruction. Occasionally, however, where the prosecutor's argument was tied in substantial part to a basic misstatement in the law (e.g., the allocation of proof), that misstatement will prove fatal. More frequently, successful challenges to prosecutorial argument have involved references (often accurate) to matters on which a judge would refuse to charge a jury if requested because they detract from its responsibility to decide the issue before it. Thus, the jury would not be told that the defendant could appeal a jury's mistake in imposing the death penalty or that the defendant would be released if the jury returned a certain verdict. Defense counsel, too, are limited to arguments relevant to the jury's determination, and are often barred from commenting on the sentencing consequences of a guilty verdict, or from giving misleading explanations of legal standards.

Personal beliefs and opinions. Courts have repeatedly noted that it is improper for a prosecutor to inform the jury of his or her personal belief in the accused's guilt or in the truth or falsity of a witness's testimony. This practice is pernicious not only because the jury may view the prosecutor's opinion as "carry[ing] with it the imprimatur of the Government," but also because such comments often convey to the jury "the impression that [there exists] evidence not presented to the jury, but known to the prosecutor." Of course, the prosecutor is not prohibited from explaining to the jury why it should conclude the defendant was guilty or accept or reject a particular witness's testimony. Where the prosecutor avoids a direct reference to phrases like "I think," "I believe," and "I know," it is often difficult to draw the line between a characterization based on the evidence and an expression of personal belief.

Comments on privileges and other assertions of rights. As discussed in § 16.5(b), prosecutorial comment on the defendant's failure to testify constitutes constitutional error in itself. Adverse references to the exercise of privileges by others ordinarily also are inappropriate, as will be the reference to the defense's failure to call a particular witness where that witness was known to be unavailable due to his exercise of the privilege. Nor are prosecutors permitted to argue to the jury that a defendant's guilt may be inferred from his failure to consent to a search, his decision to call an attorney, or his decision to remain silent at arrest. However, should the defendant take the stand, a prosecutor may question his credibility by pointing out to the jury in closing argument that the defendant's presence allowed him to listen to the other witnesses before he testified.

Appeals to emotion and prejudice. Closing arguments traditionally have included appeals to emotion. The outer limit on emotional appeals is generally stated as a prohibition against "arguments calculated to inflame the passions or prejudices of the jury." Illustrative of prohibited appeals to the prejudices of the jury are references to race or religion in characterizing the qualities of the defendant or the reliability of a witness. An illustration of a prohibited appeal to passion is the "Golden Rule" argument that asks the jury to step into the shoes of the victim. Still another is the dramatic and abusive characterization of the defendant (e.g., as a "cheap, slimy, scaly crook") or defense counsel (e.g., a "flat liar"). Yet, here too, distinctions will be drawn and courts will vary in their assessment of what goes "too far." The prosecutor may appropriately call the jury's attention to the plight of the victim and the seriousness of the crime, provided he does not take the "extra step" of asking the jurors to put themselves in the victim's position. So too, the prosecutor may characterize the defendant with disparagement that is reasonably deduced from the evidence in the case. Thus, while courts have held improper the characterization of the defendant as a "sexual fiend," or "Judas Iscariot," or as "hunting each other like animals," others will consider as fair comment (with some dramatic license) the description of the defendant as a "trafficker in human misery," or a "little lizard slipping through the underbrush," "a nine-headed, hydra-headed monster."

Injecting broader issues. The limitation that most frequently lends itself to the drawing of fine lines is that barring the injecting of issues "broader than the guilt or innocence of the accused." Courts ordinarily will allow the prosecutor to "dwell upon evil results of crime" and "urge fearless administration of the criminal law." They also have accepted arguments that a conviction would deter others from committing similar crimes, but this tends to come close to the impermissible. The impermissible is reached where the prosecutor asserts that a guilty verdict would relieve community fears or the threat to the jurors' families. Courts have also condemned appeals to jurors as the taxpayers who pay for the costs of the defendant's attorney, or, in death penalty cases, the costs of incarceration.

(d) The Invited Response. Arguments by the prosecution that would otherwise be improper are sometimes deemed appropriate (or at least "excusable") because the defense "opened the door" with its own improper argument and the prosecution merely "replied in kind." In *U.S. v. Young* (1985), the defendant challenged this "invited response" doctrine as based on the false premise that "two wrongs make a right." The Supreme Court acknowledged that it was inappropriate for the prosecution to respond to the defense's improper argument with forensic misconduct of its own. The proper response, the Court stressed, is a prosecution objection, accompanied by a "request that the [trial] court give a timely warning [to defense counsel] and curative instructions to the jury." However, because a "criminal conviction is not to be lightly overturned on the basis of a prosecutor's comments alone," even though the prosecutor did not respond in the correct manner, the reviewing court cannot avoid evaluating the prosecutor's improper, responsive comments in light of the "opening salvo" of defense counsel. Recognition of this factor, the Court noted, should not be seen as giving a "license to make otherwise improper arguments," but simply as fulfilling the task of a reviewing court, which is to determine whether the prosecutor's comments, "taken in context, unfairly prejudiced the defendant." The Court in *U.S. v. Robinson* (1988), for example, relied on the invited response doctrine to uphold a prosecutor's comment on the defendant's failure to take the stand.

(e) **Objections.** In some localities, immediate objections to improper closing arguments are expected, while others consider it a matter of common courtesy, verging on obligation, for opposing counsel not to interrupt one another's closing arguments by objections. While appellate courts recognize that the latter custom may result in a delayed objection, they do expect an objection. Without objection, the improper argument must reach the level required for a reversal under the plain error doctrine. See § 19.5. Appellate courts do not necessarily require that the objection be made in the presence of the jury. The defense should at least indicate its concern and give the trial judge the opportunity to consider the appropriate remedy, whether that be a curative instruction, a mistrial, or even granting the defense an additional opportunity to argue in response.

(f) **Due Process.** In *Darden v. Wainwright* (1986), the Court considered a closing argument in a capital case that contained numerous patently improper remarks, reflecting the prosecutor's highly emotional reaction to both the defendant and the gruesome homicide with which he was charged. Nonetheless, a majority held that there had been no violation due process. No matter how glaring the prosecutor's misconduct (the Court characterized the prosecutor's closing argument as "fully deserving the condemnation it received from every court to review it"), due process did not mandate a new trial unless that misconduct had such an impact as to deprive the defendant of a fair trial. The Court explained that various aspects of the trial, taken together, supported the lower court's conclusion that the trial " 'was not perfect—few are—but neither was it fundamentally unfair.' " These aspects included the following: the prosecutor's improper comments did not misstate or manipulate the evidence; the comments also did not implicate other specific rights of the accused; much of their objectionable content was responsive to the opening summation of the defense; the defense was able to use its final rebuttal argument (available under state rule) to portray the prosecution's argument "in a light that was more likely to engender strong disapproval than result in inflamed passions"; the trial judge instructed the jurors "several times" that their decision was to be based only on the evidence and that arguments of counsel were not evidence; and the "weight of the evidence against petitioner was heavy."

(g) Standard of Review. Jurisdictions vary in their approach under local law to the prerequisites for reversing a conviction based upon improper prosecutorial argument. Some apply what is basically the due process standard of *Darden*. Others determine initially whether the prosecution's argument was improper, and if it was, then proceed to apply the same harmless error standard that is otherwise applied in the jurisdiction for nonconstitutional errors. Still others use some separate standard of potential prejudice for this particular type of error, with that standard allowing more readily for reversal than the due process standard of *Darden*. All, however, start from the premise that there must be shown some likelihood of prejudice.

In determining whether the improper remarks were likely to have had sufficient impact to require reversal, appellate courts look to a variety of factors, including the following: (1) whether the improper remarks were particularly egregious; (2) whether the improper remarks were only isolated or brief episodes in an otherwise proper argument; (3) whether the improper remarks were balanced by the comments of the defense (either themselves improper or turning the improper remarks against the prosecution); (4) whether defense counsel made a timely and strong objection to the prosecutor's improper remarks, thereby indicating fear of prejudice; (5) whether the trial judge took appropriate corrective action, such as instructing the jury to disregard the improper remarks; (6) whether the improper remarks were combined with other trial errors; and (7) whether there was overwhelming evidence of guilt. The end result will be dependent upon a consideration of all of these factors taken together; no single factor will necessarily control in itself. Thus, where the prosecutor's comments were repeated and particularly inflammatory, a reversal might be required notwithstanding the presence of other factors that would ordinarily weigh heavily in the other direction (e.g., the presence of substantial evidence of guilt).

Appellate courts, while commonly finding a lack of prejudice flowing from improper summation by the prosecutor, have with mounting frustration expressed concern over the frequency with which such prosecutorial improprieties occur. Sometimes courts have even suggested that they might well be required to reverse convictions without a showing of prejudice in order to deter such prosecutorial misconduct, but this has been done only rarely. Critics have expressed the view that prosecutors would be effectively deterred if courts more readily reversed for misconduct in closing arguments, but others contend that this is not the case and defendants would simply receive windfall reversals, or are skeptical about the willingness of appellate courts to enforce such a remedy. Those of the latter view are more inclined to favor judicial reprimand, contempt penalties for flagrant misconduct, and disciplinary proceedings for repeated misconduct, remedies which are rarely imposed.

§ 16.8   Jury Instructions

(a) **Content of Final Instructions.** The content of the jury charge can be divided roughly into three areas: (1) the relevant principles of the substantive law of crimes; (2) the relevant principles of the law of evidence relating to proof, presumptions, and the weighing of evidence; and (3) the procedures to be followed by the jury in reaching a verdict. As to the substantive criminal law, the starting point is the elements of the offense charged. Failure to charge each of the elements may constitute cognizable error on appeal even where the defense failed to object. As for other elements of the substantive law, such as excuses and justifications, they also must be included if there is evidence in the case that would make these principles relevant and a request for the instruction is made. The principles of the law of evidence that may be covered by a jury charge. Certain basics—such as the prosecution's burden of proof beyond a reasonable doubt—will always be included. The directions relating to the jury's operations, cover such matters as the vote needed for a verdict, the general role of the jury as factfinder, and the process of deliberations (selection of a foreperson, requesting supplemental instructions, etc.) In a growing number of jurisdictions, "pattern instructions" are available that include model charges on all of the relevant principles of evidence and jury operations as well as the substantive law for many offenses.

(b) Lesser–Included Offenses Generally. No area of law relating to jury instructions has created more confusion than that governing when a court may or must put before the jury for its decision a lesser-included offense, that is, an offense not specifically charged in the accusatory pleading that is both lesser in penalty and related to the offense specifically charged. Certain offenses are so closely related in content that in the course of a trial of one offense the evidence developed may support the elements of a lesser offense. When that occurs, the trial court must consider whether, on application of one of the parties or on the court's own initiative, a charge to the jury on that lesser offense is mandatory, permissive, or prohibited. The answer to that question can vary considerably from one jurisdiction to another.

Application of the lesser-included offense doctrine rests on two basic inquiries. First, the court must determine whether a particular offense is a "lesser-included offense" to that charged in the accusatory pleading. If the offense is not lesser-included within the definition applied in the particular jurisdiction, then an instruction on that offense is neither required nor allowed (at least if either party objects). The various standards used in determining what constitutes a lesser-included offense for this purpose are considered below in subsection (c). Second, if the offense is categorized as a lesser-included offense, then the trial court must determine whether to instruct the jurors that they may consider that offense along with the higher offense. This aspect of the doctrine, which invokes differing views of the role of the jury and has certain constitutional implications, is discussed in subsection (d).

The rules regarding lesser-included offenses developed at common law to aid the prosecution in cases in which its proof may have failed as to the higher offense charged but nonetheless was sufficient to support a conviction on a lesser offense. What was at stake for the prosecution was more than just the conservation of resources by avoiding the inconvenience of a second prosecution on the lesser offense should the jury acquit on the higher offense. The prohibition against double jeopardy barred a second prosecution for the "same offense," and for that purpose, two separate crimes could be the "same offense" if the elements of the one were totally encompassed within the elements of the other. Thus, where the lesser-included offense was the "same offense" for double jeopardy purposes, which typically was the case under the definition of lesser-included offenses prevailing at common law, the prosecutor would not have had another opportunity to gain a conviction on the lesser offense. Including a jury charge on the lesser-included offense commonly presented the only opportunity the prosecution would have to gain any conviction if the higher charge were to fail. Courts have come to recognize that a lesser-included offense instruction, under some circumstances, can also be beneficial to the defense. In some situations, the instruction prompts a "compromise verdict," allowing the defense to avoid a conviction on the higher charge that may have resulted if the jury had before it only the choice between conviction on that higher offense and outright acquittal.

(c) Defining the Lesser–Included Offense. Standards for determining what constitutes a lesser-included offense can be organized around three distinct approaches. The statutory-elements approach, which was the original common law position, is used today in the federal courts and in a growing number of states. Under this approach, a crime is a lesser-included offense with respect to a higher offense only if it is "necessarily included" in that higher offense, as measured by the statutory elements of the two offenses. One offense is not necessarily included in another unless the elements of the lesser are a subset of the elements of the charged offense. Thus, the trial court must break down each offense by reference to its elements, without looking to how the offense may have been committed in the particular case, and ask whether it would be impossible to commit the higher offense without also committing the lesser offense. Only if that is the case can the offense be considered as the possible basis for a charge under the lesser-included offense doctrine. To illustrate consider the crime of assault with the intent to kill. Since an assault is a necessary element of that crime, the crime of simple assault will be a lesser-included offense. An assault with intent to kill will not, however, necessarily include a touching and therefore the crime of battery will not be a lesser-included offense and instructions on such an offense would not be authorized.

The elements test for defining lesser included offenses has the advantage of being identical to the Court's present approach for determining which offenses are the "same" under the Double Jeopardy Clause, and therefore must be tried all at once. Since the double jeopardy standard for defining the "same offense" is solely the elements test of *Blockburger* (see § 9.4(b)) any lesser offense that would be the "same offense" under *Blockburger* would also be a lesser-included offense under the statutory-elements test. For example, the Court in *Rutledge v. U.S.* (1996), concluded that the federal conspiracy statute, 18 U.S.C. § 846, "does not define an offense different from" the offense of conducting a continuing criminal enterprise, 18 U.S.C. § 848. The Court continued, "since the latter offense is the more serious of the two, and because only one of its elements is necessary to prove a § 846 conspiracy, it is appropriate to characterize § 846 as a lesser included offense of § 848." Other tests that create classes of lesser-included offenses narrower than the elements test "invite frequent questions concerning double jeopardy violations."

Another example is *Schmuck v. U.S.* (1989). The defendant in *Schmuck* was indicted under the mail fraud statute, with the government's proof at trial showing a scheme in which defendant rolled back odometers on used cars and then sold those cars to unwitting car dealers for resale to retail customers. The lower court had divided on whether the defendant was entitled to an instruction on the lesser charge of odometer tampering. Under a statutory-elements test, odometer tampering clearly was not lesser-included because the elements of mail fraud did not require odometer tampering as such, but simply any type of fraud. The Court explained:

> Because the elements approach involves a textual comparison of criminal statutes and does not depend on inferences that may be drawn from evidence introduced at trial, the elements approach permits both sides to know in advance what jury instructions will be available and to plan their trial strategies accordingly. The objective elements approach, moreover, promotes judicial economy by providing a clearer rule of decision and by permitting appellate courts to decide whether jury instructions were wrongly refused without reviewing the entire evidentiary record for nuances of inference.

An alternative, "cognate-pleadings" approach, is distinguishable from the statutory-elements approach in two respects. First, it does not insist that the elements of the lesser offense be a subset of the higher offense. It is sufficient that the lesser offense have certain elements in common with the higher offense, which thereby makes it a "cognate" or "allied" offense even though it also has other elements not essential to the greater crime. Second, the relationship between the offenses is determined not by a comparison of statutory elements in the abstract, but by reference to the pleadings in the specific case. The key ordinarily is whether the allegations in the pleading charging the higher offense include all of the elements of the lesser offense. Thus, joyriding will be a lesser-included offense to grand larceny when the pleadings allege that the item stolen was an automobile, that it was taken knowingly without permission of the owner, and that the asportation occurred by the driving away of the automobile.

The pleadings approach has also been criticized as making more difficult the task of the trial judge and counsel. Unlike the elements approach which requires only a comparison of the statutory definitions of the greater and lesser offenses, under the pleadings approach a court must examine the charging document with an eye to what offenses are hidden within its allegations and seek as well to separate those allegations. Proponents of the pleadings approach view it as a good compromise between the statutory-elements approach and a more open-ended evidentiary approach. It avoids the mechanical aspect of the elements test that excludes those lesser offenses that are commonly presented in the actual commission of a higher offense. While the prosecutor controls the initial pleading, the wording of a charging instrument can never preclude instructions on lesser offenses completely subsumed within the charged offense. Moreover, since the pleadings are the key, both parties are given notice in advance of trial of what lesser offenses may be included.

The evidentiary approach to defining lesser-included offenses looks to the actual proof submitted at trial, rather than to the pleadings alone, to assess the relationship between the lesser and higher offense. The lesser offense may have elements that are not part of the higher offense; all that is required is that some or all of the proof actually admitted to establish elements of the higher offense also establish the lesser offense. One variation of the evidentiary approach has been described as the "inherent relationship" test. An offense is lesser included when (1) the lesser offense is "established by the evidence adduced at trial on the proof of the higher offense" and (2) there is also "an inherent relationship between the greater and lesser offenses, i.e., they must relate to the protection of the same interests, and must be so related that in the general nature of these crimes * * * proof of the lesser offense is necessarily presented as part of the showing of the commission of the greater offense." So described, the inherent relationship test would seem to apply only where the lesser offense almost always is present in the commission of the higher offense. This would include, for example, joyriding under auto theft, as the driving away of the car is common to auto theft.

Critics of the evidentiary approach claim that the evidentiary focus is too flexible, as opening the door to so many potential lesser-included offenses which are often unknown at the outset of trial as to place both prosecutor and defense in an untenable position in preparing for trial. In *Schmuck*, the Supreme Court criticized the inherent relationship test, stating "If, as mandated under the inherent-relationship approach, the determination whether the offenses are sufficiently related to permit an instruction is delayed until all the evidence is developed at trial, the defendant may not have constitutionally sufficient notice to support a lesser included offense instruction requested by the prosecutor if the elements of that lesser offense are not part of the indictment." Supporters of the evidentiary approach respond that with the prosecution's proof commonly known to both parties from the outset, parties can readily anticipate what the lesser-included offenses will be. Moreover, as a safety net, courts can apply the standard only when the *defense* requests the charge and apply one of the other approaches for prosecution requests. This solution gives no unfair option to the defense over the prosecution. In most cases the prosecution can foresee whether the proof is likely to develop strongly favoring a verdict on a lesser included offense, in which event the indictment should so charge, which is the prosecutor's option. If the evidence is such that a jury can rationally choose—and is likely to choose—the lesser offense, then the interests of justice call for the defense to have the option of the lesser-included offense—whether or not the prosecution chose to put it in the indictment.

(d) Entitlement to Lesser Offense Charges. Though a lesser offense fits the jurisdiction's definition of a lesser-included offense, and though the evidence before the jury would sustain a conviction on that offense, it does not necessarily follow that the jury will be charged on that offense. Among the factors that will determine whether such a charge may or must be given are (1) the state of the evidence, (2) the presence of a request, and (3) the presence of an objection to the charge.

Courts in every jurisdiction have held that a defendant is entitled to a lesser-included offense instruction where the evidence warrants it. In some circumstances due process guarantees a criminal defendant an instruction on a lesser-included offense. In *Beck v. Ala.* (1980), the Supreme Court held that due process was violated by the operation of a state's capital punishment statute that prevented the trial court from giving the jury the option of convicting on a lesser-included, non-capital offense even though the evidence there placed in dispute that element which separated the capital offense from the non-capital offense. In elevating the rule to constitutional status, the Court noted that every state other than Alabama agreed that a defendant was entitled to a lesser-included offense instruction where the evidence warrants it, and reasoned that "the failure to give the jury the 'third option' of convicting on a lesser included offense would seem inevitably to enhance the risk of an unwarranted conviction. Such a risk cannot be tolerated in a case in which the defendant's life is at stake." The Court explained:

> On the one hand, the unavailability of the third option on convicting on a lesser included offense may encourage the jury to convict for an impermissible reason—its belief that the defendant is guilty of some serious crime and should be punished. On the other hand, the apparently mandatory nature of the death penalty [in Alabama] may encourage it to acquit for an equally impermissible reason that, whatever his crime, the defendant does not deserve death. * * * These two extraneous factors * * * introduce a level of uncertainty and unreliability

into the factfinding process that cannot be tolerated in a capital case.

In *Schad v. Ariz.* (1991), clarified that a lesser-included offense charge is required only when needed "to eliminate the distortion of the factfinding process that is created when the jury is forced into an all-or-nothing choice between capital murder and innocence." Thus, in *Schad*, the Court rejected the capital defendant's argument that his jury should have been instructed on the offenses of robbery and theft in addition to premeditated murder, felony murder, and second-degree murder. The Court explained that the second-degree murder charge had provided the third option mandated in *Beck*.

In the federal courts and most states, when there is no evidentiary basis for the lesser charge, a judge is not required to charge the jury on that offense, even when the offense would provide an alternative to either an acquittal of all offenses or conviction of a capital crime. This rule assumes that the defendant has no constitutionally protected right to present to the jury the option of nullification in the form of a lesser-included offense.

Courts have divided over if and when a jury may be told that it may convict the defendant of a lesser offense when the statute of limitations on the lesser offense has expired, barring conviction. The federal position is that "where no lesser included offense exists, a lesser included offense instruction detracts from, rather than enhances, the rationality of the process." *Spaziano v. Fla.* (1984). Thus, in order for a defendant to secure an instruction on a time-barred lesser-included offense, the defendant must first waive the limitations defense. A request for instructions on a time-barred offense may be sufficient waiver in some courts, while other courts will require that the judge inform the defendant specifically about the consequences of waiving the defense. Once a defendant has waived the defense, he cannot thereafter complain if the jury convicts him of the time-barred offense. Other states treat the statute of limitations bar as a jurisdictional prerequisite, not subject to waiver by the defense. A defendant in such a state may be equally inclined to give his jury the option of conviction on a lesser rather than a greater offense. Indeed, the evidence at trial may fit more easily the lesser offense than the greater one. State courts have demonstrated considerable imagination in their responses to this dilemma. Some bar instructions on the time-barred offense, others allow it to go to the jury but will enter judgment of acquittal.

Just as a trial judge is not required by the Constitution to instruct a capital jury concerning lesser offenses barred by the statute of limitations, the Constitution does not mandate that a trial judge instruct a capital jury on offenses that, under state law, are not considered lesser offenses of the crime charged. In *Hopkins v. Reeves* (1998), the Court rejected the defendant's claim that he was entitled to instructions on second-degree murder and manslaughter in addition to instructions on felony murder. The Court observed that state courts in Nebraska did not recognize any lesser-included homicide offenses for felony murder. Requiring the requested instructions under these circumstances, the Court reasoned, would not enhance the reliability of the conviction and would impose an unauthorized limit on the "state's prerogative to structure its criminal law."

§ 16.9　Jury Procedures

(a) **Sequestering the Jury.** Sequestration of the jury in a criminal case, that is, keeping the jury together and in seclusion, can help to reduce the risk of outside influence on the decisionmaking process. At common law, such confinement of the jury (also known as the rule against juror "separation") was undertaken in all cases as a matter of course. Sequestration was intended to prevent contamination of the jury by extraneous communications and unfair publicity, but also served to coerce agreement by withholding from the jurors their accustomed comforts and conveniences, making their confinement so unpleasant and irksome that they would be willing to end it as soon as possible. Eventually, as court reformers became concerned about the conditions of jury service and trials lengthened, most jurisdictions abandoned rules barring juror separation. In the federal courts and most states today, the trial judge has the discretion to permit a jury to disperse during trial as well as deliberations.

Understandably, "the ancient common law doctrine prohibiting jury separation is not generally thought to be such an integral part of the right to a jury trial that sequestration has constitutional status." Nor are the reasons for that doctrine so compelling that the old rule should be continued as a matter of local law. The notion that jurors should be coerced to agree by discomfort certainly is an anachronism today. Today, most agree that jurors "are more likely to perform their duty fairly and correctly when they are not subjected to extended periods of arbitrary and pointless personal confinement." Concerns about jury tampering and exposure are less pressing when judges give jurors careful and repeated admonitions to avoid publicity and other discussions of the case, and employ other steps to protect jurors from outside influence. Accordingly, sequestration typically is ordered in non-capital cases only when such steps appear inadequate to insulate the jury. When a jury sequestration order is violated, a defendant's interest in an untainted jury does not require a new trial, absent a showing that the defendant was prejudiced by the separation.

(b) Jury Questions and Note–Taking. Must jurors merely watch and listen as the trial unfolds? In most courtrooms that depends on the discretion of the trial judge. Juror questions to witnesses may assist in reducing juror confusion and inattention, but they also decrease the control of the parties over the case somewhat. A juror's ability to ask questions of witnesses, when recognized, is subject to the trial court's authority to screen questions and exclude those it deems inappropriate. Ordinarily, this authority is implemented by directing the jurors to write out any questions they may have after the witness has finished testifying and to submit those questions to the judge. If, after providing counsel the opportunity to object to the question out of hearing of the jury, the judge finds the question to be appropriate, then the judge may ask the question. If the judge concludes that the question relates to inadmissible or irrelevant matters, the judge can simply note that the question will not be asked.

Juror note-taking is much more common in criminal trials than juror questioning. The prevailing view at one time was that judges should rarely grant permission to jurors to take notes. Note-taking was thought to be an unwise practice because (1) the best note-taker would come to dominate the jury; (2) jurors, not having an overview of the case, would include in their notes interesting sidelights and ignore important (but often boring) facts; (3) a dishonest juror might falsify notes; (4) the act of taking notes would draw the juror's attention away from the demeanor of the witness and leave the juror writing rather than listening; and (5) the notes would receive undue attention during deliberations. For the most part, these problems are surmountable with appropriate instructions. Thus, jurors are warned that if they take notes, they should take care not to let note-taking distract them from hearing and observing the full testimony of the witness, they should not discuss their notes with fellow jurors until deliberations begin, they should rely on their notes as memory aids and not as a substitute for independent recollection, and a juror not taking notes should not be overly influenced by another's notes, as notes are "not entitled to any greater weight than the recollection or impression of each juror."

(c) Items Taken to the Jury Room. When the jury begins its deliberations, it ordinarily may have with it the charging instrument and written jury instructions where they are used. In most jurisdictions, the trial judge has discretion to allow the jurors to take with them other materials, such as pertinent exhibits, which have been received in evidence. Where that practice is followed, an exception ordinarily is made for depositions that have been read into the record, as they are simply another form of testimony and should not be given any greater attention than other testimony. The jury after retiring will sometimes submit to the trial judge a request to review certain testimony or evidence.

(d) The Deadlocked Jury. After the jury has been deliberating for some time, it may report to the judge that it has been unable to reach a decision. Except in a few states where statutes limit the number of times a judge may order a jury to renew deliberations, the law allows the judge to send the jury back for further deliberations once, twice, or several times. However, the court may not require or threaten to require the jury to deliberate for an unreasonable length of time. The length of the trial, the nature or complexity of the case, the volume and nature of the evidence, the presence of multiple counts or multiple defendants, and the jurors' statements to the court concerning the probability of agreement may all be considered by the court in determining the reasonableness of the deliberation period. The judge is given considerable discretion in this regard, but there are limits. If the judge declares a mistrial without making an adequate effort to ensure that the jury is incapable of reaching a verdict, the mistrial may not be justified by "manifest necessity," and double jeopardy may bar a retrial. See § 17.2.

What if the judge, in an effort to determine whether further deliberations by the jury are likely to be fruitful, inquires into the numerical division of the jury, that is, how it is divided (e.g., 6–6 or 11–1)? The Court has condemned this practice in no uncertain terms:

> We deem it essential to the fair and impartial conduct of the trial, that the inquiry itself should be regarded as ground for reversal. Such procedure serves no useful purpose that cannot be attained by questions not requiring the jury to reveal the nature or extent of its division. Its effect upon a divided jury will often depend upon circumstances which cannot properly be known to the trial judge or to the appellate courts and may vary widely in different situations, but in general its tendency is coercive. It can rarely be resorted to without bringing to bear in some degree, serious, although not measurable, improper influence upon the jury, from whose deliberations every consideration other than that of the evidence and the law as expounded in a proper charge, should be excluded. Such a practice, which is never useful and is generally harmful, is not to be sanctioned.

This decision was grounded in the Court's supervisory power over the federal courts and thus is not a constitutional rule binding upon the states.

Another troublesome issue is what steps the judge may take to "encourage" agreement by a deadlocked jury. In *Allen v. U.S.* (1896), the Supreme Court held that the trial judge had not committed error in giving a deadlocked jury the following supplemental instruction:

[A]lthough the verdict must be the verdict of each individual juror, and not a mere acquiescence in the conclusion of his fellows, yet they should examine the question submitted with candor, and with a proper regard and deference to the opinions of each other: that it was their duty to decide the case if they could conscientiously do so; that they should listen, with a disposition to be convinced, to each other's arguments: that, if much the larger number were for conviction, a dissenting juror should consider whether his doubt was a reasonable one which made no impression upon the minds of so many men, equally honest, equally intelligent with himself. If, upon the other hand, the majority were for acquittal, the minority ought to ask themselves whether they might not reasonably doubt the correctness of a judgment which was not concurred in by the majority.

This kind of instruction, commonly referred to as the "*Allen* charge" or "dynamite charge," has been used for years in state and federal courts. But many courts are inclined to require the use of more guarded language. Though most courts in turning away from *Allen* have done so on other than constitutional grounds, arguments have been made that the *Allen* charge violates due process because (1) it defeats the unanimity rule, (2) it does violence to the beyond a reasonable doubt standard, (3) the jury does not remain impartial, and (4) the jury is instructed to consider matters extraneous to the guilt or innocence of the accused.

In *Lowenfield v. Phelps* (1988), the Supreme Court upheld against constitutional challenge in a capital case a charge that did not go as far as *Allen* but arguably had more of a "coercive" quality than many lower courts would recommend. The jury in *Lowenfield* was deliberating during the penalty phase of a capital case when it requested advice from the judge, noting deadlock. After polling the jury about whether further deliberation would be helpful the judge directed the jurors to "discuss the evidence with the objective of reaching a just verdict if you can do so without violence to [your] individual judgment," but it did not include a direction to minority jurors to consider the views of majority and to ask themselves whether their position was reasonably founded in light of that taken by the majority. Rather, the charge told the jurors not to "hesitate to reexamine your own views and to change your opinion if you are convinced you are wrong," while adding a warning against "surrendering your honest belief * * * solely because of the opinion of your fellow jurors or for the mere purpose of returning a verdict.'' Within thirty minutes, the jury returned with a verdict of death. The court rejected the defense's claim that the charge had combined with other circumstances to create an unacceptable potential for coercion.

Lower courts determining whether particular instructions are impermissibly coercive typically consider all of the circumstances, particularly (1) the context of the supplemental instruction, (2) the length of the period of deliberations following the constructions, (3) the total time of deliberations, and (4) any other coercion or pressure on the jury.

(e) Polling the Jury. Once the jury reaches a verdict and that verdict is announced in court, the defendant, assuming the verdict is guilty, may wish to poll the jury. Polling is a procedure under which each juror is separately asked whether he or she concurs in the verdict. Its purpose is to determine whether the verdict announced actually reflects the conscience of each of the jurors. In the great majority of jurisdictions, the jury must be polled upon the request of a party, while elsewhere the matter is left to the discretion of the trial judge. The right to a poll is waived if not requested before the jury has dispersed, and the defendant need not be specifically advised of his right to poll the jury. The poll is conducted by the judge or the clerk of court. If a juror indicates some hesitancy or ambivalence, then it is the trial judge's duty to ascertain the juror's present intent by affording the juror the opportunity to make an unambiguous reply as to his present state of mind. If the poll reveals that there are not a sufficient number of votes for a valid verdict, then the court should have the discretion either to direct the jury to retire for further deliberations or to discharge the jury.

(f) Jury Misconduct. The term ''jury misconduct'' often is used to describe both action by jurors that is contrary to their responsibilities and conduct by others which contaminates the jury process. Much of the jury behavior considered to be misconduct is prohibited specifically in preliminary instructions. Jurors are told not to talk to each other about the case until deliberations begin; not to talk to anyone else about the case or about anything or anyone related to the case until the trial has ended; not to converse on any matter with the attorneys, witnesses, or defendant; not to read, view, or listen to any media reports of the case or anyone or anything related to it; and not to do any research or investigation on their own. Misconduct, then, includes various actions that are inconsistent with such admonitions—such as discussing the merits of the case with another juror, prior to deliberations, or with a coworker, family member, or bailiff; inspecting the scene of the crime;

reading a newspaper article about the defendant; conducting experiments; or looking on line or in a book for information about a term or concept mentioned by the judge.

Other aspects of misconduct in the jury process follow logically from the role of the jury. Efforts to intimidate, bribe, or otherwise pressure jurors are clearly inconsistent with juror independence. Presenting information to a juror outside the trial process interferes with jury's responsibility to rule on the basis of only the evidence before it. The juror who is intoxicated as he listens to testimony fails to fulfill his obligation to listen attentively to the evidence. Physically abusive behavior towards other jurors is impermissible, and racist arguments and speech by jurors, too, have been condemned. The prospective juror who lies during voir dire questioning undermines the selection process. In the end, whether motivated by good faith or bad, any action by an outsider or by a juror himself that has the potential for interfering with juror decisionmaking in accordance with the juror's responsibilities constitutes misconduct.

In shaping the proper response to juror misconduct, the court must assess its likely prejudicial impact. The method by which that assessment must take place, however, is not settled. Courts disagree, as a preliminary matter, when the defendant must prove, or the prosecutor must disprove, prejudice. In *Remmer v. U.S.* (1954), a case involving an alleged attempt to bribe a juror and a subsequent FBI investigation of that attempt, the Supreme Court described the extraneous influence upon the juror as "presumptively prejudicial." When prejudice is presumed, the burden of proof required to overcome such a presumption varies. Many courts suggest that the government must eliminate all "reasonable possibility" of prejudicial impact—a standard also expressed as requiring proof beyond a reasonable doubt that the misconduct did not influence the juror. Others suggest only that the presumption must be "overcome" and that it must be "adequately demonstrated" that there was no prejudicial impact.

The adoption of rules of evidence following the *Remmer* decision, and later opinions of the Court have persuaded many courts to reject any suggestion in *Remmer* that a presumption of prejudice is required for all types of misconduct. As discussed below, rules such as Federal Evidence Rule 606(b) prohibit the use of juror testimony by either party to impeach a verdict once delivered by the jury. This makes it difficult for the government to prove after trial that the alleged misconduct had no effect on the verdict, causing some courts to be reluctant to invoke the presumption. Also, in *Smith v. Phillips* (1982), the Court stated that the remedy for jury misconduct was "an opportunity" for the *defendant* "to prove actual bias." An increasing number of lower courts have, accordingly, required that the defendant demonstrate some "likelihood of prejudice" before the government will be assigned the burden of proving harmlessness, at least in cases that involve irregularities other than jury tampering.

The decision whether or not to hold a hearing at which witnesses may testify about the effect of the alleged misconduct is within the trial court's discretion, unless the defendant demonstrates a prima facie case of misconduct. These hearings may be held in camera, a procedure that comports with due process, at least when the trial judge solicits and reviews questions for jurors in advance with counsel, and reports the results promptly. The usual practice is for the judge to question jurors separately in the presence of counsel.

An inquiry somewhat different from whether the misconduct in question might have influenced the juror in his evaluation of case is appropriate when the misconduct consists of a juror's failure to respond accurately to a question posed on voir dire. The leading federal case on such misconduct is *McDonough Power Equipment v. Greenwood*. Although a civil case, *McDonough* has been applied by lower courts to criminal cases as well. A juror there failed to disclose that his son had been injured by an apparently defective product and the defense claimed that this falsehood had deprived it of an opportunity to intelligently exercise its peremptory challenges. The Supreme Court held, however, that a party raising such a claim "must first demonstrate that a juror failed to answer honestly a material question on voir dire, and then further show that a correct response would have provided a valid basis for a challenge for cause." Not only does this standard condition relief on party being deprived of a challenge for cause, but it also applies only where the juror answered dishonestly. A false answer produced by a juror's misunderstanding of the question would not warrant relief, nor would an answer which the juror realized only later was mistaken.

While judges are permitted, even required in some circumstances, to question jurors about misconduct when allegations of impropriety are raised during trial, access to information from jurors themselves is more limited once the jury has returned its verdict. The prevailing standard today is that set forth in Rule 606(b) of the Federal Rules of Evidence. That Rule notes initially that, upon an inquiry into the validity of a verdict, "a juror may not testify as to any matter or statement occurring during the course of the jury's deliberations or the effect of anything upon that or any other juror's mind or emotions as influencing the juror to assent to or dissent from the verdict or * * * concerning the juror's mental processes in connection therewith." For example, the rule bars efforts to demonstrate through juror testimony that the jurors discussed impermissible evidence or inferences, that smoking jurors coerced nonsmoking jurors to change their votes by refusing to obey the judge's non-smoking order, or that jurors engaged in discussions about the case prior to deliberations. This is a universally accepted prohibition, although a minority of states recognize limited exceptions, including evidence that would show the verdict was reached by lot. A second exception has been recognized by some courts for proof of racial bias during deliberations.

These rules have been premised upon sound reasons for limiting after-the-fact inquiry into jury verdicts. As the Supreme Court explained in *McDonald v. Pless* (1915), if verdicts were subject to being attacked and set aside based on the testimony of those who participated in them, then "[j]urors would be harassed and beset by the defeated party in an effort to secure from them evidence of facts which might establish misconduct sufficient to set aside a verdict." The result "would be to make what was intended to be a private deliberation the constant subject of public investigation; to the destruction of all frankness and freedom of discussion and conference."

An additional provision of the Federal Rule acknowledges certain circumstances in which impeaching testimony by a juror may be received: "a juror may testify about (1) whether extraneous prejudicial information was improperly brought to the jury's attention (2) whether any outside influence was improperly brought to bear upon any juror or (3) whether there was a mistake in entering the verdict onto the verdict form." An increasing number of state courts are following essentially this approach. Two cases decided during the mid-1960s provide illustrations of this rule. In each, the Supreme Court held that misconduct in the jury proceedings reached the level of a constitutional violation. *Turner v. La.* (1965), found that a defendant's right to an impartial jury was violated when two deputy sheriffs, who were key prosecution witnesses, were placed in charge of the jury and fraternized with the jurors throughout the proceedings. In *Parker v. Gladden* (1966), a bailiff said of defendant to a juror: "Oh, that wicked fellow, he is guilty." The Court found that the comment violated not only the defendant's right to an impartial jury, as in *Turner*, but also his right to confront witnesses against him, since the bailiff was seen as presenting evidence outside the trial process.

Parker and the Federal Rule refer only to external influences, however. The Supreme Court concluded in *Tanner v. U.S.* (1987), that no constitutional difficulties were presented by prohibiting impeaching testimony by a juror about "internal" influences. *Tanner* held that juror use of drugs and alcohol during trial was not an "external influence" within the Federal Rule 606(b) exception and therefore juror testimony about such use was barred under that

Rule. Juror intoxication was to be treated no differently than mental incompetence or inattentiveness, matters that had long been viewed as "internal" influences. The sixth amendment right to "an unimpaired jury" was adequately protected by the availability of voir dire to examine the suitability of a prospective juror, the ability of counsel and the court to observe juror behavior during the trial, the ability of jurors to report misconduct to the trial judge during the trial, and the defense's ability to impeach a verdict by use of non-juror evidence of misconduct.

The recognition of even the limited possibility of verdict impeachment through juror testimony naturally prompts the question whether it is permissible for counsel to interview the jurors after the verdict in an effort to discover grounds for challenging the verdict. As a matter of legal ethics, there is no absolute bar to such contacts, but in many jurisdictions such contacts must be first authorized by the trial judge, who can either conduct the questioning himself or pass upon the questions which may be asked by counsel.

Where the misconduct challenge is established during trial, and the applicable prejudice standard is met, the trial court has several remedial options. If the misconduct affected only one or a very few jurors, and if alternate jurors are available, the jurors affected by the misconduct can be replaced. If, as in the federal system, courts are authorized to proceed with less than the full number of jurors, the affected juror or jurors may be discharged without declaring a mistrial provided the requisite number of jurors remain. A judge should exercise great caution in removing a juror accused of misconduct when the judge learns that the juror is also a holdout for the defense. The judge's decision, however, typically will be reviewed under an abuse of discretion standard. In some instances, the court might conclude that a strong charge to the jurors will sufficiently negate the potential for prejudice. Finally, where none of the above alternatives are feasible, the trial court may order a mistrial. Where the misconduct challenge is raised after the verdict has been returned by the jury, the only remedy is the granting of a new trial.

§ 16.10 Jury Verdicts

(a) **Special Verdicts and Special Interrogatories.** "Special verdicts, where a jury returns factual findings and leaves the decision on guilt or innocence to the court, are not used in any jurisdiction. Even" special interrogatories, requiring the jury to respond to a series of fact questions in connection with the return of its verdict, are uncommon in criminal cases. The reason why this is so was explained in *U.S. v. Spock*, a court of appeals case, where the jury was called upon to answer a series of questions called "special findings" about the defendants' conduct, if it reached a verdict of guilty on the charge that the defendants conspired to counsel, aid, and abet registrants to resist the draft. In reversing the convictions, the court expressed concern

> with the subtle, and perhaps open, direct effect that answering special questions may have upon the jury's ultimate conclusion. There is no easier way to reach, and perhaps force, a verdict of guilty than to approach it step by step. A juror, wishing to acquit, may be formally catechized. By a progression of questions each of which seems to require an answer unfavorable to the defendant, a reluctant juror may be led to vote for a conviction which, in the large, he would have resisted. * * * It may be said that since the law should be logical and consistent, if the questions were proper in substance this would be a desirable rather than an undesirable result. [But in criminal cases there are other considerations, especially] the principle that the jury, as the conscience of the community, must be permitted to look at more than logic. * * * The constitutional guarantees of due process and trial by jury require that a criminal defendant be afforded the full protection of a jury unfettered, directly or indirectly.

By supplanting or supplementing the general verdict, special verdicts and special interrogatories can limit jury independence. As a result, courts have considered their use at least "suspect" as a matter of due process and typically disallow special interrogatories in criminal cases where the defendant objects to their use.

Verdict forms specifying the theory under which the jury found a defendant guilty have withstood constitutional challenge, however. When particular information about the basis of a jury's verdict is relevant to sentencing, courts have approved of special interrogatories that require the jury to specify the needed information.

(b) Inconsistent Verdicts or Findings. In the federal courts it is not necessary that the verdict returned by a jury be logically consistent in all respects. Inconsistency regarding separate counts against a single defendant was addressed in *Dunn v. U.S.* (1932). The Court declared that the "most that can be said in such cases is that the verdict shows that either in the acquittal or the conviction the jury did not speak their real conclusions, but that does not show that they were not convinced of the defendant's guilt." The point was elaborated in *U.S. v. Dotterweich* (1943), involving an inconsistency with respect to jointly tried defendants. The Court rejected one defendant's contention that he was entitled to relief because the jury had convicted him, the corporation president, but had not convicted the co-defendant corporation.

"Whether the jury's verdict was the result of carelessness or compromise or a belief that the responsible individual should suffer the penalty instead of merely increasing, as it were, the cost of running the business of the corporation, is immaterial," the Court explained. "Juries may indulge in precisely such motives or vagaries."

Written before the Court held in *Ashe v. Swenson* that collateral estoppel is a basic element of the double jeopardy protection of the Fifth Amendment, see § 9.4(a), the *Dunn* opinion reasoned that the same inconsistent verdicts would have been allowed if the different charges had been tried separately. *Ashe* undercut this assumption, as it barred attempts to reprove facts once litigated and rejected in an earlier trial. In *U.S. v. Powell* (1984), however, the Court concluded that the *Dunn* rule remained supported by "a sound rationale that is independent of the theories of res judicata." The defendant in *Powell* was convicted of using the telephone to facilitate the commission of certain felonies, but acquitted on the felony counts themselves. She argued that where a jury was told that it must find the defendant guilty of the predicate felony in order to convict on the compound offense, but then acquits on the former and convicts on the latter, the logical explanation for the inconsistency is a jury mistake adverse to the defendant. The *Powell* Court disagreed. The *Dunn* rule rested in part on the fact that "it is unclear whose ox had been gored" by an inconsistent verdict. That uncertainty presented the distinct possibility that the inconsistency *favored* the defendant. Still, it could not positively be shown that the inconsistency was a product of an error that worked either for or against the defendant. Any attempt at an "individualized assessment of the reason for the inconsistency would be based either on pure speculation or would require inquiries into the jury's deliberations that courts generally will not undertake." Considering the government's inability to appeal the acquittal, the Court concluded that "inconsistent verdicts should not be reviewable." Defendants retain the ability to challenge the sufficiency of the evidence supporting the verdict, the Court noted. Where the evidence is sufficient to sustain the conviction on the compound offense, it can hardly be said that this conviction was a "mistake" and acquittal on the predicate offense was "the one the jury 'really meant.' " Since the defendant was "given the benefit of her acquittal on the counts on which she was acquitted, * * * it is neither irrational nor illogical to require her to accept the burden of conviction on the counts on which the jury convicted."

Although most state courts have followed the same approach, a minority have taken the position that such inconsistency is grounds for overturning a conviction. In support of the latter view, it has been argued that "an enlightened jurisprudence should not thus permit the jailing of accused persons on a record exhibiting verdicts in which a jury simultaneously says 'yes' and 'no' in answer to a single critical question." In light of the difficulty posed by inconsistent verdicts, some jurisdictions have approved of the practice of refusing to accept such verdicts when first delivered. Judges in these courts resubmit the charges to the jury, explaining the inconsistency and asking the jury to reconsider its instructions. Other courts consider this refusal to accept an acquittal to be a violation of the defendant's rights under the Double Jeopardy Clause. This difference in approach is largely attributable to different understandings of when a jury's declaration becomes a verdict of acquittal triggering the double jeopardy bar.

What if the inconsistency appears in the findings of a judge who has tried the case without a jury? *Dunn* would seem to have little application in this context because it would not "enhance respect for law or for the courts by recognizing for a judge the same right to indulge in 'vagaries' in the disposition of criminal charges that, for historic reasons, has been granted the jury." But in *Harris v. Rivera* (1981), the Supreme Court refused to find that an apparent inconsistency in a trial judge's verdict requires relief as a constitutional matter. The Court noted that there were various constitutional reasons for explaining the apparent inconsistency between the finding of defendant guilty and his accomplice not guilty: (1) that the judge had "a lingering doubt" about the guilt of the accomplice which he "might not be able to articulate in a convincing manner," in which case the law should not influence him "to convict all"; (2) that the judge made an error of law concerning the acquitted defendant, which as a constitutional matter certainly need not "redound to the benefit" of the convicted defendant; and (3) that "the acquittal is the product of a lenity that judges are free to exercise at the time of sentencing but generally are forbidden to exercise when ruling on guilt or innocence," which also would not amount to a constitutional violation, for there is "nothing in the Federal Constitution that would prevent a State from empowering its judges to render verdicts of acquittal whenever they are convinced that no sentence should be imposed for reasons that are unrelated to guilt or innocence."

(c) Multi–Theory Verdicts. Is a defendant entitled to jury instructions that require that the jurors to agree on the theoretical basis of the defendant's guilt? In *Schad v. Ariz.* (1991), the Supreme Court examined the constitutional aspects of this issue. The defendant there was convicted of first-degree murder, defined by state law as murder that is "wilful, deliberate or premeditated * * * or which is committed * * * in the perpetration of, or attempt to perpetrate * * * robbery." The case was submitted to the jury under instructions that did not require unanimity on either of the available theories of premeditated murder and felony murder. In an opinion joined by three other members of the Court, Justice Souter declared that the Due Process Clause places "limits on a State's capacity to define different courses of conduct, or states of mind, as merely alternative means of committing a single offense, thereby permitting a defendant's conviction without jury agreement as to which course or state actually occurred." It was, of course, well established that "an indictment need not specify which overt act, among several named, was the means by which a crime was committed" and that juries could return "general verdicts" in such cases without agreeing upon a "single means of commission." However, due process has long been held to impose a requisite degree of specificity, so that no person is punished "save upon proof of some specific illegal conduct." That requisite degree of specificity would be compromised if the state were allowed to join separate offenses without directions to the jury to return separate verdicts on each, and the same would be true if a state were allowed to obtain a conviction under a single statutory offense "so generic" in coverage as to permit any combination of separate crimes to suffice for conviction. Thus, the critical issue was to ascertain "the point at which differences between means become so important that they may not reasonably be viewed as alternatives to a common end, but must be treated as differentiating what the Constitution requires to be treated as separate offenses."

Justice Souter concluded that in drawing the line required by due process the Court would look initially to both "history and widespread practice as guides to fundamental values." At the same time, it would proceed from a "threshold presumption of legislative competence to determine the appropriate relationship between means and ends in defining the elements of the crime." Applying this general approach, Justice Souter found that the Arizona statute provided sufficient specificity in treating premeditation and felony murder as alternative modes of establishing the "blameworthy state of mind required to prove a single offense of first-degree murder." Here "substantial historical and contemporary echoes" supported that characterization. At common law, "the intent to kill and the intent to commit a felony were alternative aspects of the single concept of 'malice aforethought.'" American jurisdictions, though modifying the common law by legislation classifying murder by degrees, had "in most cases retained premeditated murder and some form of felony murder * * * as alternative means of satisfying the mental state that first degree murder presupposes." A series of state decisions interpreting these first degree murder statutes reflected "widespread acceptance" of the concept that they simply established alternative means of satisfying the mens rea element of a single crime and therefore required unanimity only as to that ultimate element of mens rea and not as to the means themselves. Cautioning that it cannot be said "that either history or current practice is dispositive," Justice Souter also emphasized the lack of "moral disparity" in the two alternative mental states. "Whether or not everyone would agree that the mental state that precipitates death in the course of robbery is the moral equivalent of premeditation, it is clear that such equivalence could reasonably be found, which is enough to rule out the argument that this moral disparity bars treating them as alternative means to satisfy the mental element of a single offense."

Justice Scalia, providing the fifth vote for affirmance, relied solely upon the fact that the challenged practice was "as old as the common law and still in existence in the vast majority of States." He was critical of the plurality's "moral equivalence" test, and noted that if it were not for the historical and current acceptance of a general verdict in first-degree murder cases, he "might well be with the dissenters in this case."

In 1999, six justices in *Richardson v. U.S.* (1999), interpreted the federal "continuing criminal enterprise" statute to require separate, unanimous findings by the jury on each individual underlying offense making up the required "continuing series of violations," thus avoiding the question whether such an interpretation was required by the Constitution. Although the Court specifically declined to reach the constitutional question, the Court's discussion relied at points on the plurality opinion in *Schad*, and presented potentially relevant policy concerns. The statute in *Richardson* forbid any "person" from "engaging in a continuing criminal enterprise," defined as involving a violation of the drug statutes where "such violation is a part of a continuing series of violations." The Court began its discussion of statutory interpretation by noting that "[c]alling a particular kind of fact an 'element' carries certain legal consequences. * * * The consequence that matters for this case is that a jury in a federal criminal case cannot convict unless it unanimously finds that the Government has proved each element." Specifically, the Court asked whether the phrase "series of violations" creates several elements, in respect to which the jury must agree unanimously, or one "series" element, in respect to which the violations constitute mere means or facts.

Interpreting the statute to require unanimity on each separate "violation" making up the series, the Court reasoned, was consistent with "a tradition of requiring juror unanimity where the issue is whether a defendant has engaged in conduct that violates the law." This interpretation also avoids the "dangers of unfairness" posed by the alternative interpretation, considering the "word 'violations' covers many different kinds of behavior of varying degrees of seriousness." Third, because the statute invites proof of multiple offenses, failing to require agreement on each violation "significantly aggravates the risk (present at least to a small degree whenever multiple means are at issue) that jurors, unless required to focus upon specific factual detail, will fail to do so, simply concluding from testimony, say, of bad reputation, that where there is smoke there must be fire." Finally, "the Constitution itself limits a State's power to define crimes in ways that would permit juries to convict while disagreeing about means, at least where that definition risks serious unfairness and lacks support in history or tradition," the Court noted, citing *Schad*. "We have no reason to believe that Congress intended to come close to, or to test, those constitutional limits when it wrote this statute."

(d) **Partial Verdicts.** The term "partial verdict" refers to the situation in which the jury after some deliberation returns a verdict as to only some of the counts or some of the defendants prior to deciding the remaining matters before it. The return and receipt of a partial verdict as to less than all defendants or less than all counts is permitted in the federal courts, and the practice is also accepted in state procedure. A court may accept the partial verdict and then discharge the jury because of its inability to agree regarding the remaining matters, or accept the partial verdict and then require the jury to resume deliberations on matters still to be decided. Once a partial verdict has been accepted, however, it may not be reconsidered by the jury or impeached, even while the jury deliberates remaining charges.

§ 16.11 Post–Verdict Motions

(a) **Judgment of Acquittal.** A post-verdict motion asking the court to enter an acquittal, notwithstanding a contrary jury verdict, is universally available. Though jurisdictions vary in the titles they give to this motion, it operates basically as a motion for directed acquittal, which was discussed in § 16.6(b). The prevailing view is that, as in the federal system, the post-verdict motion can be made even if an earlier motion for directed acquittal was available and not made. The standard applied in reviewing the evidence is that applied to the earlier motion, as discussed in § 16.6(c). However, defense counsel recognizing pragmatically that the jury's verdict could influence the judge's application of that standard will rarely chance delaying until after the verdict the initial challenge to the evidence.

(b) **New Trial.** Motions for new trial take two forms. In many jurisdictions, the motion for new trial may challenge the verdict as against the weight of the evidence. This objection is quite distinct from the motion for judgment of acquittal when challenges the sufficiency of the evidence. It does not contend that a rational trier of fact could not reach the conclusion that the jury reached, but instead asks the trial court to become, in effect, a "thirteenth juror." As such, the trial court has the authority to grant the defense a second opportunity where that court concludes that, despite the bare sufficiency of the evidence, the conviction is against the weight of the evidence. In making that judgment, the judge is not commanded, as he would be in ruling on a motion for directed acquittal, to leave issues of credibility to the jury.

The motion may also challenge the conviction for trial error or pretrial error that would justify reversal of a conviction on appeal. Ordinarily, a defendant must raise the motion within a fairly brief period after the guilty verdict is returned. Federal Rule 33, for example, requires that such a new trial motion be made within seven days, unless the trial court grants an extension. This short period ensures that the court can move promptly to sentencing, because ordinarily any motion for new trial will be ruled upon before sentence is entered.

(c) **Newly Discovered Evidence.** All jurisdictions recognize what is often described as a delayed motion for new trial based upon newly discovered evidence. In some jurisdictions, as under Federal Rule 33, the motion must be made within a certain time period, but that time period is quite lengthy (three years under Rule 33). Other jurisdictions allow the motion to be made within 10 or 15 days. Several do not set a time limit and permit the motion to be made at any time.

In *Herrera v. Collins* (1993), the Court held that due process was not violated by a state's reliance on a time limit to refuse to consider newly discovered evidence, notwithstanding the defendant's claim that the evidence would establish his "actual innocence" of an offense for which he had been sentenced to death. State law there imposed a 60–day limit on such new trial motions, and the defendant had not presented his newly discovered evidence (affidavits of persons stating that defendant's now deceased brother had admitted that he committed the crime, including one witness who claimed he had seen the brother do the killing) until eight years after trial. The Court stated that, in light of the common law restrictions on such new trial motions to the same term of court, the state's refusal to entertain petitioner's newly discovered evidence eight years after his conviction did not transgress a principle of fundamental fairness "rooted in the traditions and conscience of our people." The Court majority also rejected defendant's claim that the Eighth Amendment would be violated by imposing the death penalty notwithstanding his alleged showing of "actual innocence." The majority noted that, "assum[ing] for the sake of

argument" that a "truly persuasive demonstration of 'actual innocence' would render the execution of defendant unconstitutional,
and warrant federal habeas relief if there were no state avenue
open to process such a claim," the "threshold showing for such an
assumed right would necessarily be extraordinarily high" and the
defendant's showing fell "far short of any such threshold."

As *Herrera* illustrates, claims of newly discovered evidence, at
least where raised after the brief period generally allowed for new
trial motions, tend to be viewed with "great caution." Courts are
naturally skeptical of claims that a defendant, fairly convicted, with
proper representation by counsel, should now be given a second
opportunity because of new information that has suddenly been
acquired. They also recognize that the "passage of time inevitably
ripens the finality of the judgment as it increases the prosecution's
difficulties of again proving a case." Accordingly, rather exacting
standards have been developed for the motion for new trial based
on newly discovered evidence. The basic points of reference are (1)
the evidence must be new to the defense, (2) the failure to learn of
the evidence earlier must not be due to a lack of proper diligence,
(3) and the evidence must reach a certain level of significance as
measured by reference to the other evidence in the trial.

The availability of DNA testing of biological evidence, which
retains its probative value for years if evidence is preserved, has
prompted some states to enact specific provisions for granting DNA
testing post-trial. With some exceptions, these laws governing post-
conviction motions for DNA testing do not limit the time in which
the prisoner must file a motion for testing. Most do limit or
prohibit repeat testing, and require some showing either that the
existence of testable evidence could not have been discovered or
that the technology for testing was not available at an earlier time.
Funding for testing when the prisoner is indigent may be ordered
by the court in many states, and some states even provide for the
appointment of counsel for the purpose of filing a motion for DNA
analysis. Testing may be limited by the statute or rule to felony
defendants, or to those who are incarcerated, or both, and may be
restricted to cases that turn on identity of perpetrator.

Some states authorize tests only in cases in which the defendant can show a favorable result would negate guilt. Doubting the
ability of judges to effectively sort the more viable claims of
innocence from the less viable, other states limit claims in a
different way, by creating disincentives for prisoners who might
otherwise file frivolous testing requests. Costs of testing are gar-
nished from the accounts of prisoners when testing confirms guilt
in several states, but critics have pointed out that the financial
consequences to prisoners with no source of income are ineffective.
Another approach is to revoke good-time credits for prisoners

whose guilt is confirmed by testing, so that a frivolous request can lead to a longer prison stay. In addition to post-conviction testing laws, some states have tried creating innocence "commissions" to address wrongful convictions.

The development of these statutes in the states played a central role in the Court's first decision evaluating the role of the Constitution in regulating post-conviction access to biological evidence for DNA testing. In *District Attorney's Office v. Osborne* (2009) an Alaska inmate claimed a constitutional right to access DNA evidence possessed by the state so that, at his own expense, he could test it using a form of testing more discriminating than methods available at the time of his trial. The Court disagreed. It acknowledged that Alaska law, which provided for post-conviction relief "if the defendant presents newly discovered evidence that establishes by clear and convincing evidence that the defendant is innocent," created "a liberty interest in demonstrating his innocence with new evidence under state law," an interest that could not be denied without due process. But the Court found "nothing inadequate" on the face of the state's procedures that regulated access to DNA evidence for those who seek to prove their innocence, procedures it concluded were similar to those adopted by other states and Congress. Alaska statutes authorized discovery of DNA evidence to pursue a claim of innocence if the evidence was "newly available, * * * diligently pursued, * * * and sufficiently material." In addition to this statutory procedure, state court decisions established access to DNA evidence supporting a claim of innocence under the State Constitution, so long as the petitioner demonstrated that the "conviction rested primarily on eyewitness identification evidence," that there was a "demonstrable doubt concerning the defendant's identification as the perpetrator," and that "scientific testing would likely be conclusive on this issue." Assuming without deciding the existence of a *federal* constitutional right to be released upon proof of "actual innocence," a right that could be the basis for federal habeas corpus relief, the Court noted that "federal procedural rules permit discovery 'for good cause,'"in habeas cases, and that Osborne did not show that this discovery was "facially inadequate," or "would be arbitrarily denied to him."

The Court also rejected Osborne's claim that he had been denied "a freestanding right to DNA evidence," citing its reluctance "to expand the concept of substantive due process because guideposts for responsible decisionmaking in this unchartered area are scarce and open-ended," and that states were making an effort to "actively confront[] the challenges DNA technology poses to our criminal justice systems and our traditional notions of finality, as well as the opportunities it affords. To suddenly constitutionalize this area would short-circuit what looks to be a prompt and considered legislative response.'' The Court also warned that recognizing such a right would force the federal courts to answer many other difficult questions including whether there is a constitutional obligation either to gather or to preserve forensic evidence that might later be tested, and if so, when that duty would begin and end, and to which types of evidence it would apply.

*

Chapter 17

DOUBLE JEOPARDY

Table of Sections

> For additional analysis of the above topics and citations to authorities supporting their discussion in this Book, consult the authors' 7-volume *Criminal Procedure* treatise, also available as Westlaw database CRIMPROC. See the Table of Cross-References in this Book.

§ 17.1 Dimensions of the Guarantee

(a) Introduction. The Double Jeopardy Clause of the Fifth
Amendment states: "Nor shall any person be subject for the same
offence to be twice put in jeopardy of life or limb." Although this
language might seem to limit only the retrial of a person for the
same crime, its influence extends far beyond that setting. As a
result, discussions of the double jeopardy limitation occur throughout this volume. The most significant and direct impact of the
Double Jeopardy Clause is in the area of retrials and that is the
aspect of double jeopardy law considered in this chapter. Sections
two, three, and four consider retrials on the same charges by the
same sovereign. Section five deals with a second prosecution by a
different sovereign. Combined with the discussion in § 9.4 of attempts by the same sovereign to punish a defendant again for
violations that may be the "same offence" for double jeopardy
purposes, this material presents the core of the double jeopardy
prohibition.

(b) Policies. As Justice Blackmun noted in *U.S. v. DiFrancesco* (1980), the preservation of the "finality of judgments" is commonly said to be a "primary" purpose of the double jeopardy bar.
Finality here is concerned less with avoiding the costs of redundant
litigation and relieving crowded dockets and more with protecting
the defendant against the oppression of prosecution. As Justice
Black explained in *Green v. U.S.* (1957):

> The constitutional prohibition against "double jeopardy"
> was designed to protect an individual from being subjected to
> the hazards of trial and possible conviction more than once for
> an alleged offense. * * * The underlying idea, one that is
> deeply ingrained in at least the Anglo–American system of
> jurisprudence, is that the State with all its resources and power
> should not be allowed to make repeated attempts to convict an
> individual for an alleged offense, thereby subjecting him to
> embarrassment, expense, and ordeal and compelling him to live
> in a continuing state of anxiety and insecurity, as well as
> enhancing the possibility that even though innocent he may be
> found guilty.

Initially, the protection of the innocent is served by the special
weight accorded to an acquittal. The "public interest in the finality
of criminal judgments" here is recognized to be "so strong that an
acquitted defendant may not be retried even though 'the acquittal
was based on an egregiously erroneous foundation.' " This "absolute finality" is "justified on the ground that however mistaken the
individual acquittal may have been there would be an unacceptably
high risk" to the innocent in allowing the government to override

such a judgment and proceed anew. To allow an acquittal to be less than final is to accept the possibility that a progression of juries could acquit, with each verdict losing its finality due to a prosecution error, until, sooner or later, some jury would finally convict. The danger of an "erroneous conviction from [such] repeated trials" is considered too great to acknowledge any exception to the absolute finality of the acquittal. Where "the innocence of the accused has been confirmed by a final judgment, the Constitution conclusively presumes [through the Double Jeopardy Clause] that a second trial would be unfair."

The threat of governmental oppression cited in *Green* poses a concern that goes beyond the threat to the innocent. There is also the unfairness of using the criminal prosecution to inflict additional burdens upon the individual, guilty or innocent, by subjecting him to "the embarrassment, expense, and ordeal" of repeated trials. The Double Jeopardy Clause protects against such unfairness by according finality to judgments of conviction as well as acquittal. A defendant who is convicted and wishes to end the matter there can do so by simply accepting that judgment. This also serves to avoid the "continual state of anxiety and insecurity" mentioned in *Green*, because one consequence of allowing the prosecution to reprosecute after a conviction would be to allow it to seek a higher sentence for the same conviction. Accordingly, as *DiFrancesco* noted, the guarantee against double jeopardy has been said to consist of three separate constitutional protections. "It protects against a second prosecution for the same offense after acquittal. It protects against a second prosecution for the same offense after conviction. And it protects against multiple punishments for the same offense."

The Supreme Court recognized at an early point that the protection of verdict finality could be subverted by actions that terminated a trial prior to verdict and thereby took away from the defendant his opportunity to gain an acquittal. If such actions allowed the prosecution to begin over again, the finality of a likely acquittal could be avoided and the prosecution would have the opportunity to regroup and try again simply by not allowing the trial to proceed to a final verdict. Thus, the Court has recognized as an aspect of bar against double jeopardy the protection of "the defendant's 'valued right' to have his trial completed by a particular tribunal." Implicit in this protection are the suggestions that not only must there be a barrier to manipulation of a trial's termination by the prosecution, but also that the termination of a trial before a verdict is returned may hurt the defendant even without such manipulation. Every jury has its own character and the initial jury may be more favorably disposed to the defendant than the next jury. Apart from any difference in the trier of fact, "if the Government may reprosecute, it gains an advantage from what it learns at the first trial about the strengths of the defense case and the weakness of its own." On the other hand, since the protection being afforded here was designed basically as a supplement to the core interest in preserving the integrity of judgments, the Court has concluded that these potential harms may be offset by other interests. The result is a case-by-case balancing approach, as compared to the more absolute standards imposed to protect the finality of verdicts. See § 17.2.

(c) Proceedings to Which Applicable. Read literally, the fifth amendment prohibition against a person being "twice put in jeopardy of life or limb" for "the same offence" would seem to be applicable only to criminal prosecutions and, only to those risking capital or corporal punishment. But the guarantee has been given a somewhat broader construction. As the Court held in *Ex parte Lange* (1873), the double jeopardy bar was based on the common law pleas of *autrefois acquit* and *autrefois convict*, was punished with death or "other punishment touching the person" when those pleas originally were pleas that were held to apply to felonies, minor crimes, and misdemeanors alike. The protection against double jeopardy applies to all criminal offenses without regard to the particular form of punishment imposed.

Generally, the prohibition has no application in noncriminal cases. Assessments of whether a civil action must be treated for double jeopardy purposes as a criminal proceeding require the application of a test developed by the Court in *Kennedy v. Mendoza–Martinez* (1963), and *U.S. v. Ward* (1980). *Kennedy* involved a challenge to a statute that divested an American of his citizenship as a penalty for draft evasion. The Court concluded that the statute was "essentially penal in character," thus requiring observance of the rights to notice, confrontation, compulsory process, trial by jury, and the assistance of counsel that are guaranteed in criminal cases by the Fifth and Sixth Amendments. The Court in *Kennedy* listed the following considerations as "relevant" to the determination of "whether an Act of Congress is penal or regulatory in character":

> [1] Whether the sanction involves an affirmative disability or restraint, [2] whether it has historically been regarded as a punishment, [3] whether it comes into play only on a finding of scienter, [4] whether its operation will promote the traditional aims of punishment-retribution and deterrence, [5] whether the behavior to which it applies is already a crime, [6] whether an alternative purpose to which it may rationally be connected is assignable for it, and [7] whether it appears excessive in relation to the alternative purpose assigned.

Because forfeiture of citizenship traditionally had been considered punishment and the legislative history of the forfeiture provisions "conclusively" showed that the measure was intended to be punitive, the Court in *Kennedy* concluded that the deprivation of citizenship was a criminal sanction requiring the procedural safeguards incident to a criminal prosecution.

In *Ward*, the Court held that a penalty provided in the Water Pollution Control Act was not a criminal sanction that would entitle a person to the protection of the Fifth Amendment's privilege against self-incrimination. The Court acknowledged that the conduct subject to penalty was also subject to criminal prosecution, but noted that this was the only factor weighing in favor of characterizing the sanction as penal. The respondent failed to offer "the 'clearest proof' that the penalty * * * is punitive in either purpose or effect."

Between 1989 and 1997, the *Kennedy-Ward* test was not the sole measure of whether defendants facing civil and criminal penalties for the same misdeed were entitled to relief under the Double Jeopardy Clause. In a unanimous decision in *U.S. v. Halper* (1989), the Court concluded that the Double Jeopardy Clause regulated the imposition of successive civil and criminal sanctions for the same offense whenever the civil sanction could be characterized as "punitive." A "punitive" civil sanction following a criminal sanction was barred, the Court held, even though the civil sanction did not amount to a "criminal" sanction under the *Kennedy* analysis. *Halper* had been convicted and sentenced for filing 65 false claims defrauding the government of a total of $585. The government then sought $130,000 in civil penalties for the same fraudulent claims under the False Claims Act. Noting the great disparity between the monetary sanction sought and the actual loss suffered, the Court held that the civil penalties could be explained only as serving the "retributive or deterrent purposes" associated with "punishment," and their imposition would violate Halper's double jeopardy rights. For several years, the *Halper* decision established a middle ground between purely criminal and purely civil sanctions: civil sanctions "punitive" enough to trigger double jeopardy protections, yet still so civil in character that their imposition need not be accompanied by other constitutional safeguards provided in criminal cases.

Eventually, in the case of *Hudson v. U.S.* (1997), the justices rejected *Halper*'s three-tiered approach to double jeopardy as "unworkable." Hudson had argued that the Double Jeopardy Clause barred the United States from pursuing criminal charges against him following a civil proceeding initiated by the Office of the Comptroller of the Currency that had resulted in monetary penalties and exclusion from participation in the affairs of any banking institution. Applying the *Kennedy-Ward* test, and overruling *Hal-*

per, the Court concluded that the prior sanctions were not criminal penalties, and thus double jeopardy did not bar the indictment. The monetary penalties had been designated by Congress as "civil," and Congress's decision to confer debarment authority upon an administrative agency was "prima facie evidence" that debarment was intended as a civil sanction. There was "very little showing, to say nothing of the 'clearest proof' required by *Ward,*" that these sanctions were actually criminal. Debarment was " 'certainly nothing approaching the "infamous punishment" of imprisonment,' " and thus did not involve "affirmative disability or restraint." Historically, neither debarment nor the monetary sanction had been viewed as punishment, and both were imposed "without regard to the violator's state of mind." The Court acknowledged that the deterrent effect of the sanctions and the existence of criminal liability for the conduct underlying the sanctions weighed in favor of a finding that the sanctions were criminal, but these features were not sufficient, given the other factors, to preempt Congress's choice to impose these sanctions outside the criminal process. "To hold that the mere presence of a deterrent purpose renders such sanctions 'criminal' for double jeopardy purposes would severely undermine the Government's ability to engage in effective regulation of institutions such as banks."

The Court has also addressed claims that double jeopardy bars confinement under a state statute that authorized the civil commitment of persons who due to a "mental abnormality" or a "personality disorder" are likely to engage in "predatory acts of sexual violence." The Court in *Kan. v. Hendricks* (1997), applied *Kennedy's* multi-factor analysis, and concluded that the defendant failed "to satisfy [the] heavy burden" of demonstrating, with "the clearest proof," that "the statutory scheme [is] so punitive either in purpose or effect as to negate [the state's] intention" to deem it "civil." Regarding the statute's purpose, the Court reasoned that the statute did "not make a criminal conviction a prerequisite for commitment," as persons acquitted or otherwise "absolved of criminal responsibility" were also eligible for confinement. Nor did the statute "affix culpability for prior criminal conduct," but instead considered such conduct as merely evidence of "mental abnormality" or "future dangerousness." Confinement under the statute did not turn on the presence of "scienter," a finding the Court stated was "evidence that confinement under the statute is not intended to be retributive." Finally, deterrence was not intended, the Court concluded, because the conditions of confinement under the statute resembled those of a mental institution, not a prison, and because persons suffering from mental abnormality or personality disorder are "unlikely to be deterred by the threat of confinement." The Court rejected defense claims that the potential of indefinite incarceration under the statute coupled with the state's failure to provide treatment rendered the statute's confinement punitive.

Justice Kennedy concurred in *Hendricks,* providing the fifth vote, but warned that if civil confinement "were to become a mechanism for retribution or general deterrence, or if it were shown that mental abnormality is too imprecise a category to offer a solid basis for concluding that civil detention is justified, our precedents would not suffice to validate it." The Court later explained in *Kan. v. Crane* (2002), that in order to prevent civil commitment from "becom[ing] a 'mechanism for retribution or general deterrence'—functions properly those of criminal law, not civil commitment"—due process requires "proof of serious difficulty in controlling behavior" before the criminal process can be sidestepped. The "lack of ability to control behavior" when considered with the nature of the psychiatric diagnosis, and the severity of the mental abnormality, "must be sufficient to distinguish the dangerous sexual offender whose serious mental illness, abnormality, or disorder subjects him to civil commitment from the dangerous but typical recidivist convicted in an ordinary criminal case."

Once a statute is adjudged to be civil, a defendant is powerless to prove that as actually applied to him the statute's effect is punitive. As a divided Court explained in *Seling v. Young* (2001), the punitive nature of a given statute must be determined on the face of the statute. The decision barred Young from challenging his confinement under a statute similar to that in *Hendricks* by proving allegations that the conditions of his confinement were punitive and did not include treatment for his personality disorder. To accept such "as applied" challenges, reasoned the Court, "would never conclusively resolve whether a particular scheme is punitive and would thereby prevent a final determination of the scheme's validity under the Double Jeopardy and Ex Post Facto Clauses."

(d) When Jeopardy Attaches. Termination of a proceeding before jeopardy has attached does not bar a second proceeding or otherwise entitle a defendant to relief under the Double Jeopardy Clause, while termination thereafter brings into play the various rules of double jeopardy.

In a jury trial, the point at which jeopardy attaches is the moment at which the entire jury has been selected and has taken the oath required for service at trial. *Crist v. Bretz* (1978). In *Crist* a mistrial was granted without sufficient reason after the jury was sworn but before the first witness was called to the stand. The lower court held that this did not prevent retrial because of a state rule that jeopardy attaches in both jury and non-jury cases only after the first witness is sworn. The state contended that the sworn-jury standard, traditionally applied in federal courts, was "no more than an arbitrarily chosen rule of convenience, similar in its lack of constitutional status to the federal requirement of a unanimous verdict of 12 jurors." Rejecting that contention, the Court recognized that although the fifth amendment guarantee was once viewed as protecting only the finality of judgment and thus came into play only after entry of a judgment of conviction or acquittal, over the years the defendant's "valued right to have his trial completed before a particular tribunal" had become an essential element of the constitutional guarantee. This meant that the commencement of jeopardy at the time the jury is sworn had become a part of that guarantee, as it "reflects and protects the defendant's interest in retaining a chosen jury."

The effect of this rule is illustrated by *Downum v. U.S.* (1963), and *Serfass v. U.S.* (1975). In *Downum*, a mistrial was declared without sufficient reason just after the jury had been sworn but before any testimony had been taken, and thus retrial was impermissible. But in *Serfass* a dismissal by the trial judge which was arguably an acquittal did not bar a later trial because the defendant had sought a jury trial and the judge entered the dismissal before the jury was selected.

In a case which is to be tried by a judge without a jury, jeopardy attaches only after the first witness has been sworn. Until evidence is actually presented, the court is free to terminate the proceedings without triggering the double jeopardy bar against a second proceeding. Thus, opening statements or other pretrial motions are not enough, but the consideration of a stipulated statement of facts is sufficient for jeopardy to attach. The different rules regarding attachment in bench and jury trials have been justified as historically grounded, and tailored to the aims of safeguarding a defendant's investment in the initial proceeding and protecting him from prosecutorial manipulation.

As for those cases ending in a guilty plea, jeopardy attaches when the court accepts the defendant's plea unconditionally and enters the judgment of conviction. In *Ohio v. Johnson* (1984), a state trial judge, over the prosecutor's objection, accepted a plea to a lesser-included offense, and sought to treat that plea as a final conviction barring prosecution on the remaining greater offense. The Court disagreed, reasoning that the defendant had no authority to subdivide the indictment, enter a plea to only one part, and then maintain that the plea ended the case. The state not having agreed and the court lacking the capacity to deny the prosecution the opportunity to prove its charge, the guilty plea could not be taken as a final judgment disposing of the higher charge. The state had not sought to present the lesser-included and higher charges in separate proceedings, and the defense could not force separate treatment and then "use the double jeopardy clause as a sword to prevent the State from completing its prosecution on the remaining charges."

(e) Termination of Jeopardy. Acquittal terminates the initial jeopardy. This means that a second trial would place the defendant twice in jeopardy. A conviction, too, is final, unless the defendant chooses to question it, as discussed in § 17.4.

If the initial jeopardy is "continuing," retrial may proceed. In *Justices of Boston Municipal Court v. Lydon* (1984), the Court found that in the context of a trial de novo system of appeal a second trial merely continued the initial jeopardy and did not violate a defendant's right to be free from a second jeopardy for the same offense. The trial in the magistrate's court and the trial de novo amounted to a two-stage continuous proceeding rather as two separate trials. Thus, the defendant's claim was no different than that of the defendant who has a motion for directed acquittal denied at the end of the prosecution's case-in-chief and then is forced to continue to the end of the trial.

When a trial is terminated without a verdict on defendant's guilt or innocence, as when a mistrial is declared, also presents a case in which jeopardy may be continuing. Thus, in *Richardson v. U.S.* (1984), the defendant claimed that he should not be forced to a second trial following a jury deadlock that resulted in a mistrial since the trial judge had erred in failing to grant defendant's motion for a judgment of acquittal based on the insufficiency of the evidence at that first trial. The Court rejected that contention as improperly viewing the first and second trials as separate subjections to jeopardy. "The failure of the jury to reach a verdict," the Court reasoned, "is not an event which terminates jeopardy." Accordingly, the government remained "entitled to resolution of the case by verdict from the jury," and the situation presented was essentially that of a completed first stage in an ongoing proceeding. Mistrials may bar retrial if not supported by manifest necessity, see § 17.2. A different result is called for if the jury necessarily rejected a fact essential to conviction on the mistried count by acquitting on a different count. In this situation, the Court held in *Yeager v. United States* (2009), even though there was no verdict on the count ending in mistrial, and therefore jeopardy continued on that mistried count, retrial is barred by the rule of *Ashe v. Swenson* (1970).

(f) The "Same Offense." Offenses for double jeopardy purposes are not necessarily defined by reference to separate titles or separate statutory sections. Two offenses may have different titles and be prohibited by different statutory sections yet constitute the "same offence" for double jeopardy purposes. As discussed in

§ 9.4(b), whether offenses are the same for double jeopardy purposes requires an inquiry into the elements of the two crimes. However, as discussed in § 9.4(a), even if the two offenses are not the same, an acquittal in the first prosecution may bar a second prosecution under the doctrine of collateral estoppel, which is also an aspect of the bar against double jeopardy.

(g) Reprosecutions: An overview. The overview that follows, at the risk of oversimplification, brings together the essence of the double jeopardy principles relevant to reprosecutions. Those principles are:

(1) Multiple initiation of a prosecution that never reached the point of bringing jeopardy into play, as where the prosecution repetitively files complaints that are subsequently rejected in judicial or grand jury screening, does not create a double jeopardy difficulty. See § 17.1(d).

(2) Multiple prosecutions that produce multiple trials are not prohibited if they are for different offenses—unless collateral estoppel applies because the first trial resulted in an acquittal based on a failure of proof as to an element also required for the offense presented in the second trial. See § 9.4(a), (b).

(3) Separate prosecutions producing separate trials on statutory offenses that are the same offense are not prohibited where the defendant, by his request or otherwise, is solely responsible for the separate trials. See § 9.4(b).

(4) Multiple trials on a single charge are not prohibited if the first trial resulted in a mistrial that was justified under the manifest necessity doctrine or was requested or consented to by the defense (absent judicial or prosecutorial overreaching that is aimed at forcing the mistrial). See § 17.2.

(5) If a prosecution is dismissed after jeopardy attached, and that dismissal is based on some preliminary error that does not permanently terminate the prosecution, but allows the prosecution to reprosecute after curing that error (as where the dismissal was based on a defective pleading), that dismissal is treated in much the same fashion as a mistrial. Where the principles governing mistrials would allow the government to cure the error and return for a retrial, the government may also seek appellate review of the dismissal and renew the prosecution if the appellate court holds that the dismissal was erroneous. See §§ 17.2(f), 19.3(d).

(6) If a prosecution is dismissed after jeopardy attached on a ground permanently terminating the prosecution (e.g., denial of a speedy trial), and the defendant moved for the dismissal, double jeopardy does not prohibit a prosecution appeal and a subsequent retrial if the dismissal is held to be erroneous. See § 17.3(a).

(7) If the jury reaches a verdict of acquittal or the judge grants a judgment of acquittal, double jeopardy bars a new trial even if it appears that the acquittal was based on an erroneous interpretation of the law. Included in the concept of an acquittal is the implied acquittal that comes when a jury returns a verdict of guilty on a lesser-included offense and fails to indicate its disposition of the higher charge. One exception to the concept that an acquittal ends all further proceedings arises when the trial judge grants a judgment of acquittal after the jury returned a guilty verdict. Here, if the appellate court should find that the judge erred in entering the acquittal, the jury verdict of conviction can be restored. See §§ 17.3, 17.4(d), 19.3(d).

(8) If there is a jury verdict of conviction, defendant may rest on the conviction, and it will bar any reprosecution on the same offense in much the same manner as an acquittal. If the defendant appeals the conviction and it is reversed, then the defendant ordinarily may be proceeded against by reprosecution without running afoul of the double jeopardy bar. The one exception is where the appellate court sets aside the conviction on the ground that the evidence of guilt was insufficient. See § 17.4.

(9) If a second trial is allowed after an overturned conviction, the court is not barred by double jeopardy from imposing a greater sentence on reconviction for the same offense than had been imposed on the original conviction. The resentenced defendant must, however, receive credit for any time served on the first sentence. Moreover, double jeopardy will not bar government appeal of a sentence when authorized by statute. See §§ 18.7, 18.8, 19.3.

(10) Multiple prosecutions that would otherwise be barred under the principles noted above are not prohibited where the prosecutions are brought by separate sovereigns (state and federal, or different states). See § 17.5.

§ 17.2   Reprosecution Following Mistrial

(a) With Defendant's Consent. This section addresses when it is constitutionally permissible to undertake another prosecution for the same offense after the trial judge has declared a mistrial.

The mistrial situation that is most straightforward in terms of the double jeopardy guarantee is that which is brought about by the request of the defendant. The leading case is *U.S. v. Dinitz* (1976), where the trial judge excluded defense counsel from the case for misconduct and then gave the defendant the choice of (1) a recess while the court of appeals passed upon the exclusion, (2) a mistrial, or (3) continuation of the trial with the assistant defense counsel. The defendant opted for mistrial. The Supreme Court held he could be retried, even though there was no "manifest necessity" for ending the trial. The Court noted that there is a significant distinction between a mistrial declared by the court sua sponte, where the "manifest necessity" test applies, and one granted at defendant's request, where "a motion by the defendant for mistrial is ordinarily assumed to remove any barrier to reprosecution, even if the defendant's motion is necessitated by prosecutorial or judicial error." As for the contention that Dinitz had not voluntarily waived his double jeopardy protection because of the "Hobson's choice" with which he was confronted, the Court responded that "traditional waiver concepts have little relevance" in this context. Rather, the "important consideration * * * is that the defendant retains primary control over the course to be followed in the event of such error."

Although in *Dinitz* the defendant actually requested a mistrial, the "consent doctrine" of that case also applies in those instances in which the defendant did not move for a mistrial but expressed agreement with the judge's announced intention to grant one. Some courts have gone so far as to suggest that silence constitutes tacit consent even where defense counsel was not asked for his views on the mistrial. But mere silence is a far cry from consent, especially when the proceedings are fast paced, the termination of the proceedings abrupt, or the defendant's opportunity to raise a meaningful objection is otherwise impaired. Moreover, the mere fact that a codefendant has moved for a mistrial should not necessarily bind the defendant joined with him for trial.

(b) The "Goaded" Mistrial Motion. As the Supreme Court recognized in *U.S. v. Jorn* (1971), even if a mistrial was brought about with the consent of the defendant, double jeopardy bars reprosecution when the circumstances prompting the mistrial were "attributable to prosecutorial or judicial overreaching." The Court in *Or. v. Kennedy* (1982), held that "[o]nly where the governmental conduct in question is intended to 'goad' the defendant into moving for a mistrial may a defendant raise the bar of Double Jeopardy to a second trial after having succeeded in aborting the first on his own motion." In such a case, "the defendant's valued right to complete his trial before the first jury would be a hollow shell if the inevitable motion for mistrial were held to prevent a later invocation of the bar of double jeopardy in all circumstances." This "intent-to-cause-mistrial" test "merely calls for the [trial] court to make a finding of fact," using the "familiar process in our criminal justice system" of "[i]nferring the existence or nonexistence of intent from objective facts and circumstances."

Four justices dissented from the Court's standard and maintained that it should be "sufficient that the court is persuaded that egregious prosecutorial misconduct has rendered unmeaningful the defendant's choice to continue or to abort the proceeding." Where the prosecution's intentional misconduct had forced the defense to seek a mistrial, the Double Jeopardy Clause should protect the defense from a retrial without regard to whether the prosecutor had intended to force the mistrial motion, to harass and embarrass the defendant, or to ensure a conviction. Several state courts, relying on their state constitutions, have adopted standards for overreaching similar to that advanced by the *Kennedy* minority.

(c) The "Manifest Necessity" Standard. When the trial judge declares a mistrial sua sponte or over the defendant's objection, retrial is barred unless the judge's ruling was supported by "manifest necessity." This standard originated in the case of *U.S. v. Perez* (1824), where a unanimous Court held that the failure of the jury to agree on a verdict of either acquittal or conviction did not bar retrial of the defendant. The Court reasoned:

> We think, that in all cases of this nature, the law has invested Courts of justice with the authority to discharge a jury from giving any verdict, whenever, in their opinion, taking all the circumstances into consideration, there is a manifest necessity for the act, or the ends of public justice would otherwise be defeated. They are to exercise a sound discretion on the subject; and it is impossible to define all the circumstances, which would render it proper to interfere. To be sure, the power ought to be used with the greatest of caution, under urgent circumstances * * *.

The "manifest necessity" standard means less than what the words might suggest on their face. As the Court stated in *Ariz. v. Washington* (1978), "The words 'manifest necessity' appropriately characterize the magnitude of the prosecutor's burden. * * * [But] it is manifest that the key word 'necessity' cannot be interpreted literally; instead, contrary to the teaching of Webster, we assume that there are degrees of necessity and we require a 'high degree' before concluding that the mistrial is appropriate."

The manifest necessity standard requires a balancing process. On the one side, the court considers the defendant's interest in having the trial completed in a single proceeding, preserving the possibility of obtaining an acquittal before that "particular tribunal." On the other side is the strength of the justification for turning to a mistrial rather than attempting to carry the trial through to a verdict. Lurking in the background is the recognition that an appellate court ruling holding that the trial judge improperly balanced these factors by ordering a mistrial operates to deprive the state of any full opportunity to establish the guilt of a person who well may be guilty.

For example, in *Ill. v. Somerville* (1973), the indictment had failed to allege the necessary mens rea element of an intent to permanently deprive, and under Illinois law, that defect was jurisdictional in nature, being neither waivable by the defense nor curable by amendment. Under that circumstance, the trial court considered continuation of the trial to be inconsistent with the ends of justice since any conviction the trial might produce would automatically be set aside by the defense. The Supreme Court majority held that this established manifest necessity for the mistrial.

The *Somerville* Court cautioned that "the declaration of a mistrial on the basis of a rule or a defective procedure that lent itself to prosecutorial manipulation would involve an entirely different question." *Downum v. U.S.* (1963), provides an example of a case in which the prosecutor's error barred retrial. The prosecutor in *Downum* had recognized on the morning of the scheduled trial that a key witness had not been subpoenaed and had not been found. Relying on the promise of the witness's spouse to let the marshall know when she found him, and apparently assuming that he would be found before the trial began that afternoon, the prosecutor went ahead with the jury selection. When the witness failed to appear in the afternoon, the prosecution moved for mistrial on the ground that the witness was critical to obtaining a conviction on two of the six counts. That motion then was granted over the objection of the defense. The Supreme Court held that the mistrial was not justified by manifest necessity. The mistrial was sought to save a case that appeared to be headed toward an acquittal because of an event the prosecutor could have anticipated. There may be situations where the prosecution can show that critical evidence suddenly became unavailable through circumstances beyond its control and reasonable anticipation (e.g., a witness's sudden illness). Where there clearly is no effort to avoid the consequences of an earlier miscalculation as to the strength of the prosecution's case, lower courts have distinguished *Downum* and sustained mistrials as consistent with the manifest necessity standard.

(d) Manifest Necessity and Alternatives to a Mistrial. Much of the case law applying the manifest necessity doctrine centers upon the proper evaluation of alternatives to a mistrial. The failure of the trial judge to consider such alternatives may, in itself, lead to a finding of a lack of manifest necessity. Illustrative is *U.S. v. Jorn* (1971), the trial judge, upon concluding that the government's witnesses did not understand the extent to which they might incriminate themselves, ordered a mistrial so as to allow the witnesses to consult with attorneys before deciding whether to testify. In finding a lack of manifest necessity, the plurality stressed that the trial judge gave absolutely "no consideration" to the alternative of a trial continuance, and " * * * acted so abruptly in discharging the jury" that the parties were given no opportunity to suggest the alternative of a continuance or to object to the jury discharge. The Court concluded that where a trial judge simply "made no effort to exercise sound discretion to assure that * * * there was a manifest necessity for the * * * sua sponte declaration of a mistrial," a "reprosecution would violate the double jeopardy provision of the Fifth Amendment." In the later case of *Ariz. v. Washington* (1978), the Court rejected the contention that the trial judge must make explicit findings as to the need for a mistrial in light of alternatives, but it did insist that the trial record demonstrate a "sufficient justification" for the mistrial ruling that reflected consideration of those alternatives.

(e) Manifest Necessity and Trial Court Discretion. In various instances, a particular circumstance clearly would justify a mistrial, and the critical issue is how much deference will be given to the trial judge's judgment as to the existence of that circumstance. The deadlocked jury, for example, presents a situation in which the trial judge must be given broad discretion. Stated the Court in *Ariz. v. Washington*, "If retrial of the defendant were barred whenever an appellate court views the 'necessity' for a mistrial differently from the trial judge, there would be a danger that the latter, cognizant of the serious societal consequences of an erroneous ruling, would employ coercive means to break the apparent deadlock." Consistent with this analysis, lower court decisions have accorded great deference to trial court rulings in hung jury cases. Lack of manifest necessity will be found nevertheless when circumstances point to a trial judge's failure to take account of the defendant's interest in obtaining a verdict in his first trial. Among the factors considered in this regard are: (1) whether the defense argued that the jury not be discharged; (2) the length of the deliberations; (3) the complexity of the issues; and (4) the nature of the communications between judge and jury.

Ariz. v. Washington itself presented still another situation in which the trial judge will be given considerable leeway. The trial court there had granted a mistrial after defense counsel in opening argument made an improper and prejudicial reference to the prosecution having withheld exculpatory evidence in an earlier trial. The Supreme Court acknowledged that "some trial judges might have proceeded with the trial after giving the jury appropriate cautionary instructions." The difficulty which led to the mistrial in this case, the Court explained, also fell within an area where "the trial judge's determination is entitled to special respect." Two reasons supported this conclusion: (1) the trial judge had heard the argument and observed the reaction of the jury, had seen and heard the jurors during voir dire, and was most familiar with the evidence and the background of the case, and thus was "far more 'conversant with the factors relevant to the determination' than any reviewing court can possibly be"; and (2) because alternative remedies would "not necessarily remove the risk of bias," a contrary result would mean that "unscrupulous defense counsel are to be allowed an unfair advantage."

(f) Dismissals Equivalent to Mistrials. In some instances, as discussed in § 17.3(a), a dismissal may permanently end all prosecution, but in other instances, a dismissal is granted in apparent contemplation of the renewal of the prosecution. Such is the case, for example, if the dismissal is based on some curable error in the course of the preliminary proceedings or an error in the charging instrument. Most often, such dismissals "without prejudice" are issued before trial, but occasionally they will occur after jeopardy has attached. The leading case on such dismissals, *Lee v. U.S.* (1977), indicates that they will be treated as the functional equivalents of mistrials, and governed by the same double jeopardy principles.

The Court in *Lee* was confronted with a situation in which the defendant had moved to dismiss the information for failure to allege allegations of intent, after the prosecutor's opening statement in a bench trial. The trial court had tentatively denied the motion subject to further study, and then at the close of the two-hour trial the court took a brief recess and granted the motion to dismiss. In holding that the defendant could be tried again, the Court rejected the contention that he should not have had to undergo the first trial because the court was made aware of the defective information before jeopardy attached. The Court concluded that the defendant "had only himself to blame" for the events as they developed, for by "the last-minute timing of his motion to dismiss, he virtually assured the attachment of jeopardy." Justice Brennan, concurring, emphasized that "an entirely different case would be presented if the petitioner had afforded the trial judge ample opportunity to rule on his motion prior to trial, and the court, in failing to take advantage of this opportunity [had] permitted the attachment of jeopardy before ordering dismissal of the information." Of particular significance was the fact that the court's initial remarks "left little doubt that the denial was subject to further consideration at an available opportunity in the proceedings—a fact of which the court reminded counsel after the close of the prosecution's evidence," following which defense counsel "made no effort to withdraw the motion." By contrast, in cases where the defendant has moved for a mistrial but has withdrawn that motion prior to the judge's ruling, lower courts have held that the *Dinitz* rule does not apply.

§ 17.3   Reprosecution Following Acquittal or Dismissal

(a) **Dismissals vs. Acquittals.** In contrast to either a mistrial or a dismissal of the type presented in *Lee*, there are dismissals that constitute a permanent bar to the prosecution of the charge. The basic standard for which dismissals will bar reprosecution and which will not was established in *U.S. v. Scott* (1978). *Scott* presented the question of the permissibility of a government appeal following the trial judge's midtrial dismissal of the prosecution on the ground of prejudicial pretrial delay. The Court explained:

> [A] defendant once acquitted may not be again subjected to trial without violating the Double Jeopardy Clause. * * * But that situation is obviously a far cry from the present case, where the Government was quite willing to continue with its production of evidence to show the defendant guilty before the jury first empaneled to try him, but the defendant elected to seek termination of the trial on grounds unrelated to guilt or innocence. [A] defendant is acquitted only when "the ruling of the judge," whatever its label, actually represents a resolution in defendant's favor, correct or not, of some or all of the factual elements of the offense charged. * * * We think that in a case such as this the defendant, by deliberately choosing to seek termination of the proceedings against him on a basis unrelated to factual guilt or innocence of the offense of which he is accused, suffers no injury cognizable under the Double Jeopardy Clause if the Government is permitted to appeal from such a ruling of the trial court in favor of the defendant [and to reprosecute if successful on appeal].

In distinguishing between a dismissal that allows retrial and may be appealed, and a dismissal that bars retrial because it is equivalent to an acquittal, the "trial judge's characterization of his own action cannot control the classification of the action." The critical question rather was whether or not the trial court's ruling was based on a failure of proof in establishing the "factual elements of the offense." For example, dismissal on the basis of insanity or entrapment would bar retrial, as these defenses go to the basic substantive element of individual "culpability," while "the dismissal for preindictment delay represents a legal judgment that a defendant, although criminally culpable, may not be punished because of a supposed constitutional violation." Thus, a trial court's ruling that the prosecution's case-in-chief failed to establish venue, though framed as a judgment of acquittal, does not preclude retrial because venue is an element "more procedural than substantive" which does not go to culpability.

If, unlike the situation in *Scott* where the defendant had moved for dismissal, the trial judge "was the instigator and the primary mover of the events that led to the dismissal of the indictment" and "took complete control of the proceedings and set off on a course over which the defendant had no control," then the "voluntary choice" which was an essential ingredient of *Scott* is not present. The dismissal there should be treated as a mistrial, allowing retrial only if the judge's action was justified by manifest necessity.

(b) The Jury Acquittal. The Supreme Court has long held that when a jury in a criminal case has returned a verdict of not guilty, the double jeopardy prohibition bars further prosecution of the defendant for the same offense. That standard was laid down in *Ball v. U.S.* (1896), and it has been accepted ever since as the cornerstone of double jeopardy jurisprudence. The Court has noted that this absolute bar finds support in the common law plea of *autrefois acquit* as well as the policy underlying the Double Jeopardy Clause. As to the latter, the most frequently cited policy justification is that set forth in *Scott*: "To permit a second trial after an acquittal, however mistaken the acquittal may have been, would present an unacceptably high risk that the Government with its vast superior resources, might wear down the defendant so that 'even though innocent, he may be found guilty.' "

The fundamental policy concern here lies not only in protection of the innocent, however. The rule grants a sense of repose to the defendant who went through a trial that produced a final decision on his guilt or innocence. The defendant who challenges a conviction is willing to put aside the finality of that verdict, but the defendant who is acquitted obviously does not desire to put aside his sense of repose. The double jeopardy bar also protects the beneficiaries of the jury's leniency, who may not be factually innocent.

(c) Acquittal by the Judge. The Court has long treated as parallel the directed acquittal entered by the judge and the jury verdict of not guilty. Critics of this position have noted that the protection of the jury's right of nullification is not at stake in the judicial acquittal, and that the protection of a factual resolution favorable to the defendant also is not necessarily at stake. While some directed acquittals are based on a judicial evaluation of the persuasiveness of the evidence, others are based solely on the trial court's view of the substantive law. Where that view is erroneous, there is no basis for arguing that the acquittal must be given finality in order to protect the innocent. The Court however, has simply noted, without extensive explanation, that the Double Jeopardy Clause "nowhere distinguishes" between bench and jury acquittals.

The leading case on judicial acquittals is *Sanabria v. U.S.* (1978). The trial judge in that case granted a judgment of acquittal that flowed from two alleged errors. First, the trial court excluded certain evidence as being legally irrelevant under its view that the indictment had failed to set forth a particular basis for liability. Second, in reviewing the evidence that remained, the trial court applied an erroneous reading of the substantive law by limiting liability for participation in illegal enterprises to persons actually engaged in the illegal activities. The Supreme Court viewed the critical issue before it as whether the trial judge's ruling was actually an acquittal. Although the trial court had looked to the indictment in striking certain evidence, it had not dismissed the indictment for failure to plead an offense, but had taken the indictment as stating an offense under a limited theory of liability, excluded evidence not consistent with that theory, and then held the remaining evidence insufficient under that theory. The Court therefore concluded:

> [W]e believe the ruling below is properly to be characterized as an erroneous evidentiary ruling, which led to an acquittal for insufficient evidence. That judgment of acquittal, however erroneous, bars further prosecution on any aspect of the count and hence bars appellate review of the trial court's error.

Whether a ruling constitutes an acquittal depends upon its substance, not its characterization (or label) under state law. *Smalis v. Pa.* (1986). If the judge determines at the end of the government's case that the evidence on one count is insufficient to sustain a conviction, the Constitution bars reconsideration of that acquittal by the judge once the trial proceeds to the defendant's introduction of evidence on the remaining counts. By contrast, the decision to grant a motion for acquittal may be reconsidered consistent with double jeopardy if that reconsideration takes place before the trial proceeds further, thus avoiding any reliance interest by the defense. *Smith v. Mass.* (2005).

(d) Pre-jeopardy "Acquittals." Even when the judge's ruling unquestionably is grounded solely on a determination that there is insufficient evidence for conviction, it does not inevitably follow that the ruling will be treated as an acquittal under *Sanabria* and *Scott*. The ruling cannot be placed in that category if it is issued in a pretrial setting, before jeopardy has attached. Once the trial has started, an acquittal will be treated as such even though it was not granted in accord with proper procedures. Thus, in *Fong Foo v. U.S.* (1962), a judge's entry of an acquittal because he viewed the government's initial witnesses as inherently incredible constituted a bar to further proceedings even though the judge went beyond the relevant Federal Rules provision by directing the acquittal before the prosecution had completed its case-in-chief.

(e) Postconviction Judgments of Acquittal. In *U.S. v. Jenkins* (1975), the Court noted: "[W]here the jury returns a verdict of guilt, but the trial court thereafter enters a judgment of acquittal, an appeal is permitted." Thus, trial judges may preserve the government's opportunity to appeal where the judge sides with the defense on a legal issue that will control as to the sufficiency of the evidence by postponing its ruling on judgment of acquittal until after the verdict. Assume for example, that an issue first arises at trial concerning the admissibility of evidence, that the evidence is crucial to the prosecution's case, and that the judge believes that it is inadmissible, but considers this position debatable and most appropriately decided finally by an appellate court. In such a situation, to preserve the prosecution's right of appeal and grant the defense the acquittal that the judge believes it deserves, the judge may allow the evidence to go before the jury, and if the jury should convict, then grant a post-verdict judgment of acquittal on the ground that the evidence is inadmissible and that without it, the prosecution's proof is insufficient. Similarly, if there is disagreement as to whether the prosecution must prove a certain element to establish a crime, the judge can send the case to the jury on instructions that do not require the finding of that element and then, if the jury convicts, grant a post-verdict judgment of acquittal on the ground that proof of the element is wanting. In a bench trial, the process is even easier, as the judge can make findings of facts and indicate that he would hold the defendant guilty except for his adoption of a certain legal interpretation that produces an acquittal. That ruling can then readily be viewed by the appellate court and if it disagrees as to the legal interpretation, remanded for entry of the judgment of guilt, which can be done without further fact finding.

§ 17.4 Reprosecution Following Conviction

(a) The General Rule. In the seminal double jeopardy decision of *Ball v. U.S.* (1896), the Supreme Court recognized an exception to the general constitutional prohibition against reprosecuting a person for an offense of which he has already been convicted. Reprosecution is allowed where the convicted defendant has managed through appeal or some other procedure to set aside his conviction on grounds other than the insufficiency of evidence. Although uncertainty existed for some time as to the doctrinal basis for this rule, the Supreme Court has stated that the "most reasonable" justification for the *Ball* rule is that advanced by Justice Harlan in *U.S. v. Tateo* (1964):

> While different theories have been advanced to support the permissibility of retrial, of greater importance than the conceptual abstractions employed to explain the *Ball* principle are the implications of that principle for the sound administration of justice. Corresponding to the right of an accused to be given a fair trial is the societal interest in punishing one whose guilt is clear after he has obtained such a trial. It would be a high price indeed for society to pay were every accused granted immunity from punishment because of any defect sufficient to constitute reversible error in the proceedings leading to conviction. From the standpoint of a defendant, it is at least doubtful that appellate courts would be as zealous as they now are in protecting against the effects of improprieties at the trial or pre-trial stage if they knew that reversal of a conviction would put the accused irrevocably beyond the reach of further prosecution. In reality, therefore, the practice of retrial serves defendants' rights as well as society's interest.

This rule is in some tension with the Court's later declaration that some misconduct by the judge or prosecution resulting in mistrial may, depending upon the circumstances, bar retrial. See § 17.2(b). Under the *Ball* rule retrial apparently will not be prohibited if the very same sort of misconduct fails to end the trial (either because defendant's mistrial motion is denied or because defendant did not move for a mistrial), a conviction results, and the conviction is reversed on appeal because of the overreaching. Moved by this seeming incongruity, a few courts have barred retrial whenever prosecutorial misconduct was sufficient for a mistrial, despite the defendant's failure to move for a mistrial. Without such a bar, these courts reason, a prosecutor apprehending an acquittal can fend off the anticipated acquittal by misconduct of which the defendant is unaware until after the verdict. The Court itself has not expressed any inclination to institute a misconduct exception to the *Ball* rule.

(b) The Evidence Insufficiency Exception. It was not until the case of *Burks v. U.S.* (1978), that the Supreme Court held that the *Ball* rule did not apply where the appellate reversal was based on the insufficiency of the evidence at trial to sustain a guilty verdict. In holding that a remand in such circumstances is inconsistent with the double jeopardy prohibition, a unanimous Court emphasized that if the trial court had done what the reviewing court said should have been done "a judgment of acquittal would have been entered and, of course, petitioner could not be retried for the same offense." Under the Double Jeopardy Clause, "it should make no difference that the *reviewing* court, rather than the trial court, determined the evidence to be insufficient."

A finding of insufficient evidence to support a conviction by either a trial court or appellate court must be distinguished from a ruling that the conviction was against the weight of the evidence. Unlike the directed acquittal, which holds that the evidence is insufficient for any reasonable juror to find guilt, the granting of a new trial on the ground that the verdict is against the weight of the evidence recognizes that the jurors could rationally reach the result that they reached, but grants the defendant another chance because the trial court has concerns, based on that judge's own evaluation of the evidence, that an injustice may have been done. For example, in *Tibbs v. Fla.* (1982), it was clear the appellate court was acting only as a "thirteenth juror," rendering a "weight of the evidence" reversal. Such a reversal, is designed primarily to "give the defendant a second chance" in "the interests of justice." It was not true, as the dissent argued, that the appellate court in practical effect was stating that the conviction would not stand without additional evidence. Precisely the same evidence could lead to an appellate court affirmance of any ensuing conviction. The *Burks* doctrine does not bar remand when a conviction is reversed by an appellate court due to other types of deficiencies, such as a charge that does not encompass the defendant's conduct, or an error in instructing the jury.

When the evidence is found on appeal to be insufficient only as to a greater offense, and the jury's actual verdict shows that it found the existence of every element of the lesser offense, the reviewing court may remand the case for entry of judgment of conviction on the lesser offense, or allow retrial of the lesser included offense. This power to modify the judgment may derive from statute, court rule, or judicial decision. Although most courts have upheld either retrial or the entry of judgment of conviction on a lesser offense whenever a conviction for a greater offense is overturned due to insufficient evidence, some states limit the remedy to retrial of the lesser offense. Even retrial in some states will be available only when the jury was actually instructed on the lesser offense at the first trial. Courts in these jurisdictions are less certain that any jury that convicts of the greater offense would necessarily have convicted of the lesser, and have argued that the state should not be able to "go for broke" at trial, hoping that without a lesser offense instruction the jury will convict on the higher offense, confident that if that conviction is overturned, conviction on the lesser offense can be had without submission to a jury. In response it has also been observed that such a limitation "creates the anomaly of forcing a defendant to make himself subject to retrial if he requests a lesser-included offense in those cases in which he challenges the sufficiency of the evidence with respect to the higher offense."

Just as appeal is permissible from a trial court's granting of a motion for acquittal after a jury verdict of guilty, the Double Jeopardy Clause does not bar review of an appellate court's conclusion that there was insufficient evidence to convict. Here too, if the government prevails, the defendant is not subject to a new trial, but to reinstatement of the trial court's judgment of conviction.

(c) The Determination of Sufficiency. When reviewing the sufficiency of evidence for conviction, a court must determine which evidence to consider. *Lockhart v. Nelson* (1988) addressed a case in which the appellate court concluded that the trial judge should have excluded evidence submitted by the government and that had the evidence been excluded, the record would have contained insufficient evidence of guilt. The Court concluded that in this situation retrial was permissible. *Burks* should bar a retrial only if *all* of the admitted evidence, even erroneously admitted evidence, was insufficient. Where that is not the case, allowing a retrial following reversal is consistent with giving the prosecution "one fair opportunity to offer whatever proof it could assemble." Had the trial court excluded the inadmissible evidence, the prosecution would have been given the opportunity to introduce other evidence on the same point.

If the appellate court determines that the trial judge erroneously *excluded* prosecution evidence, a reprosecution would not be barred if the insufficiency of the government's evidence would have been "cured" by the evidence erroneously excluded by the trial court.

When a defendant appeals a verdict of conviction and raises insufficiency of the evidence together with trial error, courts have disagreed about whether the failure to review the sufficiency of evidence bars retrial. Many lower courts have found that the failure to reverse a conviction for insufficient evidence and ordering instead a retrial is violative of the Double Jeopardy Clause, reasoning that double jeopardy protection, should not depend "on the grace of the reviewing court." Other courts have held that double jeopardy does not prohibit retrial in cases in which convictions were reversed for trial error and insufficiency claims were left unaddressed.

(d) Conviction as Implied Acquittal. The teaching of *Green v. U.S.* (1957), is that under some circumstances a conviction of one crime must, for double jeopardy purposes, be taken as an acquittal of another crime. In that case the defendant Green was charged with first-degree murder, and the jury was informed that they could find him guilty either of that crime or the lesser-included offense of

second-degree murder. The jury returned a verdict of guilty on the
lesser charge but said nothing as to the first-degree murder charge.
Green's conviction was reversed on appeal for trial error, and he
was then retried on the original first-degree murder charge and
convicted of that offense. In holding that the Double Jeopardy
Clause barred conviction on that charge, the Supreme Court explained:

> Green was in direct peril of being convicted and punished
> for first-degree murder at his first trial. He was forced to run
> the gauntlet once on that charge and the jury refused to
> convict him. When given the choice between finding him guilty
> of either first or second degree murder it chose the latter. In
> this situation the great majority of cases in this country have
> regarded the jury's verdict as an implicit acquittal on the
> charge of first degree murder. But the result in this case need
> not rest alone on the assumption, which we believe legitimate,
> that the jury for one reason or another, acquitted Green of
> murder in the first degree. For here, the jury was dismissed
> without returning any express verdict on that charge and
> without Green's consent. Yet it was given a full opportunity to
> return a verdict and no extraordinary circumstances appeared
> which prevented it from doing so. Therefore it seems clear,
> under established principles of former jeopardy, that Green's
> jeopardy for first degree murder came to an end when the jury
> was discharged so that he could not be retried for that offense.
> * * * In brief, we believe this case can be treated no different-
> ly, for purposes of former jeopardy, than if the jury had
> returned a verdict which expressly read: "We find the defen-
> dant not guilty of murder in the first degree but guilty of
> murder in the second degree."

As *Morris v. Mathews* (1986) later noted, if the jury in a second
trial convicts on a jeopardy-barred count, an adequate remedy is
simply to reduce that conviction to the lesser-included offense that
was not jeopardy-barred. In *Morris*, with the jury having convicted
on the higher, jeopardy-barred count, it necessarily found, without
any compromise, that the defendant's conduct also satisfied the
elements of the lesser-included, non-barred offense. It would be
"incongruous," said the Court, to remedy the double jeopardy
violation that occurred in trying the defendant again for the higher
offense by "ordering yet another trial" when the jury, uninfluenced
by that violation, had found defendant guilty of the lesser-included
offense that was not jeopardy-barred.

An implied acquittal is not necessarily present where the jury
has been told that it should look first at a single charge and then
not bother with the other charges if it finds guilt on that charge.
Saying nothing as to the other charges indicates only that they

were not reached. Assuming that the unreached charges were not lesser-included in the sense that conviction on the higher necessarily includes conviction on the lesser, the issue then becomes whether the jury charge that, in effect, kept defendant from receiving a verdict on the other charges is justified under the standards applied to mistrials. Also, no acquittal of a greater offense is suggested by conviction of a lesser offense when the jury is unable to reach agreement on the higher offense, and this disagreement is formally entered on the record.

When a defendant is charged with both greater and lesser offenses, an acquittal is not present where a defendant enters a guilty plea to a lesser charge over the government's objection. The acceptance of the guilty plea and even the determination that there is a factual basis for it does not constitute an inferential finding of not guilty of the higher charge.

§ 17.5   Reprosecution by a Different Sovereign

(a) **Federal Prosecution After State.** In the case of *U.S. v. Lanza* (1922), the Supreme Court promulgated what is customarily referred to as the "dual sovereignty" doctrine: "an act denounced as a crime by both national and state sovereignties is an offense against the peace and dignity of both and may be punished by each." That the dual sovereignty doctrine allows a federal prosecution notwithstanding a prior state prosecution for the same conduct was later affirmed in *Abbate v. U.S.* (1959). There, defendants who allegedly had conspired to dynamite telephone company facilities pleaded guilty to a state charge of conspiring to injure the property of another and received a three-month sentence, after which they were prosecuted in federal court for conspiring to injure those facilities that were part of a communications system "operated and controlled by the United States." The Court held that the federal conviction was not prohibited by the Double Jeopardy Clause. In declining to depart from the *Lanza* rule, the majority in *Abbate* reiterated the fears voiced in earlier cases that, "if the States are free to prosecute criminal acts violating their laws, and the resultant state prosecutions bar federal prosecutions based on the same acts, federal law enforcement must necessarily be hindered." This is especially problematic when the defendants' acts impinge more seriously on a federal interest than on a state interest.

Criticism of *Abbate* intensified after the Supreme Court held that the Double Jeopardy Clause was also applicable to the states through the Fourteenth Amendment and rejected efforts to limit other constitutional rights with "dual sovereignty" reasoning similar to that in *Abbate*. Despite this attack, the dual sovereignty doctrine has become more firmly entrenched over time.

The dual sovereignty rule also allows an Indian tribe to prosecute a defendant following a prosecution by a separate government. In *U.S. v. Lara* (2004), for example, the Court upheld a federal prosecution following a tribal prosecution for same offense after concluding that in prosecuting the defendant the Tribe did not exercise federal power, but instead acted in its capacity as a separate sovereign.

(b) State Prosecution After Federal. The reverse of the *Abbate* situation was presented in the companion case of *Bartkus v. Ill.* (1959), where after defendant's acquittal in federal court for robbery of a federally insured bank he was convicted in state court for the same bank robbery. The Court again applied the dual sovereignty doctrine and upheld the state conviction. Once more the concern was that the action of one sovereign should not cut off the enforcement of a superior interest by the other. Citing *Screws v. U.S.* (1945), a federal civil rights prosecution where the permissible punishment was but a few years while at the state level defendant's conduct was a capital offense, the Court declared that were

> the federal prosecution of a comparatively minor offense to prevent state prosecution of so grave an infraction of state law, the result would be a shocking and untoward deprivation of the historic right and obligation of the States to maintain peace and order within their confines. It would be in derogation of our federal system to displace the reserved power of States over state offenses by reason of prosecution of minor federal offenses by federal authorities beyond the control of the States.

Many states have followed *Bartkus* in interpreting their state constitutional provisions on the subject of double jeopardy, although some have held that their constitutional provisions bar a state prosecution in the *Bartkus* situation. About half of the states have adopted statutes prohibiting state prosecution for offenses that relate to a previous federal prosecution, but these statutes vary considerably as to the extent of the prohibition. Some do not allow a state prosecution based on the same offense prosecuted elsewhere, others bar subsequent prosecutions of the same conduct, or of the same "act or omission," and a few bar a state prosecution whenever based upon the "same transaction" as the prior federal prosecution. A state may also isolate a particular class of cases for protection from dual prosecutions, such as controlled substance offenses.

(c) State–State and State–Municipal. Certain criminal transactions may have a sufficient bearing on two states (usually adjoining) as to produce criminal liability in both for basically the same harm and conduct. Where such successive prosecutions are brought, as in *Heath v. Ala.* (1985), the double jeopardy bar does not apply because each state is a separate sovereign. In *Heath*, two states prosecuted the defendant for the same murder (which occurred in Georgia in the course of a kidnapping that started in Alabama and provided the grounding for a felony-murder charge in that state).

Successive municipal and state prosecutions, as in *Waller v. Fla.* (1970), are barred by the Double Jeopardy Clause. Waller had removed a mural from the city hall and had carried it through the streets until, after a scuffle with police, it was recovered in damaged condition. Following his conviction for violating two city ordinances (destruction of city property and disorderly breach of the peace), he was convicted of the felony of grand larceny in violation of state law. On the basis of the state court's assumptions that the felony charge was based on the "same acts" as the city ordinance violations and "that the ordinance violations were included offenses of the felony charge," the Supreme Court unanimously held that the second trial violated the double jeopardy prohibition. As the Court had concluded on a prior occasion, cities are not sovereign entities but rather "have been traditionally regarded as subordinate governmental instrumentalities created by the State to assist in the carrying out of state governmental functions." This meant, the Court concluded in *Waller*, that "the judicial power to try petitioner * * * in municipal court springs from the same organic law that created the state court of general jurisdiction," and thus the "dual sovereignty" doctrine has no application here.

*

Chapter 18

SENTENCING PROCEDURES

Table of Sections

For additional analysis of the above topics and citations to authorities supporting their discussion in this Book, consult the authors' 7-volume *Criminal Procedure* treatise, also available as Westlaw database CRIMPROC. See the Table of Cross-References in this Book.

---

§ 18.1   Legislative Structuring of Sentencing: Sanctions

(a) Structure and Procedure. Sentencing procedure often varies with the type of sanction under consideration. Concerns about procedural rights are heightened where the sentence involves incarceration rather than a fine or community release, and are most prominent when the penalty is death. The allocation of responsibility for determining the individual sentence also tends to shape sentencing procedure. Where that sentencing responsibility rests with the jury, sentencing procedures are most likely to resemble the rules applied at trial. Where the sentencing decision is allocated to an administrative agency (as in parole), the process is likely to be somewhat less formal than where it is allocated to a judge. Variations in the allocation of sentencing authority are discussed in § 18.2.

The degree of discretion granted to the sentencer also bears upon procedure. Where a sentence follows automatically from the establishment of a particular fact there is a tendency to look to a trial-type hearing to determine that fact. Where the range of discretion is broad and allows the judge to weigh a multitude of factors, with no single factor critical in itself, the tendency is to use a more informal process. For much of the twentieth century, the degree of discretion allocated to the judge in state sentencing systems was fairly uniform. The rehabilitative philosophy had taken hold in legislatures and courts, and by the 1970s each state followed an indeterminate sentencing scheme that offered the judge and the paroling authorities broad ranges within which to choose an appropriate sentence for individual offenders. During the past thirty years that uniformity has disappeared. Concerns about treating like cases alike, ensuring stiff penalties for certain crimes or criminals perceived to be particularly dangerous to society, and controlling corrections costs have led many legislatures to abolish parole and to impose significant constraints on judicial discretion. At the same time alternatives to incarceration have multiplied, as have the opportunities for victims to participate in the sentencing process. The fifty-two jurisdictions now follow a patchwork of approaches. Although each state is bound to comply with the Constitution's guarantees for the sentencing process, the Court has interpreted these requirements to be quite minimal, except in the context of capital sentencing. This hands-off approach to the constitutional regulation of sentencing has permitted legislatures to pursue diverse sentencing philosophies and experiment with innovative sanctions and procedures.

(b) Capital Punishment. Capital punishment is authorized by statute in all but twelve states. The death penalty has long been the subject of intense debate in the United States. Less than ten years after the Supreme Court held that the Eighth Amendment's prohibition against cruel and unusual punishment applied to the states, litigation challenging the constitutionality of capital punishment culminated in the decision *Furman v. Ga.* (1972). There, a sharply divided Court held that the death penalty was so arbitrarily and randomly imposed that it violated the Eighth Amendment. Each of the justices in the majority wrote a separate opinion and no single analysis prevailed, but the positioning of the justices left open the possibility that capital punishment could be upheld if properly structured in its application. In several cases decided in 1976, the Court upheld the post-*Furman* death sentencing provisions of three states and struck down two others, sketching an outline of the constitutional requirements for imposing the sentence of death. These cases, particularly *Gregg v. Ga.* (1976), and *Woodson v. N.C.* (1976), have guided the Court's regulation of capital punishment ever since.

In addition to the Court's close regulation of death sentencing procedure under the Constitution, special statutory requirements apply to the capital sentencing portion of the trial and to subsequent judicial review of the death sentence determination. Many contemporary capital punishment statutes build upon the basic structure of the statute upheld in *Gregg*. The Georgia statute provided: (1) capital sentencing authority rested initially with the jury; (2) a bifurcated proceeding, with the jury first determining guilt before hearing evidence on whether to recommend a death sentence; (3) specified aggravating circumstances, one of which the jury had to find was established beyond a reasonable doubt before it could consider imposing the death penalty; (4) jury consideration of mitigating circumstances, but no requirement that the jury agree to any existed in order to reject the death sentence; and (v) automatic appellate review of the sentence. The Court has upheld several variations on this pattern, including statutes that allow the judge, rather than the jury, the ultimate death-determination authority, statutes that require a sentencer to weigh aggravating circumstances.

Consistency is one of the two major concerns that have shaped the Court's death penalty jurisprudence. The Court's insistence on clear, objective standards for defining the class of offenders who are eligible for the death penalty addresses that concern. In *Woodson*, and later in *Lockett v. Ohio* (1978), the Court articulated a second goal. On the same day that it upheld Georgia's guided discretion approach to capital punishment in *Gregg,* the Court in *Woodson* struck down a North Carolina statute that mandated the sentence of death for first degree murder. Several states had enacted mandatory death penalty legislation after *Furman*, in response to the Court's condemnation in that case of the arbitrary and discriminatory application of more discretionary schemes. *Woodson* rejected this response. The Eighth Amendment, the Court declared, requires "the particularized consideration" of the offense and offender. In *Lockett*, the Court held that the Eighth Amendment requires that the sentencer must "not be precluded from considering as a mitigating factor, any aspect of a defendant's character or record and any of the circumstances of the offense that the defendant proffers as a basis for a sentence less than death." The tension between these two goals—one preserving discretion, the other limiting its exercise—permeates all sentencing procedure. Yet in capital cases, some justices have found intolerable the simultaneous pursuit of consistency and flexibility. Justice Scalia has advocated abandoning the *Woodson-Lockett* principle of individualized sentencing, while Justice Blackmun concluded that death sentencing can never be constitutional due to the difficulty of accommodating both concerns satisfactorily. At present, however, the two principles continue to find expression in the Court's death penalty decisions.

Capital sentencing hearings are subject to various trial-type restrictions designed to advance these aims, including restrictions on the evidence that can be introduced to prove mitigating and aggravating factors, and limitations on the judge's charge to the jury. Statutes and rules regarding the disclosure of evidence considered in capital sentencing may be more generous to the defense than in non-capital cases. Jury procedures in capital cases also differ from those at other trials. Common variations include the provision of additional peremptory challenges, the careful screening during voir dire for jurors capable of exercising discretion to recommend either life or death, and the mandatory sequestration of the jury during trial or deliberations.

In addition to regulating the procedures for death sentencing, the Court has narrowed the categories of offenders and offenses subject to capital punishment under the Eighth Amendment. Death is a disproportionate punishment for rape and for felony murder when the defendant was not himself a major participant in the killing. The Eighth Amendment also bars the execution of a prisoner who is insane, mentally retarded, or who was less than 18 years old at the time of the crime.

(c) Incarceration. The sanction of incarceration is a legislatively authorized punishment for nearly all offenses except a limited class of misdemeanors. Legislation authorizing incarceration provides the range of allowable incarceration for each offense, specifies whether sentences will be indeterminate (parole eligible) or determinate (no parole available), and often prescribes alternative sentences or sentence enhancements for some offenses or offenders.

The indeterminate sentence sets a maximum and minimum term of incarceration and leaves to the parole board the task of determining the precise date at which the release will actually occur. By 1975, this was the sentencing practice in every state. The primary rationale for the indeterminate sentence was that it permitted the actual term of imprisonment to fit the rehabilitative progress of an offender as it developed during his incarceration, and encouraged inmates to reform. Moreover, because a parolee continued to be subject to supervision for the remainder of his maximum term, and could be returned to prison if he violated his parole conditions, indeterminate sentencing was designed to facilitate the gradual reintegration of the inmate into society. Since the 1960s, critics of indeterminate sentencing have charged that prison programs fail to promote rehabilitation, have questioned the capacity of parole boards to predict future behavior, and have condemned the sentencing disparities that flow from the broad discretion delegated to parole authorities. As a result, Congress and a significant number of state legislatures have discarded indeterminate sentences and moved to determinate sentences—fixed terms set by the court with no allowance for discretionary early release on parole. Other states have adopted parole guidelines to reduce disparities in release practices.

The determinate sentence sets a definite term of incarceration, within the statutory maximum term, which the offender must serve. Determinate sentences have always been the norm for misdemeanors (one year or less). Although there is no parole release prior to the end of the term set by the court, "good time" provisions can result in release before the full term is served in both determinate and indeterminate jurisdictions. For most felonies, jurisdictions using determinate sentences impose an automatic period of supervision after a felon serves his term that operates in much the same way as parole supervision.

(d) Community Release. An outgrowth of the rehabilitative model of sentencing that dominated sentencing practices for the first half of the twentieth century, the supervised release of adult offenders was approved in all states by 1967. The majority of states deny probation for habitual offenders, and for serious offenses such as murder, kidnapping, sexual assault, and those involving the use of a dangerous weapon.

In some states, the relevant legislation does not provide any guidance to the court in deciding between probation and incarceration. Other jurisdictions provide some general guidance by reference to the criteria that should be used in selecting probation. Where jurisdictions use sentencing guidelines, those guidelines commonly regulate probation as well as incarceration. The statute authorizing probation often will set the permissible length of the term of probation, list mandatory conditions of probation, include a non-exclusive list of optional conditions, and set forth a general standard governing the judge's choice of probation conditions.

(e) Intermediate Sanctions. Beginning in the early 1980s, legislatures and courts began to develop various types of sanctions that are harsher than probation, but do not involve imprisonment. Boot camp, also referred to as "shock incarceration," is a correctional program that provides military-style training and discipline to offenders who are generally young, have no prior prison experience, and who have committed non-violent crimes. Home confinement—requiring offenders to remain at their residence during specified periods of the day—is another method of diverting non-violent offenders from prison. Home confinement costs less than incarceration, and allows a court to tailor the confinement period and restrictions to meet the particular needs of the offender while minimizing the threat to public safety. Correctional officers enforce compliance with restrictions through telephone calls and unannounced visits to the offender's residence or through electronic monitoring. A number of states combine probation with participation in day reporting programs as a means of increasing the surveillance of probationers and imposing upon them a more structured daily routine. Most day reporting centers offer drug treatment and education, group counseling, job-seeking training, and job placement services, and require participants to adhere to a stringent schedule including community service, routine and random drug tests, and frequent contacts with the program authorities. Another type of intermediate sanction, intensive supervision probation (ISP), includes numerous contacts with a probation officer, increased random drug testing, stricter enforcement of probation conditions, required community service, and some form of house arrest, usually evening curfews. Finally, an order to perform community service is a commonly imposed sanction, either combined with other types of sentences or included as a special condition of probation.

(f) Financial Sanctions. All jurisdictions provide for the use of fines in misdemeanor cases, and often allow the fine to be the only sanction for some misdemeanors. Fines are also authorized for many felonies and are the primary sanction for corporate defendants. Despite its widespread use, the fine is not considered as serious a penalty as incarceration for individual offenders, and is usually imposed in addition to a term of incarceration in felony cases. Where a fine is an authorized sanction, the legislature typically sets an upper limit and allows the court complete discretion to set the fine at any point up to that maximum. In most instances, the upper limit is a set dollar figure. Alternatively, the maximum fine may be stated as a multiplier of the financial gain achieved by the offender or the financial loss to the victim, or as a per diem penalty.

Before imposing a fine, a court should make findings regarding the defendant's ability to pay monetary sanctions. In *Bearden v. Ga.* (1983), the Court concluded: "If [a] probationer could not pay despite sufficient bona fide efforts to acquire the resources to do so, the court must consider alternative measures of punishment other than imprisonment. Only if alternate measures are not adequate to meet the State's interest in punishment and deterrence may the court imprison a probationer who has made sufficient bona fide efforts to pay." The Court concluded that "to do otherwise would deprive the probationer of his conditional freedom simply because through no fault of his own, he cannot pay the fine. Such a deprivation would be contrary to the fundamental fairness required by the Fourteenth Amendment."

A variety of other financial restrictions may be included in a sentence. The most common of these is restitution. Restitution may be ordered pursuant to the sentencing court's general authority to impose relevant conditions of probation or pursuant to a statutory authorization to direct any convicted defendant to pay restitution without regard to whether he is placed on probation. Before restitution may be imposed, the court must identify the "victim" entitled to restitution. This is an easy enough task where the crime inflicted immediate harm upon a particular individual, but it becomes more complicated where the offense relates to the interests of the public in general, as do many regulatory offenses. Restitution statutes generally define the "victim" as someone who has suffered actual property or pecuniary loss as a direct result of the defendant's criminal conduct, excluding those who took part in the crime. The loss that can be considered in measuring the amount of restitution is limited to "ascertainable" loss, proven by the prosecution.

A second financial directive that has gained prominence in recent years is the forfeiture order. Criminal forfeiture is a form of punishment which authorizes the government to seize certain assets of the defendant. Modern criminal forfeiture is of relatively recent origin. The Framers prohibited the English practice of "forfeiture of estate," a criminal penalty that deprived a convicted felon of the ability to transfer any of his property at death. Thereafter, criminal forfeiture disappeared almost entirely from American law until 1970 when Congress provided for the criminal forfeiture of certain specified assets as a penalty for violating RICO. Subsequently, Congress and many state legislatures have authorized criminal forfeiture as a punishment for drug offenses and various other crimes. The scope of assets subject to forfeiture is limited by statute to that property possessing a prescribed relationship with the criminal activity. Common categories of forfeitable assets include "proceeds" of the underlying criminal activity and property used to "facilitate" that activity. Some statutes permit the forfeiture of "substitute assets" of the defendant if the designated property is no longer available. Forfeiture statutes generally mandate special procedures for determining which assets are subject to forfeiture. These procedures, including notice and jury trial, tend to be more protective of the defendant's interests than those followed in typical sentencing. Yet the Supreme Court explained in *Libretti v. U.S.* (1995), that the legislature's choice to provide heightened safeguards does not alter forfeiture from a punishment into a separate, substantive crime.

§ 18.2   Legislative Structuring of Sentencing: The Allocation of Sentencing Authority

(a) Judicial Sentencing. The legislature determines not only what sanctions will be allowed and what the parameters of those sanctions will be, but also which actor will be responsible for deciding what sentence should be imposed in the individual case. The legislature's primary choice here is the trial judge. In almost every jurisdiction, the jury will have a sentencing role with respect to at least one kind of sanction and an executive agency will have a role in determining the length of terms of incarceration.

(b) Jury Sentencing. The Supreme Court has repeatedly held that there is no sixth amendment right to jury sentencing, even in capital cases, and even when the sentence within the statutory range turns on specific findings of fact. Nevertheless jury sentencing is an established feature in the processing of at least some criminal cases in most jurisdictions. Jury sentencing is most common in capital cases where it is the norm. A substantial number of jurisdictions permit the jury to determine the sentence in at least some non-capital cases as well. Many use jury sentencing only for "special offender" sentencing (e.g., recidivist) or for special sanctions (e.g., criminal forfeitures) where the sentence is conditioned upon the determination of particular historical facts. Six states, however, provide for jury sentencing in many, if not all, felony cases. Even though a state provides for jury sentencing in felony cases, the jury is likely not to be the most frequent sentencer. The jury's authority to sentence commonly is limited to cases in which the defendant goes to trial before a jury. The jury's function in a jury sentencing system is to set the terms of an sentence of incarceration, staying within the maximum and minimum limits set by the legislature. Where probation is an allowable alternative sentence for the particular offense, its imposition may be reserved to the judge, who is given the power to set aside the jury's sentence and substitute the alternative of probation or even a suspended sentence.

Jury sentencing may involve either a unitary or bifurcated trial of the guilt and sentencing issues. The Supreme Court upheld the constitutionality of the unitary trial in *Spencer v. Tex.* (1967), and *McGautha v. Cal.* (1971). The three cases consolidated in *Spencer* each involved the jury's consideration, before conviction, of prior-offense evidence relevant to sentencing but not to guilt. The Court noted that the single-stage procedure was of "longstanding and widespread use," and reflected a state's judgment as to the "best" procedure based upon "a wide variety of criteria," and concluded that the two-stage jury trial was not compelled by the Fourteenth Amendment. In *McGautha*, the Court rejected the claim by a capital defendant that the single-stage trial denied him the right to present evidence on the issue of sentence when he exercised his self-incrimination privilege not to testify on the issue of guilt. The Court concluded that "the policies of the privilege against compelled self-incrimination are not offended when a defendant in a capital case yields to the pressure to testify on the issue of punishment at the risk of damaging his case on guilt," nor must a state allow a defendant to speak to the jury at sentencing "free from any adverse consequences on the issue of guilt."

Finally, in *Marshall v. Lonberger* (1983), the Court upheld the murder conviction of a defendant whose jury had specifically determined during the guilt phase that he had been convicted before, an aggravating factor relevant to sentencing alone. Affirming the rule in *Spencer*, the majority rejected the argument of the four dissenters that the Constitution prohibits a "one-stage enhancement procedure." The Court concluded that the failure to completely segregate the guilt and penalty phases did not deprive a capital defendant of any constitutional right. In non-capital contexts where the jury may determine sentencing facts such as the defendant's habitual offender status, the forfeitability of assets, or the existence of a fact triggering a sentence enhancement, lower courts continue to hold that bifurcation is not constitutionally required.

(c) **Administrative Agency Decisions.** In jurisdictions that use indeterminate sentences of incarceration, the parole board plays an important role in determining the actual term of imprisonment. With rehabilitation as the dominant sentencing objective, some jurisdictions adopting indeterminate sentencing initially went so far as to give the parole board exclusive authority over the actual term of incarceration within the maximum term set by statute. Today, the period over which parole may be granted is more restricted. In several jurisdictions, parole boards have fashioned comprehensive guidelines, using a point allocation system to measure such basic factors as the seriousness of the defendant's criminal behavior, the probability of his recidivism, and his institutional behavior. Other states have adopted legislation setting forth general criteria for release on parole to ensure that dangerous offenders will not be released.

Occasionally, a statute will be worded so that the inmate is entitled to be released if certain criteria are met. The Supreme Court dealt with such a statute in *Greenholtz v. Inmates of Nebraska Penal & Correctional Complex* (1979), and concluded the result of that statutory structure was to vest in the inmate a due process right to limited procedural protections before release could be denied or delayed. Although "the presence of a parole system by itself does not give rise to a constitutionally protected liberty interest in parole release," the Nebraska statute did create "a protectable expectation of parole" by stating that the parole board "shall order [the inmate's] release unless it is of the opinion" that any of four conditions existed. While those conditions involved judgments that were necessarily "subjective in part and predictive in part," the mandatory structure of the provision nonetheless served to "bind" the parole board and thereby created an "expectancy of release * * * [requiring] some measure of constitutional protection." In *Board of Pardons v. Allen* (1987), the Court held that a Montana parole statute also created an expectation of parole that entitled an inmate to due process protections.

The Court retreated from this analysis in *Sandin v. Conner* (1995). In *Sandin*, the Court rejected the claim of a prisoner facing loss of the opportunity to earn good time, not parole, that he should have the right to present witnesses at his disciplinary hearing. The criticized the "methodology" used to identify such an interest that was first "foreshadowed" in *Greenholtz* and then adopted in later cases. This analysis, based on the creation of expectations, shifted the focus of the liberty interest inquiry from the "nature of the deprivation" to the "language of a particular regulation," encouraging prisoners to "comb regulations in search of mandatory language on which to base entitlements to various state conferred privileges," creating "disincentives for States to codify prison management procedures in the interest of uniform treatment," and leading to "the involvement of federal courts in the day-to-day management of prisons, often squandering judicial resources with little offsetting benefit to anyone."

The Court in *Sandin* offered a different test—those liberty interests that are protected by due process will be "generally limited to freedom from restraint which * * * imposes atypical and significant hardship on the inmate in relation to the ordinary incidents of prison life." As for the effect of its ruling on *Greenholtz* and *Allen,* the *Sandin* Court noted that its decision did not "technically require us to overrule any holding of this Court." By requiring unique hardship in order to trigger due process safeguards, however, *Sandin*'s rationale could exclude routine parole release decisions from the sphere of decisions protected by due process. On the other hand, the Court in *Sandin* distinguished the determination at issue in that case (risking lost opportunity to earn good time) from determinations that inevitably affect the duration of an inmate's sentence. The Court in *Sandin* also referred favorably to *Wolff v. McDonnell* (1974), a case which had required at least minimal procedural protections in the context of proceedings affecting already earned good time, even though the revocation of good-time credit is not an atypical hardship.

Greenholtz and *Wolff* continue to guide lower courts on the separate issue of what procedural safeguards due process requires in parole proceedings where a protectable interest is present. *Greenholtz* held that due process did not mandate a formal hearing in all cases. It was sufficient that the "Nebraska procedure affords an opportunity to be heard, and when parole is denied it informs the inmate in what respects he falls short of qualifying for parole." States commonly provide to potential parolees informal hearings or "interviews" conducted by a hearing officer or a board member. The prisoner usually will be informed of the general nature of the information in his file, or have access to that file, and will be given the opportunity to offer corrections or otherwise state his case for parole. In many jurisdictions, an inmate is entitled to a more formal hearing where he may be represented by counsel retain his own witnesses, and be present during witness testimony.

Parole boards also are assigned the responsibility of determining whether parole, once granted, should be revoked due to a violation of a parole condition. The Supreme Court in a series of cases beginning with *Morrissey v. Brewer* (1972) has set forth the due process prerequisites applicable to the revocation of parole and probation. These start with a prompt preliminary hearing following the parolee's arrest to determine whether there is probable cause to believe he has violated the parole condition (unless that is established per se by his conviction on a criminal charge). That hearing is later followed by an adversarial, trial-type hearing, with counsel appointed under some circumstances. Explaining why due process required so much more in a parole revocation proceeding, the Court in *Greenholtz* noted:

> There is a crucial distinction between being deprived of a liberty one has, as in parole, and being denied a conditional liberty that one desires. * * * [T]he parole-revocation determination actually requires two decisions: whether the parolee in fact acted in violation of one or more conditions of parole and whether the parolee should be recommitted either for his or society's benefit. "The first step in a revocation decision thus involves a wholly retrospective factual question." The parole-release decision, however, is more subtle and depends on an amalgam of elements, some of which are factual but many of which are purely subjective appraisals by the Board members.

Regardless of the availability of parole, executive agencies may reduce sentences through "good-time" credit. The executive department in charge of prisons usually has the responsibility for calculating the good-time credit, which involves applying a statutory formula to calculate the amount of credit, and determining whether the inmate's behavior qualifies him for such credit. Credit usually is calculated as a percentage of the time served or according to the "class" achieved by the prisoner. Prisoners in some states may eventually receive more than two days credit for each day served. Good time is lost by a violation of prison rules. The process due a defendant in this context is greater than that due an inmate applying for parole but less than what is required in order to revoke parole or probation.

In all jurisdictions an offender may also receive relief from a sentence through reprieve, remission, commutation, or pardon. Taken together, these devices are often described as "executive clemency." A reprieve merely delays the execution of a sentence. Remission relieves the offender of the responsibility of paying a fine or forfeiting property. Commutation reduces a term of imprisonment. The pardon absolves the defendant of guilt and thereby eliminates the basis for imposing any punishment. Clemency power in most states is shared between the governor and an administrative board or advisory group. A minority of states allow either the governor or the board the sole authority to make clemency decisions.

The discretion to grant or deny clemency is nearly absolute. The Supreme Court in *Connecticut Board of Pardons v. Dumschat* (1981), held that a prisoner has no liberty interest protected by due process in a commutation, even where seventy-five percent of the prisoners in his situation had received commutations upon application. Commutation or pardon is, the Court concluded, "simply a unilateral hope." As a result, the prisoner was not entitled to any particular procedural safeguards in the clemency process. The Court revisited the issue in *Ohio Adult Parole Authority v. Woodard* (1998). A death row prisoner seeking commutation of his sentence, the Court held, is entitled to some minimal procedural safeguards. The process provided the prisoner in *Woodard,* however, met this standard. Woodard had received notice that he was entitled to an opportunity to participate in a prehearing interview with parole board members (without counsel) three days before the interview. Participation in the clemency hearing itself by either Woodard or his counsel was permitted only at the discretion of the parole board chair.

§ 18.3   The Guidance of Judicial Discretion

(a) **Unguided Discretion.** The discretion of the sentencing judge to set a sentence within statutory maximum and minimum ranges has, until quite recently, been granted without further legislative guidance. Reluctance to provide additional statutory guidance for the court's exercise of sentencing discretion is often attributed to the need to individualize sentences so that the sentence best achieves the rehabilitation of each offender. The individualization of punishment, and the judicial discretion that makes that tailoring possible has also found support in the other goals of punishment. Deterrence, incapacitation, and even retribution may require that a judge draw distinctions between offenders who commit the same crime. Because the legislature can hardly take into consideration all of the factors that distinguish one particular offense and offender from another, a certain amount of individualization (and hence discretion) traditionally has been afforded to the judge.

(b) **The Challenge to Unguided Discretion.** This tradition of unguided judicial discretion produced variations in sentences that appeared to lack any reasonable basis. Sentences differed from locality to locality, and from judge to judge. For many years, such disparities were accepted as a necessary cost of individualization, although some trial courts experimented with procedures that sought through the exchange of views to produce greater consistency among judges. By the 1970s, a combination of factors, including concern about the potential for racial and class bias in sentencing, resulted in concerted efforts nationwide to "do something" about discretionary sentencing and the disparities it produced. Four approaches for controlling judicial discretion, each examined below, eventually gained widespread support: (1) more frequent use of mandatory minimum sentences tied to the existence of particular facts, (2) presumptive sentencing setting out specific presumed sentence levels for each offense, (3) sentence guidelines, and (4) appellate review to enforce these and other limits on judicial discretion in sentencing.

Limiting judicial discretion in sentencing cannot, of course, fully eliminate disparity in the penalties that offenders may receive. The executive, through law enforcement, charging, bargaining, parole, and clemency, retains significant, often unreviewable, power to select which offenders will be subjected to legislatively authorized penalties, as well as the amount of punishment imposed. Jurors also retain the ability to protect an offender from the penalty designated by statute in the very small percentage of cases that go to trial before a jury. As legislatures remove from judges the discretion to differentiate between offenses and offenders, the discretion of prosecutors and juries takes on added significance. It is therefore not surprising that the adoption of these limits on judicial discretion in sentencing has coincided with renewed concern among academics, judges, and legislators, about the abuse of discretion by prosecutors and juries.

(c) Mandatory Minimum and Recidivist Sentences. The mandatory minimum sentence is a form of determinate sentencing designed to control the discretion of judges and parole boards and advance the goals of deterrence and incapacitation. These statutes mandate minimum terms of imprisonment for any offender who commits a particular offense, or impose mandatory sentence enhancements for offenders who commit offenses under certain conditions. By 1994, congress and all fifty states had enacted one or more mandatory sentencing laws.

The crimes selected for mandatory minimums often have been simply those that happened to capture the public eye at a particular moment. In addition, prosecutors for the most part have remained free to circumvent mandatory minimums through charging and charge bargaining decisions. The effects of the increased application of mandatory sentences have been widely criticized as " 'imprudent, unwise, and often an unjust mechanism for sentencing.' " The proliferation of mandatory sentence enhancements has increased the significance of fact-finding at sentencing, prompting calls for procedural safeguards greater than those commonly employed in traditional discretionary sentencing. The Court has declined, however, to interpret the Constitution to require such safeguards.

Most states have enacted provisions that authorize extended terms for repeat offenders, variously labeled as "recidivists," "second offenders," "persistent violators," and "habitual criminals." In recent years, a growing number of states and the federal government have adopted "three-strikes-and-you're-out" legislation that imposes a mandatory sentence on repeat offenders. A handful of these statutes mandate a life sentence upon the third felony regardless of the classification of the prior felonies, while others require that the prior felonies involve violence, narcotics, or the use of a firearm. A small number of states have adopted two-strikes provisions for particularly serious felonies while others have adopted four-strikes provisions.

Many jurisdictions treat a defendant's prior record just like any other sentencing fact, following the theory that repeat-offender status merely enhances the sentence for the defendant's current crime and is not a separate offense. In *Almendarez-Torres v. U.S.* (1998), the Court rejected, on historical grounds, the defendant's claim that the existence of the prior conviction was an "element" that should have been charged in the indictment. The case involved a statutory provision extending to twenty years the maximum two-year penalty for unauthorized reentry into the United States, upon a finding that the initial decision to deport the defendant "was subsequent to a conviction for commission of an aggravated felony." Withholding notice of intent to seek penalties under a recidivist statute until after conviction had also been upheld by the Supreme Court in *Oyler v. Boles* (1962). Earlier cases also established that due process did not require that a jury determine the existence of a prior conviction, or that a prior conviction be proven beyond a reasonable doubt. Instead, a judicial determination of the prior offense by a preponderance of the evidence was sufficient. In light of the effect of these statutes in extending the defendant's term beyond the maximum allowed for the offense of conviction, a substantial number of jurisdictions impose more formal procedures for determining repeat-offender status including pretrial notice of intent to seek recidivist penalties, a bifurcated jury proceeding and proof of the prior conviction beyond a reasonable doubt.

(d) Presumptive Sentencing. Several states have adopted presumptive sentencing systems (sometimes termed "statutory determinate sentencing"), under which the legislature initially sets a "presumptive" term of incarceration for each offense or class of offenses within the statutory maximum term for that offense or class of offenses. That presumptive term is stated as a range of years or as a set number of years. The judge cannot set an offender's sentence lower or higher than the specified term unless mitigating or aggravating factors justify a departure. The permissible range for departures is also set by the legislature, and in some jurisdictions, relevant aggravating and mitigating circumstances are specified by the legislature, such as the use of a weapon, the vulnerability of the victim, passive participation, or, a mental condition that significantly reduces culpability. The presumptive sentencing structure substantially narrows judicial discretion by requiring specific findings that justify departures from the presumptive sentence. The Court's decision in *Cunningham v. Cal.* (2007) held that a defendant has the right to a jury finding beyond a reasonable doubt for any fact necessary for punishment exceeding the presumptive sentence.

(e) Sentencing Guidelines. In a guidelines system the presumptive sentences are set by a legislatively created sentencing commission or by the highest court, rather than by the legislature itself. Well over a dozen states and the federal government have adopted sentencing guidelines.

The presumed sentence in a guidelines system is determined through the use of a sentencing table or grid that designates the presumed sentence for the particular case. On one axis of the grid is a ranking of the criminal history of the offender by reference to past convictions. The other axis ranks the severity of the crime by reference to such factors as the harm caused, the range of the criminal activity, and the role of the offender. The severity scale utilizes a point system that starts with a certain number for the basic offense and then adds and subtracts points for specified factors. The presumptive sentence ranges tend to be fairly narrow. Presumed ranges at certain low levels will include probation as an alternative. Departure is generally permitted from the recommended guidelines range. In a mandatory guidelines system, aggravating or mitigating facts must be present before a sentence outside the presumptive range will be permitted. A fact required for an upward departure will be treated like an element of a greater offense, and must be either admitted by the defendant, or found by jury beyond a reasonable doubt before a judge may impose a sentence above the range. *Blakely v. Wash.* (2004). An advisory guidelines system does not condition the judge's ability to sentence outside the recommended range upon the finding of an aggravating factor.

Fact-finding is particularly important in guidelines sentencing. Unlike a presumptive sentencing structure that requires findings as to certain circumstances only where there is a departure from the presumed sentence, sentencing guidelines require that a series of findings be made in every case. The guidelines system accordingly requires a sentencing process that affords each side an opportunity both to submit its own information relating to the guideline factors and to challenge information before the court that is contrary to its position. The process must also provide for a fair resolution by the sentencing judge of disputes as to the presence or proper interpretation of those factors, and a record sufficient for appellate review. Compared to the federal guidelines, state sentencing guidelines systems grant more judicial discretion and involve fewer sentencing factors. Many incorporate intermediate, non-confinement penalties and tend to recommend less severe sentences than the federal guidelines. Indeed, the popularity of sentencing guidelines in the states is due in part to their success in limiting prison growth and accompanying costs.

(f) Concurrent and Consecutive Sentences. When a defendant is subject to more than one sentence, judges in most jurisdictions retain the discretion to determine whether those sentences must be served consecutively or concurrently. This choice can arise when a defendant is convicted of multiple offenses at the same trial, or is convicted while subject to a sentence for a prior offense in the same or another jurisdiction. As discussed in § 9.4, the Double Jeopardy Clause prohibits the imposition of consecutive sentences for the "same offence," and, a court may be precluded under state law from imposing consecutive sentences otherwise permissible under the Constitution.

These constraints leave considerable room for judges to "stack" sentences or run them simultaneously, discretion that could undercut legislative efforts to regularize sentence length, by allowing grossly disparate total terms of incarceration for similarly situated offenders. To guard against this sort of disparity, statutes in every jurisdiction further limit judicial discretion by establishing a presumption of either consecutive or concurrent sentences, mandating consecutive sentences for specified offense combinations, or specifying conditions under which concurrent or consecutive sentences may be imposed. The statutory guidance given judges as to what circumstances would rebut a statutory presumption varies, sometimes including checklists of factors that must be found or weighed. Sentences for crimes committed while incarcerated or on parole or probation, violations of habitual offender provisions, and firearm offenses usually must run consecutive to other sentences.

(g) Appellate Review. The traditional position in this country, as stated by the Supreme Court in *Dorszynski v. U.S.* (1974), has been that "once it is determined that a sentence is within the limits set forth in the statute under which it is imposed, appellate review is at an end." This position of no substantive review of sentences may have been a practical accommodation of the absence of any requirement that trial judges record the reasons for their sentences and the lack of standards an appellate court could invoke to determine whether a particular sentence was excessive in length or otherwise inappropriate. The constitutionality of sentencing *procedure* could be challenged by the defendant, as well as sentencing "authority" as defined by law. On occasion, even in a jurisdiction professing no substantive review, an appellate court might strike down a sentence within the statutory limits because it was so excessive as to "shock" the court.

Several states retain this very limited review of sentencing. With the advent of presumptive sentencing and sentencing guidelines, however, the landscape of appellate sentencing review in many jurisdictions has been altered dramatically. In the case of presumptive sentencing, review is likely to be focused on departures, because here the court will have a statement of grounds justifying the sentence. Under guideline sentencing, the criteria and the statement of reasons will exist for sentences within the guidelines as well as for departures, making review possible in all cases. In the federal system, sentencing procedure will be reviewed, as will factual assessments. An federal appellate court conducting "reasonableness review" of a federal sentence itself "asks whether the trial court abused its discretion," explained the Court in *Rita v. U.S.* (2007).

Allowing the government (as opposed to the defendant) to appeal a sentence was highly controversial when traditional sentencing was reviewed by only a limited "abuse" standard. With presumptive and guideline sentencing now presenting clear issues of legal interpretation as well as specific factual findings, and the Supreme Court having upheld the constitutionality appellate review of sentencing, prosecution appeals are now widely accepted.

§ 18.4 Due Process: The Framework for Sentencing Procedure

(a) *Williams v. New York.* Although decided over a half-century ago, *Williams v. N.Y.* (1949), remains the leading ruling on the content of due process as it applies to procedures in traditional discretionary sentencing. Commentators have steadily predicted that the "revolution" that transformed much of constitutional criminal procedure after *Williams* will reach sentencing as well, and that the recent developments in sentencing should render *Williams* and its reasoning obsolete. So far, such predictions have not been realized. The Supreme Court continues to cite with approval the principles expressed in Justice Black's opinion for the Court in *Williams*. Compared to the Court's fundamental refashioning of constitutional requirements for other phases of the criminal prosecution, its more conservative application of due process in sentencing appears almost frozen in time, even as sentencing itself has been transfigured by legislative reform.

Williams itself was a capital case decided at a time when the process of capital sentencing was similar to the sentencing procedure typically followed in non-capital cases decades ago. Williams had been sentenced to death by the trial judge, notwithstanding the jury's recommendation of a life sentence. In the trial court, a presentence investigation report had been compiled by the probation department following conviction and presented to the judge, apparently without disclosure to the defense. The judge had then held a brief sentencing hearing at which first the defendant and then his counsel had been allowed to address the issue of whether the judge should follow the jury's recommendation. The judge then explained why he felt the death sentence should be imposed. He pointed both to the "shocking details of the crime as shown by the trial evidence" and to information contained in the presentence report. The judge noted that the presentence investigation "had revealed many material facts concerning the appellant's background which though relevant to the question of punishment could not properly have been brought to the attention of the jury." Referring specifically to the defendant's alleged involvement in 30 other burglaries in the vicinity, he noted that although the defendant had not been convicted of those crimes, he "had information that [defendant] had confessed to some and had been identified as the perpetrator of others." The judge also referred to the report's indication that defendant possessed a "morbid sexuality" and was a "menace to society." The accuracy of the statements made by the judge as to appellant's background and past practices were not challenged by appellant, nor was the judge asked to afford appellant a chance discredit any of them by cross-examination or otherwise.

The question before the Court related to the rules of evidence applicable to the manner in which a judge may obtain information to guide him in the imposition of sentence. The defendant had challenged the judge's consideration of information about his past life and moral propensities as contrary to basic due process principles ensuring that an accused be given "reasonable notice" and be afforded "an opportunity to examine adverse witnesses." Rejecting this broad challenge, the Court noted the "wide discretion in the sources and types of evidence" granted to sentencing judges since the founding. Unlike the determinations at trial, sentencing demanded the possession of "the fullest information possible concerning the defendant's life and characteristics." This was especially true under the "modern philosophy of penology that the punishment should fit the offender and not merely the crime."

To deprive sentencing judges of the kind of individualized information contained in presentence reports would undermine modern penological procedural policies, the Court reasoned. It warned, "most of the information now relied upon by judges to guide them in the intelligent imposition of sentences would be unavailable if information were restricted to that given in open court by witnesses subject to cross-examination. * * * Such a procedure could endlessly delay criminal administration in a retrial of collateral issues."

Williams is considered the leading ruling on at least three basic elements of due process in sentencing procedure: (1) the range of the factors that a judge may consider in imposing a sentence; (2) the right of the defendant to be informed of the factors being considered by the judge and of the evidence being advanced in support of those factors; and (3) the opportunity given to the defendant to challenge the existence and relevancy of those factors. The bearing of *Williams* upon each of these elements is considered in the subsections that follow, along with modifications or reinforcement provided by post-*Williams* rulings. The defendant's opportunity to challenge sentencing information has been broken down further into four separate aspects: (1) the right to the assistance of counsel at sentencing; (2) the right to insist that sentencing information be reliable through cross-examination, corroboration, or other means; (3) the right of the defendant to speak and to submit his own evidence at the sentencing stage; and (4) the standard of proof required for facts relevant to sentencing. The Court's due process rulings on these issues form the framework for sentencing procedure in all jurisdictions. Additional requirements are provided by statute, rule, or judicial decision.

(b) The Range of Relevant Information. *Williams* clearly upholds what is now described as "real offense" sentencing—that is, sentencing that looks beyond the statutory elements of the charged offense and considers the gravity of the defendant's actual conduct. A court does not violate due process when, in setting a sentence, it considers the unrelated criminal conduct of the defendant, even if that conduct did not result in a criminal conviction (as in the case of the burglaries cited by the judge in *Williams*).

The Court has held that recidivist statutes, which provide for specific punishment enhancement based on prior convictions, do not violate double jeopardy as the enhancement "is not to be viewed as either a new jeopardy or additional penalty for the earlier crime, but instead as a stiffened penalty for the latest crime, which is considered to be an aggravated offense because a repetitive one." *Witte v. U.S.* (1995) rejected a double jeopardy objection to prosecution and punishment for an offense that had been the basis for a sentence enhancement in a prior prosecution. And in a closely divided decision in *Monge v. Cal.* (1998), the Court explained that sentence enhancements that follow from prior convictions have not been "construed as additional punishment for the previous offense;

rather they act to increase the sentence 'because of the manner in which [the defendant] committed the crime of conviction.' "

Also relevant are aspects of the defendant's life that go beyond antisocial conduct. The Court noted the need for the sentencing judge, in evaluating the "lives and personalities of convicted offenders," to draw on information concerning "every aspect of a defendant's life." Indeed, the Court cited in this connection the federal presentence report form that directed the probation officer to gather information concerning such factors as "family history," "home and neighborhood," "education," "religion," "interests and activities," "employment," and "health (physical and mental)."

Post-*Williams* rulings have held that due process does limit or even bar consideration of a small group of factors. First, the Court has limited the consideration by the sentencing judge of the defendant's exercise of procedural rights within the criminal justice process. Those rulings are discussed in a later section, § 18.4(c). Second, as discussed in the text below, judges are also prohibited from basing their sentencing decisions upon the race or gender of the defendant or victim, or upon the defendant's exercise of fundamental rights.

McCleskey v. Kemp (1987) indicates that the race of the defendant or victim is an element that simply may not be considered, negatively or positively, in sentencing. In *McCleskey*, a case in which black defendant's had been sentenced to death for killing a white victim, the Court explained that "purposeful discrimination" in sentencing based upon the race of the victim or defendant would be unconstitutional under traditional equal protection analysis. The Court insisted that the defendant carried the burden of "proving" the existence of such purposeful discrimination by "the decision-makers in his case" and that this burden could not be met by simply showing a statistical disparity across capital sentencing decisions throughout the state. In refusing to accept the statistical disparity as sufficient even to create a rebuttable presumption of discriminatory purpose, the Court distinguished its willingness to draw an inference of intentional discrimination from statistical proof in other settings (e.g., jury and grand jury venire-selection). There, the statistics related to "fewer entities" and "fewer variables [were] relevant to the challenged decisions." Thus, while race is a factor that may not be considered, the defense is unlikely to prove purposeful discrimination absent a remark of the judge or a juror referring specifically to race.

Although the race of the victim or defendant (and, presumably, the gender of the victim or defendant) cannot be the basis for setting a sentence, evidence that the defendant selected his victim because of the victim's race can be relevant, and serve as the basis for an enhanced penalty, held the Court in *Wis. v. Mitchell* (1993). At issue was a statute that increased the maximum sentence for an offense if the defendant "intentionally selects" the victim because of the "race, religion, color, disability, sexual orientation, national origin or ancestry of that person." The Court, relying upon cases upholding federal and state antidiscrimination laws, concluded that Mitchell's first amendment rights were not violated by the application of the statute. Bias-inspired conduct, the Court explained, "is thought to inflict greater individual and societal harm. * * * The state's desire to redress * * * perceived harms provides an adequate explanation for its penalty-enhancement provision over and above mere disagreement with the offender's beliefs or biases."

The first amendment rights of the defendant may be violated, however, by the sentencer's consideration of irrelevant evidence of defendant's protected beliefs or activity. In *Dawson v. Del.* (1992), the Court explained that the First and Fourteenth Amendments prohibit the introduction in a capital sentencing proceeding of evidence concerning one's beliefs and association when it is "totally without relevance" to the sentencing proceeding. In *Dawson,* the prosecution had introduced evidence that the defendant was a member of the Aryan Brotherhood, had the name of the organization as well as swastikas tattooed on his hand, and had painted a swastika on his cell wall. The Court concluded that because the prosecution had failed to demonstrate how this evidence of the defendant's "abstract beliefs" was relevant to prove or disprove any aggravating or mitigating circumstance, the introduction of this evidence was barred by the First Amendment. Evidence of political or religious association that is relevant to future dangerousness is presumably not barred by *Dawson.*

(c) Consideration of the Defendant's Exercise of Procedural Rights. A defendant may be denied due process when the sentencing court "punishes" him for exercise of a procedural right in the criminal justice process. Thus, as discussed in § 18.7, the Court agreed that a judge could not impose a higher sentence upon a defendant in retaliation for having successfully appealed his original conviction. The sentencing court may consider other choices that a defendant may make regarding trial rights. As discussed in § 14.2, the Court has repeatedly noted in its guilty plea cases that while the sentencing court may not punish with an increased sentence the defendant who goes to trial, it may accomplish the same result by rewarding with a reduced sentence the defendant who pleads guilty.

In *U.S. v. Grayson* (1978), the Court adopted a similar analysis in holding that the trial judge could weigh against the defendant his misuse of a trial right that reflected badly upon his character, specifically, his choice to perjure himself during trial. The Court rejected the defendant's claim that the sentencing judge's action impermissibly "chilled" his constitutional right to testify in his own behalf, noting that this right "is narrowly the right to testify truthfully in accordance with the oath" and that there "is no protected right to commit perjury." The Court revisited the issue in *U.S. v. Dunnigan* (1993). There, it rejected a due process challenge to the trial judge's decision to increase defendant's sentence under the federal sentencing guidelines after finding that she had perjured herself at trial. The Court cautioned that "a district court must review the evidence and make independent findings necessary to establish" perjury, before increasing a sentence for this reason. The "willingness to frustrate judicial proceedings to avoid criminal liability suggests that the need for incapacitation and retribution is heightened as compared with the defendant charged with the same crime who allows judicial proceedings to progress without resorting to perjury."

When a defendant asserts the privilege against self incrimination at sentencing regarding a factual matter, a court is prohibited from drawing an adverse inference about that factual issue from the defendant's silence, held the Court in *Mitchell v. U.S.* (1999). In *Mitchell*, the defendant pleaded guilty to several drug offenses, reserving the right to contest drug quantity at sentencing. At the sentencing hearing, the defendant did not contradict, through her own testimony, the assertions of government witnesses about the amount of drugs involved. In explaining to the defendant why he credited the testimony of the government's witnesses, the trial judge stated, "I held it against you that you didn't come forward today and tell me that you really only did this a couple of times * * *. I'm taking the position that you should come forward and explain your side of this issue." The Court concluded that the concerns underlying the *Griffin* rule against negative inferences from assertions of the privilege at trial also mandate a ban on adverse inferences from the assertion of the self-incrimination privilege at sentencing. The majority declined, however, to express a view on whether the defendant's silence at sentencing "bears on the determination of lack of remorse, or upon acceptance of responsibility" for leniency in sentencing. By limiting its opinion to inferences about facts alone, the Court left open the possibility that a valid assertion of the privilege could be considered for some purposes (assessing the defendant's character or willingness to cooperate, for example), but not other purposes (assessing the existence of particular sentencing facts).

(d) Notice. Due process also guarantees the defendant some information concerning the reasons for his sentence. The extent of that disclosure was addressed in *Williams,* where the Court held that the sentencing judge could rely on "out-of-court information" and that "no federal constitutional objection would have been possible * * * if the judge had sentenced [defendant] to death giving no reason at all."

Today the issue of notice must be analyzed in light of the Supreme Court's ruling in *Gardner v. Fla.* (1977), and later cases interpreting *Gardner.* The trial judge in *Gardner* had sentenced the defendant to death without stating on the record the substance of information in the presentence report that he might have considered material to his decision. This was held to be unconstitutional, but there was no opinion for the Court as to why. Two justices concluded that the procedure violated the Eighth Amendment, one concluded that the state's cavalier approach to the death penalty required reassessment of the constitutionality of the underlying statute, and another concurred in the reversal without opinion. Four justices concluded that there had been a violation of due process.

Twenty years after *Gardner*, in *Gray v. Netherland* (1996), the Court clarified that the scope of the notice guaranteed by *Gardner* in capital cases does not include discovery of that information *in advance* of sentencing. The petitioner in *Gray* argued that the government violated his due process rights by failing to inform him until the night before the penalty phase that it would be presenting witness testimony concerning alleged prior offenses. Previously, the prosecutor had told defense counsel that he would limit this evidence to statements of the defendant. The Court rejected the petitioner's claim to advance notice of the prosecutor's changed strategy. It likened the claim to that of the defendant in *Weatherford v. Bursey* (1977), who had argued that due process prohibited the prosecutor from presenting at trial the surprise testimony of an undercover agent. The agent, in order to preserve his cover, had told defendant and his counsel that he would not be testifying, and the Court found due process allowed his surprise testimony. Emphasizing that "there is no general constitutional right to discovery in a criminal case," the Court in *Gray* distinguished *Gardner* as a case involving "secret" not surprise testimony, noting that "Gardner literally had no opportunity to even see the confidential information [in his presentence report], let alone contest it." No constitutional violation occurred in *Gray*, reasoned the Court, when the defendant had "the opportunity to hear the testimony of [the witnesses] in open court, and to cross-examine them."

The constitutionality of failing entirely to disclose certain sentencing information to the defense in non-capital cases remains unsettled. *Gardner*, a death penalty case, may not dictate notice standards in non-capital cases. As the Court later explained in

Lankford v. Id. (1991), where it held that a capital defendant is entitled to adequate notice that a judge might sentence him to death, the "threatened loss" in a capital case is "so severe" that "the need for notice is even more pronounced" than in non-capital cases. Significant too is the Court's statement in *O'Dell v. Netherland* (1997), that Justice White's concurring opinion in *Gardner* states the holding in that case. Justice White concurred in *Gardner* on a basis that would not in all likelihood require the same outcome in a non-capital case—that reliance upon secret information in sentencing a defendant to death violated the Eighth Amendment, not due process. On the other hand, most of the arguments that the Court rejected in *Gardner*, and most of the concerns that it expressed there regarding the subversion of reliable factfinding, apply equally to nondisclosure in non-capital sentencing under modern presumptive sentencing schemes prevalent today. Just as a death sentence must be justified by reference to statutorily identified aggravating factors and subject to appellate scrutiny, similar fact-dependent inquiries and extensive review are now integral to many modern non-capital sentencing systems.

Assuming due process might require the disclosure to the defendant of sentencing information used by a judge in non-capital cases, the appropriate analysis for assessing what due process requires has been the subject of debate. The balancing test of *Mathews v. Eldridge* (1976), a case decided by the Court a year before *Gardner,* has been advanced as one analysis for determining the extent to which notice is required by due process in the context of sentencing. Under *Mathews*, the disclosure required may vary with the type of information at issue and the circumstances of the case. This approach was adopted by three justices of the Supreme Court dissenting in *Burns v. U.S.* (1991). There, the defendant had received his presentence report, but was not told that the court was contemplating an upward departure from the guidelines range. The majority avoided addressing whether due process required such notice by concluding that such disclosure was required by Rule 32. The dissenters, however, concluded that Congress did not intend to mandate such disclosure, nor was disclosure required as a matter of due process. Examining the particular disclosure in its specific context of sentencing under the federal guidelines, the dissenting justices applied the balancing test of *Mathews* and decided that "the risk of error under the procedures already required and the probable value of a further notice requirement are sufficiently low" that failure to require advance notice of the court's intent to depart "passes constitutional muster." The very next term, in *Medina v. Cal.* (1992), a majority of justices disapproved of the use of the *Mathews* test in the criminal setting. "The Bill of Rights speaks in explicit terms to many aspects of criminal procedure, and the expansion of those constitutional guarantees under the open-ended rubric of the Due Process Clause invites undue interference with both considered legislative judgments and the careful balance that the Constitution strikes between liberty and order." Instead, a state law defining procedure in criminal cases must be tested by the "less intrusive" analysis in *Patterson v. N.Y.* (1977), which provides that such a statute is "not subject to proscription under the Due Process Clause unless it offends some principle of justice so rooted in the traditions and conscience of our people as to be ranked as fundamental."

Even while the contours of the constitutional right to notice of sentencing information remain less than clear, a defendant's statutory entitlement to review such information is well-established in most jurisdictions. Typically judges are required by statute or court rule to state the reasons for a sentence at sentencing. As discussed in § 18.5(b), presentence reports commonly are made available to defendant, providing defendants with some opportunity to review and object to factual allegations that may influence the sentence.

(e) The Right to the Assistance of Counsel. One of the most fundamental features of fair procedure in the trial setting is the right to the assistance of counsel. *Mempa v. Rhay* (1967), established that the Sixth Amendment guaranteed a defendant the assistance of counsel at his combined probation revocation and sentencing hearing. The Court noted that sentencing is a "stage of a criminal proceeding where substantial rights of a criminal accused may be affected." Subsequently, the Supreme Court has reiterated that the sixth amendment right to the effective assistance of counsel extends through the sentencing phase of a criminal prosecution.

Due process may require the provision of counsel at post-trial proceedings that fall outside the scope of the Sixth Amendment, such as parole or probation revocation proceedings. Some states have extended the scope of their state guarantees to provide defendants with counsel at sentencings which do not involve imprisonment, or at all probation revocation hearings.

Proceedings prior to sentencing, too, may be protected by the sixth amendment right to counsel. In *Estelle v. Smith* (1981), the Supreme Court held that a psychiatrist's examination of the defendant for "future dangerousness," a factual prerequisite for the sentence of death in Texas, was a "critical stage" at which the right to counsel attached. The Court held that the statements elicited from the defendant in that case could not be used in his capital sentencing hearing. Lower courts, however, have distinguished the situation in *Estelle* from other efforts to obtain sentencing information during the typical presentence interview by a probation officer, reasoning that the probation officer is a neutral party, and the non-adversarial interview is not a "critical stage" requiring the assistance of counsel. Although counsel is not required at these interviews, a jurisdiction may permit counsel's attendance.

(f) Ensuring the Reliability of Sentencing Information. The Court in *Williams* stated flatly that due process did not require that a "sentencing judge * * * be denied an opportunity to obtain pertinent information [as] a requirement of rigid adherence to restrictive rules of evidence properly applicable to the trial." In response to the defendant's claim that he was entitled to examine adverse witnesses at sentencing, the *Williams* Court explained that cross-examination would be "totally impractical if not impossible" in the sentencing context. Lower courts generally rely on *Williams* to reject defense demands for evidentiary hearings with trial-type testing of sentencing information.

Due process may require some reliability in factfinding, short of that level ensured by trial-type procedures, regarding prior convictions. In *U.S. v. Tucker* (1972), the Court held that the defendant's sentence could not stand where the judge had relied upon defendant's prior felony convictions without knowledge that those convictions were constitutionally infirm because defendant had been denied his constitutional right to appointed counsel in the proceedings that produced the convictions. The prisoner was sentenced on the basis of assumptions concerning his criminal record which were materially untrue. The Court subsequently has interpreted *Tucker* to provide relief only for those defendants who can show they were denied counsel altogether on a prior felony charge. Challenges to prior convictions based on other types of constitutional defects cannot be raised as a basis for attacking the use of those convictions in sentencing. Defendants must instead seek collateral relief from the prior convictions in state court, then, if successful, "apply for reopening of any federal sentence enhanced by the state sentences." In capital cases, a defendant's constitutional right to challenge prior convictions that are used by the government to support the penalty of death may be broader than the limited entitlement established by *Tucker*. As the Court recognized in *Johnson v. Miss.* (1988), there is "a special 'need for reliability' in the determination that death is the appropriate punishment" in capital cases.

As to other types of information considered at sentencing, due process guarantees only that a defendant not be sentenced based upon "materially untrue" assumptions and that sentencing information carry a "sufficient indicia of reliability" to support its probable accuracy. Hearsay information of the type included in presentence reports is typically allowed over constitutional objection, and the reliability of challenged statements may be established by corroborating evidence. Some courts have insisted that due process bars reliance on particular types of questionable information (e.g., the hearsay statements of an unidentified informant) unless corroborative evidence or some other factor provides a reasonable basis for assuming it is trustworthy. Many jurisdictions allow the judge to indicate that a contested matter will not be taken into account as an alternative to determining whether the fact exists.

(g) The Right to be Heard: Allocution and the Right to Offer Rebuttal Evidence. While some opportunity to object to the sentencing information relied upon by the court is generally considered part of the due process guaranteed to criminal defendants under the Constitution, that opportunity, at least in non-capital cases, does not necessarily include either the right to present evidence, or the right to make a personal unsworn statement to the sentencer, otherwise known as the right of allocution.

In capital cases the defendant must be given the opportunity to present mitigating evidence on his own behalf at sentencing. In *Gardner*, the Court found that a capital defendant had been denied this right where his counsel was given no opportunity "to challenge the accuracy or materiality" of information relied upon by the judge. The same principle was invoked in *Mempa v. Rhay* (1967), a non-capital case, where the Court explained that "counsel was necessary to assist defendant in marshaling the facts, *introducing evidence of mitigating circumstances* and * * * present[ing] his case as to sentence * * *." In addition, the Court's recognition of a due process right to present evidence in proceedings for parole and probation revocation, situations in which the defendant's liberty interests as well as the risks of error are certainly no higher than they are during the initial sentencing proceeding, would also support constitutional protection for the defendant's ability to present evidence at the sentencing hearing. Some contrary authority can be found. In *McGautha v. Cal.* (1971), the Court noted: "This Court has not directly determined whether or to what extent the concept of due process of law requires that a criminal defendant wishing to present evidence or argument presumably relevant to the issues involved in sentencing should be permitted to do so."

Notwithstanding these conflicting signals about the necessity of providing to the defendant an opportunity to submit sentencing information to the court, judges traditionally have afforded defendants this opportunity. Defense submissions may be rejected when the defendant fails to raise a timely and specific objection to sentencing information, or absents himself from sentencing. A court may also reject a defendant's submission whenever it rules that the disputed fact will not be taken into account in sentencing. Courts also may limit the form that a defense presentation may take. Due process does not necessarily require formal hearings at sentencing during which the parties may present evidence on disputed facts. An entitlement to an evidentiary hearing is still viewed by many courts as "compromising the flexibility of the sentencing process." Many states give judges the discretion to grant or deny evidentiary hearings. Often, formal hearings will be required by statute for certain types of penalties, such as restitution or forfeiture.

The right of a defendant to make an unsworn statement on his own behalf at sentencing, known as the right of *allocution*, is recognized in most jurisdictions by court rule or statute and in some states by the state constitution. The right has its origins in the common law practice of allowing a defendant to state legal reasons why his sentence should not be imposed. This tradition arose at a time when the defendant had no right to be represented by counsel or to testify on his own behalf. Today, with counsel to speak for him and the ability to testify under oath, the defendant's need to make an unsworn statement in order to get across his side of the story to the sentencer is considerably less pressing. But the opportunity to personally address the sentencer retains both symbolic and practical significance. It may increase for some defendants the perceived equity of the process. Moreover, as the Supreme Court noted in *Green v. U.S.* (1961), a case which held that merely affording counsel a chance to speak fails to fulfill the allocution requirement in the federal rules, there are times when a plea in mitigation can best be presented by the defendant: "The most persuasive counsel may not be able to speak for a defendant as the defendant might, with halting eloquence, speak for himself." Allocution today typically includes any reason why the defendant feels a particular sentence should not be pronounced, but may be limited by the court to comments of a reasonable duration, to comments directed to the judge not the jury, or, in some jurisdictions, to "a plea for mercy" rather than a statement of historical fact.

Despite this widespread acceptance, the Supreme Court has not yet decided whether silencing a defendant who wishes to speak at sentencing is constitutional error. In *Hill v. U.S.* (1962), the Court held that where defendant is represented by counsel, absent "aggravating circumstances," the failure of a judge to comply with Rule 32 of the Federal Rules of Criminal Procedure and ask the defendant whether he wished to say anything before imposition of sentence "is not a fundamental defect which inherently results in a complete miscarriage of justice" necessitating that the sentence be vacated. Also relevant is the Court's decision in *McGautha*, where a petitioner claimed that because the sentencing in his capital case was left to the jury and because the state had refused to utilize a bifurcated trial, he had lost his right to present evidence on the issue of sentence when he exercised his self-incrimination privilege not to testify at trial. Rejecting this claim, the Court noted that even assuming a criminal defendant had a right to present evidence or argument relevant to sentencing, there was no denial of the right in that case. The Court explained that defense *counsel* was given the opportunity to argue for leniency, and that the state is not required to provide an opportunity for the defendant to speak to the jury free from any adverse consequences on the issue of guilt. Citing *McGautha*, some lower courts have upheld a judge's insistence that defendants be sworn as witnesses and be subject to cross-examination in order to speak at sentencing. The risk that the defendant's statements at sentencing may be used against him later may deter a defendant from exercising any allocution opportunity. To eliminate this "hard testimonial choice," some courts have advocated use immunity for statements made by defendants during sentencing proceedings.

(h) Burden of Proof. When a sentence depends upon particular facts, the degree of certainty by which the existence of those facts must be established during sentencing is also an important element of due process. In *McMillan v. Pa.* (1986), the Court considered this issue in a case involving sentencing under a statute that mandated a minimum sentence of five years upon proof that defendant visibly possessed a weapon during the commission of his offense. The statute directed the sentencing judge to determine whether possession was established by a preponderance of the evidence introduced at the trial and sentencing hearing. The defendant challenged this scheme as constitutionally deficient. The Court initially rejected defendant's reliance upon decisions requiring proof beyond a reasonable doubt in criminal cases, as that standard had been held to be required by due process only as to the elements defining the crime. The preponderance standard was sufficient for sentencing facts, the Court explained. The Court rejected the contention that at least a clear and convincing evidence standard should be required where, as here, the sentencing factor in question had a mandatory consequence. The preponderance standard, it noted, was constitutionally acceptable at trial for proof of defenses and mitigating factors that do not negate elements of the crime. Additionally, the court observed, "sentencing courts have traditionally heard evidence and found facts without any prescribed burden at all." The Court again upheld the preponderance standard for facts triggering higher sentence floors, but not higher sentencing ceilings, in *Harris v. U.S.* (2002). In *U.S. v. Watts* (1997), the Court in a per curiam opinion rejected the claim that due process is compromised whenever a sentencing court increases a sentence based upon conduct for which the defendant had been previously tried and acquitted. Citing *Williams* and *McMillan*, the Court reasoned that "application of the preponderance standard at sentencing generally satisfies due process" and that "a jury's verdict of acquittal does not prevent the sentencing court from considering conduct underlying the acquitted charge, so long as that conduct has been proved by a preponderance of the evidence."

Standards less exacting than the preponderance standard may be consistent with due process when adjudicating facts that may prompt a more lenient sentence. In *Walton v. Ariz.* (1990), a plurality of justices reasoned that a state may require a capital defendant to prove mitigating circumstances relevant to sentencing by a preponderance, so long as the prosecution first proves the elements of the offense and the existence of aggravating circumstances. When the Court later repudiated a separate holding in *Walton* that upheld as complying with the Sixth Amendment the state's law authorizing judicial rather than jury determination of *aggravating* facts necessary for the death sentence, it expressly left open the constitutional requirements for establishing mitigating factors in sentencing.

The Court later relied upon *Walton*'s approval of placing on the defendant the burden of proving mitigating factors, when, in *Kansas v. Marsh*, it upheld a state statute that required that the death penalty be imposed when a jury determined that the aggravating and mitigating factors were in equipoise. It follows from *Walton*'s approval of placing on the defendant the burden to prove mitigating factors in capital cases that due process would permit legislatures to place upon the defendant the burden of proving mitigating factors in non-capital cases as well. The extent of the burden— whether the defendant may be required to prove up mitigating facts by more than a preponderance, for example, remains uncertain.

(i) Enhancements That Constitute Separate Offenses. The previous subsection addressed the burdens of proof required by the Constitution for factors used to set the defendant's sentence. There are, however, limits to a legislature's ability to characterize certain facts as mere sentence factors rather than as elements of separate, aggravated offenses. The Court evaluated these limits in a series of cases beginning in the late 1960s, and eventually settled on a bright line rule. In *Apprendi N.J.* (2000) the Court held that any fact, other than the fact of prior conviction, that increases the penalty for a crime beyond the maximum penalty authorized for the conviction offense must be submitted to a jury, and proved beyond a reasonable doubt. Apprendi had been charged with several weapons offenses after firing shots into the home of an African–American family. A New Jersey "hate-crime" statute provided a higher sentence maximum for any crime, once a judge determine by a preponderance that the defendant "in committing the crime acted with a purpose to intimidate an individual or group of individuals because of race, color, gender, handicap, religion, sexual orientation or ethnicity." In Apprendi's case, it meant that the potential sentence maximum would double, from ten years for the underlying offense of possession of a weapon for an unlawful purpose, to twenty years. The Supreme Court found that Apprendi had been denied his right to a jury determination, with proof beyond a reasonable doubt, of each offense element. The Court rested its conclusion upon precedent as well as historical practice.

In *Ring v. Ariz.* (2002), a majority of justices overruled a portion of the Court's earlier decision in *Walton v. Ariz.* (1990), and held that because Arizona law required an additional finding of an aggravating fact before a death sentence could be imposed, that additional fact, after *Apprendi*, must be found by a jury beyond a reasonable doubt. But in *Harris v. U.S.* (2002), the Court refused to extend *Apprendi* to facts that raise a defendant's *minimum* sentence, rather than his maximum exposure. The Court rejected arguments that the legislature's decision to attach specific sentencing consequences to a particular fact triggered the rights to jury trial and proof beyond a reasonable doubt. Instead, Justice Kennedy, writing for a plurality of four justices, reasoned that while "any fact extending the defendant's sentence beyond the maximum authorized by the jury's verdict would have been considered an element of an aggravated crime—and thus the domain of the jury—by those who framed the Bill of Rights, [t]he same cannot be said of a fact increasing the mandatory minimum (but not extending the sentence beyond the statutory maximum), for the jury's verdict has authorized the judge to impose the minimum with or without the finding." Justice Breyer, concurring, maintained that *Apprendi* was wrongly decided and joined the Court's opinion only "to the extent that it holds that *Apprendi* does not apply to mandatory minimums."

In *Blakely v. Wash.* (2004), the Court extended the logic of *Apprendi* to invalidate a sentence imposed under the presumptive sentencing guideline system in Washington State, tightening the constitutional constraints on legislative power to create graduated penalties for crime through sentencing reform. The trial judge in *Blakely* had rejected the prosecutor's recommendation of a sentence within the standard presumptive sentencing range of 49 to 53 months, found that Blakely had acted with "deliberate cruelty," a statutorily enumerated ground for departure, and imposed a sentence of 90 months. The Supreme Court found that this sentence violated Blakely's rights under *Apprendi* because the fact supporting the finding that authorized the higher penalty was neither admitted by him nor found by a jury. The Court explained:

> [T]he "statutory maximum" for *Apprendi* purposes is the maximum sentence a judge may impose solely on the basis of the facts reflected in the jury verdict or admitted by the defendant. In other words, the relevant "statutory maximum" is not the maximum sentence a judge may impose after finding additional facts, but the maximum he may impose without any additional findings.

The Court soon held that there was no distinction of constitutional significance between the federal guidelines and the Washington procedures, and held in *U.S. v. Booker* (2005) that the federal sentencing guidelines violated *Apprendi* as well. A different majority of the Court decided upon a remedy of "excising" the provision of the federal act that *required* judges to impose a sentence within the applicable Guidelines range as well as the provision on appellate standards, making the guidelines "effectively advisory." As the Court later explained, the key question "is whether the law *forbids* a judge to increase a defendant's sentence *unless* the judge finds facts the jury did not find (and the offender did not concede)." By rendering the Sentencing Guidelines no longer mandatory, *Booker* preserved judicial fact finding for guideline factors.

Lower courts also divided over the effect of *Apprendi* on factual determinations required by state statute prior to running sentences for multiple crimes consecutively. The Court reached the issue in *Oregon v. Ice* (2009) and declined to extend *Apprendi* to fact-finding that is required by law before judges can require multiple sentences to be served consecutively instead of concurrently. "[S]pecification of the regime for administering multiple sentences has long been considered the prerogative of state legislatures," concluded the Court, and the decision to impose sentences consecutively is "not within the traditional jury function." The Court also recounted a number of reasons other than historical practice for its decision: (1) that it "would make scant sense" to permit states to make consecutive sentences the rule and concurrent sentences the exception but not the reverse; (2) that a contrary decision may lead to the extension of *Apprendi*'s rule into findings such as "the length of supervised release following service of a prison sentence; required attendance at drug rehabilitation programs or terms of community service; and the imposition of statutorily prescribed fines and orders of restitution"; and (3) that bifurcated or trifurcated trials might be required in order to avoid prejudice to the defense at the guilt phase of trial. Justice Scalia, writing for four justices in dissent, protested that the majority opinion relied upon arguments "dead and buried by prior cases."

Because of its widespread reach, the rule in *Apprendi* has become one of the most important developments in sentencing law since the criminal procedure revolution of the mid-twentieth Century. On the other hand, the rule does not change constitutional limitations on sentencing procedure, so much as it defines what processes count as sentencing in the first place. The rule in *Apprendi/Blakely* separates those graded punishments that may be determined by judges under the loose framework applied in *Williams*, from those graded punishments that must be treated as separate offenses. It does not affect sentencing procedure in states that have not enacted rigid constraints on judicial discretion. For example, in states with voluntary sentencing guidelines, judges will continue to determine facts setting guidelines ranges using a standard of proof that is less than the beyond a reasonable doubt standard required for elements of an offense. Also, the Court exempted prior convictions from the *Apprendi* rule, leaving undisturbed *Almendarez-Torres v. U.S.* (1998), which permitted a judicial finding of prior conviction to boost a maximum sentence from two to twenty years. Thus, the *Apprendi/Blakely* rule does not affect a legislature's ability to graduate punishments based on the criminal history of the offender. Finally, legislatures remain free under *McMillan* and *Harris* to calibrate punishment using mandatory minimum sentence provisions.

§ 18.5 Sentencing Information

(a) **Evidentiary Standards.** The traditional policy regarding the range and nature of the information that may be considered by a sentencing judge is succinctly stated in 18 U.S.C.A. § 3661: "No limitation shall be placed on the information concerning the background, character, and conduct of a person convicted of an offense which a court of the United States may receive and consider for the purpose of imposing an appropriate sentence." This policy finds support in the Supreme Court's reasoning in *Williams v. N.Y.* (1949), (discussed in § 18.4) and its comment there that "modern concepts individualizing punishment have made it all the more necessary that a sentencing judge not be denied an opportunity to obtain pertinent information by a requirement of rigid adherence to restrictive rules of evidence properly applicable to the trial." The Federal Rules of Evidence incorporate this traditional position in Rule 1101(d), which provides that "the rules (other than with respect to privileges) do not apply" in "sentencing." Similar provisions are found in many states.

Evidence obtained in violation of the Fourth Amendment and thus barred from trial use may be considered at sentencing as well. Statements elicited in violation of a defendant's sixth amendment right to counsel must be excluded, however, as well as statements elicited in violation of the defendant's rights under the Fifth Amendment.

(b) The Presentence Report. The presentence report is a singularly important document for the sentencing and correctional processes. While the presentence report is often supplemented by trial evidence, victims' statements, the defendant's allocution, or other submissions by defense and prosecution, it often serves as the primary source of information about the defendant and the offense. The report is prepared by a probation officer and represents the product of the officer's presentence investigation. The report provides information bearing upon the choice between probation and imprisonment, upon the probation conditions that should be imposed if the former alternative is chosen, and upon the length of the prison term that should be imposed if the latter alternative is selected. In addition, the report is a major source of information for other significant decisions: the probation officer's determination of the appropriate level of supervision if the defendant is placed on probation; and if the defendant is incarcerated, decisions regarding the institution at which he will be held, his classification within the institution, his release on parole, and his supervision during parole.

A probation officer usually prepares a presentence report after an in-depth interview with the defendant in order to obtain his account of the offense and information about the defendant's background and circumstances, interviews with law enforcement agents connected with the case in order to get their version of the offense and other information they may have about defendant's activities, examination of the defendant's prior criminal record, and contact with various individuals and agencies who might provide additional information about the defendant, such as members of his family, present and past employers, the victim of the crime, and medical, educational, financial, and military institutions with whom the defendant has had dealings. In its final form, the presentence report usually contains information about a defendant's prior criminal record, financial condition, and any circumstances affecting defendant's behavior that may be helpful in sentencing or correctional treatment. The inclusion of a detailed description of the crime is especially important where the defendant pleads guilty, as the court will not have the trial evidence to look to in applying the various distinctions relevant to characterizing the offense.

In the federal system and in some states, the presentence report may be prepared prior to the defendant's guilty plea or conviction. There are several reasons for delaying preparation of the presentence report until after the determination of guilt, most importantly the danger that otherwise prior to conviction the contents of the report might come to the attention of the court, the prosecution, or the jury. It may often be wise, however, for the defense to give its consent to having the judge inspect the report earlier, so that the judge will have a basis for determining whether he will concur in a plea agreement which has been reached by the parties.

Many jurisdictions make the use of the presentence report mandatory for all felony cases. Others require a report unless the judge makes a specific finding that the evidence on the record is sufficient to stand alone. Many states leave the decision to order a presentence report to the discretion of the judge, but require it for certain dispositions (e.g., probation).

At one time, there was a presumption against disclosure of the presentence report to the defense due to concerns that disclosure would (1) impair the collection of vital information from persons afraid of reprisal or public notoriety, and (2) damage the defendant's rehabilitation by adversely affecting his relationships with family, friends, or the probation officer who might supervise his community release. Today the vast majority of jurisdictions have adopted, by statute, court rule, or judicial decision, a mandatory requirement for disclosure of at least a portion of the presentence report to the defendant, as well as to defense counsel and the prosecution. Most jurisdictions have provisions authorizing the court to withhold portions of the report under certain circumstances. Federal Rule 32 is typical. It provides that the report must not include (1) "any diagnoses that, if disclosed, might seriously disrupt a rehabilitation program," (2) "sources of information obtained upon a promise of confidentiality," or (3) "any other information that, if disclosed, might result in physical or other harm to the defendant or others."

The timing of disclosure is often regulated by statute or rule. Recognizing that early disclosure is needed in order to provide the defense an opportunity to check the accuracy of the report, particularly in jurisdictions employing guidelines or other presumptive sentencing systems in which each fact may mean added prison time, many provisions require disclosure of the report well in advance of the sentencing hearing. Where there are no specific timing requirements, courts require that the report be disclosed early enough to provide the defendant and his counsel a reasonable opportunity to review the report before sentencing.

Information in the presentence report is often shared with corrections agencies and used after sentencing in connection with various correctional decisions such as the appropriate living quarters and work assignments. In addition, paroling authorities use the report to provide information about the offense and the offender in their parole decisions. The fact that the presentence report is used at the correctional stage in these ways suggests that defense counsel should ensure that the factual allegations in the report are correct even if the sentencing judge states he is not taking a particular allegation into account.

Access to presentence reports by third parties is strictly limited by courts. The person seeking disclosure usually must demonstrate a particularized compelling need, similar to the showing required for access to grand jury proceedings, in order to protect the privacy and safety of defendants, victims, and other sources of sentencing information.

(c) Victim Impact Statements. Over the past several decades most jurisdictions have adopted statutes or constitutional provisions that authorize or require consideration of victim impact statements during the sentencing stage. These provisions typically allow victims the right to make an oral statement at sentencing or provide that the victim's written statement appear in the presentence report, or both. The victim is usually defined as any individual who suffers direct or threatened physical, emotional, or financial harm as a result of the crime. The function of the victim statement is to provide information about the financial, emotional, and physical effects of the crime on the victim and the victim's family. It may also include information regarding the circumstances surrounding the crime and the manner in which it was perpetrated as well as, in some states, the victim's views on the appropriate sentence. Unlike the presentence report, which would only summarize the probation officer's interview of the victim, the victim impact statement is sometimes presented in the victim's own words. Where there are numerous victims and obtaining a statement from each would not be feasible, one or more representative statements may be used. Of course, the victim is not required to make an impact statement, and some evidence suggests that victims often fail to exercise their opportunity to do so. Some courts require that victim statements be made under oath to meet minimal standards of reliability, or permit a judge to exclude statements that are too prejudicial.

The use of victim statements has been particularly controversial in capital cases. Four years after holding that the Eighth Amendment barred the use of victim impact statements in capital cases as irrelevant to the sentencing decision, the Court in *Payne v. Tenn.* (1991), reversed itself. The Court reasoned that the use of victim impact evidence serves the legitimate purpose of illustrating the harm caused by a defendant's crime and is "surely relevant in determining [a defendant's] blameworthiness." Despite the Court's endorsement in *Payne* of the constitutionality of victim evidence, several states continue to limit its introduction in capital cases.

§ 18.6   Resentencing: Double Jeopardy

(a) Resentencing Following Reconviction and the *Bullington* Rule. Where the conviction of a defendant is overturned on appeal under circumstances permitting reprosecution, and the second prosecution results in a valid conviction, the question arises as what weight must be given to the original sentence under the Double Jeopardy Clause. One aspect of that question, addressed by the Supreme Court in *N.C. v. Pearce* (1969), is "whether, in computing the new sentence, the Constitution requires that credit must be given for that part of the original sentence already served." Emphasizing that one of the protections of the Double Jeopardy Clause is "against multiple punishments for the same offense," a unanimous Court answered that question in the affirmative.

A second issue presented in *Pearce* was whether, assuming proper credit is given for time already served, double jeopardy prevents the trial court from imposing a longer sentence on reconviction than was imposed following the original conviction. The Court rejected this claim, declining to depart from the longstanding rule "that a corollary of the power to retry a defendant is the power, upon the defendant's reconviction, to impose whatever sentence may be legally authorized, whether or not it is greater than the sentence imposed after the first conviction." This was a sensible rule, the *Pearce* majority asserted, for "it rests ultimately upon the premise that the original conviction has, at the defendant's behest, been wholly nullified and the slate wiped clean."

The rule is different in capital cases. In *Bullington v. Mo.* (1981), a divided Court held that a state could not seek the death penalty on a retrial where the original jury had decided against imposing capital punishment following a trial-type sentencing procedure. The majority noted that under Missouri law the jury determination as to capital punishment involved application of specific factual standards, relating to the presence of aggravating and mitigating factors, following an extensive trial-type hearing in which the prosecution bore the burden of proof beyond a reasonable doubt. The original jury's determination not to impose capital punishment was therefore comparable to a trial acquittal as to the issue of the death penalty, rather than to the traditional sentencing determination. *Ariz. v. Rumsey* (1984), too, held that the sentencing judge's imposition of a life sentence for want of proof of any aggravating circumstances, though prompted by his erroneous interpretation of the statute defining those circumstances, barred later resentencing of death in light of the Court's earlier cases holding "that an acquittal on the merits bars retrial even if based on legal error." Where the sentencing judge never holds that the state "failed to prove its case" as to the death penalty, resentencing is permitted. Similarly, if a sentencing jury deadlocks on sentencing, held the Court in neither judge nor jury has "acquitted" the defendant and the government is free to seek the death sentence in a retrial.

The analogy drawn by the *Bullington* Court between a trial acquittal and a sentencing determination made by the trier of fact under guidelines that refer to specific factors so far has been applied by the Supreme Court only to capital sentencing, and even there has been limited to situations in which there was a clear ruling that the prosecution had failed to make its case. In *Monge v. Cal.* (1998), for example, the Court held that Double Jeopardy Clause does not preclude retrial of a prior conviction allegation in non-capital sentencing proceedings. "Even assuming," that Court reasoned, "that the proceeding on the prior conviction allegation has the 'hallmarks' of a trial that we identified in *Bullington,* a critical component of our reasoning in that case was the capital sentencing context."

(b) Resentencing and Sentencing Appeals. In jurisdictions that allow appellate review of sentences, two situations may produce a more severe sentence following appeal. First, where the defendant's appeal is viewed as opening the door to appellate court assessment of all aspects of the sentence, the appellate court may decide not only that the defendant's complaint is not well taken, but that the sentence is too low and should be raised. Second, where the prosecution is allowed to appeal a sentence, the appellate court may sustain the prosecution's challenge and impose a higher sentence, or remand for consideration of a higher sentence. The leading double jeopardy decision, *U.S. v. DiFrancesco* (1980), involved the latter situation. Functionally, the Court stressed, resentencing here would be quite different from a retrial on guilt:

> The basic design of the double jeopardy provision, * * * is, as a bar against repeated attempts to convict, with consequent subjection of the defendant to embarrassment, expense, anxiety, and insecurity, and the possibility that he may be found guilty even though innocent. These considerations, however, have no significant application to the prosecution's statutorily granted right to review a sentence. This limited appeal does not involve a retrial or approximate the ordeal of a trial on the basic issue of guilt or innocence. * * * The defendant, of course, is charged with knowledge of the statute and its appeal provisions, and has no expectation of finality in his sentence until the appeal is concluded or the time to appeal has expired.

(c) Resentencing by the Trial Judge. Yet another group of double jeopardy issues are presented where the trial judge, in a system utilizing traditional judicial sentencing, initially imposes a particular sentence and then, learning of some deficiency in that original sentence, alters the sentence to the prejudice of the defendant. Double jeopardy bars modification in the government's favor if the second sentence would constitute multiple punishment for the "same offense" or if defendant had a legitimate expectation of finality in the initial sentence. *Ex Parte Lange* (1874).

In *Lange*, the applicable penal statute authorized a sentence of a fine *or* imprisonment, but the trial court erroneously imposed a sentence consisting of both the maximum term of imprisonment (one year) and the maximum fine ($200). After having paid the fine and having served five days in prison, the defendant petitioned the trial court for relief, demanding his immediate release on the ground that the imprisonment portion of the sentence could not be imposed along with the fine. Recognizing its error in imposing both a fine and imprisonment, the trial court vacated the original sentence and imposed a new sentence limited to imprisonment for the maximum term of one year. The Supreme Court held that the new sentence violated a double jeopardy prohibition against imposing "multiple punishments" for the same offense, and the defendant therefore was entitled to his release, as he had fully satisfied one of the two allowable alternative sentences by paying the fine. It stressed that the end result of the resentencing before it was to impose upon the defendant punishment beyond that authorized by statute.

Double Jeopardy does not bar resentencing that falls within statutory limits where defendant receives full credit for the time served under the original sentence. In *Jones v. Thomas* (1989), the defendant had been convicted of felony murder and the underlying felony of attempted robbery, both charges being tried in the same proceeding as they presented the same offense for double jeopardy purposes. The trial court originally had sentenced defendant to consecutive terms of fifteen years for the attempted robbery and life imprisonment for the felony murder. After the initial sentence for the attempted robbery had been satisfied (due to several years' incarceration and a subsequent commutation), the state's highest court held that the felony murder statute did not authorize separate punishments for the felony murder and the underlying felony. The trial court then vacated the attempted robbery sentence, leaving only the felony murder sentence, and gave the defendant credit for the entire time of his incarceration under the vacated sentence as against the remaining life sentence for felony murder. Defendant claimed that the credit was not sufficient, that he had fully satisfied one of two sentences allowable under state law, and that imposition of further imprisonment pursuant to the trial court's modification of the sentence would constitute multiple punishment contrary to *Lange*. Rejecting defendant's reliance upon *Lange*, the Supreme Court majority noted that here, unlike *Lange*, the consequence of upholding the modified sentence was not to impose punishment in excess of that authorized by statute.

Jones also noted that another interest protected by the double jeopardy prohibition—a defendant's "legitimate expectation of finality" in an imposed sentence—could also stand as a bar to resentencing. As an illustration of an unconstitutional resentencing, notwithstanding an ultimate sentence less than the authorized maximum—the Court discussed a case "where a judge imposes only a 15–year sentence under a statute that permitted 15 years to life, has second thoughts after the defendant serves the sentence, and calls him back to impose another 10 years." In *DiFrancesco*, the Court similarly had taken note of defendant's legitimate expectation of finality, but had concluded that the sentencing procedure there gave rise to no such expectation. *DiFrancesco* reasoned that the double jeopardy protection of such an interest did not preclude the use of an appeal procedure, known to defendant at the outset, as that procedure forewarned the defendant that the final determination of his sentence would not come until after that appeal and the defendant had no constitutional right to the initial setting of a final sentence. Lower courts have suggested that a defendant could not rely on a legitimate expectation of finality where the subsequent upward modification responded to defendant's intentional deception in the original sentencing proceeding.

§ 18.7   Resentencing: The Prohibition Against Vindictiveness

(a) **Presumed Vindictiveness: The *Pearce* Ruling.** In *N.C. v. Pearce* (1969), the petitioners successfully overturned their original convictions in post-conviction proceedings, were retried and convicted on the same charges, and then were sentenced to imprisonment terms that were longer than those imposed on the original convictions. The petitioners claimed that the trial courts had imposed heavier sentences in order to punish them for having challenged their original convictions. The Supreme Court unanimously concluded that such a sentencing purpose violates due process, noting Justice Stewart's opinion that a court is "without right to put a price on an appeal" and that "vindictiveness against a defendant for having successfully attacked his first conviction" could "play no part" in the sentencing on retrial.

Due process required that a "defendant be freed of apprehension of such a retaliatory motivation on the part of the sentencing judge," since that apprehension could itself "deter a defendant's exercise of the right to appeal or collaterally attack his first conviction." Accordingly, the majority reasoned, where a higher sentence was imposed following a successful defense challenge to a conviction (and subsequent reconviction and resentencing), it would presume vindictiveness and impose upon the resentencing judge the burden of rebutting that presumption with reasons "based upon objective information concerning identifiable conduct on the part of the defendant occurring after the time of the original sentencing proceeding."

(b) Rebutting the *Pearce* Presumption. The Court has refused to restrict the rebuttal of the *Pearce* presumption of vindictiveness to "identifiable conduct of the defendant occurring after the time of the original proceeding." The trial judge in *Wasman v. U.S.* (1984), had noted when imposing the original sentence that no consideration would be given to those criminal charges then pending against the defendant; it was that court's policy to consider only the prior convictions of a defendant. Following a successful appeal, retrial, and reconviction, the same judge imposed a second sentence higher than the first, based upon a conviction (on a previously pending charge) that had occurred during the interim between the first and second sentence. Allowing consideration of an intervening conviction, the Court reasoned, did not open the door to vindictive sentencing. At retrial *Tex. v. McCullough* (1986) allowed an increased sentence to be based on any new, "objective information" not considered in the initial sentencing. Two new witnesses, combined with the fact that McCullough had been released from confinement only four months before the murder, "amply justified McCullough's increased sentence." Some states have retained statutes prohibiting increased sentences after appeal in the absence of intervening conduct of the defendant.

(c) Applying the *Pearce* Presumption in Other Resentencing Settings. The vindictiveness presumption of *Pearce* does not apply to all settings presenting a resentencing following a reversed conviction and subsequent reconviction. In *Colten v. Ky.* (1972), the Supreme Court held that a Kentucky trial court, when sentencing a defendant following a trial de novo "appeal" of a misdemeanor conviction, did not have to set forth reasons justifying a sentence higher than that which had been imposed by the magistrate. Accordingly, there was no basis for assuming that "defendants convicted in Kentucky's inferior courts would be deterred from seeking a second trial out of fear of judicial vindictiveness." Three factors, in particular, were stressed: (1) because the court which conducted the trial de novo and imposed the second sentence was not the same court as had tried the case initially, this was not a case of a court being "asked to do over what it had thought it had already done correctly"; (2) the de novo court was not being asked to "find error in another court's work," but simply to provide the defendant with the same trial that would have been provided if his case had begun in that court; and (3) the attitude of the Kentucky courts was that the inferior courts were not "designed or equipped to conduct error-free trials," but were "courts of convenience," so there was no suggestion that a defendant "ought to be satisfied" with the informal proceeding provided by an inferior court.

Chaffin v. Stynchcombe (1973) held that the prophylactic rule of *Pearce* also did not apply to jury sentencing. A closely divided Court concluded that, unlike the situation in *Pearce*, the potential for vindictive sentencing by a jury was "*de minimis* in a properly controlled retrial." The jury sitting in the second trial would not know of the earlier sentence, and because the jury had no personal stake in the earlier proceeding, it "is unlikely to be sensitive to the institutional interests that might occasion higher sentences by a judge desirous of discouraging what he regards as meritless appeals."

Nor does the presumption of vindictiveness apply when a different judge sentences on retrial, or when a judge sentences after initial sentencing by a jury. Although the second trial judge arguably would have an "institutional interest" in discouraging appeals from the trial court's rulings, in *McCullough*, the Supreme Court suggested that such an "institutional interest" was too speculative a basis for imposing the *Pearce* presumption. In such situations, the trial judge has "no motivation" to engage in "self-vindication."

In *Ala. v. Smith* (1989), the Court further held that "when a greater penalty is imposed after trial than was imposed after a prior guilty plea," the presumption should not apply, "for the increase in sentence is not more likely than not attributable to the vindictiveness on the part of the sentencing judge." Because the information considered by the judge in accepting a guilty plea "will usually be far less than that brought out in a full trial on the merits," the judge imposing a second sentence after that trial is likely to have had "a fuller appreciation of the nature and extent of the crime charged." The defendant's conduct during trial may also have given the judge "insights into his moral character and suitability for rehabilitation." Moreover, "after trial, the factors that may indicate leniency as consideration for the guilty plea are no longer present." Finally, since the trial court had originally accepted a guilty plea and then conducted a trial after that plea was vacated, it would not be in a position of "simply 'doing over what it thought it had already done correctly.'"

*

Chapter 19

APPEALS

Table of Sections

> For additional analysis of the above topics and citations to authorities supporting their discussion in this Book, consult the authors' 7-volume *Criminal Procedure* treatise, also available as Westlaw database CRIMPROC. See the Table of Cross-References in this Book.

§ 19.1 Constitutional Protection of the Defendant's Right to Appeal

(a) No Federal Constitutional Right. Following dictum written over a century ago, the Supreme Court has consistently maintained that the due process guaranteed to the accused by the Constitution does not include access to appellate review of criminal convictions. In 1894, the Court in *McKane v. Durston* (1894) upheld a state's denial of bail pending appeal, reasoning that the state had no constitutional obligation to provide appellate review at all. It stated:

> An appeal from a judgment of conviction is not a matter of absolute right, independently of [state] constitutional or statutory provisions allowing such appeal. A review by an appellate court of the final judgment in a criminal case, however grave the offense of which the accused is convicted, was not at common law, and is not now, a necessary element of due process of law. It is wholly within the discretion of the state to allow or not to allow such a review.

McKane was written at a time when appellate review had only recently been introduced into the federal judicial structure. Congress did not grant circuit courts the authority to review federal criminal convictions until 1879, and did not give the Supreme Court jurisdiction to entertain writs of error in federal criminal cases until 1889. The appellate review process in the state courts also remained quite limited well into the mid–1800s.

Today in the federal system and in most states, statutes or state constitutional provisions guarantee defendants in all felony cases a right to appellate review. In a small number of states, review of felony convictions remains at the discretion of the state's highest court. In misdemeanor cases, defendants commonly have a right of review in the general trial court (in some states, by trial de novo) with subsequent discretionary appellate review. Although the significance of appellate review for the enforcement of constitutional rights of the accused has led some commentators and judges to advocate a constitutional conclusion different from that expressed in *McKane*, the Court has yet to reconsider its position.

(b) Constitutional Protection of the Statutory Right of Appeal. Various strands of constitutional doctrine protect the defendant's access to the appellate review that is provided under state law. In *Griffin v. Ill.* (1956), *Douglas v. Cal.* (1963), and *Halbert v. Mich.* (2005) the Court relied on equal protection to ensure the indigent defendant "meaningful access" to the appellate process. *Anders v. Cal.* (1967) added to this protection by ensuring that appointed counsel could not withdraw from that obligation by mere assertion that the appeal would be frivolous.

The prohibition against vindictiveness in sentencing also serves to safeguard the defendant's right of appeal under state law. In *N.C. v. Pearce*, discussed in § 18.7, the Court was unanimous in holding that due process was denied where a sentencing judge sought to punish a defendant for having taken an appeal by imposing a more severe sentence following reconviction. As in *Griffin*, though a state had no duty to establish avenues of appellate review, it could not subject those avenues, once established, to "unreasoned distinctions" that would deter a defendant's "free and unfettered" exercise of his right to challenge his conviction.

§ 19.2   Defense Appeals and the Final Judgment Rule

(a) The Statutory Requirement of a Final Judgment. Appellate review typically is limited to claims that challenge trial court decisions that can be characterized as "final judgments" or that fit within an exception to the final judgment rule. The statutory provisions that govern defense appeals uniformly reflect the view that piecemeal appellate review of litigation is generally inappropriate and therefore appeals ordinarily should be allowed only from a final judgment. Special double jeopardy concerns guide the implementation of this policy in the context of prosecution appeals, which are discussed in § 19.3. This section considers the final judgment rule as it applies to appeals by defendants, potential defendants (e.g., grand jury targets), and third parties (e.g., witnesses).

In many jurisdictions defense appeals in criminal cases are governed by the same statutes that regulate civil appeals. The federal provision, 28 U.S.C. § 1291, is typical. It provides that the "courts of appeals * * * shall have jurisdiction of appeals from all final decisions of the district courts * * *." Counterpart state statutes often refer to appeals from "final orders." In those states with separate statutes governing defense appeals in criminal cases the statutes commonly refer to a "final judgment of conviction." Notwithstanding such references to "convictions," the prevailing view is that an appealable final judgment does not come with conviction alone, but requires the imposition of a sentence for that conviction.

(b) Underlying Policies and Statutory Exceptions. The final judgment rule reflects a determination that, on balance, postponing an appeal until a final judgment is reached best protects the interests of the litigants in a fair and accessible process while conserving judicial resources. Weighing against the final judgment rule is the possibility that not allowing an interlocutory appeal from a potentially erroneous pretrial ruling may result in a final judgment that will be reversed on appeal, forcing the litigants to start over with a repeat trial.

Yet the costs of permitting interlocutory appeals are thought to be greater. Permitting parties to postpone a trial with interlocutory appeals is likely to result in even greater delay in final adjudication than allowing appeals only from final judgment. Interlocutory review would be especially wasteful, it is argued, because most trial court rulings are correct and even those that are incorrect are unlikely, in the end, to taint the final judgment. Freely allowing interlocutory appeals would in the end cause greater injustice to litigants overall than the unfairness occasioned by that small portion of cases in which trials must be repeated because appellate review was delayed until after final judgment was reached. That injustice would be particularly likely when the adversaries had unequal resources and interests in securing or avoiding a prompt disposition of the case. The party interested in a prompt adjudication would be at the mercy of an opponent willing and able to delay litigation by appealing adverse pretrial rulings.

The advantages of the final judgment rule in securing efficient judicial administration are even more apparent. A major responsibility of the trial court is self correction, and the delay of appellate review until final judgment permits the trial court to reassess its decisions in light of later trial developments. From the perspective of the appellate court, rulings also are better judged in light of the completed proceeding when more information is available, and a single appeal may consider more than one error. Most significantly, rulings often become moot when the party adversely affected by the erroneous ruling ultimately gains a favorable jury verdict.

The delay that can accompany interlocutory appeals is especially pernicious in the criminal justice process, where a speedy trial advances a "societal interest * * * which exists separate from * * * the interests of the accused." In his frequently quoted opinion in *Cobbledick v. U.S.* (1940), Justice Frankfurter emphasized the dangers of delay in urging strict adherence to the final judgment rule in criminal cases. He noted:

An accused is entitled to scrupulous observance of constitutional safeguards. But encouragement of delay is fatal to the vindication of the criminal law. Bearing the discomfiture and cost of a prosecution for crime even by an innocent person is one of the painful obligations of citizenship. The correctness of a trial court's rejection even of a constitutional claim made by the accused in the process of prosecution must await his conviction before its reconsideration by an appellate tribunal.

The viewpoint expressed in *Cobbledick* has dominated the federal statutory scheme for defense appeals in criminal cases. While Congress has adopted several statutory provisions allowing interlocutory appeals in civil cases, only two federal statutes authorize interlocutory appeals in criminal cases. One, 18 U.S.C. § 3731, is quite narrow and carefully limited to prosecution appeals; the other, 18 U.S.C. § 3154(c), provides both the defense and the prosecution with a right to appeal orders concerning pretrial release or detention.

A substantial number of states have much broader provisions permitting interlocutory appeals by defendants in criminal cases on a discretionary basis. Several have adopted provisions similar to 28 U.S.C. § 1291(b) that apply to criminal as well as civil cases, and require that the trial judge certify that immediate appeal is warranted. Others simply provide for interlocutory appeal by leave of the appellate court, without requiring certification by the trial judge. Such provisions often identify a series of factors to be considered by the appellate court in determining whether to grant review, such as whether immediate review will "clarify an issue of general importance in the administration of justice" or "protect the petitioner from substantial or irreparable injury."

(c) Collateral Orders. The final judgment rule has been subject to considerable judicial development in both criminal and civil cases. One major "exception" to the final judgment rule is the collateral order doctrine, established in the civil case of *Cohen v. Beneficial Industrial Loan Corp.* (1949). In that case, the defendant in a stockholder's derivative suit sought to appeal a district court's pretrial ruling refusing to direct the plaintiffs to post a security bond. The Supreme Court held that the ruling was appealable under 28 U.S.C. § 1291. A final decision, the Court noted, did not necessarily have to terminate an action. Given a "practical rather than technical construction," the final judgment concept also encompassed certain orders collateral to the basic litigation. As the Court later stated:

To come within the "small class" of decisions excepted from the final judgment rule by *Cohen*, the order must conclusively determine the disputed question, resolve an important issue completely separate from the merits of the action, and be effectively unreviewable on appeal from a final judgment.

The first of these three prerequisites demands that the trial court ruling not be "tentative, informal, or incomplete," but constitute a firm and final decision on the issue. As to the second prerequisite, if the trial court ruling is not "independent of the cause" itself, determining rights "separable from and collateral to [those] rights asserted in the action," then review prior to the ultimate disposition constitutes a wasteful use of appellate resources. Depending upon the disposition of the case, permitting appeal will produce either an unnecessary review or a review that will only be repeated, possibly in a new light that would require the appellate court to withdraw from an earlier ruling. The second prerequisite also requires that the issue resolved by the trial court be not only independent but "important." Thus, in *Cohen* the Court noted that the trial court order there might not have been appealable if the only issue presented was one of the proper exercise of the trial court's discretion. Finally, the third prerequisite insists that interlocutory appeal be withheld if review on appeal following the final disposition would provide a satisfactory remedy.

The Supreme Court first applied the collateral order doctrine to a criminal case in *Stack v. Boyle* (1951). The defendants there were unable to make bail and sought habeas corpus relief after the trial court denied their motion to reduce bail. The Court said very little about why the bail ruling met the prerequisites of *Cohen*. It noted only that, as in *Cohen*, the rejected motion "did not merely invoke the discretion of the district court," as it "challenged the bail as violating statutory and constitutional standards." In a concurring opinion, Justice Jackson, the author of *Cohen*, added a brief explanation. "An order fixing bail," he noted, "can be reviewed without halting the main trial—its issues are entirely independent of the issues to be tried-and unless it can be reviewed before sentence, it can never be reviewed at all."

In *Abney v. U.S.* (1977), the Supreme Court added an additional ruling to the list of orders deemed collateral. The Court there held appealable the denial of a pretrial defense motion seeking dismissal of an indictment on double jeopardy grounds. The denial of the motion to dismiss had constituted a "complete, formal and * * * final rejection" of the defendant's double jeopardy claim; the double jeopardy issue was "collateral to, and separable from, the principal issue at the accused's impending criminal trial, i.e., whether or not the accused is guilty of the offense charged;" and "the rights conferred upon the criminal accused by the Double Jeopardy Clause would be significantly undermined if appellate review of double jeopardy claims were postponed until after conviction and sentence." The function of the Double Jeopardy Clause, the Court stressed, was not simply to insulate the defendant against being subjected to double punishment, but also to protect the defendant against being forced "to endure the personal strain, public embarrassment, and expense of a criminal trial more than once for the same offense." Reversal on appeal from a conviction following a second trial was too late to afford protection against "being twice put to trial for the same offense."

In *Helstoski v. Meanor* (1979), the Court found appealable an order denying a former Congressman's claim that the indictment against him violated the Speech or Debate Clause (which provides that "for any speech or debate," a Congressperson "shall not be questioned in any Place"). But in *U.S. v. MacDonald* (1978), and *U.S. v. Hollywood Motor Car Company* (1982), the Court concluded that trial court orders rejecting speedy trial and vindictive prosecution claims prior to trial did not have the special qualities needed to fall under the "collateral order exception," which was to be construed "with the utmost strictness in criminal cases."

A critical factor distinguishing *Abney* and *Helstoski* on the one hand, and *MacDonald* and *Hollywood Motor Car* on the other, was the Court's characterization of the nature of the claim presented by defendant's pretrial motion. *Helstoski* held that the constitutional right of a Congressperson not to "be questioned" encompassed a protection against trial itself, not just conviction, and therefore was analogous to the double jeopardy claim presented in *Abney*. The claims presented in *Hollywood Motor Car* and *MacDonald* did not include the right not to be tried at all. The dissenters in *Hollywood Motor Car* argued that the constitutional prohibition against vindictive prosecution should encompass protection against the burdens of trial, but the majority viewed the scope of the right quite differently. The petitioner's claim was not characterized as presenting "a right not to be tried," but only as "a right whose remedy requires the dismissal of charges." As in the case of other challenges to the validity of a charge, such as a challenge to the constitutionality of the statute on which a charge is based, dismissal on an appeal following a conviction constituted an adequate remedy. In *MacDonald*, a unanimous Court similarly characterized a defendant's speedy trial claim as not encompassing a "right not to be tried." It was "the delay before trial, not the trial itself that offends the constitutional guarantee." Indeed, to present an appeal prior to trial would threaten many of the interests protected by the Speedy Trial Clause.

MacDonald also distinguished *Abney* on other grounds. The determination as to whether there had been a denial of a speedy trial is often dependent upon an assessment of the prejudice caused by the delay, which could best be considered "only after the relevant facts had been developed at trial." Unlike the double jeopardy claim presented in Abney, which required an initial showing of prior jeopardy, there was "nothing about * * * a speedy trial claim which inherently limits the availability of the claim." If a right to immediate appeal were recognized, "any defendant" could raise such a claim in anticipation of a dilatory pretrial appeal.

Most further attempts to expand the "very few" instances in which pretrial rulings come within *Cohen* have been rejected by the Court. *Flanagan v. U.S.* (1984) presented a defendant's attempt to appeal an order disqualifying defense counsel on conflict grounds under Federal Rule 44(c). The Court concluded that the second condition of *Cohen*—"that the order be truly collateral"—was not satisfied. Assuming that a constitutional violation was tied to a finding of prejudice, a disqualification order could hardly be said to be "independent of the issues to be tried." The "effect of the disqualification on the defense, and hence whether the asserted right had been violated, cannot be fairly assessed until the substance of the prosecution's and defendant's case is known." In this respect, the petitioner's claim was analogous to the speedy trial claim presented in *MacDonald*.

In *Midland Asphalt Corp. v. U.S.* (1989), the defendant had stronger grounds for arguing that his constitutional claim would be "effectively unreviewable on appeal from a conviction," but the Court held that the ruling below still fell outside the *Cohen* exception because the very quality that made it unreviewable on appeal also established that it was not truly collateral to a decision on the merits of the case. The trial court in *Midland Asphalt* had denied the defendant's motion to dismiss the indictment based on an alleged violation of Federal Rule 6(e). The Supreme Court reasoned that if, under *Mechanik v. U.S.*, discussed § 15.6(e), such a ruling would be considered harmless error after conviction due to the subsequent petit jury finding of guilt beyond a reasonable doubt, the trial court's denial did not "resolve an important issue completely separate from the merits of the action." Instead, the trial court's ruling would "involve considerations 'enmeshed in the merits of the dispute' * * * [that] would * * * 'be affected by' the decision on the merits."

The Court did add to its short list of collateral orders subject to appeal a trial court's decision to forcibly medicate a defendant into competency for trial. "By the time of trial," the Court reasoned in *Sell v. U.S.* (2003), the defendant "will have undergone forced medication—the very harm that he seeks to avoid. He cannot undo that harm if he is acquitted. Indeed, if he is acquitted, there will be no appeal through which he might obtain review." This, combined with "the severity of the intrusion and corresponding importance of the constitutional issue, readily distinguish" the order authorizing forced medication from the examples given by the dissenting justices, concluded the Court.

The collateral order doctrine of *Cohen* is applied in many states, and several others apply doctrines that are similar. Many jurisdictions generally reach the same results as the federal courts, and often follow closely the leading Supreme Court rulings. Another group of states, however, does not recognize even the narrow exception to the final judgment concept recognized in *Cohen*. In most of these jurisdictions, alternative routes are available to defendants for obtaining immediate review of the few orders that the federal courts would describe as collateral.

(d) Independent Proceedings. The collateral order doctrine permits an immediate appeal from orders that clearly are a part of the ongoing litigation. Certain proceedings, though related to ongoing or contemplated litigation, may be viewed as sufficiently separate from that litigation so that an order terminating that proceeding is itself a final judgment and therefore appealable. The crucial question here, the Supreme Court has noted, is whether the proceeding is "independent * * * or merely a step in the trial of the criminal case."

Perhaps the clearest illustration of an independent proceeding is the third party challenge to an order issued in a criminal case. Consider, for example, a news organization's objection to a trial court ruling that portions of a trial will be closed to the public. If the defendant, rather than a news organization, had objected to the closure, the trial court's rejection of that objection would be part of the criminal case and its immediate appeal subject to the limitations of the *Cohen* doctrine. When a third party such as a news organization brings an action to vindicate its alleged right to be present at the proceedings, that action is deemed independent and the denial of its challenge is appealable by that party as a final judgment without applying the *Cohen* standards. Similarly, while the denial of a defense motion to strike surplusage in an indictment would not be appealable by the defendant, an unindicted co conspirator may appeal from an order rejecting his motion to strike his name from the indictment.

Where the party seeking to appeal is a defendant or a potential defendant who has sought relief that would have a direct bearing on the criminal trial, both federal and state courts are much less likely to find that the denial of such relief is subject to immediate appeal. The leading case on the application of the independent proceeding doctrine in this context is *DiBella v. U.S.* (1962). A unanimous Supreme Court there held nonappealable the denial of a defense motion to suppress that had been filed before the defendant was indicted but after he had been arrested. The Court, per

Frankfurter, J., reasoned that the factors that led to the characterization of a post-indictment suppression ruling as an interlocutory order were equally applicable to a pre-indictment ruling. Because the disposition of the motion, whether made before or after indictment, would "necessarily determine the conduct of the [eventual] trial," the ruling was not "fairly severable from the context of a larger litigious process." Appellate intervention prior to trial would result in a "truncated presentation of the issue of admissibility because the legality of the search too often cannot truly be determined until the evidence at the trial has brought all circumstances to light."

(e) Grand Jury Proceedings. Application of both the independent proceeding and collateral order doctrines has proven especially troublesome in the analysis of court orders growing out of grand jury proceedings. Even though the absence of indictment makes each grand jury proceeding "party less," courts have refused to treat all challenges by witnesses and others to grand jury orders as independent proceedings subject to appeal prior to resolution of the criminal case. In *Cobbledick v. U.S.* (1940), the Supreme Court held that the denial of a witness's motion to quash a grand jury subpoena was not appealable. The Court distinguished the proceeding to enforce an administrative subpoena which is commonly regarded as an independent action for agency discovery, thereby rendering orders granting or quashing an agency subpoena final and appealable. The ongoing grand jury proceeding, *Cobbledick* noted, was instead part of the ongoing prosecution:

> The proceeding before a grand jury constitutes "a judicial inquiry" * * * of the most ancient lineage. The duration of its life, frequently short, is limited by statute. It is no less important to safeguard against undue interruption the inquiry instituted by a grand jury than to protect from delay the progress of the trial after an indictment has been found. * * * That a grand jury proceeding has no defined litigants and that none may emerge from it, is irrelevant to the issue.

The Court did recognize one avenue for appeal by a grand jury witness, however. In the context of a trial, the Court had held that the rejection of a witness's objection to a subpoena was not a final order. To gain appellate review, the witness had to refuse to comply and be held in contempt, which did produce a final order. The same requirement, *Cobbledick* held, was applicable to the grand jury witness.

In addition, an exception to the contempt prerequisite exists when a subpoena duces tecum is directed at a person other than the appellant and that person cannot be expected to risk contempt for the purpose of protecting the appellant's interest in the property or information subpoenaed. This exception was established in *Perlman v. U.S.* (1918). In *Perlman*, the clerk of a federal court was directed to produce before a grand jury documents that Perlman had deposited with the clerk in connection with a patent infringement suit. Claiming a continuing right to those documents, Perlman challenged the order directed to the clerk and subsequently appealed from the denial of that challenge. As later explained in *U.S. v. Ryan* (1971), Perlman's appeal was allowed without the witness (the clerk) meeting the contempt prerequisite of *Cobbledick* because the witness did not share Perlman's interest in challenging the order. Without immediate review, Perlman would have been "powerless to avert the mischief of the [challenged] order." The lower courts have applied the exception to a variety of situations. For example, appeals have been allowed from an order denying an appellant's motion to quash subpoenas directing her treating physician to turn over her medical records, an order upholding a subpoena to a grand jury target's supervisor, an order denying a bank depositor's motion to quash a grand jury subpoena issued to his bank, and an order denying a record custodian's motion to quash a subpoena issued to a corporation.

Where the challenge to ongoing grand jury proceedings does not relate to the appearance of a witness, the contempt alternative of *Cobbledick* may not be available. In such cases, courts focus on whether the person seeking to appeal (who is usually the target of the investigation) will have a subsequently available appellate remedy if an immediate appeal from his denied request for relief is not available. Thus, if the target is objecting to the alleged use of the grand jury to develop evidence for a civil case, a court is likely to hold that an immediate appeal is not permissible since a later objection (and appeal) is available if the government should seek to transfer any such evidence to a potential civil litigant or to use it in a civil proceeding. Similarly, if the target claims that the grand jury proceeding is being tainted by misconduct, a court may hold that such an objection can be advanced when (and if) an indictment is issued and an appeal can then be taken when (and if) the target is convicted. Once the grand jury investigation has ended, a petitioner seeking relief unrelated to an ongoing prosecution can more readily claim that his request involves an independent proceeding. Thus, an appeal can be taken from the grant or denial of a Rule 6(e) motion for disclosure of grand jury minutes for use in an unrelated proceeding.

§ 19.3 Prosecution Appeals

(a) **Constitutional Constraints.** Throughout much of the nineteenth century, most states denied the government an opportunity to appeal an acquittal through writ of error, and many states disallowed writs of error for the state in criminal cases altogether. Government appeals of acquittals were considered a violation of the defendant's freedom from double jeopardy, a right originally guaranteed to most state defendants by state constitutional provisions and to federal defendants by the Fifth Amendment. As discussed in more detail in Chapter 17, double jeopardy continues to bar the government from appealing a variety of rulings.

(b) The Need for Specific Statutory Authorization. Absent specific statutory authorization, the prosecution lacks the right to appeal an adverse ruling in a criminal case. The policy underlying that position was set forth by the Supreme Court's ruling in *U.S. v. Sanges* (1892). Congress had granted federal defendants the statutory right to apply for writs of error in criminal cases, but had not extended the same opportunity to the government. Consequently, the Court concluded, "the defendant, having been once put upon his trial and discharged by the court, is not to be again vexed for the same cause, unless the legislature, acting within its constitutional authority, has made express provision for a review of the judgment at the instance of the government."

After Congress adopted in 1907 a statute allowing government appeals under specified circumstances, the Supreme Court, consistent with *Sanges*, strictly limited such appeals to the letter of that provision. Government attempts to gain more expansive appellate review using the general appeals statute, 18 U.S.C. § 1291 (allowing for appeals from final decisions), were rejected. In *Ariz. v. Manypenny* (1981), the Court reviewed the basis for this limitation, noting that the Court's "continuing refusal to assume that the United States possesses any inherent right to appeal" reflects the need "to check the Federal Government's possible misuse of its enormous prosecutorial powers." Requiring Congress "to speak with a clear voice when extending to the Executive a right to expand criminal prosecutions" through appeal places the responsibility for "such assertions of authority over citizens in the democratically elected Legislature where it belongs." This philosophy is repeated frequently in state as well as federal decisions. All of the states now have provisions allowing prosecution appeals from at least a limited class of orders in criminal cases. These provisions, like the Criminal Appeals Act governing federal criminal cases (18 U.S.C. § 3731), typically list which interlocutory and final orders may be appealed by the prosecution. In many jurisdictions, these provisions narrow the government's right to appeal considerably, well beyond the limitations on appeal imposed by the final judgment rule and the Double Jeopardy Clause.

(c) Pretrial Rulings. *Final judgments.* As to final judgments entered prior to trial, some statutes refer broadly to appeals from all "final judgments," or, as in the federal provision, from all "dismissals of an indictment or information * * * as to one or more counts." These provisions encompass dismissals based upon such grounds as the insufficiency of the accusatory pleading, prior jeopardy, denial of a speedy trial, lack of sufficient evidence to support a bindover, prosecutorial misconduct, and the unconstitutionality of the underlying statute. Other jurisdictions restrict the category of appealable final judgments to dismissals based on a deficiency in the pleading itself. A few states have even more restrictive provisions, providing a prosecution appeal as of right only from a ruling holding unconstitutional the statute forming the basis for the charges.

Interlocutory pretrial rulings generally. The states also vary in their treatment of prosecution appeals from interlocutory pretrial rulings. As noted in § 19.2, with some exceptions, a defendant typically cannot appeal an adverse interlocutory order, but can gain review of the adverse pretrial ruling on appeal if he is convicted. The prosecution, however, is in a quite different position. If the government is not allowed an immediate appeal from an adverse interlocutory ruling, there will be no opportunity for later appellate review should the defendant be acquitted, since the double jeopardy prohibition then bars further prosecution. This circumstance has led a few jurisdictions to provide the prosecution with the opportunity to appeal nearly any adverse pretrial interlocutory order. Most jurisdictions, however, have stopped short of conferring such broad authority, and allow the prosecution to appeal from designated categories of pretrial interlocutory orders.

Suppression Orders. The federal government and most states have adopted legislation providing for review of suppression orders as a matter of right. Two grounds are advanced in support of allowing the prosecution to appeal from a trial court's decision to grant a defendant's motion to suppress evidence. One justification is the special need for appellate court rulings on legal issues relating to searches and seizures and interrogation. The law in this area is so uncertain, it has been argued, that law enforcement officers dissatisfied with the rulings of individual trial judges will persist in a challenged practice until they obtain a favorable decision from another trial judge, and perhaps a favorable ruling on appeal after a resulting conviction. The better rule, it is argued, is to give the prosecution the opportunity to gain immediate review of those trial court rulings that it considers questionable. Perhaps for this reason, several state provisions authorizing the appeal of suppression orders by the government limit that authority to the appeal of orders relating to illegal practices by police in obtaining evidence.

Other statutes, such as 18 U.S.C. § 3731, speak generally of orders "suppressing or excluding" evidence, and have been held applicable to a broad range of pretrial orders limiting the government's proof at trial. The broader review extended to prosecutors under these statutes builds upon the second justification for allowing the prosecution to appeal suppression orders, namely the recognition that the practical effect of such an order is, in many cases, equivalent to dismissal. A ruling suppressing evidence often eliminates the heart of the prosecution's case. With the opportunity to appeal such rulings, even those that result from its own motions in limine, the prosecution may have the opportunity to gain appellate review of a wide range of orders that otherwise would be subsumed in an acquittal. Consistent with this case ending justification for review, several states condition appeal on a prosecutor's certification that the suppression order will eliminate any "reasonable possibility" of a successful prosecution. The federal statute and a number of state provisions, for example, require certification that "the appeal is not taken for the purpose of delay and that the [suppressed] evidence is a substantial part of the proof of the charge pending against the defendant."

Other interlocutory orders. Many jurisdictions allowing prosecution appeals from pretrial interlocutory orders do not extend that authority beyond orders suppressing evidence. Several jurisdictions, however, also authorize appeals from one or more additional categories of interlocutory rulings as specified by statute. Thus, the 1984 Bail Reform Act allows a prosecution appeal from a district court's pretrial release order. Rather than designate particular categories of orders that a prosecutor may appeal as of right, some states limit the prosecution's ability to appeal using the standards that apply to defense requests for interlocutory review, or rely on the discretion of the court. At least one state grants a right to appeal if the interlocutory ruling will have a "reasonable likelihood of causing either serious impairment to or a termination of the prosecution."

(d) Post–Jeopardy Rulings. Statutory provisions authorizing government appeals typically include one or more provisions applicable to rulings issued after jeopardy has attached. Most allow a prosecution appeal from "an order arresting judgment." These provisions have not met significant opposition because (1) the order arresting judgment clearly constitutes a final judgment; (2) since the defendant has been found guilty prior to the issuance of the order, reversal on appeal does not require a new trial but simply requires reinstituting the original verdict; and (3) the order arresting judgment commonly must be based on grounds that are unrelated to the factual innocence of the defendant (e.g., lack of jurisdiction).

While only the second factor cited above applies to the grant of a new trial following a conviction, the federal system and a substantial number of states allow the prosecution to appeal from a new trial order. Such an appeal permits the prosecution to challenge underlying rulings that could not have been appealed if they had been made before or during trial. The new trial order might be based, for example, on a trial court's post-verdict determination that the trial had been marred by improper joinder or an erroneous charge to the jury. If the trial court had originally ruled in favor of the defendant on the same points, the end result would have been a mistrial (on the joinder issue) or perhaps an acquittal (depending upon the influence of the jury charge), and the prosecution would not have had the opportunity to appeal either ruling.

Statutory provisions that allow the prosecutor to appeal from the dismissal of an indictment or information may also provide a basis for a post-jeopardy appeal. Although some of these provisions refer specifically to dismissals prior to trial, most do not contain that limitation. Where the dismissal occurred after jeopardy attached, but before a verdict was reached, reprosecution will be barred by the double jeopardy prohibition if the "dismissal" was in fact an "acquittal" or constituted the equivalent of a mistrial not justified by either "manifest necessity" or a defense request.

Because the provisions authorizing the government to appeal from suppression orders apply only to *pretrial* suppression rulings, conceivably a defendant could cut off appellate review by delaying his motion to suppress until after jeopardy has attached. In the case of the typical suppression motion claiming the unconstitutional acquisition of evidence, however, statutes ordinarily require that such a motion be presented before trial.

Several states have also adopted provisions specifically allowing appeals from acquittals entered by the trial court following a guilty verdict. Finally, prosecutors in most jurisdictions are allowed to appeal sentences, as well.

§ 19.4 Review by Writ

(a) **Extraordinary Writs Generally.** Where a trial court's order is not appealable, the defense or prosecution may seek higher court review through an application for one of the writs commonly described as "extraordinary" writs. These include the writ of habeas corpus, described more fully in Chapter 20, the writ of mandamus, and the writ of prohibition.

(b) Prohibition and Mandamus: Traditional Limits and Modern Extensions. The writs of prohibition and mandamus traditionally were available only to control jurisdictional excesses. Prohibition was used to confine a lower court to the lawful exercise of its prescribed jurisdiction and mandamus was used to compel it to exercise that jurisdiction. When raising jurisdictional issues, the writs serve to protect the "interests of the judicial system as a whole" by correcting action or inaction contrary to the structural limits that control the system. Other decisions employed the writs in cases that were properly before a court, issuing the writ of mandamus to require a lower court to take action that it had no discretion to avoid (action commonly described as "ministerial" in nature), and the writ of prohibition to bar an order that the lower court lacked authority to issue under any set of circumstances. Although some states continue to adhere to these traditional limits, most have moved substantially beyond them.

Among the factors that courts consider in determining whether the writs should apply to non-jurisdictional claims, the availability of an alternative means of obtaining relief (e.g., through a subsequent appeal) is prominent. Nevertheless, if the harm to the petitioner is unlikely to be remedied by a later appeal, if the issue presented is of great significance, or if there is a need to preclude recurring error, the appellate court may conclude that the advantages of immediate disposition outweigh the policies of finality.

Even in those jurisdictions that reach a broad range of issues under the writs, courts continue to stress that the writs should be sparingly allowed. This reluctance reflects both the apprehension that the writs could be used so frequently that their use would imperil the policies that limit the right of appeal, particularly the final judgment rule.

(c) Defense Petitions. In addition to allegations that the lower court lacked jurisdiction over the proceeding, review by writ also has been available where the grand jury or prosecutor lacked authority to initiate prosecution of a particular crime, venue was improper, or the lower court otherwise lacked authority to try the particular offense. Also reviewed are claims thought to address impending harm that is either irreparable, or goes beyond the hardship of a possibly needless or flawed trial, such as alleged violations of the right to a speedy trial, the right to be free from double jeopardy, or challenges to orders that would cause a loss of privilege which would not be remedied by a ruling excluding the evidence from trial.

In some jurisdictions, appellate courts will consider on a application by writ a defendants challenge directed at almost any pretrial ruling, provided the legal issue presented has some general significance.

(d) **Prosecution Applications.** Prosecutors have sought to use the extraordinary writs to gain appellate review of a wide variety of orders issued at various stages of the criminal process, including interlocutory rulings, pretrial dismissals, and unappealable rulings entered after a jury returns a guilty verdict. In jurisdictions in which the prosecution does not have a right to appeal a sentence, the writs have been used to challenge sentences allegedly imposed without statutory authorization.

Some courts hold that the writ will be available to the prosecution only when the lower court "acted in excess of its jurisdiction" by issuing an order that it had no authority to issue under any circumstances or by failing to issue an order that it had no discretion under any circumstances not to issue. Other courts have held that the writ will issue to correct a gross abuse of discretion where a significant prosecution interest is at stake, or will review any ruling that raises a legal question of general significance. Federal courts generally limit the government's access to mandamus to "rare cases" in which the lower court's order falls outside the limits of judicial power and poses irreparable harm, but they have also recognized mandamus can be appropriate when an application presents an issue that is "novel, of great importance, and likely to recur."

There are two concerns that may lead a court to apply more stringent standards to prosecution petitions than are applied to either civil cases or defense petitions in criminal cases. Courts frequently note the need to approach the prosecution's use of the writs with "an awareness * * * that a man is entitled to a speedy trial." Courts also express concern that the writs not be used so as to undermine the limitations that the legislature has placed on the prosecution's right to appeal.

§ 19.5   The Scope of Appellate Review

(a) **Mootness.** An appellate court will not review a lower court decision, in either a civil or criminal case, where post trial events have rendered the claim moot. One such event is the death of the defendant. Should the defendant die pending discretionary or collateral review, courts typically will simply dismiss the petition or appeal and let the underlying judgment or ruling stand. When a defendant dies pending direct review, however, most courts are willing to take further action. Many courts will set aside the conviction and dismiss the indictment or information. Such abatement is premised on the theory that without it, the defendant would be deprived of his statutory right to review, and that abatement prevents both recovery against the decedent's estate (if there is a fine) and the use of the conviction in civil litigation against the estate. Other courts, reasoning that "it seems unreasonable automatically to * * * pretend the defendant was never indicted, tried, and found guilty," choose instead to dismiss the appeal and vacate the conviction only if the deceased's personal representative or the state moves for the substitution of another person for the deceased party pursuant to court rule, enabling the appeal to go ahead. Heightened concern for the rights of victims has also persuaded some judges that abatement is inappropriate, as it "creates an unacceptable and ultimately painful legal fiction for the surviving victims which implies that the defendants have somehow been exonerated."

Traditionally, a criminal appeal was considered moot once the defendant fulfilled his sentence. Nevertheless, important "exceptions" to the fully-satisfied-sentence standard permit review. The most significant exception is known as the "collateral consequences" exception. Under this doctrine a case is not moot, notwithstanding full satisfaction of the sentence, if the defendant is still subject to a collateral legal disability as a result of his conviction. In *Sibron v. N.Y.* (1968), the Supreme Court that the "mere possibility" that there would be "adverse collateral legal consequences" was sufficient to keep a case "from ending 'ignominiously in the limbo of mootness.'" Because New York statutes allowed Sibron's conviction to be used to impeach him if he should become a witness in a future trial, and required that the conviction be considered in sentencing should he be convicted of a future offense, his appeal was not moot. Building upon *Sibron*, courts have taken the position that the possibility of adverse collateral consequences from a criminal conviction will be " 'presumed' as an 'obvious fact of life.' " Even where a conviction is for a low-level misdemeanor, a careful search of state law is likely to turn up some provision through which the conviction could come back to haunt the defendant. In those misdemeanor cases in which appeals have been held moot, defendant apparently sought to rely on the consequences of adverse treatment by private parties rather than disabilities that flowed from state or federal law.

In *Spencer v. Kemna,* the Court limited this willingness to presume adverse consequences sufficient to defeat a claim of mootness to challenges raised to convictions. In *Spencer*, the Court refused to presume that a defendant who has served his sentence and challenges not his conviction, but rather the revocation of his parole, continues to suffer collateral consequences from the revocation sufficient to keep his habeas corpus proceeding alive after he was released from the confinement brought about by the revocation. The Court distinguished *Sibron*, observing that while "the presumption of significant collateral consequences is likely to comport with reality" when a defendant challenges a conviction, the same cannot be said when a defendant challenges the revocation of parole. The appellant's predictions of harm from an unreviewed revocation proceeding were speculative, the Court in *Spencer* concluded, for the parole violation would be only one factor among many that would be considered by a parole board in any future parole decision, and even then would only become relevant if the defendant at some future date committed a crime and was returned to prison. The Court also went on to reject as speculative any apprehension that the revocation would be used to impeach the defendant, or introduced as substantive evidence, should the defendant appear in a future criminal proceeding. Moreover, the Court discounted possible employment or sentencing repercussions from the parole violation as "insufficient to keep the controversy alive."

A second major exception allows review of a case in which the defendant has completed his sentence when the issue raised on appeal is "capable of repetition, yet evading review." In the federal courts, this doctrine applies only where "(1) the challenged action [is] in its duration too short to be fully litigated prior to cessation or expiration, and (2) there [is] a reasonable expectation that the same complaining party [will] be subject to the same action again." States do not necessarily insist on such an exacting showing, and may require only a likelihood that *other* litigants will confront the same issues, accompanied by some barrier to review. Most states, however, also require that in order for a court to reach an otherwise moot, but recurring question, the question must be important or of "broad public interest." The issues that courts have addressed under this exception are quite varied, and include press access to court proceedings and documents, the meaning or constitutionality of new statutes, issues regarding release from custody prior to trial or pending appeal, and a variety of sentencing issues.

(b) The Concurrent Sentence Doctrine. Where a defendant receives concurrent sentences on each of several counts of an indictment, and the appellate court finds no error in the conviction on any one count carrying a sentence at least equal to a remaining challenged count, the validity of the conviction remaining on the count will not be reviewed in a minority of jurisdictions that continue to adhere to what is commonly termed the "concurrent sentence doctrine." In *Ray v. U.S.* (1987), however, the Court held that because Ray was obligated to pay a $50 "special assessment" for each count of conviction, the sentences were not truly concurrent, precluding application of the concurrent sentencing doctrine and mandating review. *Ray* has essentially abolished the doctrine for direct review of federal convictions, since a separate monetary assessment is mandated by statute for each count of conviction. Those state courts that continue to apply the concurrent sentence doctrine stress its value in preserving scarce judicial resources and in avoiding the unnecessary consideration of potentially difficult legal questions.

(c) **Waiver or Forfeiture of the Right to Appeal.** Some appeals are barred because the defendant expressly waives his right to appeal. With increasing frequency, negotiated plea bargains include an express waiver of the right to appeal. A defendant may agree to waive the right to appeal only his sentence, waive his right to appeal his conviction after trial in return for a favorable sentence recommendation, or give up the right to appeal both conviction and sentence. Most courts uphold appeal waivers, so long as the waiver is made voluntarily and with an understanding of the consequences. These courts are persuaded that because other important constitutional rights of the defendant may be waived by plea agreement, the right to appeal, which is not even guaranteed by the Constitution, but by statute, should also be subject to waiver. Courts also point to the importance of plea bargaining, the value of saving appellate resources, and the advantages gained by the defendant in entering the agreement. Some courts disallow such waivers in cases carrying the sentence of death, or allow waiver, but impose more stringent requirements for ensuring that a defendant's waiver of appellate rights is informed and voluntary. Moreover, courts that otherwise honor waivers have noted that an appeal waiver cannot foreclose appellate review of allegations that the trial court relied on a constitutionally impermissible factor, such as race, in setting the defendant's sentence, or that a sentence was imposed in violation of the plea bargain, or that in agreeing to the waiver, defendant lacked the effective assistance of counsel.

The right to appeal may be relinquished by less deliberate means as well. As the Court explained in *Ortega–Rodriguez v. U.S.* (1993), "it has been settled for well over a century that an appellate court may dismiss the appeal of a defendant who is a fugitive from justice during the pendency of his appeal." This rule is aptly termed the "fugitive disentitlement doctrine." Not only would any judgment reached on appeal be unenforceable against an absent appellant, dismissal discourages escape, encourages voluntary surrender, and advances "an interest in efficient, dignified appellate practice." This justification explains the Court's decisions to uphold state rules providing for the dismissal of the appeals of prisoners who escape during the pendency of their appeal, but are recaptured, while rejecting the sanction of dismissal for an appellant who escapes *prior* to filing his appeal. Escape and recapture prior to invoking appellate jurisdiction, the Court concluded in *Ortega–*

Rodriguez, does not interrupt proceedings in the court of appeals, and flouts not the authority of the court of appeals, but only the authority of the District Court. The District Court can tailor a response to deter such misconduct that is "more finely calibrated" than "the blunderbuss of dismissal" available to the court of appeals. Moreover, the Court feared that dismissal would be invoked inappropriately as a response to much less egregious misconduct prior to appeal. Even though the limits imposed in *Ortega-Rodriguez* were an exercise of the Court's supervisory powers over the federal courts and were not mandated by the Constitution, many states also reject automatic dismissal of appeals filed by former fugitives, reserving dismissal for cases in which the defendant's conduct significantly interferes with the appellate process.

Perhaps no standard governing the scope of appellate review is more frequently applied than the rule that "an error not raised and preserved at trial will not be considered on appeal." Even a constitutional right "may be forfeited in criminal as well as civil cases by the failure to make timely assertion of the right." The "raise-or-waive" rule is supported by the need to recognize our adversary system in which issues are framed by the litigants and presented to a court; to insist that a litigant advance his contentions at a time when there is an opportunity to respond to them factually, if his opponent chooses to; to promote efficient trial proceedings; and to present the trial court with the opportunity to make a correct ruling. Judicial economy is advanced when the parties and public are not put to the expense of retrial that could have been avoided had an objection been made. All jurisdictions recognize one or more situations in which issues not raised below will be considered on appeal. The plain error rule, discussed in the next subsection, is clearly the most important of these "exceptions" to the raise-or-waive rule.

Where the defendant lacked an opportunity to present his objection before the trial court in compliance with the jurisdiction's procedural rules, the defendant's failure to raise his objection below is likely to be excused. The clearest case for considering an issue not raised in accordance with a particular procedural requirement occurs when that requirement fails to allow the defense a reasonable time within which to raise the issue. In other situations the general timing requirements may be fair, but the defendant may be in a special situation where the failure to comply was excusable. A claim lack of jurisdiction will also be reviewed even if unraised below. However, courts tend to utilize a definition of a jurisdictional defect for this purpose that is quite narrow, including challenges to subject matter jurisdiction or that the offense occurred outside the territorial jurisdiction of the state. While several appellate courts allow a first time challenge to the constitutionality of the statute on which the prosecution is based, most hold that such an objection also is not jurisdictional and therefore cannot be raised unless it fits within some other exception to the raise-or-waive rule. Finally, in many jurisdictions, claims of ineffective assistance typically need not be raised at trial, or even on direct appeal, but may be raised for the first time on collateral review.

(d) Plain Error. All but a few jurisdictions recognize the authority of an appellate court to reverse on the basis of a plain error even though that error was not properly raised and preserved at the trial level. The plain error exception is recognized in Federal Rule 52(b) and in similar provisions in most states. Others have adopted it as a common law exception to the raise-or-waive rule, based upon the appellate court's inherent authority to prevent a "miscarriage of justice." The doctrine usually extends to all types of errors. In some jurisdictions, however, the doctrine is restricted to a limited class of "plain errors." Thus, one state limits review to unpreserved errors that are discoverable "by a mere inspection of the pleadings and proceedings * * * without inspection of the evidence." Another includes only errors that could not have been cured by the trial judge if an objection had been made at trial. Several apply it only to the most flagrant constitutional violations.

In *U.S. v. Olano* (1993), and *Johnson v. U.S.* (1997), the Supreme Court developed a four-step analysis for determining whether an error is subject to review as "plain error" under Federal Rule 52(b), an analysis subsequently adopted by many states. As the Court summarized in *Johnson*, an appellate court can correct an error not raised at trial only if there is (1) error, (2) that is plain, (3) that "affects substantial rights," and (4) "seriously affects the fairness, integrity, or public reputation of judicial proceedings." Applying this analysis, the Court held that neither the trial court's violation of Federal Rule 24(c) in *Olano*, allowing alternate jurors to be present during jury deliberations, nor the failure to submit the question of materiality to the jury in a perjury prosecution in *Johnson*, required correction under Federal Rule 52.

Initially, the appellant must have "forfeited" his right to appellate review of an error by failing to make a timely objection. Review is not available to a defendant who expressly "waived" his right to review or for an error that has been intentionally relinquished or abandoned. Second, the error must be "plain," which "is synonymous with 'clear,' or equivalently 'obvious.'" It is enough that an error be "plain" at the time of appellate consideration, at least in a case where "the law at the time of trial was settled and clearly contrary to the law at the time of appeal." Otherwise, defense counsel would "inevitably" make "a long and virtually useless laundry list of objections to rulings that were plainly supported by existing precedent," explained the Court in *Johnson.*

Third, to "affec[t] substantial rights," the error "must have been prejudicial" in the sense of "affect[ing] the outcome" of the lower court proceedings. Here, however, in contrast to a harmless error inquiry, "the defendant rather than the Government bears the burden of persuasion with respect to prejudice." In *Olano,* the Court concluded that the erroneous presence of alternate jurors during deliberations did not meet this requirement, noting that the defendants had not shown that the error had prejudiced them and refusing to find that the error was "inherently prejudicial." The Court in *U.S. v. Dominguez Benitez* (2004) held that a defendant who seeks relief for plain error for a violation of Rule 11 must show "a reasonable probability that, but for the error, he would not have entered the plea." This standard, the Court noted, "should not be confused with a requirement that a defendant prove by a preponderance of the evidence that but for error things would have been different."

The Court has so far declined to address whether prejudice should be presumed under the third prong of *Olano* for "structural" errors that require relief without regard to prejudice if adequately preserved for appeal. But in *Puckett v. United States* (2009) the Court did clarify that plain error relief under Rule 52(b) does require a showing of prejudice for at least some claims that, had they been raised on time in the trial court, would have received relief under Rule 52(a) without regard to prejudice. In *Puckett,* the prosecutor at sentencing had refused to request a sentence reduction as promised in the plea agreement, noting that the the defendant had engaged in additional criminal activity since his conviction. The judge imposed the minimum sentence under the applicable guideline range rather than the reduced sentence. Puckett, who had not objected to the breach at sentencing, argued on appeal that relief was required without regard to its likely impact on the sentence, both because breach was a structural error and because the breach rendered the agreement void. The Court affirmed the decision of the court of appeals that Puckett had failed to meet *Olano*'s third prong. Automatic reversal when a defendant raises a timely objection to a plea breach, the Court explained, "rested not upon the premise that plea-breach errors are (like "structural" errors) somehow not *susceptible,* or not *amenable,* to review for harmlessness," but rather "upon a policy interest in establishing the trust between defendants and prosecutors that is necessary to sustain plea bargaining—an 'essential' and 'highly desirable' part of the criminal process." The rule of contemporaneous objection, the Court continued, "is equally essential and desirable, and when the two collide we see no need to relieve the defendant of his usual burden of showing prejudice." The Court also rejected the argument that breach eliminates the knowing and voluntary character of the plea, "retroactively" invalidating a valid agreement.

Finally, Federal Rule 52(b) is "permissive rather than mandatory," allowing rather than requiring correction when an error is found to be "plain" and "affecting substantial rights." In previous cases the Court had indicated that this discretion should be employed "in those circumstances in which a miscarriage of justice would otherwise result." However, in contrast to the position taken in its habeas corpus jurisprudence, this use of "miscarriage of justice" in plain-error cases was not meant to restrict plain error review to only those errors that caused "the conviction or sentencing of an actually innocent defendant." An appellate court should, in addition, "correct a plain forfeited error affecting substantial rights if the error 'seriously affects the fairness, integrity, or public reputation of judicial proceedings.' " In *Johnson*, the record showed that the error in question—failure to submit the element of materiality to the jury—did not seriously affect either the outcome, or the "fairness, integrity, or public reputation of judicial proceedings" because the evidence supporting materiality was "overwhelming." "Indeed," the Court ventured, "it would be the reversal of a conviction such as this which would have that effect." The Court in *Puckett* also rejected the defendant's argument that failing to remedy a plea breach should always satisfy this aspect of the *Olano* test. "The fourth prong is meant to be applied on a case-specific and fact-intensive basis. * * * It is true enough that when the Government reneges on a plea deal, the integrity of the system may be called into question, but there may well be countervailing factors in particular cases. Puckett is again a good example: Given that he obviously did not cease his life of crime, receipt of a sentencing reduction for *acceptance of responsibility* would have been so ludicrous as itself to compromise the public reputation of judicial proceedings."

The Court's unanimous decision in *U.S. v. Cotton* (2002), in which defendants objected on appeal to the government's failure to allege an element of the greater drug offense for which they were sentenced, illustrates how difficult this analysis is to overcome if proof of guilt is strong. The *Cotton* Court refused to grant relief, noting the "overwhelming and uncontroverted evidence" that the defendants were guilty of the greater offense.

A rare case where unraised error required relief despite no showing of prejudice, was *Nguyen v. U.S.* (2003). There the court sidestepped the *Olano* analysis, preferring instead to vacate, under the Court's supervisory powers, an appellate order upholding the convictions of two drug defendants, because the appellate panel included a non-Article III judge. The majority reasoned that neither the failure to object nor an express stipulation of the parties could have created authority that Congress carefully withheld. Rejecting in a footnote the dissenters' argument that under *Olano* no relief was required, the majority noted that allowing the judgment to stand would "call into serious question the integrity as well as the public reputation of judicial proceedings * * * for *no one* other than a properly constituted panel of Article III judges was empowered to exercise appellate jurisdiction in these cases."

(e) **Standard of Review.** Assuming that review is not precluded by the doctrines examined in the preceding sections, a reviewing court must decide how much deference to accord the trial court's decision in order to determine whether or not that decision was erroneous. As in civil cases, different standards of review are used by appellate courts to examine different types of trial court decisions. The Supreme Court has summed up the law on this topic succinctly: "For purposes of standard of review, decisions by judges are traditionally divided into three categories, denominated questions of law (reviewable de novo), questions of fact (reviewable for clear error) and matters of discretion (reviewable for 'abuse of discretion')." When not specified by statute, courts will choose the standard to apply. Deferential standards of review are used when the trial judge is likely to have more information or expertise than reviewing judges, or when uniform rules to guide trial courts are not essential. Although states are free to adopt standards of direct review for federal constitutional issues that are more exacting than those adopted by federal courts, because the standard of review (like the applicability of harmless error) is part and parcel of the federal right itself, a state court may be prohibited from adopting standards of review that are more deferential than the standards adopted by federal courts.

Abuse of discretion review. Some trial court decisions are considered erroneous only if the reviewing court determines that the trial court "abused its discretion." This most lenient oversight is applied to decisions to admit or exclude evidence, to rulings on motions for recusal, substitution of counsel, continuance, severance, discovery, jury instructions, specific performance of plea agreements, as well as motions for mistrial. Sentencing decisions in some jurisdictions remain subject to review for abuse of discretion. More stringent review is often provided for findings of fact, statutory interpretations, or decisions weighing aggravating and mitigating factors in capital cases.

Decisions reviewed for abuse of discretion share one or more common characteristics. They often depend upon the trial judge's first-hand observations of the litigants and the evidence, observations that cannot be replicated by reviewing judges who have access only to the written record. Second, they often involve the judge's ability to control the trial proceedings. Third, decisions reviewed for abuse of discretion often address issues about which the trial judge has a greater understanding than an appellate judge. Finally, discretionary decisions tend to be context specific and resistant to general rules.

Clearly erroneous review. Factual findings by trial judges may form the basis for relief on appeal if found to be "clearly erroneous." A finding of fact is clearly erroneous when "a court is left with a firm and definite conviction that a mistake has been committed." The differences between this standard and the abuse of discretion standard are somewhat elusive, to say the least. This type of review is common for decisions concerning the presence or absence of discriminatory intent, the competency of a defendant, the breach of plea agreements, the intelligence and voluntariness of waivers, and factual decisions underlying rulings on motions to suppress.

Appeals based on insufficient of evidence of guilt are evaluated by asking, "whether, after viewing the evidence in the light most favorable to the prosecution, any rational trier of fact could have found the essential elements beyond a reasonable doubt."

De novo review. While the trial judge's better vantage point for making factual assessments warrants greater deference to the factual findings of a trial judge, appellate judges are equally well situated to decide legal questions. Appellate judges also benefit from deliberation as a panel, which can reduce the risk of error. Consequently, no weight is given to the legal conclusions of the trial judge. De novo review also promotes uniformity and predictability. Questions reviewed in this manner include questions of statutory or constitutional interpretation, and questions concerning the scope of the attorney client privilege.

Mixed questions of law and fact requiring the application of legal principles to historical fact usually receive do novo review. For example, whether or not there was probable cause to justify a warrantless search, whether a defendant had received the notice required by due process was denied the effective assistance of counsel, or whether a statute as applied to a defendant violates the First Amendment are all questions reviewed de novo on appeal.

§ 19.6 Harmless Error

(a) **Origins of Harmless Error Review.** During the mid–1800s the English courts adopted a rule of appellate review that became known as the Exchequer Rule. Under that rule, a trial error as to the admission of evidence was presumed to have caused prejudice and therefore required a new trial. The presumption of prejudice was designed to ensure that the appellate court did not encroach upon the jury's fact finding function by discounting the improperly admitted evidence and sustaining the verdict on its belief that the remaining evidence established guilt. Early American courts adopted the Exchequer Rule from English law, extending it to a wide range of trial errors. Retrials for seemingly insignificant errors mounted, and appellate courts were criticized as "impregnable citadels of technicality." Reformers urged adoption of harmless error legislation. Their efforts began to bear fruit during the early 1900s when a substantial number of states adopted such legislation. By the 1960s all 50 states had harmless error statutes or rules. The federal statute, adopted in 1919, provided the model for much of the state legislation. It required a federal appellate court to "give judgment after an examination of the entire record before the court, without regard to technical errors, defects, or exceptions which do not affect the substantial rights of the parties."

(b) Harmless Error Review of Nonconstitutional Errors. American appellate courts initially applied harmless error legislation to nonconstitutional error alone. Some American courts reviewing nonconstitutional errors today continue to use two modes of analysis when applying harmless error statutes. For rights that might loosely be described as concerned with the structure of the proceeding, courts have looked to whether the error was merely a technical violation or took from the defendant the substantive protection of the right. A violation of the substance of such a right automatically requires a new trial, so that the strength of the evidence supporting the conviction is irrelevant. Examples of this automatic-reversal analysis include decisions reviewing errors in jury selection and changes of venue. A second analysis, which considers the likely impact of the error on case outcome, is applied to trial errors that determine what evidence is presented to the jury, such as rulings on admissibility and joinder. It also is applied to erroneous pretrial rulings that have an impact upon the presentation of evidence, such as rulings on discovery, and to actions of the judge and prosecutor that may have influenced the jury in its evaluation of the evidence, such as erroneous jury instructions or trial misconduct by the prosecutor. Finally, this impact-on-outcome analysis is applied to violations of rules regulating plea bargaining and plea taking, and to errors in sentencing.

In the federal courts Federal Rule 52(a) sets out the harmless error rule. For example, in *U.S. v. Lane* (1986), the Court stated that "Rule 52(a) admits of no broad exceptions to its applicability," rejecting "bright-line per se rules whether to conduct harmless error analysis." The Court in *Lane* applied harmless error analysis to a misjoinder of parties in violation of Federal Rule 8(b). In *U.S. v. Mechanik* (1986), the Court rejected defendant's claim that certain grand jury errors should be exempt from harmless error review under Rule 52(a). According to the Court, most grand jury error is necessarily harmless beyond a reasonable doubt if followed by an otherwise valid conviction. The Court explained that a subsequent guilty verdict renders harmless any error in failing to dismiss an indictment due to a violation of Federal Rule 6(d). However, if the error during the grand jury process is raised in a motion to dismiss and considered by the trial court prior to trial, relief may be available, but only if the traditional standard for harmless error was satisfied. In explaining this pretrial application of harmless error review to grand jury error, the Court in *Bank of Nova Scotia v. U.S.* (1988) emphasized that "a federal court may not invoke supervisory power to circumvent the harmless error inquiry prescribed by" Rule 52(a). The Court explained, "federal courts have no more discretion to disregard the Rule's mandate than they do to disregard constitutional or statutory provisions." In *Zedner v. U.S.* (2006), the Court found that the text of the Speedy Trial Act precluded the application of harmless error review under Rule 52 to a judge's failure to make on-the-record findings for an ends-of-justice continuance.

Once an appellate court concludes that an error is subject to harmless error review, the court must identify the proper standard for measuring the impact of the error on the outcome of the proceeding. The Supreme Court in *Kotteakos v. U.S.* (1946) offered the following standard:

> If * * * the error did not influence the jury, or had but very slight effect, the verdict and the judgment should stand, except perhaps where the departure is from a constitutional norm or a specific command of Congress. But if one cannot say, with fair assurance, after pondering all that happened without stripping the erroneous action from the whole, that the judgment was not substantially swayed by the error, it is impossible to conclude that substantial rights were not affected.

As various courts have acknowledged, the principle that the error should be judged by its likely impact on the jury's judgment, whatever the standard as to requisite probability of impact, is only the first step of the harmless error inquiry. Courts have also sought, with varying success, to identify the *process* for determining whether a particular error is so unlikely to have influenced the jury's judgment that it meets the applicable probability standard. Considerable attention has been given, for example, to the allocation of the burden of showing potential prejudice. In *Kotteakos*, the Supreme Court rejected the idea of uniformly placing the burden on either party. Any presumptions of prejudice, shifting the burden to one side or the other, should "aris[e] from the nature of the error and its 'natural effect' for or against prejudice in the particular setting."

Another significant issue is what weight should be assigned to overwhelming evidence of guilt in determining the impact of a trial error. Once it is agreed that the impact of an error must be measured in light of all of the evidence before the jury, it does not follow that an overwhelming prosecution case will inevitably render the error harmless. In *O'Neal v. McAninch* (1995), a case concerning the application of the *Kotteakos* standard on collateral review, the Court described the appropriate inquiry as whether the error "had substantial and injurious effect or influence in determining the jury's verdict," not whether, despite the error, the jury reached the right result. One method of measuring that impact, and ensuring that the weight of the state's evidence does not become determinative, is to match the potential element of prejudice against the state's evidence. For example, to render harmless the erroneous admission of potentially prejudicial evidence, it would have to be shown that the government had properly introduced other, more persuasive evidence on the same point. Most courts, however, view a requirement that the prosecution's evidence independently establish the same fact as the inadmissible evidence as unduly restrictive. Even without a "perfect match," strong prosecution evidence may indicate that a particular error was most unlikely to have contributed to the jury's verdict. For example, erroneously admitted evidence may have been the only evidence casting doubt upon defendant's reputation for honesty, but it may nevertheless have been inconsequential in light of strong eyewitness testimony clearly establishing that the defendant had committed the crime.

(c) Application to Constitutional Violations. Prior to the 1960s, it was assumed that constitutional violations could never be regarded as harmless error. This assumption was called into question by the due process revolution of the 1960s and its dramatic expansion of federal constitutional regulation of state procedures. In the case of *Fahy v. Conn.* (1963) the Court was faced with the possible application of the harmless error rule to a violation of one of the leading "expansionist" decisions of the 1960s. The state court there had held harmless a violation of the *Mapp v. Ohio* requirement that evidence obtained through an unconstitutional search not be admitted into evidence at trial. The Supreme Court majority found it unnecessary to decide whether the harmless error rule applied to *Mapp* violations. If it was assumed arguendo that the rule applied, the state court had still erred in its analysis of the alleged harmlessness of the *Mapp* violation in this particular case. Four years later, in *Chapman v. Cal.* (1967), the Court majority resolved the issue left open in *Fahy*. *Chapman* involved a clear violation of the Court's recent decision in *Griffin v. Cal.* prohibiting comment on the defendant's failure to testify at trial. The California Supreme Court, stressing the overwhelming evidence of guilt, had held the *Griffin* violation harmless. Before the Supreme Court, the defendant contended that no constitutional error could be harmless, while the prosecution claimed that the state court could appropriately apply to a constitutional violation the same harmless error standard it applied to nonconstitutional errors. The Court majority rejected both arguments.

The *Chapman* majority held initially that federal rather than state law determined whether the harmless error rule applied to constitutional violations, and whether a particular constitutional violation was harmless. "Whether a conviction for a crime should stand when a state had failed to accord federally constitutionally guaranteed rights" was as much a matter of constitutional law as the definition of the constitutional right itself. The Court then turned to the question of whether the Constitution required automatic reversal as to all constitutional errors. It was true, the Court noted, that a rule of automatic reversal had been applied to certain constitutional errors in the past, but that did not mean constitutional errors could never be treated as harmless. A proper harmless error standard could appropriately be applied to some constitutional violations, including a violation of the *Griffin* ruling. That standard required the appellate court to be convinced "beyond a reasonable doubt that the error complained of did not contribute to the verdict obtained."

The *Chapman* opinion presents a two-step analysis for an appellate court dealing with a constitutional error. First, the court must determine if the error falls in that category of violations subject to the harmless error rule or instead falls in that category of errors requiring automatic reversal. Second, if the harmless error rule is applicable, the court must determine the impact of the error in the case before it under the federal standard laid down in *Chapman*. These two determinations are examined in the subsections that follow.

(d) Harmless Error or Automatic Reversal. The *Chapman* opinion focused primarily on responding to the contention that the harmless error rule should never apply to constitutional error. The Court found no basis in theory or past precedent for granting constitutional errors a blanket exemption from this rule of appellate review. It acknowledged that prior cases had indicated "that there are some constitutional rights so basic to a fair trial that their infraction can never be treated as harmless error." A footnote to this statement cited and described three illustrative cases: "*Payne* *v. Ark.* (coerced confessions) (1958); *Gideon v. Wainwright* (right to counsel) (1963); [and] *Tumey v. Ohio* (impartial judge) (1927)." The Court made no attempt to identify the characteristics that distinguished these constitutional errors from the *Griffin* violation before it. An improper comment on defendant's silence was the type of "trial error" as to which a harmless error analysis traditionally had been applied, and the Court apparently concluded that once it was decided that "some constitutional errors" could be deemed harmless, the *Griffin* violation clearly fell within that group.

The logic of *Chapman* did exclude from the outset two very different types of constitutional violations. The very nature of the harmless error inquiry made harmless error analysis irrelevant to one major group of constitutional violations. Where the constitutional error is one that requires the remedy of barring reprosecution, reversal is automatic upon concluding that there was such a violation. That is the case, for example, where defendant establishes a violation of his right to a speedy trial or the bar against double jeopardy.

An additional group of violations were destined not to be subject to the *Chapman's* harmless error test because they were harmful by definition, inherently incapable of meeting the rigorous *Chapman* prerequisite for finding an error to be harmless. *Chapman* insisted upon a judicial finding of lack of prejudicial impact "beyond a reasonable doubt." As a result, it would be wasted effort to look to *Chapman* where the constitutional violation is one of those that already requires—as an element of the violation—a finding of likely prejudicial impact. Typically, those violations do not exist unless the challenged behavior presented a "reasonable probability" of having affected the outcome of the proceeding. Examples include a finding that counsel's representation was ineffective under the *Strickland* standard, or that nondisclosed exculpatory evidence was material under the *Bagley* standard. As the Court explained in *Kyles v. Whitley* (1995), "once a reviewing court applying Bagley has found constitutional error there is no need for further harmless error review."

Leaving aside those constitutional violations that bar reprosecution and those that already require a finding of probable impact upon outcome, the *Chapman* harmless error analysis still offered the potential of applying to a broad range of constitutional errors. In the years after *Chapman*, that potential was fully realized. *Chapman's* harmless error standard has now been held by the Supreme Court to apply to each of the following constitutional violations: improper comment on the defendant's failure to testify; admission of evidence obtained in violation of the Fourth Amendment; admission of evidence obtained in violation of an accused's right to counsel; admission at trial of an out-of-court statement of a non-testifying codefendant in violation of the Sixth Amendment's Confrontation Clause; admission of evidence at the sentencing stage of a capital case in violation of the right to counsel; erroneous use during trial of defendant's silence following *Miranda* warnings; a restriction on a defendant's right to cross-examine in violation of the Sixth Amendment's Confrontation Clause; denial of the right to present exculpatory evidence, denial of the right to be present during a trial proceeding; shackling of defendant in front of a jury in violation of due process; denial of an indigent's right to appointed counsel at a preliminary hearing; a jury instruction containing an unconstitutional rebuttable presumption; a jury instruction containing an unconstitutional conclusive presumption; an unconstitutionally overbroad jury instruction in a capital case; the submission of an invalid aggravating factor to the jury in a capital sentencing proceeding, and even a the omission of an element of the offense in the instructions to the jury. In its decision in *Ariz. v. Fulminante* (1991) the Court overruled one of *Chapman's* three illustrations of errors requiring automatic reversal, holding that harmless error analysis is applicable to the admission of a coerced confession.

The Court has said that "[W]hile there are some errors to which *Chapman* does not apply, they are the exception and not the rule." These "exceptions," in which harmless error is not applied, extend beyond the Court's classic examples of the denial of an impartial adjudicator or the denial of counsel. Following *Chapman*, the rule of automatic reversal has been held by the Court to apply to the denial of defendant's constitutional right to self-representation; the denial of the right to select counsel of one's choice discrimination in the selection of the petit jury; the improper exclusion of a juror because of his views on capital punishment; racial discrimination in the selection of the grand jury; the violation of the *Anders* standards governing the withdrawal of appointed appellate counsel; the denial of consultation between defendant and his counsel during an overnight trial recess; the denial of a defendant's right to a public trial; an erroneous reasonable doubt instruction to the jury; representation by counsel acting under an actual conflict of interest that adversely affects his performance; and the failure of the trial court to make an appropriate inquiry into a possible conflict of interest under those special circumstances that constitutionally mandate such an inquiry.

In *Ariz. v. Fulminante*, the majority characterized those errors placed within the automatic reversal category as involving "structural defect[s] affecting the framework within which the trial proceeds, rather than simply an error in the trial process itself." Their nature was quite distinct, the Court noted, from those errors held subject to the *Chapman* harmless error standard. The latter group of violations were tied together by the "common thread" of "involv[ing] 'trial error'—error which occurred during the presentation of the case to the jury and which may therefore be quantitatively assessed in the context of other evidence presented in order to determine whether its admission was harmless beyond a reasonable doubt." Although the Court has later discounted the idea of a "rigid dichotomy," preferring to refer to the difference as a "spectrum of constitutional errors," it has also continued to cite to *Fulminante's* classification scheme as authoritative.

In some instances, constitutional violations have fallen in the automatic reversal category because the right violated is not primarily concerned with ensuring reliable verdicts, but serves an entirely different function. The refusal to apply *Chapman* to a denial of defendant's right to proceed pro se was so explained in *McKaskle v. Wiggins* (1984). That right, the Court noted, is designed to permit the defendant to control his own destiny, even though its exercise "usually increases the likelihood of a trial outcome unfavorable to the defendant"; accordingly, "its denial is not amenable to 'harmless error' analysis." The broader function of the right violated may also explain, in part, the Court's refusal to apply a harmless-error analysis in the jury selection cases. The Court in *Batson v. Ky.* (1986) required automatic reversal even where a single juror was excluded unconstitutionally and there was no suggestion of bias on the part of the jurors actually selected. This position may follow from those functions of the jury trial guarantees (e.g., community participation) that extend beyond simply providing the defendant with a factfinding process that is reliable. Indeed, the Court in its post-*Batson* decisions has characterized jury discrimination as impairing not the rights of defendants, but the rights of potential jurors.

Of course, the recognition that a constitutional right serves a function other than promoting the reliability of verdicts does not in itself place that error beyond the reach of *Chapman*. The self incrimination privilege serves a variety of functions beyond the protection of the innocent, yet *Chapman* itself applied the harmless error standard to an infringement of that right. The key may be that unlike some of the other rights which, when violated warrant a rule of automatic reversal, the self incrimination privilege operates solely as a prohibition against the use of evidence.

Closely linked to the idea that some errors require reversal in order to vindicate an interest other than verdict reliability are the Court's references to the need to protect the integrity of the judicial process. This "judicial integrity" rationale has been cited as an explanation for the requirements of automatic-reversal in both the jury selection cases and in *Tumey*, the paradigmatic example of a biased judge. Finally the need for deterrence of error may play a role in the decision to require relief regardless of harm, particularly when other rationales for requiring reversal are wanting. Thus, the Court has noted "that racial discrimination in the selection of grand jurors is so pernicious, and other remedies so impractical, that the remedy of automatic reversal was necessary as a prophylactic means of deterring grand jury discrimination in the future."

Another critical factor in determining the applicability of harmless error analysis is the impact of allowing harmless error review upon the function that the right is designed to achieve. Consider, for example, the withdrawal of appellate counsel without the procedures specified by *Anders*. Here, a subsequent analysis could determine that the appeal truly was frivolous and that defendant was not hurt since counsel would have been allowed to withdraw after filing an *Anders* brief. But as the court noted in *Penson v. Ohio* (1988), applying *Chapman* to an *Anders* violation would leave the defendant without the very protection that *Anders* sought to provide when it barred withdrawal on counsel's bare assertion that the appeal was frivolous. In applying a harmless error analysis, *Penson* noted, the appellate court would be required to assess the potential merits of the defendant's appeal, finding the error harmless or not harmless according to its view as to whether a reversal on the merits would be required. To allow such an analysis would thereby "render * * * meaningless the protections afforded * * * by *Anders*."

Undoubtedly the characteristic of "structural" violations that is most frequently mentioned by the Supreme Court is the "inherently indeterminate" impact of the violation upon the outcome of the trial. Unlike most errors at trial, such errors do not relate to the introduction or evaluation of particular items of evidence. Thus, in *U.S. v. Gonzalez-Lopez* (2006), the Court explained that its conclusion that the denial of the right to counsel of one's choice was structural error rested "upon the difficulty of assessing the effect of the error." In *Sullivan v. La.* (1993), the Court deemed "structural" and requiring automatic reversal a constitutional error in charging the jury on the reasonable doubt standard. *Chapman* directs a reviewing court to ask whether the jury's verdict "was surely unattributable to the error." Here since there never was a jury verdict of guilty beyond a reasonable doubt, the "most an appellate court could conclude is that a jury surely would have found petitioner guilty beyond a reasonable doubt," an inquiry *Chapman* prohibits. The Court distinguished cases involving unconstitutional jury instructions relating to presumptions, reasoning that a court reviewing such error is able to assess the bearing of the presumption upon the jury's verdict by reference to the various findings the jury did make. "But the essential connection to a 'beyond a reasonable doubt' factual finding cannot be made where the instructional error consists of a misdescription of the burden of proof which vitiates all the jury's findings."

Sullivan's reasoning appeared to prohibit harmless error review of a judge's complete failure to submit an element to the jury, but in *Neder v. U.S.* (1999), the Court interpreted *Sullivan* differently. Neder had been convicted of several charges of fraud as well as filing a false tax return. The trial judge, in accordance with the Court of Appeals precedent at the time and over the objection of the defendant, did not include materiality as an element of these crimes in its charge to the jury. Subsequent Supreme Court precedent refuted the trial judge's assumption that materiality was a question for the court, not the jury, raising in Neder's case the question whether the failure to instruct the jury on this element could be considered harmless. The Supreme Court in *Neder* admitted that it would not be "illogical to extend the reasoning of *Sullivan*" to this case, but concluded that "[w]e do not think the Sixth Amendment requires us to veer away from settled precedent to reach such a result." Assessments of the harmlessness of an omitted instruction, the Court reasoned, do not differ from assessments the harmlessness of instructions that erroneously describe an element or that involve an unconstitutional presumption—all foreclose independent jury consideration of whether the facts proved establish beyond a reasonable doubt the element in question. By contrast, the Court continued, the error in *Sullivan* "vitiate[d] all of the jury's findings."

After the Court's decisions in *Apprendi, Blakely,* and *Booker,* thousands of defendants claimed on appeal a violation of the right to have a jury, not a judge, determine the existence of an aggravating sentence factor. The Court in *Wash. v. Recuenco* (2006) held that this type of claim was indistinguishable from Neder's, and was subject to harmless error analysis. The failure to submit a fact triggering a higher sentencing maximum to the jury, like the failure to submit any other element to the jury, is not structural error.

In *Puckett v. United States* (2009) the Court summed up the nature of a "structural" error and also confirmed that policy concerns can justify dispensing with harmless error review for errors that are not "structural." First rejecting the defendant's argument that breach of a plea agreement was "structural," the Court noted that a breach shared none of the common features of "structural errors." Breach does not "necessarily render a criminal trial fundamentally unfair or an unreliable vehicle for determining guilt or innocence," does not " 'defy analysis by "harmless-error" standards' by affecting the entire adjudicatory framework," nor is the " 'difficulty of assessing the effect of the error' greater than with respect to other procedural errors" subject to harmlessness review. Instead, the Court explained, its decision to grant relief on appeal without regard to harmlessness when a defendant raises a timely objection to a plea breach rested "upon a policy interest in establishing the trust between defendants and prosecutors that is necessary to sustain plea bargaining—an 'essential' and 'highly desirable' part of the criminal process."

(e) Applying the Reasonable Doubt Standard for Constitutional Errors. When the Court in *Chapman* sought to fashion a federal harmless error standard for constitutional errors, it looked to the analysis it had adopted earlier in *Fahy v. Conn.* In a passage that is generally viewed as the key to *Chapman* ruling, the *Chapman* Court reasoned:

> "The question is whether there is a reasonable possibility that the evidence complained of might have contributed to the conviction." * * * An error in admitting plainly relevant evidence which possibly influenced the jury adversely to a litigant cannot, under *Fahy*, be conceived of as harmless. Certainly error, constitutional error, in illegally admitting highly prejudicial evidence or comments, casts on someone other than the person prejudiced by it a burden to show that it was harmless. It is for that reason that the original common law harmless error rule put the burden on the beneficiary of the error either to prove that there was no injury or to suffer a reversal of his erroneously obtained judgment. There is little, if any, difference between our statement in *Fahy* about "whether there is a reasonable possibility that the evidence complained of might have contributed to the conviction" and requiring the beneficiary of a constitutional error to prove beyond a reasonable doubt that the error complained of did not contribute to the verdict obtained. We, therefore, do no more than adhere to the meaning of our *Fahy* case when we hold, as we now do, that before a federal constitutional error can be held harmless, the court must be able to declare a belief that it was harmless beyond a reasonable doubt.

The *Chapman* standard looked not to whether the jury could have convicted without regard to the error, or whether the appellate court itself would have convicted without the error, but to whether the error had influenced the jury in reaching its verdict. It required that the appellate court be convinced "beyond a reasonable doubt" that there was no "reasonable possibility" that the error contributed to the jury's verdict. The *Chapman* opinion did not clearly indicate, however, precisely what weight was to be given to the presence of overwhelming untainted evidence in making that judgment. Later in *Neder*, the Court stated that "where a reviewing court concludes beyond a reasonable doubt that the omitted element was uncontested and supported by overwhelming evidence, such that the jury verdict would have been the same absent the error, the erroneous instruction is properly found to be harmless." "If," after "a thorough examination of the record," the reviewing court "cannot conclude beyond a reasonable doubt that the jury verdict would have been the same absent the error—for example, where the defendant contested the omitted element and raised evidence sufficient to support a contrary finding—it should not find the error harmless." Similarly, when the Court in *Wash. v. Recuenco* (2006) found harmless the judge's failure to submit a fact raising the maximum sentence to the jury, it again followed the approach of asking what the outcome would have been had the trial error not occurred, rather than assessing the effect of the error on the trial that took place, as in *Sullivan.*

*

Chapter 20

POST CONVICTION REVIEW: COLLATERAL REMEDIES

Table of Sections

> For additional analysis of the above topics and citations to authorities supporting their discussion in this Book, consult the authors' 7-volume *Criminal Procedure* treatise, also available as Westlaw database CRIMPROC. See the Table of Cross-References in this Book.

§ 20.1 Current Collateral Remedies and Historical Antecedents

(a) **The Nature of Collateral Remedies.** Every jurisdiction has one or more procedures through which defendants can present post-appeal challenges to their convictions on at least limited grounds. In addition, through the federal writ of habeas corpus, a state defendant may challenge his state conviction on federal constitutional grounds in the federal courts. The various state and federal procedures for presenting post-appeal challenges are commonly described as "collateral remedies." Many common collateral remedies today are derived from the common law writs of habeas corpus and coram nobis. The common law habeas proceeding was a separate civil action in which a petitioner challenged his continued detention by attacking the conviction on which his detention was based. Because the petitioner sought release from custody, the petition was filed in the court having jurisdiction over the official who held the petitioner in custody (e.g., the prison warden), rather than the court that had entered judgment of conviction. The writ of coram nobis directly attacked the conviction and was pursued in the court of conviction, but it also was commonly viewed as an independent civil action.

This chapter focuses on the contemporary federal writ of habeas corpus. Federal habeas is the one collateral remedy available to all state prisoners. It also provides the doctrinal framework for the primary post-conviction remedy for federal prisoners challenging their convictions: the motion to vacate a sentence under 28 U.S.C. § 2255. In addition, many states have modeled their own collateral remedies upon the federal writ.

(b) **The Common Law Writ of Habeas Corpus.** The common law writ of habeas corpus, simply defined, is a judicial order directing a person to have the body of another brought before a tribunal at a certain time and place. The writ apparently takes its name from its directive, originally stated in Latin, that the court would "have the body." As initially developed sometime before the thirteenth century, the writ was a process by which courts compelled the attendance of parties whose presence would facilitate their proceedings. It was not until the mid-fourteenth century that it came to be used as an independent proceeding designed to challenge illegal detention. The subsequent sixteenth-century characterization of habeas corpus as the Great Writ of Liberty—the alleged procedural underpinning of the guarantees of the Magna Carta—stemmed primarily from battles fought in establishing its effectiveness against imprisonment by the King's agents without judicial authorization. The celebrated Habeas Corpus Act of 1679 reinforced judicial authority to use the writ to release persons illegally detained by the Crown, but specifically excluded from its coverage persons confined as a result of criminal conviction. As a remedy for persons detained upon a conviction, the writ historically had very limited utility.

English habeas corpus jurisprudence was transplanted to post-colonial America, the Constitution included a provision limiting the suspension of the writ, and the Judiciary Act of 1789 granted federal courts limited habeas review. During Reconstruction, Congress passed the Habeas Corpus Act of 1867, which broadened significantly federal power to review the judgments of state courts. For the first time federal courts were given the power to grant writs of habeas corpus when any person, including one convicted of crime, was held "in violation of the Constitution." Despite the significant changes in the statute that have occurred since that era, the history of the writ and its use in federal courts during the nineteenth century continue to inform the Court's application of the Suspension Clause and contemporary commands of Congress.

§ 20.2   The Statutory Structure and Habeas Policy

(a) **Constitutional Right or Legislative Grace.** In the Suspension Clause, Article I of the United States Constitution states: "[T]he Privilege of the Writ of Habeas Corpus shall not be suspended, unless when in Cases of Rebellion or Invasion the Public Safety may require it." On its face, this provision suggests that federal courts have the inherent authority to issue the writ in the absence of a valid suspension. Such a reading would establish, in effect, a constitutional right to habeas relief, at least to the extent such relief was available at common law, for persons held in custody.

The Court in *Felker v. Turpin* (1996), unanimously rejected the contention that the Clause was violated by those provisions of the Antiterrorism and Effective Death Penalty Act of 1996 that sharply limit habeas relief for petitioners filing successive petitions. Chief

Justice Rehnquist's opinion for the Court initially noted that "the writ of habeas corpus known to the Framers was quite different from that which exists today" as the writ at that time was available "only to prisoners confined under the authority of the United States, not under state authority" and "[t]he class of judicial actions reviewable by the writ was more restricted as well." It "was not until 1867 that Congress made the writ generally available * * * [to state prisoners,] [a]nd it was not until well into this century that this Court interpreted that provision to allow a final judgment of conviction in a state court to be collaterally attacked." The *Felker* Court assumed, however, for purposes of its decision, "that the Suspension Clause of the Constitution refers to the writ as it exists today, rather than as it existed in 1789." The Court had long recognized that "judgments about the proper scope of the writ are 'normally for Congress to make.'" In enacting new restrictions on successive petitions in 1996, Congress dealt with an area of habeas law which the Court had previously described as the product of "a complex and evolving body of equitable principles informed and controlled by historical usage, statutory developments and judicial decisions." The new limitations were "well within the compass of this evolutionary process." Noting that the 1996 Act did not repeal the authority of the Supreme Court to entertain original habeas petitions filed under 28 U.S.C.A. § 2241, the Court concluded that the limitations on successive petitions did "not amount to a suspension of the writ contrary to Article I, § 9."

Although not involving constitutional limitations on congressional efforts to restrict federal habeas review of state-convicted prisoners, the decision in *Boumediene v. Bush* (2008) contained dicta that may be relevant to future interpretations of the scope of the Clause in that context. In *Boumediene,* a closely divided Court concluded that the Military Commissions Act of 2006 effected an unconstitutional suspension of the writ because it stripped the federal courts of habeas jurisdiction over claims of illegal custody filed by detainees at the U. S. Naval Station at Guantanamo Bay, Cuba, and did not provide an adequate substitute for habeas corpus review. Under the Suspension Clause, the Court explained, "the necessary scope of habeas review in part depends upon the rigor of any earlier proceedings." In *Boumediene,* the earlier proceedings were determinations by Combatant Status Review Tribunals (CSRTs) that the detainees were "enemy combatants." Because the CSRTs provided only limited safeguards, the Court found, they presented "a considerable risk of error in the tribunal's findings of fact." Accordingly, the substitute for habeas review of these decisions had to provide not only "the power to order the conditional release of an individual unlawfully detained," but also "some authority to assess the sufficiency of the Government's evidence against the detainee," and "the authority to admit and consider relevant exculpatory evidence that was not introduced during the earlier proceeding." Even if construed to provide for the remedy of release, the review process Congress had provided—in the Court of Appeals for the District of Columbia—"f[ell] short of being a constitutionally adequate substitute, for the detainee still would have no opportunity to present evidence discovered after the CSRT proceedings concluded." Moreover, the Court reasoned, the Deputy Secretary's wholly discretionary determination whether to initiate new proceedings "is an insufficient replacement for the factual review these detainees are entitled to receive through habeas corpus." Most importantly for assessing potential limitations on habeas review of convicted prisoners, the Court was careful to distinguish the statutory scheme it addressed from the review of a sentence after conviction, noting, "A criminal conviction in the usual course occurs after a judicial hearing before a tribunal disinterested in the outcome and committed to procedures designed to ensure its own independence. These dynamics are not inherent in executive detention orders or executive review procedures." The Court stated, for example, that although "limiting the scope of collateral review to a record that may not be accurate or complete" was unconstitutional in the context before it, "[i]n other contexts, *e.g.*, in post-trial habeas cases where the prisoner already has had a full and fair opportunity to develop the factual predicate of his claims, similar limitations on the scope of habeas review may be appropriate." Should Congress in the future significantly restrict federal habeas review of constitutional claims raised by prisoners serving state sentences, this discussion in *Boumediene* will surely be referenced in any debate over whether the resulting statutory remedy provides an adequate "substitute" under the Suspension Clause.

(b) Statutory Structure: From the 1867 Act to the 1996 Act. For over a century, the Habeas Corpus Act of 1867 provided the basic statutory framework for federal habeas relief on behalf of state prisoners. Although several key provisions have now been superseded by provisions of the 1996 Antiterrorism and Effective Death Penalty Act, an understanding of the earlier statute is an essential backdrop to litigation under the new provisions.

The 1867 Act provided habeas relief for any person "restrained of his or her liberty," including state prisoners, who had been excluded under the 1789 Act. Accordingly, the 1867 Act specified that relief could be granted from only those restraints imposed in violation of federal law—the Constitution, treaties, and statutes of the United States. A narrow reading of the Act assumed that the Act incorporated the "historical meaning and scope" of the writ, including earlier cases that had limited habeas review to a determination of whether the convicting court had jurisdiction over the person and the subject matter. The competing, broader view of the 1867 Act would have extended the writ beyond jurisdictional defects.

By the 1960s the Court had adopted this broader interpretation of the Act's purpose in several expansive decisions, noting that the writ was capable of growth to meet "changed conceptions of the kind of criminal proceedings so fundamentally defective as to make imprisonment pursuant to them constitutionally intolerable." But by the mid–1970s the tide had turned, and the Court's interpretations of the habeas statute narrowed. Still, the Court continued to apply the writ substantially beyond the review of jurisdictional defects. Meanwhile, Congress offered little further direction, adding various provisions to the habeas statute over the years, none of which modified the core statutory authorization set forth in the 1867 Act. In 1976 habeas cases became subject to the "Rules Governing 2254 Cases in the United States District Courts," supplementing the statutory provisions.

(c) The Current Statute. In 1996, Congress enacted the Antiterrorism and Effective Death Penalty Act (AEDPA), substantially changing the basic provisions of the habeas statute. The current statutory provisions governing the writ are found in 28 U.S.C.A. §§ 2241–2266. What follows is a very brief outline of the most important provisions governing the writ for persons in state custody, provisions that will be examined in more detail in later sections of this chapter.

Section 2241 contains the basic authorization for the federal courts to issue the writ, with its subsection (c) setting forth the conditions under which the writ may "extend to a prisoner." Subsection (c)(3) provides that the writ may issue when the prisoner "is in custody in violation of the Constitution or laws or treaties of the United States." Section 2241 also provides authority for the Supreme Court to grant a petition filed originally with the High Court, although Rule 20.4(a) of the Supreme Court Rules limits such relief to "exceptional circumstances."

Section 2243 deals primarily with matters of procedure but ends by noting that the habeas court shall "dispose of the matter as law and justice require." This provision has been cited by the Supreme Court as evidencing the "equitable nature" of the habeas remedy.

Section 2244 sets forth circumstances under which a judge may refuse to consider a petition on the basis of the disposition of an earlier petition. It also includes a one-year limitations period during which a petitioner may apply for a writ of habeas corpus.

Sections 2254(b) and (c) contain the requirement that a state prisoner exhaust state remedies before federal relief may be granted. Section § 2254(d) defines the circumstances under which a writ may be granted when the petitioner's claim was adjudicated on the merits in state court. Section § 2254(e) governs factfinding and evidentiary hearings, and includes a presumption concerning state factfinding.

Sections §§ 2261 through 2266 impose special restrictive standards for considering habeas petitions by state prisoners sentenced to death in states which have been certified as having adopted a "mechanism for the appointment, compensation, and payment of reasonable litigation expenses of competent counsel in State post-conviction proceedings brought by indigent prisoners whose capital sentences have been upheld on direct review." Attempts to qualify for these standards by several states have all been rejected by the courts, so that these standards have yet to be applied.

(d) Balancing Within the Statutory Framework. Except where the language of the statute is quite specific, the Court generally has considered its task in interpreting the habeas statute as one of achieving the appropriate balance between the value of expansive habeas review and the costs of providing such review. Although the 1996 Act has restricted the circumstances under which the Court is free to balance such interests, and has tipped that balance distinctly in the direction of narrowing relief, plenty of room for judicial policy analysis remains under the revised statute.

The benefits of expansive collateral review for both state and federal prisoners have been advocated most forcefully in the opinions of Justice Brennan. Plenary review of constitutional claims on collateral attack is essential to fulfilling the historic function of habeas corpus—providing relief against the detention of persons in violation of their fundamental liberties. An open-ended mechanism, he stated, is needed, in particular, to consider claims that were not presented in the original proceeding that led to conviction, often through no fault of the defendant himself. Since the Supreme Court lacks the resources necessary to review more than a few of the state cases in which direct review is sought, the lower federal courts must serve as its functional surrogate in providing federal habeas review. This role of the federal habeas courts, it is argued, also provides greater uniformity in constitutional interpretation. The demand for a federal forum is not based on any doubts as to the personal integrity of state judges, but rather on the recognition of the institutional limitations under which state judges operate. "State judges popularly elected may have difficulty resisting popular pressures not experienced by federal judges given lifetime ten-ure designed to immunize them from such influences."

The Court, however, has questioned the assumption that insti-tutional factors render state judges less receptive to federal consti-tutional claims than federal judges. Justice O'Connor has noted, for example, that many states utilize merit selection systems that give state judges security against "majoritarian pressures" comparable to that provided by the life tenure afforded federal judges. Without substantial evidence of concerted failure by state courts to abide by their obligations, several Justices have argued, it should not be assumed that federal habeas courts must review federal claims notwithstanding entirely adequate state procedures for considering those claims. "[T]here is 'no intrinsic reason why the fact that a man is a federal judge should make him more competent, or conscientious, or learned with respect to the [consideration of Fourth Amendment claims] than his neighbor in the state court-house.' "

In addition, expansive federal habeas review of state cases carries three costs. First, broad habeas review is said to result in an unwise expenditure of scarce federal judicial resources. Second, systematic habeas review of state decisions is said to be inconsis-tent with the "constitutional balance upon which the doctrine of federalism is founded." Finally, plenary habeas review is said to work against the important objective of achieving a rational point of finality in the criminal justice process.

(e) Competing Models of Habeas Review. How should the Court balance the costs and benefits of habeas review? The basic contours of several distinct but not necessarily conflicting theories are set forth below.

Ensuring responsible state court adjudication of constitutional rights: the "one fair chance" model. One of the narrowest models of habeas review still exerting considerable influence is that which views the primary function of the writ as ensuring that the state judicial systems fulfill their obligation to apply in a responsible manner the prevailing constitutional doctrine. Such a model, sup-plemented by the traditional review of jurisdictional defects, fur-nished the foundation for the standards that governed habeas review for a good part of the first half of the twentieth century. Utilizing what was later described as a "due process" approach to habeas review, those standards looked to whether the state process had afforded the habeas petitioner an adequate opportunity to gain a fair determination of his constitutional claim.

Two developments in federal habeas doctrine prior to the 1996 Act followed this model. *Stone v. Powell* (1976) barred habeas relitigation of a fourth amendment claim provided the state procedure granted the defendant a "full and fair opportunity" for litigating that claim. More significantly, *Teague v. Lane* (1989) held that to deter state courts from disregarding federal constitutional precedent, the federal habeas court need only apply constitutional doctrine as it stood when the state courts applied it. Amended § 2254(d) now codifies this general approach, barring relief for claims litigated on their merits in state court unless the state court decision was contrary to or involved an "unreasonable" application of "clearly established Federal law." See § 20.6(f).

Surrogate supreme courts. Another model of federal habeas review considers the federal habeas courts as primarily quasi-appellate courts, serving as a replacement for a Supreme Court that can review only a small fraction of all petitions for certiorari presented to it. The initial focus of this "surrogate" model was the importance of development and interpretation of federal constitutional guarantees by federal, not state, courts. This model found its strongest support in decisions of the 1950s and early '60s, but was weakened by the Court's decision in *Teague v. Lane*, which forbid habeas courts from expanding the rights of criminal defendants. *Teague* barred the announcement of new rules in habeas cases, except in a few narrow circumstances. The 1996 amendments narrowed those circumstances further still. So circumscribed, habeas litigation is no longer a vehicle for developing federal law. Still, to the limited extent that habeas courts supplement Supreme Court review in correcting error in state courts, the surrogate model retains vitality.

The "fundamental fairness" model. Justice Stevens, in a series of opinions in the 1980s, advanced a "fundamental fairness" model of habeas review. Justice Stevens's position was that "constitutional errors are not fungible," at least with respect to remedies. Just as there are some errors that call for automatic reversal and some that call for reversal on appeal only if deemed not to have been harmless, there are some errors "important enough" to require reversal on direct appeal but not important enough to require the overturning of a conviction on collateral review, and some errors so significant that they should be recognized on habeas review under almost any circumstance. In this latter category, Justice Stevens placed "errors so fundamental that they infect the validity of the underlying judgment itself, or the integrity by which that judgment was obtained," such as a trial dominated by mob violence, the prosecutor's knowing use of perjured testimony, or the admission of a confession "extorted from the defendant by brutal methods." While Justice Stevens agreed courts must be cautious when considering claims that were not raised at trial (in part on the premise that the tardiness in their presentation suggests in itself their likely irrelevance), he was willing to push aside even weighty state interests in procedural regularity when a clear denial of fundamental fairness was presented. Although neither the Court majority nor Congress accepted Justice Stevens's fundamental fairness doctrine, both adopted the basic premise that certain claims should prevail over limits that would otherwise bar habeas review.

Protection of the "innocent." In 1969 Justice Black, in a brief dissent from a majority ruling granting collateral relief based on a fourth amendment violation, noted: "I would always require that the convicted defendant raise the kind of constitutional claim that casts some shadow of a doubt on his guilt." This comment was expanded upon in a highly influential article by Judge Henry Friendly, with the provocative title "Is Innocence Irrelevant?" Judge Friendly argued that "with a few important exceptions," "convictions should be subject to collateral attack only when the prisoner supplements his constitutional plea with a colorable claim of innocence." There were important distinctions in the manner in which Judge Friendly and Justice Black would have used habeas review as a safety net for the innocent. Justice Black focused on the general nature of the constitutional claim, asking whether its basic function is to protect the innocent by safeguarding the reliability of the guilt determining process. Judge Friendly, on the other hand, focused on actual factual innocence on a case-by-case basis. The defendant would have to show factual innocence that may have gone unrecognized due to a constitutional violation that affected the determination of guilt.

Both versions of habeas review as a safety net for the innocent have been incorporated into various aspects of habeas law. Innocence has not, however, become the exclusive theme of habeas review. With one exception, see § 20.3(e), habeas review remains focused on the question of whether a constitutional right was violated, not whether a petitioner is in fact innocent. On the other hand, whether or not a claim affects the reliability of a guilty verdict may be critical in determining whether review will be available notwithstanding a failure by the petitioner or his counsel to raise the claim in a timely manner, a failure that would otherwise bar review. The Court's holding in *Stone v. Powell* that claims of fourth amendment error ordinarily are not cognizable on habeas review is based in part on the recognition that such error does not jeopardize the reliability of a conviction.

Current law, as the above discussion indicates, does not exclusively follow any one model of habeas review. Rather, the statute and the doctrinal landscape against which it must be interpreted contain elements, sometimes inconsistent, of several different models. In part, this is a product of stare decisis, and the failure of any single model to capture the full support of a majority of the Court, or Congress.

§ 20.3   Cognizable Claims

(a) **Cognizable Claimants: The Custody Requirement.** The federal habeas corpus statutes, from the 1789 Act to today's statute, have all provided that the writ extend to a person "in custody." Presently, §§ 2241 and 2254 provide that the writ is limited to persons "in custody in violation of the Constitution or laws or treaties of the United States." Not surprisingly, as the Court expanded the scope of the writ in its treatment of such matters as the range of cognizable claims during the 1960s, it also broadened the element of custody. Subsequent decisions continue to interpret generously the initial jurisdictional requirement of custody, despite markedly restrictive readings of other requirements for habeas relief. "Custody" may exist not only when a petitioner is incarcerated, but also when a petitioner suffers certain significant "present restraints."

The decision of *Jones v. Cunningham* (1963) was the critical ruling extending the concept of "custody" beyond actual incarceration. The Court there held, in an opinion by Justice Black, that a petitioner subject to typical conditions of parole was "in custody" for the purposes of § 2254. Justice Black concluded "there are other restraints on a man's liberty, restraints not shared by the public generally, which have been thought sufficient in the English-speaking world to support the issuance of habeas corpus." For example, he noted, the writ had been made available to an alien seeking entry into the United States, or to a person contesting the legality of induction into the military service. The parolee was subject to special regulations which restricted other aspects of his liberty, including the requirements that he obtain special permission before operating an automobile and that he report regularly to his parole officer. He was threatened with reincarceration for the duration of his original sentence for even the most insignificant violation of the parole regulations. Moreover, he could be ordered back to prison for violation of parole without a judicial hearing. Taken together these elements were "enough to invoke the help of The Great Writ."

In *Hensley v. Municipal Court* (1973), *Jones* was held applicable to a habeas petitioner who was at large on his own recognizance pending execution of the sentence on his misdemeanor conviction. Due to an unusual combination of stays, the petitioner had been able to pursue his appeals within the state system and present his habeas application before starting to serve his one-year sentence. Petitioner continued to be bound by the conditions imposed during his pretrial release. He had agreed to "appear at all times and places" as ordered by the court, to waive extradition if he failed to appear and was apprehended outside the state, and to be subject to a court order at any time that could revoke his release. Although these conditions were less restrictive than those imposed on the petitioner in *Jones* the petitioner was "in custody" within the meaning of the habeas statute. Justice Brennan's opinion for the Court concluded that Hensley was subject to "restraints not shared by the public generally" which placed his freedom of movement "in the hands of judicial officers who may demand his presence at any time." Later the Court held that a person released on his own recognizance pending a trial *de novo* was in custody, at least where the terms of the recognizance imposed restraints roughly similar to those found in *Hensley,* such that the petitioner was subject to restraints "not shared by the public generally." Restraints attending probation are sufficient to establish custody as well. Similar treatment is due the suspended sentence that poses a threat of future imprisonment if the petitioner fails to comply with a condition.

In *Carafas v. LaVallee* (1968), the petitioner filed his habeas application while still in prison, but he was unconditionally discharged (upon completion of his sentence) while the habeas court's denial of relief was on appeal. The Court found that so long as the applicant was in custody when the writ was filed, the habeas court has jurisdiction, which it retains pending a final disposition of the case. A contrary view, the Court noted, would "only aggravate the hardships that may result from the 'intolerable delays in affording justice.' " A habeas petitioner "should not be thwarted * * * simply because the path of litigation has been so long * * * that he served his sentence." The Court later extended the concept of custody to a prisoner serving the first of two consecutive sentences who attacks in his habeas petition the second conviction or sentence; a prisoner in one jurisdiction attacking a pending prosecution in another; and a petitioner challenging a conviction underlying a sentence already served, when that petitioner is incarcerated under consecutive sentences.

Many disadvantages flowing from conviction do not constitute custody for purposes of habeas review, however. In *Maleng v. Cook* (1989), for example, the Court rejected the petitioner's contention that he remained in custody at the time he had filed his petition, notwithstanding the prior expiration of his sentence, because of the "possibility" that the conviction "will be used to enhance the sentences imposed for any subsequent crimes of which he is convicted." The Court responded that since almost all states have habitual offender statutes, acceptance of such a contention "would read the 'in custody' requirement out of the statute." In addition to

the mere possibility of a future enhanced sentence, other consequences deemed insufficient to establish custody include the payment of a fine (despite the possibility of physical restraint as a
penalty for nonpayment), the revocation of professional licenses,
the suspension of drivers licenses, the prohibition against possessing firearms, and the inability to hold public office.

(b) Cognizable Claims—From Jurisdictional Defects to *Stone v. Powell.*

Stone v. Powell. Petitioners "in custody" who seek habeas relief
must also demonstrate that they are in custody in violation of
federal law. For over a century, first under the 1789 Act and later
under the 1867 Act, Supreme Court rulings limited federal habeas
review for convicted prisoners to those claims that challenged the
jurisdiction of the court of conviction. Federal habeas review is no
longer so limited. Beginning with *Ex parte Lange* in 1873, the Court
initiated what has been described as "a long process of expansion of
the concept of a lack of jurisdiction" from a narrow view of
jurisdiction to one stretched beyond recognition. Lange contended
that he had been twice sentenced for the same offense, in violation
of the Fifth Amendment's Double Jeopardy Clause, when he had
been resentenced to a term of imprisonment after having paid the
fine originally imposed. Carefully disclaiming the use of habeas as a
writ of error, the Supreme Court ordered Lange released from
imprisonment because the lower court's jurisdiction terminated
upon the satisfaction of the original sentence.

Soon the Court found jurisdictional error included the failure
to secure an indictment, conviction under an unconstitutional statute, conviction after a mob-dominated trial, and the failure to
provide appointed counsel. The Court in *Waley v. Johnston* (1942),
faced on habeas review a constitutional claim that it could not so
readily characterize as undermining the structure of the proceeding
and therefore causing the trial court to "lose jurisdiction," the
petitioner claimed that his guilty plea had been coerced by an F.B.I.
agent. In a per curiam opinion, the Court concluded the writ

> is not restricted to those cases where the judgment of convic-
> tion is void for want of jurisdiction of the trial court to render
> it. It extends also to those exceptional cases where the convic-
> tion has been in disregard of the constitutional rights of the
> accused, and where the writ is the only effective means of
> preserving his rights.

As various commentators have noted, *Waley* "finally dispensed with
the fiction of 'jurisdiction.' " But it did not go so far as to hold that
all constitutional claims were subject to habeas review. The Court
had stressed that petitioner's claim rested on facts outside the
record. It was not the type of claim that petitioner could readily
have raised in the original proceeding that produced his conviction

or on appeal. Accordingly, if the claim was ever to be reviewed by a federal court, that review would have to come on collateral attack. It was not until 1953, in *Brown v. Allen* (1953), that the Court extended review to claims raised in state court. At issue in *Brown* was whether a federal habeas court could review the petitioner's claims of grand jury and trial jury discrimination and the admission of a coerced confession, claims fully litigated and decided against the petitioner in the state courts. A majority agreed that the habeas court should have the "final say" on federal claims. The habeas writ guaranteed federal review of the petitioner's federal claim, not simply a fair state consideration of the claim, for such consideration "may have misconceived a federal constitutional right."

At least one type of constitutional error is not cognizable in habeas. In *Stone v. Powell* (1976), the Court held that "where the State has provided an opportunity for full and fair litigation of a Fourth Amendment claim, the Constitution does not require that a state prisoner be granted federal habeas corpus relief on the ground that the evidence obtained in an unconstitutional search and seizure was introduced at his trial." Justice Powell's opinion in *Stone* emphasized the exclusionary rule was not a "personal constitutional right," but a "judicially created means of effectuating rights secured by the Fourth Amendment," which had a "primary function" of deterring police illegality. The majority concluded that "the additional contribution, if any, of the consideration of search-and-seizure claims of state prisoners in collateral review" to deterrence of police misconduct "is small in relation to the costs."

In reaching this conclusion, Justice Powell proceeded from the premise that the deterrent function of the exclusionary rule was served effectively by enforcement at trial and on direct appeal. He rejected petitioners' argument that state courts might not enforce the Fourth Amendment as rigorously as federal courts, and the effectiveness of the exclusionary remedy as a deterrent therefore depended upon police awareness that "federal habeas might reveal flaws in a search or seizure that went undetected" in the state proceedings.

Turning to the other side of its cost/benefit ledger, the *Stone* majority first noted that the exclusionary rule necessarily "deflects the truthfinding application of the process and often frees the guilty." While these costs were justified by the deterrence gained from applying the rule in the original proceedings, they could not be sustained by the marginal increase in deterrence that might be provided by the rule's application in a collateral proceeding. Moreover, "resort to habeas corpus, especially for purposes other than to assure that no innocent person suffers an unconstitutional loss of liberties," entailed additional costs, including the consumption of scarce federal judicial resources, the delayed finality of criminal proceedings, and the frustration of good-faith state court efforts to fulfill their responsibilities to honor federal constitutional rights.

(c) **Post-*Stone* Rulings.** The Court has considered, and rejected, the possible extension of *Stone* to claims other than fourth amendment violations on four separate occasions. In *Jackson v. Va.* (1979), the Court examined whether a federal habeas court, considering a due process challenge to the sufficiency of the evidence before the state trier of fact, had to look to the *In re Winship* (1970) standard of proof beyond a reasonable doubt, or to a lesser standard, taken from a pre-*Winship* ruling, that would hold due process violated only when the record was "wholly devoid of any relevant evidence of a crucial element of the offense charged." The state argued that *Winship* review was unwarranted on habeas once the petitioner had received a "full and fair hearing" on his insufficient evidence claim in the state's appellate court. Responding to these contentions, the majority noted the constitutional issue presented here was "far different" from that presented in *Stone*: "The question whether a defendant has been convicted upon inadequate evidence is central to the basic question of guilt or innocence."

In *Rose v. Mitchell* (1979) the Court again refused to extend *Stone,* this time to a constitutional claim that the justices agreed had no bearing on the reliability of the truth-finding process at trial. The habeas petitioner in *Mitchell* claimed that the foreman of the indicting grand jury had been selected on the basis of racial discrimination in violation of the Equal Protection Clause of the Fourteenth Amendment. The defendant had been found guilty by a fairly drawn petit jury, following a fair trial, so the claim clearly did not involve the "protect[ion] of the innocent from incarceration."

The *Mitchell* majority offered several reasons for not extending *Stone* to bar habeas review of grand jury discrimination claims. Initially, the Court noted that while *Stone* assumed that state courts were as capable as federal courts in dealing with fourth amendment claims, the same could not be said of grand jury discrimination claims. Such a claim required the state bench to review its own procedures rather than the actions of police. In most cases, the trial court that initially rules on the claim will be the same court that has responsibility for the grand jury selection process. These differences, the Court noted, led it "to doubt that claims of [grand jury discrimination] in general will receive the type of full and fair hearings deemed essential to the holding of *Stone*." For similar reasons, it could not be said here, as it was said in *Stone,* that federal habeas review would have no significant "educative and deterrent effect." There was "strong reason to believe that federal review would indeed reveal flaws not appreciated by state judges perhaps too close to the day-to-day operation of the system." While *Stone* doubted that habeas rulings would have a substantial additional deterrent or educative impact with respect to the police, the responsible state officials here, the courts and their employees, were very likely to take note of the federal decisions and respond accordingly. Moreover, the "costs associated with quashing an indictment returned by an improperly constituted grand jury" were "significantly less than those associated with suppressing evidence." A prisoner who "is guilty in fact" is "less likely to go free" since the prosecution, after reindictment, can retry the defendant on the same evidence. Finally, the "constitutional interests" that are vindicated in rectifying grand jury discrimination were characterized as "substantially more compelling than those at issue in *Stone*." Racial discrimination "strikes at the core concerns of the Fourteenth Amendment and at fundamental values of our society and our legal system." The "harm is not only to the accused," but "to society as a whole."

In *Kimmelman v. Morrison* (1986), the state contended that the reasoning of *Stone* barred habeas review of the petitioner's claim of ineffective assistance of counsel where counsel's incompetency lay solely in failing at trial to properly present an objection to the introduction of damaging evidence that had been seized in violation of the Fourth Amendment. Rejecting that argument, the Court held that a claim of ineffective assistance is based on a separate constitutional right and therefore is cognizable even though the alleged incompetency consisted of counsel's mishandling of a fourth amendment objection. Habeas review served to vindicate the defendant's right to a fair trial within the structure of an adversary system, not merely the exclusionary rule.

Taken together, *Jackson*, *Kimmelman*, and *Mitchell* suggested that if *Stone* was to be extended to any other constitutional claim, the most likely candidate would be a prophylactic rule of comparatively recent vintage, aimed at controlling police behavior, and resulting in the exclusion of reliable evidence. However, in *Withrow v. Williams* (1993), a closely divided Court refused to extend *Stone* to the one claim that seemingly had the best chance of being placed in this category—a violation of *Miranda*. Several features of *Miranda* violations, the majority reasoned, distinguished those violations from the *Mapp* violations considered in *Stone*. First, *Miranda*, "prophylactic though it may be, in protecting a defendant's fifth amendment privilege, * * * safeguards a fundamental trial right [of the individual]." Second, unlike *Mapp*'s exclusionary rule, *Miranda* did not serve only "some value necessarily divorced from the correct ascertainment of guilt." Rather, by "bracing against the possibility of unreliable statements in every instance of in-custody interrogation, *Miranda* serves to guard against the use of unreliable statements at trial." Finally, "eliminating [habeas] review of

Miranda claims would not significantly benefit the federal courts in their exercise of habeas jurisdiction or advance the cause of federalism in any substantial way, * * * as it would not prevent a state prisoner from simply converting his barred *Miranda* claim into a due process [voluntariness] claim" that would still be cognizable on habeas review.

(d) The Opportunity for Full and Fair Litigation. Consistent with its assumption that state courts would conscientiously enforce fourth amendment rights, the *Stone* Court held that federal habeas review would be available if the state had not provided the petitioner an "opportunity for full and fair litigation." This "exception" arguably is broader than what would be needed simply to serve *Stone's* view of the deterrent function of the exclusionary rule. Certainly, if a state regularly fails to provide an adequate litigation opportunity, its enforcement of the exclusionary rule would not provide a substantial deterrent and habeas review would then provide more than a marginal increment in deterrence. The *Stone* exception, however, focuses on the individual case. Thus, the *Stone* majority apparently concluded that even though the exclusionary rule is a "judicially created" remedy rather than a "personal constitutional right," the defendant is entitled to at least one opportunity for a "full and fair consideration" of his claim.

The *Stone* opinion offered little by way of definition of its full and fair opportunity standard. Lower courts assessing the adequacy of state procedures often apply a two-step inquiry asking (1) whether the state procedural mechanism is satisfactory in the abstract, and (2) whether there was a failure of the mechanism in the individual case. A finding of inadequacy is most likely to come under the second inquiry, such as when counsel was appointed one day before the expiration of the time period for presenting a suppression motion and when in denying counsel's oral request for an extension the trial court applied an unwritten local rule mandating a written application. Similarly, a petitioner was denied an adequate opportunity to present his claim where the state appellate court rejected the claim based on a recent decision which had not been raised by the state.

An erroneous application of the Fourth Amendment, without more, does not constitute a denial of an opportunity for full and fair litigation. It is said to be "of no consequence whether the state courts employed an incorrect legal standard, misapplied the correct standard, or erred in finding the underlying facts."

(e) "Bare Innocence" Claims. Until quite recently the Court has insisted that habeas relief was limited to petitioners who could demonstrate some flaw in the process by which they were

convicted or that the punishment was otherwise imposed in violation of federal law. A showing of innocence alone was not a basis for
relief, as the writ was designed to ensure that state court processes
comply with the Constitution, not to enlist federal courts to duplicate guilt-innocence determinations. Indeed, nothing would seem to
upset more the interests in finality and comity than the prospect of
allowing a defendant, fairly convicted in state court upon constitutionally sufficient evidence, to reopen his conviction with "new"
evidence of innocence discovered years after trial, especially when
the state itself carefully confines its own forum for such claims. As
the Court narrowed access to the writ in the 1970s and '80s, a
showing of possible or probable innocence became a common ingredient of habeas relief as interpreted by the Court, but only as a
gateway to habeas review of a separate constitutional claim. For
example, a petitioner who could persuade a federal court that he
may be innocent could overcome a procedural default for which he
could not show "cause and prejudice," or pursue in a second
petition a claim he had failed to bring the first time.

In *Herrera v. Collins* (1993), the Court considered whether
habeas relief was available for claims of "bare innocence," and if so,
when such claims required relief. Herrera had been convicted of
murder and sentenced to death, but claimed that several new
affidavits demonstrated that his brother, and not himself, committed the crime. State law required defendants to bring motions for
new trial based on newly discovered evidence within thirty days of
trial; Herrera had missed this deadline, so a state challenge to his
conviction and sentence was unavailable. He argued in federal court
that the execution of an innocent man would violate the Eighth and
Fourteenth Amendments, although he alleged no constitutional
violation during the state prosecution. Despite considerable ambiguity in their opinions, most of the justices seemed to agree that in
extremely unusual circumstances, a claim of innocence, even one
unaccompanied by a separate constitutional claim, could compel
relief. Justice Rehnquist wrote: "We may assume, for the sake of
argument in deciding this case, that in a capital case a truly
persuasive demonstration of 'actual innocence' made after trial
would render the execution of a defendant unconstitutional, and
warrants federal habeas relief if there were no state avenue open to
process such a claim." The showing required "would necessarily be
extraordinarily high."

New DNA testing, with its extraordinary ability to exonerate
those wrongly convicted, presents a realistic possibility of meeting
this hypothetical standard. The Court has, since *Herrera*, addressed
two cases in which a prisoner has sought to establish innocence
using DNA testing. In each, the Court again declined to decide
whether federal courts have authority to review a freestanding

claim of innocence as a basis for invalidating a state conviction or death sentence. In *House v. Bell* (2006), death row inmate House had managed to gather DNA and other forensic evidence that "cast considerable doubt on his guilt—doubt sufficient to satisfy [the] standard for obtaining federal review despite a state procedural default," his was "not a case of conclusive exoneration." His showing fell "short of the threshold implied in *Herrera*." The Court again assumed, but did not decide, the existence of a federal constitutional right to be released upon proof of "actual innocence" in *District Attorney's Office v. Osborne* (2009). There, the Court, in the course of rejecting the prisoner's argument that he was denied his constitutional right to access evidence for DNA testing, stated that whether a "federal constitutional right to be released upon proof of 'actual innocence' " exists "is an open question."

The chances that such a claim will succeed are extremely small, and the questions such a claim raises are numerous and daunting. First, exactly what type of showing of innocence is required? The justices in *Herrera* stated only that the showing of innocence must be "truly persuasive." The Court's discussion appeared to contemplate a demonstration more stringent than one that would leave a factfinder to believe the petitioner is "probably" innocent, perhaps requiring proof of innocence "beyond a reasonable doubt." Second, the meaning of the Court's requirement that there be "no state avenue open to process such a claim" is unclear. If the state's provision of even the most limited, rarely exercised clemency relief is sufficient to preclude a claim of bare innocence in habeas court, then bare innocence claims are truly hypothetical. Third, the Court's opinion spoke of a showing of innocence that would make an *execution* unconstitutional, suggesting that the claim is open only to defendants sentenced to death. Yet, if punishment of the factually innocent is what the Constitution forbids, limiting relief to capital defendants is difficult to justify. With innocence of the offense as the focus, the petitioner who concedes he committed the crime but disputes the factual allegations that make him eligible for the death penalty may also be barred from raising a *Herrera* claim.

(f) Harmless Error on Habeas Review. In *Brecht v. Abrahamson* (1993), the Court held the *Chapman* harmless error standard was too stringent to apply on habeas review. It reasoned: "Overturning final and presumptively correct convictions on collateral review because the State cannot prove that an error is harmless under *Chapman* undermines the States' interest in finality and infringes upon their sovereignty over criminal matters. Moreover, granting habeas relief merely because there is a ' "reasonable possibility" ' that trial error contributed to the verdict [the *Chapman* standard] is at odds with the historic meaning of habeas corpus—to afford relief to those whom society has 'grievously wronged.' " Concluding that the "imbalance of the costs and benefits of applying the *Chapman* harmless-error standard on collateral review counsels in favor of applying a less onerous standard on habeas review," the *Brecht* majority opted for application of the *Kotteakos* standard, which federal appellate courts have traditionally applied on direct review to non-constitutional errors. "Under this standard," habeas petitioners "are not entitled to habeas relief based on trial error unless they can establish that it resulted in 'actual prejudice.' " As the Court explained later in *Calderon v. Coleman* (1998), the standard "protects the State's sovereign interest in punishing offenders and its good-faith attempts to honor constitutional rights." Noting the "significant" social costs of retrial or resentencing, the Court has decided that the states should not be forced to bear those costs "based on mere speculation that the defendant was prejudiced by trial error; the court must find that the defendant was actually prejudiced by the error."

In *O'Neal v. McAninch* (1995), the Court majority rejected the government's contention that the habeas petitioner bore the "burden of establishing" that a constitutional error was "prejudicial" under the *Brecht-Kotteakos* harmless-error standard. According to the Court, a judge better puts the question as whether "I, the judge, think that the error substantially influenced the jury's decision?" If the judge is left with a "grave doubt" that the error may have had a "substantial influence," then the "conviction cannot stand." There are at least two situations in which a habeas court need not apply the *Brecht* standard. First, harmless analysis is unnecessary whenever a petitioner establishes certain constitutional violations that already require a showing of prejudice (e.g., *Brady; Strickland*). Second, "structural errors" that would not be subject to harmless error analysis on direct review require relief on habeas review without a showing of harm or prejudice, just as they do on direct appeal.

§ 20.4 Claims Foreclosed by State Procedural Defaults

(a) Claims "Defaulted" in State Court—The Policy Debate. When a petitioner has failed to present his claim in the state proceedings in accordance with applicable state procedural requirements, and the state has held that this lapse bars consideration of the claim on the merits, the issue presented to the habeas court is under what conditions, if any, should that state procedural default also bar federal habeas review. Although the 1996 amendments specify the consequences of state procedural default in a particular class of capital cases, the consequence of default in other cases is not addressed by the amendments, nor was procedural default addressed by the statute prior to the 1996 amendments. In the absence of controlling language from Congress, federal courts apply rules for reviewing defaulted claims that have evolved over decades in a wavering course of decisions of the Supreme Court.

These decisions reflect deep differences of opinion over the significance of two sets of competing interests. On the one hand is the petitioner's interest in obtaining review of a federal constitutional claim at least once and the public interest in ensuring that constitutional commands are followed in state proceedings. On the other hand, the state has a stake in the finality of the judgments of its courts, and in the effective enforcement of its procedural rules. Also weighing against habeas review of a claim forfeited in state court for failure to comply with a procedural rule is the risk that federal review will require initial factfinding long after the critical event has passed. Depending on the type of claim raised by the petitioner, delay may result in the loss of the opportunity to punish admitted offenders since the erosion of memory and dispersion of witnesses render retrial difficult or impossible. The Supreme Court has also expressed concern that habeas review not reward what has been described as "sandbagging" tactics by defense counsel, holding a claim in reserve as a means of obtaining a new trial through the writ if the trial should result in a conviction. Another concern repeatedly noted by the Court is that federal review after a state court's efforts to enforce its own procedural rules demonstrates a lack of respect for the state justice system. "Comity," it is argued, may require deference to such state decisions, in order to maintain the appropriate federal balance and prevent strained federal-state relations.

(b) Which Defaults Count: The "Adequate State Ground" Standard. The present standards for determining which defaulted claims are reviewable in habeas proceedings and which are not are discussed in § 20.4(c)-(d). The different issue addressed in this subsection is when federal court will recognize that there has been a default in state court, so that such standards will be applicable.

The Court had long held that on direct review it would not reach the merits of an appellant's constitutional claim if the court below had relied upon an "adequate state ground." If the state court ruling based on state law, independent of the federal constitutional claim, then that law would necessarily control the outcome of the case. Even if the Court were to find that there had been a constitutional violation, it lacked authority to review the question of state law and the state court's ruling would therefore have to be affirmed. Although this analysis was developed initially in connection with state rulings based on substantive grounds, it soon was held applicable to rulings involving procedural grounds as well. Application of the same principle on habeas review was viewed as consistent with the role of the habeas court as a functional surrogate of the Supreme Court in providing a federal forum for federal claims. Thus, a defendant not excused by the state court could only be excused by the habeas courts if the state procedural ruling did not constitute an adequate state ground.

Daniels v. Allen (1953) offers a dramatic example of the effect of this adequate state ground standard on habeas review. Daniels had raised at trial constitutional challenges to the composition of the jury and to the use of an allegedly coerced confession. Daniels' counsel, however, had failed to file a timely appeal. The trial court had granted the defense 60 days in which to prepare and serve its statement of the case on appeal, but that statement was not delivered until the 61st day. The state appellate court refused to hear the appeal even though, if the papers had been mailed on the 60th day, as permitted under court rules, they would not have arrived any earlier. A divided Supreme Court held that the procedural default barred federal habeas review of the petitioner's claims.

Although habeas review may be available despite an adequate and independent state procedural ground for default, the adequacy of the state's application of its procedural rule remains a threshold issue in any case in which procedural default is raised as a defense. The test for adequacy, as explained in *Dugger v. Adams* (1989), looks to whether the procedural rule serves a "legitimate state interest," and to the evenhandedness of its application by state courts. The state may not manipulate its rules to evade federal rights, or exercise its procedural discretion to discriminate against the presentation of such rights. For example, a state procedural rule that was not firmly established at the time of a defendant's trial cannot be applied retroactively as a basis for deeming untimely his objection to jury selection. State procedural rulings are also inadequate when applied in such an arbitrary manner as to "force resort to arid ritual of meaningless form." A rule must be "regularly" and "consistently" applied by state courts to be considered an adequate ground for barring habeas review. A federal court may also review a petitioner's federal claim if the petitioner substantially complied with the essential requirements of the state's procedural rule, and "nothing would [have] be[en] gained by requiring" more exacting adherence to the rule.

In order for a state to rely on the defense of procedural default in a habeas action, not only must it show that the state court's reason for rejecting the petitioner's claim was "adequate," the state must also show that the court's reason was "independent," that is, based on *state* law, not federal. A state court's decision is not "independent" of federal law if either 1) the " 'resolution of [a] state procedural law question depends on a federal constitutional ruling,' " or 2) the state court decision actually rested on such a ruling.

(c) **The Cause-and-Prejudice Standard.** For more than a decade before it settled on the current "cause-and-prejudice" test for determining which claims not properly raised in state court could be reviewed in habeas proceedings, the Court applied an approach more favorable to petitioners known as the "deliberate bypass" standard. Established in *Fay v. Noia* (1963), the "deliberate bypass" standard excused procedural defaults and allowed for federal review unless the default was a product of a "deliberate bypassing" of "the orderly procedure of the state courts." If an applicant who "understandingly and knowingly forewent the privilege of seeking to vindicate his federal claims in the State courts, whether for strategic, tactical, or any other reasons that can fairly be described as the deliberate bypassing of state procedures, then it is open to the federal court on habeas to deny him all relief if the state courts refused to entertain his federal claims on the merits."

The protections of *Fay v. Noia* were soon eroded. In *Henry v. Miss.* (1965), the Court indicated that review may be barred even without the defendant's personal participation in the decision that led to the default. *Murch v. Mottram* (1972), added that a deliberate bypass by counsel did not require knowledge that the tactical maneuver would result in a procedural default under state law, provided counsel had "reasonable warning" that he ran that risk. In *Davis v. U.S.* (1973), the Court considered a claim of racial discrimination in the selection of a grand jury, raised by a federal defendant in a collateral attack on his conviction under 28 U.S.C. § 2255 filed three years after his trial. The Supreme Court rejected Davis's argument that his failure to raise that claim at trial should be judged under the deliberate bypass standard. The Court noted that if Davis's case had come before it on direct review, it would have been decided under Federal Rule 12(b). That Rule provided that the failure to raise before trial a defect in the institution of the prosecution, such as grand jury discrimination, would "constitute a waiver, but the court for cause shown may grant relief from the waiver." The Court found it "inconceivable" that Congress, having foreclosed such a claim from review in the initial proceeding, meant to allow it nonetheless to be presented on collateral attack. Accordingly, the Rule 12(b) standard was held to apply under § 2255 as well as in the original proceeding. This meant that the petitioner could have his claim considered only if his failure to object was justified by "cause shown." Here the district court specifically had held that "cause" was not shown, noting both the defendant's lack of explanation for failing to comply with Rule 12(b) and the lack of any showing of actual prejudice. *Francis v. Henderson* (1976) held that the standard announced in *Davis*—now described as requiring a showing of "cause" and "actual prejudice"—was applicable when reviewing a state prisoner's defaulted claim of grand jury discrimination. The state requirement of a pretrial objection, the Court noted, served many of the same salutary purposes as Federal Rule 12(b). "Surely," the Court concluded, "considerations of comity and federalism require that * * * [habeas courts] give no less effect to the same clear interests when asked to overturn state convictions."

In *Wainwright v. Sykes* (1977), the Court expanded the test to all trial errors. The petitioner Sykes had sought habeas relief on the ground that his conviction had been based on a confession obtained without his full understanding of the *Miranda* warnings. There had been no objection before or during the trial. The *Sykes* opinion offered three reasons for preferring the *Francis* test over *Noia's* deliberate bypass standard. The "contemporaneous-objection" rule applied in the state court deserved "greater respect" than the deliberate bypass standard would give it, the Court reasoned, both because "it is employed by a coordinate jurisdiction within the federal system" and because of the many valid interests it served. The Court also criticized the deliberate bypass rule for detracting from the appropriate role of the trial. The "failure of the federal habeas courts generally to require compliance with a contemporaneous-objection rule [would] tend to detract from the perception of the trial in a criminal case * * * as a decisive and portentous event." The "adoption of the *Francis* rule," on the other hand, would have "the salutary effect of making the trial on the merits the 'main event,' so to speak, rather than a 'tryout on the road' for what will later be the determinative federal habeas hearing." Responding to the dissenters, the majority also stressed that the cause and prejudice test would still serve the basic function of habeas review, and "not prevent a federal habeas court from adjudicating for the first time the federal constitutional claim of a defendant who in the absence of such an adjudication will be the victim of a miscarriage of justice."

Eventually, in *Coleman v. Thompson* (1991), Justice O'Connor finally put *Noia* to rest, stating: "We now make it explicit: In all cases in which a state prisoner has defaulted his federal claims in state court pursuant to an independent and adequate state procedural rule, federal habeas review of the claim is barred unless the prisoner can demonstrate cause for the default and actual prejudice as a result of the alleged violation of federal law, or demonstrates that failure to consider the claims will result in a fundamental miscarriage of justice."

Ineffective Assistance of Counsel as Cause. "Cause" that would excuse default includes the failure by the state to ensure the effective assistance of counsel for the defendant. A defendant must bear the cost of his counsel's error in failing to raise a claim properly in state court, unless the error amounts to a violation of the right of effective assistance of counsel under the Sixth Amendment. As Justice O'Connor explained in *Coleman:*

> Attorney error that constitutes ineffective assistance of counsel is cause * * * not because * * * the error is so bad that "the lawyer ceases to be an agent of the petitioner." Rather, * * * "if the procedural default is the result of ineffective assistance of counsel, the Sixth Amendment itself requires that responsibility for the default be imputed to the State." In other words, it is not the gravity of the attorney's error that matters, but that it constitutes a violation of petitioner's right to counsel, so that the error must be seen as an external factor, i.e., "imputed to the State." * * * Where a petitioner defaults a claim as a result of the denial of the right to effective assistance of counsel, the State, which is responsible for the denial as a constitutional matter, must bear the cost of any resulting default and the harm to state interests that federal habeas review entails.

As the Court explained in *Murray v. Carrier* (1986), however, the "mere fact that counsel failed to recognize the factual or legal basis for a claim, or failed to raise the claim despite recognizing it, does not constitute cause for a procedural default." "So long as defendant is represented by counsel whose performance is not constitutionally ineffective," the Court concluded, "we discern no inequity in requiring him to bear the risk of attorney error that results in a procedural default."

Even attorney incompetence equivalent to that required under *Strickland* will not be sufficient to establish cause if counsel's failure takes place in a phase of the criminal process during which the defendant has no sixth amendment right to the effective assistance of counsel. In *Coleman,* defense counsel had failed to file a timely notice of appeal from a denial of a state habeas corpus petition. Because the defendant had no constitutional right to the assistance of counsel in such a collateral proceeding, the incompetency of his attorney could not give rise to a constitutional claim of ineffective assistance. Such incompetency, not amounting to a constitutional violation in itself, did not constitute cause. "[I]n those circumstances where the State has no responsibility to ensure that the petitioner was represented by competent counsel," Justice O'Connor explained, "it is the petitioner" not the state "who must bear the burden of a failure to follow state procedural rules."

Rather than pursue the underlying constitutional claim forfeited by his attorney's failings, a petitioner may choose to seek relief on the basis of the sixth amendment violation itself. This will work to defendant's advantage where counsel's failures extend beyond the default on the cognizable constitutional claim. Even where counsel's only error related to the default, as the Court noted in *Carrier*, "the right to effective assistance of counsel * * * may in a particular case be violated by even an isolated error of counsel if that error is sufficiently egregious and prejudicial." Indeed, if the defaulted claim involves a violation of rights under the Fourth Amendment, a petitioner will not receive review unless he casts his claim as a denial of the sixth amendment right to the effective assistance of counsel.

Unlike most constitutional claims, a claim of ineffective assistance of counsel in most states need not be raised until after a prisoner's direct appeal, in a state post-conviction proceeding. The Court explained the rationale for adopting this rule for federal appeals in *Massaro v. U.S.* (2003). The trial court is "the forum best suited to developing the facts necessary to determining the adequacy of representation during an entire trial. The court may take testimony from witnesses from witnesses * * * and from the counsel alleged to have rendered the deficient performance." When presented in the trial court, rather than on appeal, a claim of ineffective assistance "often will be ruled upon by the same * * * judge who presided at trial, [who] should have an advantageous perspective for determining the effectiveness of counsel's conduct and whether any deficiencies were prejudicial." Were defendants required to raise ineffectiveness claims on appeal, the Court explained, "trial counsel [would] be unwilling to help appellate counsel familiarize himself with a record for the purpose of understanding how it reflects trial counsel's own incompetence," and "[a]ppellate courts would waste time and resources attempting to address some claims that were meritless and other claims that, though colorable, would be handled more efficiently if addressed in the first instance" by the trial court.

State Interference as Cause. Another circumstance that constitutes "cause" was noted in *Carrier*. The Court there explained that absent ineffective assistance of counsel, the "existence of cause for a procedural default must ordinarily turn on whether the prisoner can show some objective factor external to the defense impeded counsel's efforts to comply with the state's procedural rule." A showing of " 'some interference by officials' that made compliance impracticable" would constitute cause, such as a warden's suppression of a prisoner's timely appeal papers. *Amadeo v. Zant* (1988), for example, involved the state's concealment of a prosecutor's request to jury commissioners to underrepresent African Americans and women. This constituted cause for defense counsel's failure to object to the composition of the jury at trial. *Strickler v. Greene* (1999) provided another example of governmental interference with a defendant's ability to raise a claim. The petitioner there had failed to raise his *Brady* claim in state court. The Court found that he established cause for this failure "because (a) the prosecution withheld exculpatory evidence; (b) petitioner reasonably relied on the prosecution's open file policy as fulfilling the prosecution's duty to disclose such evidence; and (c) the Commonwealth confirmed petitioner's reliance on the open file policy by asserting during state habeas proceedings that the petitioner had already received 'everything known to the government.' " As the Court explained in *Banks v. Dretke* (2004), another case in which the government had lied when it assured the defense it had produced all *Brady* material then maintained that the defense had not been diligent in uncovering its claim in state court, "Our decisions lend no support to the notion that defendants must scavenge for hints of undisclosed *Brady* material when the prosecution represents that all such material has been disclosed."

In order to amount to cause the state's interference must actually have impeded the defendant's efforts to comply with procedural rules. In *McCleskey v. Zant* (1991), for example, the Court held that the prosecution's failure to disclose a recorded statement of an informant prior to a second habeas petition did not constitute "cause" and therefore did not relieve the petitioner of the forfeiture that occurred when counsel failed to include in the first petition a sixth amendment challenge to the use of the informant's statement at trial. The recorded statement was not "critical" to the substance of petitioner's sixth amendment challenge (which had been raised in an earlier state habeas proceeding), and the petitioner had sufficient information to raise the claim in his first petition in any event. A petitioner's inability to obtain relevant evidence "fails to establish cause if other known or discoverable evidence could have supported the claim," and that the failure to assert the claim "will not be excused merely because evidence discovered later might also have supported or strengthened the claim." Delay in providing a defendant with a transcript of trial proceedings also will not constitute cause for failing to raise a claim unless the petitioner was prevented by that delay from making the claim. This will not be the case when the factual and legal basis for the claim was apparent at the time of trial, or was known to the defendant prior to receiving the transcript.

Assuming that cause is established, what type of showing will establish "actual prejudice?" In *Kyles v. Whitley* (1995), and *Strickler v. Greene* (1999), the Court clarified that in order to establish prejudice under *Sykes*, a petitioner must demonstrate that there is a "reasonable probability that the result of the trial would have

been different." A "reasonable probability" is described as a probability sufficient to "undermine confidence in the verdict." This
produces consistency in cases where the defendant seeks to convert
the procedural default into a sixth amendment claim of ineffective
assistance of counsel, because the reasonable probability standard
is also used to measure the prejudice prong of such sixth amendment claims.

(d) The "Miscarriage of Justice" Exception. An exception
to the cause-and-prejudice requirement was noted in *Sykes* when
the Court stated that the standard developed there would not bar
habeas relief for a victim of a "miscarriage of justice."

The Court initially discussed this exception as applying "in an
extraordinary case, where a constitutional violation has probably
resulted in the conviction of one who is actually innocent," as
distinct from "legal[ly] innocen[t]."

The Court in *Schlup v. Delo* (1995) clarified that where the
alleged constitutional violation would have resulted in the failure of
the factfinder to have before it additional evidence that was both
reliable and exculpatory, the habeas petitioner has to show only
that "it is more likely than not that no reasonable juror would have
convicted him in light of the new evidence." *Sawyer v. Whitley*
(1992) held, however, that the petitioner sentenced to death who
claims that a procedurally defaulted constitutional error in capital
sentencing resulted in a capital sentence when he was "actually
innocent of the death penalty," must "show by clear and convincing evidence that but for a constitutional error no reasonable juror
would find the petitioner eligible for the death penalty."

In *House v. Bell* (2006), a majority of justices agreed that a
death row petitioner's showing entitled him to pass through the
Schlup "innocence gateway" and receive federal review of his
defaulted claims of ineffective assistance of counsel and prosecutorial misconduct. The Court emphasized that in evaluating whether a
petitioner has demonstrated that "more likely than not any reasonable juror would have reasonable doubt," a habeas court must
consider all the evidence, "old and new, incriminating and exculpatory, without regard to whether it would necessarily be admitted
[at trial]." The petitioner's "new reliable evidence" of innocence,
included (1) forensic evidence indicating that blood from the victim
found on petitioner's jeans was spilled on them from vials of blood
taken from the victim at her autopsy; (2) DNA evidence demonstrating that the semen found on the victim's clothing was from her
husband, not the petitioner; and (3) testimony by several witnesses
describing a confession to the killing by the victim's husband, the
indifferent reception one of these witnesses encountered when
reporting the confession to authorities, a history of abuse of the
victim by her husband, and an attempt by the husband to construct

a false alibi. The Court found that "the central forensic proof connecting House to the crime * * * has been called into question, and House has put forward substantial evidence pointing to a different suspect. * * * [T]his is the rare case where—had the jury heard all the conflicting testimony—it is more likely than not that no reasonable juror viewing the record as a whole would lack reasonable doubt."

Interpreting the "miscarriage of justice" exception to provide an opportunity for reviewing only those claims of error that implicate actual innocence may prevent habeas review of defaulted claims of error that would not affect the accuracy of a jury's verdict of guilt or eligibility for the death sentence. Such claims include grand jury error preceding a valid conviction, violations of the prohibition against double jeopardy, and denials of speedy or public trials. Also excluded are claims based on the introduction of reliable evidence obtained in violation of a defendant's right to counsel or privilege against self-incrimination, claims that a petitioner's jury venire was selected in violation of the Sixth or Fourteenth Amendments, as well as claims of selective prosecution. In other words, once defaulted in state court, claims unrelated to factual innocence do not receive the same protection in federal court as claims that may prevent the incarceration or execution of a factually innocent individual. The Court's willingness to restrict collateral review of such claims suggests that it has concluded that sufficient incentive to comply with these particular constitutional requirements is provided by litigation on behalf of those defendants who, while still in state court, manage to learn of and effectively raise such claims. As *Schlup* explained, "Explicitly tying the miscarriage of justice exception to innocence thus accommodates both the systemic interests in finality, comity, and conservation of judicial resources, and the overriding individual interest in doing justice in the 'extraordinary case.'"

For a petitioner who is seeking relief from a conviction following a plea of guilty, actual innocence means "factual innocence," based on "any admissible evidence of petitioner's guilt even if that evidence was not presented during petitioner's plea colloquy," declared the Court in *Bousley v. U.S.* (1998). Furthermore, in cases when there is "record evidence" that "the government has foregone more serious charges in the course of plea bargaining, petitioner's showing of actual innocence must also extend to those charges."

§ 20.5 Claims Foreclosed Due to Premature, Successive, or Delayed Applications

(a) **Exhaustion of State Remedies.** *Overview and origins.* The "exhaustion doctrine" presently codified in § 2254, requires the petitioner before seeking federal relief, to "exhaust" his available state remedies. It is " 'principally designed to protect the state courts' role in the enforcement of federal law and prevent the disruption of state judicial proceedings.' " Over half of all of the habeas petitions filed are dismissed initially for failure to exhaust state remedies.

Both the "equitable nature" of the doctrine and the considerations underlying its exercise were set in place by the Court's seminal opinion in *Ex parte Royall* (1886), one of the first cases under the 1867 Habeas Act to reach the Supreme Court. The petitioner there, while awaiting trial in his state case, sought federal habeas relief on the ground that the pending state prosecution was based on an unconstitutional statute. Sustaining the lower court's denial of the writ, the Supreme Court noted:

> The [statute's] injunction to hear the case summarily, and thereupon "to dispose of the party as law and justice require" does not deprive the court of discretion as to the time and mode in which it will exert the powers conferred upon it. That discretion should be exercised in the light of the relations existing, under our system of government, between the judicial tribunals of the Union and of the States, and in recognition of the fact that the public good requires that those relations be not disturbed by unnecessary conflict between courts equally bound to guard and protect rights secured by the Constitution.

By 1944, the Court was able to announce as settled law that "ordinarily an application for habeas corpus by one detained under a state court judgment of conviction will be entertained * * * only after all state remedies available, including all appellate remedies in the state courts and in this Court by appeal or writ of certiorari have been exhausted."

Today § 2254(b)(1) sets forth the general requirement of exhaustion: "An application for a writ of habeas corpus on behalf of a person in custody pursuant to the judgment of a State court shall not be granted unless it appears that (A) the applicant has exhausted the remedies available in the courts of the State, or (B)(i) there is either an absence of available State corrective process or (ii) circumstances exist that render such process ineffective to protect the rights of the applicant." Section 2254(c) also provides that an applicant may not be deemed to have exhausted his remedies "if he has a right under the law of the State to raise, by any available procedure, the question presented."

A petitioner who has fully pursued his claim on direct appeal from his conviction is not thereafter required to repeat the process through state collateral remedies. The statute does not require repeated attempts to invoke the same remedy nor more than one attempt where there are alternative remedies. Some situations may require a petitioner to present the same claim more than once to the state's highest court. An intervening Supreme Court decision which casts petitioner's claim in a new light may require him to reapply for state relief if still available. On the other hand, when the highest state court changes its view of preexisting Supreme Court precedent, the petitioner need not return to the state courts, since the state's opportunity to reach the correct result when it first heard petitioner's case had not been altered. Nor must a petitioner return to the state courts after later state decisions held invalid the statute under which he was prosecuted.

Exceptions to exhaustion. The exhaustion requirement has been characterized as "an unnecessary price to exact from a person, in the name of comity or judicial economy, where state procedures offer no practical hope of swift vindication of his federal claim." Section 2254(b) recognizes this position in noting that further state review is not required where there is either "an absence of available state corrective process" or "circumstances * * * render such process ineffective to protect the rights of the prisoner."

First, the petitioner will be deemed to have exhausted a state remedy that is no longer available to him because of a procedural bar. For example, if a defendant fails to take advantage of a state remedy within the time specified by state law, the remedy will be considered unavailable to him. In this situation the petitioner will have to establish cause for his default in order to get beyond the procedural bar. As one court put it, "Having avoided the Scylla of exhaustion, [the petitioner] must also steer by the Charybdis of procedural default before his petition can be heard on the merits."

Second, futile or uncertain remedies constitute "ineffective" avenues under the statute and need not be exhausted. A theoretical system of relief need not be pursued. A state remedy can also be rendered "ineffective" if there has been inordinate delay in the administration of that remedy. Of course, the fault for the delay must rest with the state rather than the petitioner. Even then, the delay found to be inordinate is usually one full year or longer.

Mixed petitions. Prior to the 1996 amendments, the Court in *Rose v. Lundy* (1982) concluded that when a petition contained both exhausted and unexhausted claims, there were only two alternatives: either (1) dismiss the mixed petition without prejudice so that the petitioner could return to the state courts to exhaust remaining claims, then present all his claims together later in a single petition or (2) allow the petitioner to drop his unexhausted claims.

With the addition of a strict statute of limitations in 1996, the Court revisited this approach. As the Court observed in *Pliler v.*

Ford (2004) requiring dismissal of "mixed petitions" could result in a loss of all claims, even those already exhausted, because the limitations period could expire during the time a petitioner returns to state court to exhaust his unexhausted claims. In *Rhines v. Weber* (2005) the Court held that a district court has discretion to stay a mixed petition holding the exhausted claims in abeyance while allowing a petitioner to present his unexhausted claims to the state court and then return to federal court for review of his perfected petition, without risking being time barred. This "stay and abeyance" procedure, however, is appropriate only when three conditions are met. First, the petitioner's claims must not be "plainly meritless." Second, the petitioner must have had good cause for failing to exhaust his claims in state court—there must be no indication that the petitioner engaged in intentionally dilatory litigation tactics. Finally, the judge should "place reasonable time limits on the petitioner's trip to state court and back." If "employed too frequently," the Supreme Court warned, the procedure has the potential to undermine the goals of promoting finality and reducing delay in habeas litigation.

Providing a "fair opportunity"—presenting the claim to the state courts. In order to provide the state with a fair opportunity to decide his claim, a petitioner must (1) present to the state courts a claim substantially equivalent to the claim he raises in his federal petition and (2) allow the state courts to complete their review of that claim.

As the Supreme Court noted in *Picard v. Connor* (1971), the exhaustion requirement "would serve no purpose if it could be satisfied by raising one claim in the state courts and another in the federal courts." A petitioner must present to the state court "the substance" of his claim in a manner sufficient to give that court "a fair opportunity" to rule upon it. *Picard* itself illustrates a situation in which there was so much variation between the theories advanced before the state and federal courts that the state court never had "a fair opportunity" to rule on the contention in the federal courts. That case involved a state practice under which the grand jury originally indicted a named individual and a fictitious "John Doe," with the true name of the alleged accomplice then added by amendment following his arrest. Before the state courts, petitioner argued that amendment of the indictment to substitute his name for John Doe violated his right to be prosecuted only upon an indictment actually issued by the grand jury. On habeas review, the federal court held for petitioner but relied on a different theory. The amendment of the indictment did not violate due process since the state had no constitutional obligation to proceed by indictment; but once having granted the protection of a grand jury indictment to defendants generally, the state had denied petitioner equal protection by utilizing the John Doe indictment. The Supreme Court held that while the same facts were before both state and federal courts, the state court could not be expected to consider the equal protection claim sua sponte, and it had not been cited in any fashion before the state courts. While a claim could be presented without citing "book and verse in the federal constitution," it could not be said that the original challenge was the "substantial equivalent" of the unconstitutional discrimination claim.

In *Anderson v. Harless* (1982), *Duncan v. Henry* (1995), *Baldwin v. Reese* (2004), and *Gray v. Netherland* (1996), the Court reached similar conclusions. When the petitioner in *Anderson* challenged in the state courts a jury charge on "malice," he characterized it as simply "erroneous" and cited a state case that referred only to a due process requirement that the jury instructions "properly explain" the law. This was not sufficient indication of the theory advanced in the federal courts that the charge created a mandatory presumption contrary to the prosecution's constitutional obligation to prove guilt beyond a reasonable doubt. In *Duncan,* the Court concluded that arguing a claim raised under state law does not satisfy the exhaustion requirement as the claim must be clearly identified as one made under federal law and the "mere similarity of claims is insufficient to exhaust." Nor did the petitioner in *Baldwin* "fairly present" his constitutional claim to the state court when that court would have had to read beyond the petition and brief in order to find a lower court opinion alerting it to the presence of a federal claim. So too, in *Gray*, the petitioner did not fairly present to the state courts his claim that the state misled him about evidence it intended to introduce, when he had referred in the state courts to a broad federal due process right and cited cases that forbid the use of secret testimony. The cases cited by petitioner in state court and those he later cited in federal court, the Court explained, "arise in widely differing contexts."

Just as different legal claims or claims originating in state law will not suffice as a fair presentation to the state court, neither will factual claims significantly different than those advanced in federal court. Where a petitioner presents newly discovered evidence "such as to place the case in a significantly different and stronger evidentiary posture than it was when the state courts considered it," that the petitioner must first give the state courts an opportunity to consider the evidence.

Speaking to the second element of the state's fair opportunity to review a claim—allowing a state to complete its review—*O'Sullivan v. Boerckel* (1999) held that although a petitioner need not invoke "extraordinary remedies when those remedies are alternatives to the standard review process and where the state courts have not provided relief through those remedies in the past," a petitioner is required to invoke "one full round of the State's established appellate review process." When that process includes discretionary review by the state supreme court, a petitioner must pursue this remedy before seeking relief in federal court.

(b) Time Limits for Filing Petitions. Although a petition with unexhausted claims is filed too early, a petition may also be filed too late. Prior to the enactment of the Antiterrorism and Effective Death Penalty Act in 1996, the only time limitation imposed on the filing of a federal habeas petition was that flowing from the application of the laches doctrine contained in Rule 9 of the Rules Governing Section 2254 Cases, which provided that a petition may be dismissed if "the state has been prejudiced in its ability to respond to the petition by delay in filing unless the petitioner shows that it is based on grounds of which he could not have had knowledge by the exercise of reasonable diligence before the circumstances prejudicial to the state occurred." If the petition was not filed until many years after conviction, that was of no consequence, unless the state could show that delay prejudiced its ability to respond to the petition.

The 1996 legislation included, for the first time, a specific time limitation for the filing of federal habeas petitions. Section 2244(d) imposes a one-year period for filing a habeas petition, running from the date on which the judgment challenged "became final by the conclusion of direct review or the expiration of the time for seeking such review," and excluding any period during which a properly filed collateral attack was pending before the state courts. A later starting point is provided where: (1) state action in violation of the Constitution or other federal law impeded the timely filing of the habeas petition; (2) the petition relies on a constitutional right that was both recognized by the Supreme Court after the date of finality and held to be retroactive in application; or (3) the petition relies on a constitutional claim as to which the factual predicate could not have been discovered at the date of finality by the exercise of due diligence.

Due to the pro se petitioner's lack of control over the filing of documents, the petition will be deemed filed at the moment petitioner delivers it to prison officials for mailing to the district court.

The statute excludes from the one-year filing period any time during which a "properly filed" collateral attack was pending before the state courts. The time a petition for certiorari is pending before the United States Supreme Court is not excluded from the limitations period, however. To be properly filed, a collateral proceeding must comply with state filing deadlines. When state law does not define a definite filing period, federal courts must determine if the petitioner sought state remedies with reasonable diligence, so as to stop the limitations period from running. If the petitioner's delay in seeking state relief was unreasonable, as it was in *Evans v. Chavis* (2006), tolling is not available. Three years and one month had elapsed between a lower court's denial of the Evans's state habeas petition and the filing of notice of appeal from that decision. Although Evans claimed that hindrances on library access and lockdowns prevented him from filing his request for appeal sooner, the Court found that no evidence refuted the state's showing that for a period of at least six months he had full access to the library without lockdowns. Because six months is far longer than the period of 30 to 60 days that most states provide for an appeal to the state supreme court, the delay in filing was unreasonable.

Lower courts have also interpreted the statute to allow for "equitable tolling" of the limitations period in extraordinary circumstances, despite the lack of any reference to such an exception in the statute itself. Equitable tolling has yet to be endorsed by the Supreme Court, although in *Lawrence v. Fla.* (2007), the Court "assume[d] without deciding" that equitable tolling would be available given showing of "extraordinary circumstances." The errors in *Lawrence* made by state-appointed post-conviction counsel in calculating deadlines did not meet this threshold.

(c) Successive Petitions: Claims Advanced in Prior Applications. Under the current statute a habeas petitioner may raise any given claim only once. This limitation is a significant departure from the common law rule that the doctrine of res judicata did not apply to the rulings of the habeas court. Denied relief by one judge, a prisoner could simply turn to another, seeking the same relief on the same grounds. Although numerous explanations are plausible, the refusal of the common law to limit habeas applications through the doctrine of res judicata is most frequently attributed to the absence of direct appellate review of writ denials.

The 1996 Act now states: "A claim presented in second or successive habeas corpus application under section 2254 that was presented in a prior application shall be dismissed." The statute removes the prior authority of federal courts to consider again a claim by a petitioner who could supplement his previously presented constitutional claim with a newly discovered evidence of "actual innocence."

(d) Abuse of the Writ: New Claims in Second or Successive Petitions. Prior to the 1996 Act, a new claim in a successive petition was treated much like a claim that the petitioner failed to raise properly in state court. Former § 2244 provided that the federal habeas court "need not entertain" a successive petition "unless the application alleges and is predicted on a factual or other ground not adjudicated on the hearing of the earlier application * * * and unless the court * * * is satisfied that the applicant has in the earlier application deliberately withheld the newly asserted ground or otherwise abused the writ." Rule 9(b) of the § 2254 Rules added that the habeas court may dismiss the application if it finds "the failure of the petitioner to assert those [new and different] grounds in a prior petition constituted an abuse of writ."

The 1996 Act now directs that a second or successive application advancing a "claim" not presented in a prior application "shall be dismissed" unless one of two specified exceptions is found applicable.

The first exception, contained in § 2244(b)(2)(A), allows for review if the claim relies on a new rule of constitutional law, previously unavailable, that the Supreme Court has made retroactively applicable on collateral review. In *Tyler v. Cain* (2001), the Court interpreted this provision to require a successive petitioner to identify a decision from the Court itself that holds that the new rule is retroactively applicable to cases on collateral review. It is not sufficient to point to a decision that either 1) "establishes principles of retroactivity and leaves the application of those principles to lower courts," or 2) suggests in dictum that the new rule is retroactively applicable, the Court explained. The Court rejected Tyler's claim that this interpretation would have the effect of blocking relief entirely for petitioners seeking to raise a valid claim in a second petition, noting, "we do not have license to question" the decision of Congress to establish stringent procedural requirements for retroactive application of new rules.

The second exception, recognized in § 2244(b)(2)(B), allows for the review of certain successive claims based on newly discovered evidence. This exception has two requirements. The factual predicate for the new claim must be one that could not have been discovered previously through "due diligence." Second, the "facts underlying the claim, if proven and viewed in light of the evidence as a whole" must be "sufficient to establish by clear and convincing evidence that but for the constitutional error, no reasonable factfinder would have found the applicant guilty of the underlying offense." Because this provision permits relief only for petitioners who can show that no reasonable factfinder would have found the petitioner guilty of "the underlying offense," it conceivably prohibits review of sentencing errors, as well as errors that do not affect the factfinder's assessment of guilt, such as the introduction of evidence obtained in violation of the defendant's right to counsel, jury discrimination, double jeopardy, or selective prosecution. This scheme seems to be based on the assumption that sufficient incentive to comply with these innocence-neutral constitutional requirements is provided by scrutiny of the claims of defendants who manage to discover and effectively raise such claims while still in state court.

(e) The "Gatekeeping" Provision. Another innovation of § 2244(b) is its subdivision (3) making the court of appeals the "gatekeeper" in applying the standards described above for second or successive petitions. The applicant must seek from the court of appeals an order authorizing the district court to consider the second or successive application. The new statute states that a three-judge panel must rule on whether the "application makes a prima facie showing" that it will satisfy the standard for filing a second or successive petition, and make that ruling within 30 days. Under the new statute, the panel's decision granting or denying the application is "not appealable" and "shall not be the subject of a petition for rehearing or for a writ of certiorari." Thus, at this point, if the application is denied, the petitioner cannot seek further judicial action, apart from an original petition to the Supreme Court.

§ 20.6 Constitutional Interpretation on Habeas Review

(a) The Changing Role of Federal Habeas Courts. Both of the separate opinions for the Court in *Brown v. Allen* (1953) flatly rejected the contention that a state court's interpretation of the Constitution should be binding on the federal habeas court. *Brown* directed federal habeas courts to "independently apply the correct constitutional standards" to a petitioner's claim "no matter how fair and completely the claim had been litigated in state courts." The function of the 1867 Habeas Act, characterized by Justice Frankfurter, was to give to federal courts the "final say" on the merits of a state prisoner's federal constitutional claim. In exercising de novo review of constitutional questions, the federal habeas court was to give the state court's adjudication no more "weight" than what "federal practice [commonly] gives to the conclusion of a court of last resort of another jurisdiction on federal constitutional issues." Almost forty years after *Brown*, *Teague v. Lane* (1989) substantially altered the nature of that "final say" given to the federal habeas courts. Following *Teague*, the task of the federal habeas court was not to ask how it would interpret the Constitution, but to ask whether the state court's interpretation was a reasonable reading of the Supreme Court precedent prevailing when the opportunity for direct review of the prisoner's conviction ended.

The passage of the 1996 Act altered habeas review of state court decisions further still, as § 2254(d) now bars relief unless "the adjudication of the claim by the State court * * * resulted in a decision that was contrary to, or involved an unreasonable application of, clearly established Federal Law as determined by the Supreme Court of the United States * * *." This new standard for reviewing state court decisions appears to incorporate several aspects of the *Teague* inquiry, but it did not displace *Teague*. As the Court explained in *Horn v. Banks* (2002), "[T]he AEDPA and *Teague* inquiries are distinct * * *. [I]n addition to performing any analysis required by the AEDPA, a federal court considering a habeas petition must conduct a threshold *Teague* analysis when the issue is properly raised by the state."

(b) *Teague* and the Application of New Rules to State Convictions. The habeas petitioner in *Teague* raised a constitutional objection to the prosecutor's use of peremptory challenges to exclude African Americans from his jury. While his habeas petition was working its way through the federal appellate process, the Supreme Court decided *Batson v. Ky.*, which established an equal protection safeguard against racial discrimination in the use of peremptory challenges. The petitioner in *Teague* argued that *Batson* sustained his constitutional claim. He further argued that even if *Batson* had come too late for him to take advantage of the *Batson* ruling itself, a similar prohibition should be incorporated into the sixth amendment right to a jury venire selected from a fair cross-section of the community.

The Court considered whether a habeas petitioner could gain the benefit of a Supreme Court ruling that had come after the exhaustion of the direct appellate review of his conviction and had clearly expanded constitutional protection beyond what previous precedent had required. A majority agreed that, subject to certain exceptions, a habeas petitioner's conviction should be reviewed by reference to the "law prevailing at the time [his] conviction became final."

Justice O'Connor's plurality opinion derived this "law-at-the-time" principle from what was described as the "deterrence function" of the habeas writ. A central function of federal habeas review, it was argued, is ensuring that the state courts faithfully apply the prevailing "constitutional principles" as announced by the Supreme Court. Because the Supreme Court's docket limitations preclude its review of all but a small number of state court departures from prevailing constitutional principles, habeas review in the lower federal courts was needed to deter state courts from taking advantage of the likelihood that their departures from prevailing precedents would escape Supreme Court review. Federal habeas review was to "serve as a necessary incentive for trial and appellate judges * * * to conduct their proceedings in a manner consistent with established constitutional principles." Such a "deterrence function" requires only that the conviction be reviewed by reference to the law prevailing at the time of its final review in the state system. The state courts can hardly be required to apply constitutional principles that do not yet exist. Hence, a federal habeas court, as a general principle, should not invalidate a conviction based upon a "new ruling" of constitutional law issued after that point. The *Teague* plurality opinion recognized two exceptions to the "law-at-the-time" principle, which are discussed in subsection (e).

Unless the exceptions apply, a habeas petitioner could not obtain the benefit of either 1) a "new" Supreme Court ruling decided after his conviction became final, or 2) a "new" expansion of the protection established by preexisting precedent (i.e., the Supreme Court rulings prevailing at the time the conviction became final). Thus, the Court concluded that a habeas court could neither apply retroactively the *Batson* decision, which came after the defendant's conviction had become final, itself establish a new ruling by reading a similar prohibition into a series of sixth amendment cases which came before the defendant's conviction became final.

Having applied *Teague* in a dozen different cases, the Court has distilled the "*Teague* inquiry" into "three steps." First, the habeas court must determine the date on which the petitioner's conviction became final. Second, the habeas court must consider "whether 'a state court considering [the petitioner's] claim at the time his conviction became final would have felt compelled by existing precedent to conclude that the rule [he] seeks was required by the Constitution.' " If not, then the rule is new, and as a third step the "court must determine whether the rule nonetheless falls within one of the two narrow exceptions to the *Teague* doctrine."

(c) Determining When a State Conviction Becomes Final. A petitioner's state conviction is final only after the time for filing a petition for certiorari from the state judgment affirming the conviction has expired, or after the Court has denied certiorari. This point in time is arguably inconsistent with the deterrence rationale of *Teague*, since the opportunity of the state courts to evade federal law normally ends prior to the time defendant seeks certiorari review in the United States Supreme Court. The assumption may be that if certiorari were sought, the Court could remand the case to the state court for reconsideration in light of its new rule, so that the state appellate court would have an opportunity to apply any new ruling handed down between the time of its decision and the Supreme Court's disposal of a petition for certiorari. Even where the defense fails to seek certiorari the defendant is likely to have had a chance to petition the state court for a rehearing prior to the exhaustion of the time period for filing for certiorari.

(d) The "New Rule" Concept. The second step in applying *Teague* is the determination of whether the rule on which the petitioner relies is a "new" rule of criminal procedure. Speaking for a plurality in *Teague*, Justice O'Connor advanced a broad definition of a new ruling that was later extended to include applications of prior precedent that would not have been classified as new rulings under the Supreme Court's previous retroactivity decisions.

> [I]n general * * * a case announces a new rule when it breaks new ground or imposes a new obligation on the States or the Federal Government. * * * To put it differently, a case announces a new rule if the result was not dictated by precedent existing at the time the defendant's conviction became final.

In *Penry v. Lynaugh* (1989), the Court suggested that what was "dictated" should not be read too narrowly, and that it would include the application of the logic of the earlier precedent to an analogous situation. The case involved a petitioner's challenge that the Texas capital sentencing scheme unconstitutionally limited the jury's consideration of mitigating evidence. The Court concluded that upholding petitioner's challenge did not demand a new rule as it "merely asked the State to fulfill the assurances upon which [the Court's prior precedent] was based" by applying a general prohibition that was "clear" under earlier rulings. Similarly in *Stringer v. Black* (1992), the Court held that the rule of *Clemons v. Miss.* (1990), which applied a rule concerning invalid aggravating factors in death sentencing to "weighing" states, was not "new" under *Teague*. The majority noted: "The purpose of the new rule doctrine is to validate reasonable interpretations of existing precedents. Reasonableness in this, as in many other contexts, is an objective standard, and the ultimate decision * * * [must be] based on an objective reading of the relevant cases."

More frequently, however, the Court has found that the rule advanced by a petitioner is new, precluding habeas relief. In *Butler v. McKellar* (1990), for example, the Court rejected the petitioner's claim that the rule upon which he relied fell within the "logical compass" of an earlier precedent and as a result was not a new rule. There had been a significant difference among the lower courts as to whether the rule advanced by the petitioner followed from that precedent, and that division in itself provided proof that the state court in rejecting the rule had adopted a position "susceptible to debate among reasonable minds."

The Court in *Beard v. Banks* (2004) also suggested that if the Supreme Court decision announcing the rule at issue is closely divided on the merits, the rule is not likely to apply retroactively.

Banks held that the rule in *Mills v. Md.* (1988) was "new," because it "broke new ground" and was not "mandate[d]" by precedent. Pointing out that four justices dissented in *Mills,* at least one of whom protested that the decision was "stretching" precedent beyond proper bounds, the *Banks* majority concluded that "reasonable jurists differed" as to whether the rule the petitioner asked to be applied to him was "compel[led]" by existing precedent.

(e) The *Teague* Exceptions. Two exceptions to the prohibition against applying new rules on habeas review were recognized in *Teague.*

Rules establishing constitutionally protected conduct. The first exception encompasses rulings that "place certain kinds of primary, private individual conduct beyond the power of the criminal lawmaking authority." A prior example of such a rule was a holding that a statute creating an offense violated the self-incrimination privilege; all defendants previously convicted of that offense were entitled to the benefit of that new ruling. Since *Teague,* the Court has reserved this exception for rules that either "decriminalize a class of conduct" or "prohibit the imposition of capital punishment on a particular class of persons." As a result, few rules have qualified.

Rules of fundamental fairness protecting accuracy. New rulings that implicate "fundamental fairness" by mandating procedures "central to an accurate determination of innocence or guilt" also will be applied retroactively. Speaking for the plurality, Justice O'Connor stated in *Teague* that procedures "central to an accurate determination of innocence or guilt" were best illustrated by what Justice Stevens had once described as the "classic" grounds for habeas review—the mob-dominated trial, the knowing use of perjured testimony, and conviction based on a confession "extorted from defendant by brutal methods." The plurality opinion added that it seemed "unlikely that many such components of basic due process have yet to emerge."

Holding out the decision in *Gideon* as the "paradigmatic example of a watershed rule of criminal procedure," the Court has yet to find another rule that meets this exception. Some rulings fail the requirement that they affect the accuracy of a criminal judgment. Consider, for example, the new ruling advanced by the petitioner in *Teague*—an innovative reading of the Sixth Amendment's cross-section requirement that would have provided a *Batson*-like prohibition against racially discriminatory use of peremptory challenges. Though a *Batson*-type rule might promote accuracy in a systemic sense, it did not necessarily affect accuracy in any particular case, and it therefore fell outside of *Teague*'s second exception.

Other new rules fail the exception because they are not sufficiently fundamental, "less sweeping" than *Gideon*, which established an affirmative right to counsel in all felony cases. In *Sawyer v. Smith* (1990), the "new rule" in question was one prohibiting a prosecutorial closing argument which suggested that the ultimate responsibility for determining the appropriateness of the death penalty rested on the appellate court and thereby reduced the jury's sense of responsibility. This rule certainly was "aimed at improving the accuracy of the trial." It was not, however, a "watershed ruling" in this regard; it did not "alter our understanding of the *bedrock procedural elements* essential to the fairness of the proceeding." Rather it was a per se prohibition of a particular type of argument that served basically to supplement the traditional due process prohibition against closing arguments that "so infected the trial with unfairness" as to violate due process. Other rules rejected by the Court as insufficiently fundamental include: a rule providing to capital defendants jury instructions concerning "mitigating evidence of youth, family background, and positive character traits"; a rule barring jury instructions that do not warn the jury that it could not find the defendant guilty of murder without even considering voluntary manslaughter; a double jeopardy bar limiting successive noncapital sentencing proceedings; a rule prohibiting states from requiring capital sentencing juries to disregard mitigating factors not found unanimously; the rule that entitles a capital defendant to a jury determination of facts that state law provides must be found before a death sentence may be imposed; and a rule that would have required notice of evidence to be used at sentencing. None of these rules satisfied the two-pronged test requiring that the rule both "relate to the accuracy of the conviction" and "alter our understanding of the 'bedrock procedural elements' essential to the fundamental fairness of a proceeding."

(f) Review of State Court Decisions Under § 2254(d). Section 2254(d)(1) states that relief is permissible only when the state decision is "contrary to, or involved an unreasonable application of, clearly established Federal law as determined by the Supreme Court of the United States." Interpreting this provision in *(Terry) Williams v. Taylor* (2000), the Court held that under "the 'contrary to' clause, a federal habeas court may grant the writ if the state court arrives at a conclusion opposite to that reached by this Court on a question of law or if the state court decides a case differently than this Court has on a set of materially indistinguishable facts." The "unreasonable application" clause limits relief to cases in which "the state court identifies the correct governing legal principle from this court's decision but unreasonably applies that principle to the facts of the prisoner's case." The inquiry into reasonableness is objective, and does not turn on whether "one of the Nation's jurists has applied the relevant federal law in the same manner the state court did in the habeas petitioner's case." Furthermore, stated the Court, "an unreasonable application of federal law is different from an incorrect application of federal law." It is not enough that a state court decision applying federal law was erroneous, "that application must also be unreasonable."

Six justices in *Williams* agreed that the state court decision in that case was "both contrary to and involved an unreasonable application of this Court's clearly established precedent." First, the Virginia Supreme Court misinterpreted the Court's decision in *Strickland*, erroneously assuming that a later decision of the Court had modified the test for prejudice to require more than "mere outcome determination." Second, because it failed to "consider the totality of the omitted mitigation evidence," the state court unreasonably applied *Strickland* to Williams' case when it found that the grossly deficient performance did not prejudice Williams.

Applications of the § 2254 standard by the Court have often been closely divided, and have produced very few general principles. "[E]valuating whether a rule application was unreasonable requires considering the rule's specificity," explained the five-justice majority in *Yarborough v. Alvarado* (2004). "The more general the rule, the more leeway courts have in reaching outcomes in case by case determinations." The *Alvarado* majority found that the rule for when a suspect is in custody for purposes of *Miranda* was "general," and the state court's application of that rule—finding no custody and refusing to consider the suspect's age and inexperience—fit "within the matrix of our prior decisions."

A narrow holding, too, permits more freedom to state courts in distinguishing the decision as not controlling. Consider, for example, the Court's decision in *Carey v. Musladin* (2006). The Court found that a state court did not unreasonably apply clearly established law when, in a case involving prejudicial spectator conduct, the state court did not include in its analysis Supreme Court precedent regulating other prejudicial circumstances—requiring a defendant to wear prison clothes and seating four uniformed troopers behind the defendant at trial. Those holdings involved government-compelled practices, reasoned the majority, unlike the spectator practices at issue. The Court has also rejected efforts to equate the § 2254 standard with "clear error," noting that "the gloss of clear error fails to give proper deference to state courts by conflating error (even clear error) with reasonableness."

*"Clearly established * * * by the Supreme Court."* The language "clearly established Federal law, as determined by the Supreme Court of the United States," was interpreted in *Williams* as restricting "the source of clearly established law to this Court's

jurisprudence." The provision refers to "the holdings, as opposed to the dicta, of this Court's decisions as of the time of the relevant state-court decision." This standard differs from *Teague* in two ways. First, the date on which federal law must be assessed is different. After *Teague*, a petitioner could obtain relief from a state court decision only if that decision was not in accordance with federal law existing at the time when the defendant's ability to apply for review in the Supreme Court expired or when Supreme Court denied the defendant's petition for certiorari. Under § 2254(d), the Court's decisions in place at the time of the relevant state decision govern. Second, § 2254(d) allows consideration only of the holdings of the Court, while *Teague* arguably permits consideration of even dicta.

Adjudicated on the Merits. The deferential standard of review in Section 2254(d) applies only to claims "adjudicated on the merits" in state court. If a claim was rejected on procedural grounds rather than on the "merits," pre-1996 de novo standards of review are applied. Lower courts have divided over whether summary decisions disposing of federal claims without comment should qualify as "on the merits" rulings triggering deferential review, with most granting terse denials the same deference as that given to rulings accompanied by reasoning.

§ 20.7 Fact-finding and Evidentiary Hearings

(a) Presuming the Correctness of State Court Determinations of Fact. The present rules regarding federal review of state court fact-finding and the provision of evidentiary hearings in federal habeas proceedings have evolved from a 1963 decision, *Townsend v. Sain.* In *Townsend,* the Court addressed the question when a petitioner was entitled to an evidentiary hearing and concluded that a habeas court must hold an evidentiary hearing if the habeas applicant did not receive a "full and fair" evidentiary hearing in a state court, either at the time of trial or in a collateral proceeding. Specifically, the Court explained, a hearing was required if:

> (1) the merits of the factual dispute were not resolved in the state hearing; (2) the state factual determination is not fairly supported by the record as a whole; (3) the fact-finding procedure employed by the state court was not adequate to afford a full and fair hearing; (4) there is a substantial allegation of newly discovered evidence; (5) the material facts were not adequately developed at the state court hearing; or (6) for any reason it appears that the state trier of fact did not afford the habeas applicant a full and fair hearing.

Former § 2254(d), enacted in 1966 to regulate fact-finding in habeas proceedings, appeared to track much of *Townsend.* The 1996 Act, however, substantially altered the treatment of state fact-finding in habeas proceedings.

The 1996 Act replaced former § 2254(d) with two provisions: § 2254(d)(2) and § 2254(e)(1). New § 2254(e)(1) provides that "a determination of a factual issue by a State court shall be presumed to be correct," with the petitioner having the "burden of rebutting the presumption of correctness by clear and convincing evidence." New § 2254(d)(2) provides that relief shall not be granted for any claim adjudicated on the merits in state court unless the state decision "was based on an unreasonable determination of the facts in light of the evidence presented in the state court proceeding."

As the Court explained in *Miller-El v. Dretke* (2005), under the statute a federal court must "presume the [state] court's factual findings to be sound unless [the petitioner] rebuts the 'presumption of correctness by clear and convincing evidence.' " *Miller-El* was a case in which the petitioner did just that. Referring to evidence before the state court "too powerful to conclude anything but discrimination" in violation of *Batson,* the Court found the state's conclusion "wrong to a clear and convincing degree * * * unreasonable as well as erroneous."

Although the 1996 Act no longer includes as a prerequisite to federal court deference under §§ 2254(d)(2) or (e)(1) a "full and fair hearing" on the facts in state court, lower courts have concluded that the fact finding process afforded the defendant in state courts remains relevant in determining whether or not a petitioner has met his burden of demonstrating that the state finding was unreasonable. Indeed, the fact-finding process used by the state court can itself violate constitutional command, so that the factual conclusions reached through that process do not warrant the deference state court factual findings would otherwise receive. In *Panetti v. Quarterman* (2007), the Court refused to defer to the state court's conclusion that a death row petitioner was competent to be executed because that conclusion had been reached after failing to provide petitioner with procedures mandated by the Constitution, including "an adequate means by which to submit expert psychiatric evidence in response to the evidence that had been solicited by the state court."

(b) Distinguishing Mixed Determinations of Law and Fact from Fact–Finding. The Supreme Court has noted on several occasions that the rules governing state court findings of fact in the former § 2254(d) applied only to a state court's determination of "historic fact" as opposed to "a mixed determination of law and fact that requires the application of legal principles to the historical facts." The 1996 amendments appear to maintain this distinction, using essentially the same language: "determination of a factual issue" compared to "determination of the facts" under prior law. Thus, the reach of the presumption of correctness contained in § 2254(e)(1), like the presumption under its predecessor, former § 2254(d), seems to be limited to pure questions of historical fact.

The Court has not always found the distinction between a "factual" and a "mixed" determination easy to apply. Its ruling in *Sumner v. Mata* (1982) is illustrative. The Court held that "the ultimate question as to the constitutionality of the pretrial identification procedures used in this case is a mixed question of law and fact that is not governed by § 2254." But, the Court went on, "the questions of fact that underlie this ultimate conclusion," including whether the witnesses "had an opportunity to observe the crime or were too distracted; whether the witnesses gave a detailed, accurate description; and whether the witnesses were under pressure" were "questions of fact as to which the statutory presumption applies."

In *Patton v. Yount* (1984), the presumption of correctness did not apply to a state court's finding as to whether prejudicial publicity had made a fair trial impossible, but it did apply to the finding, based on a juror's responses on voir dire, that the individual juror was not biased. Similarly, *Rushen v. Spain* (1983) held that former § 2254(d) was applicable to a finding that a juror's ex parte communication with the judge had no bearing on the juror's impartiality, and in *Wainwright v. Witt* (1985), the Court applied former § 2254(d) to a finding that a prospective juror's opposition to capital punishment would substantially impair her ability to comply with the trial court's instructions.

Recognizing the sharp division within the Court, Justice O'Connor in *Miller v. Fenton* (1985) observed "that the decision to label an issue a 'question of law,' a 'question of fact' or a 'mixed question of law and fact' is sometimes as much a matter of allocation as it is of analysis. * * * At least in those instances in which Congress has not spoken and in which the issue falls somewhere between a pristine legal standard and a simple historical fact, the fact/law distinction at times has turned on a determination that, as a matter of the sound administration of justice, one judicial actor is better positioned than another to decide the issue in question."

The ruling in *Miller v. Fenton* itself reflected the broad range of factors that may enter into the characterization of a particular issue as one within or without the presumption of correctness. The Court there held that the voluntariness of a confession was a "legal inquiry requiring plenary federal review." "Subsidiary factual questions," such as whether a drug had certain properties or whether the police used certain interrogation tactics, are considered questions of fact alone, but not the "ultimate question whether, under the totality of the circumstances, the challenged confession was obtained in a manner compatible with the requirements of the Constitution." Voluntariness was held in *Miller* to be an issue beyond the presumption of correctness due to the combined influence of *stare decisis*, congressional intent, the "uniquely legal dimension" of the voluntariness determination, and "practical considerations" that favored "independent federal review" as necessary to "protec[t] the rights at stake."

Admitting that it has found the characterization of a question as one of law or fact "sometimes slippery" the Court in *Thompson v. Keohane* (1995) reviewed its earlier decisions in the area and held that a state court determination of whether or not a defendant was "in custody" for *Miranda* purposes is a mixed question of law and fact that is not subject to the presumption of correctness under former § 2254(d). The question of custody turns on whether there was a "formal arrest or restraint on freedom of movement, of the degree associated with a formal arrest." As in *Miller*, the Court reasoned that assessments of credibility were not crucial to the proper assessment of this issue.

(c) Obtaining Evidentiary Hearings. Prior to the 1996 amendments, a petitioner's failure to develop facts in state court would require a federal hearing only if a petitioner could show "cause" for and "prejudice" from his failure to develop those facts. New § 2254(e)(2) states that the federal habeas court shall not hold an evidentiary hearing on a claim as to which there was "a failure to develop the factual basis" in state court proceedings, unless that claim rests on either (1) an intervening new rule held to apply retroactively; *or* (2) a factual predicate not previously discoverable with due diligence, and the facts underlying the claim would be sufficient to "establish by clear and convincing evidence that but for the constitutional error, no reasonable factfinder would have found the applicant guilty of the underlying offense."

In *(Michael) Williams v. Taylor* (2000), the Court construed this provision to govern only cases in which the failure to develop the factual basis of a claim was due to some fault of the petitioner or his counsel. If a claim had been "pursued with diligence but remained undeveloped in state court because, for instance, the prosecution concealed the facts, a prisoner lacking clear and convincing evidence of innocence could be barred from a hearing on the claim even if he could satisfy § 2254(d) * * * [The clause] does not bear this harsh reading." "Diligence for purpose of the opening clause depends upon whether the prisoner made a reasonable attempt, in light of the information available at the time, to investigate and pursue claims in state court; it does not depend * * * upon whether those efforts could have been successful." Diligence, the Court continued, "will require in the usual case that the prisoner, at a minimum, seek an evidentiary hearing in state court in the manner prescribed by state law." If petitioner had been diligent, an evidentiary hearing is not barred by § 2254(e). Applying this provision in *Williams,* the Court found that Williams was diligent in his efforts to develop the facts supporting his juror bias and prosecutorial misconduct claims in state court. The facts supporting juror bias were not revealed during state proceedings because the allegedly biased juror's answers to questions posed to her by the court and counsel during voir dire were misleading, and because the prosecutor had "completely forgotten" his earlier representation of the juror in her divorce from the state's witness. "Counsel had no reason to believe" the juror had been married to the state's witness or had been represented by the prosecutor. The "standards of trial practice" did not require "counsel to check public records containing personal information pertaining to each and every juror." Williams had not been diligent, ruled the Court, in developing the basis for his *Brady* claim in state court. Petitioner's state habeas counsel had notice of the existence and materiality of the psychiatric report in question, but made no effort to find the report other than a making a general request for all psychological tests. "Given knowledge of the report's existence and potential importance, a diligent attorney would have done more." Because he was not diligent in developing the factual basis for this claim, an evidentiary hearing on the claim was unavailable unless the stringent requirements of § 2254(e) were met.

Under § 2254(e), a petitioner must show that "the legal or factual basis of the claims did not exist at the time of the state court proceedings," either by showing that his claim was based on a "new rule of constitutional law" not available at the time of the earlier proceedings (§ 2254(e)(2)(A)(i)) or by showing that had he exercised due diligence, "the factual predicate could not have been discovered" (§ 2254(e)(2)(A)(ii)). Second, § 2254(e)(2)(B) requires the petitioner to show that the new facts, if proven, "would be sufficient to establish by clear and convincing evidence" that "no reasonable factfinder would have found the [petitioner] guilty of the underlying offense" if the constitutional error had not occurred. In *Williams*, the petitioner conceded he could not show "by clear and convincing evidence, that no reasonable factfinder would have found [him] guilty of capital murder but for" the *Brady* error.

Evidentiary Hearings in Other Cases. If not barred by § 2254(e), an evidentiary hearing may be ordered by the district court in the exercise of its discretion. In *Schriro v. Landrigan*

(2007), the Court stated that in "deciding whether to grant an evidentiary hearing, a federal court must consider whether such a hearing could enable an applicant to prove the petition's factual allegations, which, if true, would entitle the applicant to federal habeas relief ... [I]f the record refutes the applicant's factual allegations or otherwise precludes habeas relief, a district court is not required to hold an evidentiary hearing." In *Landrigan*, the Court found that because the petitioner would not have been entitled to relief even if all the facts he alleged were true, the district court did not abuse its discretion by denying the petitioner the opportunity to prove those facts at an evidentiary hearing. Despite the discretion to order evidentiary hearings, district courts rarely hold them in non-capital cases, and most capital cases are resolved without hearings.

(d) Discovery. Discovery in habeas proceedings is more limited than discovery in other civil proceedings in federal court. Rule 6 of the Rules Governing § 2254 Cases allows discovery under the Federal Rules of Civil Procedure "if, and to the extent that, the judge in the exercise of his discretion and for good cause shown grants leave to do so." In *Bracy v. Gramley* (1997), the Court considered this Rule in the context of a case in which the petitioner had been sentenced to death by a judge who was later convicted of taking bribes from other defendants to fix their cases. The petitioner argued that the judge had convicted him and sentenced him to death in order to "cover up" for this illegal activity. The Court held that this was "good cause" for discovery since the allegations provided "reason to believe that the petitioner may, if the facts are fully developed, be able to demonstrate that he is * * * entitled to relief," and that it was "an abuse of discretion not to permit any discovery."

*

Table of Cases

A

G

N

O

*

Index

†